797,885 Books
are available to read at

Forgotten Books

www.ForgottenBooks.com

Forgotten Books' App
Available for mobile, tablet & eReader

ISBN 978-1-333-66169-4
PIBN 10532536

This book is a reproduction of an important historical work. Forgotten Books uses state-of-the-art technology to digitally reconstruct the work, preserving the original format whilst repairing imperfections present in the aged copy. In rare cases, an imperfection in the original, such as a blemish or missing page, may be replicated in our edition. We do, however, repair the vast majority of imperfections successfully; any imperfections that remain are intentionally left to preserve the state of such historical works.

Forgotten Books is a registered trademark of FB &c Ltd.
Copyright © 2015 FB &c Ltd.
FB &c Ltd, Dalton House, 60 Windsor Avenue, London, SW19 2RR.
Company number 08720141. Registered in England and Wales.

For support please visit www.forgottenbooks.com

1 MONTH OF FREE READING

at

www.ForgottenBooks.com

By purchasing this book you are eligible for one month membership to ForgottenBooks.com, giving you unlimited access to our entire collection of over 700,000 titles via our web site and mobile apps.

To claim your free month visit:

www.forgottenbooks.com/free532536

* Offer is valid for 45 days from date of purchase. Terms and conditions apply.

English
Français
Deutsche
Italiano
Español
Português

www.forgottenbooks.com

Mythology Photography **Fiction** Fishing Christianity **Art** Cooking Essays Buddhism Freemasonry Medicine **Biology** Music **Ancient Egypt** Evolution Carpentry Physics Dance Geology **Mathematics** Fitness Shakespeare **Folklore** Yoga Marketing **Confidence** Immortality Biographies Poetry **Psychology** Witchcraft Electronics Chemistry History **Law** Accounting **Philosophy** Anthropology Alchemy Drama Quantum Mechanics Atheism Sexual Health **Ancient History Entrepreneurship** Languages Sport Paleontology Needlework Islam **Metaphysics** Investment Archaeology Parenting Statistics Criminology **Motivational**

IROQUOIAN COSMOLOGY

(FIRST PART)

BY

J. N. B. HEWITT

EXTRACT FROM THE TWENTY-FIRST ANNUAL REPORT OF THE
BUREAU OF AMERICAN ETHNOLOGY

WASHINGTON
GOVERNMENT PRINTING OFFICE
1904

IROQUOIAN COSMOLOGY

FIRST PART

BY

J. N. B. HEWITT

CONTENTS

	Page
Introduction	133
An Onondaga version	141
A Seneca version	224
A Mohawk version	255

ILLUSTRATIONS

		Page
Plate LXIV.	William Henry Fishcarrier, a Cayuga chief (age 88), Canada..	340
LXV.	Robert David (Gadjinonda'he'), a Cayuga chief, Canada.....	340
LXVI.	William Sandy, William Henry Fishcarrier, Alexander Hill, Robert David...	340
LXVII.	William Sandy (born Fishcarrier), Cayuga warrior, Canada..	340
LXVIII.	John Buck, Onondaga chief and fire-keeper, Canada.........	340
LXIX.	William Wedge, Cayuga head chief and fire-keeper, Canada..	340

IROQUOIAN COSMOLOGY

FIRST PART

By J. N. B. Hewitt

INTRODUCTION

The term Iroquoian is derived from the name Iroquois, which, adapted from the Algonquian Indian language by the early French explorers, was applied originally to a group of five tribes then united in a permanent confederacy for offense and defense, and inhabiting the central and eastern portions of the region now comprised within the State of New York. Among other names they were called the Five Nations, and the League of the Iroquois, and, after their adoption of the Tuscaroras, in 1722, the Six Nations. These five tribes attained the zenith of their remarkable career during the latter part of the seventeenth century, when, by the exploitation of the fundamental principles of the constitution of their League, they dominated by force of arms the greater part of the watershed of the Great lakes. Never very numerous, they reached this commanding position by an incisive and unexcelled diplomacy, by an effective political organization founded on maternal blood relationship, both real and fictitious, and by an aptitude for coordinate political action, all due to a mentality superior to that of the surrounding tribes.

The sophiology—that is, the body of opinions—of a people such as the Iroquois is necessarily interesting and very abundant. It would be an almost interminable work to collect these opinions exhaustively and to publish them in a body, so in the accompanying texts only narratives relating to the genesis of things are included. The following comments may serve to aid the scholar who would study these narratives at first hand, giving him what the author regards as the most apparent viewpoints of their relators and originators:

It must not be overlooked that these texts represent largely the spoken language of to-day, conveying the modern thought of the people, although there are many survivals in both word and concept from older generations and past planes of thought. These archaisms when encountered appear enigmatic and quaint, and are not understood by the uninformed. The relators themselves often do not know the signification of the terms they employ. The author has attempted, where it appeared needful, to reduce evident metaphors to statements of concrete things which gave rise originally to the figures of speech.

The attempts of a primitive people to give in the form of a narrative the origins and to expound the causes of things, the sum of which constitutes their philosophy, assume in time the form of cosmologic legends or myths. In these legends are stored the combined wisdom and speculations of their wise men, their ancients, their prophets, and their soothsayers.

By primitive man all motions and activities were interpreted as manifestations of life and will. Things animate and things inanimate were comprised in one heterogeneous class, sharing a common nature. All things, therefore, were thought to have life and to exercise will, whose behests were accomplished through orenda—that is, through magic power, reputed to be inherent in all things. Thus, all phenomena, all states, all changes, and all activity were interpreted as the results of the exercise of magic power directed by some controlling mind. The various beings and bodies and operations of environing nature were interpreted strictly in terms of the subjective self. Into the known world self was projected. The wind was the breath of some person. The lightning was the winking of some person's eyes. The generative or reproductive power in nature was personified, and life and growth were in the fostering care of this personage.

Upon the concepts evolved from their impressions of things and from their experience with the bodies of their environment rest the authority for men's doctrines and the reasons for their rites and ceremonies. Hence arises the great importance of recording, translating, and interpreting from the vernacular the legends constituting the cosmology of peoples still largely dominated by the thoughts peculiar to the cultural stage of imputative and self-centered reasoning. The great difficulty of accurately defining and interpreting the ideas of primitive man without a deep and detailed study and a close translation of the words embodying these ideas renders it imperative for their correct apprehension that they be carefully recorded in the vernacular, and that there be made not only a free but also a literal rendering of the record, in such wise that the highly subjective thought of barbaric man may be cast, so far as is possible, into the more objective phraseology of science and enlightenment. By this means it is possible to obtain a juster and more accurate comprehension and interpretation of the thoughts and conceptions underlying and interwoven with the cosmologic and other legends of primitive man than that obtained by the ordinary method of recording only a free and popular version of them.

INTRODUCTION

A fact of great importance made evident in these texts is that anthropic persons, called man-beings in the accompanying translations, were, in Iroquoian thought, the primal beings. They were the first to exercise the functions and to experience the lot of their several kinds. Sometimes these first beings have been called the prototypes of the things of like kind which are to-day. Some of these beings were mere fictions, figures of speech made concrete and objective. They were not beasts, but they belonged to a rather vague class, of which man was the characteristic type. To speak with the logicians, no other deduction from the intension and the extension of the term oñgwe, man-being, appears sufficiently broad to set forth the true interpretation of the personages the narrative of whose lives and acts constitutes the subject matter of these texts. Among these primal beings may be named Daylight, Earthquake, Winter, Medicine, Wind, or Air, Life (germination), and Flower. So it seems evident from this fact that beast powers, the so-called beast gods, were not the first beings or chief actors at the beginning of time.

Beast gods appear later. In the development of Iroquoian thought, beasts and animals, plants and trees, rocks, and streams of water, having human or other effective attributes or properties in a paramount measure, were naturally regarded as the controllers of those attributes or properties, which could be made available by orenda or magic power. And thus began the reign of the beast gods, plant gods, tree gods, and their kind. The signification of the Iroquoian term usually rendered into English by the term "god" is "disposer," or "controller." This definition supplies the reason that the reputed controllers of the operations of nature received worship and prayers. To the Iroquois god and controller are synonymous terms.

From the very nature of the subject-matter and the slow acquirement of new ideas and development of concepts, the content of a cosmologic myth or legend must be the result of a gradual combination and readjustment of diverse materials, which, in the flux of time, are recast many times into new forms to satisfy the growing knowledge and wider experience and deeper research of the people among whom the myth is current. In different branches of a cognate group of peoples the old materials, the old ideas and concepts, modified by acculturational influences and by new and alien ideas, may be combined and arranged in quite unlike forms, and hence arise varying versions of a cosmogonic legend. These different versions modify the thought contemporary with them, and are in turn still further changed by acculturational influences and motives arising from the activities of the people. And in later times, when they no longer constitute the chief body of the philosophy of the people, these legends and stories concerning the causes and beginnings of things are called myths.

As has been suggested, the development of legend is not always internal, from the activities of the people dealing with the materials supplied by the legend itself, but often, and naturally, from alien material, from ideas and concepts consciously or unconsciously adopted from other peoples. And thus older forms and concepts, the ancient dogmas, are displaced or changed by accultural influences and by a more definite knowledge of nature acquired through a wider experience, a closer observation, and a more discriminating interpretation and apprehension of environing phenomena. Cosmologies, therefore, are composite, representing the accumulated explanations of many things by many generations in diverse times. The correct and fundamental analysis must therefore seek by a wide comparison of materials to separate the accultural from the autochthonous product. This analysis, however, can bring to light only such material as still exhibits by some marked token of incongruity its alien origin; for it is obvious that accultural matter in time becomes so thoroughly assimilated and recast that a more or less complete congruity is established between it and the cosmologic material with which it is joined, but to which it is, in fact, alien. Furthermore, where reason demands it, metaphor and personification must be reduced to concrete statements of objective facts upon which the original figurative expressions were founded; in short, the process resulting in metaphor and personification must be carefully retraced, so far as it may be possible so to do from the materials in hand.

It must not be overlooked that although these legends concerning the beginnings of things are usually called myths, creation stories, or cosmogonies, the terms myth and creation are, in fact, misnomers. In all of these narratives, except such as are of modern date, creation in the modern acceptation of the word is never signified, nor is it even conceived; and when these legends or narratives are called myths, it is because a full comprehension and a correct interpretation of them have to a large extent been lost or because they have been supplanted by more accurate knowledge, and they are related without a clear conception of what they were designed to signify, and rather from custom than as the source of the major portion of the customs and ceremonies and opinions in vogue among the people relating them.

Five different versions of the Iroquoian cosmology have been recorded by the author at different times from 1889 to 1900. Of these only three appear in the following pages, namely, one Onondaga, one Mohawk, and one Seneca legend.

The first text is an Onondaga version of the Iroquoian cosmology, obtained in 1889 on the Grand River reservation, Canada, from the late chief and fire-keeper, John Buck, of the Onondaga tribe. Afterward, in 1897, it was revised and somewhat enlarged by the aid of Mr Joshua Buck, a son of the first relator. It is not as long as the Mohawk text printed herewith because the relator seemed averse to telling more than a brief outline of the legend. A version in the Onondaga, much longer and fuller than any herewith printed, has been recorded from the mouth of Chief John Arthur Gibson, and will be printed in a later report of the Bureau.

The second text is a Seneca version of the cosmologic legend, obtained in 1896 on the Cattaraugus reservation, in the western part of the State of New York, from the late Mr John Armstrong, of Seneca-Delaware-English mixed blood, an intelligent and conscientious annalist. Later, at various times, it was revised in this office with the assistance of Mr Andrew John.

The last text in order is a Mohawk version, obtained in 1896 and 1897 on the Grand River reservation in Canada from Mr Seth Newhouse, an intelligent and educated member of the Mohawk tribe.

In general outlines the legend, as related here, is identical with that found among all of the northern tribes of the Iroquoian stock of languages. It is told partly in the language of tradition and ceremony, which is formal, sometimes quaint, sometimes archaic, frequently mystical, and largely metaphorical. But the figures of speech are made concrete by the elementary thought of the Iroquois, and the metaphor is regarded as a fact.

Regarding the subject-matter of these texts, it may be said that it is in the main of aboriginal origin. The most marked post-Columbian modification is found in the portion relating to the formation of the physical bodies of man and of the animals and plants, in that relating to the idea of a hell, and in the adaptation of the rib story from the ancient Hebrew mythology in connection with the creation of woman. These alien elements are retained in the texts to show by concrete examples how such foreign material may be adopted and recast to conform to the requirements of its new setting. In the translation some of the quaintness of the original is retained, as well as some of its seeming tautology. No liberty, however, has been taken with the texts either in the way of emendation or addition or in rendering them into English. They are given exactly as related. It may possibly be objected that the interlinear and the free translations are too literal; but the aboriginal thought, however commonplace, figurative, poetical, is set forth as simply and with as strict a rendering of the original as the matter and thought contained in it permit. It is no ready task to embody in the language of enlightenment the thought of barbarism. The viewpoint of the one plane of thought differs much from that of the other.

The idea that the bodies of man and of the animals were created directly out of specific portions of the earth by Tharonhiawakon[a] is a comparatively modern and erroneous interpretation of the original

---

[a] "He grasps the sky (by memory)."

concept. The error is due largely to the influence of the declaration of like import in the Semitic mythology, found in the Hebrew Scriptures, the figurative character of which is usually not apprehended. The thought originally expressed by the ancient teachers of the Iroquoian and other barbaric peoples was that the earth through the life, or life power, innate and immanent in its substance—the life personated by Tharonhiawakon[a]—by feeding itself to them produces plants and fruits and vegetables which serve as food for birds and animals, all which in their turn become food for men, a process whereby the life of the earth is transmuted into that of man and of all living things. Hence, the Iroquois consistently say, in addressing the earth, "Eithinoha," "our Mother." Thus in 1896 the author's late friend, Mr David Stephens, a grave Seneca priest and philosopher, declared to him that the earth or ground is living matter, and that the tender plantlet of the bean and the sprouting germ of the corn nestling therein receive through their delicate rootlets the life substance from the earth; that, thus, the earth indeed feeds itself to them; that, since what is supplied to them is living matter, life in them is produced and conserved, and that as food the ripened corn and bean and their kinds, thus produced, create and develop the life of man and of all living things. Hence it is seen that only in this metaphorical manner Tharonhiawakon, the personified life immanent in the matter of the earth, creates daily, and did in the beginning of time create man and all living things out of the earth. But the fiat creation of man and things from nothing or from definite portions of clay or earth, as the potter makes pottery, never is involved in the earliest known conceptions of the beginning of things. In the quaint protology, or science of first things, of the Iroquois things are derived from things through transformation and evolution. The manner in which the earth or dry land itself was formed, as detailed in the Onondaga and the Mohawk texts, is an apt example of this statement.

Another misapprehended figure of speech is expressed in the popular dogma of the virgin, or parthenogenetic, conception, which in this as in other cosmologies, affects one of the chief persons. This is, however, a metaphor as old as the earliest philosophies of man. And some of the most beautiful and touching thoughts and activities of both barbaric and enlightened man rest on the too literal acceptation of the figurative statement of a great fact of life, attested by all human experience, namely, that breath (spirit, air, wind, atmos, atman) is the principle of life and feeling, and that without it there can be no manifestation of life. This is the key to the riddle of the virgin, or parthenogenetic, conception. It is made very clear in the

---

[a] He is also called Odendonnia, Sprout, or Sapling, and Ioskaha, having apparently the same meaning.

Onondaga version. The fact and the idea are matters of experience in all times and in all lands.

While in general outlines and in the sum of incidents comprised in them the several versions of the cosmologic story of the Iroquois substantially accord, there are nevertheless marked divergences in both structure and matter, which in time, by further development from accultural and other potent causes, would necessarily cause them to be regarded as quite different legends in source and meaning; and this emphasizes the great and fundamental fact that all legends are the gradual result of combination from many sources by many minds in many generations.

Most of the characteristic incidents related in these legends are widely prevalent over the American continent, occurring among peoples speaking tongues of widely different linguistic stocks and dwelling in widely separated habitats. It should not be assumed that these coincidences are indubitably due to accultur…al influences, but rather that they indicate universality of the natural phenomena from which the incidents embodied are drawn. Among these coincidences may be mentioned that of the seclusion of the members of the animal world in a vast cave in by one of the chief characters of the legends, Winter, the man-being of frosts and snow and ice. This episode evidently portrays the annual hibernation of the animals and insects and the migration of the birds caused by the winter power, which is called Tawiskaron by the Mohawks,[a] Ohaä by the Onondagas, and Othä'kwenda' by the Senecas.

The author desires to acknowledge his many obligations to the officers and staff of the Bureau of American Ethnology for most kindly advice, wise counsel, and many valuable suggestions, especially to the late Director, Major John Wesley Powell; to Professor W J McGee, formerly Ethnologist in Charge; to Professor William Henry Holmes, the present Chief of the Bureau, and to Herbert Spencer Wood, editor, who has also kindly performed the irksome task of correcting the proofs of the texts and translations while they were passing through the press.

Alphabet and abbreviations

a	as in far, father; Gm. haben; Sp. ramo.
ā	the same sound prolonged.
ȧ	as in what; Gr. man.
ä	as in hat, man.
ǟ	the same sound prolonged.

---

[a] The Mohawk epithet is commonly interpreted "flint," but its literal and original meaning is "crystal-clad" or "ice-clad," the two significations being normal, as crystal, flint and ice have a similar aspect and fracture. The original denotation is singularly appropriate for Winter. The last two names do not connote ice, but simply denote flint.

â	as in haw, all; Fr. o in or.
ai	as in aisle, as i in pine, find; Gr. Hain.
au	as ou in out, as ow in how; Gm. haus; Sp. auto.
c	as sh in shall; Gm. sch in schellen; Fr. ch in charrer
ç	as th in health.
d	pronounced with the tip of the tongue touching the upper teeth as in enunciating the English th; this is the only sound of d in this language.
e	as in they; Gm. Dehnung; Fr. né; Sp. qué.
ĕ	as in then, met; Gr. denn; Fr. sienne; Sp. comen
f	as in waif
g	as in gig; Gr. geben; Fr. goût; Sp. gozar.
h	as in has, he; Gm. haben.
i	as in pique, machine.
ı	the same sound prolonged
ĭ	as in pick, pit.
k	as in kick.
n	as in nun, run.
ñ	as ng in sing, ring.
o	as in note, rote.
q	as ch in Gm. ich
r	slightly trilled; but in Mohawk it closely approximates an l sound.
s	as in sop, see.
t	pronounced with the tip of the tongue touching the upper teeth as in enunciating the English th; this is the only sound of t in this language.
u	as in rule; Gr. du; Fr. ou in doux; Sp. uno.
ŭ	as in rut, shut.
w	as in wit, witch.
y	as in yes, yet.
dj	as j in judge.
hw	as wh in what.
tc	as ch in church
ⁿ	marks nasalized vowels, thus, e^n, o^n, ai^n, $ĕ^n$, $ä^n$.
‘	indicates an aspiration or soft emission of breath, which is initial or final, thus, ‘h, $ĕ^{n‘}$, o‘
’	marks a sudden closure of the glottis, preceding or following a sound, thus, ’a, o’, ä’, $ä^{n’}$
′	marks the accented syllable of every word.
th	in this combination t and h are always pronounced separately.

In the literal (interlinear) translation the following abbreviations denoting gender have been used: z.=zoïc; anthr.=anthropic; m.=masculine; fem.=feminine; indef.=indefinite.

AN ONONDAGA VERSION

The Manner in W ̣ic ̣ it Established Itself, in W ̣ic ̣ it Formed Itself, in W ̣ic ̣, in Ancient Ti ̣ ̣e, it Ca ̣e about t ̣at the Earth Beca ̣e Extant

He who was my grandfather was wont to relate that, verily, he had heard the legend as it was customarily told by five generations of grandsires, and this is what he hi ̣self was in the habit of telling. He custo ̣arily said: Man-beings dwell in the sky, on the farther side of the visible sky [the ground separating this from the world above it].

Tca''	Dediodieä'da·'gwi‘	Tca''	Deio'dĕndä''i·	Tca''	Wä'wadoñ'niä'	
The where	Therefrom it it employed Therefor	The where	It was established	The where	It itself formed	1
Tca''	Io^s‘hwĕñdjiä'de‘	Wä'wa'do^s‘	Ne''	O^u'hwagä'io .		
The where	It earth extant is	It came to be	The	It matter (is) ancient		2
Ksodä‘hä‘-gĕⁿ‘‘hä‘,	hwi'ks	nwä'hoñdiä'di·''sä‘	tca''	hodikstĕñ'ä·-		
My grand-father	was,	five	so many they matured in body	the where	they ancient	3
gĕⁿ‘‘hä‘	nä'ie‘	ne''	hoñthoiä‘hä·''gwä‘	ne''	hi'iä‘ gĕⁿ's hothoñ'de‘	
were	that (it is)	the	they it tell did habitually	the	verily custom-arily be it heard	4
tca''	ni·hadii·ho''dĕⁿ‘,	nä'ie‘	ne''	haoⁿ·'hwä‘	oⁿ·'kŏⁿ' hathoiä	
the where	such their relation (is) kind of.	that (it is)	the	he himself	next in order he it tell	5
‘hä·'gwä‘.	I·ha'doⁿk	gĕⁿ's:	Enä'gee‘	ne''	oñ'gwe‘ ^a gaoⁿ hi. gɔñ'wä‘	
did.	He it said habitually	custom-arily:	They abide	the	man-being it sky in	6

^aThe classific conceptual term oñgwe‘, having no discernable grammatic affix, is what grammarians call a primitive word, and has both a singular and a collective denotation. It signifies "mankind, man, human beings; a human being, a person." But its original meaning was "man-being" or "primal being," which signified collectively those beings who preceded man in existence and exceeded him in wisdom and effective power, the personified bodies and elements of nature, the gods and demigods of later myth and legend, who were endowed by an imputative mode of reasoning with anthropic form and attributes additional to those normally characteristic of the particular bodies or elements that they represented. But, after the recognition of man as a species different from all others, consequent upon wider human experience and more exact knowledge, and after these had pushed back from the immediate fireside and community most of the reified fictions of savage mentation, a time came when it became needful to distinguish between the man-being, a human being, and the man-being, a reified personification of a body or element of nature; in short, to distinguish between what human experience had found to be "real, genuine, native," and what was the converse. Hence, the limiting term oñwe‘, signifying "native, real, genuine, original," was combined with oñgwe‘, thus forming oñgwe‘-oñwe‘, which signifies "native, real, or genuine man-being," hence, "man, human being." But after the advent of trans-Atlantic peoples the antithesis was transferred unconsciously from the "primal being," or "man-being," the reified concepts of myth and legend, to "white human being," denotive of any trans-Atlantic person. So, in this legend, when applied to times previous to the advent of man the word oñgwe‘ usually denotes a man-being that is a personification, one of the gods of the myths, one of that vague class of primal beings of which man was regarded by Iroquoian and other sages as a characteristic type.

The lodges they severally possess are customarily long. In the end of the lodges there are spread out strips of rough bark whereon lie the several rats (beds). There it is that, verily, all pass the night.

Early in the morning the warriors are in the habit of going to hunt and, as is their custom, they return every evening.

In that place there lived two persons, both down-fended, and both persons of worth. Verily, one of these persons was a woman-being, a person of worth, and down-fended; besides her there was a man-being, a person of worth, and down-fended.

In the end of the lodge there was a doorway. On the one side of it the woman-being abode, and on the other side of it the man-being abode.

1	si"	hăgwā'dĭ'	tca"	gaĕⁿ'hiā'de'.	Ganoⁿ'se'djĭ's	gĕⁿ's	tca"
	far yonder	side of it	the where	it sky is extant.	It lodge long plurally (are)	custom- arily	the where
2	hodinoⁿ'sāiĕñ'doⁿ'.		Tca"	heiotnoⁿ'so"kdă'	ne"tho'	gĕⁿ'sowāiĕñdā'die'	
	they lodge have plurally.		The where	there it lodge ends	there	it rough bark is spread along	
3	tca"	ne"tho'	ganakdăge''bĕñdoⁿ'.		Ne"tho'	hi'iă'	gagwe'gĭ'
	the where	there	it mat lay plurally.		There	verily,	it all (entire)
4	hoñnoⁿ'hwe'sthă'.						
	they (m.) stay over night.						
5	Nă'ie'	ne"	hĕⁿ'ge·'djĭk	hoⁿ'dĕñdioñ'gwăs	ne"	hodi'sgĕⁿ'äge''dă',	
	That (it is)	the	early in the morning	hence they depart repeatedly	the	they (are) warriors (mat-bearers),	
6	hoñdowä'thă'	gĕⁿ's.	Shadi'ioⁿk	o'ga''hoⁿk	gĕⁿ's		
	they go to hunt habitually	custom- arily.	They returned home habitually	evening after evening	custom- arily.		
7	Nă'ie'	ne"	ne"tho'	de'hni''dĕñ',	dehiiă'dăge'',	de'hninoä'doⁿ',[a]	
	That (it is)	the	there	they (m.) two abode,	they (m.) two are persons,	they (m.) two are down-fended,	
8	de'hiiă'dano'wĕⁿ'.		Nă'ie'	ne"	hi'iă'	tcieiă''dădă'	agoñ'gwe'
	they (m.) two are persons of worth.		That (it is)	the	verily	she is one person	she man-being (is)
9	e"dĕñ',	eiă'dăno'wĕⁿ'.		deienoä'doⁿ';	'a·''soⁿ'	ne"	shāiă''dădă,
	she abides,	she is a person of worth,		she (is) down-fended;	still,	the	he one person (is)
10	hoñ'gwe'	hĕⁿ'dĕñ',	hāiă'dăno'wĕⁿ',	de'hanoä'doⁿ'.			
	he man-being (is)	he abides,	he is a person of worth.	he (is) down-fended.			
11	Tca"	heiotnoⁿ'so"kdă'	ne"tho'	ga'nhoga·'hĕñ'dă'.	Sgagä'dĭ'		
	The where	there it lodge ends	there	it is doorway.	One side on		
12	hagwā'dĭ'	ne"tho'	e"dĕñ'	ne"	agoñ'gwe';	sgagä'dĭ'	hagwā'dĭ'
	side of it	there	she abides	the	she man-being (is);	one side on	side of it
13	ne"tho'	ne"	na"	ne"	boñ'gwe'	hĕⁿ'dĕñ'.	
	there	the that	that one	the that	he man-being (is)	he abides.	

[a] Down-fended. This compound approximately describes a feature characteristic of a primitive Iroquoian custom, which required that certain children should be strictly hidden from the sight of all persons save a trustee until they reached the age of puberty. The better to guard the ward from access the down of the cat-tail flag was carefully scattered about the place of concealment, so that no person could pass into the forbidden place without first disturbing the down and so indicating invasion of the guarded precinct; hence, it is proposed to apply a literal rendering of the Iroquoian term "down-fended" to a person so concealed. Persons so hidden were regarded as uncanny and as endowed with an unusual measure of orenda, or magic potence.

So1eti1e afte1wa1d, the1, this ca1e to pass. As soo1 as all the man-bei1gs had se\e1all) depa1ted this wo1a1-bei1g ca1e fo1th and we1t thithe1 and, 1o1eo\e1, a111\ed at the place whe1e the man-bei1g abode, and she ca111ed a co1b with her. She said: "Do thou a1ise; let me dise1ta1gle th) hai1." Now, \e1il), he a1ose, and the1, 1o1eo\e1, she dise1ta1gled his hai1, and st1aighte1ed it out. It co1-ti1ued in this 1a11e1 day afte1 day.

So1eti1e afte1wa1d her kindred we1e su1p1ised. It see1s that the life of the 1aide1 was 1ow cha1ged. Day afte1 day it beca1e 1o1e and 1o1e 1a1ifest that now she would gi\e bi1th to a child. Now, 1o1eo\e1, her 1othe1, the a1cie1t one, beca1e awa1e of it. The1, \e1il), she questio1ed her, say1g to the maide1: "Mo1eo\e1, what 1a11e1 of pe1so1 is to be jo11t pa1e1t with thee?" The 1aide1 said

Gaiñ'gwă'	nwă'oñni'she'	o'nĕⁿ'	tho'nĕⁿ'	nwă'awĕⁿ''hă'.	Ganio''	
Some (time)	so (long) it lasted	now	thus (here)	so it came to pass.	So soon as	1
gagwe'gĭ'	wă'hoñ'dĕñdioñ'gwă'	o'nĕⁿ'	dagăiagĕⁿ''nhă'	nĕñ'gĕⁿ'		
it all (entire)	they departed plurally	now	thence she (z.) came forth	this (it is)		2
ne''	agoñ'gwe'	ne''tho'	nhwă''we',	ne''tho'	dĭ''	hwă'gā'ioⁿ'	
the	she man-being (is)	there	thither she (z.) went	there	besides	there she (z.) arrived	3
tca''	noñ'we'	hĕⁿ''dĕñ'	ne''	hĕñ'gwe',	1ă'ie'	ne''	c'ha'wi'	ne''	
the where	the place	he is (abides)	the	he man-being (is)	that (it is)	the	she it bearing is	the	4
ga1a''dă'.	Wă'gĕⁿ''hĕñ':	"Satgĕⁿ''hă'.	Dagoñio'dai''siă'."	O'nĕⁿ'	
it comb (is).	She (z.) said:	"Do thou arise.	Let me dress thy hair."	Now,	5
bi'iă	da'hatgĕⁿ''hă'.	tho'ge'	o'nĕⁿ'	dĭ''	bi'iă'	wă'thoio'dai''siă',	
of course,	thence he did arise,	at that (time)	now,	besides,	of course,	she his hair did dress,	6
wă'tgaga''tciă'	ne''	hoge''ă'.	Nă'ie'	ne''	o'hĕⁿ''sĕñk	ne''tho'	
she (z.) it untangled	the	his hair (it is).	That (it is)	the	day after day	there	7
ni'io't.						
so it continued to be.						8
Gaiñ'gwă'	nwă'oñni'she'	o'nĕⁿ'	wă'hoñdiĕñ''hă'	gwă''	ne''	
Some (time)	so (long) t lasted	now	they were surprised	seemingly	the	9
agaoñgwe''dă'	tca''	o'iă'	o'nĕⁿ'	ni'io't	tca''	ago'n'he'	ne''	
her people	the where	(it is) other	now	so it is	the where	she lives (is alive)	the	10
eksă'go'nă'.	Tca''	o'hĕⁿ''sĕñk	heiotgoñdă''gwĭ'	dăiotgĕⁿ''i'ha'die'	
she maid (large child).	The where	day after day	it is unceasing	thence it becomes manifest more and more	11
tca''	oiĕñ'det	o'nĕⁿ'	tca''	ĕⁿiowiăiĕñdă''nhă'.	O'nĕⁿ'	dĭ''	
the where	it is knowable	now	the where	she (z.) child will have.	Now,	besides,	12
wă'oñtdo'kă'	ne''	gok'stĕñ'ă'.	Tho''ge'	o'nĕⁿ'	hi'iă'	wă'oñdadei'-	
she it noticed	the	she elder one (is).	At that (time)	now,	of course,	she her questioned	13
hwanĕñ'doⁿ'	ne''	eksă'go'nă',	wă'ă''hĕñ':	"Soñ''	dĭ''	1oñwa'-	
repeatedly	the	she maid (large child)	she it said:	"Who	besides	kind of	14
ho''dĕⁿ'	djiade'doⁿ''ne'?"	Hiiă''	stĕⁿ''	de'aga'wĕⁿ'	ne''	eksă'go'nă'	
thing	ye two are going to have offspring?"	Not (it is)	anything	she it said	the	she maid (large child).	15

nothing in reply. So, now, at that time, the man-being noticed that he began to be ill. For some time it continued thus, when, verily, his mother came to the place where he lay. She said: "Where is the place wherein thou art ill?" Then the man-being said in reply: "Oh, my mother! I will now tell thee that I, alas, am about to die." And his mother replied, saying: "What manner of thing is meant by thy saying 'I shall die?'"

It is said that they who dwelt there did not know what it is for one to say "I shall die." And the reason of it was that no one living there on the sky had ever theretofore died. At that time he said: "And, verily, this will come to pass when I die: My life will go forth. Moreover, my body will become cold. Oh, my

1	Da′,	tho″gĕ‘	o′nĕⁿ‘	ne″·	heñ′gwe‘	wă‘batdo″kă’	tca″	o′nĕⁿ‘
	So	at that (time)	now	the	he man-being (is)	he it noticed	the where	now
2	wă‘‘honoⁿ‘hwăk′dĕⁿ.		Gaiñ′gwă’	nwă‘oñni′she‘		ne″tho‘	ni′io‘t	
	he became ill.		Some (time)	so (long) it lasted		there	so it is	
3	o′nĕⁿ‘	bi′iă’	ne″	hono‘‘hă’	ne″tho‘	wă‘e′ioⁿ	tca″	noñ′we‘
	now,	of course, verily	the	his mother	there	she arrived	the where	the place
4	hĕñdă′gă’.	Wă‘ă‘‘hĕñ’:	"Gaiñ″	noñ′we‘	nisanoⁿ‘hwăk′dănĭ‘?"			
	he lay.	She it said:	"Where (is)	the place	so it thee pain (illness) causes?"			
5	O′nĕⁿ·	ne″	hĕñ′gwe‘	ni‘hă′wĕñ’:	"Ageno‘‘hă’,	o′nĕⁿ‘	ĕⁿgoñia	
	Now	the	he man-being (is)	so he replied:	"Oh, my mother,	now	I thee it will tell	
6	tho′iĕⁿ’	· nă′ie’	ne″	ni′ă‘	gi‘heioⁿ‘′sē′."	Nă′ie’	ne″	gă′wĕn‘
	that (it is)	the	I personally	I am going to die."	That (it is)	the	she it has said	
7	ne″	hono‘‘hă’,	wă‘ă‘‘hĕñ’:	"Ho′t	noñwă‘ho″dĕⁿ	gĕñ′dă’	tca″	
	the	his mother,	she it said:	‘What (is it)	kind of thing	it signifies	the where	
8	i‘să′doⁿk:	‘Ĕⁿgi‘he′iă’?'"						
	thou it art saying:	‘I will die?'"						
9	Nă′ie’	ne″,	iă′kĕⁿ,	tca″	hadină′gee’	biiă″	de‘hadiiĕñde′i‘	
	That (it is)	the,	it is said,	the where	they (m.) dwell	not	they it know	
10	ne″	soñ″	noñwă‘ho″dĕⁿ	aia′‘hĕñ’:	"Ĕⁿgi‘he′iă’."	Nă′ie’	gāi‘-	
	the	what (who)	kind of thing (it is)	one it should say·	"I will die."	That (it is)	it	
11	hoñnią′‘hă’	ne″	biiă″	bwĕñ′doⁿ‘	de‘agawĕⁿ‘he′ioⁿ‘	tca″	hadină′gee’	
	it causes (makes matter)	the	not (it is)	ever	one has died	the where	they (m.) dwell	
12	ne″	ne″tho‘	gaoⁿ‘hiă′ge‘.	O′nĕⁿ‘	hi′iă’	tho‘′ge‘	wă‘hĕⁿ‘‘hĕñ’:	
	the	there	· it sky on.	Now,	of course,	at that time,	he it said:	
13	"Nă′ie’	ne″	tho′nĕⁿ‘	nĕⁿiawĕⁿ‘‘hă’	ne″	o′nĕⁿ‘	ĕⁿgi‘he′iă’.	
	"That (it is)	the	here (this way)	so it will come to pass	the	now (when)	I will die.	
14	Nă′ie’	ne″	ĕⁿgāiagĕⁿ‘nhă″	ne″	agadon‘he′‘sä’.	Ĕⁿgană′no′sdă’		
	That (it is)	the	it will go out	the	my life (lifehood).	It will become cold		
15	dī″	ne″	giă‘dī′ge‘.	Ageno‘‘hă’,	tho′nĕⁿ‘	nĕⁿsieä″	ne″	kgă‘-
	besides	the	my body on.	My mother,	this way	so thou it wilt do	the	my

mother! thus shalt thou do on my eyes: Thou must lay both thy hands on both sides. And, moreover, thou must keep thy eyes fixed thereon when thou thinkest that now he is [I am] nearly dead. So soon as thou seest that my breathing is being made to become less, then, and not till then, must thou think that now it is that he is about to die. And then, moreover, thou wilt place thy two hands on both my eyes. Now, I shall tell thee another thing. Ye must make a burial-case. When ye finish the task of making it, then, moreover, ye must place my body therein, and, moreover, ye must lay it up in a high place."

Now, verily, she, the ancient one, had her eyes fixed on him. So soon as she believed that now he was about to die, she placed both her hands on his eyes. Just so soon as she did this she began to weep. Moreover, all those who abode in the lodge were also affected in the same way; they all wept. Sometime after he had died they set

hi″ge‘.	Dĕⁿ‘sĕⁿniä'‘hĕñ‘	dedjaoⁿ″gwī‘.	Ne″tho‘	dī″	nĕⁿskä‘hä″k	1
eyes on.	Thou thy two hands on (them) wilt lay	on both sides.	There	besides	there it thy eyes will be on	
ne″	o'nĕⁿ‘ ĕⁿ‘se'ä' o'nĕⁿ‘	tho'‘hä‘	ĕⁿgi‘he'iä'.	Ganio″	ĕⁿsatgat'-	2
the	now thou wilt now decide	almost	I will die.	So soon as	thou it wilt	
hwä‘	tea″ gadoñ'ie's	dĕⁿdiosthwä‘di‘hä'die'	o'nĕⁿ‘	ha‘'sä‘	ĕⁿ‘se'ä'	3
see	the I am breath- where ing	it will continue to grow less	now	just then	thou wilt decide	
o'nĕⁿ‘-khĕⁿ‘'	tho'‘hä‘	ĕⁿ‘hĕⁿ‘he'iä'.	O'nĕⁿ‘	dī″	kgä‘hi″ge‘	dĕⁿ‘- 4
now is it	nearly	he will die.	Now	besides	my eyes on	thou
sĕⁿniä'‘hĕñ‘	dedjaoⁿ″gwī‘.	O'nĕⁿ‘	o'iä‘	ĕⁿgoñiatho'iĕⁿ‘.	Nä'ie‘	5
thy two hands on (them) wilt lay	on both sides.	Now	it is other	will I thee tell it.	That (it is)	
ne″	ĕⁿswa‘soñ'niä' ne″ ga‘boⁿ″'sä'.	Ne″	o'nĕⁿ‘	ĕⁿ‘swadiĕñno″kdĕⁿ‘	6	
the	will ye it make the it case (burial-case).	The	now	will ye task finish		
né″tho‘	dī″ ĕⁿ‘sgwäiä'doñ'däk,	he‘tkĕⁿ‘'	dī″	ĕⁿswa‘'hĕñ‘ "		
there	be- ye my body will incase, sides	up high	be- sides	ye it will up-lay."		
O'nĕⁿ‘	ne″ gok'stĕñ'ä‘	ne″tho‘	hi'iä‘	de‘hogä'‘hä'.	Ganio″	8
Now	the she elder one (is)	there,	verily,	she(z.) had her eyes on him.	So soon as	
wä‘eñä″	o'nĕⁿ‘ hi'ä'	tho'‘hä‘	a‘hĕⁿ‘he'iä‘,	tho″ge‘	o'nĕⁿ‘	9
she decided	now, verily,	nearly	he would die,	at that (time)	now	
wä‘dioⁿniä'‘hĕñ‘	ne″	haga‘hi″ge‘.	Agwa's	ganio″	ne″tho‘	10
she laid her two hands on them	the	his eyes on.	very	so soon as	thus	
nwä‘eie'ä‘	o'nĕⁿ‘ wä‘dioⁿ‘shĕñt'hwä'.	Gagwe'gī‘	dī″	tea″	nioⁿ‘'	11
so she it did	now she wept.	It all	be- sides	the where	so it (is) many	
ganoⁿsgoñ'wä‘	e″dĕñ‘ ne″tho‘ o″	nwä‘awĕⁿ″‘hä',	wä‘dioⁿshĕñthw	12		
it lodge in	they (in- there too def.) abode	so it came to pass,	they (indef.) plurally			
ä'‘hoⁿ‘	gagwe'gī‘.	Gaiñ'gwä'	nwä‘oñni'she‘	hawĕⁿ‘he'ioⁿ‘	o'nĕⁿ‘	13
wept	it all.	Some (time)	so it lasted	he is dead	now	

the 1 sel\es to wo1k, 1 aking a bu1ial-case. Mo1eo\e1, so soon as they had finished thei1 task the) placed his body the1ein, and also laid it up in a high place.

So1eti1e afte1 they had laid the bu1ial-case in the high place, the 1 aiden, now a wo1an-being, ga\e bi1th to a child, which was a fe1ale, a wo1an-being. Then the ancient one [elde1 one, the 1othe1 of the 1aiden] said: "Moreo\e1, what 1anne1 of pe1son is the fathe1 of the child?" The 1aiden said nothing in 1eply.

The gi1l child g1ew 1apidly in size. It was not long afte1 this that the gi1l child was 1unning about. Suddenly, it see1s, the gi1l child began to weep. It was i1possible to stop her. Five are the numbe1 of days, it is said, that the gi1l child continued to weep. Then the elde1 one [her g1and1othe1] said: "Do ye show her the bu1ial-case lying there in the high place." Now, \e1ily, they ca11ied

1 wä'hodiio'dĕⁿ'·hä', wä'hadi'soñ'niä' ne'' ga'hoⁿ'·sä'. Ganio'' dī'
they (m.) worked, they (m.) it made the it case (burial-case). So soon as besides

2 o'nĕⁿ· wä'hoñdiiĕñno''kdĕⁿ o'nĕⁿ· ne''tho· wä'honwäiä'doñ'dak,
now they (their) task finished now there they his body incased,

3 he''tkĕⁿ· o''nī' wä'hadi''hĕñ'
up high also they (m.) it up-laid.

4 Gaiñ'gwä' nwä'oñni'she' ne'' he''tkĕⁿ· he'hodi''hä' o'nĕⁿ·
Some (time) so (long) it lasted the up high they it had up-laid now

5 tho·'ge· ne'' eksä'go'nä·, ne'' agoñ'gwe· o'nĕⁿ·, wä'agoksä'·
at that (time) the she maiden, the she man-being (is) then, she became possessed

6 daiĕñdä''nhä', e''hĕⁿ·, agon'gwe· ne'' eksä''a·. Tho·'ge o'nĕⁿ
of an infant she (is) female she (is) man-being the she infant (is). At that (time) now

7 ne'' gok'stĕñ'ä· wä'ä·hĕñ'': "Soñ'' dī'' nonwa'ho'dĕⁿ ne''
the she elder one she it said: "Who (is it) be-sides kind of person the

8 eksä''ä· ago'ni''hä·?" Hiiä'' stĕⁿ'' de'aga'wĕñ· ne'' eksä'go'nä .
she infant (is) her father (it is)?" Not (it is) any-thing she it has said the she maiden. (is)

9 Godi'sno'we' tca'' gododi'ha'die' ne'' eksä''ä·. Hiiä''
She grew rapidly the where she continued to grow in size the she infant (is). Not (it is)

10 de'aoᵢmishe''i· o'nĕⁿ· ne''tho· eda'khe's ne'' eksä''ä·. Diĕñ'·hä'
it lasted (long) now at that place she ran about the she infant. Suddenly

11 gwä'' o'nĕⁿ· ne'' eksä''ä· wä'oⁿ·sa'wĕⁿ wä'dioⁿ·shĕñt'hwä'. Hiiä''
it seems now the she child she began she wept. Not (it is)

12 de'a'wet äioñni'qhĕⁿ. Hwi'ks niwĕñdäge'', iä'gĕⁿ, deioⁿ·shĕñt-
it is possible she it would stop. Five so many it day in number (is), it is said, she goes about

13 hwä''he's ne' eksä''ä·. Tho·'ge· o'nĕⁿ· wä'ä·hĕñ'' ne''
weeping the she child. (is) At that (time) now she it said the

14 gok'stĕñ'ä·: "Etchinä''doⁿs tca'' tga'hoⁿ·sä''hä'." O'nĕⁿ· bi'iä'
she elder one: "Do ye it show to her the where there it case up-lies." Now, of course (verily),

her person, and caused her to stand up high there. Then the girl child looked at it [the corpse], and then she ceased her weeping, and also she was pleased. It was a long time before they withdrew her; and it was not a long time before she again began to weep. Now, verily, they again carried her person, and, moreover, they caused her to stand there again. So, it continued thus, that, day after day, they were in the habit of carrying her, and causing her to stand there on the high place. It was not long before she by her own efforts was able to climb up to the place where lay the dead man-being. Thus it continued to be that she at all times went to view it.

So sometime afterward it thus came to pass that she came down again bringing with her what was called an armlet, that being the kind of thing that the dead man-being had clasped about his arms, and, being of the wampum variety, it was, it is said, fine-looking.

wä'hodiiä'dĕⁿ''häwä'	ne''tho'	be''tkĕⁿ'		wä'dioñdatdĕⁿ'sdä'.	O'nĕⁿ'	1
they her person carried	there	up high		they (indef.) her caused to stand.	Now (it is)	
wä'oñtgat'hwä'	ne''	eksä''ä';	tho''ge'	o'nĕⁿ'	wä'oñni'qhĕⁿ' tca''	2
she it looked at	the	she child (is):	at that (time)	now	she it ceased the where	
deioⁿ'shĕñt'hwäs,	wä'oñtcĕññoñ'niä'	o''nï'.	Aoñni'she'i'		o'nĕⁿ'	3
she is weeping.	she was pleased	also:	It lasted (long)		now	
sarondadiä'doⁿ''tkä'.	Nä'ie'	ne''	hiiä''	de'aoñni'she'i'	o'nĕⁿ'	4
again they her person withdrew.	That (it is)	the	not	it lasted (long)	now	
he''	doñsäioⁿ'shĕñt'hwä'.	O'nĕⁿ'	hi'iä'	säshagodiiä'dĕⁿ''häwä',		5
again	again she wept.	Now,	of course, verily,	again they her person carried,		
ne''tho'	dï''	he''tkĕⁿ'	wä'shagodidĕⁿ'sdä'.	O'nĕⁿ'	ne''tho'	6
there	besides	up high	they her caused to stand.	Now	there	
ni'io't	o'hĕⁿ'sĕñk	shagodiiä'dĕⁿ''häwäs	he''tkĕⁿ'	o''nï'	shagodi	7
so it is	day after day	they her person carried customarily	up high	also	they her caused	
dĕⁿ'sthä'.	Hiiä''	de'aoñni'she'i'	o'nĕⁿ'	ga'oⁿ'hwä'	wä'oñdadie'nä-	8
to stand.	Not	it lasted (long)	now	she herself	she herself helped to do it	
wä's	wä'eiä''thĕⁿ'	tca''	noñ'we'	tga''hä'	ne''	hawĕⁿ'he'ioⁿ'. 9
herself	she climbed up	the where	the place	there it up-lay	the	he is dead.
Ne''tho'	ni'io't	ekdoⁿ''ne's	diiot'goñt.			10
There	so it is	she it customarily went to see	at all times.			
Gaiñ'gwä'	nwä'oñni'she'	o'nĕⁿ'	ne''tho'	nwä'awĕⁿ''hä'	doñda	11
Some (time)	so it lasted	now	thus	so it came to pass	thence	
ioⁿ'kwe'nĕⁿ''dä'	tcie'hä'wï'	iĕⁿ'nĕñtcha'nhäs'thä'	gara'djï',	nä''		12
again she descended	she it brought again	one it uses for armlet	it is called,	that one		
noñwä'ho''dĕⁿ'	hi'iä'	hotnĕñtcha'nhä''hoⁿ'	ne''	hawĕⁿ'he'ioⁿ',		13
kind of thing,	verily,	he his arm has wrapped around (plurally)	the	he is dead,		
otko''ä'	nonwä'ho''dĕⁿ,	oiä'ne',	iä'kĕⁿ'.	Wä'ä'hĕñ''	ne''	14
it wampum	kind of thing,	it (is) fine,	it is said.	She it said	the	

The elder one said: "What manner of thing caused thee to remove it?" The girl child replied, saying: "My father said: 'Do thou remove it. It will belong to thee. I, verily, am thy parent.'" The elder one said nothing more. It continued thus that customarily, as soon as another day came, she would again climb to the place where the burial-case lay. So, now, verily, all those who were in the lodge paid no more attention to her, merely watching her grow in size. Thus it continued that day after day, at all times, she continued to go to see it [the corpse]. They heard them conversing, it is said, and they also heard, it is told, what the two said. After a while she again came down bringing with her a necklace which the dead man-being had had around his neck, and which she had removed. She, it is reported, said: "Oh, my grandmother! My father gave this to me; that is the reason I

1	gok'stĕñ'ä': she elder one:	"Ho't "What (is it)	noñwä'ho''dĕⁿ' kind of thing	dāioi'hwä''khe' it is reason of it	tca'' the where	wäskä'' thou didst
2	tciä'?" remove it."	Dāiei'hwä'sä'gwä' She it replied	ne'' the	eksä''ä' she child	wä'ä''hĕñ': she it said:	"G'ni'hä'' "My father
3	wä'bĕⁿ'hĕñ'', he it said,	'Sgä''tciä'. 'Do thou it remove.	I's Thou	ĕⁿsa'wĕⁿk. thou it wilt own.	I' I (it is),	bi'iä' verily,	goñ'hä'wä'.'" I thy parent am.'"
4	Hiiä'' Not (it is)	stĕⁿ'' anything	de'tciaga'wĕⁿ' again she it said	ne'' the	gok'stĕñ'ä'. she elder-one.	Ne''tho' Thus	ni'io't so it is
5	gĕⁿ's customarily	ganio'' so soon as	wä'o'hĕⁿ''nhä' it day became	o'nĕⁿ' now	he'' again	sāieä''thĕⁿ' again she climbed up	tca'' the where	noñ'we' the place
6	tga'hoⁿ'sä''hä'. there it case up-lay.	Da', So,	o'nĕⁿ' now,	hi'iä' verily,	tca'' the where	ni'hĕñ'nädī' so they (m.) are many in number	nĕ'' the
7	ganoⁿ'sgoñ'wä' it lodge in	hĕñni''dĕñ' they (m.) abide	hiiä'' not	de'shoññasdei'sdī', they (m.) again pay attention to it,	ne''tho' there
8	gĕñ'gwä' only	de'hadiga''hä' they (m.) their eyes had on it	tca'' the where	gododi'ha'die'. she continued to grow.	Ne''tho' There	ni'io't so it is
9	diiot'goñt at all times	heioñtgat'hwäs thither she went to see it	o'hĕⁿ''sĕñk. day after day.	Hoññathoñ'de', They (m.) it heard,	iä'kĕⁿ, it is said,
10	de'hodi'thä', they (m.) conversed,	hoññathoñ'de' they (m.) it heard	o''nī', also,	iä'kĕⁿ, it is said,	ne'' the	stĕⁿ'' anything	gwä'' seemingly
11	noñwä'ho''dĕⁿ kind of thing	de'hia'doⁿk. they two (m.) kept saying.	Diĕñ''hä' Suddenly,	gwä'' seemingly,	o'nĕⁿ' now	he'' again
12	doñdāioⁿ'kwe'nĕⁿ''dä' thence she again descended	tcie'ha'wī' she it brought again	ne'' the	ioⁿ'ni'diäs'thä' one uses it as a necklace	ne'' the
13	ho'diĕñ''nä' he had had it around his neck	ne'' the	hawĕⁿ'he'ioⁿ', he is dead,	nä'ie' that (it is)	oⁿ''kĕⁿ this time,	gogä'tciĕñ'ha'die'. she came, having removed it.
14	Wä'ä'hĕñ'', She it said,	iä'kĕⁿ: it is said:	"Gso'dä'hä', "My grandmother,	g'ni'hä'' my father	wä'ha'gwĕⁿ he it gave to me	nĕñ'gĕⁿ' this (it is);
15	nä'ie' that (it is)	gäi'hoññiä''hä' it it causes	wä'kgä''tciä'." I it removed."	O'nĕⁿ,' Now,	iä'kĕⁿ, it is said,	tca'' the where

re loved it." So, it is reported, until the time she was full-grown she was in the habit of going to view the place where lay the burial-case.

At that time, it is reported, her father said: "Now, my child, verily, thou hast grown to maturity. Moreover, I will decide upon the time when thou shalt marry." Some time afterward he said: "Thou must tell thy mother, saying: 'My father said to me, "Now thou must marry."' Now, moreover, verily, thy mother must bake loaves of bread, and it must fill a large forehead-strap-borne basket. Now, moreover, thou must take the bread, and thou must have it ready by the time it becomes night."

Truly, it this came to pass. It became night, and, verily, the elder one had it all ready. She said: "I have now made it ready. The basket is even now full of bread." Now, the maiden again climbed

nwä'oñni'she'	heiagodo'dï'	ne''tho'	ekdo^n''ne's.	tca''	ıoñ'we'	1
so (long) it lasted	thither she grew to full size	there.	she it went habitually to see	the where	the place	
tga''hä'	ne''	ga'ho^n''sä'.				2
there it up-lay	the	it case (burial-case).				
Tho''ge',	iä'kĕ^n',	o'nĕ$^{n\iota}$	wä'hĕ$^{n\iota}$hĕñ''	ne''	ago'ni''hä':	"O'nĕ$^{n\iota}$	3
At that (time),	it is said,	now	he it said	the	her father:	"Now (it is)	
ɔi'iä'	goñ'ha'wä'	wä'sadodiä'gä'.	I''	di''	ĕ^{n}tgĕñno$^{n\iota}$'do^n	gaiñ''	4
verily,	I thy parent am	thou hast grown up.	I (it is)	more-over	I it shall will (decide it).	where	
niga'ha'wï'	tca''	ĕ^{n}sania'khe'."	Gaiñ'gwä'	nwä'oñni'she'	o'nĕ$^{n\iota}$	5
there it bears it (the time)	the where	thou wilt marry."	Some (time)	so (long) it lasted	now	
wä'hĕ^n'hĕñ'':	"Ĕ^n'sheiatho'iĕ^n'	ne''	sano''hä'	ĕ^n'si'hĕñ'',	'Wä'ha-	6
he it said:	"Thou her wilt tell	the	thy mother	wilt thou it say,	'He addressed	
goñ'hăs	g'ni'hä''.	O'nĕ$^{n\iota}$	ĕ^{n}sania'khe'.'"	O'nĕ$^{n\iota}$	di''	hi'iä'	7
me, saying,	my father.	Now	wilt thou marry.'"	Now,	more-over,	verily,	
ĕ^{n}ie'hä'goñniä''hĕñ'	ne''	sano''hä',	iä'ie''	ne''	ĕ^{n}gä'ä''seik	8
she bread will make repeatedly	the	thy mother,	that (it is)	the	it will fill a basket	
oñtge'da's'thä'	gä'ä''sä'.	O'nĕ$^{n\iota}$	di''	ĕ^{n}shä'goñ'niä'	ĕ^{n}säiĕñnĕñdä''ik	9
one bears it by the forehead-strap	it basket.	Now,	more-over,	thou bread wilt make	thou it wilt have ready	
tca''	niga'ha'wï'	ne''	ĕ^{n}io''gak"			10
the where	there it it bears (time)	the	it will be dark."			
Do'gĕ^{n}s	ne''tho'	ıwä'awĕ^n''hä'	Wä'o''gak	o'nĕ$^{n\iota}$	hi'iä'	11
It is true	thus	so it came to pass.	It became might	now,	verily,	
gagwe'gï'	gäiĕñnĕñdä''ï'	ne''	gok'stĕñ'ä'.	Wä'ä'hĕñ'':	"O'nĕ$^{n\iota}$	12
it all	she it had ready	the	she elder one (is).	She it said:	"Now	
wä'gadadeiĕñnĕñdä''nhä'.	O'nĕ$^{n\iota}$	gä'ä''sei'	ne''	o'hä''gwä'"		13
I my preparations have finished.	Now	it basket (is) full	the	it bread."		
O'nĕ$^{n\iota}$	ne''	nä''	ne''	eksä'go'nä'	säieä''thĕ^n'	tca''	noñ'we'	14
Now	that one	the that	that one	she maiden	again she up-climbed	the where	the place	

up to the place where lay the burial-case. At that time they heard her say: "My mother has now made everything ready." He then replied: "To-morrow thou must depart; early in the morning thou must depart. The distance from here to the place where lives the one whom thou wilt marry is such that thou wilt spend one night on thy way thither. And he is a chief whom thou art to marry, and his name, by repute, is He-holds-the-earth."

Now the next day she dressed herself. As soon as she was ready she then again ran, going again to the place where lay the dead man-being. Then she told him, saying: "The time for me to depart has arrived." Now, at that time he told her, saying: "Do thou have courage. Thy pathway throughout its course is terrifying, and the reason that it is so is that many man-beings are traveling to and fro along this pathway. Do not, moreover, speak in reply if

1	tga'hon'sä''hä'. there it burial-case up-lies.	O'nĕn' Now	hoñnathoñ'de' they (m.) it heard	tca'' the where	wă'ă'hĕñ'': she it said:	"O'nĕn' "Now
2	wă'eiĕñnĕñdä''nhä' she her preparations has finished	ne'' the	agro'·bă'.'' my mother."	Tho''ge' At that (time)	o'nĕn' now	ni'ha'wĕñ'· thence he replied:
3	"Ĕnio'hĕn''nhä' "It will become day (tomorrow)	o'nĕn' now	ĕnsa'dĕñ'diă'. thou wilt depart.	Hĕn'ge''djĭk Early in the morning	o'nĕn' now	ĕnsa' thou wilt
4	dĕñ'diă'. depart.	Sga'dă' One it is	ĕnsĕñnon·hwe'tciă' thou wilt stay over night	tca'' the where	niio'we' so it is distant ·	tganadā'iĕn' there it village lies
5	tca'' the where	noñ'we· the place	thana'gee' there he dwells	ne'' the	ĕndjinia'khe'. ye two will marry.	Hä'sĕñnowa'nĕn' He is a chief
6	rā'ie' that (it is)	ne'' the	ĕndjinia'khe', ye two will marry.	Haon·hwĕñdjiawä''gĭ' He-it-earth-holds		ni'ha'sĕñ'no''dĕn'." such his name (is) kind of."
7	Wă'o'hĕn''nhä' It became day	tho''ge· at that (time)	o'nĕn' now	wă'oñde·sĕñ'niă'. she herself dressed.	Ganio'' So soon as	wă'oñ- she made
8	de''să herself ready	o'nĕn' now	tho''ge· at that (time)	doñsāioñā''dat thither again she ran	ne''tho' there	nhoñsā'iĕn' tca' thither again the she went where
9	noñ'we· the place	tga'hon'sä''hä' there it burial-case up-lies	ne'' the	hawĕn'he'ion·. he is dead.	Tho''ge' At that (time)	wă'honwa · she told
10	tho'iĕn' him	wă'ă'hĕñ'': she it said:	"O'nĕn' "Now	hwä'ga'he''g it has arrived	tca'' the where	o'nĕn' ŏnga'- now . I shall
11	dĕñ'diă'." depart."	Tho''ge· At that (time)	o'nĕn' now	wă'shagotho'iĕn' he her told	wă'hĕn'hĕñ'': she it said:	"Djia'kĕn'. "Do thou have courage.
12	Deiodenon·hiani''dĭ' It is terrifying	tca'' the where	roñ'we· the place	nheiotha'hi'noñ· thither it path has its course	nā'ie' that (it is)	ne'' the
13	nā'ie· that (it is)	găi·hoñniă''hă' it it causes	tca'' the where	ne''tho' there	ni'io't so it is	tca'' deiagoñnada- the they (anthr.) travel where
14	wĕñ'ie· in numbers	tca'' the where	roñ'we' the place	nheiotha'hi'noñ' thither it path has its course	hoñnatgă'de' they are numerous	ne'' oñ'gwe'. the man-being.

so 1 e ɔeɪsoɪ. whoeʌeɪ he may be, addɪesses woɪds to thee. Aɪd wheɪ thoʋ hast goɪe one half of thy joɪɪney, thou wilt coɪe to a ɪiʌeɪ theɪe, and, ɪoɪeoʌeɪ, the floatiɪg log wheɪeoɪ ɔeɪsoɪs cross is ɪaple. Wheɪ thoʋ dost aɪɪiʌe theɪe, theɪ thoʋ wilt kɪow that thoʋ art halfway oʋ thy joɪɪney. Theɪ thoʋ wilt cɪoss the ɪiʌeɪ, and also pass oɪ. Thoʋ ɪʋst coɪtiɪʋe to tɪaʌel withoʋt iɪteɪɪʋɔtioɪ. Aɪd thoʋ wilt haʋe tɪaʌeled soɪe tiɪe ɔefoɪe thoʋ arrivest at the place wheɪe thoʋ wilt see a laɪge field. Thoʋ wilt see theɪe, ɪoɪeoʌeɪ, a lodge staɪdiɪg ɪot far away. Aɪd theɪe beside the lodge staɪds the tɪee that is called Tooth.[a] Noɪeoʌeɪ, the ɔlossoɪs this staɪdiɪg tɪee ɔeaɪs caʋse that woʋld to be light, ɪakiɪg it light foɪ the man-beiɪgs dwelliɪg theɪe.

'Ä́'gwi·	dī''	dĕⁿtcada'diä·	do'gä·t	hi'iä·	ĕⁿiesawĕñna''nhä·	ne''	1
Do it not,	more-over,	thou wilt speak in reply	if it be so,	verily,	one thee words will address to	the	
soñ·'	gwä''	noñwa·ho''dĕⁿ·.	Nä'ie·	ne''	tca·'	dewa·sĕñ'noⁿ·	tca·''	2
who	seemingly	kind of person.	That (it is)	the	the where	it half is	the where	
niio'we·	nhĕⁿ·'se·	ne''tho·	tgĕⁿ·biⁿoⁿ·hwädä'die·,	ɪä'ie·	dī''	ne''	3
so it is distant	thither thou wilt be going	there	there it river extends itself along,	that (it is)	more-over	the	
o·hwa·''dä·	ne·''	gaĕñ'do·	tca·''	ɪoñ'we·	deieia·hiä''kthä·.	Ne''	4
it maple	the	it log floats	the where	the place	one uses it stream to cross.	The	
o'nĕⁿ·	ne''tho·	ɔĕⁿ·'sioⁿ·	o'nĕⁿ·	ĕⁿ·seä''	o'nĕⁿ·	tca·''	dewa·sĕñ'noⁿ·	5
now	there	there thou wilt arrive	now	thou wilt conclude	now	the where	it middle is	
nhwä''ge·.	Tho''ge·	o'nĕⁿ·	dĕⁿ·'siia''hiä·k.	ĕⁿsadoñgo''dä·	o'nī·.		6
there I am going.	At that (time)	now	thou stream wilt cross,	thou wilt pass on	also.		
Heɪotgoñdä·''gwī·	ĕⁿ·sa·'dĕñdioñ·hä'die·.	Nä'ie·	ne''	gaiñ'gwä·			7
Without interruption	thou wilt continue to travel on.	That (it is)	the	some (time)			
nĕⁿioñni'she·	tca·''	hĕⁿsatha·hi'ne·	o'nĕⁿ··	ha·'sä·	ne''tho·	hĕⁿ·'sioⁿ·		8
so it will last	the where	thither thou wilt be traveling	now	just then	there	there thou wilt arrive		
tca·''	ɪoñ'we·	ĕⁿsatgat·hwä·',	ĕⁿshĕñdagĕⁿ·''nhä·	ɪä'ie·	ne''	tga-		9
the where	the place	thou it wilt see,	thou a clearing (field) wilt see	that (it is)	the	there		
·hĕñdäiĕⁿ·'gowa'nĕⁿ·.	Ĕⁿsgĕⁿ·''nhä·	dī''	ne''tho·	gwä·''tho·	tganoⁿ·-		10
it field lies great.	Thou it wilt see,	more-over,	there	near by	there it		
sä'iĕⁿ·.	Nä'ie·	ne''	ganoⁿ·'säk'dä·	ne''tho·	gä·'he·	ɪä'ie·	ne''	11
lodge lies.	That (it is)	the	it lodge beside	there	it tree stands	that (it is)	the	
Oɪo''djä·[a]	gaĕñdäia'djī·.	Nä'ie·	ne''	dī''	tca·''	awĕⁿ·ha·ha'gī·		12
It Tooth	it tree (is) called.	That (it is)	the	more-over	the where	it is full of flowers		
nĕñ'gĕⁿ·	gä·'he·	tca·''	ne''tho·	diioⁿ·hwĕñdjiä'de·	deio·hathe''dī·,		13
this (it is)	it tree stands	the where	there	there it world (earth) is present	it it causes to be light,		
ɪä'ie'	ne''	ɪä'ie·	de·hodi·hathe''däni·	tca·''	ne''tho·	ena'gee·		14
that (it is)	the	that (it is)	it it them causes to be light for	the where	there	they dwell		
ne''	oñ'gwe·							15
the	man-being.							

---

[a] Probably the yellow dog-tooth violet, Erythronium americanum.

"Such, in kind, is the tree that stands beside the lodge. Just there is the lodge of the chief whom thou art to marry, and whom his people call He-holds-the-earth. When thou enterest the lodge, thou wilt look and see there in the middle of the lodge a mat spread, and there, on the mat, the chief lying down. Now, at that time, thou shalt lay thy basket down at his feet, and, moreover, thou shalt say: 'Thou and I marry.' He will say nothing. When it becomes night, he who is lying down will spread for thee a skin robe at the foot of his mat. There thou wilt stay over night. As soon as it is day again, he will say: 'Do thou arise; do thou work. Customarily one who lives in the lodge of her spouse works.' Then, verily, thou must work. He will lay down a string of corn ears and, moreover, he will say: 'Thou must soak the corn and thou must make mush.' At that time

1	"Ne"tho' Thus	nigaëndo''dĕⁿ' so it tree (is) kind of	tca" the where	ganonˢăk'dă' it lodge beside	gă''he'. it tree stands.	Ne"tho' There
2	gwă" seemingly	ni'hononˢă'iĕⁿ' there his lodge stands	ne" the	ha'sĕñnowa'nĕⁿ' he chief (is)	ne" the	ĕⁿdjinia'khe', ye two will marry,
3	Haoⁿ'hwĕñdjiawă''gī' He-it-earth-holds		hoñwană'doⁿ''khwă' they him designate thereby	ne" the	haoñgwe'dă'. his people.	Ne" The
4	o'nĕⁿ' now	ne"tho' there	ɔĕⁿ''sioⁿ' there thou wilt arrive	ne" the	ganoⁿsgoñ'wă' it lodge in	ĕⁿsatgat'hwă' thou it wilt see	tca" the where
5	hă'deganoⁿs'hĕⁿ' just it lodge in middle of	ĕⁿsgĕⁿ''nhă' thou it wilt see	ne"tho' there	ganak'doⁿ', it mat (bed) is spread,	nă'ie' that (it is)	ne" the
6	ne"tho' there	ganakdă''ge' it mat on	hĕndă'gă' he lies	ne" the	ha'sĕñnowa'nĕⁿ'. he chief.	Tho''ge' At that time
7	o'nĕⁿ' now	ne"tho' there	ĕⁿsat'ă'ˢă'iĕñ' thou thy basket wilt lay	tca" the where	ioñ'we' the place	hă'de'ha'si'dăge''hĕñ', just (where) his two feet are lying,
8	ĕⁿ'si'hĕñ'' thou it wilt say,	di'': moreover:	' Wă'oñginia'khe'.' 'Thou I marry now'	Hiiă'' Not (it is)	stĕⁿ'' anything	tha'hĕⁿ''hĕñ''. he it will say.
9	Ne" The	o'nĕⁿ' now	ĕⁿio''gak it will become night	ră'ie' that (it is)	ne" the	tca" the where	hĕndă'gă' he lies	ie'tho' there	ĕⁿhiĕⁿ'sō'wäs he will spread for thee a mat (bark)
10	tca" the where	ioñ'we' the place	hă'de'ha'si'dade'nioⁿ'. just where his two feet end.	Ne"tho' There,	di'' moreover,	ĕⁿsĕñnoⁿ''hwet thou wilt stay over night.
11	Ganio'' So soon as	ĕⁿio'hĕⁿ''nhă' it will be day	o'nĕⁿ' now	se" it is a matter of fact	ĕⁿ'hĕⁿ'hĕñ'': he it will say:	' Satgĕⁿ''hă'. ' Do thou arise.
12	Săio'dĕⁿ''hă'. Do thou work.	Goio''de' She works	gĕⁿ's customarily	tca" the where	e'hnĕⁿ''hwăs'hĕⁿ'.' she abides with her husband's family.'	Tho''ge' At that (time)
13	o'ɪĕn' now,	ɔi'iă' verily	ĕⁿsăio'dĕⁿ''hă'. thou wilt work.	Onĕⁿ''hă' It corn	ĕⁿ'ba'stĕⁿ'ˢă'iĕñ', he a string of it will lay down,	ĕⁿ'hĕⁿ'hĕñ'' he it will say,
14	di'': moreover:	' Ĕⁿsenĕⁿ'banawĕⁿ''dă', 'Thou it corn wilt soak,		ĕⁿsdjisgoñ'nia'.' thou mush wilt make.'	Tho''ge' At that (time)	odjisdă''ge' it fire on

there will be a kettle of water set on the fire. As soon as it boils
so that it is terrifying, thou must dissolve the real therein. It must
be boiling when thou takest the rush. He himself will speak,
saying: 'Do thou undress thyself.' Moreover, thou must there
undress thyself. Thou must be in thy bare skin. Nowhere wilt thou
have any garment on thy body. Now, the rush will be boiling, and
the rush will be hot. Verily, on thy body will fall in places the
spattering mush. He will say: 'Thou must not shrink back from
it;' moreover, he will have his eyes fixed on thee there. Do not
shrink back from it. So soon as it is cooked, thou shalt speak,
saying: 'Now, verily, it is cooked; the rush is done.' He will arise,
and, moreover, he will remove the kettle, and set it aside. Then,
he will say: 'Do thou seat thyself on this side.' Now then, he
will say: 'My slaves, ye dogs, do ye two come hither.' They two are

o'hne'ganos̈	ěⁿganä'djio'dak.	Ganio''	ěⁿdiowiiä‘hěⁿ‘‘hä'		ne''tho‘	1
It water (fresh)	It kettle will sit.	So soon as	It will up-boil		there	
tca''	deiodenoⁿ‘hiani‘''di‘	o'něⁿ‘	ne''tho‘	ne''	othe''tchä'	2
the where	It is terrifying	now	there	the	it meal (flour)	
hěⁿ‘‘sok.	Děⁿdiowiiä‘hěⁿ‘‘sek	ne''	o'něⁿ‘	ěⁿsdjĭsgoñ'niä'	Ha'oⁿ‘	3
there thou it wilt immerse.	It will be up-boiling	the	now	thou mush wilt make.	He himself	
hwä'	ěⁿthadä'diä'	ěⁿ‘hěⁿ‘hěñ'';	'Sadadiä'dawi'dä‘''siä‘.'		Ne''tho‘	4
	he will speak	he it will say:	'Do thou thyself disrobe.'		There	
dī''	ěⁿsadadiä'dawi'dä‘''siä'.	Sa'nesda'goⁿks	ěⁿgěñ'k.	Hiiä‘''	gat'kä'	5
moreover.	thou thyself wilt disrobe.	Thou thy bare skin wilt be in	it will be.	Not (it is)	anywhere	
dä'děⁿdjisadiä'dawi''dĭk.	O'něⁿ‘	ne''	odjĭs‘gwä'	ěⁿdiowiiä‘hěⁿ‘‘sek,		6
thou wilt be robed.	Now	the	it mush	it will be up-boiling,		
o‘dai‘‘hěñ‘	ěⁿgěⁿ‘ks	ne''	odjĭs‘gwä'.	Siä'di''ge‘	hi'iä'	hěⁿgaä''	7
it is hot	it will be	the	it mush.	Thy body on	of course	it will become at-	
sěñ'	tca''	ěⁿwatdjĭsgwadoñ'gwä'.	Ěⁿ‘hěⁿ‘hěñ'';	'Hiiä‘''	thoñdäsa	8
tached the to it	where	it itself mush will splatter.	He it will say:	'Not (it is)	thou shouldst	
doⁿ''tkä‘.'	Ne''tho‘	dī''	děⁿiesagä‘''hä'k.	'Ä''gwī'	thoñdä‘sadoⁿ''tkä‘	9
flinch from it.'	There,	moreover,	he his two eyes will have on thee.	Do not do it	thou shouldst flinch from it.	
Ganio''	ěⁿgä'ik	o'něⁿ‘	děⁿtcada'diä'	ěⁿsi‘‘hěñ'';	'O'něⁿ‘	hi'iä'	10
So soon as	it will be cooked	now	thou wilt speak	thou wilt say:	'Now,	verily,	
wä'gä'ik,	wä'gadjĭs‘gwäik.'	Děⁿthatgěⁿ‘''hä',	o'něⁿ‘	dī''	ěⁿhonä'-	11
it is cooked,	it mush is cooked.'	Thence he will up-rise,	now	moreover	he will remove	
djioda'gwä',	si''	bägwä'dī‘	ěⁿ‘hä'iěⁿ‘.	Tho''ge‘	o'něⁿ‘	ěⁿ‘hěⁿ‘-	12
the set kettle,	yonder far	side of it	he it will set down.	At that (time)	now	he it will	
hěñ'';	"Sadiěñ‘'	něⁿ‘'	bägwä'dī‘.''	Tho‘'ge‘	o'něⁿ‘	ěⁿ‘hěⁿ‘hěñ''.	13
say:	"Do thou sit	here	side of it."	At that (time)	now	he it will say:	
'Agetchěněⁿ''shoⁿ',	dji‘hä',	gä'e‘	doñde'sne‘.'	Agwa's	degni		14
'My slaves several,	dogs,	hither	do ye two come.'	Very	they (z.) two		

very large. As soon as they two arrive he will say: 'Do ye two lick her body where the rush has fallen on it.' And their tongues are like rough bark. They will lick thee, going over thy whole body, all along thy body. Blood will drop from the places where they will lick. Do not allow thy body to flinch therefrom. As soon as they two finish this task he will say: 'Now, do thou again put on thy raiment.' Now, moreover, thou must again dress thyself completely At that time he will take the basket and set it down, saying, moreover: 'Now, thou and I marry.' So now, so far as they are concerned, the dogs, his slaves, they two will eat." That is what the dead man being told her.

It became night. Now, at that time, they verily laid their bodies down, and they slept. It became day, and the sun was present yonder when the maiden departed. She bore on her back by the forehead strap her basket of bread. Now, verily, she traveled with a rapid

	gowa'nĕⁿ‘.	Ganio"	dĕⁿgni'ioⁿ·	o'nĕⁿ·	ĕⁿ‘hĕⁿ‘hĕñ":	'Etchikā'nĕñt
1	are large.	So soon as	they two will arrive	now	he it will say:	'Do ye two lick her
2	nā'ie' that (it is)	ne" the	iagodjĭsgwă‘hi"soⁿ·' it mush has fallen on her in places.'	Nā'ie' That (it is)	ne" the	tca" the where	awĕⁿ'na·'să' (their) tongues
3	gaĕñ'wā' it rough bark (file)	ni'io‘t. so it is.	Ĕⁿsakā'nĕñt They thee will lick	ĕⁿgni'să' they (z.) it two will finish	ne" the	siă'dagwe'gĭ‘, thy body entire,	
4	siă'dă'ge"shoⁿ·. thy body on along.	Dĕⁿtgatkwĕⁿ'sa‘hi"nhă' Thence it blood will drop	tca" the where	noñ'we· the place	ĕⁿgnikā'nĕñt. they (z.) two will lick (it).		
5	'Ă‘'gwĭ· Do it not,	dĭ" moreover,	dĕⁿtcadadiă'doⁿ"tkă‘. thou wilt flinch from it with thy body.	Ganio" So soon as	ĕⁿgni"să they (z.) two will finish it	o'nĕⁿ now	
6	ĕⁿ‘hĕⁿ‘hĕñ": he it will say:	'O'nĕⁿ‘ 'Now	sasadiă'dawi"dă‘.' again do thou dress thyself.'	O'nĕⁿ‘ Now	dĭ" moreover,	ĕⁿtca'sei"să' thou thyself wilt re-dress	
7	gagwe'gĭ‘. it all.	Tho"ge‘ At that (time)	o'nĕⁿ‘ now	dĕⁿ‘hă'ă'să"gwă' he it basket will take up	si" yonder far	hăgwā'dĭ' side of it	
8	ĕⁿ‘hā'iĕⁿ", he it will set,	ĕⁿ‘hĕⁿ‘hĕñ" he it will say	dĭ": more-over,	'O'nĕⁿ‘ 'Now	wă'oñginia'khe·.' thou I marry.'	Da', So,	o'nĕⁿ‘ now
9	ne" the	nă" that one that	ne" the	dji‘‘hă‘ dogs	·ne" the	hotchenĕⁿ"shoⁿ· his slaves several	dĕⁿgiadekhoñ'niă·." they (z.) two will eat."
10	Nă" That (it is)	wă‘hĕⁿ‘hĕñ" he it said	ne" the	hawĕⁿ‘he'ioⁿ‘. he is dead.			
11	Wă'o"gak. It became night.	Tho"ge‘ At that (time)	o'nĕⁿ‘ now	bi'iă' verily	wă'hoñdiiă'dăge"hĕñ', they their bodies laid down,	o'nĕⁿ, now	
12	wă'hoñnă"gak. they (m.) went to sleep.	Wă'o‘hĕⁿ"nhă' It became day	si" yonder	tgaä"gwă' there it orb of light rested	tho"ge‘ at that (time)	o'nĕⁿ‘ now	
13	go'dĕñ'dioñ‘ she departed	ne" the	eksă'go'nă‘. she maiden.	Wă'oñtge"dat She bore it by the forehead-strap,	bi'iă' verily,	ne" the	go'ă"să' her basket
14	ne" the	o‘hä"gwă'. it bread.	O'nĕⁿ‘ Now,	hi'iă' verily,	oñtha‘hi'ne' she traveled onward	eianoä'die'. her gait was rapid.	Hiiă" Not (it is)

gait. It was not long before she was surprised to find a river. There beside the river she stood, thinking, verily, "I have lost my way." At that time she started back. Not long afterward those who abode in the home lodge were surprised that the maiden returned. She said: "I believe I have lost my way." Now she laid her basket on the mat, and, moreover, she again ran thither and again climbed up to the place where lay the burial-case. So soon as she reached it she said: "Oh, father! I believe that I lost my way." He said: "What is the character of the land where thou believest that thou lost thy way?" "Where people habitually cross the river, thence I returned," said the maiden. She told him everything. She said: "A maple log floats at the place where they habitually cross the river." He said: "Thou hast not lost thy way." She replied: "I think the distance to the place where the river is seen is too short, and that is the reason that I think

---

de'aoñni'she'ï'	o'nĕⁿ·	wä'oñdiĕñ''hä'	gwä''	ne''tho'	gĕⁿ·hioⁿ·hwä-	1
it lasted (long)	now	she was surprised	seemingly	there	it river had its course	
dä'die'.	O'nĕⁿ·	ne''tho'	gĕⁿ·hioⁿ·hwäk'dä'	wä'diedä''nhä'	ne''	2
along (there).	Now	there	it river beside	she stopped	the	
wä'eñ'ä'	o'nĕⁿ·	hi'iä'	wä'gadiä'dä''doⁿ.	Tho''ge'	o'nĕⁿ·	säioⁿk'dä'	3
she did believe	now,	verily,	I my way (my person) have lost.	At that (time)	now	she turned back.
Hiiä''	de'aoñnis'he'ï·	o'nĕⁿ·	ne''	tca''	tganoⁿsä'iĕⁿ·	theñni''dĕñ'	4
Not (it is)	it lasted (long)	now	the	the where	there it lodge	there they (m.) abide
wä'hoñdiĕñ''hä'	gwä''	säie'ioⁿ·	ne''	eksä'go'nä'.	Wä'ä·hĕñ'':	5
they (m.) were surprised	seemingly	again she returned	the	she maiden (is).	She it said:	
"Ge''he'	wä'gadiä'dä''doⁿ.''	Onĕⁿ·	ganakdä''ge'	wä'oñt'ä'sä'iĕñ',	6
"I it think	I lost my way (my person).''	Now	it mat on	she her basket laid.	
ne''tho·	di'.	tciedäk'he',	säieä''thĕⁿ·	tca''	noñ'we'	tga·hoⁿsä''hä'.	7
there	moreover	again she ran,	again she climbed up	the where	the place	there it case up-lies.
Ganio''	ne''tho·	hwä'e'ioⁿ·	o'nĕⁿ·	wä'ä·hĕñ'':	"G'ni'hä'',	ge''he'	8
So soon as	there	there she arrived	now	she it said:	"My father,	I it think
wä'gadiä'dä''doⁿ.''	Wä'hĕⁿ·hĕñ'':	"Ho't	niioⁿ·hwĕñdjio''dĕⁿ·	tca''	9
I lost my way (my person).''	He it said:	"What (it is)	so it earth is kind of	the where	
noñ''we·	tca''	se''he',	Wä'gadiä'dä''doⁿ?''	"Didieia·hiak'thä'	tca''	10
the place	the where	thou it thinkest,	I lost my way (my person)?''	"There where they use it to cross river	the where	
tgĕⁿ·hioⁿ·hwädä'die'	ne''tho·	doñdagäk'dä'.	wä'ä·hĕñ''	ne''	eksä'-	11
there it river has its course	there	thence I turned back again,''	she it said,	the	she	
go'nä'.	Gagwe'gï·	wä'oñtho'iä.	Wä'ä·hĕñ'':	"O·hwä'dä''	ne''	12
maiden, (is).	It all (is)	she it told.	She it said:	"It maple	the	
gaĕñ'do·	tca''	noñ'we·	deieia·hiak'thä'.''	Wä'hĕⁿ·hĕñ'':	"Hiiä''	13
it log floats	the where	the place	one it uses to cross river.''	He it said:	"Not (it is)	
de'säiä'dä''doⁿ·.''	Wä'ä·hĕñ'':	"Ge''he'	swä'djï'k	dosgĕⁿ·hä'	nigĕⁿ·'	14
thou hast lost thy way (thy person).''	She it said:	"I it think	too much	near (it is)	so it is far	

that I lost my way." At that time he said: "The place that I had indicated is far. But thy person is so endowed with magic potence, thou hast in thee so much orenda that it causes thy pace to be swift. Verily, so soon as thou arrivest at the river, thou shalt cross it and also shalt pass on." At that time the maiden said: "Oh, my father, now I depart." "So be it. Moreover, do thou take courage," said the dead man-being in reply. Now she again descended and again went into the lodge.

There then she placed her basket of bread on her back by means of the forehead strap. It was early in the morning when she departed. She had been traveling some time when she was surprised to hear a man-being speak to her, saying: "Do thou stand, verily." She did not stop. Aurora Borealis it was who was talking. She had passed

1. niio'we' tca'' tgĕⁿ'hioⁿ'hwădā'die', nā'ie' gāi'hoñniä''hă' tca''
   so it is / the / there it river has its course, / that (it is) / it it causes / the where

2. ge''he' wă'gadiä'dă''doⁿ'." Tho''ge' wŭ'hĕⁿ'hĕñ'': "I'noⁿ' tca''
   I it think / I lost my way (my person)." / At that (time) / he it said: / "Far (it is) / the where

3. noñ'we' hewagnä''doⁿ'. Ne''tho' gwä'' tca'' nisäiä'dat'goⁿ',
   the place / there I it indicated. / There / seemingly / the where / so thy body (is) magically potent

4. disaëñnoñ'de', nā'ie' gāi'hoñniä''hă' ne'' siano'we'. Ganio'' bi'iä'
   so thou art magical (hast orenda), / that (it is) / it it causes / the / thy gait is rapid. / So soon as / verily

5. hĕⁿ''sioⁿ' tca' noñ'we' tgĕⁿ'hioⁿ'hwădā'die' dĕⁿsia''hiä'k ĕⁿsa
   there thou arrivest / the where / the place / there it river has it course / thou wilt cross river / thou

6. doñgo''dä' o''nī'." Tho''ge' ne'' eksä'go'nä' wä'ä'hĕñ'': "G'ni'hä'',
   wilt pass on / also." / At that (time) / the / she maiden / she it said: / "My father,

7. o'nĕⁿ' wă'ga'dĕñ'diä'." "Nio''. Djia'kĕⁿ' dī'', " ni'ha'wĕñ' ne''
   now / I depart." / "So be it. / Do thou lake courage, / moreover," / so he said in reply / the

8. hawĕⁿ'he'io''' O'nĕⁿ' doñdāioⁿ'kwe'nĕⁿ''dä', ganoⁿsgoñ'wă'
   he is dead. / Now / thence she descended, / it lodge in

9. nhoⁿsä'iĕⁿ'.
   thither again she went.

10. O'nĕⁿ' ne''tho' go'ă''sä' ne'' o'hä''gwä' wă'oñtge''dat
    Now / there / her basket / the / it bread / she bore it by the forehead-strap on her back.

11. Hĕⁿ'ge''djĭk o'nĕⁿ' go'dĕñ'dioñ' Gaiñ'gwä' nwä'oñnis'he' oñtha'
    Early in the morning / now / she departed. / Some (time) / so (long) it lasted / she is

12. hi'ne' o'nĕⁿ' wă'oñdiĕñ''hă' gwä'' oñ'gwe' gothoñ'de' tca''
    traveling / now / she was surprised / seemingly / man-being / she it heard / the where

13. da'hadā'diä', i'ha'doⁿk: "Desdä''nhă' hi'iä'." Hiiä'' dä'deiagodä''ĭ'
    thence he spoke, / he kept saying: / "Do thou stand verily." / Not (it is) / she did stop.

14. Hodoñni''ä', nā'ie' thot'hä'. Gaiñ'gwä' niio'we' godoñgo''dī'
    He Aurora Borealis / that (it is) / thence he is talking. / Somewhat / so it is distant / she passed on

on some distance when she heard another man-being talking to her, saying: "I am thankful that thou hast now again returned home, my child. I am hungry, desiring to eat food." She did not stop. It was Fire Dragon of the Storm who was speaking to her. Sometime after she was again at the place where people customarily crossed the river. Now, at that place, he, the chief himself, stood, desiring to try her mind, saying: "Verily, thou shouldst stop here; verily, thou shouldst rest thyself." She did not stop. She only kept right on, and, moreover, she at once crossed the river there

She traveled on for some time, and when the sun was at yonder height she was surprised that there was spread out there a large field. At that time, verily, she stopped beside the field. Now she looked, and there in the distance she saw a lodge—the lodge of the

o'nĕⁿ·	he''	o'iä'	gothoñ'de'	oñ'gwe‘	tho'thä',	i·ha'doⁿk:	1
now	again	it is other one	she it heard	man-being	thence he is talking	he kept saying:	
"Niiawĕⁿ''·hä'	o'nĕⁿ·	sa·''sioⁿ'',	goñ·ha'wä'.	Aksi's,		ge''·he'	2
"I am thankful (so let it come)	now	again thou hast returned,	I am thy parent.	I am hungry.		I it desire	
agadekhoñ'niä'.''	Hiiä·''	dä'deiagodä''ï‘.		Hadawine'thä'		ne''	nä''	3
I should eat.''	Not (it is)	she did stop.		He Fire-Dragon of Storm		the that	that one	
tho'thä'.	Gaiñ'wä'	nwä'oñni'she'	o'nĕⁿ·	ne''tho·	doñsäiedä''nhä'	4
thence he is talking	Somewhat	so long it lasted	now	there	there again she stood	
tca''	noñ'we‘	deieia·hia'kthä'.	O'nĕⁿ·	ne''tho·	ne''	ha'oⁿhwä'	5
the where	the place	one it uses to ford stream.	Now	there	the	he himself	
ne''	ha·señnowa'nĕⁿ·	ne''tho·	he·ha'dä'',	he·''he'	dä·shago'ni-	6
the	he chief (is)	there	there he stands, .	he desires	he trouble should give	
goⁿ·hä'ĕñ'	ne''	eksä·go'nä',	i·ha'doⁿk:	''Tho'nĕⁿ·	bi'iä'	däsdä''nhä';	7
to her mind	the	she maiden (is).	he kept saying·	"Here (it is)	verily,	thou shouldst stand;	
a·sadoñwi'shĕñ·	hi'iä'.''	Hiiä·''	dä'deiagodä'ï‘.	Nä'ie'	gĕñ'gwä'	8
thou thyself shouldst rest	verily.''	Not (it is)	she did stop.	That (it is)	only	
go‘déñdioñ·ha'die',	iogoñda'die'	dï''	wä'dieia''hiä'k	tca''	ne''tho·	9
she walked right on,	without stopping	more-over	she river crossed	the where	there	
tgĕⁿ·hioⁿ·hwĕdä'die'.						10
there it river has its course.						
Gaiñ'gwä'	nwä'oñnis'be'	oñtha·hi'ne'	o'nĕⁿ·	dï''	si·'	gwä''	11
Somewhat	so long it lasted	she travels on	now	more-over	yonder	seem-ingly	
hegaä·gwä'·hä'	o'nĕⁿ·	wä'oñdiĕñ·'hä'	gwä'.'	ne''tho·	gwä''	12
there it orb of light (sun) rests	now	she was surprised	seem-ingly	there	seem-ingly	
ga·hĕñdädĕⁿ·'dä'	ga·hĕñdowa'nĕⁿ‘.	Tho''ge‘	o'nĕⁿ·	hi'iä'	ga·'-	13
it plain is spread out	it plain large (is)	At that (time)	now	verily	it	
hĕñdäk'dä'	ne''tho·	wä'dieda''nhä'.	O'nĕⁿ·	ne''tho·	wä'oñtgat'-	14
plain beside	there	she stood,	Now	there	she looked	
hwä'	si·'	tganoⁿ·sä'iĕⁿ'	tca''	honoⁿ·sä'iĕⁿ''	ne''	ha·señnowa'nĕⁿ·.	15
yonder		there it lodge lies	the where	his lodge lies	the	he chief (is).	

chief. Verily, she went thither. When she arrived there, she looked, and saw that it was true that beside the lodge stood the tree Tooth, whose flowers were the source of the light of the earth there present, and also of the man-beings dwelling there. Verily, she then entered the lodge. Then she looked, and saw that in the middle of the lodge a mat was spread, and that thereon, moreover, lay the chief. Now, at that time, she removed her pack-strap burden, and then she also set the basket before him, and then, moreover, she said: "Thou and I marry," and then, moreover, she handed the basket to him. He said nothing. When it became night, he spread a mat for her at the foot of his mat, and then, moreover, he said: "Verily, here thou wilt stay overnight." Moreover, it thus came to pass. Now, verily, they laid their bodies down and they slept.

1	Ne''tho‘	hi'iä'	heiagawe'nonˀ.	Ne''	o'nĕⁿ·	ne''tho‘	hwä'e'ionˀ
	There	verily	thither she went.	The	now	there	there she arrived
2	o'nĕⁿ‘	wä'oñtgat'hwä'	ne''tho‘	do'gĕⁿs	gä·'he'	tca''	ganoⁿ'säk'dä'
	now	she looked	there	it is true	it tree stands	the where	it lodge beside
3	ne''	Ono''djä'	nwä'gaeñdo''dĕⁿ'',	nä'ie'	ne''	tca''	deiawĕⁿ·hä·bä'gĭ‘
	the	It Tooth	such it tree kind of is,	that (it is)	the	the where	it full-blown flowers has
4	nä'ie'	deio·hathe'dä''gwĭ‘	tca''	ne''tho‘	diioⁿ·hwĕñdjiä'de',	ne''tho‘
	that (it is)	it uses it to cause it to be light	the where	there	there it earth is present,	there
5	gwä''	o''	ne''	ne''tho‘	enä'gee'	ne''ᵢ	oñ'gwe‘.	O'nĕⁿ·	hi'iä'
	seemingly,	too	the	there	they (indef.) dwell	the	man-being.	Now	verily
6	hwä'e'ionˀ	ne''	ganoⁿ'sgoñ'wä‘.	O'nĕⁿ·	ne''tho‘	wä'oñtga'thwä'
	there she entered	the	it lodge in	Now	there	she it saw
7	tca''	deganoⁿ·'shĕⁿ·	ne''tho·	ganäk'doⁿ''	ne''tho‘	dĭ''	heñdä'gä'
	the where	it lodge center of	there	it mat (bed) is spread	there	moreover	he lay
8	ne''	ba‘señnowa'nĕⁿ‘.	Tho''ge‘	o'nĕⁿ·	wä'oñtge‘da''siä',	o'nĕⁿ‘
	the	he chief (is). (he great-named).	At that (time)	now	she removed her forehead-band	now
9	o·'nĭ	wä'hoñwä'ä‘säiĕñ''häs,	o'nĕⁿ·	dĭ''	wä'ä·hĕñ'':	"Wä'oñginiak'-
	also	she him set basket for,	now	moreover	she it said:	"We two marry,"
10	he‘,"	o'nĕⁿ·	dĭ''	wä'hoñwä'ä‘set'häs	Hiiä·'	stĕⁿ''	de'ha'wĕñ·.	Ne''
		now	moreover	she him handed basket.	Not (it is)	anything	he it said.	The
11	o'nĕⁿ‘	wä'o·'gak	o'nĕⁿ‘	wä'shago·so'·has	tca''	noñ'we‘	hä'de‘bä‘
	now	it became night	now	he for her a mat spread	the where	the place	just his (where)
12	si'däge''hĕñ',	o'nĕⁿ·	dĭ''	wä'hĕⁿ·hĕñ''·	"Tho'nĕⁿ‘	bi'iä'
	feet lie,	now	moreover	he it said:	"Here (it is)	verily
13	ĕⁿsĕñnoⁿ''hwet.''	Ne''tho‘	dĭ''	nwä'awĕⁿ''hä'.	O'nĕⁿ‘	hi'iä'
	thou wilt stay over night."	Thus	moreover,	so it came to pass.	Now	verily
14	wä'hoñdiä'däge''hĕñ',	wä'hoñnä''gak
	they their bodies laid down (to sleep),	they went to sleep.

When day came to the 1, the chief then said: "Do thou arise. Do thou work, moreover. It is customary for one to work who is living in the family of her spouse. Thou must soak corn. Thou must set a pot on the fire. And when it boils, then thou must put the corn therein. Moreover, when it boils, then thou must again remove the pot, and thou must wash the corn. As soon as thou finishest the task thou must then, moreover, pound it so that it will become meal. Now, moreover, thou must make mush. And during the time that it is boiling thou must continue to stir it; thou must do so without interruption after thou hast begun it. Moreover, do not allow thy body to shrink back when the mush spatters. That, moreover, will come to pass. Thou must undress thyself when thou workest. I, as to the rest, will say: 'Now it is cooked.'"

At that time he laid down there a string of corn ears, and the corn was white. So now, verily, she began her work. She undressed her-

Ne"	o'nĕⁿ‘	wa‘hodi‘hĕⁿ"'nha'	o'nĕⁿ‘	wa‘hĕⁿ‘hĕñ"	ne"	ha‘-	1
The	now	it them became day for	now	he it said	the	he-	
sĕnnowa'nĕⁿ‘:	"Satgĕⁿ"'ha'.	Saio‘dĕⁿ"‘ha‘	di'.	Goio‘de'	gĕⁿ's		2
chief (is):	"Do thou arise.	Do thou labor	more-over.	She labors	customarily		
ne"	tca"	e‘hnĕⁿ‘hwas‘hĕⁿ".	Ěⁿsnĕⁿ‘hanawĕⁿ"'da'.	Ěⁿsna‘dja‘‘hĕñ'			3
the	the where	she family of her spouse abides with.	Thou wilt soak corn.	Thou wilt set a kettle			
odjisda"'ge‘.	Ne"	o'nĕⁿ‘	ĕⁿdiowiia‘hĕⁿ"‘ha'	o'nĕⁿ‘	ne"tho‘		4
it fire on.	The	now	it will up-boil	then	there		
hĕⁿsnĕⁿ"‘bok	Ne"	o'nĕⁿ‘	di"	ĕⁿdiowiia‘hĕⁿ"‘ha'	o'nĕⁿ‘	ĕⁿtcna‘dja	5
there thou corn wilt immerse.	The	now	more-over	it will up-boil	now	thou wilt again	
'ha'gwa',	ĕⁿsnĕⁿ‘ho‘ha'e‘.	Ganio"	ĕⁿseiĕnnĕnda"'nha'	o'nĕⁿ‘	di"		6
remove the kettle,	thou corn wilt wash.	So soon as	thou task wilt finish	now	more-over		
ĕⁿsetbe"'da';	othe"'tca'	ĕⁿwa'doⁿ".	O'nĕⁿ‘	bi'ia'	ĕⁿsdjisgoñ'nia'.		7
thou it wilt pound,	it meal	it will become.	Now	verily	thou mush wilt make.		
Na'ie'	ne"	tca"	niga‘ha'wi"	ne"	ĕⁿdiowiia‘hĕⁿ"'sek	dijot'goñt	8
That (it is)	the	the where	there it bears it (time)	the	it will be up-boiling	without stopping	
dĕⁿsawĕñ'iek,	heiotgoñda"'gwi"	ne"	na'ie'	ne"	o'nĕⁿ‘	dĕⁿtca‘-	9
thou wilt keep stirring it,	hence it will be without interruption	the	that (it is)	the	now	there thou it	
sa'wĕⁿ".	'A‘'gwi"	di"	doñda‘sadoⁿ"'tki"	ne"	o'nĕⁿ‘	ĕⁿwasdjisgwa-	10
wilt begin	Do it not	more-over	thence thou shouldst flinch	the	now	it mush will	
doñ'gwa'.	Na'ie'	di"	tca"	nĕniawĕⁿ"'ha'.	Ěⁿsa‘sĕnnia"'sia"	tca"	11
spatter.	That (it is)	more-over	the	so it will come to pass.	Thou thyself wilt undress	the where	
o'nĕⁿ‘	ĕⁿsaio‘dĕⁿ"‘ha'.	I"	ne"	na"	ĕⁿgi‘hĕñ",	'O'nĕⁿ‘	wa‘ga‘ik.'"	12
time	thou wilt work.	I	the	that that one‘	I it will say,	'Now	it is cooked.'"	
Tho‘'ge‘	o'nĕⁿ‘	ne"tho‘	wa‘ha‘stĕⁿ"sa'iĕñ'	ne"	onĕⁿ"‘ha'	na'ie'	13
At that (time)	now	there	he laid corn-string	the	it corn	that (it is)	
ne"	ganĕⁿ"hagĕñ'ada‘.	Da'.	o'nĕⁿ‘	hi'ia'	wa'oⁿ"sa'wĕⁿ".	Wa‘oñdia‘-	14
the	it corn white (is).	So	now	verily	she it began.	She undressed herself,	

self, and now, verily, she was naked. She soaked the corn, and she also washed the corn, and also pounded it, and she also made meal of it, and, now, moreover, in the pot she had set on the fire she made mush. She stirred it without interruption. But, nevertheless, it was so that she was suffering, for, verily, now there was nothing anywhere on her body. And now, moreover, it was evident that it was hot, as the mush spattered repeatedly. Some time after she was surprised that the chief said: "Now, verily, the mush which thou art making is cooked." At that time he arose to a standing position, and also removed the pot, and also set it on yonder side. At that time he said: "Do thou sit here." Now he went forward, and, taking up the basket, he took the bread therefrom, out of her basket. At that time

1 dawi'dä"siä',   o'nĕⁿ‘   hi'iä'   go'nesda'goⁿ'.   Wä'enĕⁿ‘hanawĕⁿ‘'dä'
              now   verily   she is fully naked.   She the corn soaked,

2 wä'enĕⁿ‘ho‘hä'e'   o"nī',   wä'ethe"dä'   o"nī',   wä'ethe'tchi"sä'   o"nī',
   she the corn washed   also   she it pounded   also   she meal finished   also

3 o'nĕⁿ‘   dī"   tca"   gonä'djä'‘hä'   tca"   odjīsdä"ge‘   deiodenoⁿ‘hia
   now   more- the   she had set kettle   the   it fire on   it is terrifying
            over   where   up   where

4 ni"dī‘   diiowiiä'‘hĕⁿs,   o'nĕⁿ‘   hi'iä'   ne"tho‘   wä'edjīsgoñ'niä'.
            it is up-boiling, now   verily   there   she mush made.

5 Heiotgoñdä"gwī‘   deiagowĕñ'ie‘.   Ne"tho‘   ne"   nä'ie'   ni'io‘t   tca"
   Hence it is without   she it stirred.   There   the   that   so it is   the
   interruption   (it is)   where

6 goĕⁿ‘hia'gĕⁿ‘,   o'nĕⁿ‘   hi'iä'   hiiä"   gat'kä'   dä'detga'de'   ne"
   she is suffering. now   verily   not   anywhere   it it is shielding   the
                                        (it is)

7 eiä'di"ge‘.   O'nĕⁿ‘   dī"   ne"tho‘   ni'io‘t   otgĕⁿ"ī‘   o'dai'‘hĕⁿ‘   tca"
   her body on. Now   more- thus   so it is   it is plain   it is hot   the
                          over   where

8 wasdjīsgwadoñ'gwäs.   Gaiñ'sgwä'   nwä'oñnis'he'   o'nĕⁿ‘   wä'oñdiĕñ'‘hä'
   it mush is spattering.   Some (time)   so it lasted   now   she was surprised

9 gwä"   o'nĕⁿ‘   ne"   ha‘sĕñnowa'nĕⁿ‘   wä'hĕⁿ‘hĕñ":   "O'nĕⁿ‘   bi'iä'
   seem-   now   the   he chief is   he it said: "Now   verily
   ingly

10 wä'gadjīs'gwāik   tca"   sadjīsgoñ'ni‘."   Tho"ge‘   o'nĕⁿ‘   doñdä'‘ha-
   it mush is cooked the   thou mush art   At that   now   thence he
                      where   making."   (time)

11 dä"nhä',   wä'banä'djä'‘hä'gwä'   o"nī',   si"   hägwä'dī‘   wä'hä'iĕⁿ"
   arose,   he kettle removed   also,   yon-   side of it   he it set
                                                  der

12 o"nī'.   Tho"ge‘   o'nĕⁿ‘   wä'hĕⁿ‘hĕñ":   "Tho'nĕⁿ"   sadiĕñ"."   O'nĕⁿ‘
   also.   At that   now   be it said: Here   do thou seat   Now
            (time)   thyself."

13 wä'ha'dĕñ'diä',   wä'thä'ä'sä"gwä',   wä'ha'‘hä'gwädä"gwä'   ne"
   he departed,   he basket took up   he bread took out of it   the

14 go'ä'sägoñ'wä'   wädä"gwä'.   Tho"ge‘   o'nĕⁿ‘   ha'wĕñ‘:   "O'nĕⁿ‘
   her basket in   it had been   At that   now   he it has   "Now
                    contained.   (time)   said:

he said: "Now, thou and I marry. Verily, so it seems, thou wert able to do it. Hitherto, no one from anywhere has been able to do it."
Now, at that time he shouted, saying: "My slaves, ye two dogs, do ye two come hither. It is necessary for me that ye two should lick this person abiding here clean of the rush that has fallen on her." Verily, she now looked and saw come forth two dogs, pure white in color and terrifying in size. So now, they two arrived at the place where she was. Now, verily, they two licked her entire body. The tongues of these two were like rough bark. So now, moreover, in whatsoever places they two licked over and along her body blood exuded therefrom. And the maiden did fortify her mind against it, and so she did not flinch from it. As soon as they two completed the task, then he himself took up sunflower oil, and with that, moreover,

---

wā'oṅginia'khe'. thou and I marry.	Wā'sgwe'niă' Thou wast able to do it	hi'iă' verily	nige'·khĕⁿ·'. forsooth is it.	Hiiă'' Not (it is)	gat'kā' any- where	1
de'agogwe'nioñ· one has been able to do it	tca'' the where	nwā'oññis'he'." . so long it has lasted."				2
Tho''ge· At that time	o'nĕⁿ· now	wā'tho'hĕñe''dā' he called aloud		wā'hĕⁿ·hĕñ'': he it said:	"Agetche- " My several	3
nĕⁿ''shoⁿ· slaves,	dji''hā', dogs.	ga'e' hither	doñde'sne' thence do ye two come.	Dewagadoⁿ·hwĕñdjio'niks It is necessary to me		4
aetchika'nĕñt ye two her should lick	tho'nĕⁿ· here	e''dĕñ she abides	godjīsgwā'hi''soⁿ·." it mush on her has fallen iteratively."		O'nĕⁿ· Now	hi'iă' verily	5
wā'oñtgat'hwā' she it saw	dagniiagĕⁿ''nhā' thence they (z.) two came forth	owā'he'sdo'goⁿ· it white pure (is)		thā'tgniiă'do''dĕⁿ· such their (z.) two bod- ies are in kind		6
dji''hā· dogs	deiodenoⁿ·hiani''dī· it is terrifying	degnigowa'nĕⁿ·. they (z.) two (are) large.		Da', So	o'nĕⁿ· now	7
nĕ''tho· there	wā'tgni'ioⁿ· they two arrived	tca'' the where	noñ'we' the place	e''dĕñ. she abides.	O'nĕⁿ· Now	bi'iă' verily	8
wā'tgnika'nĕñt they (z.) it two licked	gagwe'gī· it all	eiā'di'ge''shoⁿ. her body on along.	Nā'ie' That (it is)	ne'' the	gni'nă'si'ge', their (z.) two tongues on	9
ne''tho· there	ni'io't so it is	tca'' the where	ga'ĕñ'wā·. it rough bark (is).	Da', So	o'nĕⁿ· now	dī'' more- over	dagatkwĕⁿ·so thence it blood oozed out	10
doñ'nioñ· plurally	tca'' the where	noñ'we' the place	wā'tgnika'nĕñt they (z.) two licked	eiā'di'ge''shoⁿ. her body on along.	Nā'ie' That (it is)	11
ne'' the	eksā'go'nă' she maiden (is)	godat'nigoⁿ·hä·ni''dī', she has fortified her mind,		hiiă'' not (it is)	dā'dāioñdoⁿ''tkā'. thence she should flinch.	12
Ganio'' So soon as	wā'tgni·'sā' they (z.) two it finished	o'nĕⁿ· now	ne'' ,the	ha'oⁿ·hwā' he himself	wā'tha''gwā' he it took up	ne', the	13
oä'wĕⁿ·'sā' it sunflower	o'·hnā' it oil	nā'ie' that (it is)	dī'' more- over	ne'' the	wā'has'dā' he it used	wā'shago·hno''gā'k. he her skin smeared.	14

he anointed her body. As soon as he had finished this task he said "Now, verily, do thou again dress thyself." Now she redressed herself entirely, and she was again clothed with raiment.
When it became night, he spread a mat for her at the foot of his mat. There they two passed two more nights. And the third day that came to them the chief said to her: "Now thou must again depart. Thou must go again to the place whence thou didst start." Then he took up the basket of the maiden and went then to the place where he kept meat of all kinds hanging in quarters. Now, verily, he took up the dried meat of the spotted fawn and put it into her basket. All the various kinds of meat he placed therein. As soon as the basket was full, he shook the basket to cause its contents to settle down. When he did shake it, there was seemingly just a little room left in it. Seven times, it is said, he shook the basket before he completely

1	Ganio″ So soon as	wăʻhāiĕññĕńdă″ʻnhă′ he task completed	wăʻhĕⁿʻhĕñ′: he it said:	"O′nĕⁿʻ "Now	hi′iă′ verily
2	sasadiă′dawi″dăʻ." again do thou thyself dress."	O′nĕⁿʻ Now	sāioⁿʻsĕñ′niă′ again she herself dressed	gagwe′gĭʻ, it all	sāioⁿʻsei″să′. again she herself rearranged.
3	Ne″ The	o′nĕⁿ· time	wăʻo″gak it became dark	tcă″ the where	deʻhaʻsi′dăgeʻʻhĕñ two his feet lie	ne″thoʻ there
4	wăʻshagoʻʻso″ʻhăs. he for her a mat spread.	Ne″thoʻ There	de′gniʻ two (it is)	wăʻdiĕñnoⁿʻhwe′t. they two stayed over night.	Nă′ie′ That (it is)	ne″ the
5	′ă·′sĕⁿʻ three	wadoⁿʻtḣă′ it became	tcă″ the where	wăʻhodiʻhĕⁿ″ʻnhă′ it day became for them	o′nĕⁿʻ now	wăʻhĕⁿʻhĕñ″ he it said
6	ne″ the	haʻsĕñnowa′nĕⁿʻ: he chief is:	"O′nĕⁿ· "Now	ĕⁿtcaʻdĕñ′diă′. again thou wilt depart.	Ne″thoʻ There	bĕⁿtcheʻ there again thou wilt go
7	tcă″ the where	noñ′weʻ the place	nidisaʻdĕñ′dioⁿʻ." there whence thou hast departed."	O′nĕⁿʻ Now	wăʻthă′ă·să″gwă′ he (the) basket took up	ne″ the
8	goʻă·′să· her basket	ne″ the	eksă′goʻnă· she (is) maiden	ne″thoʻ there	nhwăʻhe″ thither he went	tcă″ the where	noñ′weʻ the place
9	niʻhă·wăʻhăiĕñdăk′hwă′, there he uses it to keep meat,	nă′ie′ that (it is)	ne″ the	hăʻdiioʻwăʻʻhăgeʻ every it meat is in number (in kind)	ne″tho there
10	găʻwăʻhăniioñ′doⁿ·. it meat hangs plurally.	O′nĕⁿʻ Now	bi′iă′ verily	ne″thoʻ there	wăʻtha″gwă′ he it took up	ne″ the
11	tcīsdăʻthiĕñ′·hăʻ spotted fawn	o′wăʻbăthĕⁿʻ, it meat dry (is)	o′nĕⁿʻ now	o″nĭʻ also	goʻăʻsăgoñ′wăʻ her basket in
12	wăʻhoñ′dak. he it placed.	Gagwe′gĭʻ It all	hăʻdiioʻwăʻhăgeʻ″ every it meat is in number (in kind)	ne″thoʻ there	wăʻhoñ′dak he it placed in.
13	Ganio″ So soon as	wăʻgăʻă″scik it basket was filled	o′nĕⁿʻ now	wăʻhowăk′dă′ he it shook	ne″ the	găʻă·′să·. it basket.	Tcă″ The where
14	nigaʻhaʻwĭʻ there it bears it (time)	wăʻhowăʻkdă′ he it shook	nĕⁿʻʻ this, here	gwă″ seemingly	năʻdetgă′ă′. just there it is contained.	Tciaʻdăk, Seven (it is),

filled it. At that time he said: "Now thou must again depart. Do not, moreover, stand anywhere in the course of thy path homeward. And, moreover, when thou dost arrive there, thou must tell the people dwelling there that they, one and all, must remove the roofs from their several lodges. By and by it will become light and I will send that which is called corn. In so far as that thing is concerned, that is what man-beings will next in time live upon. This kind of thing will continue to be in existence for all time." At that time he took up the basket and also said: "Now, verily, thou shouldst hear it on thy back by means of the forehead strap." Now, at that time she departed.

Now again, as she traveled, she heard a man-being talking, saying: "Come, do thou stand." She did not stand. It was Aurora Borealis who was talking to her. She traveled on for some time, when she again

iā'kĕⁿ', it is said,	nwā'howăk'dā' so many me it shook	o'nĕⁿ· now	hā''sā' not before	wā'hā'ā''seik. he basket filled.	Tho''ge· At that (time)	1
wā'hĕⁿ''hĕñ'': he it said:	"O'nĕⁿ· "Now	ĕⁿtca·dĕñ'diā'. again thou wilt depart.	'Ă·'gwī' Do it not	dī'' more-over	dĕⁿsdā''nhā' thou wilt stand	2
tca'' the where	niio'we' there it is distant	heiotha·hi'noñ·. thither it path has course.	Nā'ie' That (it is)	dī'' more-over	ne'' the	ĕⁿsheiatho'iĕⁿ' thou them wilt tell	3
tca'' the where	ne''tho· there	thadina'gee' there they (m.) dwell	ne'' the	o'nĕⁿ· now	ne''tho· there	hĕⁿ''sioⁿ', there thou wilt arrive,	tca· the where	4
gagwe'gī· it all	ĕⁿiegā·teio·īgwā''hoⁿ· they will undo them severally	ne'' the	gaioⁿ·sā''ge· it lodge on	mā'ie' that (it is)	ne'' the	5
ĕⁿ·hoñsgwā·hĕñ'gwā·hoⁿ· they (m.) will remove the bark roofs severally	tca'' the where	hodinoⁿ·sāiĕñ'do''. they (m.) have lodges severally.	Gĕⁿ·dji'k By and by	6
ĕⁿio''gak it will become night	ĕⁿgadĕñnie·'dā' I it will send	ne'' the	onĕⁿ''hā' it corn	gāia·djī·. it is called.	Nā'ie' That (it is)	ne'' the that	7
mā'' that one	ne'' the that	oⁿ·'kĕⁿ' next in time	ĕⁿiagon·he·'gwik they it will use to live	ne'' the	oñ'gwe·. man-being.	Ĕⁿioi·hwāda'die' It matter will be continuing	8
ĕⁿgāiĕñ'dăk it will remain	ne'' the	nĕñ'gĕⁿ· this one	noñwā·ho''dĕⁿ·'' kind of thing."	Tho''ge· At that (time)	o'nĕⁿ· now	9
wā·thā'ā·sā·'gwā· he (the) basket took up	wā·hĕⁿ''hĕñ'' ne it said	o''nī·: also:	"O'nĕⁿ· "Now	hi'iā' verily	ā·'satge''dat.'' thou shouldst bear it on thy back by the forehead strap."	10
O'nĕⁿ· Now	tho''ge· at that (time)	go·'dĕñ'dioñ·. she departed.				11
O'nĕⁿ· Now	he'' again	tca'' the where	oñtha·hi'ne· she travels onward	ne''tho· there	gothoñ'de' she it heard	oñ'gwe·. a man-being	12
i·ha'doⁿk: he kept saying:	"Hau'', "Come,	o'nĕⁿ· now	desdā''nhā·.'' do thou stand."	Hiiā'' Not (it is)	dā'deiagodā''ī·. she did stop.	13
Hodoñni''ā· He Aurora Borealis	mā'ie' that (it is)	thot'hā'. thence he is speaking.	Gaiñ'gwā Some (time)	nwā·oñni'she· so (long) it lasted	oñtha·hi'ne she travels onward	14

heard a man-being talking, saying: "Verily, do thou stand. Now, verily, thou hast returned home. I am hungry. My child, I desire to eat food." She did not stop. In so far as he is concerned, it was White Fire Dragon who was talking to her. Now, she again arrived where she had crossed the river, and there again, beside the river, she stood. Now, moreover, she heard again a man-being saying: "Do thou stand. I desire that thou and I should converse together." She did not stop. It was the chief who was standing here seeking to tempt her mind. At once she crossed the river on the floating maple log. It was just midday when she again arrived at the place whence she departed, and she went directly into the lodge. As soon as she laid her burden down, she said: "Oh, my mother, now, hither I have returned." She, the elder one, spoke, saying: "I am thankful that

	o'nĕⁿ·	he''	gothoñ'de'.	i·ha'doⁿk·	" Desdä''nhă'	hi'iä'.	O'rĕⁿ'
1	now	again	she it heard	he kept saying:	"Do thou stand,	verily.	Now,
	hi'iä'	sa''sioⁿ'.	Agsi's·	ge·he''	agadekhoñ'niä',	goñ·ha'wä'.'	
2	verily,	again thou hast returned.	I am hungry,	I it desire	I food should eat,	I am thy parent.''	
	Hiiä''	dä·deiagodä''ï·.	Ga·ha·sĕñdie'thä·	owä·he''sdä·	ni·hāiä·do''		
3	Not (it is)	she did stand.	Fire-Dragon (it casts fire)	it white (is)	thus his body (is)		
	dĕⁿ·	mä'ie·	ne''	mä''	tho'thä'.	O'rĕⁿ·	ne''tho'	säie'ioⁿ'	tca''
4	in kind	that (it is)	the that	that one	thence he is talking.	Now	there	again she arrived	the where
	moñ'we·	deiagoia·hiä''gï·,	ne''tho·	he''	doñsäiedä''nhä'	ne''	
5	the place	she river crossed,	there	again	there again she stood	the	
	gĕⁿ·hioⁿ'hwäk'dä'.	O'nĕⁿ·	dï''	he''	gothoñ'de·	ne''	oñ'gwe',
6	it river beside.	Now,	moreover,	again	she it heard	the	man-being
	i·ha'doⁿk:	" Desdä''nhä'.	Dewagadoⁿ·hwĕñdjioñ'niks	daedithä'ĕñ' ''
7	he kept saying:	" Do thou stand.	It me is necessary to	thou should converse.''
	Hiiä''	dä·deiagodä''ï·.	Ha·sĕñnowa'nĕⁿ·	ne''	mä''	ne''tho'
8	Not (it is)	she did stand.	He chief is	the that	that one	there
	he·ha'dä',	he·'he·	hi'iä'	dĕⁿshago'nigoⁿ·hä'ĕñ'.	Goñdadie''	wä·
9	there he stands,	he it verily,	desires,	he her mind will give trouble to.	At once	she
	dieia''hiä'k	tca''	o·'hwä''dä'	gaĕn'do'.	Agwä's	gaĕⁿ·hiä'·hĕⁿ'
10	river crossed where	the	it maple	it log floats.	Just	it sky center (is) (noontide)
	ne''	o'rĕⁿ·	hoñsäie'ioⁿ'	tca''	noñ'we·	diiago·'dĕñ'dioⁿ',	eiä'dä-
11	the	now	there again she arrived	the where	the place	thence she departed,	her body went
	goñda'die·	ne''	ganoⁿsgoñ'wä·	hoñsäie'ioⁿ'.	Ganio''	wä·oñthe'-
12	right on	the	it lodge in	there again she reentered.	So soon as	she her burden laid
	nä'iĕⁿ'	wä'ä·hĕñ'':	" Agno'·hä',	o'nĕⁿ·	ne''	nĕⁿ·'	sagioⁿ'.''	Ne''
13	down	she it said·	" My mother,	now	the	this (is)	again I have returned.''	The
	gokstĕñ''ä'	o'nĕⁿ·	däiewĕñnitgĕⁿ''nhä'	wä'ä·hĕñ'':	" Niiawĕⁿ'·hä'
14	she elder one	now	thence she word spoke	she it said:	" I am thankful

thou hast arrived in peace." Then the maiden again spoke and said: "Ye severally must make preparations by severally removing the roofs from your lodges. There is an abundance of meat and corn also coming, as animals do come, when it becomes night, by and by." And at that time she at once went to the place where lay the burial-case of her dead father, and now, moreover, she again climbed up there. As soon as she reached the place, she said: "Oh, my father, I have now returned home." He said, in replying: "How fared it? Was he willing to do it?" She said: "He was willing." Now, again, he spoke, saying: "I am thankful that thou wast able to do it, as it seems. Thou art fortunate in this matter. And it seems, moreover, good, that thou shouldst, perhaps, at once return home, for the reason, verily, that the chief is immune to magic potence, that nothing can affect the orenda of Chief-who-has-the-standing-tree-called-Tooth, and who some call He-holds-the-earth."

tcaˑ"	skĕñ'nonˑ	wäˑsionˑ."	O'nĕnˑ	tcieda'diäˑ	ne"	eksäˑgo'näˑ	1
the where	well (it is)	thou hast arrived."	Now	again she spoke	the	she maiden (is)	
wäˑäˑhĕñ"ˑ	"Ĕⁿswadogĕⁿs'däˑ		ĕⁿswasgwäˑhĕñ'gwäˑ"hoⁿˑ		tcaˑ"	2
she it said:	"Ye it will prepare well		ye hark roof will take off plurally		the where	
swanoⁿ'säiĕñ'doⁿ.	Odoˑhĕñ'doⁿ	O'wäˑ'häˑ,	o'nĕⁿˑ'häˑ	o"'niˑ,	3
ye lodges have plurally.	It is abundant	it meat,	it corn	also,	
dagoñ'ne'	ne"	o'nĕⁿˑ	gĕⁿ'djĭ'k	ĕⁿio"'gak."	Tho"'geˑ	o'nĕⁿˑ	goñda-	4
thence they (z.) are coming	the	now	by and by	will it become night."	At that (time)	now	at once	
die"	ne"'thoˑ	nhwäˑ'ĕⁿˑ	tcaˑ"	noñ'weˑ	tgaˑhoⁿˑsäˑ'häˑ	ne"	goˑniˑhäˑ-	5
	there	thither she went	the where	the place	there it case up-lies	the	her father	
gĕⁿˑ'häˑ,	o'nĕⁿˑ	dĭ"	ne"'thoˑ	hoñsäieäˑ'thĕⁿˑ.	Ganio"	hwäˑe'ioⁿˑ	6
it was,	now	more-over	there	thither again she climbed.	So soon as	there she arrived	
o'nĕⁿˑ	wäˑäˑhĕñ"ˑ:	"Gˑniˑhäˑ'	o'nĕⁿˑ	sagioⁿˑ."	Niˑha'wĕñˑ	tcaˑ"	7
now	she it said	"My father,	now	again I have returned."	Thence he it said	the where	
däˑhäiˑhwäˑsäˑ'gwäˑ:	"Hate'gwiˑ,	wäˑhokāiĕⁿˑ'häˑ-khĕⁿˑ'?"	Wäˑäˑhĕñ":	8
he answered:	"How is it,	he was willing, was he?"	She it said:	
"Wäˑhokāiĕⁿˑ'häˑ."	O'nĕⁿˑ	heˑ"	daˑhawĕñnitgĕⁿˑ'nhäˑ	wäˑhĕⁿˑhĕñ":	9
"He was willing"	Now	again	thence he word spoke	he it said:	
"Niiawĕⁿˑ'häˑ	tcaˑ"	wäˑsgwe'niäˑ	nige"'khĕⁿˑ'.	Weˑ'swadääˑ'shwiios'-	10
"I am thankful	the where	thou wast able to do it	it would seem, does it not (forsooth)	It prospers your (pl.) fortune.	
däˑ'.	Näˑ'ieˑ	dĭ"	oiäˑ'neˑ	oⁿˑ"	ne"	goñdadie"	hoñsaˑ'saˑdĕñ'diäˑ,	11
	That (it is)	more-over	it is good	proba-bly	the	at once	hence again thou 'shouldst depart,	
swäˑ'djĭkˑ'	bi'iäˑ'	. biiäˑ'	stĕⁿˑˑ	noñwäˑho"'dĕⁿ	deˑhonäˑ'gō'wäs	ne"	12
because (too much)	verily,	not (it is)	any-thing	kind of thing	it affects him (he is immune to orenda)	the	
nĕñ'gĕⁿˑ	ne"	Haˑsĕñnowa'nĕⁿˑ	ne"	Hodäˑ'heˑ	näˑ'ieˑ	ne"	Ono"	13
this one	the	He chief (is)	the	He has a standing tree	that (it is)	the	It	
djäˑ'	nwäˑgaĕndo"'dĕⁿˑ;	näˑ'icˑ	ne"	o'diäˑk	Haoⁿˑhwĕñdjiäwäˑ"giˑ	14
tooth	such it tree kind of (is);	that (it is)	the	some	He-earth-holds	
hoñwanäˑ'doⁿˑ'khwäˑ."						15
they it use to designate him."						

At that time all those who dwelt there undid their lodges by removing the roofs from all severally. Then, verily, when it became night, as soon as the darkness became settled, they heard the sounds made by the raining of corn, which fell in the lodges. Then they went to sleep. When it became day, they looked and saw that in the lodges corn lay piled up, quite filling them. Now, moreover, their chief said: "Do ye severally repair your lodges. And, moreover, ye must care for it and greatly esteem it; the thing has visited our village which He-who-has-the-standing-tree-called-Tooth has given you to share with him."

In a short time they were surprised, seemingly, that the maiden was nowhere to be found. She had again departed. They knew that she had again gone to the place where stood the lodge of the chief

1	Tho"ge· *o'nĕⁿ*· *At that time*	*ne"* *now*	hadina'gee' *the*	gagwe'gī· *they (m.) are dwelling*		wä'hadigä'tciä"hoⁿ· *it all* *they (m.) them undid plurally*
2	tca" *the where*	hodinoⁿ·sāiĕñ'doⁿ·, *they (m.) plurally lodges have,*		wä'hoñsgwä·hĕñgwä'·hoⁿ· *they (m.) bark roofs removed plurally*		gagwe'gī· *it all.*
3	O'nĕⁿ· *Now*	bi'iä· *verily*	ne" *the*	o'nĕⁿ· *now*	wä'o"gak, *it became night,*	ganio" *so soon as*	wä'dwa·soñdāiĕñdä"nhä' *it night became settled*
4	o'nĕⁿ· *now*	hoñnathoñ'de· *they (m.) it heard*	o'nĕⁿ· *now*	wä'o·kä'e·hä' *it noise made*		tca" *the where*	wä'o·staiñ'dī' *it showered*
5	ne" *the*	onĕⁿ"·hä' *it corn*	ne" *the*	tca" *the where*	ganoⁿsgoñwä'·shoⁿ· *it lodge in along*	ĕⁿ·sĕⁿ"nhä'. *it fell.*	O'nĕⁿ· *Now*
6	wä'hoñnä"gak. *they (m.) slept.*	Ne" *The*	o'nĕⁿ· *now*	wä'o·bĕⁿ"nhä' *It day became*	wä'hoñtgat'hwä', *they (m.) it looked at*		wä'ha- *they (m.)*
7	di'gĕⁿ· *saw it*	tca" *the where*	ganoⁿsgoñwä'·shoⁿ· *it lodge in along*	dega'·hĕñ· *it is full*	gage'·heⁿ· *it is heaped*	ne" *the*	onĕⁿ"·hä' *it corn.*
8	O'nĕⁿ· *Now*	dī" *moreover*	ne" *the*	hoñwa·sĕñ'noⁿ· *their (m.) chief*	wä'hĕⁿ·hĕñ": *he it said:*	"O'nĕⁿ· *"Now*	sasni·soñ *again do ye them repair*
9	niä'·hĕñ· *plurally*	(saswa·soñniä'·hĕñ·) *(again do ye them plurally repair)*	tca" *the where*		swanoⁿ·sāiĕñ'doⁿ·. *ye (pl.) lodges have plurally*	Nä'ie· *That (it is)*	dī" *moreover*
10	ne" *the*	ĕⁿswadeiĕñnoñ'niä', *ye it good care will give,*		ĕⁿswanoⁿsdek', *ye will continue to esteem it greatly,*	hi'iä' *verily,*	tca" *the where*	noñwa·ho"dĕⁿ· *kind of thing*
11	wä'oñgwanadowĕⁿ"nhä' *it has found (visited) our village*		ne" *the*	tca" *the where*	wä'etchinoñ'dä" *one it has shared with you*	ne" *the*	Ono"djä· *It tooth*
12	Hodä"·he·." *He has standing tree."*						
13	Niioi·hwăgwä·hä" *Just it is short matter (time)*		o'nĕⁿ· *now*	wä'hoñdiĕñ'hä' *they (m.) were surprised*	gwä" *seemingly*	hiiä" *not (it is)*	ga'tkä' *anywhere*
14	de"tciĕⁿ"'s *she goes about*	ne" *the*	eksä'go'nä·. *she (is) maiden*	Tciago·dĕñ'dioñ·. *Again she had departed.*		Hoñnĕnnoⁿ"do", *They (m.) it knew,*	
15	iä'kĕⁿ·, *it is said,*	tca" *the where*	ne"tho· *there*	hetciagawe'noñ· *thither again she has gone*	tca" *the where*	noñ'we· *the place*	thonoⁿ·sä'iĕⁿ· *there his lodge lies*

who was her consort. Now, verily, in reference to him he himself in turn was surprised to see her return home. When it became day again, the chief noticed that seemingly it appeared that the life of the maiden, his spouse, had changed.[a] Thus it was that, day after day and night after night, he still considered the matter. The conditions were such that he did not know what thing was the cause that it [his spouse's condition] was thus, so he merely marveled that it had thus come to pass.

It is certain, it is said, that it formed itself there where they two conversed, where they two breathed together; that, verily, his breath is what the maiden caught, and it is that which was the cause of the change in the life of the maiden. And, moreover, that is the child to which she gave birth. And since then, from the time that he [her

---

ne″ the	ha·sĕñnowa′nĕⁿ· he chief is	ne″ the	gado′gĕⁿ· it is certain (place)	de·hia′di·. they (m.) two are one.	O′nĕⁿ· Now	hi′iă′ verily		1
ne″ the that	nă′ that one·	ha′oⁿ·bwă′ he himself	oⁿ″′kĕⁿ next in turn	wă′hadiĕñ′·hă′ he was surprised	gwă′ seemingly	o′nĕⁿ· now	săie′ioⁿ· again she returned.	2
Ne″ The	o′nĕⁿ· now	wă′o·hĕⁿ″′nhă′ it day became		o′nĕⁿ· now	wă′hatdo′gă′ he it noticed	ne″ the	ha‘sĕñno he	3
wa′nĕⁿ· chief is	tca″ the where	ne″tho· there	ni′io·t so it is	tca″ the where	ăiĕñ′ă′ one would think	tca″ the where	o′nĕⁿ· now	o′iă′ it is other	4
ni′io·t so it is	tca″ the where	ago′n·he· she is living	ne″ the	eksă′go′nă· she maiden	ne″ the	he′nă. his spouse.	Ne″tho· There	5
ni′io·t so it is	tca″ the where	wĕñdade′nioⁿ· day after day	wă·soñdade′nioⁿ· night after night	o″′nĭ′ also	de·hoiă′dowe″′di·. he it is considering.			6
Ne″tho· There	ni′io·t so it is	hiiă″′ not (it is)	de·honoⁿ″′doⁿ· he it knows	ho′t what	noñwa·ho″′dĕⁿ· kind of thing	dăioi′- thence it is		7
hwă″′khe· reason	tca″ the where	ne″tho· there	ni′io·t, so it is,	nă′ie· that (it is)	gĕñ′gwă′ only	hoi·hwane·hă′gwăs he matter marvels at		8
tca″ the where	nwă′awĕⁿ″·hă′. so it came to pass.							9
Ne″tho· There	gāi·hwado′gĕⁿ·, it is definite matter,	iă′kĕⁿ″, it is said,	wă′wadoñ′niă′ it itself formed	tca″ the where	de·hodi′thă′ they conversed together			10
tca″ the where	hiiadoñ′ie·s they two (m.) breathed	ne″ the	aoñwi″′să′ it breath (is)	nă′ie· that (it is)	hi′iă′ verily	wă′eie′nă′ she it caught	ne″ the	11
eksă′go′nă·, she maiden (is),	nă′ie· that (it is)	hi′iă′ verily	dagăi·hoñ′niă′ thence it matter caused	tca″ the where	o′iă′ it is other one	nwă′awĕⁿ″·hă′ so it came to pass		12
tca″ the where	ago′n·he· she is living	ne″ the	eksă′go′nă·. she maiden (is)	Nă′ie· That (it is)	ne″ the that	nă″ that one	di′ more-over	wă′ago she became	13
ksă′dăiĕñdă″′nhă′. possessed of a child (gave birth to it).	Nă′ie· That (it is)	ne″ the	tca″ the where	gă′e· hither	dăga·hawi″′dă′ thence it bore (the time)	tca″ the where		14

[a] The expression "life has changed" is employed usually as a euphemism for "is pregnant."

spouse] let man-beings go here on the earth, the manner in which man-beings are paired has transformed itself. This is the manner in which it will continue to be; this will be its manner of being done, whereby it will be possible for the man-beings dwelling on the earth to produce ohwachiras of posterity. Thus, too, it seems, it came to pass in regard to the beast-world, their bodies all shared in the change of the manner in which they would be able to produce ohwachiras of offspring here on the earth.

Thus it was that, without interruption, it became more and more evident that the maiden would give birth to a child. At that time the chief became convinced of it, and he said: "What is the matter that thy life has changed? Verily, thou art about to have a child. Never, moreover, have thou and I shared the same mat. I believe that it is not I who is the cause that thy life has changed. Dost thou thyself

1	nigaʻhaʼwĭ̈ there it it hore (the time)	onʻhwĕñdjiäʼʼgeʻ it earth on	wäʼshagotʼgäʼk he them let go	neʼʼ the	oñʼgweʻ man-being	oʼnĕⁿʻ now
2	deiotdeʼnioñʻ it itself changed	tcaʼʼ the where	nigäiĕñnoʼʼdĕⁿʻ there its kind of doing (its method of action)	tcaʼʼ the where	wäʼshagoäneʼgöⁿʻ he them places together	neʼʼ the
3	oñʼgweʻ. man-being.	Thoʼnĕⁿʻ Here	hiʼiäʼ verily	onʻʼkĕⁿ next in time	nĕⁿioʼʼdĭk, so it will continue to be,	nĕⁿgäiĕñnoʼʼdĕⁿk, such its method of being done will be,
4	näʼieʼ that (it is)	neʼʼ the	čⁿgagweʼniäʼ it will be able to do it	ĕⁿioñthwadjiĕñʼnĭ̈ʼ they will produce ohwachiras (families)	neʼʼ the	oñʼgweʻ man-being	tcaʼʼ the where
5	onʻhwĕñdjiäʼʼgeʻ it earth on	enaʼgeeʻ. they dwell.	Neʼʼthoʻ There	gwäʼʼ seemingly	oʼ too	nwäʼawĕⁿʻʻhäʼ so it came to pass	neʼʼ the
6	goñdiʼioʼ, they (z.) animals,	gagweʼgĭ̈ʻ it all	wäʼodiiäʼdadiioʼʼäs their bodies shared its fate	tcaʼʼ the where	nwäʼgäiĕñnoʼʼdĕⁿʻ such its manner of being done became		
7	neʼʼ the	tcaʼʼ the where	dĕⁿgoñthwädjiʼiäʼk they (z.) will produce ohwachiras	neʼʼ the	thoʼnĕⁿʻ here	onʻhwĕñdjiäʼdeʼ. it earth is present.	
8	Neʼʼthoʻ There	niʼioʻt so it is	heiotgoñdaʻʼgwĭ̈ʻ hence it is unceasing	däiotgĕⁿʼiʻhäʼdieʼ it became more and more manifest	tcaʼʼ the where	ĕⁿia she	
9	gowiäiĕñdäʼʼnhäʼ will have a child	neʼʼ the	eksäʼgoʼnäʻ. she maiden. (is)	Thoʼʼgeʻ At that (time)	oʼnĕⁿʻ now	doʼgĕⁿs it is true	wäʼ- he
10	hatdoʼkäʼ it noticed	neʼʼ the	haʻsĕñnowaʼnĕⁿʻ, he chief (is),	wäʼhĕⁿʻhĕñʼʼ he it said,	dĭʼʼ: moreover:	"Hoʼt "What	
11	noñwaʻhoʼʼdĕⁿ kind of thing	niʼioʻt so it is	tcaʼʼ the where	oʼiäʼ it is other	niʼioʻt so it is	tcaʼʼ the where	soʼnʻheʼ? thou art living?
12	Saksäʼdäiĕñdäʼʼseʼ Thou art about to have a child	biʼiäʼ. verily.	Hiiäʻʼ Not (it is)	hwĕñʼdoⁿʻ ever	dĭʼʼ moreover	deʼoñgiaäʼdĭʻ. thou I have lain together.	
13	Geʻheʼʼ I it think	biiäʼʼ not (it is)	iʼʼ I (am)	deʼgĕñʻʼ it is	neʼʼ the	tcaʼʼ the where	oʼiäʼʼ it is other	niʼioʻt so it is	tcaʼʼ the where	soʼnʻheʼ. thou art living.
14	Sĕñnoⁿʻʼdoⁿʻ-khĕⁿʻʼ Thou it knowest, dost thou	soñʼʼ, who (it is),	neʼʼ the	iʼsʼʼ? thou?"	Hiiäʻʼ Not (it is)	stĕⁿʼʼ anything	deʼagoʼnigoⁿ - she it under-

know who it is?" She did not understand the meaning of what he said.

Now, at that time, the chief began to be ill. Suddenly, it seems, she herself now became aware that her life had changed. Then she said, addressing the chief: "I believe that there is, perhaps, something the matter, as my life at the present time is not at all pleasant." He did not make any reply. Not long thereafter she again said: "My thoughts are not at all pleasant." Again he said nothing. So it continued thus that she did nothing but consider the matter, believing that something must be the matter, perhaps, that the condition of her body was such as it was. It became more and more evident that she was pregnant. Now it was evident that she was big with child.

Sometime afterward she again resolved to ask him still once more. She said: "As a matter of fact, there must be something the matter,

haiĕñdå"ï	ho't	noñwaho"dĕⁿ"	gĕñ'då'	tca"'	noñwaho"dĕⁿ"	
stood	what (it is)	kind of thing	it means	the where	kind of thing	1
wa'hada'diä'						2
he it spoke.						
Tho"'ge'	o'nĕⁿ'	wä'wa'så'wĕⁿ'	wä'honoⁿ'hwǎk'dĕⁿ'	ne"	ha'-	3
At that (time)	now	it began	he became ill	the	he	
sĕñnowa'nĕⁿ'.	Diĕñ"'hä'	gwä"	o'nĕⁿ'	wä'oñtdo'gä'	ga'oⁿ'hwä'	4
chief [is].	After a while	seemingly	now	she it noticed	she herself	
tca"'	o'iä"	ni'io't	tca'	ago'n'he'.	O'nĕⁿ'	tho"'ge'	wä'ä'hĕñ',	5
the where	it is other	so it is	the where	she is living.	Now	at that (time)	she it said,	
wä'hawĕⁿ"'has	ne"	ha'sĕñnowa'nĕⁿ':	"Ge"'he'	stĕⁿ"'	gwä"	6
she him addressed	the	he chief [is]:	"I it think	something	seemingly	
noñwaho"dĕⁿ'	oñ"'	ni'io't,	tca"'	hiiä"'	de'awĕñtga'de'	tca"'	7
kind of thing	perhaps	so it is,	the where	not	it is pleasant	the where	
go'n'he'	ne"	oⁿ"'kĕⁿ'?"	Hiiä"'	stĕⁿ"'	de'ha'wĕñ'.	Hiiä"'	de'	8
I am living	the	at present?"	Not (it is)	anything	he it has said.	Not (it is)	it	
aoñni'she'ï'	o'nĕⁿ'	he"	wä'ä'hĕñ':	"Hiiä"'	skĕñ'noⁿ"	de'gĕñnoⁿ'-	9
lasted (long)	now	again	she it said:	"Not (it is)	peaceful (it is)	I am think-	
doñ'nioⁿk."	Hiiä"'	he"	stĕⁿ"'	de'ha'wĕñ'.	O'nĕⁿ'	ne"'tho'	10
ing repeatedly."	Not (it is)	again	anything	he it has said.	Now	there	
ni'io't	deiagoiä'dowe"'dï'	gĕñ'gwä',	ĕñ'´'he'	stĕⁿ"'	gwä"	noñwa'-	11
so it is	she it is considering	only,	she it thinks	something	seemingly	kind of	
ho"dĕⁿ'	oñ"'	ni'io't,	tca"'	tho'nĕⁿ'	ni'io't	tca"'	giä'di"'ge'."	12
thing	probably	so it is,	the where	here. this way	so it is	the where	my body on."	
Dāiotgĕⁿ'ï'hä'die'	tca"'	ene'ioⁿ'.	O'nĕⁿ'	otgĕⁿ"'ï'	egowa'nĕⁿ'	13
It became more and more manifest	the where	she is pregnant.	Now	it is evident	she large (is).	
Gaiñ'gwä'	nwä'oñni'she'	o'nĕⁿ'	he"	wä'ĕñ'ä'	ĕⁿsheiä'hĕñ'doⁿ'	14
Some (time)	so long it lasted	now	again	she it thought	again I him will ask	
'ä"'soⁿ'.	Wä'ä'hĕñ':	"Ho't	noñwaho"dĕⁿ'	oñ"'	se"	ni'io't	tca"'	15
once more.	She it said:	"What	kind of thing	probably	it is matter of fact	so it is	the where	

perhaps, that my body is in this condition. And the thoughts of my mind are not at all pleasant. One would think that there can be no doubt that, seemingly, something is about to happen, because my life is so exceedingly unpleasant." Again he said nothing. When it became night, then, verily, they laid their bodies down and they slept. So now, verily, he there repeatedly considered the matter. Now, in so far as the maiden was concerned, she still did not understand what was about to take place from the changed condition of her body. Sometime afterward the chief spoke to her, saying: "As a matter of fact, a man-being (or rather woman-being) will arrive, and she is a man-being child, and thou must care for her. She will grow in size rapidly, and her name is Zephyrs."[a] The maiden said nothing, for the reason that she did not understand what her spouse told her.

#								
1	tho′nĕⁿˑ here	ni′io‘t so it is	ne′′ the	giä′di′′ge‘, my body on, (it is)	nä′ie’ that	ne′¹ the	g′nigoⁿˑhä′ge· my mind on	hi′iä′′ not (it is)
2	skĕñ′noⁿˑ peaceful (it is)	de‘gĕñnoⁿˑdoñ′nioⁿk? I am thinking repeatedly?		Gäi‘hwado′gĕⁿˑ It matter certain (is)	äiĕñ′ä‘ it seems		stĕⁿ′′ something	gwä′′ seemingly
3	niiawĕⁿ′′se’, so it is going to happen,	swä′djĭk′ because	dĕⁿgi′′ exceedingly	biä′′ not (it is)		de‘awĕñtga′de· it is pleasant		tea′′ the where
4	go′n‘he‘." I am living."	Hiiä′′ Not (it is)	he‘ again	stĕⁿ′′ anything	de‘ha′wĕñ· he it has said.	Ne′′ The	o′nĕⁿˑ now	wä′o′′gak it became night
5	o′nĕⁿ‘ now	bi′iä’ verily	wä‘hoñdiä′dage‘·hĕñ’, they (m.) laid their several bodies down,			wä‘hoñnä′′gak. they (m.) went to sleep.	Da′, So,	o′nĕⁿˑ now
6	bi′iä· verily	ne′′tho· there	hĕñnoⁿˑdoñ′nioⁿk. he is thinking repeatedly.		O′nĕⁿˑ Now	ne′′ the that	nä′ that one	eksä′go′nä· she maiden (is)	hiiä′′ not
7	’ä′′soⁿˑ still	de‘äiago‘nigoⁿˑhäiĕñdä′′nhä’ she it comes to understand			ho′t what (is)	noñwa‘ho′′dĕⁿˑ kind of thing		niiawĕⁿ′′se’ so it is about to happen
8	tea′′ the where	o′iä‘ it is other	ni′lo·t so it is	eiä′di′′ge·. her body on.	Gaiñ′gwä’ Some (time)	nwä′oñni′she’ so it lasted		ne′′tho‘ there
9	ni′io‘t so it is	o′nĕⁿˑ now	ne′′ the	ha‘sĕñnowa′nĕⁿˑ he chief (is)		da‘hada′diä’, thence he spoke,		wä‘hĕⁿˑhĕñ′′: he it said:
10	"Ĕⁿie′ioⁿ "She will arrive	se′′ it is matter of fact,	oñ′gwe‘, a man-being,	eksä′ä′′, she child (is),	nä′ie’ that (it is)	ne′′ the	nä′ie’ that (it is)	dĕⁿshe‘- wilt thou
11	snie′′nhä’. care well for her.	Gode‘sno′we· She grows rapidly		di′′, more over.	Gaĕnde·′soⁿk It-wind-goes-plurally (Gusts-of-wind)		eiä′dji·." she is named."	Hiiä′′ Not (it is)
12	stĕⁿ′′ anything	de‘aga′wĕñ· she it said	ne′′ the	eksä′go′nä‘ she maiden (is)	nä′ie’ that (it is)	ne′′ the	däioi‘hwä′′khe’ thence it is reason	
13	tea′′ the where	biä′′ not (it is)	de‘ago‘nigoⁿˑhäiĕñdä′′i‘ she it understood		ne′′ the	noñwa‘ho′′dĕⁿ kind of thing		gĕñ′dä it means

[a] This name Zephyrs merely approximates the meaning of the original, which signifies the warm springtide zephyrs that sometimes take the form of small whirlwinds or eddies of warm air.

Not long afterward, then, verily, she gave birth to a child. She paid no attention to it. The only thing she did was to lay it on the place where the chief customarily passed the night. After ten days' time she again took it up therefrom.

Sometime afterward the chief became aware that he began to be ill. His suffering became more and more severe. All the persons dwelling in the village came to visit him. There he lay, and sang, saying: "Ye must pull up this standing tree that is called Tooth. The earth will be torn open, and there beside the abyss ye must lay me down. And, moreover, there where my head lies, there must sit my spouse." That is what he, the Ancient One, sang. Then the man-beings dwelling there became aware that their chief was ill.

tca′	wa`shagotho′iĕⁿ·	ne′′	de·hia′di·	Hiiā·′	de′oi·hwishe′′i·		1
the where	he her told	the	they (m.) two are one.	Not (it is)	it long matter became		
o′nĕⁿ·	bi′iā·	wa`agoksā`dāiĕñdā′′nhā′.		Hiiā·′	de`agosde′isdi·		2
now	verily	she became possessed of a child.		Not (it is)	she it paid attention to.		
Nā′ie·	gĕñ′gwā·	ne′′tho·	hwā′e·′hĕñ′	tca′′	noñ′we·	ni·hĕñnoⁿ·-	3
That (it is)	only	there	there she it laid	the where	the place	there he it uses	
hwes′thā·	ne′′	ha·sĕñnowa′nĕⁿ·.	Washĕⁿ·′	niwĕñdage·′′	nwā·oⁿ-		4
to sleep on	the	he chief (is).	Ten (it is)	so it day (is) in number	so it		
ni′she·	o′nĕⁿ·	hā`doñsāie′′gwā·					5
lasted	now	thence again she it took.					
Gaiñ′gwā·	nwā′oñni′she·	o′nĕⁿ·	ne′′	ha·sĕñnowa′nĕⁿ··	wā`hat		6
Some (time)	so it lasted (long)	now	the	he chief (is)	he it noticed		
do′gā·	ne′′	tca′′	o′nĕⁿ·	wā`wa·sa′wĕⁿ·	o′nĕⁿ·	wā`honoⁿ·hwāk′dĕⁿ·	7
	the that	the where	now	it began	now	he became ill.	
Dāiotgĕⁿ·i·hā′die·	tca′′	ni·hoĕⁿ·hia′gĕⁿ·.	Gagwe′gī·	tca′′	gana		8
It became more and more manifest (severe)	the where	so he is suffering.	It all	the where	it village		
dā′iĕⁿ·	ena′gee·	hadik′doⁿk.	Ne′′tho·	hĕñdā′gā·,	hodĕñnō′dā·,		9
lies	they dwell	they (m.) come to see (him).	There	he lay,	he is singing,		
i·ha′doⁿk:	"Ĕⁿswaĕñdodā′gwā·	nĕñ′gĕⁿ·	gā·′he·.	ono·′djā·	gāia′djī·.		10
he kept saying:	"Ye standing tree will pull up	this one (it is)	it tree stands,	it tooth	it is called.		
Ĕⁿwadoⁿ·hwĕñdjiādet′hā·.	ne′′tho·	o·sadāgĕⁿ·hia′dā·	hĕⁿsgwĕñ				11
Will it earth open,	there	it abyss edge of	there will ye				
dā′gāñ·.	Nā′ie·	dī′	ne′′	tca′′	noñ′we·	hā·degnoⁿ·hā′iĕⁿ·	ne′′tho·	12
me lay.	That (it is)	more-over	the	the where	the place	just my head (scalp) lies	there
ĕⁿietgo′dak	ne′′	deiagni′′dĕñ·."	Nā′ie·	hodĕñnō′dā·	ne′′		13
she will sit	the	one I abide together."	That (it is)	he is singing	the		
hokstĕñ′′ā·.	O′nĕⁿ·	ne′′	oñ′gwe·	ne′′	ne′′tho·	hadina′gee·	14
he elder one.	Now	the	man-beings	the	there	they (m.) dwell	
wā`hoñtdo′gā·	tca′′	honoⁿ·hwāk′dāni·	ne′′	ha·sĕñnowa′nĕⁿ·.			15
they it noticed	the where	he is ill	the	he chief (is).			

Now, verily, all came to visit him. They questioned him repeatedly, seeking to divine his Word, what thing, seemingly, was needful for him, what kind of thing, seemingly, he expected through a dream. Thus, day after day, it continued that they sought to find his Word. After a time the female man-being child was of fair size. She was then able to run about from place to place. But it thus continued that they kept on seeking to divine his Word. After a while, seemingly, one of the persons succeeded in finding his Word, and he said: "Now, perhaps, I myself have divined the Word of him, the ordure, our chief." He who is called Aurora Borealis said this. And when he told the chief what manner of thing his soul craved, the chief was very pleased. And when he divined his Word, he said: "Is it not this that thy dream is saying, namely, that it is direful, if it so be that no person should divine thy Word, and that it will become still more

1	O'něⁿ·	bi'iă'	gagwe'gǐ·	hadigwa'thwăs.	Hoñwa·hěñ'doⁿk
	Now	verily	it all	they (m.) visit severally.	They him question
2	hoñwawěnni''saks	stěⁿ''	gwă''	noñwa·ho''děⁿ'	de·hodoⁿ·hwěñd
	they his Word seek to divine	anything	seemingly	kind of thing	it is necessary
3	jioñ'nǐks,	stěⁿ''	gwă''	nonwa·ho''děⁿ'	hotgāiěⁿ·'dǐ·.	Ne''tho'
	for him,	anything	seemingly	kind of thing	he desires through a dream.	There
4	ni'io·t	hoñwawěnni''saks	o·hěⁿ'sěñk.	Diěñ'·hă'	gwă''	o'něⁿ'
	so it is	they seek his Word repeatedly	day after day.	After a while,	seemingly,	now
5	gaiñ'gwă'	niiă'gă'	ne''	eksă'ă''.	O'něⁿ'	hă'degāie'ǐ'	ne''tho'
	somewhat	so she is large	the	she child. (is)	Now	just it is sufficient	there
6	edăk'he's.	Ne''tho·	ni'io·t	hegagondă·'gwǐ'	hoñwawěnni''saks
	she runs about.	There	so it is	hence it is unceasing	they his word seek to divine.
7	Diěñ'·hă'	gwă''	o'něⁿ·	shāiă''dat	o'něⁿ·	wă'hoñwawěnnowěⁿ''nhă',
	After a while	seemingly,	now	he person one is	now	he his word divined,
8	wă'hěⁿ·hěñ'':	"O'něⁿ·	hoñ''	ni''ă·	wă'he·dawěnnowěⁿ''nhă'	ne''
	he it said:	"Now	probably	I personally	his, ordure's, Word have found	the
9	shedwa'sěñ'noⁿ.''	Hodoñni''ă·	hoñwanā·doⁿ·'khwă'	nă''	wă'hěⁿ'
	he our chief (is).''	He Aurora Borealis	they (m.) designate him thereby	that one	he it
10	hěñ''.	Nă'ie'	ne''	o'něⁿ'	wă·hoñwatho'iěⁿ'	ne''	ha'sěnnowa'něⁿ'
	said.	That (it is)	the	now	he him told	the	he chief (is)
11	tea''	nonwa·ho''děⁿ'	wadădjǐs'thă'	ne''	hothwā'i·	wă'hatcěn
	the where	kind of thing	it it craves	the	his soul	he was
12	noñ'niă'.	Nă'ie'	ne''	o'něⁿ'	wă'hoñwawěnnowěⁿ''nhă'	wă'hěⁿ·hěñ'':
	pleased.	That (it is)	the	now	he his Word divined	he it said:
13	"Nă'ie'-khěⁿ·''	iwa'doⁿ·	ne''	sadă'ă'shwă'	nă'ie'	gano'wěⁿ,	nă'ie'
	"That it is,	is it	it it says	the	thy dream (luck)	that (it is)	it direful (is),	that (it is)
14	ěⁿganowěⁿ''khe',	nă'ie'	gi'shěⁿ'	ne''	biiă''	thāiesawěnnowěⁿ''nhă'.
	it direful will become	that it is)	it may be (that)	the	not (it is)	they thy Word should divine

direful? And yet, moreover, it is not certain that this is what thy soul craves; that its eyes may have seen thy standing tree, Tooth as to kind, pulled up, in order that the earth be torn open, and that there be an abyss that pierces the earth, and, moreover, that there beside the abyss one shall lay thee, and at thy head thy spouse shall be seated with her legs hanging down into the abyss." At that time the chief said: "Ku".[a] I am thankful! Now, verily, the whole matter has been fulfilled by thy divining my Word."

During this time [the duration of the dream feast], a large body of man-beings,[b] paid a visit there. He, the Deer, paid a visit there. He, the Great-horned Deer [the Buck], paid a visit there. He, the Spotted Fawn, paid a visit, and was there seeking to divine the Word of the

Nā′ie′	dī″	ne″	biä″	de'oi'hwado′gĕⁿ‧	īā′ie′	wadädjĭs'thä′	ne″	
That (it is)	more-over	the	not (it is)	it matter certain (is)	that (it is)	it it craves	the	1
sathwä′i‧,	īā′ie′	dāioga'hä″ik	ne″	tca″	agaĕndodä′gwĕⁿk		ne″	
thy soul,	that (it is)	its two eyes should have fallen on it	the	the where	one should uproot standing tree		the	2
sadĕndo′dä′	ne″	ono″djä′	nwä′gaĕndo″dĕⁿ,	īā′ie′	diioi‘hwä′			
thou thyself tree hast set for	the	it tooth	such it tree (is) kind of.	that (it is)	thence it is reason			3
awado″·hwĕndjiadet′hä′		āio‘sadĕⁿ‘hä′	hä′dāiaoⁿ·hwĕndjiongo′‘dä‧					
it itself earth should cause to gape		it cave should come to be	just it earth should transpierce.					4
Nā′ie′	ne″	ne″tho‘	dī″	o'sadagĕⁿ·hia′dä‧	hĕⁿiesĕndä′gäⁿ′		ne″tho	
That (it is)	the	there	more-over	it cave edge of	there they thee will lay		·there	5
dī″	tca″	hesroⁿ·hä′iĕⁿ'	ne″tho‧	o'sadagoñ′wä'	hä′dĕⁿiago'si′dĕⁿ-			
more-over	the where	there thy scalp lies	there	it cave in	just her two feet will			6
doñ′nioⁿk	ne″	dedjia′di‧."	Tho″ge‧	ne″	ha'sĕnnowa′nĕⁿ‘			
severally hang	the	one thou are one."	At that (time)	the	he chief (is)			7
wä′hĕⁿ·bĕñ″:	"Ku″.	Niiawĕⁿ″'hä‧'.	O′ⁿĕⁿ‘	bi′iä‧'	wä′gäi‘hwäiei″khe‘			
he it said:	"Ku".	I am thankful.	Now	verily	it matter is fulfilled			8
hegagwe′gr‧	ne″	tca″	wä'sgwawĕnnowĕⁿ″nhä′."					
entirely (it all)	the	the where	ye my Word have divined."					9
Nā′ie′	ne″	gĕndio'gowa′nĕⁿ‘	hodigwat′hwĭ‧	tca″	nwä′oñni′she′.			
That it is	the	it body of persons large (is)	they (m.) visited	the where	so long it lasted.			10
Skĕnnoñdoⁿ′	wä′hagwat′hwä′.		Onä′gaĕndoⁿ·go′nä‧	Skĕnnoñdoⁿ′				
Deer	he visited (there).		It has great horns	Deer				11
wä′hagwat′hwä′.	Tcisdä′thiĕñ′‘hä‧		wä′hagwat′hwä‧,		ne″tho‧			
he visited (there).	Spotted Fawn		he visited (there)		there			12
hoñwawĕnni·′saks	ne″	ha'sĕnnowa′nĕⁿ‘.		O'gwäi″	o″nĭ′	wä′ha		
he sought to divine his Word	the	He chief (is).		Bear	also	he		13

[a] This is an exclamation expressing gratification at having one's dream or vision divined and satisfied.

[b] The relator of this version stated that there was a reputed connection between the visits of these different personages and the presence of their kinds in the new world beneath the sky land, but he had forgotten it.

chief. He, the Bear, also paid a visit. Now, he also, the Beaver, paid a visit. And he, the Wind-who-roves-about-from-place-to-place, paid a visit also. And now, also, he, the Daylight, paid a visit. Now she also, the Night, the Thick Night, paid a visit. Now also she, the Star, paid a visit. Now, also, he, the Light-orb [the sun] paid a visit. And, too, the Water-of-springs, she paid a visit. Now, also, she, the Corn, paid a visit. Now, also, she, the Bean, paid a visit. Now, also, she, the Squash, paid a visit. Now, also, she, the Sunflower, paid a visit. Now, also, the Fire Dragon with the body of pure white color, he paid a visit. Now, also, the Rattle paid a visit. Now, also, he, the Red Meteor, paid a visit. Now, also, he, the Spring Wind, paid a visit. Now, also, he, the Great Turtle, paid a visit. Now, also, he, the Otter, paid a visit. Now, also, he, the Wolf, paid

#						
1	gwa'thwä'. visited (there).	O'něn‘ Now	o‘'nĭ‘ also	Nagaiä''gĭ' Beaver	wä'hagwat'hwä'. he visited (there).	Tca'' The where
2	Gaeñ'de's It Wind Goes About	o‘'nĭ‘ also	wä'hagwat'hwä'. he visited (there).	O'něn‘ Now	o‘'nĭ‘ also	ne'' the	Hä'deio'- It
3	hat'hek Light of Day	wä'hagwat'hwä'. he visited (there).	O'něn‘ Now	o‘'nĭ‘ also	ne'' the	A‘soñ''he‘, It Night,	Deioda'- It
4	soñdä'igĭ' Black Darkness	wä'egwat'hwä'. she visited (there).	O'něn‘ Now	o‘'nĭ‘ also	ne'' the	Odjĭsdäno''gwä' It Star (spot)
5	wä'egwat'hwä'. she visited (there).	O'něn‘ Now	o‘'nĭ‘ also	tca'' the where	Gaä''gwä' It Orb of Light (Sun)	wä'hagwat'hwä' he visited (there).
6	Nä'ie‘ That (it is)	o'' too	tca'' the where	Ga‘hne'go‘ It Embedded Water	wä'egwat'hwä'. she visited (there).	O'něn‘ Now	o‘'nĭ‘ also	ne'' the
7	Oněn'‘hä' It Corn	wä'egwat'hwä'. she visited (there).	O'něn‘ Now	o‘'nĭ‘ also	ne'' the	O‘sa‘he''dä‘ It Bean	wä'egwat' she visited (there).
8	hwä'.	O'něn‘ Now	o‘'nĭ‘ also	ne'' the	O‘hnion‘'sä' It Squash	wä'egwat'hwä'. She visited (there).	O'něn‘ Now
9	o‘'nĭ‘ also	ne'' the	Oä'wěn'‘sä' It Sunflower	wä'egwat'hwä'. she visited (there).	O'něn‘ Now	o‘'nĭ‘ also	Ga‘ha‘señ It
10	die'thä' Fire-dragon	owä‘he‘sdo'gon' it white pure (is)	ni‘häiä'do''děn‘ such his body kind of (is)	wä'hagwat'hwä'. he visited (there).	O'něn‘ Now
11	o‘'nĭ‘ also	ne'' the	Ga‘stawěn'‘sä' It Rattle	wä'hagwat'hwä'. he visited (there).	O'něn‘ Now	o‘'nĭ‘ also	ne'' the
12	Hadawine'thä' He (Red) Meteor	wä'hagwat'hwä'. he visited (there).	O'něn‘ Now	o‘'nĭ‘ also	ne'' the	Daga‘shwi- It Spring Wind
13	ne''dä'	wä'hagwat'hwä'. he visited (there).	O'něn‘ Now	o‘'nĭ‘ also	ne'' the	Hania'děn‘go'nä He Great Turtle
14	wä'hagwat'hwä'. he visited (there).	O'něn‘ Now	o‘'nĭ‘ also	ne'' the	Skwä'iěn‘ Otter	wä'hagwat'hwä'. he visited (there).

a visit. Now, also, he, the Duck, paid a visit. Now, also, he, the Fresh Water, paid a visit. Now, also, he, the Yellowhammer, paid a visit. Now, also, he, the Medicine, paid a visit. Moreover, all things that are produced by themselves, that produce themselves, that is, the animals, and, next to them, the small animals, the flying things, of every species, all paid a visit. Now, sometime afterward, he, the Aurora Borealis, paid a visit. And, verily, he it was who divined the Word of the chief. Verily, he said: "The great standing tree, the Tooth, must be uprooted. And wherever it has a root there severally they must stand, and they must severally lay hold of each several root. And just then, and not before, shall they be able to uproot the standing tree. The earth will be torn open. Moreover, all persons must look therein. And there, beside the abyss, they

O'něⁿ⸲	o⸲'nĭ⸲	ne''	Tha‛hioñ'nĭ⸲	wă‛hagwat'hwă⸲.		O'něⁿ⸲	o⸲'nĭ⸲	1
Now	also	the	Wolf	he visited (there).		Now	also
ne''	So'wĕk	wă‛hagwat'hwă⸲.	O'něⁿ⸲	o⸲'nĭ⸲	ne''	O‛hne'ganos		2
the	Duck	he visited (there).	Now	also	the	It Fresh Water
wă‛hagwat'hwă⸲.	O'něⁿ⸲	o⸲'nĭ⸲	ne''	Gwěⁿ⸲'gwěⁿ⸲'	wă‛hagwat'hwă⸲'			3
he visited (there).	Now	also	the	Yellow-hammer	he visited (there).
O'něⁿ⸲	o⸲'nĭ⸲	ne''	Onoⁿ‛gwă''tchă⸲	wă‛hagwat'hwă⸲.	Gagwe'gĭ⸲			4
Now	also	the	It Medicine	he visited (there).	It all
dĭ''	ne''	stěⁿ⸲'	gwă''	noñwa‛ho''děⁿ⸲	ne''	odadoñ'nĭ⸲,	wadoñ'ni	5
more- over	the that	any- thing	seem- ingly	kind of thing	the	it has grown (It has produced itself),	it grows (it pro-
ă''‛hă⸲,	nă'ie⸲	ne''	goñdi'io⸲.	nă'ie⸲	gwă''tho⸲	ne''	goñdiio'shoⁿ''ă⸲	6
duces itself),	that (It is)	the	they (z.) are animals,	that (it is)	next in order	the	they (z.) are small animals (birds)
ne''	goñdi'děⁿ⸲,	nhwă‛diiodi‛se'äge⸲,	gagwe'gĭ⸲	wă‛goñdigwat'hwă⸲'				7
the	they (z.) fly habitually,	every they (z.) are species in number,	it all	they (z.) visited (there)
O'něⁿ⸲	gaiñ'gwă⸲	nwă‛oñni'she⸲	o'něⁿ⸲	wă‛hagwat'hwă⸲	ne''			8
Now	some (time)	so (long) it lasted	now	he visited (there),	the
Hodoñnĭ'ă⸲.	Nă'ie⸲	bi'iă⸲	wă‛hoñwawěñnowěⁿ''nhă⸲	ne''	Ha‛			9
He Aurora Borealis.	That (it is)	verily	he his word divined	the	he
sěñnowa'něⁿ⸲.	Nă'ie⸲	ne''	hĭiă⸲	wă‛hěⁿ‛hěñ'':	"Eⁿgaěñdodă'-			10
chief (is).	That (it is)	the	verily	he it said:	"It tree will be uprooted
gwěⁿk	ne''	gă‛he'gowa'něⁿ⸲	ne''	Ono''djă⸲.	Nă'ie⸲	ne''	tca''	11
	the	it tree standing great (is)	the	It Tooth.	That (it is)	the	the where
noñ'we⸲	niiokde‛häde'nioⁿ	ne''tho⸲	děⁿ‛hadidă''nhă⸲,	děⁿ‛hadiie-				12
the place	there it roots project plurally	there	they (m.) will stand,	they (m.) will plurally
nauⁿ‛hoⁿ	ne''	djokde‛hăt'shoⁿ⸲.	O'něⁿ⸲	ha⸲'să⸲	ěⁿ‛hadigwe'niă⸲			13
lay hold of it	the	each it root is one.	Now	just then, (not before)	they (m.) will be able to do it
ěⁿ‛hadiěñdoda'gwă⸲.	Ěⁿwado⸲‛hwěñdjiadet'hă⸲.	Gagwe'gĭ⸲	dĭ''					14
they (m.) tree will uproot.	It itself earth will open roughly.	It all	more- over
ne''tho⸲	hěⁿioñtgat'hwă⸲.	O⸲sadagěⁿ‛hia'dă⸲	ne''tho⸲	hěⁿiesěñ-				15
there	hence will one look.	It abyss edge of	there	hence one thee will

must lay thee. Now, moreover, there at thy head she with whom thou dost abide must sit with her legs hanging down into the abyss." Then, verily, the chief replied, saying: "Kuʻ. I am thankful that ye have divined my word. Now all things have been fulfilled."

Verily, it did thus come to pass that they did uproot the standing tree, Tooth, that grew beside the lodge of the chief. And all the inhabitants of that place came thither with the intention of looking into the abyss. It did thus come to pass that everyone that dwelt there did look therein. At that time the chief then said, addressing his spouse: "Now, too, let us two look into the abyss. Thou must bear her, Zephyrs, on thy back. Thou must wrap thyself with care." Now, moreover, he gave to her three ears of corn, and, next in

---

1 däʹgän̄ʻ.   Oʹiĕⁿʻ   diʹʼ   tcaʼʼ   non̄ʹweʻ   nisnonʻhäʹiĕⁿʻ   neʼʼthoʻ   ĕⁿiet
   lay.   Now   more-   the   the   there thy scalp   there   she
                          over   where   place   lies   will

2 goʹdak   neʼʼ   desniʻʹdĕn̄ʻ,   oʻsadagon̄ʹwäʻ   häʻdĕⁿiagoʻsiʻdĕⁿʻdon̄nionʻ-
   sit   the   ye two abide   it abyss in   just her two feet will
                          together,   severally hang."

3 ʻhek.ʻʼ   Oʹnĕⁿʻ   hiʹiäʻ   neʼʼ   haʻsĕn̄nowanĕⁿʻ   niʻhaʻwĕn̄ʻ: "Kuʻʹ.   iia-
              Now   verily   the   he chief (is)   thence he   "Kuʻ,   I am
                                                                replied:

4 wĕⁿʼʻhäʻ   wäʻsgwĕn̄nowĕⁿʼʼnhäʻ.   Oʹnĕⁿʻ   gagweʹgĭʻ   wäʻgäiʻhwa-
   thankful   thou my word hast divined. Now   it all   it matter
                                                                   has been

5 ieiʼʼkheʻ.ʼʼ
   fulfilled.ʼʼ

6 Neʼʼthoʻ   biʹiäʻ   niiawĕⁿʼʼĭʻ   neʼʼ   tcaʼʼ   hodiĕn̄dodäʹgwĕⁿʻʻ   neʼʼ
   There   verily   so it came   the   the   they (m.) tree   the
                           to pass   where   uprooted

7 Onoʼʼdjäʻ   tcaʼʼ   gäʻʻheʼ   neʼʼ   honoⁿʻsäʹkdäʻ   neʼʼ   haʻsĕn̄nowaʹnĕⁿʻ.
   it tooth   the   it tree   the   his lodge be-   the   he chief (is)
                where   stands   side it

8 Oʹiĕⁿ   tcaʼʼ   enaʹgeeʻ   gagweʹgĭʻ   neʼʼthoʻ   däʹiĕⁿʻ   gaweiʻhäʹdie
   Now   the   they dwell   it all   there   hither one one came desiring it
             where   (they) came (for the purpose of it)

9 neʼʼthoʻ   hegatgatʻhwäʻ   tcaʼʼ   oʻsadagon̄ʹwäʻ.   Neʼʼthoʻ   iwäʻ-
   there   thither let me   the   it abyss in.   There   so it
                look   where

10 awĕⁿʼʻhäʻ   tcaʼʼ   hwäʻhodiʻheʼʼg   tcaʼʼ   niʹionʻ   enaʹgeeʻ   neʼʼthoʻ
   came to   the   it exhausted their the   so it is much they (indef.) there
   pass   where   number   where   (many)   dwell

11 hwäʻhon̄tgatʻhwäʻ.   Thoʼʼgeʻ   oʹiĕⁿ   neʼʼ   haʻsĕn̄nowanĕⁿʻ,   wäʻ-
   thither they (m.)   At that   now   the   he chief (is)   he
   looked.   (time)

12 shagawĕⁿʼʻhäs   neʼʼ   heʹiäʻ   wäʻhĕⁿʻhĕn̄ʼʼ: "Oʹnĕⁿʻ   oʼʼ   niʼʼ
   her addressed   the   his   he it said: "Now   too   the
                              spouse   we

13 hĕⁿdiatgatʻhwäʻ   tcaʼ   oʻsaʹdeʻ   Dĕⁿʻsadäksaʹdĕⁿʻ   neʼʼ   ĕⁿsheiäʹdĕⁿʻ-
   thither we two will the   it abyss is Thou wilt bear on   the   thou her person
   look   where   present.   thy back   wilt bear

14 ʻhäwäʻ   neʼʼ   Gaĕn̄deʼʼsoⁿk.   Ĕⁿʻsaʼʼgwas   ĕⁿʻsatdogĕⁿʼʼsdäʻ."   Oʹnĕⁿʻ
   the   Gusts-of-wind.   Thou thyself   thou thyself wilt   Now
                       Zephyrs.   wilt wrap   make ready."

15 diʼʼ   dashagäʹoⁿʻ   neʼʼ   onĕⁿʼʻhäʻ,   äʻʼsĕⁿʻ   nionoⁿʻkwĕⁿʼʼiägeʻ,   näʼʼie
   more-   he it to her   the   it corn.   three   so it ear is in num-   that
   over,   gave   ber,   (it is)

order, the dried meat of the spotted fawn, and now, moreover, he said: "This ye two will have for provision." Now he also broke off three fagots of wood, which, moreover, he gave to her. She put them into her bosom, under her garments. Then, verily, they went thither to the place. They arrived at the spot where the earth was torn up, and then he said: "Do thou sit here." There, verily, she sat where the earth was broken off. There she hung both legs severally into the abyss. Now, in so far as he was concerned, he, the chief, was looking into the abyss, and there his spouse sat. Now, at that time he upraised himself, and said: "Do thou look hence into the abyss." Then she did in this manner, holding with her teeth her robe with its burden. Moreover, there along the edge of the abyss she seized with her hands, and, now, moreover, she bent over to look. He said: "Do

gwä″tho,	tcīsdä'thieñ″'ä'	o'wa'hät'he^n',	o'nĕ^n'	di''	wä'hĕ^n'hĕñ'':	1
next in order,	spotted fawn	it meat dry (is),	now	moreover	he it said:	
"Na'ie'	nĕñ'gĕ^n'	ĕ^{n}djadĕnnä″dä'."	O'nĕ^n'	o'nï'	wä'thäiä″kho^n'	2
"That (it is)	this one	ye two will take for provisions."	Now	also	he iteratively broke them	
'ä'sĕ^n'	niioko^n'kho''nage'	ne''	oiĕñ'dä',	ıä'ie' di''	shago'wi'.	3
three	so many it wood sticks are in number	the	it wood (fuel),	that moreover it is	he gave (them) to her.	Ena's
gwagoñ'wä'	heiago'sĕ^n''di'.	O'nĕ^n'	hi'iä'	ne''tho'	nhe'hoñne'noñ'	4
Her bosom in	thither she them slipped.	Now,	verily,	there	thither they (m.) went.	
Wä'hni'io^n'	tca''	noñ'we'	iodo^n'hwĕñdjiadethä'ĕñ',	o'nĕ^n'	wä'hĕ^n'	5
They two (m.) arrived	the where	the place	it earth is roughly opened,	now	he it said:	
hĕñ'':	"Tho'nĕ^n'	sadiĕñ''."	Ne''tho' bi'iä'	wä'oñ'diĕñ''	tca'' noñ'we'	6
	"Here	do thou sit down."	There, verily,	she sat down	the the place where	
odo^n'hwĕñdjiiä″gï'.	Ne''tho'	wä'dioñdno^n'dĕ^n'do^n'gwä'		ne''	o'sa	7
it earth is sundered.	There	she hung her legs thereby		the	it	
dagoñ'wä',	o'sadagoñ'wä'	heiagono^n'dĕ^n'doñ'nio^{n}k.		O'nĕ^n'	ne''	8
abyss in,	it abyss in	thither her leg is hanging severally.		Now	the that	
ıä''	o'sadagoñ'wä'	hä'de'haga''hä'	ne''	ha'sĕñnowa'nĕ^n',	ne''tho'	9
that one	it abyss in	hence he his eyes has fixed on it	the	he chief (is),	there	
ne''	nä''	etgo'dä'	ne'' he'ıä'.	O'ıĕ^n' tho''ge'	wä'hatgetc'gwä'	10
the that that one	that	she sat	the his wife.	Now at that time	he himself raised up	
wä'hĕ^n'hĕñ'':	"Hwä'satgat'hwä'	o'sadagoñ'wä'."		O'nĕ^n'	doñdäie'ä'	11
he it said:	"Hence do thou look	it abyss in."		Now	just she did it	
nĕ^n''	ne''	goiĕñ''sä'	wä'o^n'tco''hik	tca''	deioñda'kse'.	Ne''tho'	12
this way	the	her robe	she took it in her mouth	the where	she bore it on her back.	There
di''	o'sadagĕ^n'hiadä''sbo^n'	wä'eienauñ'gwä',		o'nĕ^n' di''	wä'dioñ	13
moreover	it abyss edge of it along	she it laid hold of severally,		now moreover	she bent	
tcä'k'dä'	hwä'oñtgat'hwä'.	Wä'hĕ^n'hĕñ'':	"Otgĕ^n'ï'		i''sowä'	14
forward	hence she looked.	He it said:	"It is plain		it (is) much	

thou bend much and plainly over." So she did do thus. As soon as she bent forward very much he seized the nape of her neck and pushed her into the abyss. Verily, now at that time she fell down thence. Now, verily, the man-being child and the man-being mother of it became one again. When she arrived on earth, the child was again born. At that time the chief himself arose and said, moreover: "Now, verily, I have become myself again; I am well again. Now, moreover, do ye again set up the tree."

And the chief was jealous, and that was the cause that he became ill. He was jealous of Aurora Borealis, and, in the next place, of the Fire Dragon with the pure white body. This latter gave him much mental trouble during the time that he, the chief, whom some call He-holds-the-earth, was married.

1	hwă'desattcă'k'dă'." hence do thou bend forward."	O'něnʻ No v	ne"thoʻ there	nwă'eie'ă'. thus she it did.	Ganio" So soon as	i"sowă' it (is) much	
2	wă'dioñttcă"kdă' she bent forward	o'něnʻ now	wă'hăie'nă' he it took hold of	ne" the	e'se'dă"ge' her nape of the neck on	hwă'shago'- hence he	
3	tcia'ěn" shoved her	o'sadagoñ'wă'. it abyss in.	Tho"'geʻ At that (time)	bi'iă' verily	o'něnʻ no v	diiagoiă'děn"'ī'. thence her body fell down.	
4	O'něnʻ No v	bi'iă' verily	hă'doñsagiadies'dă' just again they two (z.) became commingled	ne" the	eksă'ă"' she child	o"'nī' also	ne" the
5	ono'ʻhă' its mother.	O'něnʻ No v	tca" the where	e'ion" she arrived	ne" the	on"hweñdjiă"ge' it earth on	o'něnʻ now	he" again
6	săioñna'gät again she is born	ne" the	eksă"ă'. she child. (is)	Tho"'geʻ At that time	o'něnʻ no v	ne" the	ha'on"hwă' he himself	ne" the
7	ha'seññowa'něnʻ he chief (is)	sa'hatgěn"'ʻhă' again he arose	o'něnʻ no v	dī" moreover	wă'hěn"hěñ": he it said:	"O'něnʻ "No v		
8	sagă'don" again I am well,	bi'iă'. verily.	O'něnʻ No v	dī" moreover	sadjiiěñdo'děnʻ." do ye reset tree."			
9	Nă'ie' That (it is)	ne" the	ha'seññowa'něnʻ he chief (is)	ho'ga'ʻhěn's he is jealous	iă'ie' that (it is)	gāi'hoññiă'ʻhă' it it causes		
10	tca" the where	wă'honon"hwăk'děn". he became ill.	Nă'ie' That (it is)	ne" the	ho'ga'hă'sek' he him is jealous of	ne" the	Hodoñ- He Aurora	
11	ni'ʻă', Borealis,	iă'ie' that (it is)	gwă"thoʻ next in order	ne" the	Ga'ha'señdie'thă' It Fire-dragon	owă'ʻhe"'sdo'gon" it white pure (is)		
12	ni'hăiă'do'děnʻ, so his body (is) kind of,	iă'ie' that (it is)	gwă"thoʻ next in order	ne" the	Hadawine'thă'. He Red Meteor.	Nă'ie' That (it is)		
13	de'hă'nigon"hā'ʻhă' he gave trouble to the mind	tca" the where	nwă'oñni'she' so it lasted long	o'něnʻ no v	tca" the where	wă'thadäne'gěn" he was married		
14	ne" the	ha'seññowa'něnʻ. he chief (is).	Haon"hweñdjiawă"gī' He-it-earth-holds	o'diă'k some (persons)	hoñwană'don"'khwă'. they him designate thereby.			

So now, verily, her body continued to fall. Her body was falling some time before it emerged. Now, she was surprised, seemingly, that there was light below, of a blue color. She looked, and there seemed to be a lake at the spot toward which she was falling. There was nowhere any earth. There she saw many ducks on the lake [sea], whereon they, being waterfowl of all their kinds, floated severally about. Without interruption the body of the woman-being continued to fall.

Now, at that time the waterfowl, called the Loon shouted, saying: "Do ye look, a woman-being is coming in the depths of the water, her body is floating up hither." They said: "Verily, it is even so." Now, verily, in a short time the waterfowl [duck] called Bittern [Whose eyes-are-ever-gazing-upward], said: "It is true that ye believe that her body is floating up from the depths of the water. Do ye,

Da', *So,*	o'nĕⁿ' *now,*	bi'iă' *verily,*	hwă'eiă'doñ'die' *thither her body falls onward*	ne" *the*	agoñ'gwe'. *she man-being.*	Gaiñ'gwă' *Somewhat*	1
nwă'oñni'she' *so it long lasted*	eiă'doñ'die' *her body was falling*	o'nĕⁿ' *now*		hwă'gūiagĕⁿ"'nhă. *thence it emerged.*		O'nĕⁿ' *Now*	2
wă'oñdiĕñ"'hă' *she was surprised*	gwă" *seemingly*	deio'hă'thek *it is light*	ne" *the*	e'dă"'ge' *below*	oĕⁿ"'hiă' *it (sky) blue (is)*	ni'io't *so it is.*	3
Wă'oūtgat'hwă' *She it looked at*	nā'ie' *that (it is)*	gwă" *seemingly*	ganiă'dae' *it lake is present*	tca" *the where*	bagwă" *direction*	nhwă'aga-wenoñ'hă'die'. *whither she was continuing to go.*	4
	Hiiă" *Not (it is)*	gat'kă' *anywhere*	de'oⁿ'hwĕñdjiă'de'. *it earth is present.*		Ne"tho' *There*	wă'e'gĕⁿ *she it saw*	5
oñnatgă"'de' *they (z.) are numerous*	ne" *the*	so'wek *duck(s)*	ganiadae"'ge' *it lake is present on*	ne"tho' *there*		goñdi'sgo'gă'hă' *they (z.) float about*	6
nhwă'tga'sowă"tchäge'. *every it duck kind in number is (waterfowl).*		Heiotgoñdā"'gwĭ' *Hence it continues*		tca" *the where*	eiă'doñ'die' *her body is falling*	ne" *the*	7
agoñ'gwe' *she man-being (is).*							8
Tho"'ge' *At that time*	o'nĕⁿ' *now*	wă'tho'hĕñe"'dă' *he shouted*		ne" *the*	so'wek. *duck.*	Ha'ho'wĕⁿ' *Loon*	9
hāia'djĭ', *he is named.*	wă'hĕⁿ'hĕñ": *he it said:*	"Tciatgat'hwă' *"Do ye look*		ganonwagon'wă' *it depths of water in*		oñ'gwe', *man-being,*	10
tdā'ioⁿ, *hence she s'coming,*	dāieiă'doñ'die'." *thence her body is flying."*		Wă'hĕñni'hĕñ": *They (m.) it said:*		"Do'gĕⁿs *"It is true*	hi'iă'." *verily."*	11
Ñioi'hwăgwă'hă" *So it matter is short (in a short time)*	o'nĕⁿ' *now,*	bi'iă' *verily,*	wă'tho'hĕñe"'dă' *he shouted*		ne" *the*	so'wek, *duck (?), waterfowl,*	12
Goⁿ'ga"'hwă' *Bittern*	hāia'djĭ' *he is named*	(diiotgoñ't *(at all times*		he'tgĕⁿ'/ *up above*	hă'de'haga'/hă) *thither his two eyes are fixed)*		13
wă'hĕⁿ'hĕñ": *he it said:*	"Swe"'be' *"Ye it do think*	do'gĕⁿs *it is true*	ganoñwagon'wă' *it water depths in*		dāieiă'doñ'die' *thence her body is approaching.*		14

however, look upward." All looked upward, and all, ɔreovei, said:
"Verily, it is true." They next said: "What manner of thing shall
we do?" One of the persons said: "It seems, then, that there must
be land in the depths of the water." At that time the Loon said·
"Moreover, let us first seek to find someone who will be able to bear
the earth on his back by means of the forehead pack strap." All said
seemingly: "I shall be able to bear the earth by means of the forehead pack strap." He replied: "Let us just try; it seems best."
Otter, it seems, was the first to make the attempt. As soon, then,
as a large bulk of them mounted on his back, verily, he sank. In
so far as he was concerned, he was not able to do anything. And
they said: "Thou canst do nothing." Now many of them made the
attempt. All failed to do it. Then he, the Carapace, the Great Turtle,

#						
1	He'tgĕⁿʻ' Up high	hwă'tciatgat'hwă'." thither do ye look."		Gagwe'gĭʻ It all		hwă'hoñtgat'hwă' thither they (m.) looked.
2	gagwe'gĭʻ it all	dĭ'' more- over	wă'hĕñni'hĕñ'': they (m.) it said:	"Do'gĕⁿs "It is true	hi'iă'." verily."	Wă'hĕññi'hĕñ'' They it said
3	gwă''tho'ʻ: next in order:	"Ho't "What (is it)	nonwa'ho''dĕⁿ· kind of thing	nĕⁿdwăie'ä'?" so will we it do?"		Wă'hĕⁿ'hĕñ'' He it said	ne'' the
4	shaiä''dădă'ʻ: he one person	"Diioⁿ'hwĕñdjiä'de' "There it earth is present		nige''-khĕⁿʻ' so it is it must be, (not)	ne'' the	ganonwa- it depths of
5	goñ'wă'?" water in?"	Tho''ge' At that (time)	wă'hĕⁿ'hĕñ'' he it said	ne'' the	Ha'ho'wĕⁿ·: Loon:	"Nă'ie' "That it is	dĭ'' more- over
6	dwadieĕⁿ''dă'ʻ let us it first do,	dwe'ʻsak let us it seek	soñ'' who	nonwa'ho''dĕⁿ· kind of person	ĕⁿ'hagwe'niä' he will be able	ĕⁿ'ba- he will
7	doⁿ'hwĕñdjiage''dat.'' bear earth on his back by means of the forehead strap."	Gwă'' Seem- ingly	thigagwe'gĭʻ just it whole (is)	wă'hĕññi'hĕñ'': they it said:		"I'' "I
8	ĕⁿkgwe'niä' I will be able to do it	ĕⁿgadoⁿ'hwĕñdjiage''dat.'' I will bear the earth on my back (by means of the forehead strap)."		Wă'hĕⁿ'hĕñ''· He it said:		"Gwă'' "Just,
9	gi'shĕⁿʻ' perhaps, (I think)	dwade'niĕñ'dĕⁿʻ.'' let us it try "	Skwă'iĕⁿʻ Otter	gi'shĕⁿʻ I think	da'hadieĕⁿ''dă'ʻ he first was
10	tca'' the where	wă'hade'niĕñ'dĕⁿ·. he it attempted to do.	Ganio'' So soon as	iawe'dowa'nĕⁿʻ it bulk large is	hwă'hoñdawĕⁿ''hät thither they (m.) it got upon
11	hă'nowă''ge'ʻ his back on	o'nĕⁿʻ now	bi'iă' verily	wă'honowiĕ''dă'ʻ he sank into the water.	Hiiă'' Not (it is)	stĕⁿ'' any- thing
12	de'hogwe'nioñʻ he it was able to do	ne'' the that	nä''. that one.	Wă'hĕññi'hĕñ'': They it said:	"Hiiă'' "Not (it is)	stĕⁿ'' any- thing
13	thasgwe'niä'.'' thou it art able to do."	O'nĕⁿ· Now	hoñnatgä''de' they (m.) are numerous	wă'hoñde'niĕñ'dĕⁿ·. they (m.) it attempted.	Gagwe'gĭʻ It all
14	wă'hodino'wĕⁿ·. they it failed to do.	Tho''ge'ʻ At that time	o'nĕⁿʻ now	ne'' the	Hania'dĕⁿ'go'nă'ʻ He Turtle Great, (is)	Hă'no'wă', He Cara- pace (is)

said: "Next in turn, let me make the attempt." Then, verily, a large bulk of the mounted on his back. He was able to bear the all on his back. Then they said: "He it is who will be able to bear the earth on his back." Now, at that time, they said: "Do ye go to seek earth in the depths of the water." There were many of them who were not able to obtain earth. After a while it seems that he, the Muskrat, also made the attempt. He was able to get the ground thence. Muskrat is he who found earth. When he came up again, he rose dead, holding earth in his jaws, and earth was also in his mouth. They placed all of it upon the carapace of the Turtle. Now their chief said: "Do ye hurry, and hasten yourselves in your work." Now a large number of muskrats continued to dive into the depths of the water. As fast as they floated to the surface they placed the earth on the

wā'hĕⁿ‧hĕñ': he it said:	"I" "I	oⁿ'/kĕⁿ‧ next in turn	agade'nieñ'dĕⁿ'." let me it attempt to do."	O'nĕⁿ‧ Now	hi'iă' verily	1
hwā'hoñdawĕⁿ'hät' thither they (m.) got upon it (his back)	iawe'dowa'nĕⁿ‧ it bulk large (is).		Wā'hagwe'niă' He it was able to do	gagwe'gĭ‧ it all		2
wā'hatge''dat. he it bore on the back by the forehead strap.	O'nĕⁿ‧ Now	wā'hĕñni‧hĕñ': they (m.) it said:	"Nā'ie' "That (it is)	ne' the	ĕⁿ'hagwe'niă' he it will be able to do	3
ĕⁿ'hadoⁿ‧hwĕñdjiage''dat." he will bear earth on the back by the forehead strap."	Tho''ge‧ At that time	o'nĕⁿ‧ now	wā'hĕñni‧hĕñ': they it said	"Sne'- "Do ye two it		4
sak'hă'ᵃ go to seek	(swesak'hă‧?) (do ye it go to seek?)	ne'' the	ganoñwagoñ'wā‧ it water depths in	ne'' the	o'he''dā'." it earth (ground)."	5
Oñnatgā''de' They (z.) are not numerous	hiiă'' not (it is)	de'hodigwe'nioñ‧ they it were able to do	a'hadihe'dā'gwā'. could they earth get.	Dĭĕñ''hă' After a while,		6
gwā'' seemingly,	o'nĕⁿ‧ now	ne'' the	Hano'gie'' He Muskrat	o'nĕⁿ‧ now	o''nĭ' also	wā'hade'nieñ'dĕⁿ". he it attempted to do.	7
Nā'ie' That (it is)	wā'hagwe'niă' he it was able to do		hwā'ha‧he'dā'gwā'. thither he earth (ground) fetched.	Hano'gie'' He Muskrat	wā'ha‧he'dā- he found ground.	8
tcĕñ'nĭ'	Sawĕñdā'gä''gwā' Again it floated		hăwĕⁿ‧heioⁿ‧hā'die', he came up dead,		ho‧tciagwe'noñni'- he came with his paws closed	9
hā'die' (on it)	ne'' the	o‧he‧'dā', it ground,	ha'sagoñ'wā‧ his mouth in	o''nĭ' also	wadak'he‧. it came contained in it.	Gagwe'gĭ‧ It all	10
ga'nowā''ge‧ it carapace on	wā'hadi'hĕñ'. they (m.) laid it.	O'nĕⁿ‧ Now	ne'' the	hoñwa'sĕñ'noⁿ" their chief	wā'hĕⁿ‧hĕñ''‧ he it said:	11
"Tciăsno'wĕⁿ‧ᵇ, "Do ye two make haste,		deswā'nowāiă‧hĕⁿ''‧hă' do ye hurry yourselves		swāio'dĕⁿ''hă‧ " do ye work."	O'nĕⁿ‧ Now	12
gĕⁿdio'gowa'nĕⁿ‧ it body of persons large (is)		hano'gie'' muskrat	hoñna'doñe''hwi‧ they (m.) continued to dive		ganoñwagoñ'wā‧. it depths of water in.	13
Ganio'' So soon as	swĕⁿdā'gää''gwā' again it floated habitually		nā'ie' that (it is)	niio‧sno'we' so it is rapid	ga'nowā''ge‧ it carapace on	hadi'he‧- they (m.) are laying the	14

ᵃ This is a dual form employed in the place of a plural, which follows it in parentheses.
ᵇ This is a dual form used for a plural.

back of the Turtle. Sometime thereafter then, verily, they finished covering the carapace with earth. Now, at that time, the carapace began to grow, and the earth with which they had covered it became the Earth.

Now, also, they said: "Now, moreover, do ye go to see and to meet this woman-being whose body is falling hither." At once a great number of the large waterfowl flew hence, joining their bodies together, and there on their joined bodies her person impinged. Then slowly the large waterfowl descended, and also they placed the woman-being there on the carapace. Moreover, the carapace had now grown much in size. Now, moreover, they said: "Now, verily, we are pleased that we have attended to the female man-being who has appeared in the same place with us."

1	da‘hä´‘hă’. earth on it.	Gaiñ´gwä’ Some (time)	nwä’oñni’she’ so (long) it lasted	o’nĕⁿ‘ now	hi’iă’ verily	wä’hadi‘‘sä’ they (m.) it finished
2	ga’nowä´’ge‘ it carapace on	wä’hadi‘he‘do‘‘gä’. they (m.) it with earth coated.		Tho‘‘ge‘ At that time	o’nĕⁿ‘ now	wä’wadodia’gä’ it grew in size
3	ne’’ the	ga’no´wä’ it carapace	nä’ie’ that (it is)	ne’’ the	oⁿ‘hwĕñ’djiä’’ it earth	wä’wa’doⁿ’ it it became	ne’’ the
4	hodi‘he‘do´‘hwi‘. they (m.) it with earth had covered.					
5	O’nĕⁿ‘ Now	dī’’ moreover	wä’heñni‘heñ’’: they it said:	"O’nĕⁿ‘ "Now	dī’’ moreover	swakdoⁿ´‘nă‘, do ye go to see it,	deiétciiä’dää‘dä‘‘nă‘ do ye her body to meet go
6	ne’’ the	nĕñ’gĕⁿ‘ this (it is)	agoñ’gwe‘ she man-being	däieiä’doñ’die’." thence her body is falling."		Goñ At
7	dä’die’ once	o’nĕⁿ‘ now	wä’tgoñdi’dĕⁿ’ they (z.) flew	nä’ie’ a (it is)	ne’’ the	goñdigo’wănĕⁿs they (z.) large ones
8	oññatgä´’de‘ they (z.) are many	nä’ie’ that (it is)	ne’’ the	wä’tgoñdidiä’däik‘hoⁿ’, they (z.) their bodies conjoined severally,		ne’’tho‘ there	hi’iă’ verily
9	he’’tgĕⁿ‘ up high	däieiä’da‘hä’’nhă’. there her body alighted.		O’nĕⁿ‘ Now	skĕñnoⁿ’’ă‘ slowly	dagoñdä’sĕⁿ‘‘dä’ thence they let themselves down	ne’’ the
10	so’wek duck(s)	goñdigo’wănĕⁿs, they (z.) large ones,		nä’ie’ that (it is)	dī’’ moreover	ne’’tho‘ there	ga’nowä´’ge‘ it turtle on
11	wä’shagoni´’dĕñ’ they her placed	ne’’ the	agoñ’gwe‘. she man-being.	O’ĕⁿ‘ Now	dī’’ moreover	ne’’ the	ga’no’wä’ it turtle
12	gowa’ẽⁿ‘ it much	iodo’di‘. it has grown.	O’ẽⁿ‘ Now	dī’’ moreover	wä’heñni‘heñ’’: they (m.) it said:	"O’nĕⁿ‘ "Now	hi’iă’ verily,
13	we‘dwatcĕñnoñ’nia’ we are glad	ne’’ the	tca’’ the where	wä’dioñkhi‘snie’’nhă’ we her have cared for		ne’’ the	oñ’gwe‘ man-being
14	nä’ie’ that (it is)	ne’’ the	gado’gĕⁿ‘ in a certain place	wä’oñgwagoⁿso’’dä’." we (and she) have appeared."			

ONONDAGA VERSION

The next day came, and she looked and saw lying there a deer, also fire and firebrands, and also a heap of wood, all of which had been brought thither. At that time she kindled a fire, using for this purpose the three fagots which she had slipt into the bosom of her garment, and of which he [the chief] had said: "Ye two will have this for a provision." At that time she laid hands on the body of the deer. She broke up its body, some of which she roasted for food. She passed three nights there, when she again gave birth, again becoming possessed of a child. The child was a female. That, verily, was the rebirth of Zephyrs. Now the elder woman-being erected a booth, thatching it with grasses. There the mother and daughter remained, one being the parent of the other.

Now the earth was large and was continually increasing in size. It was now plain where the river courses would be. There they two remained, the mother attending to the child, who increased in size

Wä'o·hĕⁿ''nhä',	wä'oñtgat'hwä'	ne''tho'	gĕñda'gä'	ne''	skĕñ-
It became day,	she it saw	there	it lay	the	deer 1
noñdo''' odjĭs'dä'	o''nĭ'	ne''tho'	gagoⁿ'hetchäge''hĕñ',		oiĕñ'dä'
it fire	also	there	it brands lay heaped,		it fuel 2
o''nĭ' o·sotcio'dä'	ne''tho'	ga''hä.	Tho''ge o'nĕⁿ'		wä'oñdegä''dä',
also it heap stands	there	one it has brought.	At that (time) now		she kindled (a fire), 3
na'ie' wä'oñtc'dä'	ne''	enä'sgwagoñ'wä'	ä''sĕⁿ'		niiokoⁿ'kho''näge'
that she it used (it is)	the	her bosom in	three		so many it fagot in number (is) 4
heiago'sĕⁿ''dĭ',	nä'ie' ne''	ha'wĕñ':	"Ĕⁿtciadĕⁿnä''dä'."		Tho''ge
there she them had dropped.	that (it is) the	he it said:	"Ye two will take provision."		At that (time) 5
o'nĕⁿ' wä'dioⁿnia''hĕñ'	gäiä'di''ge'	ne''	skĕñnoñdoⁿ'.		Wä'dieiä'
now she her two hands to it put	its body on	the	deer.		She its body 6
da'hi''dä', nä'ie'	wä'oñde'skoñ'dĕⁿ'	ne''	ĕⁿioñdekhoñ'niä'.		'Ä''sĕⁿ'
broke up, that (it is)	she it roasted for herself	the	she it will eat.		Three 7
niiagonoⁿ'hwe'dĭ· o'nĕⁿ'	he''	säioñde''doñ',	wä'agowiäiĕñdä''nhä',		
so many she remained over night now	again	again she was confined	she infant became possessed of.		8
e''hĕⁿ' ne''	eksä'ä''.	Nä'ie'	bi'iä' ne''	säioñna'gät	ne''
she female the (is)	she child.	That (it is)	verily the	again she is born	the 9
Gaĕñde''soⁿ'k.	O'nĕⁿ'	ne''	gokstĕñ''ä'	wä'eno'shĕⁿ'',	wä'die'-
It-winds-go-about (Gusts-of-wind)	Now	the	she ancient one	she set up a bower	she 10
sthoñdä'doⁿ'.	Ne''tho'	degni''dĕñ',	oñdat'hawä'.		
thatched it with grass.	There	they (z.) abode,	one parent of the other (was)		11
O'nĕⁿ' gowa'nĕⁿ'	ododi'hä'die'	ne''	oⁿ'hwĕñ'djiä'		O'nĕⁿ'
Now it much (is)	it continues to grow	the	it earth.		Now 12
oiĕñ'det tca'' noñ'we'	ĕⁿgĕⁿ'hioⁿ'hwäde'nioñk.		Ne''tho'		degni''dĕñ''
it is cognizable the the place where	it river will have its course severally.		There		they (z.) two abode. 13
deioñdade''snie' ne''	eksä'ä''.	Agwa's	ne''	nä'ie'	godi'sno'we'
she her cared for the	she child.	Exceedingly	the	that (it is)	she grew rapidly 14

very rapidly. So 1e ti 1e afterward she then became a maiden. And they two continued to re 1ain there.

After a while, see 1ingly, the elder wo 1an-being heard her offspring talking with so 1eone. Now, verily, the elder wo 1an-being was thinking about this 1atter, wondering: "Whence may it be that a man-being could co 1e to talk with her." She addressed her, saying: "Who is it, 1oreover, who visits thee?" The 1aiden said nothing in reply. As soon as it beca 1e night and the darkness was co 1plete, he, the man-being, again arrived. And just as the day dawned the elder wo 1an-being heard hi 1 say: "I will not co 1e again." Verily he then departed.

Not long after this the life of the 1aiden was changed. Moreover, it beca 1e evident that she was about to give birth to a child. After

1	gododi'hā'die'. she continues to grow.	Gaiñ'gwă' Some (time)	nwă'oñni'she' so long	o'něⁿ‘ it lasted	now	eksă'dăse''ă‘ she small maiden (is)
2	wă'wa'doⁿ'. it it became.	Ne''tho‘ There	ni'io't so it is	tca'' the where	degni''děñ. they (z.) two abode.		
3	Dień''hă' After a while,	gwă'' seemingly,	o'něⁿ‘ now	gwă'' seemingly	othoñ'de' she (z.) heard it	ne'' the	gok'stěñ'ă‘ she ancient one	ne'' the
4	deiagot'hā' she is talking with one	ne'' the	dat'hawă‘. her offspring.	O'něⁿ‘ Now	bi'iă' verily	wă'weñnoⁿ‘doñ'nioⁿ she (z.) it thought about repeatedly		
5	ne'' the	gok'stěñ'ă‘ she ancient one	wă'we'ă': she (z.) it thought:	"Gaiñ'' "Where	hoñ'' probably	noñ'we‘ the place	noñda'iěⁿ thence one should come	
6	ne'' the	oñ'gwe‘ manbeing	deiagot'hā'. she is talking with one,	Wă'agoweñnā''nhă', She addressed words to her,	wă'gěⁿ''‘hěñ': she (z.) it said:		
7	"Goñ‘ha'wă‘, "I am thy parent,	soñ'' who (is it)	dī'' moreover	noñwa‘ho''děⁿ kind of person	hiianada‘hěñ''sek?" he thy mat visits?''		
8	Hiiă'' Not (it is)	stěⁿ'' anything	de'aga'weñ‘ she it said	ne'' the	eksă'go'nă‘. she maiden.	Ganio'' So soon as	wă'o''gak, it became night,
9	nā'ie' that (it is)	ne'' the	wă'dwa‘soñdāiěñdă''nhă' it thick night became	o'něⁿ‘ now	ne'' the	sa‘hā'ioⁿ'. again he arrived.	Agwa's Just as
10	o'něⁿ‘ now	dāio‘hěⁿ'ī‘hā'die' there it is coming to be day	o'něⁿ‘ now	ne'' the	gok'stěñ'ă‘ she ancient one	gothoñ'de' she it heard	
11	tca'' the where	wă‘hěⁿ‘hěñ'': he it said:	"Hiiă'' "Not (it is)	he'' again	dă'doñda'ge'." again I will come."	O'něⁿ‘ Now	bi'iă' verily
12	sho‘děñ'dioñ‘. again he departed.						
13	Hiiă'' Not (it is)	de'oi‘hwishe''ī‘ it matter long (is)	o'něⁿ‘ now	o'iă' it other (is)	ni'io't so it is	tca'' the where	ago'n‘he' she living (is)	ne'' the
14	eksă'go'nă‘. she maiden. (is)	O'něⁿ‘ Now	dī' moreover	oiěñ'det. it is recognizable	tca'' the where	ěⁿiagoksă'dāiěñdă''nhă'. she will become possessed of a child.	

a time, when, seemingly, the maiden had only a few more days to go, she was surprised, seemingly, to hear two male man-beings talking in her body. One of the persons said: "There is no doubt that the time when man-beings will emerge to be born has now arrived." The other person replied: "Where, moreover, does it seem that thou and I should emerge?" He replied, saying: "This way, moreover, thou and I will go." Now, again, one of them spoke, saying: "It is too far. This way, right here, is near, and, seemingly, quite transparent." At that time he added, saying: "Do thou go then; so be it." Now, he started and was born. The child was a male. Then, so far as the other was concerned, he came out here through her armpit. And now, verily, he killed his mother. The grandmother saw that the child that was born first was unsurpassedly fine-looking.

Dien̈''hä'	gwă''	o'něⁿ'	gwă''	dogā''ă'	ěⁿtciago'hěⁿ''sěn̄'	o'něⁿ'	1
After a while	seemingly,	now	seemingly,	a few in number	will it her days dawn on	now	
ne''	eksă'go'nă'	wă'on̄dien̈''hä'	gwă''	o'něⁿ'	gothon̄'de'	de'hodi'-	2
the	she maiden	she was surprised	seemingly	now	she it heard	they (two) were conversing	
thä'	tca''	eiă'dagon̄'wă'.	I'ha'doⁿk	ne''	shāiă''dădă':	"O'něⁿ'	3
the where		her body in.	He said repeatedly	the	he one person is:	"Now	
gāi'hwado'gěⁿ'	ne''	tca''	hwă'ga'he''g	tca''	non̄'we'	ěⁿieia	4
it is a matter of certainty	the	the where	it (time) has arrived	the where	the place	one will	
gěⁿ''nbă'	ne''	on̄'gwe'	nā'ie'	ne''	ěⁿion̄nagăt'."	Ni'ha'wěn̄'	5
emerge	the	man-being	that (it is)	the	will one be born."	Thence he it said	
ne''	shāiă'dădă':	"Gain̄''	gwă''	dī''	non̄'we'	hěⁿ'dene'?"	Da'.	6
the	he one person is:	"Where,	seemingly,	moreover,	the place	hence we two will go?"	He	
hāi'hwă'sä'gwă'	wă'hěⁿ'hěn̄'':	"Tho'něⁿ'	dī''	hěⁿ'dene'."	O'něⁿ'		7
answered	he it said:	"Here (it is)	moreover	hence we two will go."	Now		
he''	ne''	shāiă''dădă'	wă'hawěn̄nitgěⁿ''nbă',	wă'hěⁿ'hěn̄''.			8
again	the	he one person is	he spoke (uttered word),	he it said:			
"Swă'djĭk'	i'noⁿ'.	Tho'něⁿ'	gwă''tho'	dosgěⁿ''hă',	gwă''		9
"Excessively	far (it is).	This way	just here	(it is) near,	seemingly,		
deio'hat'bek."	Tho''ge'	wă'hěⁿ'hěn̄'':	"Wă'se'',	nio''."	O'něⁿ'		10
it is light (i. e., transparent)."	At that (time)	he it said:	"Thither do thou go,	so be it."	Now		
wă'ha'děn̄'diă',	wă'hěn̄nagät'	ne''	shāiă''dădă'.	Hadji'na'	ne''		11
he started,	he was born	the	he one person is.	He male (is)	the		
haksă'ă''.	Tho''ge'	nă''	ne''	shāiă'dădă'	tho'něⁿ'	e'sioⁿ'dă''ge'	12
be child.	At that (time)	that one	the that	he one person is	here	her side at	
da'hāiagěⁿ''nbă'.	O'něⁿ'	bi'iă'	wă'shago'iio'	ne''	hono''hä'.		13
thence he came forth.	Now	verily	he her killed	the	his mother.		
Heiawěn̄go''dī'	haksă'di'io	ne''	tca''	wă'watgat'hwă'	ne''	ho'sodă'hä''	14
Unsurpassedly (thoroughly)	he fine child (is)	the	the where	she (z.) it looked at	the	his grandmother	

At that time she asked, saying: "Who, moreover, killed your mother, now dead?" Now, he who did it replied, saying: "This one here." Verily, he told a falsehood. Now, the elder woman-being seized the other one by the arm and cast his body far beyond, where he fell among grasses. Now, she there attended to the other one. It is said that they grew rapidly in size. After a while, seemingly, he was in the habit of going out, and there running about from place to place. In like manner they two grew very rapidly.

Now the child who lived out of doors kept saying: "Do thou tell thy grandmother, who, verily, is grandmother to us two, that she should make me a bow, and also an arrow." Now, verily, he told her what manner of thing the other person desired. The only

	ne''	da'hadieĕⁿ·'dä'	wä'hĕñnagät'.	Tho''ge·	o'nĕⁿ·	wä'ei'hwa-
1	the	there he did it (first) was the	he was born.	At that (time)	now	she asked questions repeatedly
2	ıĕñ'doⁿ	wä'ä'hĕñ'':	"Soñ''	noñwa'ho''dĕⁿ	dï''	wä'shago'io'	ne''
		she it said:	"Who	kind of person,	moreover,	he her killed	the
3	etchino''hä'-gĕⁿ''hä'?''	Da'hĕⁿ'hĕñ''	ne''	ne''tho·	ni'hoie'ĕⁿ··	
	she your two mother—it was?''	Thence he it said	the	there	so he it did:	
4	"Nĕñ'gĕⁿ·.''	Wä'hĕñnoiĕⁿ''dä'	hi'iä'.	O'nĕⁿ·	ne''	gok'stĕñ'ä'
	"This (one) it is.''	He told a falsehood	verily.	Now	the	she ancient one,
5	da'honĕñtchä''	ne''	shäiä'dädä·	si''	ia'hoiä'doñ'dï',	awĕñnu'gä
	thence she his arm seized	the	he one person is	yonder (far)	hence she cast his body,	it grass (weeds)
6	goñ'wä·	hwä'hĕñdägä''nhä'.	O'nĕⁿ·	ne'tho'	de'ho'snie'	ne''
	among	there he fell on his back.	Now	there	she him cared for	the
7	shäiä''dädä'.	Agwa's,	iä'kĕⁿ',	de'hodisno'we'.	Diĕñ''hä'	gwä''
	he one person is.	Very,	it is said,	they two grew rapidly.	After a while,	seemingly
8	o'nĕⁿ·	he'häia'gĕⁿ's,	ne''tho'	hadak'he's.	Hiiĕⁿ'noiĕⁿ'hä'	ne''
	now	hence he goes out of doors,	there	he ran about habitually.	They two played together	the
9	deiadĕⁿ'hnoñ'dä'.	Shä'de'io't	hoñnadisno'we'.			
	they two are brothers.	It two is alike	they (m.) grew rapidly.			
10	O'nĕⁿ·	i'ha'doⁿk	ne''	haksä'ä''	ıä'ie'	ne''	äsde''	bägwä''
	Now	he it kept saying	the	he child	that (it is)	the	out of doors	toward, side of it
11	hana'gee':	"Sheiatho'iĕⁿ·	ne''	sa'sodä'hä''	ıä'ie'	ne''	bi'iä'
	he dwells:	"Do thou her tell	the	thy grandmother	that (It is)	the	verily
12	shedi''sodä'hä·	ne''	äioñge'sĕñ'niĕⁿ'	nĕ''	a'ĕñ'ıä'	ga'hes'ga'
	she our two grandmother is	the	she me should it make for	the	it bow	it arrow
13	o''ıi'.''	O'nĕⁿ·	bi'iä'	wä'shagotho'iĕⁿ·	tca''	noñwa'ho''dĕⁿ	ne''
	also.''	Now,	verily,	he her it told	the where	kind of thing	the
14	de'hodoⁿ'hwĕñdjioñ'niks	ne''	shäiä''dädä'.	Nä'ie'	ne''	dāionä'-
	it him is necessary for	the	he one person is.	That (it is)	the	there she

result was that she got angry, saying: "Never will I take him a bow and also an arrow. It is he, verily, who killed her who was the mother of you two."

It continued thus that the two brothers played together. They were in the habit of making a circuit of the island[a] floating there. And, as rapidly as they made a circuit of it, so rapidly did the earth increase in size. When, it is said, the island had grown to a great size, then he who had been cast out of doors kept saying: "Man-beings[b] are about to dwell here." The other person kept saying: "What manner of thing is the reason that thou dost keep saying, 'Man-beings are about to dwell here?'" He said: "The reason that I say that is that it is a matter of fact that man-beings are about to

---

khwĕⁿ'·hā'	gĕñ'gwä',	iioñ'doⁿk.	"Hiiă'	hwĕñ'doⁿ·	thakhe'sĕñ'niĕⁿ'	1
became angry	only.	she it kept saying:	"Not (it is)	ever	I him it will make for	
ne"	a'ĕñ'ıă'	ga·hes'ga'	o"'ıi'.	Nă'ie'	bi'iă' shago'io'	ne'¹ 2
the	it bow	it arrow	also.	That (it is),	verily, he her killed	the
she·snino'·hā'."						3
she (is) your two mother."						
Ne"tho'	ni'io't	hiiĕⁿ'noiĕⁿ'·hā'	de'biadĕⁿ'hnoñ'dä'.	De·hiiathwä	4
There	so it is	they (m.) two played together	they (m.) two are brothers.	The (m.) two made customarily a	
da'ses	tca"	ga·hwe"'no'.	Nă'ie'	ne"	tca"	niio'sno'we' ne" 5
circuit of it	the where	it island floats.	That (it is)	the	the where	so it is rapid the
wä'hiathwäda'se'	gĕⁿ's	he"	niio'sno'we'	wä'wadodia'gă'	tca" 6
they two made a circuit of it	customarily	so	so it is rapid	it grew in size	the where
oⁿ·hwĕñdjiä'de'.	O'nĕⁿ',	iä'kĕⁿ",	gowa'ıĕⁿ·	wä'ododi·ha'die'	ne" 7
it earth is present.	Now,	it is said,	it much (is)	hence it continued to grow in size	the
tca"	ga·hwe·'no'	tho"ge'	o'nĕⁿ·	i·ha'doⁿk.	nĕñ'gĕⁿ·	ă'wet äsde" 8
the where	it island floats	at that time	now	he it kept saying	this one (it is)	it can be out of doors
hoiä'doñ'dioⁿ·:	"Oñ'gwe·	oñnagät'he'	ne"	tho'nĕⁿ·."	I·ha'doⁿk 9
she his body cast:	"Man-being	they are about to dwell	the	here."	He it kept saying
ne'¹	shäiä"dädä'·	"Ho't	noñwa·ho"dĕⁿ'	diioi·"hwä'	tca" 10
the	he one person is:	"What	kind of thing	there its matter (is) (=is the reason)	the where
i·sa'doⁿk:	"Oñ'gwe·	oñnagät'he'	ne"	tho'nĕⁿ·?"	Wä·hĕⁿ"hĕñ": 11
thou art saying:	"Man-being	they are about to dwell	the	here?"	He it said:
"Nă'ie'	ne"	diioi·"hwä'	ne"	nä'ie'	igä'doⁿk	ne" do'gĕⁿs se'¹ 12
"That (it is)	the	there its matter (is) (=is the reason)	the	that (it is)	I keep saying it	the it is true as a matter of fact
oñ'gwe·	ĕⁿioñnagät'	ne"	tho'ıĕⁿ·.	I"	nä"	igä'doⁿk	ne" Odĕñdoñ- 13
man-being	they (indef.) will dwell	the	here.	I	that one	I keep saying it	the It Sap-

---

[a] Hence arose the idea so prevalent among Amerindian peoples that the earth is an island, floating on the primal sea.
[b] Here man-being means human being.

dwell here. And it is I, the Sapling, who say it." So then, this other person began to say: "I shall be called Flint."

When they two had really grown to maturity, it is said, then he, the Sapling, made himself a lodge, erecting a booth. And when he had completed it, he departed. He went to hunt. He shot at a bird, but he missed it, and his arrow fell into the water. Verily, he then resolved: "I will take it out of the water again." Now, there into the water he cast himself, plunging into the water. He was surprised that, seemingly, he fell there beside a doorway. Then, moreover, from the inside of the lodge a man-being spoke to him, saying: "Do thou come in, my child; I am thankful that thou hast visited my lodge. I purposely caused thee to visit the place where my lodge stands. And the reason that it has thus come to pass is that my mind was so affected by what thy grandmother keeps saying. And, moreover, I

---

1. Iiʼäʻ / ling — eⁿgiaʼdjĭk." / will I be named." — Daʼ, / So, — oʼnĕⁿʻ / nov — nĕñʼgĕⁿʻ / this one (it is) — shaiäʼʼdădăʻ / he one person is — wäʼhaʻsaʼwĕⁿʼ / he it began

2. tcaʼʼ / the where — iʻhaʼdoⁿk: / he it kept saying: — "Oʻhaʼäʼ / "It Flint — năʼʼ / that one — neʼʼ / the that — iʻ / I — eⁿgiaʼdjĭk " / will I be named."

3. Oʼnĕⁿʻ / Now — thoʼʻhăʻ, / nearly — iăʼkĕⁿ, / it is said, — aʻhiadodiaʼgăʼ / they two would grow up — oʼnĕⁿʻ / now — hotnoⁿʼsoñʼniʻ / he himself made a lodge

4. wăʼhanosʼhĕⁿʼ / he made a bower — neʼʼ / the — Odĕñdoñniʼʼăʻ. / It Sapling. — Năʼie' / That (it is) — neʼʼ / the — oʼnĕⁿʻ / now — wăʼhadiĕñ / he completed his

5. noʼʼkdĕⁿʼ / task — oʼnĕⁿʻ / now — hoʻdĕñʼdioñʻ. / he departed. — Wăʼhadowătʼhăʼ. / He went to hunt. — Wăʼbăʼaʼgwăʼ / He (it) shot

6. neʼʼ / the — goñdiioʼshoⁿʼʼăʻ / they (z.) birds (are) (=small animals) — saʻhatʼwăʼʼdăʼ / he it missed — awĕⁿʼʼgeʻ / it water in — hwăʼoʼnhăʼ / thither it was immersed — neʼʼ / the

7. hoʻhesʼgăʼ. / his arrow. — Oʼnĕⁿʻ, / Now, — hiʼiăʼ / verily, — wăʼheʼăʼ: / he it thought: — "Ĕⁿsgoʼgwăʼ." / "will I it take out of the water." — Oʼnĕⁿʻ / Now — neʼʼthoʻ / there

8. awĕⁿʼʼgeʻ / it water on (in) — wăʻhadiăʼdoʼʼiak / he cast his body — wăʻhadeʼsʼgok. / he plunged himself in it. — Wăʻhadiĕñʼʼhăʼ / He was surprised — gwăʼʼ / seemingly,

9. ieʼʼthoʻ / there — hwăʻhĕñdagäʼʼnhaʼ / there he fell on his back — ganhoʻhwăkʼdăʼ. / it doorway beside. — Oʼnĕⁿʻ / Now — diʼʼ / moreover — ganoⁿsʼ / it lodge

10. goñʼwăʻ / in — oñʼgweʻ / man-being — daʻhadaʼdiăʼ / thence he spoke — wăʻhĕⁿʻhĕñʼʼ: / he it said: — "Dădjioⁿʼʼ, / "Do thou come in, — goñʻhaʼwăʻ / I am thy parent.

11. Niiawĕⁿʼʼhăʻ / I am thankful — wăʻsguoⁿʻsoweⁿʼʼnhăʼ. / thou my lodge hast found. — Tcaʼʼ / The where — geʼqdăʼ / I it did purposely — tcaʼʼ / the where — wăʻsgwatʼhwă / thou dost pay a visit

12. tcaʼʼ / the where — noñʼweʻ / the place — agenoⁿʻsäʼieⁿʼ. / I lodge have. — Năʼeʼ / That (it is) — neʼʼ / the — diioiʼʻhwăʼ / there its reason (is) — tcaʼʼ / the where — ieʼʼthoʻ / thus

13. nwăʼawĕⁿʼʼhăʼ / so it came to pass — neʼʼ / the — akʻnigoⁿʼʼhăʼ / my mind — neʼʼ / the — tcaʼʼ / the where — noñwaʻhoʼʼdĕⁿʼ / kind of thing — iioñʼ / she it kept saying

14. doⁿk / the — neʼʼ / your two grandmother. — etchiʼsoʼdăʻhăʼ. / That (it is) — Năʼieʼ / moreover — diʼʼ / I it intended — ageʼiʻʻ / the — neʼʼ / I thee it will give — eⁿgoñʼieⁿʼ / the

desired to give thee a bow and also an arrow which thou dost need, and which, by and by, thy brother will see, and then he will ask, saying: 'Whence didst thou get this?' Thou must say: 'My father has given it to me.'" Now, further ore, he gave both to him. At this time he bestowed another thing; it was corn. At that time he said: "This corn, as soon as thou arrivest at home, thou must at once roast for food for thyself; and at that time thou must continue to say: 'In this manner will it continue to be that man-beings, who are about to dwell here on the earth, will be in the habit of eating it. Thy brother will visit thy lodge, and at that time Flint will ask, saying: 'Whence didst thou get this kind of thing?' Thou must say, moreover: 'My father has given it to me.'"

Moreover, it did thus come to pass when he arrived at his home At that time he husked the ear of corn and also laid it beside the fire;

a'ĕñ'nä'	ga·hes'gā'	o"nĭ',	nä'ie·	ne"	de'sadoⁿ·hwĕñdjio'nĭks.	
(it) bow	it arrow	also,	that (it is)	the	it thee is necessary for.	1
Nä'ie·	ne"	gĕⁿ'djĭk	ĕⁿ·hatgat'hwä'		ne"	detciadĕⁿ·bnoñ'dä'	
That (it is)	the	by and by	he it will see		the	thou he are brothers	2
ĕⁿ·hĕⁿ·hĕñ":	"Gaiñ'"	noñ'we'	däs'hawä'?"	Ĕⁿ·si·hĕñ':	"G'ni·hä·"	
he will say:	"Where	the place	thence thou it didst bring?"	Thou it wilt say:	"My father	3
haga'wi'."	O'nĕⁿ·	dĭ"	däshagaoⁿ"	dedjia'oⁿ'.	O'nĕⁿ·	dĭ"	he"
he it gave to me."	Now	moreover	he it gave to him	both.	Now.	moreover,	again	4
o'iä'	doñda'hat'gä'k,	nä'	ne"	onĕⁿ'·hä'.	Tho"ge'	o'nĕⁿ·	
it is other one	thence again he bestowed it	that one	the that	it corn.	At that (time)	now	5
wa'hĕⁿ·hĕñ":	"Nĕñ'gĕⁿ'	o'nĕⁿ'·hä'	ganio"	hĕⁿ'tcioⁿ'	goñdadie"	
he it said:	"This one (it is)	it corn	so soon as	there thou wilt again arrive	at once	6
ĕⁿsadade'skoñt'häs	ĕⁿsadekhoñ'niä',	o'nĕⁿ·	ne'tho"ge'	ĕⁿ'sadoⁿ'-	
thou wilt roast it for thyself	thou wilt eat,	now	the at that (time)	thou wilt continue	7
'hek:	"Tho'nĕⁿ·	nĕⁿio"dĭk	ĕⁿiek'sek	ne"	oñ'gwe'	gĕⁿ"djĭk	
to say:	"Here	so it will continue to be	they (indef.) will continue to eat it	the	man-being	by and by	8
tho'nĕⁿ·	oñnagät'he'	tca"	oⁿ·hwĕñdjiä'de' "	Ĕⁿ·bianoⁿ·sowĕⁿ"nhä'	
here	they are about to dwell	the where	it earth is present."	Will he thy lodge visit	9
ne"	detciadĕⁿ·bnoñ'dä'	O·ha'ä'.	Tho"ge·	o'nĕⁿ·	ĕⁿ·häi·hwanĕñ'	
the	thou he are brothers	It Flint.	At that (time)	now	will he ask questions	10
doⁿ":	ĕⁿ·hĕⁿ·hĕñ":	"Gaiñ'"	noñ'we',	dĭ"	das'hawä'	nĕñ'gĕⁿ·	
	will he it say:	"Where (is)	the place	moreover	thence thou didst bring it	this one (it is)	11
nonwa·bo"dĕⁿ'?"	Ĕⁿ·si·hĕñ'	dĭ':	"G'ni·hä"	thagawi'."	
kind of thing?"	Thou it wilt say	moreover:	"My father	thence he me it gave."	12
Ne'tho·	dĭ"	niiawĕⁿ"ĭ·	ne"	o'nĕⁿ·	hesho'ioⁿ·.	Tho"ge'	
There	moreover	so it came to pass	the	now	there again he had arrived.	At that (time)	13
o'nĕⁿ·	wä'hanoio"sä'	ne"	onĕⁿ'·hä',	odjĭsdäk'dä'	wä'hä'iĕⁿ"	o"nĭ'	
now	he it ear husked	the	it corn,	it fire beside	he it laid	also	14

he roasted the ear. So soon as it became hot, it emitted an odor which was exceedingly appetizing. They, his grandmother's people, smelled it. She said: "Flint, do thou go to see what the Sapling is roasting for himself, moreover." He, the Flint, arose at once, and he ran thither. When he arrived there, he said: "Whence didst thou get that which thou art roasting for thyself?" He said in replying: "It is a matter of fact that my father gave it to me. And it is this that the man-beings who are about to dwell here on the earth will be in the habit of eating." Then Flint said: "My grandmother has said that thou shouldst share some with her." The Sapling replied, saying: "I am not able to do it, and the reason is that she desires to spoil it all. I desire, as a matter of fact, that man-beings, who are about to dwell here on the earth shall continue to eat it, and that it shall continue to be good." Then, verily, the lad returned home. When

1	wă'hade'tcień''hěⁿ'. he it roasted.	Ganio'' So soon as	wă'o'dāi'hěⁿ'·hă' it became hot	o'něⁿ‛ now	wă'waděⁿ‛sä'ěⁿ' it scent emitted
2	nā'ie' that (it is)	ne'' the	heiodoñgo''dĭ‛ it is exceeding	wěⁿ‛säga''wĭ‛. it odor is appetizing.	Wă'odis'hwă' They (z.) it smelled	ne'' the
3	ho‛sodă'hă'' his grandmother.	Wă'gěⁿ‛hěñ'': She (z.) it said:	"O‛ha'ä', "It Flint,	sekdoⁿ‛'nă‛ do thou it go to see	dĭ'' moreover	ho't what (it is)
4	noñwa‛ho''děⁿ kind of thing	hode'skoñ'dă' he himself is roasting for	ne'' the	Oděñdoñni''ă‛." It Sapling."	Dă'haděⁿsdā'tcĭ', He arose at once.	
5	o'něⁿ‛ now	ne''tho‛ there	iă'thaä''dat hence he ran	ne'' the	O‛ha'ä'. It Flint.	Ne'' The	o'něⁿ‛ now	ne''tho‛ there
6	hwă'hā'ioⁿ' thither he arrived	wă'hěⁿ‛hěñ'': he it said:	"Gaiñ'' "Where	noñ'we‛ the place	dăs'hawă' thence thou it didst bring	tca'' the where
7	noñwa‛ho''děⁿ kind of thing	sade'skoñ'dă'?" thou it art roasting for thyself?"	Da'hāi‛hwă'sä'gwă' Thence he replied	ni'ha'wěñ‛· there he it has said:		
8	"G'ni‛hă'' "My father	se'' as a matter of fact	thagawi‛'. thence he gave it to me.	Nā'ie' That (it is)	ěⁿie'ksek they (indef.) will habitually eat it	ne'' the	oñ'gwe‛ manbeing(s)
9	oñnagät'he‛ they (indef.) are about to dwell	ne'' the	tho'něⁿ‛ here (it is)	oⁿ‛hwěñdjiä'de''." it earth is present."	O'něⁿ‛ Now	ne'' the	O‛ha'ä' It Flint
10	wă'hěⁿ‛hěñ'': He it said·	"Gawěñ'' "She it has said	ksodă'hă'' my grandfather	a‛shenoñ'dă'?" thou it shouldst share with her?"	Da'hāi‛hwă' Thence he	
11	sä'gwă' answered	ne'' the	Oděñdoñni''ă‛ It Sapling	wă'hěⁿ‛hěñ'': he it said:	"Hiiă'' "Not (it is)	thakgwe'nĭă', I it am able to do,
12	nā'ie' that (it is)	ne'' the	diioi‛'hwă' so its reason is	ne'' the	tca'' the where	ěñ‛'he' she it desires	ěⁿkhetgěⁿ''dă' I it shall spoil'
13	gagwe'gĭ‛. it entire.	Ge‛he'' I it desire	se'' as a matter of fact	ne'' the	ěⁿiek'sek they (indef.) will habitually eat	ěⁿioia'nek it will continue to be good	oñnagät'he‛ they (indef.) are about to dwell
14	ne'' the	oñ'gwe‛ man-being(s)	ne'' the	tho'něⁿ‛ here (it is)	oⁿ‛hwěñdjiä'ge‛." it earth on."	O'něⁿ‛ Now	bi'ĭă' verily

he arrived there, he told what he had learned, saying: "The Sapling did not consent to it." She arose at once and went thither to the place where the booth of the Sapling stood. Arriving there, she said: "What kind of thing is it that thou art roasting for thyself?" He replied, saying: "It is corn." She demanded: "Where is the place whence thou didst get it?" He said: "My father gave it to me. And it is this which the man-beings who are about to dwell here on this earth will continue to eat." She said: "Thou shouldst give a share, verily, to me." He answered and said: "I can not do it, and the reason is that thou desirest to spoil it." At that time she said: "It is but a small matter, and thou shouldst pluck off a single grain of corn and give it to me." He said: "I can not do it." She said: "It is a small matter, if thou shouldst give me the nubbin end of the corn ear." He said: "I can not do it. I desire that it shall all be

---

sho‘dĕñ′dioñ·	ne″	haksä′ä″.	Ne″.	o′nĕⁿ·	hoñsa‘hä′ioⁿ″	wä′-
again he departed	the	he child. (is)	The	now	there again he arrived	he

1

hatho′iä’	wä‘hĕⁿ"hĕñ″·	"Hiiä"′	thogäiĕⁿ″i·	ne″	Odĕñdoñni″ä·.
it told	he it said:	"Not (it is)	there he was willing	the	It Sapling.

2

Doñdagadĕⁿs′dä’	ne″	ho‘sodä‘hä″	ne″tho‘	nhwä″ĕⁿ	tca″	noñ′we·
Thence she (z.) sprang up at once	the	his grandmother	there	thither she went	the where	the place

3

ni‘hodĕⁿnos′hĕⁿ″	ne″	Odĕñdoñni″ä·.	Hwä′e′ioⁿ″	wä′ä‘hĕñ″:	"Ho′t
there his thatched bower (is)	the	It Sapling.	There she arrived	she it said:	"What (it is)

4

noñwa‘ho″dĕⁿ″	sade’skoñ′dä’?"	Da‘hada′diä’	wä‘hĕⁿ"hĕñ″:	"Oneⁿ′
kind of thing	thou thyself art roasting for?"	He spoke in reply	he it said·	"It corn."

5

‘hä’."	Wä‘gĕⁿ"hĕñ″:	"Gaiñ″	noñ′we·	däs′hawä’?"	Wä‘hĕⁿ"hĕñ″·
	She (z.) it said:	"Where (it is)	the place	thence thou it didst bring?"	He it said:

6

"G′ni‘hä″	thagawi‘.	Nä′ie’	ĕⁿiek′sek	ne″	oñ′gwe· oñnagät′he·
"My father	there he it gave it to me.	That (it is)	they (indef.) will continue to eat it	the	man-being(s) they (indef.) are about to dwell

7

ne″	tho′nĕⁿ·	oⁿ‘hwĕñdjiä″geʼ."	Wä‘gĕⁿ"hĕñ″:	"Ä‘sgenoñ′dä’
the	here (it is)	it earth on."	She (z.) it said:	"Thou shouldst share it with me

8

hi′iä’."	Da‘häi‘hwä‘sä′gwä·	wä‘hĕⁿ"hĕñ″:	"Hiiä″	thäkgwe′niä·
verily."	Thence he answered	he it said:	"Not (it is)	I it am able to do.

9

Nä′ie’	diioi′‘hwä·	tca″	se‘he″	ĕⁿkhetgĕⁿ″dä’."	Tho″ge· o′nĕⁿ·
That (it is)	there its reason (is)	the where	thou it intendest	I it will spoil."	At that (time) now

10

wä‘gĕⁿ"hĕñ″:	"Nigäi‘hwä″ä·	ne″	teionĕⁿ″hädä·	ä‘se‘niodä′gwä·
she (z.) it said:	"Just it matter small (is)	the	it grain of corn single	thou it shouldst pluck out

11

nä′ie’	doñdas′gwĕⁿ″."	Wä‘hĕⁿ"hĕñ″:	"Hiiä″	thäkgwe′niä’."
that (it is)	thou it shouldst give to me."	He it said:	"Not	I it am able to do."

12

Wä‘gĕⁿ"hĕñ″·	"Nigäi‘hwä″ä·	ne″	doñdas′gwĕⁿ″	ne″	okoⁿ·-
She (z.) it said:	"Just it matter small (is)	the	thence thou it shouldst give to me	the	it immature end

13

seĕⁿ″dä’."	Wä‘hĕⁿ"hĕñ″:	"Hiiä″	thäkgwe′niä.	Ge‘he″ gagwe′gī·
(of the corn-ear)."	He it said:	"Not (it is)	I it am able to do.	I it desire. it whole

14

good, so that the man-beings shall continue to eat it." At that time she became angry and she came forward, and, taking up some ashes, cast them on what he was roasting, and that was now spoiled. She said: "Thou desirest that that which they will continue to eat shall continue to be good. There, it will now be different." Thrice did she repeat the act that spoiled it. Then the Sapling said: "Why hast thou done that deed?"

Now again, another thing: he had a pot wherein he heated water. Then from the ear of corn he plucked a single grain of corn, and he put it therein, saying: "Thus shall man-beings be in the habit of doing when they prepare food for eating." Then he placed the corn in a mortar, and also said: "In this manner also shall man-beings, who are about to dwell here on the earth, continue to do." Then he took from its stand the pounder and brought it down once, and it became

---

1	ěⁿioia'nek it will be good	ěⁿiek'sek they (indef.) it will continue to eat	ne'' the	oñ'gweʻ." man-being(s)."	Tho''geʻ At that (time)	o'něⁿʻ now	wă'onă' she (z.)
2	khwěⁿ''ʻhă', became angry,	dawa'děñ'diă' thence she (z.) started forward	wă'tgaʻ''gwă' she (z.) it took up	ne'' the	o'gěⁿ''ʻhă' it ashes		ne''thoʻ there
3	wă'gāiěⁿʻ''dă' she (z.) it dashed against	tca'' the where	hode'skoñ'dă' he it is roasting for himself so	o'iěⁿʻ now	ne'' the that	iă'' that one	wă'gaʻhetgěⁿʻ''dă'. she (z.) it spoiled.
4	Wă'gěⁿʻběñ'': She (z.) it said:	"Seʻhe'' "Thou it intendest	ěⁿioia'nek it will be ever good	tca'' the where	ěⁿiek'sek. they (indef.) will habitually eat it.	Tho'' There,	o'něⁿʻ now	
5	o'iă' it is other	něⁿio''dĭk. so it will continue to be."	'Ă''sěⁿʻ Three	nwă'wadiet''ă' so many	tca'' she (z.) it repeated	wă'gaʻhetgěⁿʻ''dă' the where	she (z.) it spoiled.	
6	O'něⁿʻ Now	ne'' the	Oděñdoñni'ăʻ It Sapling	wă'hěⁿʻhěñ'': he it said:	"Hoʻt "What (why)	iă'' that one	ne''thoʻ there	
7	iwă'sieʻă'?'' so thou it didst do?"							
8	O'něⁿʻ Now	he'' again	o'iă' it is other	hotnă'djā'iěⁿʻ he has a kettle set for himself	ne''thoʻ there	wă'haʻhnekadaiʻhă''dă'. he water heated.		
9	Tho''geʻ At that (time)	o'něⁿʻ now	onoⁿʻkwěⁿ''iă''geʻ it ear of corn on	tcioněⁿ''ʻhădăʻ it grain of corn one (is)	wă'haʻnioda'gwă' he plucked it off,			
10	ne''thoʻ there	hwă'hokʻ, thither he it immersed,	wă'běⁿʻhěñ'': he it said:	"Ne''thoʻ "Thus	oñ'gweʻ man-being(s)	něⁿieiěŭno' such their method of doing kind of will		
11	děⁿʻk continue to be	něⁿieieʻʻhăk so they it will continue to do	ne'' the	ěⁿiekhoñ'niă' one food will prepare	ne'' the	ěⁿioñdekhoñ'niă'.'' one food will eat."		
12	Tho''geʻ At that (time)	ga'nigaʻdagoñ'wăʻ it mortar in	wă'haʻěⁿʻ he it put in	ne'' the	oněⁿʻ''ʻhă', it corn,	wă'hěⁿʻhěñ'' he it said		
13	o''nĭ': also:	"Thoněⁿʻ "This way	něⁿieieʻʻhăk so one it will continue to do	ne'' the	oñ'gweʻ man-being(s)	oñnagätʻheʻ they (indef.) are about to dwell	ne'' the	
14	thoʻiěⁿʻ here	oⁿʻhwěñdjiăʻdeʻ.'' it earth is present."	O'něⁿʻ Now	wă'haʻnioda'gwă' he it took from standing	ne'' the	ioñtheʻ- one it uses to pound		

finished perfect real. He said: "Thus it shall continue to be; thus shall be the manner of preparing real along the man-beings who are about to dwell here on the earth." At that time she, his grandmother, came forward and heard what he was saying. She arrived there, and said: "Sapling, thou desirest that the man-beings shall be exceedingly happy." She went forward, and, taking off the pot from the fire, put ashes into the hot water. Now, moreover, she took the ear of corn, shelled it, and put the corn into the hot water. She said: "This, moreover, shall be their manner of doing, the method of the man-beings." At that time the Sapling said: "Thou shouldst not do thus." His grandmother did not obey him. Thence, it is said, originated the evil that causes persons customarily to speak ill when

dä´´gwä˙	sgu´dä˙	da‘hä˙sĕⁿ´´dä’	gāiĕññĕndä´´ï˙	gathe˙tchi˙sä´´ï˙	1
	one it is	he it brought down	it is finished	one it meal has finished
wä˙wa´doⁿ.	Wä˙hĕⁿ‘hĕñ´´:	"Ne´´tho‘	nĕⁿio´´dĭk,	ne´´tho‘	2
it became.	He it said:	"There	so it will continue to be,	thus
nĕⁿgāiĕñno´´dĕⁿk	ne´´	ĕⁿiethe˙tchoñ´nia’	ne´´	oñ´gwe˙ ne´´	3
so its method of doing will continue to be	the	one it meal will make	the	man-being(s) the
tho‘nĕⁿ˙	oññagät´he˙	oⁿ‘hwĕñdjiä´´ge˙."	Tho´´ge˙	o’nĕⁿ˙ dawa‘dĕñ´	4
here	they (indef.) are about to dwell	it earth on."	At that (time)	now thence she started
diä˙,	da´we˙ ne´´	ho˙sodä‘hä´´	gothoñ´de˙	ne´´ ıä´ie’ i‘ha´doⁿk	5
forward,	thence the she (z.) came	his grandmother	she it heard	the that (it is) he it kept saying.
Ne˙´tho˙	wä˙gä´ioⁿ´	wä˙gĕⁿ‘hĕñ´´˙	"Odĕñdoñni´´ä˙	se‘he´´	6
There	she (z.) arrived	she (z.) it said:	"It Sapling	thou it intendest
ĕⁿiagotcĕññoñ´nik	ne´´	oñ´gwe˙	ıä´ie’ ne´´	heiawĕñgo´´dï˙ "	7
they (indef.) will continue to be happy.	the	man-being(s)	that (it is) the	it is exceeding."
Wä˙wa‘dĕñ´diä’	wä´ganä˙djiodä´gwä’	ne´´	odjĭsdä´´ge˙	ganä´´djiot	8
She (z.) started forward	she (z.) it kettle took up	the	it fire on	it kettle stands
o‘gĕⁿ˙‘hä˙	wä˙´ok tca´´	io‘hnegadai´‘hĕñ˙.	O’ıĕⁿ˙’ dï´´	onĕⁿ´´‘hä˙	9
it ashes	she (z.) it immerged in the where	it water (is) hot.	Now moreover	it corn
wä˙tga´´gwä˙	wä˙ganĕⁿ‘hogĕñ´iä’	ne´´tho‘	o´´ hwä˙´ok	tca´´	10
she (z.) it took up	she (z.) it corn shelled	there	too thence she (z.) it immersed	the where
noñ´we˙	o‘hnegadai´‘hĕñ˙.	Wä˙gĕⁿ‘hĕñ´´:	"Tho’nĕⁿ˙ dï´´	nĕⁿieie´-	11
the place	it water is hot.	She (z.) it said:	"This way moreover,	so they (indef.) it will
‘häk	nĕⁿieiĕñno´´dĕⁿk	ne´´ oñ´gwe˙ "	Tho´´ge˙	o’nĕⁿ˙ ne´´	12
continue to do	so their method of doing will be in kind	the man-being(s)."	At that (time)	now the
Odĕñdoñni´´ä˙	wä˙hĕⁿ‘hĕñ´´:	"Ä´´gwi’ ne´´tho‘	nä˙sie´´ä˙."	Hiiä´´	13
It Sapling	he it said:	"Do it not thus	so thou it shouldst do."	Not (it is)
de˙agogäiĕⁿ´´ï˙	ne´´	ho˙sodä˙hä´´.	Tho´´ge‘,	iä˙kĕⁿ´, nidio˙nhi´´ï˙	14
she it consented to	the	his grandmother.	At that (time),	it is said, there it went wrong
ıä´ie’	ne´´	wä˙he˙tgĕⁿ´´	gĕⁿ’s de‘hodi´thä’	tca´´ niga˙ha´wĭ˙ ne´´	15
that (it is)	the	it is evil	customarily they are talking	the where there it bears it (the time) the

they prepare food. And, it is said, she stated her wish, thus: "This, as a matter of fact, shall be the manner of doing of the man-beings." It so continued to be. The Sapling kept saying: "The way in which thou hast done this is not good, for I desire that the man-beings shall be exceedingly happy, who are about to dwell here on this earth."

Now at that time the Sapling traveled about over the earth. Now there was a large expanse of earth visible. There was a mountain large, visible river courses, and a high clay bank, near which he passed. Now, verily, he there pondered many times. Then he made the bodies of the small game, the bodies of birds. All were in twos, and were mated, in all the clans [kinds] of birds. · The volume of the sound made by all the various kinds of bird voices as they talked together was terrifying. And the Sapling kept saying: "Thus this shall continue to be, whereby the man-beings shall habitually be made

	iekhoñnia̋"hă'.	Nă'ie'	ne"	wă'ă'heñ"·	"Nĕ"tho'	se"	nĕⁿieiĕñno"-
1	they (indef.) prepare food.	That (it is)	the	she it said:	"There	as a matter of fact	so their method of doing

	dĕⁿk	ne"	oñ'gwe'."	Wă'dwatgoñ'dĕⁿ'	ne"tho'	ni'io't.	I'ha'doⁿk
2	will be in kind	the	man-being(s)."	It became fixed (thus)	there	so it is.	He it kept saying

	ne"	Odĕñdoñni"ă':	"Hiiă''	de'oia'ne'	tca"	nwă'sie'ă'.	Ge'he"
3	the	It Sapling:	"Not (it is)	it is good	the where	so thou it didst do.	I it desire

	heiotgoñdă''gwĭ'	skĕñ'noⁿ'	ĕⁿiagotcĕñnoñ'nik	ne"	oñ'gwe'
4	it will be immeasurably	well (it is)	they (indef.) will be happy.	the	man-being(s)

	tho'nĕⁿ'	oⁿ'hwĕñdjiă'de'	oññagät'he'."
5	here (it is)	it earth is present	they (indef.) are about to dwell."

	Tho"ge'	o'nĕⁿ'	ne"	Odĕñdoñni"ă'	wă'thadawĕñ'ie'	tca"
6	At that (time)	now	the	It Sapling	he traveled about	the where

	oⁿ'hwĕñdjiă'de'.	O'nĕⁿ'	gowa'ıĕⁿ'	tca"	oⁿ'hwĕñdjiă'de'.	Onoñda'-
7	it earth is present.	Now	it much (is)	the where	it earth is present.	It mountain

	hă'die',	gĕⁿ'bioⁿ'hwăde'nioⁿ',	degă'daetci''hă'die'	ne"tho'	wă'ha
8	rises extending along,	it stream stands forth severally,	it clay tall extends along	there	he it

	doñgo''dă'.	O'nĕⁿ'	bi'iă'	ne"tho'	wă'hĕñnoⁿ'doñ'nioⁿ'.	O'nĕⁿ'
9	passed.	Now	verily	there	he thought repeatedly.	Now

	wă'hăiă'doñ'niă'	ne"	goñdi'io'	nigoñdiio'dă's'ă".	Gagwe'gĭ'
10	he its (their) body made	the	they (z.) animals	so they (z.) are small bodied.	It all

	degni'hă'die',	odinia'gĭ',	gagwe'gĭ'	tca"	niiodi'seä'ge'	ne"
11	two they two are each,	they (z.) are married,	it all	the where	so it breed is in many number	the

	goñdi'io'.	Deiodenoⁿ'hiani''dĭ'	tca"	nigăi'sdowa'nĕⁿ'	ne"
12	they (z.) are animals.	It is terrifying	the where	so it noise large (is)	the

	goñdi'io'	nhwă'tgoñdiwĕñnage''	odit'hă'.	Nă'ie'	ne"	Odĕñ
13	they (z.) animals	every their (z.) language in number (is)	they (z.) are talking.	That (it is)	the	It

	doñıi"ă'	hot'hă'	i'ha'doⁿk:	"Nă'ie'	nĕⁿio'dĭk	ne"	oñ'gwe
14	Sapling	he is talking	ne it is saying:	"That (it is)	so it will continue to be	the	man-being(s)

happy." And now he made the bodies of the large game animals. He finished the bodies of two deer, and the two were mates. "There, that is sufficient to fill the whole earth," he said. He made all the various kinds of animals severally. All were in twos, and they, each pair, were mates [male and female].

At that time he, the Sapling, again traveled. Now the earth had grown to a very great size, and continued to grow. So now Flint became aware that the animals were ranging about. After a while then Flint concealed all the bodies of the animals. There in the high mountain was a rock cavern whereinto he drove all the animals. And then he closed it with a stone. Then Sapling became aware that the animals no longer roamed from place to place. Now, at this time, he again traveled over the entire earth. He saw on this side a

ĕⁿiaga′wĕñtgade′dä′′gwĭk." it them will make happy thereby."	Nā′ie′ That (it is)	ne′′ the	nā′ie′ that (it is)	oⁿ′′kĕⁿ′ next in time	ne′′ the	goñdi- they (z.) are	1
go′wănĕⁿ's large in size	ne′′ the	goñdi′io′ they (z.) are animals	wä′hāiä′doñniä′′hĕñ′. he their several bodies formed.			Skĕñnoñdoⁿ′′ Deer	2
degiiä′dage′′ they two body in number (are)	odinia′gĭ′ they (z.) are married	wä′thas′′ä′. he them two finished.	"Ne′′tho′ "There (it is)			hä′degāie′ĭ′ just it is sufficient	3
dĕⁿga′hĕñ′′nhä′ it will be filled	tca′′ the where	niioⁿ′′hwĕñ′djiä′," so it earth is large."	wä′hĕⁿ′hĕñ′′. he it said.			Gagwe′gĭ, It all	4
hä′deganio′′däge′ just it animal in every number is	wä′hāiä′doñniä′′hĕñ′. he its body formed severally.		Gagwe′gĭ′ It all			degniiä′dage′- they (z.) two body (is) each in	5
hā′die′ number	odiniäk′sĕⁿ′ they (z.) are severally married.						6
Tho′′ge′ At that time	o′nĕⁿ′ now	he′′ again	doñsa′hadawĕñ′ie′ there again he traveled	ne′′ the	Odĕñdoñni′′ä′. It Sapling.		7
O′nĕⁿ′ Now	gowa′nĕⁿ′ it much (is)	tca′′ the where	oⁿ′′hwĕñdjiä′de′ it earth is present	ododi′hā′die′. it is growing in size.	Da′, So,		8
o′nĕⁿ′ now	wä′hatdo′gä′ he it noticed	ne′′ the	O′ha′ä′ It Flint	tca′′ the where	deioñnadawĕñ′ie′ they (z.) are traveling	ne′′ the	9
goñdi′io′. they (z.) are animals (game).	Diĕñ′′hä′ After a while	gwä′′ seemingly	o′nĕⁿ′ now	ne′′ the	O′ha′ä′ It Flint	wä′hāiä′da′se′′dä′ he their bodies concealed	10
gagwe′gĭ′. it all.	Ne′′tho′ There	tca′′ the where	onoñda′hä′gowa′nĕ′′′ it mountain rises great		ne′′tho′ there	ostĕⁿ′′hä it rock	11
ga′hĕñ′dä′ cavern has	ne′′tho′ there	gagwe′gĭ′ it all	wä′hāiä′dinioⁿ′′dä′ he their bodies impounded		ne′′ the	goñdi′io′ they (z.) are animals.	12
O′nĕⁿ′ Now	ne′′ the	ostĕⁿ′′bä′ it rock	da′hadji′heda′′gwä′. there he it used to close it.		O′nĕⁿ′ Now	wä′hatdo′gä′ he it noticed	13
ne′′ the	Odĕñdoñni′′ä′ It Sapling	tca′′ the where	biiä′′ not (it is)	de′sgoñ′ne′s again they (z.) go about habitually	ne′′ the	goñdi′io′. they (z.) are animal.	14
Tho′′ge′ At that (time)	o′nĕⁿ′ now	wä′thadawĕñ′ie′ he traveled	tca′′ the where	niioⁿ′′hwĕñ′djiä′. so it earth is large.		Wä′ha- He looked	15

mountain range. He went thither, and he arrived where the opening of the cavern was. And he then took up the great stone and opened it again. Now, he looked therein and saw that the animals abode in that place. "Do ye again go out of this place," he said. Then they came out again. And it was done very quickly. And all those that fly took the lead in coming out. At that time they, his grandmother and Flint, also noticed that the animals again became numerous. And then Flint ran, running to the place where the rock cavern was. He reached the place while they were still coming out. And he, by at once pulling down the stone again, stopped up the cavern. Verily, some of them failed, and they did not get out, and at the present time they are still there. And it came to pass that they

	tgat'hwă'	nĕⁿ''	ͻăgwă'''	diionoñdă''hă'.		Ne''tho'	nhwă'he'',
1	about	this way	toward	there it mountain rises.		There	thither he went,

	hwă'hā''ioⁿ'	ne''tho'	gwă''	oga'hĕñ'dă'	tca''	ne''tho'	io'sa'de'
2	there he arrived	there	seem- ingly	it has an opening	the where	there	it cavern present is.

	Wă'tha''gwă'	ne''	gastĕⁿ'hä'gowa'nĕⁿ'		wă'hadji'hedā'gwă'.		O'nĕⁿ'
3	He it took up	the	it rock large (is)		be it unclosed.		Now

	ne''tho'	wă'hatgat'hwă'	wă'ha'gĕⁿ	ne''tho'	goñni''dĕñ	ne''	gā'io'.
4	there	he looked	he it saw	there	they (z.) abide,	the	it game (animals).

	"Saswāiagĕⁿ'''nhă'	ne''	tho'nĕⁿ',"	wă'hĕⁿ'hĕñ''.	Tho''ge'	o'nĕⁿ'
5	"Again do ye emerge	the	here,"	he it said.	At that (time)	now

	sagondiiagĕⁿ'''nhă'.	Agwa's	tca''	niio'sno'we'.	Nā'ie'	dagoñdi'
6	again they emerged.	Just as much as possible	the where	so it is rapid.	That (it is)	thence they (z.) came

	'hĕñt	tca''	niioñ''	degoñdidĕⁿ''hă'.	Gagwe'gĭ'	sagoñdiiagĕⁿ'''nhă'
7	ahead	the where	so it is much (many).	they (z.) fly.	It all	again they emerged.

	Tho''ge'	o'nĕⁿ'	wă'hiiatdo'gă'	ne''	ho'sodă'hă''	ne''	O'ha'ä'
8	At that (time)	now	they two it noticed	the	his grandmother	the	It Flint

	o''nĭ'	ne''	tca''	sāioñnatgă'dĕⁿ''hă'	ne''	goñdi'io'.	O'nĕⁿ'	tho''ge'
9	also	the	the where	again they (z.) became numerous	the	they (z.) are animal.	Now	at that (time)

	wă'thaä''dat	ne''	O'ha'ä'	ne''tho'	nhwă'hadak'he'	tca''	noñ'we,
10	he ran	the	It Flint	there	thither he ran	the where	the place

	diiostĕⁿ'häga'hĕñ'dă'.	Hwă'hā'ioⁿ'	tca''	non'we'	diiodiiagĕⁿ''ĭ'.
11	there it rock opening has.	There he arrived	the where	the place	there they (z.) were coming forth

	Nā'ie'	ne''	hāiă'dagoñdă'die'	doñda'hă'sĕⁿ''dă'	ne''	ostĕⁿ''hă'
12	That (it is)	the	his body kept right on	thence again he it dropped	the	it rock

	sa'hadji'he'dĕⁿ'.	Ne''tho'	hi'iă'	o'diă'k	dăiodino'wĕñ',	hiiă'
13	again he it closed up.	There	verily	they are some	there they failed	not (it is)

	de'tciodiiagĕⁿ''ĭ',	ne''tho'	ne''	oⁿ''kĕⁿ'	tgoñni''dĕñ.	Ne''tho'
14	again they (z.) emerged.	there	the	at present	there they (z.) abide.	There

weie chaıged, ɔecoɪıŋg otgoɪ [malefic], and the reason that it thıs caɪe to ɔass is that soɪe cɪstoɪaɪılɪ put foɪth theiɪ oɪeɪda foɪ the puɪpose of eɪdiɪg the days of the man-ɔeiŋgs; and, ɪoɪeo\ei, they still haɪɪt the iɪside of the eaɪth.

At this tiɪe Saɔliɪg agaiɪ traveled aboɪt. Theɪ he was sɪɔɪised that, seeɪiɪglɪ, a man-beiɪg caɪe towaɪd hiɪ, and his ɪaɪe was Hadɪ'i'. They two met. The man-ɔeiɪg Hadu'i', said: "Where is the place wheɪce thoɪ dost coɪe?" The Sapliɪg said: "I am goiɪg aɔoɪt \iewiɪg the eaɪth heɪe ɔɪeseɪt. Where is the ɔlace wheɪce thoɪ dost coɪe?" Hadu'i' said: "Fɪoɪ heɪe do I coɪe. I am

niiawĕⁿ'ï'	tca"	wă'dwatde'nï'	o'tgoⁿ'ᵃ	wă'wa'doⁿ,	ɪă'ie'	dāioi'-	1
so it came to pass	the where	it (they) changed themselves	otgon	it (they) became,	that (it is)	it was	
hwă'k'he'	tca"	ne"tho'	nwă'awĕⁿ''hă'	ɪă'ie'	ne"	o'diă'k	ɪă'ie'	2
reason	the where	there	so it came to pass	that (it is)	the	they (z.) are some	that (it is)	
deioññadĕññoñdă''gwĭ'	ne"	āiagawĕⁿ'ni'sei'kdă''gwĕⁿ		ne"	oñ'gwe',		3
they (z.) are emitting orenda for it	the	they (z.) would cause days to end for them		the	man-being(s),		
ɪă'ie'	ne"	dï"	ne"	oⁿ'hwĕñdjiagoñ'wă'	tgoñ'ne's.		4
that (it is)	the	more-over	the	it earth in (side)	there they (z.) go about habitually.		
Ne"tho'	nigĕⁿ''	o'nĕⁿ'	he"	doñsa'hadawĕñ'ie'	ne"	Odĕñdoñ	5
There	so it is distant	now	again	there again he trav-cled about	the	It Sapling.	
ni"ă'.	Tho"'ge'	o'nĕⁿ'	wă'hadiĕñ''hă'	gwă"	da''he'	ne"	hĕñ'gwe',	6
At that (time)	now	he was surprised, seemingly,		is coming	thence he	the	he man-being (is),	
ɪă'ie'	ne"	Hadu"'i'ᵇ	hăia'djï'.	Wă'thiadă''nhă'.	Wă'hĕⁿ'hĕñ"	ne"	7
that (it is)	the	Hadu''i' -	he is called.	They two met.	He said	the	
hĕñ'gwe'	ne"	Hadu"'i':	"Gaiñ''	ɪoñ'we'	noñda'se"? "	Wă'hĕⁿ	8
he man-being	the	Hadu''i'	"Where	the place	thence thou didst come?"	He said	
'hĕñ"	ne"	Odĕñdoñni''ă':	"Agekdoññioñ'die's	tca"	ioⁿ'hwĕñdji		9
	the	It Sapling:	"I them am going about viewing	the	it earth is present.		
ā'de'.	Gaiñ''	ɪi's	ɪoñ'we'	noñda''se'? "	Wă'hĕⁿ'hĕñ''	ne"	10
Where	the	thou	the place	thence thou didst come?"	He it said	the	
Hadu"'i':	"Tho'nĕⁿ'	noñda'ge'	dewagadawĕnie'hā'die'.	I"	hi'iă'		11
Hadu''i'	"Here	thence I did come	I am traveling about.	I	verily		

ᵃ In English there is no approximately exact equivalent of the term otgon, which is an adjective form denotive of the deadly, malefic, or pernicious use of orenda or magic power reputed to be inherent in all beings and bodies. It usually signifies deadly in deed and monstrous in aspect.

ᵇ The Onondagas call this personage Hadu'i'', the Senecas, Shagodiiowe'gowă, and the Ɉohawks, Akoñwăra'. The Onondaga name is evidently connected with the expression hadu'ă', signifying "he is hunch-backed," in reference to the stooping or crouching posture assumed by the impersonator, to depict old age. The Seneca name means, "He, the Great One, who protects them (= human beings)," and the Ɉohawk name, "The Mask," or "It, the Mask." All these names are clearly of late origin, for they refer evidently to the being as depicted ceremonially in the festival for the new year. The orenda or magic power of this being was believed to be efficacious in warding off and driving away disease and pestilence, as promised in this legend, and hence the Seneca name. The Ɉohawk epithet arose from the fact that the impersonator usually wears a mask of wood. But these etymologies do not give a definite suggestion as to what natural object gave rise to this personification, this concept. But from a careful synthesis of the chief characteristics of this personage, it seems very probable that the whirlwind lies at the foundation of the conception.

going about traveling. Verily, it is I who am the master of the earth here present." At that time the Sapling said: "I it is who finished the earth here present. If it so be that thou art the master of the earth here present, art thou able to cause yonder mountain to move itself hither?" Hadu'i' said: "I can do it." At that time he said: "Do thou, yonder mountain, come hither." Then they two faced about. Sometime afterward they two now faced back, and, moreover, saw that the mountain had not changed its position. At that time Sapling said: "Verily, thou art not the master of the earth here present. I, as matter of fact, am master of it. Now, next in time, I will speak." He said: "Do thou, yonder mountain, come hither." Now they two faced about. And as quickly as they two faced about again the mountain stood at their backs. The Sapling said: "What sayst thou? Am I master of it?" Then Hadu'i' said: "It

1	giä'dagwe'ni'io'	tca''	oⁿ'hweñdjiă''ge'."		Tho''ge'	wä'hěⁿ'hěñ''
	I it am master of	the where	it earth on."		At that time	he it said
2	ne'' Odĕñdoñni''ă':	"I''	aksă''i'	tca''	ioⁿ'hweñdjiä'de'.	Tho''
	the It Sapling:	"I	I it finished	the where	it earth is present.	Thus,
3	gwă'' ěñ'k do'gěⁿs	i's	siä'dagwe'ni'io'	tca''	ioⁿ'hweñdjiä'de',	
	seemingly, it may be it is true	thou	thou it art master of	the where	it earth is present,	
4	sagwenioñ'-kběⁿ''	gä'e'	nonda'we'	tca''	sigěⁿ''	diionoñdä''hä'?"
	thou it art able to do . art thou	hither	thence it would come	the where	yonder it is	there it mountain rises?"
5	Wä'hěⁿ'hěñ'' ne''	Hadu''i':	"Ěⁿkgwe'niä'."		Tho''ge'	o'něⁿ'
	He it said the	Hadu''i':	"I it will be able to do."		At that time	now
6	wä'hěⁿ'hěñ'': "Gä'e'	nonda''se'	sigěⁿ''		diionoñda''hä'.	Tho''ge'
	he it said: "Hither	thence do thou come	yonder it is		there it mountain rises up."	At that (time)
7	wä'hiatga'hade'nï'.	Gaiñ'gwä'	nwä'oñni'she'	o'něⁿ'	doñsa'hiatga'ha	
	they two faced about.	Some (time)	So (long) it lasted	now	again they two faced back	
8	de'ri' o'něⁿ' dï''	hoñsa'hiatgat'hwä'	gadogěⁿ''	ïi'dio't	tca''	onoñ
	now moreover	again hence they two looked	it unchanged (is)	so there it is	the where	it moun-
9	dä''hä'. Tho''ge'	ne'' Odĕñdoñni''ă'	wä'hěⁿ'hěñ'':	"Hiiă''		bi'iä'
	tain rises up. At that (time)	the It Sapling	he it said:	"Not		verily, (it is)
10	de'siä'dagwe'ni'io'	tca''	oⁿ'hweñdjiä'de'.	I'' se''		giä'dagwe'ni'io'
	thou it art master of	the where	it earth is present.	I it is a matter of fact		I it am master of.
11	O'něⁿ' i'' oⁿ''kěⁿ'	děⁿtgada'diä''."	Wä'hěⁿ'hěñ'':		"Gä'e'	noñ
	Now I next in turn	I will talk out."	He it said:		"Hither	thence do
12	da''se' sigěⁿ''	disnoñda''hä'.	O'něⁿ'	wä'hiatga'hade'nï'.		Ne''tho
	thou yonder come it is	there thou mountain art rising up."	Now	they two faced about.		There
13	niio'sno'we'	deshoñnatga'hade'nioñ'	o'něⁿ'	ni'sho''ne'		diionoñ
	so it is rapid	they two again faced back	now	there their two backs at		there it mountain
14	da''hä'. Wä'hěⁿ'hěñ''	ne''	Odĕñdoñni''ă':	"Hatc'kwi',	i''	gweñ-
	rises up. He it said	the	It Sapling:	"What sayst thou,	I	I it am

is true that thou art master of it. Thou hast finished the earth here present. Thou shouldst have pity on me that I may be suffered to live. I will aid thee, moreover. Verily, thou dost keep saying: 'Man-beings are about to dwell here on the earth here present.' In this matter, moreover, will it continue to be that I shall aid and assist thee. Moreover, I will aid the man-beings. Seeing that my body is full of orenda and even otgon, as a matter of fact, by and by the man-beings will be affected with mysterious ills. Moreover, it will be possible for them to recover if they will make an imitation of the form of my body. I, who was the first to travel over the earth here present, infected it with my orenda. And, verily, it will magically conform itself to [be marked by] the lineaments of my body. Moreover, this will come to pass. If it so be that a man-being becomes ill by the contagion of this magic power, it is here that I will aid thee. And the man-beings will then live in contentment. And,

ni'io'."	Tho"ge'	wä'hĕⁿ'hĕñ"	ne"	Hadu''i':	"Do'gĕⁿs	i's
master of."	At that time	he it said	the	Hadu''i':	"It is true	thou

swĕñni'io'.	I's	sāiĕñnĕñdä''ï'	tca"	ioⁿ'hwĕñdjiä'de'.	Ä'sgidĕñ'ä'
thou it art master of.	Thou	thou it hast finished	the where	it earth is present.	Thou shouldst have mercy on me

ago'n'hek.	Ĕⁿgoñiä'dage''nhä'	di".	I'sa'doⁿk	bi'iä'	oñ'gwe'
I should continue to live.	I thee will aid	moreover.	Thou it art saying	verily	man-beings

hoñnagät'he'	ne"	tho'nĕⁿ'	ioⁿ'hwĕñdjiä'de'.	Tho'nĕⁿ'	di"
they (z.) are about to dwell	the	here	it earth is present.	Here	moreover

nĕⁿio''dik	ĕⁿgoñie'näwä's	ĕⁿgoñiä'dăge''nhä'.	Ĕⁿkheiä'dage''nhä'
so it will continue to be	I thee will assist	I thee will aid.	I them will aid

di"	ne"	oñ'gwe'.	Nä'ie'	ne"	ioĕñ'dāe'	o'tgoⁿ'	di"	se"
moreover	the	man-beings.	That (it is)	the	it orenda is possessed of	otgon (it is)	moreover	as a matter of fact

ne"	giä'di''ge'.	Gĕⁿ'djï'k	ĕⁿiagodianĕñ''nhä'	ne"	oñ'gwe'.	Ĕⁿwa'doⁿ'
the	my body on.	By and by	they will be affected by mystic ills	the	man-beings.	It will be possible

di"	ne"	ĕⁿtcioñ'doⁿ'	dogä''t-khĕⁿ'	dĕⁿioñde'niĕñdĕⁿs'dä'	tca"
moreover	the	again one will recover one's self	if it so be,	is it,	one it will make in the pattern of it.	the where

nigiä'do''dĕⁿ'.	Agadiĕñtgä''hwï'	dwagadieĕⁿ''di'	dewagadawĕñie''
such as my body is in kind.	My body has affected it (with orenda)	I was the first one	I traveled about

tca"	oⁿ'hwĕñdjiä'de'.	Nä'ie'	ne"	bi'iä'	ĕⁿioñä'gĕ'ĕⁿ'	tca"
the where	it earth is present.	That	the	verily	it it will pattern after	the where

nigiä'do''dĕⁿ'.	Tho'nĕⁿ'	di"	nĕⁿiawĕⁿ''hä'.	Dogä''t	ĕⁿiagodiĕⁿsĕⁿ'
such as my body is in kind.	Here	moreover	so it will come to pass.	If it so be	one will become ill from magic

gaiⁿ''nhä'	ne"	oñ'gwe'	nä'ie'	ne"	ne''tho'	noñ'we'	ĕⁿgoñie'
potence	the	man-being	that (it is)	the	there	the place	I thee will

näwä's.	Skĕñ'noⁿ'	ĕⁿioñnoⁿ'doñnioⁿ''hek	nĕ"	oñ'gwe'.	Nä'ie'	di"
assist.	Well (it is)	they will continue to think repeatedly	the	man-beings.	That (it is)	moreover

moreover, they must customarily greet me by a kinship term, saying: ' my Grandfather.' And when, customarily, the man-beings speak of me they must customarily say: 'our Grandfather'; thereby must they designate me. And I shall call the man-beings on my part by a kinship term, saying: ' my Grandchildren.' And they must make customarily a thing of wood which shall be in my likeness, being wrought thus, that will enable them to go to the several lodges, and, moreover, they who thus personate me shall be hondu'i'.[a] They must employ for this purpose tobacco [native tobacco]. It will be able to cause those who have become ill to recover. There, moreover, I shall take up my abode where the ground is wild and rough, and where, too, there are rock cliffs. Moreover, nothing at all obstructs me [in seeing and hearing or power]. So long as the earth shall be extant so long shall I remain there. I shall

1. dĕⁿioñknoⁿ'hĕñ'‘khwăk ne‘’ ĕⁿia‘hĕñ’’ gĕⁿ’s: ‘Ksodă‘hă‘’.’
   they (indef.) will greet me by the one it will customarily: ‘My Grandfather.’
   the relationship term   say

2. Nā'ie’ ne‘’ o’nĕⁿ‘ gĕⁿ’s i‘’ ĕⁿioñgwatho'iă’ ĕⁿia‘hĕñ’’ gĕⁿ’s:
   That the now customarily I one me will tell of one it will say customarily:
   (it is)

3. ‘Shedwa‘sodă‘,’ iă'ie’ ĕⁿioñgnă'doⁿ‘khwăk ne‘’ oñ'gwe‘. O'nĕⁿ‘
   ‘Our Grandfather,’ that (it is) they (indef.) me will use it to designate the man-beings. Now

4. ne‘’ i‘’ ne‘’ oñ'gwe‘: ‘Kheiade'shoⁿ‘‘ă‘,’ dĕⁿkhenoⁿ‘hĕñ‘‘khwăk
   the I the man-being: ‘My Grandchildren several,’ I them will greet by the relationship term.

5. Nā'ie’ di‘’ ne‘’ ĕⁿie‘sĕñ'niă’ gĕⁿ’s ne‘’ tca‘’ nigiă'do’’dĕⁿ‘ ne‘’
   That (it is) moreover the one it will make customarily the the where such my body (is) as in kind the

6. o‘hwĕñ’’gă’ dĕⁿgāiĕñdă‘’gwĭk, iă'ie’ ĕⁿgagwe'niă’ iă'ie’ tca‘’ goioⁿ‘-
   it wood it it will resemble, that (it is) it it will be able to do that (it is) the where they (indef.)

7. sāiĕñ'doⁿ‘ ne‘’tho‘ nhĕⁿ‘hĕñ'ne’, ne‘’tho‘ di‘’ nĕⁿ‘hadiie'ă’ ne‘’
   lodges have severally there thither they (m.) will go there moreover so they (m.) it will do the

8. boñdu'i' ne‘’ i‘’ ĕⁿioñgadiă'doñda‘’gwă’ tca‘’ nigiă'do’’dĕⁿ‘. Oiĕⁿ’-
   they (m.) are badu'i' the I they (indef.) my person will represent thereby the where such my body is as in kind. It

9. gwă'oñ'we‘ gĕⁿ’s ĕⁿioñdieă'dă‘’gwă’. Ĕⁿgagwe'niă’ ĕⁿdjoñ'doⁿ’
   tobacco native customarily one it it will use to do. It it will be able to do again one will be well (=become one's self again)

10. ne‘’ gonoⁿ‘hwăk'dănĭk. Ne‘’tho‘ di‘’ noñ'we‘ nĕⁿgadiĕñ’’ ne‘’ tca‘’
    the they (indef.) ill are severally. There moreover the place I myself will place the the where

11. noñ'we‘ odoⁿ‘hwĕñdjiat'gĭ's tca‘’ o‘’ degastĕⁿ‘he'nioⁿ‘. Hiă‘’
    the place it earth is wild severally the where too it rock rises severally. Not (it is)

12. stĕⁿ’’ di‘’ de'wagadawĕⁿ‘‘das. Nā'ie’ di‘’ tca‘’ iĕⁿioñni'she’
    any-thing moreover it me obstructs (my sight, hearing, or power). That (it is) moreover the where so it will last long

13. ĕⁿioⁿ‘hwĕñdjiā'dek ne‘’tho‘ ĕⁿgi'dĕñ'dak. Ĕⁿkheiă'dage‘’nhĕⁿk di‘’
    it earth will be present there I will continue to abide. I them will continue to aid more over

---

[a] Masculine plural of hadu'i'.

continue to aid the man-beings for that length of time." There, it is said, is the place wherein all kinds of deadly ills begot themselves—fevers, consumptions, headaches—all were caused by Hadu'i'.

Now, at that time the Sapling again traveled. He again arrived at his lodge, and he marveled that his grandmother was angry. She took from its fastening the head, which had been cut off, of his—the Sapling's—dead mother, and she carried it away also. She bore the head away with her. When she had prepared the head, it became the sun, and the body of flesh became the nocturnal light orb. As soon as it became night, the elder woman-being and, next in order, Flint departed, going in an easterly direction. At the end of three days, then said Sapling: "I will go after the diurnal orb of

ne″	oñ'gwe‘	ne″tho‘	nigāi‘‘hwes."	Ne″tho‘,	iā'kĕⁿ˙,	noñ'we‘	1
the	man-beings	there	so it matter is long."	There (it is)	it is said,	the place	
diiodadoñni‘'		ne″	nwä'tganoⁿ'sodä'tchäge‘';		ĕⁿiago'do"'gwăk,		2
there it formed itself		the	every it disease is in number:		one fever will have,		
dĕⁿiago‘hwä'e'sdä',			ĕniagonoⁿ'wanoⁿ'‘hwăk		ıä'ie'	ıe″tho‘	3
colic, the gripes (it will pierce one's body),			one pain in the head will have,		that (it is)	there	
ni‘hoie'ĕⁿ‘	ne″	Hadu″i'.					4
so he it has done	the	Hadn″i'.					
Tho″ge‘	o'nĕⁿ‘	he″	doūsa‘hadawĕñ'ie'	ne″	Odĕñdoñni″ä˙.		5
At that (time)	now	again	again he traveled	the·	It Sapling.		
Hoñsa‘hä'ioⁿ'	tca″	ıoñ'we‘	thonoⁿ‘sä'iĕⁿ'.	O'nĕⁿ‘	wä'hoi‘hwane‘-		6
There again he arrived	the where	the place	there his lodge lies.	Now	he marveled at the		
hä'gwä˙	tca″	o'nĕⁿ‘	gonä'khwĕⁿ″ı‘	ne″	ho‘sodä‘hä‘'	Wä˙e˙hä'gwä˙	7
matter	the where	now	she is angry	the	his grandmother.	She it took off	
tca″	gannondä‘'gwä˙	ne″	onoⁿ″wä˙	ne″	tca″	oñdat‘hniä'djiä″gī‘	8
the where	it had been fastened up	the	it head	the	the where	one her head had cut off	
ne″	hono‘‘hä'-gĕⁿ‘‘hä˙	ne″	Odĕñdoñni″ä‘	hwä'e‘‘hwä˙	o″ni̇˙		9
the	his mother	it was	the	It Sapling	hence she it carried away	also.	
Heiago‘hauⁿ‘'	ne″	onoⁿ″wä'.	Tca″	wä‘eiĕñnĕñdä″nhä˙	ne″		10
Hence she carried it away	the	it head.	The where	she finished the way of it	the		
onoⁿ″wä'	gää‘'gwä˙	wä'wa'doⁿ,	o'nĕⁿ‘	ne″	oieĕⁿ″dä'	ne″	nä˙	11
it head	it sun (luminary)	it it became,	now	the	it flesh	the that	that one	
a‘soñek'hä˙	gää‘'gwä˙	wä'wa'doⁿ.	Gaulo″	däio″gak	o'nĕⁿ‘		12
nocturnal (it is)	it moon (luminary)	it it became	So soon as	thence it became night	now		
wä‘hiia‘dĕñ'diä˙	ne″	gok'stĕñ'ä‘	ıäie‘	gwä″tho˙	ne″	O‘ha'ä˙	13
they two departed	the	she ancient one (is)	that (it is)	next in place	the	It Flint (is)	
tgaä‘'gwi'tgĕⁿ';	nhwä'hniieä″dä˙.	Nä'ie‘	ne″	ä'sĕⁿ‘	niwĕñdage‘'		14
there it sun rises	thither they two (m.) directed their course.	That (it is)	the	three	so it day (is) in number		
nwä'oñni'she‘	o'nĕⁿ‘	ne″	Odĕñdoñni″ä‘	wä'hĕⁿ‘hĕñ″:	··O'nĕⁿ‘		15
so long it lasted	now	the	It Sapling	he it said:	"Now		

light. Verily, it is not good that the human beings who are about to dwell here on the earth should continue to go about in darkness. Who, moreover, will accompany me?" A man-being, named Fisher, spoke in reply, saying: "I will accompany thee." A man-being, another person, said: "I, too, will accompany thee." It was the Raccoon who said this. Another man-being, whose name is Fox, said: "I, too, will accompany thee." There were several others, several man-beings, who, one and all, volunteered to aid Sapling. At that time Sapling said: "Moreover, who will work at the canoe?" The Beaver said: "Verily, I will make it." Another man-being, whose name was Yellowhammer, said: "I will make the hollow of it." At that time there were several others who also gave their attention to it. And then they worked at it, making

1 hĕⁿsgegwă'‘hă’ ne" gaä"gwā’ ĕndek'hă’. Hiiă'’, bi'iă’ de’oia'ne’
   hence I it will go to the it orb of diurnal Not verily, it is good
   bring   light   (it is). (it is),

2 dāio’gās'dĭk tca" noñ'we‘ āionˮ'sek ne" oñ'gwe‘ oñnagäthe"
   it should con- the the place they should con- the human they (indef.) are
   tinue to be night where tinue to go about being about to dwell

3 ne" tho'nĕⁿ‘ oⁿ‘hwĕndjiä"ge‘. Soñ" dĭ" noñwa‘ho"dĕⁿ hĕⁿia'gne’?"
   the here it earth on. Who more- kind of person one and I will go
                            (is it), over,   together?"

4 Hĕñ'gwe‘, Sgāia'nis hāia'djĭ‘, dă‘hada'diă’ wă'hĕⁿ‘hĕñ": "I"
   He man- Fisher he is he talked in he it said: "I
   being, (Long-track) called, reply

5 hĕⁿdne"." Hĕñ'gwe‘, thi‘hāiă’da'de’ wă'hĕⁿ‘hĕñ": "I" o"
   thou and I He man- just his body is projecting he it said: "I too
   will go." being (is) (he is another person)

6 ĕⁿdwe"." Tcokda'gĭ’ ne" nă" wă'hĕⁿ‘hĕñ". Hĕñ'gwe‘ thi‘hawe will go." Raccoon the that one he it said. He man- just his
                         that   being (is) body is

7 iă'da'de’, Sgĕⁿ‘hnă'ksĕⁿ’ hāia'djĭ‘ wă'hĕⁿ‘hĕñ": "I" o" ĕⁿdwe’."
   projecting (he is Fox he is he it said: "I too we will go
   another person), (It Has Bad Fur) called   together."

8 Thi‘hadiiă’dade'nioⁿ" hĕñnoñgwe‘shoⁿˮoⁿ‘ gagwe'gĭ‘ wă'hoñthoñ
   They (m.) other (are) they (m.) man-being it all they (m.)
   severally   (are) severally   made their

9 gā'iă'k ne" tca" ĕⁿ‘hoñwāie'năwă’s ne" Odĕñdoñni"ă‘. O'nĕⁿ
   scores (vol- the the they (m.) him will assist the It Sapling. Now
   unteered) where

10 tho"ge‘ ne" Odĕñdoñni"ă‘ wă'hĕⁿ‘hĕñ": "Soñ" dĭ" noñwa‘ho"
   at that the It Sapling he it said: "Who more- kind of person
   (time)   (is it) over

11 dĕⁿ’ ĕⁿ‘hoio‘dĕⁿ"‘hă’ ne" ga‘hoñ'wă’?" Wă'hĕⁿ‘hĕñ" ne"
   he it will work at the it canoe?" He it said the

12 Nagāiă"gĭ’: "I" hi'iă’ ĕⁿge‘sĕñ'niă’." Hĕñ'gwe‘ thi‘hāiă’da'de’,
   Beaver "I verily I it will make." He man- he another
   (Stick-cutter)   being (is) person is,

13 Kwĕⁿ"kwĕⁿ‘ ni‘ha‘sĕñno"dĕⁿ‘ nă'ie" ne" wă'hĕⁿ‘hĕñ": "I"
   Yellowhammer such his name (is) that the he it said: "I
                 in kind   (it is)

14 ĕⁿksădoñ'niă’ " Tho"ge‘ o'nĕⁿ‘ thigoñdiiă’dade'nioⁿ o"nĭ’ wă'ha-
   I trough (hol- At that now they (z.) other individuals also they (m.)
   low)." will make (time)   severally (are)

the canoe. There Sapling kept saying: "Do ye make haste in the work." In a short time, now, verily, they finished it, making a canoe. Quickly, now, they prepared themselves. At that time they launched the canoe into the water. Then Sapling said: "Moreover, who shall steer the canoe?" Beaver said: "I will volunteer to do it." Otter also said: "I, too." Now they went aboard and departed. Then Sapling said: "In steering the canoe, thou must guide it eastward." Now, it ran swiftly as they paddled it onward. It was night; it was in thick darkness; in black night they propelled the canoe onward. After a while, seemingly, they then looked and saw that daylight was approaching. And when they arrived at the place whither they were going it was then daylight. They saw that there

diiʻhwasteis'dă'. the matter gave attention to.	Tho''ge' At that (time)	o'nĕⁿ' now	wăʻhodiio'dĕⁿ'ʻhă' they (m.) it worked at	wăʻhadiʻhoñ they (m.) made	1
ioñ'niă'. the canoe.	Ne''tho' There	iʻha'doⁿk he it kept saying	ne'' the	Odĕñdoñni''ă': It Sapling:	"Hau'', "Come, 2
deswă'nowāiăʻhĕⁿʻhă'.'' do ye make haste (make your backs boil).''		Niioiʻhwăgwăʻhă'' So it is a short matter	o'nĕⁿ' now	biʻiă' verily	wăʻhoñdi they (m.) 3
ĕnnoʻk'dĕⁿ' it task finished	wăʻhadiʻhoñioñ'niă'. they (m.) it canoe made.	Wă'dwakdă''ă' It is a short space	o'nĕⁿ' now	wăʻhoñde''să' they made themselves ready.	4
Tho''ge' At that (time)	o'nĕⁿ' now	awĕⁿ''ge' water on (in)	hwăʻhoñna'dī' thither they (m.) it cast	ne'' the	gaʻhoñ'wă' it canoe. 5
Tho''ge' At that (time)	wăʻhĕⁿʻhĕñ'' he it said	ne'' the	Odĕñdoñni''ă': It Sapling:	"Soñ'' "Who	dī'' moreover 6
noñwaʻho''dĕⁿ' kind of person	ĕⁿthĕññidĕñwă''dă'?'' he be the canoe will guide?''		Nagāiă''gī' Beaver (Stick-Cutter)		wăʻhĕⁿʻhĕñ'': he it said: 7
"I'' "I	ĕⁿgathoñgā'iăʻk.'' I will volunteer.''	Skwā'iĕⁿ' Otter	wăʻhĕⁿʻhĕñ'': he it said:	"I'' "I	o''nī'.'' also.'' 8
Tho''ge' At that (time)	o'nĕⁿ' now	wăʻhoñdi'dak, they (m.) got aboard,	o'nĕⁿ' now	wăʻhoñʻdĕñ'diă'. they (m.) departed.	O'nĕⁿ' Now (it is) 9
ne'' the	Odĕñdoñni''ă· It Sapling	wăʻhĕⁿʻhĕñ'': he it said:	"Tgaäʻgwi'tgĕⁿ's "There it sun rises		nĕⁿsieä''dă' thither thou it wilt direct 10
tca'' the where	ĕⁿseññidĕñ'wă''dă'.'' thou wilt guide the canoe.''	O'nĕⁿ' Now	hi'iă' verily	deioä''dădi· it is running	tca'' hodiga- the they (m.) where 11
weʻha'die'. go along rowing.	Deio''gas, It is night,	deiodaʻsoñdāi'goⁿ, two it darkness to darkness (pitch-dark) is joined,		oʻsoñdagoñwăʻshoⁿʻgowa'- it blackness (night) in along great	12
ne' there	ne''tho· they (m.) go along propelling the canoe.	hadiʻhoñioñ'die'.	Diĕñ'ʻhă' Suddenly,	gwă'' seemingly,	o'nĕⁿ' wăʻhoñtgat'hwă' now they (m.) looked 13
o'nĕⁿ' now	ĕnde·' day (daylight),	dāioʻdoⁿʻhā'die'. thence so it is coming along.	Ne' The	o'nĕⁿ' now	wăʻhadi'ioⁿ' ne'' tca'' they (m.) arrived the the where 14
noñ'we' the place	hwăʻhĕñ'ne' thither they (m.) are going	ĕnde'' daylight (it is)	o'nĕⁿ'. now.	Wăʻhoñtgat'hwă' They (m.) looked at it	ne''tho· there 15

was there, seemingly, an island, and they saw that the trees standing there were very tall, and that some of them were bent over, inclining far over the sea, and there in the water where the tree tops ended the canoe stopped. Then Sapling said: "Moreover, who will go to unfasten the light orb [the sun] from its bonds yonder on the tree top?" Then Fisher said: "I will volunteer." Then Fox said: "I, too [will volunteer]." At that time Fisher climbed up high, and passed along above [the ground]. He crossed from tree to tree, going along on the branches, making his way to the place where the diurnal light orb was made fast; thither he was making his course. But, in regard to Fox, he ran along below on the ground. In a short time Fisher then arrived at the place where the diurnal light orb was made fast.

1. gwä″ tgä·hwe″'no', wä·hadi'gĕⁿ' ne″tho‘ gä·hi'doⁿ' agwa's
seemingly, there it island floats, they (m.) it saw there it tree stands plurally very (it is)

2. gaĕñ·he'djï's agwa's deiotcha·kdoñ'nioⁿ', hä'deiodĕñ·hä·k'doñnioñ'
it tree trunks (are) long (tall), very (just) they (z.) are bent severally, just it tree trunks are bent over toward it

3. gwĕⁿ‘ ne″ gania'dä·ge″'shoⁿ' hägwa'dï‘, ne″tho‘ tca″ noñ'we‘
the it lake (sea) on along side of it, there the where the place

4. awĕⁿ'ge″' begaĕñ·hade'nioⁿ' ne″tho‘ doñdagadä″'nhä' ne″
it water on (in) there it trees end severally there there it stopped the

5. ga·hoñ'wä'. Tho″'ge‘ o'nĕⁿ'. wä·hĕⁿ‘hĕñ″' ne″ Odĕñdoñni″'ä‘·
it canoe. At that (time) now he it said the It Sapling:

6. "Soñ″' dï″' noñwa·ho″'dĕⁿ' ĕⁿ‘haniioñdagwa″'hä' si″' tganiioñ'dä'
"Who (is it) more-over kind of person he it will go to unfasten yonder there it is fastened

7. ne″ tca″ hegaĕñ·hagĕⁿ‘bia'dä' ne″ gaä″'gwä″? Sgäia'nis
the the where there it tree top ends the it sun (orb of light)?" Fisher

8. wä·hĕⁿ‘hĕñ″: "I", ĕⁿgathoñgä'iä'k." Sgĕⁿ'hnäk'sĕⁿ' wä·hĕⁿ‘hĕñ″:
he it said: "I, I will volunteer." Fox he it said:

9. "I" o″'nï″." Tho″'ge‘ o'nĕⁿ' wä·haä″'thĕⁿ' ne″ Sgäia'nis
"I also." At that (time) now he it climbed the Fisher

10. he'tgĕⁿ‘″' ni·hodoñgo'dï·hä'die'. Wä·haĕñ·hiiä″'khoⁿ', o‘sgo‘ha'ge″'-
up high there he passed along. He tree tops crossed over, severally it bough on along

11. shoⁿ' ne″tho‘ ni·hat·ha·hi'ne' ne″tho‘ nhwä·he″ tca″ noñ'we‘
there there he traveled along, there thither he was going the where the place

12. tganiioñ'dä‘ ne″ ĕñdek·hä' gaä″'gwä', ne″tho‘ nhwä·hawenoñ'hä'-
there it is fastened up the diurnal it sun (orb of light), there thither he was making his way.

13. die' Ne″ nä' Sgĕⁿ·bnä'ksĕⁿ' e‘dä″'ge‘ ni·hadäk'he'.
The that that one Fox down (on the ground) there he ran.

14. Wä'dwäkdä″'ä‘ o'nĕⁿ' ne″ Sgäia'nis o'nĕⁿ' hwä·hä'ioⁿ' tca″
In a short time (it is close apart) now the Fisher now there he arrived the where

15. noñ'we‘ tganiioñ'dä‘ ne″ gaä″'gwä'. Goñdadie″ wä·hatcho·hi'-
the place there it is fastened up the it sun. At once he it bit repeatedly

At once he repeatedly bit that by which it was secured, and, severing it, he removed the sun. Now, moreover, he cast it down to his friend, Fox, who stood near beneath him. He caught it, and now, moreover, they two fled. When they two had run half the way across the island, then Flint's grandmother noticed what had taken place. She became angry and wept, saying: "What, moreover, is the reason, O Sapling, that thou hast done this in this manner?" Then she, the elder woman-being, arose at once, and began to run in pursuit of the two persons. Fox ran along on the ground and, in turn, Fisher crossed from tree to tree, running along the branches. Now, the elder woman-being was running close behind, and now she was about to sieze Fox, who now, moreover, being wearied, cast the sun up above. Then Fisher caught it. Now, next

'hon'‑ ne'' the	tca'' the where	ganiioñdä''gwĕn', it it fastened by it,		wă'hä'iă'k he it severed	wă'haniioñda'gwă' he it unfastened	1
ne'' the	gaä''gwā'. it sun.	O'nĕn' Now	dī'' more-over	e'dä''ge' down below	hwă'ho'dī' thither he it threw	hwă'hoñwa'diĕn's thither he it threw to him	2
ne'' the	hoñna'tchī' they are friends	ne'' the	Sgĕn'hnăk'sĕn' Fox	ne''tho' there	dosgĕn''hă' near by	thā'dă'. there he stands.	3
Nä'ie' That (it is)	ne'' the	da'hāie'nä' there he it caught	o'nĕn' now	dī'' more-over	wă'hiade''gwā'. they two (m.) fled.	Tca'' The where	4
dewa'sĕñ'non' it is the middle (half)	tca'' the where	niga'hwe''nä' so it island (is.) large	ne''tho' there		hă'doñ'sa'hnidăk'he' just there again they two (m.) are running		5
o'nĕn' now	wă'oñtdo'gä' she it noticed	ne'' the	ho'sodä'hă'' his grandmother	ne'' the	O'ha'ä'. It Flint.	Wă'agoñä''- She became	6
khwĕn''hă', angry,	wă'dion'shĕñt'hwä', she wept,	wā'ä''hĕñ'': she it said:	"Ho't "What (is it)	dī'' more-over	noñwa'ho''- kind of thing		7
dĕn'	dāioi'hwä''khe' thence it was the reason	ne'' the	tho'nĕn' thus	nwă'sie'ä' so thou it didst do	Odĕñdoñni''ä·?'' It Sapling?''		8
O'nĕn' Now	doñdāiedĕn'sdä'djī' thence she leapt up		wă'dioñä''dat she ran	ne'' the	gok'stĕñ'ä' she ancient one	wă'hoñwa- she them pursued.	9
di''se'k.	Nä'ie' That (it is)	ne'' the	Sgĕn'hnă'ksĕn' Fox	e'dä''ge' ground on	ni'hadăk'he' there he ran	nä'ie' that (it is)	10
ne'' the	on''kĕn' next in time	ne'' the	Sgāia'nis Fisher	he'tgĕn'' up high	de'haĕñ'hiiă'khon''ne' he tree tops is crossing severally		11
o'sgo'ha''ge''sho' it boughs on along	ni'hadăk'he'. there he is running.		O'nĕn' Now	dosgĕn''hă' near by	dāiedăk'he' there she came running		12
ne'' the	gok'stĕñ'ä', she ancient one,	o'nĕn' now	tho''hă' almost	a'hoñwāie'nä' she him could seize	o'nĕn' now	ne'' the	13
Sgĕn'hnă'ksĕn' Fox	wă'hatchĕn''dä' he became wearied	o'nĕn' now	dī'' more-over	he'tgĕn'' up high	hwă'ho'dī' thither he it threw		14
ne'' the	gaä''gwā'. it sun.	Sgāia'nis Fisher	da'hāie'nä'. there he it caught.	Nä'ie' That (it is)	ne'' the	on''kĕn' next in time	15

in turn, she pursued him. And he, next in turn, when she came running close behind him and was about to seize him, being in his turn wearied, cast the sun down, and then Fox in his turn caught it. Thus, verily, it continued. Fisher was in the lead, and he at once boarded the canoe. And close behind him was Fox, holding the sun in his mouth, and he, too, at once got aboard of the canoe. Now, moreover, the canoe withdrew, and, turning around, it started away. Now, moreover, it was running far away as they paddled it onward when the elder woman-being arrived at the shore of the sea; and she there shouted, saying: "O Sapling, what, moreover, is the reason that thou hast done this thing in this manner? Thou shouldst pity me, verily, in that the sun should continue to pass thence, going thither [in its orbit, giving day and night]." He, Sapling, said noth-

1	wă'hoñwa'se''k. she him pursued.	Nā'ie' That (it is)	oⁿ''kĕⁿ' next in time	ne'' the	o'nĕⁿ' now	dosgĕⁿ''hă' near by
2	dāiedăk'he', there she came running,	o'nĕⁿ' now	tho''hă' almost	a'hoñwāie'nă' she him could seize	o'nĕⁿ' now	ne'' the that	oⁿ'kĕⁿ next in time
3	wă'hatchĕⁿ''dă' he became wearied	e'dă''ge' down below	hwă'ho'dĭ', thither he it cast.	Sgĕⁿ'hnă'ksĕⁿ' Fox	oⁿ'kĕⁿ next in time
4	da'hāie'nă'. there he it caught.	Nā'ie' That (it is)	bi'iă' verily	niio'di'hā'die'. so it continued to be.	Ha'bĕñ'de' He is in the lead	ne'' the
5	Sgāia'nis Fisher	na'ie' that (it is)	hāiă'dagoñdā'die' his body did not stop	sa'hadi'dăk again he got aboard	gă'hoñwăgoñ'wă'. it canoe in.
6	O'nĕⁿ' Now	ne''tho' there	gwă''tho' next in place	ne'' the	Sgĕⁿ'hnă'ksĕⁿ' Fox	ho'nhoñdā'die' he came holding it in his mouth	ne'' the
7	gaä''gwă', it sun.	nā'ie' That (it is)	-o'' too	hāiă'dagoñdā'die' his body did not stop	sa'hadi'dăk again he got aboard	ne'' the	ga'hoñwăgoñ'wă'. it canoe in.
8	O'nĕⁿ' Now	dĭ'' moreover	ne'' the	ga'hoñ'wă' it canoe	dawadoⁿ''tgă' thence it withdrew itself	wă'dwatga'ha- it turned around
9	dĕ'nĭ' sawathoñwanĕñdă''siă'. again it canoe disjoined itself (from the landing).	O'nĕⁿ' Now	dĭ'' moreover	i'noⁿ' far	sagadăk'he' again it is running	ne'' the
10	tca'' the where	hodigawe'hā'die' they (m.) go paddling onward	ne'' the	o'nĕⁿ' now	dāie'ioⁿ' there she arrived	ganiadăk'dă' it sea (lake) beside	ne'' the
11	gok'stĕñ'ă', she ancient one,	o'nĕⁿ' now	dĭ'' moreover	ne''tho' there	wă'diago'bĕñe''dă', she shouted,	wă'ă'hĕñ'': she it said:
12	"Odĕñdoñni''ă', "It Sapling,	ho't what (is it)	dĭ'' moreover	noñwa'ho'dĕⁿ' kind of thing	diioi''hwă' it is reason	tca'' the where
13	tho'nĕⁿ' here	uwă'sie'ă'? so thou it hast done?	Ă'sgidĕñ'ă' Thou me shouldst pity	bi'iă', verily,	ne'' the	tca'' the where	doñdawet'hak thence it should continue to pass thither
14	ne'' the	gaä''gwă'." it sun."	Hiiă'' Not (it is)	stĕⁿ'' anything	de'ha'wĕñ' he it said	ne'' the	Odĕñdoñni''ă'. It Sapling.	Ă''sĕⁿ' Three

ing. She said this three times in succession. Now she exclaimed: "O thou, Fox, effuse thy orenda to cause the sun to pass habitually thence, going thither." Fox said nothing in reply. Thrice, too, did she repeat this speech. Now, again, she said: "O thou, Fisher, effuse thy orenda whereby thou canst make the sun to pass habitually thence, going thither." He said nothing. Thrice did she repeat this saying. And all the other persons, too, said nothing. She said: "O thou, Beaver, thou shouldst at this time have pity on me; do thou effuse thy orenda; moreover, thou hast the potence to cause the sun to pass thence habitually, going thither." He said nothing. Thrice, too, did she repeat this speech. All said nothing. Now, there was there a person, a man-being, whose orenda she overmatched. She said: "O thou, Otter, thou art a fine person, do thou effuse thy orenda

nwă'oñdiet''ă'	ne"	iă'ie'	iioñ'doⁿk.	O'něⁿ·	wă'gěⁿ·hěñ'':	"Sgěⁿ·-	1
so many she it repeated	the	that (it is)	she it kept saying.	Now	she (z.) it said:	"Fox	
hnă'ksěⁿ·	desaděññoñ'děⁿ·		tca''	sa'shaskděⁿ'sä'iěⁿ''		ěⁿ'sgwe'niă'	2
do thou thyself in thy orenda array			the where	thou hast potency		thou it art able to do	
doñdawet'hak	ne''	gaä''gwă'.''	Hiiă''	stěⁿ''	de'ha'wěñ·	ne''	3
thence it should continue to pass thither	the	it sun.''	Not (it is)	anything	he it said	the	
Sgěⁿ·hnă'ksěⁿ·.	'Ă·'sěⁿ·	o''	nwă'oñdiet''ă'	iă'ie'	iioñ'doⁿk.	O'něⁿ·	4
Fox.	Three	too	so many she it repeated	that (it is)	she it kept saying	Now	
he	o'iă'	wă'gěⁿ·hěñ'':	"Sgāia'nis	desaděññoñ'děⁿ·	tca''	sa'sha	5
again	it other (is)	she (z.) it said:	"Fisher	do thou thyself in thy orenda array	the where	thou hast	
sděⁿ'sä'iěⁿ''	ne''	tca''	ěⁿ'sgwe'niă'	doñdawet'hak	ne''	gaä''gwă'.''	6
potency	the	the where	thou it art able to do	thence it should continue to pass thither	the	it sun.''	
Hiiă''	stěⁿ''	de'ha'wěñ·.	'Ă·'sěⁿ·	o''	nwă'oñdiet''ă'	iă'ie'	7
Not (it is)	anything	he it said.	Three	too	so many she it repeated	that (it is)	
iioñ'doⁿk.	Nă'ie'	o''	ne''	thi'hadiiă'dade'nioⁿ''	gagwe'gī·	biiă''	8
she it kept saying.	That (it is)	too	the	just they (m.) are different ones	it all	not (it is)	
stěⁿ''	de'hoñ'něñ·.	Wă'gěⁿ·hěñ''·	"Nagāiă''gī',	i's	ne''	oⁿ·'kěⁿ'	9
anything	they (m.) it said.	She (z.) it said:	"Beaver,	thou	the	present time	
ă'sgiděñ'ă';	desaděññoñ'děⁿ·	di'',	sa'shaskděⁿ'sä'iěⁿ''	tca''	ěⁿ'sgwe'		10
thou me shouldst pity;	do thou thyself in thy orenda array	moreover,	thou potency hast	the where	thou wilt be able		
niă'	ne''	tca''	doñdawet'hak	ne''	gaä''gwă'.''	Hiiă''	stěⁿ''	11
to do	the	the where	thence it should continue to pass thither	the	it sun.''	Not (it is)	anything	
de'ha'wěñ·.	'Ă·'sěⁿ·	o''	nwă'oñdiet''ă'	iă'ie'	iioñ'doⁿk.	Gagwe'gī·	12
he it said.	Three	too	so many she it repeated	that (it is)	she it kept saying.	It all	
biiă''	stěⁿ''	de'hoñ'něñ·.	O'něⁿ·	ne''tho·	ne''	hěñ'gwe·	shăiă'-	13
not (it is)	anything	they (m.) it said.	Now	there	the	he man-being	he is a	
dădă·	wă'thoñwaěñ'gěñ'niă'.		Wă'gěⁿ·hěñ'':	"Skwă'iěⁿ·,	i's	soñ-		14
person	she his orenda overmatched.		She (z.) it said:	"Otter,	thou	thou art a		

wherein thou hast the potence to ordain [forethink] that the sun thence shall come to pass, going thither." He said: "So be it." Instantly accompanying it was her word, saying: "I am thankful." At that time Beaver said: "Now, verily, it is a direful thing, wherein thou hast done wrong." And now, moreover, he took the paddle out of the water and with it he struck poor Otter in the face, flattening his face thereby.

As soon as they arrived home Sapling said: "I am pleased that now we have returned well and successful. Now, I will fasten it up high; on high shall the sun remain fixed hereafter." At that time he then said: "Now, the sun shall pass over the sky that is visible. It shall continue to give light to the earth." Thus, moreover, it too came to pass in regard to the nocturnal light orb [the moon].

1	gwe'di'io', good person,	desadĕñnoñ'dĕⁿ' do thou thyself in thy orenda array	tca" the where	sa'shasdĕⁿ'sä'iĕⁿ" thou hast potency	ne" the	tca" the where
2	ĕⁿsgwe'niä' thou it wilt be able to do	ne" the	ĕⁿtcĕñnoⁿ'doⁿ thou thyself will will it	tca" the where	doñdawet'hak thence it will continue to pass	ne" the	gaä'- it
3	gwä'." sun."	Wä'hĕⁿ'hĕñ": He it said:	"Niio". "So let it be."	Ne"tho' There	gawĕñnaniioñdä'die' as soon as it was said (it word came fastened to it)		
4	wä'gĕⁿ'hĕñ": she (z.) it said:	"Niiawĕⁿ'hä'. "I am thankful."	Tho"ge' At that (time)	o'nĕⁿ' now	ne" the	Nagäiä'gi' Beaver	
5	wä'hĕⁿ'hĕñ": he it said:	"O'nĕⁿ' "Now	hi'iä' verily	gano'wĕⁿ it is dire	tca" the v here	sa'sadei'hwat'wa'dä'," again thou hast done wrong (mistaken a matter),	
6	o'nĕⁿ' now	di" moreover	da'hagawe'sotciĕⁿ"dä', instantly he took paddle out of water,		hagoⁿ'si"ge' his face on	wä'häiĕⁿ"dä', he it struck,	
7	da'ha'hwä'e'gwä' thence he battered it (flattened it)	ne" the	Skwäiĕⁿ'-gĕn'hä'. Otter it was (poor it is).				
8	Ganiio" So soon as	sa'hadi'ioⁿ" again they (m.) returned	o'nĕⁿ' now	ne" the	Odĕñdoñni"ä' It Sapling	wä'hĕⁿ'hĕñ": he it said:	
9	"O'nĕⁿ' "Now	wä'gatcĕñnoñ'niä' I am glad	tca" the where	o'nĕⁿ' now	skĕñ'noⁿ well (it is)	tca" the where	sedwä'ioⁿ". again we have returned.
10	O'nĕⁿ' Now	di" moreover	he'tgĕⁿ'' up high	ĕⁿgniioñ'dĕⁿ, I it will fasten,	he'tgĕⁿ'' up high	hĕⁿioñtgoñdä"gwĕⁿ it will be unchanging	
11	ĕⁿganiioñ'dak it will be fast	tca" the where	gaä"gwä'." it sun."	Tho"ge' At that (time)	o'nĕⁿ' now	wä'hĕⁿ'hĕñ" she (z.) it said:	
12	"O'nĕⁿ' "Now	dĕⁿwet'hak thence it will continue to pass thither	ne" the	gaä"gwä' it sun	gaĕⁿ'hia'de'. it sky (is) present.	Dĕⁿio'hathe"dik It will cause it to be light	
13	tca" the where	oⁿ'hwĕñdjiä"ge'." it earth on."	Ne"tho' There	di" moreover	nwä'awĕⁿ'hä' so it came to pass	tca" the v here	a'soñek'hä' it night pertaining to
14	gaä"gwä'. it moon. (it luminary)						

Now, Sapling traveled over the visible earth. There was in one place a river course, and he stood beside the river. There he went to work and he formed the body of a human man-being.[a] He completed his body and then he blew into his mouth. Thereupon, the human man-being became alive. Sapling said: "Thou thyself ownest all this that is made." So, now, verily, he repeatedly looked around, and there was there a grove whose fruit was large, and there, moreover, the sound of the birds talking together was great. So, now came another thing. Thus, in his condition he watched him, and he thought that, perhaps, he was lonesome. Now, verily, he again went to work, and he made another human man-being. Next in time he made a human woman-being. He completed her body, and then he blew into her mouth, and then she, too, became alive. He said, addressing the male man-being: "Now, this woman-being and thou

O'nĕⁿ'	de'hodawĕñie''	tca''	oⁿ'hwĕñdjiă'de'	ne''	Odĕñdoñni''ă'	1
Now	he traveled	the where	it earth is present	the	It Sapling.	
Gĕⁿ'hioⁿ'hwădă'die'	ne''tho'	gĕⁿ'hioⁿ'hwăk'dă'	wă'thadă''nhă'.		Ne''tho'	2
It river is present in a course	there	it river beside	he came to stand.		There	
wă'hoio'dĕⁿ''hă'	wă'hoiă'doñ'niă'	ne''	oñ'gwe'.[b]		Wă'hoiă'di''să'	3
he went to work	he his body made	the	human being.		He his body finished	
o'nĕⁿ'	wă'hăĕñ''dăt	ne''	ha'sagoñ'wă'.	Tho''ge'	o'nĕⁿ' wă'ha	4
now	he blew (wind uttered)	the	his mouth in	At that (time)	now he	
do'n'het	ne''	oñ'gwe'.	Odĕñdoñni''ă'	wă'hĕⁿ'hĕñ'':	." I's sa'wĕⁿ'	5
became alive	the	human being.	It Sapling	he it said	"Thou thou it ownest	
nĕñ'gĕⁿ'	tca''	niiodie'ĕⁿ'."	Da',	o'nĕⁿ'	bi'iă' de'hotga'doñ'nioⁿ'k	6
this one	the where	so it is done."	So.	now	verily he is looking repeatedly about	
ne''tho'	o'hoñ'dă'iĕⁿ'	ne''	swa'hio'nă',	ne''tho'	di'' gāi'sdowa'nĕⁿ'	7
there	it brush (shrubs) are (lie)	the	it fruit (are) large,	there	more- over it sound (is) large	
goñdiio'shoⁿ''ă'	odit'hă'.	Da',	o'nĕⁿ'	he'' o'iă'.	Ne''tho' ni'io't	8
they (z.) animals small (birds)	they (z.) are talking.	So,	now	again it another (thing).	There so it is	
tca''	de'hoga''hă	wă'he'ă'	hagwa'dă's	hoñ''.	O'nĕⁿ' hi'iă'	9
the where	he him had his eyes fixed on	he it thought	he is becoming lonesome	per- haps.	Now verily	
sa'hoio'dĕⁿ''hă'	o'nĕⁿ'	he''	o'iă'	sa'ha'soñ'niă'	ne'' oñ'gwe'	10
again he went to work	now	again	It an- other	again he it made	the human being.	
Agoñ'gwe'	oⁿ''kĕⁿ'	ne''	sa'ha'soñ'niă'.	Wă'shagoiă'di''să'	o'nĕⁿ'	11
She human being	next in time	the	again he it made.	He her body com- pleted	now	
wă'hăĕñ''dăt	ne''	e'sagoñ'wă',	o'nĕⁿ'	o'' nă''	wă'oñdo'n'het.	12
he blew	the	her mouth in,	now	too that one	she became alive.	
Wă'hĕⁿ'hĕñ'',	wă'hoñwĕⁿ''hăs	ne''	hadji'nă':	"Nā'ie'	ne''	13
He it said,	he it said to him	the	he (is) male:	"That (it is)	the	

[a] From this paragraph to the end of this version there is more or less admixture of trans-Atlantic ideas.
[b] Here oñ'gwe' denotes a human being. See footnote on page 141.

ra11y. Do thou not ever cause her mind to be grieved. Thou must at all times hold her dear." At that time he said, addressing her who was there: "This human man-being and thou now marry. Thou must hold him dear. And ye two shall abide together for a time that will continue until death shall separate you two. Always ye two must hold one the other dear. Ye two must care for the grove bearing large fruit. For there are only a few trees that belong to you two." He said: "Moreover, do ye two not touch those which do not belong to you two. Ye two will do evil if it so be that you two touch those which do not belong to you two."

Thus, in this manner, they two remained together, the man-being paying no attention to the woman-being. The male human man-being cared not for the female human man-being. Customarily, they two laid themselves down and they two slept. Now sometime afterward, he who had completed their bodies was again passing that way, and,

1. nĕñ'gĕⁿ'hă' (this one) ne" (the) agoñ'gwe' (she human being) wedjinia'khe'. (ye two marry.) 'A"gwi' (Do not do it) hwĕñ'doⁿ' (ever)

2. a'she'nigoⁿ'hähetgĕⁿ'dă'. (thou her mind shouldst hurt (grieve her mind).) Ĕⁿshenoĕⁿ'khwăk (Thou her shalt hold dear ever) diiot'goñt." (always.") Tho"ge' (At that (time))

3. wă'hĕⁿ'hĕñ", (he it said,) wă'shagowĕⁿ'hăs (he her addressed) ne" (the) ne"tho' (there) e"dĕñ': (she abode:) "Wedjini ("Ye two

4. ak'be' (marry) nĕñgĕⁿ'hă' (this one) hoñ'gwe'. (he human being.) Ĕⁿshenoĕⁿ'khwăk. (Thou him shalt hold dear ever.) Ne"tho' (There

5. nigăi'hwe's (so it matter long (is)) ne" (the) gado'gĕⁿ (it certain place (is)) ĕⁿtciā'diĕñ' (ye two will abide) tca" (the where) nigĕⁿ' (so it is far) o'nĕⁿ' (no) ne" (the

6. gĕⁿ'he'ioⁿ' (it death) dĕⁿdjisnikhă"siă'. (again it you two will separate.) Diiot'goñt (Always) dĕⁿdjiadadatnoĕⁿ'khwăk. (ye two shall hold one the other dear ever.)

7. O'hĕndā'iĕⁿ' (It grove lies) swa'hio'nă' (it fruit large (is)) ĕⁿsni'nigoⁿ'hä"k. (ye two it will care for.) Dogā"ă' (Few in number) niio'hoñdo'dă' (so many) (it shrubs stand)

8. tca" (the where) is' (ye) tcia'wĕⁿ'." (ye two own them.") Wă'hĕⁿ'hĕñ" (He it said) dī'': (more-over:) "'A"gwi ("Do it not, dī" (more-over,) ne" (the that) nă" (that one)

9. nĕⁿ' (this way) nhĕⁿdjiie'ä' (thither ye two it will do (touch it)) tca" (the where) biiă" (not (it is)) is' (ye) de'tcia'wĕⁿ'. (ye two it own.) Ĕⁿsnii'hwăne'a'gwă' (Ye two will make a mistake

10. sĕñ'a' (at all events) gwă" (seem-ingly) ne" (the) biiă" (not (it is)) is' (ye) de'tcia'wĕⁿ' (ye two own it) nĕⁿ' (this way) nhĕⁿdjiie'ä'." (thither ye two will do (touch it).")

11. Ne"tho' (There) ni'io't (so it is) de'hni"dĕñ' (they two (m.) abode together) biiă" (not (it is)) stĕⁿ' (any-thing) de'hoñwasteis'thă' (he her paid any atten-tion to) ne" (the

12. hoñ'gwe' (he human being) ne" (the) agoñ'gwe'. (she human being (is).) Hiiă" (Not (it is)) ne" (the) hadji'nă' (he male (is)) de'shagosteis'thă' (he her paid any atten-tion to)

13. ne" (the) e'hĕⁿ'. (she fe-male (is).) De'hnidā'gä', (They two (m.) lay down together,) de'hnidă"wi' (they two (m.) sleep together) gĕⁿ's. (cus-tomarily.) O'nĕⁿ' (Now) gaiñ'gwă' (some (time))

seeing the condition of things, thought of what he might do to arouse the minds of the two persons. Then he went forward to the place where lay the male person sleeping, and having arrived there he removed a rib from the male person, and then, next in turn, he removed a small rib from the sleeping female man-being. And now, changing the ribs, he placed the rib of the woman-being in the male human man-being, and the rib of the male human man-being he set in the human woman-being. He changed both alike. At that time the woman-being awoke. As soon as she sat up she at once seized the place where was fixed the rib that had been hers. And, as soon as she did this, then the man-being, too, awoke. And now, verily, they both addressed words the one to the other. Then Sapling was highly

---

nwä'oñni'she'	ne''tho'	is'he'	nĕñ'gĕⁿ'	ne''	shagodiiä̆'di·sä̆''ī'	1
so long it lasted	there	again he passed	this one (it is)	the	he their two bodies formed	
wä'hatgat'hwä'	tca''	niiodie'ĕⁿ'	o'nĕⁿ'	wä'hĕñnoⁿ'doñ'nioⁿ'	ho't	2
he it looked at	the where	so it has done	now	he it thought repeatedly	what (it is)	
noñwa'ho''dĕⁿ'	nä'häie'ä'	tca''	dä'hodi'nigoⁿ'häwĕñ'ie'.	Tho''ge'		3
kind of thing	so he it should do	the where	it their two minds should amuse.	At that (time)		
wä'ha'dĕñ'diä'	ne''tho'	nhwä'he''	tca''	noñ'we'	hĕndä̆'gä'	ne''	4
he started	there	thither he went	the where	the place	he lay	the	
hadji'nä'	hodä̆''wi'.	Wä'hä'ioⁿ'	ne''tho'	o'nĕⁿ'	wä'ha'niodä̆'gwä'		5
he male (is)	he slept (was asleep).	He arrived	there	now	he it unfixed (it removed)		
sgä'dä̆'	o'stiĕⁿ''dä'	o'de''gä',	o'nĕⁿ'	ne''	oⁿ''kĕⁿ'	ne''	e''hĕⁿ'	6
one it is	it bone	it rib,	now	the	next in time	the	she female	
tca''	godä̆''wi'	o'nĕⁿ'	ne''	nä̆''	wä'ha'niodä̆'gwä'	ago'de''gä	7
the where	she asleep was	now	the	that one	he it unfixed (it removed)	her rib	
tca''	niwä'a''.	O'nĕⁿ'	ne''tho'	wä'thade'nī'	ne''	o'de''gä';	8
the where	so it is small in size.	Now	there	he them exchanged	the	it rib(s);	
nä'ie'	ne''	e''hĕⁿ'	ago'de''gä'	ne''	hadji'nä'	wä'ho'de'gae'dĕⁿ'',	9
that (it is)	the	she female	her rib	the	he male	he him set rib in,	
o'nĕⁿ'	dī''	ne''	hadji'nä'	bo'de''gä'	ne''	e''hĕⁿ'	wä'shago'de'-	10
now,	moreover,	the	he male	his rib	the	she female	he her set rib	
ga'edĕⁿ'.	Dedjia'oⁿ'	shä̆'thäie'ä'	wä'thade'nī'.	Tho''ge'	o'nĕⁿ',		11
in.	Both	alike he it did	he changed the two.	At that (time)	now		
ne''	agoñ'gwe'	wä'e'iek.	Ganiio''	wä'oñtgetc'gwä'	ne''tho'		12
the	she human being	she awoke.	So soon as	she sat up (arose)	there		
gondä'die'	hwä'eie'nä'	tca''	noñ'we'	heio'nio'dä̆'	ne''	ago'de''gä'-	13
at once	thither she it seized	the where	the place	there it stands fixed	the	her rib	
gĕⁿ''hä'.	Ganiio''	ne''tho'	nwä'eie'ä'	o'nĕⁿ'	wä'hä'iek	o''	ne''	14
it was (had been)	So soon as	thus	so she it did	now	he awoke	too	the	
boñ'gwe'	ne''	hadji'nä'.	O'nĕⁿ'	hi'iä'	dedjia'oⁿ'	skĕñ'noⁿ'	15
he human being	the	he male. (is)	Now	verily	both	peaceful (it is)	

pleased. He said: "Now I tell you both that, in peace, without ceasing ye both must hold one the other dear. Thou wilt do evil shouldst thou address unkind words to the one who abides with thee in this particular place. And, next in turn, he addressed the male human man-being, saying: "Do not thou ever come to dislike her with whom thou dost abide. The two human man-beings that I have made are sufficient. The ohwachira [blood-family], offspring of one another] which ye two will produce will fill the whole earth." Then he again separated from them.

It thus came to pass that he noticed that his brother, Flint, was at work far away. Then he ordered one, saying: "Go thou after him who is at work yonder; he is my brother, Flint." At that time a person went thither, and said: "I have come for thee. Thy brother,

1	de‘hiadadwĕñnaa’’sĕñk. they conversed together repeatedly.	Tho‘’ge‘ At that (time)	o’nĕⁿ‘ now	agwa’s very	wä’hatcĕññoñ’nia’ he was glad	
2	ne’’ the	Odĕñdoñni’’a‘. It Sapling.	Wä’hĕⁿ‘hĕñ’’: He it said:	"O’nĕⁿ‘ "Now	skĕn’noⁿ’ peaceful (it is)	wä’- I
3	giatho’iĕⁿ’ you two tell	tea’’ the where	heiotgoñda‘’gwï‘ hence it is unending (unceasing)	dĕⁿtciadadnoĕⁿ’’khwäk. ye two will each other hold dear.		Ĕⁿsei‘ Thou
4	hwäne’a‘gwä’ wilt err	dogä’’t if it so be	ne’’ the	gawĕnna‘het’gĕⁿ’ it word evil is	ĕⁿ‘he‘sĕñ’’häs thou her wilt say to	ne’’ the
5	gado’gĕⁿ‘ it is a certain (place)	desni’’dĕñ’.’’ ye two abide."	Nä’ie’ That (it is)	oⁿ’’kĕⁿ’ next in time	ne’’ the	hadji’nä‘ he male	wä’ho- he him
6	wĕⁿ’’häs addressed	wä’hĕⁿ‘hĕñ’’: he it said:	"Ä’’gwi‘ "Do it not	hwĕñ’doⁿ‘ ever	ä‘sheshwä‘hĕⁿ‘hä’ thou shouldst hate her	
7	ne’’ the	de‘sni’’dĕñ’. ye two abide together.	Ne’’tho‘ There	hä’degāie’ï’ just it is sufficient	degui‘’ two it is	wä’tge‘sĕñ’nia I them two have made
8	ne’’ the	oñ’gwe‘. human being(s).	Dĕⁿga‘hĕñ’’nhä’ It will become filled	tea’’ the where	niioⁿ‘hwĕñ’djia’, so it earth is large,	nä’ie’ that (it is)	ne’’ the
9	i’s ye	ĕⁿtciathwadjiĕn’nia’.’’ ye two will make ohwachira."	O’nĕⁿ‘ Now	deshoññadekhä‘’sioñ. again they (m.) have separated themselves.		
10	Ne’’tho‘ There	di’’ moreover	niiawĕⁿ’’ï‘ so it came to pass	tea’’ the where	o’nĕⁿ‘ now	wä’hatdo’gä‘ he noticed	tea’’ the where	si’’ yonder
11	thoio’’de‘ there he is working	ne’’ the	de‘hiadĕⁿ‘hnoñ’dä’ they two are brothers	ne’’ the	O‘ha’ä’. It Flint.	O’nĕⁿ‘ Now	wä’ha- he one
12	dĕⁿ’nhä’nhä’ commanded	wä’hĕⁿ‘hĕñ’’: he it said:	"Hetchi‘hno’’kse‘ There go ye after him	ne’’ the	si’’ yonder	thoio’’de‘ there he is working
13	deiagiadĕⁿ‘hnoñ’dä’ one I are brothers	ne’’ the	O‘ha’ä’.’’ It Flint."	Tho‘’ge‘ At that time	o’nĕⁿ‘ now	ne’’tho‘ there
14	nhwä’he’’ thither he went	ne’’ the	shäiä’’dädä‘ he is one person	wä’hĕⁿ‘hĕñ’’: he it said:	"Dagoñ‘hno’’kse’ "Thence I thee have come for.	

Sapling, has sent me to bring thee with me. Then Flint said: "I am at work. By and by I shall complete it, and then, and not before, will I go thither." He again departed. He arrived home, and moreover, he brought word that Flint had said: "I am at work. I shall complete it by and by, and then, not before, will I go thither to that place." He said: "Go thou thither again. I have a matter about which I wish to converse with him." Again he arrived there, and he said: "He would that thou and he should talk together." He replied, saying: "Verily, I must first complete my work, and not until that time will I go thither." Then he again departed thence. Again he arrived home, and he said: "He yonder did not consent to come." At that time Sapling said: "He himself, forsooth, is a little more important than I. Moreover, I verily shall go thither." Thereupon Sapling went to that place. Flint did not notice it. When he arrived

Hage·nhä'i'hā'die'	neʸ	dedjiadĕⁿ'hnoñ'dä'	neʸ	Odĕñdoñni''ä'."		1
He me has ordered in coming	the	he thou are brothers	the	It Sapling."		
O'nĕⁿ'	neʸ	O'ha'ä'	wä'hĕⁿ'hĕñ'':	"Wagio''de'.	Ěⁿgeiĕñnĕñdä''nhä'	2
Now	the	It Flint	he it said:	"I am working.	I task will finish	
gĕⁿ'djĭk',	o'nĕⁿ'	hä''sä'	ne''tho'	nhĕñ'ge'."	Sa'ha'dĕñ'dia'	3
by and by,	now	just then (not before)	there	thither I will go."	Again he departed.	
Sa'hā'ioⁿ,	o'nĕⁿ'	dī''	sa'hatho'iä'	tca'	noñwa'ho''dĕⁿ'	wä'hĕⁿ'	4
Again he returned,	now	more-over	again he it told	the where	kind of thing	he it	
hĕñ'',	nä'ie'	ne'':	"Wagio''de'.	Ěⁿgeiĕñnĕñdä''nhä'	gĕⁿ'djĭk'	5
said,	that (it is)	the: that	"I am at work.	I task will finish	by and by	
o'neⁿ'	hä''sä'	ne''tho'	nhĕñ'ge'."	Wä'hĕⁿ'hĕñ'':	"Ne''tho',	6.
now	just then, (not before)	there	thither I will go."	He it said:	"There	
hoñsa'se'.	Agei'hwä'ieⁿ	tca''	ge'he'	dāiagitba'ĕñ'."	Hoñsa'-	7
there again do thou go.	I a matter have	the where	I it desire	he and I it should converse about."	There again	
hā'ioⁿ,	wä'hĕⁿ'hĕñ'':	"De'hodoⁿ'hwĕñdjioñ'niks	daesnitha'ĕñ'."			8
he arrived,	he it said:	"It him is necessary for	ye two should converse together."			
Da'hāi'hwä'sä'gwä'	wä'hĕⁿ'hĕñ'':	"Ěⁿgadiĕñno''kdĕⁿ'	bi'iä'	hia'c',	9
He replied	he it said:	"I my task will finish	verily	In the first place,	
o'nĕⁿ'	ha''sä'	ne''tho'	nhĕⁿ'ge'."	Doñda'ha'dĕñ'dia'.	Sa'hā'ioⁿ	10
now	just then, (not before)	there	thither I will go."	Thence again he departed.	Again he returned	
wä'hĕⁿ'hĕñ'':	"Hiiä'	de'thogäiĕⁿ''ī'."	Tho''ge'	O'nĕⁿ'	wä'hĕⁿ'hĕñ''	ne''	11
he it said:	"Not (it is)	there he it consented to."	At that (time)	now	he it said	the	
Odĕñdoñni''ä':	"Ha'oⁿ'hwä'	si''hägwä'	bi'iä'	ni'hāiä'dano'wĕⁿ'	12
It Sapling:	"He himself	farther	verily	so his body is precious.	
I''	dī''	hi'iä'	ne''tho'	nhĕñ'ge'."	O'nĕⁿ'	ne''tho'	nhe'hawe'noñ'.	13
I	more-over	verily	there	thither I will go."	Now	there	thither he went.	
Hiiä''	de'hotdo'gĕⁿ'	ne''	O'ha'ä'.	Ne''	o'nĕⁿ'	hwä'ha'ioⁿ	wä'hĕⁿ'-	14
Not (it is)	he it noticed	the	It Flint.	The	now	there he arrived	he it	

there, he said: "Thou art working for thyself, art thou, in thy work?" He replied, saying: "I am working. I desire to assist thee, for that it will take a long time for the man-beings to become numerous, since thou hast made only two." At that time Sapling said: "Verily, as a matter of fact, the two man-beings that I have completed are sufficient. And, in so far as thou art concerned, thou art not able to make a human man-being. Look! Verily, that which thou believest to be a man-being is not a true one." He saw standing there a long file of things which were not man-beings. There sat the beast with the face of a man-being, a monkey;[a] there next to him sat the ape;[a] and there sat the great horned owl. And there were other things also seated there. Then they all changed, and the reason of it is that they were not man-beings. Sapling said, when he overmatched their

1	hĕñ": said:	"Sadadio'dĕⁿ'se'-khĕⁿ'', "Thou art working for thyself,	tca'' art thou,	sāio''de'?'' the thou art at where work?''	Da'hāi'hwă'sä'gwă' He replied	
2	wă'hĕⁿ'hĕñ'': he it said:	"Wăgio''de'. "I am working.	Ge'he'' I it desire	ĕⁿgoñie'năwă's. I thee will aid,	swă'djĭk' because (too much)	
3	ĕⁿioñni'she' it will last (long)	ĕⁿ'hoñnatgă'dĕⁿ''hă' they (m.) will become numerous	tca'' the where	degni'' two they (are)	gĕñ'gwă only	wă'tci''să' thou two completedst them
4	ne'' oñ'gwe'.'' the human beings.''	Tho''ge' At that (time)	wă'hĕⁿ'hĕñ'' he it said	ne'' the	Odĕñdoñni''ă': It Sapling:	"Ne''tho' "There
5	se'' as matter of fact	hi'iă' verily	hă'degāie'i' just it is sufficient	tca'' the where	degni'' two they (are)	wă'tge''să' two I them finished	ne'' the	oñ'gwe' human beings.
6	Hiiă'' Not (it is)	hi'iă' verily	nĕⁿ'' this here	ne'' the	i's thasgwe'niă' thou thou art able to do it	ne'' the	oñ'gwe' human being	a'se'sĕñ'niă' thou it shouldst make.
7	Satgat'hwă', Do thou look,	biiă'' not (it is)	hi'iă' verily	de'tgāie'i' it is correct	tca'' the where	se'he'' thou dost think	oñ'gwe'.'' human being.''	Wă'- He
8	hatgat'hwă' looked	tca'' the where	deiodinĕⁿ'he's they (z.) are in rank	ne''tho' there	goñni''dĕñ' they (z.) abide	biiă'' not (it is)		
9	oñ'gwe' human being	de'gĕñ'. it is (are).	Ne''tho' There	hatgo'dă' he sits	ne'' the	gadji'k'daks it eats lice (= monkey)	(nă'ie' (that it is)	
10	ne'' the	gā'io' it is animal	oi'gwe' human being	gagoⁿ'soīdă''gwĭ'), it has the face of),	ne''tho' there	gwă''tho' next in place	ne'' the	
11	gĕⁿ'noⁿ''hă'. it ape.	Nā'ie' That (it is)	o''nĭ' also	ne''tho' there	hatgo'dă' he sits	ne'' the	degĕñs'ge'. horned owl.	
12	Thigoñdiiă'dade'nioⁿ' Just they (z.) are different others	o''nĭ'. also.	Ne''tho' There	wă'dwatde'nĭ' they (indef.) changed in kind	gagwe'gĭ', it all,			
13	nă'ie' that (it is)	dāioi'hwă''khe' it is reason of it	tca'' the where	ne''tho' there	nwă'awĕⁿ''hă' so it came to pass	tca'' the where	biiă'' not (it is)	
14	oñ'gwe' human being	de'gĕñ'. it is.	Wă'hĕⁿ'hĕñ'' He it said	ne'' the	Odĕñdoñni''ă' It Sapling	ne'' the	o'nĕⁿ' now	

[a] The monkey and the ape were probably quite unknown to the Iroquois.

oienda: "Verily, it is good that thou, Flint, shouldst cease thy work. It is a direful thing, verily, that has come to pass." He did not consent to stop. Then Sapling said: "It is a marvelously great matter wherein thou hast erred in not obeying me when I forbade thy working." At that time Flint said: "I will not stop working, because I believe that it is necessary for me to work." Then Sapling said: "Moreover, I now forsake thee. Hence wilt thou go to the place where the earth is divided in two. Moreover, the place whither thou wilt go is a fine place."

At that time he cast him down, and he fell backward into the depths of the earth. There a fire was burning, and into the fire he fell supine; it was exceedingly hot. After a while Flint said: "Oh, Sapling! Thou wouldst consent, wouldst thou not, that thou and I should converse

wă'thaĕñ'gĕñ'niă': he their orenda overmatched:	"Oia'ne' "It is good	hi'iă' verily	ne" the	a'sĕñni'ʻhĕⁿ', thou it shouldst cease,	O'ha'ă', It Flint,	1
tca" the where	săio"de'. thou art at work.	Gano'wĕⁿ' It is direful	bi'iă' verily	tca" the where	nwă'awĕⁿ'ʻhă'." so it has come to pass."	Hiiă" Not (it is)	2
de'hogăiĕⁿ"'ĭ'. he it consented to.	O'nĕⁿ' Now	ne" the	Odĕñdoñni"ă' It Sapling	wă'hĕⁿʻhĕñ"· he it said:	"Oi' "It is a		3
hwaneʻhä'gwăt marvelous matter	oiʻhowa'nĕⁿ' it is an important matter	wă'seiʻhwaneʻa'gwă' thou hast done wrong		tca" the where	hiiă" not (it is)	4
de'sathoñda'dĭ' thou it hast consented to	tca" the where	goñiaʻhis'thă' I thee forbid doing	tca" the	săio"de' " thou art at work."	Tho"ge' At that time	5
o'nĕⁿ', nov	ne" the	O'ha'ă' It Flint	wă'hĕⁿʻhĕñ": he it said:	"Hiiă" "Not (it is)	thagĕñni'ʻhĕⁿ' I it should cease	tca" the where	6
wagio"de' I am at work	swă'djĭk' because (too much)	geʻhe' I am thinking	deiodoⁿʻhwĕñdjio'ʻhwĭ' it is necessary	tca" the where	wagio" I am at work."	7
de'."	Tho"ge' At that (time)	o'nĕⁿ' nov	ne" the	Odĕñdoñni"ă' It Sapling	wă'hĕⁿʻhĕñ": he it said:	"O'nĕⁿ' "Nov	8
dĭ" moreover	wă'goñiadwĕnde"dă'. I thee forsake.	Tho'nĕⁿ' Here	nhĕⁿʻse" thither thou shalt go	tca" the where	noñ'we' the place	9
dediioⁿʻhwĕñdjio'gĕⁿ'. there two it earth is divided in.	Ganakdi'io' It place fine (is)	dĭ" moreover	ne"tho' there	nhĕⁿʻse"." thither thou shalt go."		10
Tho"ge' At that (time)	o'nĕⁿ' nov	ne"tho' there.	heʻhoñwăiă'dĕⁿ"dĭ' there he his body cast down	ne" the	oⁿʻhwĕñdjiagoñ'wă' it earth in	11
goñ'wă'	ne"tho' there	heʻhodagă'ʻĭ'. there he fell supine.	Ne"tho' There	diiodek'hă' there it is burning	odjĭsdagoñ'wă' it fire in	12
ne"tho' there	heʻhodagă"ʻĭ'. there he fell supine.	Heiawĕñgo"dĭ' There it surpassing is	o'dai'ʻhĕñ'. it is hot.	Gaiñ'gwă' Some (time)		13
nwă'oñni'she' it lasted long	wă'hĕⁿʻhĕñ" he it said	ne" the	O'ha'ă'· It Flint:	"Odĕñdoñni"ă', "It Sapling,		14
a'sathoñ'dat-khĕⁿ' thou wouldst consent	'ă'soⁿ' wouldst thou	still	doñsednitha'ĕñ'?" once again thou and I should converse together?	Odĕñdoñni"ă' It Sapling	wă' he	15

once more together?" Sapling replied, saying: "Truly, it shall thus come to pass. Moreover, I will appoint the place of meeting to be the place where the earth is divided in two." And Flint was able to come forth from the fire. At that time then Sapling went thither, going to the point designated by him. He arrived there, and, moreover, he stood there and looked around him. He looked and saw afar a cloud floating away whereon Flint was standing. Sapling said: "What manner of thing has come to pass that thou art departing hence away?" Flint answered: "I myself did not will it." Sapling said: "Do thou come thence, hitherward." At that time the cloud that was floating away returned, and again approached the place where Sapling stood. Then this one said: "How did it happen that it started away?" Flint, replying, said: "It is not possible that I personally should have willed

1. hĕⁿ‘hĕñ": "Do'gĕⁿs ne"tho‘ nĕⁿiawĕⁿ'‘hă'. Ne"tho‘ dĭ" wă'gnă'doⁿ"
   it said· "It is true there so it will come There more- I it appoint
   to pass. over

2. tca" deioⁿ‘hwĕñdjio'gĕⁿ‘ ne"tho' dĕⁿdiadă"nhă'." Wă'hagwe'niă'
   the two it earth is divided in there thou and I will He was able to
   where meet." do it

3. ne" O‘ha'ă' da‘hāiagĕⁿ"nhă' tca" odjĭsdagoñ'wă‘. Tho"ge‘
   the It Flint thence he emerged the it fire in. At that
   where time

4. o'ⁱĕⁿ‘ ⁱe"tho‘ he‘hawe'noñ‘ ne" Odĕñdoñni"ă‘ tca" noñ'we‘
   now there there he went the It Sapling the the place
   where

5. ni‘hoñnă"doⁿ'. Wă'hă'ioⁿ' ne"tho‘ dĭ" wă'thadă"nhă' wă'thatga‘-
   there he it has He arrived there more- he stood he looked
   appointed. over about

6. doñ'nioⁿ'. Wă'ha'gĕⁿ' i'ⁱoⁿ‘ wă'o‘dĕñdioñ‘hă'die' wă'o‘dji'gă'die
   repeatedly. He it saw far thither it is going along thither it cloud is
   (it is) going on

7. ne"tho‘ hada'die' ne" O‘ha'ă'. Odĕñdoñni"ă‘ wă'hĕⁿ‘hĕñ":
   there he is riding the It Flint. It Sapling he it said:
   on it

8. "Ho't noñwa‘bo"dĕⁿ' nwă'awĕⁿ'‘hă' tca" we'sa‘dĕñdioñ‘hă'die'?"
   "What kind of thing so it came to the thither thou art going
   (it is) pass where along?"

9. Wă'hĕⁿ‘hĕñ" ne" O‘ha'ă': "Hiiă" ne" i" dagĕñnoⁿ'doⁿ'."
   He it said the It Flint: "Not the I I it willed."
   (it is)

10. Wă'hĕⁿ‘hĕñ" ne" Odĕñdoñni"ă‘: "Gă'e' ⁱă" doñda"se‘."
    He it said the It Sapling: "Hither that thence do
    one thou come."

11. Tho"ge‘ o'ⁱĕⁿ‘ sawăk'dă' tca"ⁱ o‘dji'gă'die‘, ne"tho‘ saga'ioⁿ
    At that now again it the it cloud is float- there again it
    time turned back where ing along, arrived

12. tca" non'we‘ ⁱi‘ha'dă' ne" Odĕñdoñni"ă‘. O'nĕⁿ‘ nĕñ'gĕⁿ‘
    the the place there he is the It Sapling. Now this one
    where standing

13. wă'hĕⁿ‘hĕñ": "Ho't nwă'awĕⁿ'‘hă' tca" wă'wa‘dĕñ'diă'?" Wă'
    he it said: "What so it came to the it started? He
    (is it) pass where onward?

14. hĕⁿ‘hĕñ" ne" O‘ha'ă' da‘hadadiă': "Hiiă" de'a'wet ⁱi"ă‘
    it said the It Flint he spoke in "Not it is possi- the I
    reply: (it is) ble personally

it." Sapling rejoined: "How did it happen that thou didst not will
it?" Then Flint said: "I did not do that." Sapling said: "It is true
that it is impossible for thee to do it. Moreover, thou and I, verily,
are again talking together. What kind of thing desirest thou? What
is it that thou needest, that thou and I should again converse
together?" Flint then said: "It is this; I thought that, perhaps,
thou wouldst consent that the place where I shall continue to be may
be less rigorous. And thou didst say: 'Thou art going to a very fine
place.' And I desire that the place where thou wilt again put me be
less rigorous than the former." Sapling said: "It shall thus come
to pass. I had hoped that, it may be, thou wouldst say, 'I now
repent.' As a matter of fact it did not thus come to pass. Thy
mind is unchanged. So, now, I shall again send thee hence. I shall

dońdageñnon''don''.		Odeñdonni''ă'	wă'hĕn'hĕñ'':		"Ho't	nwă'	1
there I it could will."		It Sapling	he it said:		"What (is it)	so it came	
awĕn''hă'	tca'' biiă'' de'a'wet i's	doñda'sĕñnon''don''?		Tho''ge'			2
to pass	the where not (it is) it is possible thou	there thou it couldst will?"		At that time			
wă'hĕn'hĕñ''	ne'' O'ha'ă': "Hiiă''	de'ne''	thă'gie'ă.''	Odeñdoñ			3
he it said	the It Fint: "Not (it is)	the that	thus I did do it.''	It Sapling			
ni''ă'	wă'hĕn'hĕñ'': "Do'gĕns biiă''	de'a'wet	a'sgwe'niă'.	O'nĕn'			4
	he it said: "It is true not (it is)	it is possible	thou couldst be able to do it.	Now			
di''	bi'iă' detcioñgni'thă' o'nĕn'.	Ho't	noñwa'ho''dĕn''	se'he''?			5
more-over	verily again thou and I are talking together now.	What (is it)	kind of thing	thou it desirest?			
Ho't	noñwa'ho''dĕn'' desadon'hwĕñdjioñ'ni'	tca''	doñsednitha'ĕñ'?''				6
What (is it)	kind of thing thou it needst	the where	once again thou and I should converse together?''				
Wă'hĕn'hĕñ''	ne'' O'ha'ă': "Nă'ie'	ne''	wă'ge'ă'	do'gă't			7
He it said	the It Flint: "That (it is)	the	I it thought	if perhaps (it may be)			
a'sathoñ'dat	thagĕnk'ă' tca'' naganakdo''dĕnk	tca''	noñ'we				8
thou it shouldst consent to	it should be less the where such it place be in kind	the where	the place				
ĕngi'dioñ'dak.	Nă'ie' ne'' tca''	wă'si'hĕñ'':	'Ne''tho'	nhĕn'se''			9
I will abide continuously.	That (it is) the the where	thou it didst say:	'There	thither thou shalt go			
tca''	noñ'we' tganakdi'io'.'	Nă'ie'	ge'he''	thagĕnk'ă'	tca''		10
the where	the place there it place (is) fine.'	That (it is)	I it desire	it should be less (severe)	the where		
naganakdo''dĕnk	tca'' noñ'we' hoñsasgi''dĕñ''.	Odeñdonni''ă'	wă'-				11
such it place be in kind	the where the place there again thou me shouldst place.''	It Sapling	he				
bĕn'bĕñ'':	"Ne''tho' nĕn'iawĕn''hă'.	Nă'ie' ne''	ge'he''gwă'	diĕñ''hă'			12
it said:	"There so it will come to pass.	That (it is) the	I it had thought	after a while,			
gwă''	ĕn'si'hĕñ'': 'Sagadathewa''dă'' o'nĕn'.'	Hiiă''	se''	ne''tho'			13
seemingly,	thou it wilt say: 'I myself repent now.'	Not (it is)	as a matter of fact	there			
dwă'awĕn''hă'.	Te'nigon'hägoñ'dă'.	Da'',	o'nĕn'	di''	hĕnsgoñia		14
so it came to pass.	Thence thy mind is unchanged.	So	now,	moreover,	hence again I thee will		

send thee to the bottom of the place where it is hot." Now, at that time his body again fell downward. The place where he fell was exceedingly hot. At that time Sapling said: "Not another time shalt thou come forth thence." Then Sapling bound poor Flint with a hair. And he bound him with it that he should remain in the fire as long as the earth shall continue to be. Not until the time arrives when the earth shall come to an end will he then again break the bonds. Then Sapling departed thence.

Moreover, it is said that this Sapling, in the manner in which he has life, has this to befall him recurrently, that he becomes old in body, and that when, in fact, his body becomes ancient normally, he then retransforms his body in such wise that he becomes a new man-being again and again recovers his youth, so that one would think

1	dĕñnie''dă'. send	Ne''tho' There	hĕⁿsgoñiadĕñnie''dă' hence again I thee will send	ne'' the	ga'noⁿ'deä'ᵛge' it bottom on
2	tca'' the where	noñ'we' the place	diio'dai''hĕñ'.'' there it is hot.''	Tho''ge' At that (time)	o'nĕⁿ' now	heshoiä'dĕⁿ''ï' there again his body fell down in it
3	o'nĕⁿ'. now.	Ogĕñi'sdï' It is exceeding	o'dai''hĕñ' it is hot	tca'' the	noñ''we' the place	he'hodagä'ï'. there he fell supine.
4	Tho''ge' At that (time)	o'nĕⁿ' now	ne'' the	Odĕñdoñni''ă' It Sapling	wă'hĕⁿ'hĕñ'': he it said:	"Hiiä'' "Not (it is)	ne'' the
5	o'iä' it other (is)	doⁿsasiagĕⁿ''nhă' '' again thou shalt come out.''	Tho''ge' At that (time)	wă'hoñwashaiñ'dĕⁿ' he bound him	onoⁿ'khwe''ä' it hair
6	wă'has'dă' he used it	ne'' the	Odĕñdoñni''ă' It Sapling	ne'' the	O'ha'ä'-gĕⁿ''hä' It Flint it was.	Nä'ie' That (it is)	ne'' the
7	nă'' the one that	wă'hoñwashaiñda''gwă' he it used to bind him	tca'' the where	nĕⁿioñni'she' so long it will last	ĕⁿioⁿ'hwĕñdjiä'dek it earth will continue to be present
8	ne''tho' there	hĕⁿ'hĕⁿ'dĕñ'dăk there he will continue to be	odjĭsdagoñ'wă'. it fire in.	Ne''tho' There	nigĕⁿ'' so it is far	tca'' the where
9	ĕⁿwadoⁿ'hwĕñdjio''kdĕⁿ' it earth itself will end.	o'nĕⁿ' now	dĕⁿshadeshä'iă'k. he will break the tether.	Tho''ge' At that (time)	o'nĕⁿ' now
10	ne'' the	Odĕñdoñni''ă' It Sapling	sho'dĕñ'dioñ'. again he departed.
11	Nä'ie' That (it is)	dï'' more- over	ne'' that	nä'ie' that (it is)	ne'' the	nĕñgĕⁿ''hă' this (it is)	ne'' the	Odĕñdoñni''ă' It Sapling
12	ne''tho', thus,	iä'kĕⁿ', it is said,	ni'io't so it is	ne'' the	tcă'' where	ho'n'he'' he is alive	ne''tho' thus	niiä'wĕⁿs so it comes to pass
13	ne'' the	tcă'' the where	hok'stĕñ'ă' he old in age	wadoⁿ'hă' it becomes iteratively	heiotgoñdä''gwï', it is unceasing,	nä'ie' that (it is)	ne'' the
14	nä'ie' that (it is)	se'' in fact	ne'' the	o'nĕⁿ' now	gĕⁿ's customarily	hāiä'dăgĕⁿ''tcï' his body ancient	wă'wä'doⁿ' it has become	o'nĕⁿ' now
15	gĕⁿ's customarily	doⁿsa'hadiä'dăde'nï', again he changes his body (transforms it),	nä'ie' that (it is)	ne'' the	gĕⁿ's customarily	sa'hadoñgwe'' again he becomes man-being	ne'' the

that he had just then grown to the size which a man-being customarily has when he reaches the youth of man-beings, as manifested by the change of voice at the age of puberty.

Moreover, it is so that continuously the orenda immanent in his body—the orenda with which he suffuses his person, the orenda which he projects or exhibits, through which he is possessed of force and potency—is ever full, undiminished, and all-sufficient; and, in the next place, nothing that is otkon[a] or deadly, nor, in the next place, even the Great Destroyer, otkon in itself and faceless, has any effect on him, he being perfectly immune to its orenda; and, in the next place, there is nothing that can bar his way or veil his faculties.

Moreover, it is verily thus with all the things that are contained in the earth here present, that they severally retransform or exchange their bodies. It is thus with all the things [zoic] that sprout and grow, and, in the next place, with all things [actively zoic] that produce

tcă″	hoñgwe'dă'se″ă'	sawā'doⁿ',	nā'ie'	ne″	āień'ă'	ne″tho'	hă''să'	
where	he man-being new	again it is become,	that (it is)	the	one would think,	thus (there)	just then	1
nithodō'dĭ'	ne″	tcă″	ni'io't	gěⁿ's	ne″	hă''să'	de'hodwěñna-	
so there he has grown	the	where	so it is	customarily	the	just then	his voice has	2
de'nioⁿ'	ne″	hoñgwe'dă'se″ă'	ne″	oñ'gwe'.				
changed	the	he man-being new small	the	man-being.				3
Ne″tho'	nā'ie'	dĭ'	ni'io't	ne″	tcă″	tgāie'ĭ'	diiotgoñt	ne″
Thus	that (it is)	moreover	so it is	the	where	there it is full and sufficient	always	the 4
tcă″	ni'hoiă'daěñ'nāe'	ne″	tcă″	hadeñnodă″'gwă',	ne″tho'	gwă″-		
where	so his body has orenda	the	the where	he his orenda exhibits,	there	next to		5
tho'	haděñnoñdă″'gwă'	ne″	tcă″	hā'qhwă'	ne″	gă'shasděⁿ'să',		
it	he himself with orenda embodies by which,	the	the where	he it holds	the	it potency (power, force)		6
ne″tho'	gwă″tho'	ne″	hiiă″	stěⁿ	noñwă'ho″děⁿ	ne″	o'tgoⁿ',[a]	
there	next to it	the	not it is	anything	kind of thing	the	otkon (monstrous),	7
ne″tho'	gwă″tho'	ne″	O'soñdoă'go'nă'	O'ni'dat'goⁿ	Hiiă″			
there	next to it	the	It Great Destroyer	Otkon in itself	not it is			8
De'gagoⁿ''soñde',	de'honă'go'wăs,	ne″tho'	gwă″tho'	biiă″	stěⁿ'			
It has a face,	(not) it affects (wears on) him,	there	next to it	not (it is)	anything			9
noñwă'ho″děⁿ	de'hodawěⁿ·'das.	Ne″tho'	hi'iă'	dĭ″	ni'io't	tcă″		
kind of thing	it him bars (shuts) out.	Thus,	verily,	moreover	so it is	where		10
niioñ'	ga'qhwă'	ne″	tcă″	oⁿ'hwěñdjiă'de'	dewadiă'dade'nioⁿ's,			
so it is much (many)	it it holds	the	where	it earth is present	it changes its body iteratively,			11
gagwe'gĭ'	ne″tho'	ni'io't	ne″	wadoñniă'·hă',	ne″tho'	gwă″tho'		
it all	thus	so it is	the	it (z.) produces itself,	there	next to it		12

---

[a] See footnote on page 197.

themselves and grow, and, in the next place all the man-beings. All these are affected in the same manner, that they severally transform their bodies, and, in the next place, that they (actively zoic) retransform their bodies, severally, without cessation.

1. ne″ goñdoñniä′‛hă′,   ne″tho‛   gwä″tho‛   ne″   oñ′gwe‛.   Gagwe′gï‛
   the   they (act. z.) pro-   there   next to it   the   man-   It all
         duce themselves,   being(s).

2. ne″tho‛   nigāie′‛hă′   deswadiä′dade′nio^n‛s,   nā′ie′   gwä″tho‛   des-
   there   so it acts   it changes its body   that   next to it   they
                          iteratively,   (it is)   (act. z.)

3. goñdiä′dade′nio^n‛s   heiotgoñdä″′gwï‛.
   'again change their   it is unceasing.
    bodies iteratively

A SENECA VERSION

There were, it seems, so it is said, man-beings dwelling on the other side of the sky. So, just in the center of their village the lodge of the chief stood, wherein lived his family, consisting of his spouse and one child, a girl, that they two had.

He was surprised that then he began to become lonesome. Now, furthermore, he, the Ancient, was very lean, his bones having become dried; and the cause of this condition was that he was displeased that they two had the child, and one would think, judging from the circumstances, that he was jealous.

So now this condition of things continued until the time that he, the Ancient, indicated that they, the people, should seek to divine his Word; that is, that they should have a dream feast for the purpose of ascertaining the secret yearning of his soul [produced by its own

---

Ne″	gwä́′,	gi″oⁿ‵,	hadi′noñge‵	ne″	sgäoñ‵iädï″	ne″	heñ′noñ′-	
That,	it seems,	it is said,	they dwell	the	one other side of the sky	the	they (m), man-beings.	1
gwe‵.	Da′,	shä′degano′ndäěⁿ‵		ne″ho‵	ni‵honoⁿ‵sō′t	ne″	hä‵señ-	
	So,	just in the center of the village		there	just his lodge stands	the	he Chief (great)	2
nowä́′něⁿ‵,	ne″ho‵	häwadjiä′iěⁿ″,	ne″	ne′io‵	ne″	kho″	ne″	
name),	there	his ohwachira lies,	the	his spouse	that	and	the	3
sgä′t	hodiksä‵dä′iěⁿ″,	ie′oⁿ‵	ne″	ieksä″ä‵				
one it is	they child have,	she the female (is)		she child.				4
Waädieñgwä″shoñ‵		o′něⁿ‵	ho′wä″säwěⁿ‵		ne″	hägweñdä″s		
He was surprised,		now	it began		that	he became lonesome.		5
O′něⁿ‵	dï′q	we′so′	ho′neñ′iatheñ‵	ne″	Hageⁿ″′tcï;	ne″	gai′ioññï,	
Now	more-over	much	his bones are dry (= he is very lean)	the	He Ancient One;	that	it it causes	6
theⁿ″ěⁿ‵	deo′nigoñ″īō‵	he″	odiksä‵dä′iěⁿ″,	äiěñ″	ne″	noñ″		
not (it is)	his mind happy is	(because)	they child have,	one would think	that	perhaps.		7
heniio″děñ‵	ne″	ne″	hosheie′oⁿ‵.					
so it is in state	that	the	he is jealous.					8
Da′,	o′něⁿ‵	ne‵ho″shoñ‵	niio′děñ′andie‵	he″	niio′we‵	o′něⁿ‵		
So,	now	only thus	so it continued to be	where	so it is distant	now		9
waⁿoñwänděⁿ″	ne″	Hageⁿ″′tcï	ne″	ne″	äⁿauⁿwaⁿweññï″sak		Da′,	
he pointed it out	the	he Ancient One	the	that	they should seek to divine his word.		So,	10
o′něⁿ‵	gagwe′goⁿ‵	ne″	heññoñgwe‵shoñ″oⁿ‵		ne‵ho″shoñ‵	hodii		
now	it all	the	they (m.) man-being individully (are)		only thus	they (m.) habitually		11

221

motion]. So now all the people severally continued to do nothing else but to assemble there. Now they there continually sought to divine his Word. They severally designated all manner of things that they severally thought that he desired. After the lapse of some time, then, one of these persons said: "Now, perhaps, I myself have divined the Word of our chief, the excrement. And the thing that he desires is that the standing tree belonging to him should be uprooted, this tree that stands hard by his lodge." The chief said: "Gwă'" [expressing his thanks].

So now the man-beings said: "We must be in full number and we must aid one another when we uproot this standing tree; that is, there must be a few to grasp each several root." So now they uprooted it and set it up elsewhere. Now the place whence they had uprooted the tree fell through, forming an opening through the sky earth. So now, moreover, all the man-beings inspected it. It was curious;

1	e'is. assemble.	Diiawĕⁿ''oⁿ' Constantly	o'nĕⁿ' now	ie''ho' there	hoñwaⁿwĕññĭ''sas; they (m.) sought to divine his word	ganio'shoⁿ'' it anything whatsoever
2	he'' where	nă''ot such kind of thing	hĕññoñwañ'thă' they (m.) it point out	ne'' that	nă''ot such kind of thing	deodoĕñdjoñ'nĭ'. he it needs.	Gain' Some-
3	gwă' what	nă'ioññishe''t so it lasted	o'nĕⁿ' now	shāiă''dăt he (is) one person	waĕñ''· he it said:	"O'nĕⁿ' "Now it is,	noñ'' perhaps,
4	ii''ă' I personally	wae'dawanoñ'wĕⁿ''t I have divined excrement's word.	ne'' the	sedwă'sĕñ'noⁿ'. he (is) our chief.	Ne'' That it is,	noñ'' perhaps	ne'' the
5	deodoĕñdjoñ'nĭ' he it needs,	noñ'' perhaps,	ne'' the	hagāniodagwĕñ'oñg one it should uproot	nĕñ'gĕñ' this is it		ne'' the
6	hodă'it, he has for himself standing tree,	nĕñ'gĕñ' this is it	dosgĕñ'oⁿ' it is near	gă'it it tree stands	heoñ'we' where	ni'honoⁿ''so't " so his lodge stands."	
7	"Gwă'," "Thanks,"	waĕñ'' he it said	ne'' the	hă'sĕñnowa'nĕⁿ'. he chief (is)			
8	Da', So,	o'nĕⁿ' now	waĕñ'nĭ': they it said:	"Ĕⁿdwagwego'oñg, "We will be in full number,		dĕⁿdwāie'nâñ' we will assist one another	
9	no'nĕⁿ' the time	ĕⁿdwa'niodāgo' we it will uproot	nĕñ'gĕñ' this it is	gă'it. it tree stands.	Ne'' That it is	ne'' the	do''gā'ă' few it is
10	niioñgwe'dăgea'die' so they man-being in number to each	ne'' the	ĕⁿadiie'nâñ' they it will grasp	ne'' the	djokde'ăshoⁿ.'' each it root several."	Da', So,	
11	o'nĕⁿ' now	waādiniodā'go' they it uprooted	oiă''djĭ' else where	ie''ho' there	saādinio'dĕⁿ'. again they (m.) it set up.	O'nĕⁿ' Now,	
12	di'q moreover,	ho'wă''sĕñ't hence it fell down	he'oñwe' where	hodiniodā'gwĕⁿ', they it have uprooted,		auñdjăga'ĕñt it earth perforated	
13	o'wā'doⁿ'. it became.	Da', So,	o'nĕⁿ' now	di'q moreover,	na'e' verily,	gagwe'goⁿ' it all	ne'' the	oñ'gwe' man-being(s)

below the 1 the aspect was green and nothing else in color. As soon as the man-beings had had their turns at inspecting it, then the chief said to his spouse: "Come now, let us two go to inspect it." Now she took her child astride of her back. Thither now he made his way with difficulty. He moved slowly. They two arrived at the place where the cavern was. Now he, the Ancient, himself inspected it. When he wearied of it, he said to his spouse: "Now it is thy turn. Come." "Age'," she said, "myself, I fear it." "Come now, so be it," he said, "do thou inspect it." So now she took in her mouth the ends of the rattle which she wore, and she rested herself on her hand on the right side, and she rested herself on the other side also, closing her hand on either side and grasping the earth thereby. So now she looked down below. Just as soon as she bent her neck, he seized her leg and pushed her body down thither. Now, moreover, there [i. e., in the hole] floated the body of the Fire-dragon with the white body, and,

waĕñnatchi'waĕñ'.	Odianoñ't‘	ganä‘daikhoⁿ''shoñ‘	niio''dĕñ‘	nĕ''		1
they (m.) looked at it.	It curious (is),	it green only (is)	so it is	the		
naⁿ'goñ'.	Ganio''	o'tho'diä‘ho'	nĕ''	hĕñnoñtchī'wā''hä',	o'nĕⁿ‘	2
below (inside).	So soon as	they had their turns to look	the	they it were looking at,	then	
hä'e'gwă‘	nĕ''	hă‘sĕñnowā'nĕⁿ‘	waĕñ'':	"Hau'',	o'nĕⁿ‘ gwā''	3
also	the	he chief (is),	he it said:	"Come,	now, it seems,	
noñ''	ī''	diiatchi'wā'noⁿ‘.''	O'nĕⁿ‘	wä'ago‘sā'dĕⁿ'	nĕ'' goa'wăk.	4
perhaps,	we	let us two it go to look at.''	Now	she her took astride of own back	the her child.	
O'nĕⁿ‘	sĕⁿ‘ge''	ne''ho‘	wā'e'.	Skĕñnoⁿ''oñ‘	i'ē'. Wāni'ioⁿ'	5
Now	with difficulty	there	thither he went.	Slowly	he walked. They two arrived	
he'oñwe‘	oia'de'.	O'nĕⁿ‘	waätchi'wa'ĕñ'	nĕ''	ha'oñhwaⁿ' nĕ''	6
where	it abyss stands.	Now	he it looked at,	the	he himself the	
Hagĕⁿ''tcĭ.	Ganio'	waogäñ'dĕⁿ'	o'nĕⁿ‘	waĕñ'':	"I's ne'wā'	7
He Ancient One.	So soon as	he it was weary of	now	he it said:	"Thou next in turn	
satchi'wa'ĕñ‘	gwā''.''	"Age''!''	wä'a'gĕⁿ':	"Ge‘shā'nis	nī''ă‘.''	8
do it thou look at	just.''	"Age!''	she it said:	"I it fear	I personally.''	
"Hau'',	nĕñ‘',	nio'',''	waĕñ'',	"satchi'wa'ĕñ‘.''	Da', o'nĕⁿ‘	9
"Come.	now,	so let it be,''	he it said,	"do thou it look at.''	So, now	
wă'oⁿ‘sho'go'	nĕ''	i'ios	nĕ''	goē',	o'nĕⁿ‘-kho‘ o'dioⁿ''tchĭ‘	10
she it took in her mouth	the	mantle	the	she it wore,	now and she rested herself on her hand	
nĕ''	ieiĕñsdoñ'-gwā‘,	o'nĕⁿ‘-kho‘	nĕ''	sgagā'dĭ‘	ba'e'gwă‘	11
the	her right side,	now and	the	(the one side), the other side,	also	
o'dioⁿ''tchĭ‘,	o'dioⁿ''tchăgwe'noñ'nĭ'		dedji'aoⁿ-gwā''	he''	ieienaⁿ-	12
she herself rested on her hand,	she her hands closed		both side	where	she it held	
waⁿ'khoⁿ'.	Da'.	o'nĕⁿ‘	naⁿ'goñ‘	wä‘oñtgät'ho'.	Ganio'shoñ''	13
severally.	So,	now	below (inside)	she it looked at.	Just so soon as	

verily, he it was who i the Ancient regarded with jealousy. Now Fire-dragon took out an ear of corn, and verily he gave it to her. As soon as she received it she placed it in her bosom. Now, another thing, the next in order, a small mortar and also the upper mortar [pestle] he gave to her. So now, again, another thing he took out of his bosom, which was a small pot. Now, again, another thing, he gave her in the next place, a bone. Now, he said: "This, verily, is what thou wilt continue to eat."

Now it was so, that below [her] all manner of otgon [malefic] male man-beings abode; of this number were the Fire-dragon, whose body was pure white in color, the Wind, and the Thick Night.

---

1 o'die'noñniä'k dä'shago'si'nä', o'nĕⁿ'-kho' ie"ho' ho'shagoiä"dĕn
   she bent her head   he her leg seized,   now and   there   hence he her body cast down.

2 Da', o'nĕⁿ' ie"ho' ieiä'doñ'die'. O'nĕⁿ' di'q ie"ho' häiä'doñ'
   So,   now   there   her body was falling.   Now more-over there   his body floated

3 die' ne" Gaha'ciĕndie'thä' Onoñwaⁿ'dä"äⁿ Ni'häiä'do"dĕⁿ ne"
   along the It Fire Dragon   it (is) white   so his body is in kind that

4 nigĕⁿ" kho" nä'e' ne" hoñwaⁿ'sheä'se'äk ne" Hagĕⁿ"tci. O'nĕⁿ'
   that it is and verily, the he was jealous of him the He Ancient One. Now

5 ie"ho' waäda"go' ne" o'ni'sdä' ne" onĕñ'oⁿ', o'nĕⁿ'-kho' nä'e'
   there he it took out the it ear the it corn, now and, verily,

6 o'shaga'oñ'. Ganioⁿ" wä'eie'nä' o'nĕⁿ' ie"ho' ieniäs'dägoñ' wä'-auñ'iä't.
   he her it gave. So soon as she them took now there her bosom in she them placed

7 O'nĕⁿ' o'iä' ie'wä' ne" ne" gä'niga"dä' niwä"ä',
   Now it next in order that the it mortar so it is small in size,

8 ne"-kho' ne" hetgĕñ'oñ" ne" gä'niga"dä', dedjiä'oⁿ' o'shaga'oñ'.
   that and the upper (one) the it pestle (= it mortar), both he her gave them to.

9 Da', o'nĕⁿ' a'e' o'iä' daäda"go' haniäsdagoñ", ne" ie'wä'
   So, now again it other (is) he it took out his bosom in, that next in order

10 ne" ganaⁿ"djä' niwä"ä'. O'nĕⁿ' a'e' o'iä'-kho' ne" ie'wä"
   the it pot so it small in size is. Now again it and other the next in order

11 ne" o'iĕi'iä' o'nĕⁿ' o'shaga'oñ'. O'nĕⁿ' waĕñ": "Ne" na'e'
   the it bone (is) now he it her gave to Now he it said: "That, verily,

12 ĕⁿ'seg'seg."
   thou it wilt be in the habit of eating."

13 Da', o'nĕⁿ' he" niiodie'ĕⁿ' ne" e'dä"ge' hadi'naⁿge' ne"
   So, now where so it is being done the below they (m.) are dwelling the

14 hoñnondiä'dät'goⁿ's ho'dio"dĕⁿ"; ne" ne" Ga'ha'ciĕndie'thä'
   they are otgon-bodied (are malefic) of all kinds; that the It Fire Dragon

15 Onoñwaⁿ'dä"äⁿ Ni'häiä'do"dĕⁿ', kho" ne" Gä'hä', ne" gwä"ho'
   it white (is) so his body is in kind, and the It Wind, that next to it

16 ne" Deiodä'sondäi'koⁿ'.
   the It Thick Night.

Now, they, the male man-beings, counseled together, and they said: "Well, is it not probably possible for us to give aid to the woman-being whose body is falling thence toward us?" Now every one of the man-beings spoke, saying: "I, perhaps, would be able to aid her." Black Bass said: "I, perhaps, could do it." They, the man-beings, said: "Not the least, perhaps, art thou able to do it, seeing that thou hast no sense [reason]." The Pickerel next in turn said: "I, perhaps, could do it." Then the man-beings said: "And again we say, thou canst not do even a little, because thy throat is too long [thou art a glutton]." So now Turtle spoke, saying: "Moreover, perhaps, I would be able to give aid to the person of the woman-being." Now all the man-beings confirmed this proposal. Now, moreover, Turtle floated there at the point directly toward which the body of the woman-being was falling thence. So now, on the Turtle's carapace she, the woman-being, alighted. And she, the woman-being, wept there. So the time

Da′,	o′nĕⁿ·	waādiās′hĕñ.	Waĕñ′nī′:	"Gwĕ′,	gĕñ′	nŏñ″	1
So,	now	they (m.) held a council.	They it said:	"Well,	can it be	perhaps	
dä′a′ŏñ·	aedwagwe′nī·	aethiiä′dage′·hä′	ni′gĕⁿ·	ne·′	iagoñ′gwe·		2
not it possible (is)	we should be able it to do	we her should aid	such it is	the	she man-being (is)		
dāieiä′doñ′die·?"	O′nĕⁿ·	hä′de′ioñ	hadi′sɪie's,	hĕñnoñ′doⁿ·:	"I"		3
thence her body is falling?"	Now	every one of them	they (m.) spoke,	they (m.) it said:	"I,		
nŏñ″	agegwe′nī·.	akheiä′dage′·hä′."	Oga′·gwä′	waĕñ″:	"I",		4
perhaps,	I it could do	I her could aid."	It Black Bass,	he it said:	"I,		
nŏñ″	agegwe′nī·."	Waĕñ′nī′:	"De′osthoñ″	ioñ″	de′sagwe′nioñ·		5
perhaps,	I it could do."	They it said·	"Not a little,	perhaps	thou art able to do it,		
so″djī·	de′sa′ni′goⁿt."	Ne·′	ie′wä′	ne·′	Sgĕñdjes′	waĕñ″:	6
because (too utterly)	thou hast no sense."	That	next in order	the	It Pickerel (=it fish long)	he it said:	
"I,"	ioñ″	agegwe′nī·."	Waĕñ′nī′	kho″	a′e·:	"De′osthoñ″	7
"I,	perhaps,	I it could do."	They it said	and	again:	"Not a little	
de′sagwe′nioñ·,	so″djī·	saniä′do′wis."	Da′,	o′nĕⁿ·	ne·′	ne′wä'	8
thou hast no sense,	because (too utterly)	thou art a glutton."	So,	now	that	next in order	
waā′sniet	ne·′	ha′no′wa·	waĕñ″·	"I"	dī′q	nŏñ″	agegwe′nī·	9
he spoke	the	It turtle	he it said:	,'I,	moreover,	perhaps,	I it could do	
akheiä′dage′·hä′	ne·′	iagoñ′gwe·."	O′nĕⁿ·	gagwe′goⁿ·	waādii·-		10
I her could aid	the	she man-being (is)."	Now	it all	they confirmed		
wäni′äd.	O′nĕⁿ·	dī′q	ie″ho·	ha″sko′	he′oñwe·	odogĕⁿ′doⁿ·	ne·′	11
(the) matter.	Now,	moreover,	there	he floated	the where	it is objective point	the	
dāieiä′doñ′die·	ne·′	iagoñ′gwe·.	Da′,	o′nĕⁿ·	ie″ho·	ga′nowä′′ge·		21
thence her body is falling	the	she man-being is.	So,	now	there	it turtle on		
o′die′dioñ′dä·t.	O′nĕⁿ·	dī′q	ie″ho·	wä′oⁿs′daĕñ′	ne·′	iagoñ′gwe·.		13
she alighting stepped.	Now,	moreover,	there	she wept	the	she man-being is.		

afterward she   bered that see ingly she still held [in her hands] earth. Now she opened her hands, and, moreover, she scattered the earth over Turtle. As soon as she did this, then it seems that this earth grew in size. So now she did thus, scattering the earth very many times [much]. In a short time the earth had become of a considerable size. Now she herself became aware that it was she herself, alone seemingly, who was forming this earth here present. So now, verily, it was her custom to travel about from place to place continually. She knew, verily, that when she traveled to and fro the earth increased in size. So now it was not long, verily, before the various kinds of shrubs grew up and also every kind of grass and reeds. In a short time she saw there entwined a vine of the wild potato. There out of doors the woman-being stood up and said: "Now, seemingly, will be present the orb of light [the sun], which shall be called the

1	Gaiñ'gwă'	nă'ioñ'nĭshe't	o'nĕⁿ'	wă'agoshăă"t	ne''	ie'ā'	gwa''
	Somewhat	so long it lasted	now	she it remembered	the	she it held,	seemingly
2	ne''	oe''dă'.	O'nĕⁿ'	wă'oⁿ'tcagwai''sī',	o'nĕⁿ'-kho'	di'q	ıe''ho'
	the	it earth.	Now	she her hand opened,	now and	moreover	there
3	o'dioñdo'gwăt	ne''	ga'no'wä'ge'.	Ganio'	ıe''ho'	ıă'e'ie'	agwă's
	she it scattered	the	it turtle on.	So soon as	thus	so she it did	very (just)
4	gwa''	na'e'	o'wado'diak	nĕñ'gĕñ'	ne''	oe''dă'.	Da',	o'nĕⁿ'
	seemingly	verily,	it grew	this it is	the	it earth.	So,	now
5	we'so'	ıe''ho'	ıă'e'ie'	o'dioñdo'gwăt	ne''	oe''dă'	Dă'djiă''shoñ
	much (it is)	thus	so she it did	she it scattered	the	it earth.	In a very short time only
6	o'nĕⁿ'	gaiñ'gwă'	niioĕñ'djă'	o'wā'doⁿ'.	O'nĕⁿ'	wă'ĕñni'naⁿdog
	now	somewhat	so it earth is large	it became.	Now	she it noticed
7	he''	gaoñ'hoñ''	gwa''shoñ	ie'cioñ'nĭ's	nĕñ'gĕñ'	ne''	ioĕñ'djă'de'
	where	she herself	seemingly only	she it makes	this it is	the	it earth is present.
8	Da',	o'nĕⁿ'	na'e'	gĕñ's	deiagodawĕñ'nie'	diiawĕⁿ''oⁿ'.	Gonoⁿ''doⁿ'
	So,	now,	verily,	customarily	she is traveling about	without ceasing.	She it knew
9	ne''	na'e'	o'wado'diak	gauio''	deiagodawĕñ'nie'.	Da',	o'nĕⁿ'
	that,	verily,	it grew	so soon as	she would travel about.	So,	now,
10	dī'q	de'aoñni'she'oñ'	o'ıĕⁿ'	na'e'	o'skawă'shoñ''oⁿ'	o'wĕñıaⁿ
	moreover,	it did not last long	now,	verily,	it bush of various kinds	they (z.)
11	do'diak,	ne''-kho'	ne''	hă'deio'eo''dage'.	Dă'djiă''shoñ'	o'nĕⁿ'
	grew up,	that and	the	every grass (plant) in number.	In a very short time only	now
12	wă'e'gĕⁿ'	owadăse''	ne''	onĕñ'noⁿ'dă'-oñ'we'	o'oⁿ''sa'.	O'nĕⁿ',	ne''
	she it saw	it is entvined	the	it wild potato (native)	it vine.	Now,	the
13	iăgoñ'gwe'	ıe''ho'	a'sde'	o'die'dă't,	o'nĕⁿ'-kho'	wă'a'gĕⁿ':	"O'nĕⁿ'
	she man-being (is)	there	out of doors	she stood up,	Now and	she it said:	"Now,
14	gwă''	ĕⁿgää'gwă'ă'k	ne''	ĕñdek'ha'	ĕⁿgāiasō'oñg."	Dogĕⁿ's	sede''-
	seemingly,	it luminary will be present,	the	day pertaining to	it will be called."	It is true	early in

diurnal one." Truly now, early in the morning, the orb of light arose, and now, moreover, it started and went thither toward the place where the orb of light goes down [sets]. Verily, when the orb of light went down [set] it then became night, or dark. Now again, there out of doors she stood up, and she said, moreover: "Now, seemingly, next in order, there will be a star [spot] present here and there in many places where the sky is present [i. e., on the surface of the sky]." Now, truly, it thus came to pass. So now, there out of doors where she stood she there pointed and told, moreover, what kind of thing those stars would be called. Toward the north there are certain stars, severally present there, of which she said: "They-are-pursuing-the-bear they will be called." So now, next in order, she said another thing: "There will be a large star in existence, and it will rise customarily just before it becomes day, and it will be called, 'It-brings-the-day.'" Now, again she pointed, and again she said: "That cluster of stars yonder will be called 'the Group Visible.' And they, verily,

---

djiă'	o'nĕⁿ'	dagää'gwit'gĕⁿ't,	o'nĕⁿ'	dĭ'q	ho'wa'děñ'dĭ'	he''	gä'ä'-	1
morning	now	thence it luminary came forth	now	moreover	it started	where	it luminary	
gwĕⁿ's-gwă'	ho''we'.	Ne''	no'nĕⁿ'	ho'gä'ä'gwĕⁿ't	o'nĕⁿ'	wai''		2
sets direction	thither it went.	That	the time	thither it orb of light set	now	of course		
wä'o''gä'.	O'nĕⁿ'	a'e'	ne''ho'	a'sde'	o'die'dä't,	wä'a'gĕⁿ	dĭ'q:	3
it became night.	Now	again	there	out of doors	she stood up,	she it said	more over:-	
"O'nĕⁿ'	gwă'	ne'wä'	ěⁿgadjĭ'soⁿ''deoññioñg	he''	gäoⁿhia'de'.''			4
"Now	seemingly	next in order	it star will be present plurally	where	it sky is present."			
O'nĕⁿ'	dogĕⁿ's	ne''ho'	niiawĕⁿ''oⁿ'.	Da',	o'nĕⁿ'	as'de'	he'oñwe' i'iet	5
Now	it is true, indeed,	thus	so it came to pass.	So,	now	out of the place doors where	she stood	
ne''ho'	wä'oⁿ''tcadĕⁿ',	wä'a'gĕⁿ	dĭ'q	ne''	naⁿ''ot	ěⁿgaiaso'oñg	hoi'-	6
there	she pointed with her finger,	she it said	moreover	that	such kind of thing	it will be called	those	
gĕñ'	gadjĭ'soⁿ''dä''shoⁿ'.	Otho'we'ge'-gwă'	ne''ho'	gadogĕñ'noⁿ'	ne''			7
it star is severally	It is cold direction	there	it is certain one the severally					
gadjĭ'soⁿ''de'oññioⁿ'	ne''	ne''	"Nia'gwai'	hadĭshe''	ěⁿgāiaso'oñg,''			8
it star is present (fixed) plurally	that	the	"Bear	they (m.) are pursuing it	it will be called,''			
wä'a'gĕⁿ.	Da',	o'nĕⁿ'	o'iă'	ne'wä'	wä'a'gĕⁿ:	"Ne''	ne''	9
she it said.	So,	now	it other (is)	next in order	she it said:	"That	it is	
ěⁿgowanĕñ'oñg	gadjĭ'soⁿ''dä	ěⁿgĕⁿ'k,	ěⁿtgä'ä'gwitgĕⁿ'seg	tho''hă'				10
it will be large	it star	it will be	it will be in the habit of rising	nearly				
gĕñ's	ne''	ěⁿio''hĕñ't	ne''	ěⁿgāiaso'oñg	Tgĕñdĕñ'withä'.''	O'nĕⁿ'		11
customarily	the	it will become day	that	it will be called	It day brings.''	Now		
o'iă'	wä'oⁿ''tcadĕⁿ',	a'e'-kho'	wä'a'gĕⁿ:	"Ne''	hi'gĕñ'	wä'go''sot		12
it other (is)	she pointed her finger,	again and	she it said:	"That	that one it is	it group is present.		
odjĭ'soⁿ''dä''shoⁿ'	ne''	ěⁿgāiaso'oñg,	Gatgwă''dä'.	Ne''	na'e,			13
it star (is) severally	that	it will be called,	It cluster is present.	That,	verily			

will know [will be the sign of] the time of the year [at all times]. And that [group] is called 'They-are-dancing.'" So now, still once more, she spoke of that [which is called] "She-is-sitting." [She said]: "Verily, these will accompany them [i. e., those who form a group]. 'Beaver-its-skin-is-spread-out,' is what these shall be called. As soon, customarily, as one journeys, traveling at night, one will watch this [group]." Some time after this, she, the Ancient-bodied, again spoke repeatedly, saying: "There will dwell in a place far away man-beings. So now, also, another thing; beavers will dwell in that place where there are streams of water." Indeed, it did thus come to pass; and the cause that brought it about is that she, the Ancient-bodied, is, as a matter of fact, a controller [a god].

So now, sometime afterward, the girl man-being, the offspring of the Ancient-bodied, had grown large in size. And so now there was also much forest lying extant. Now near by there was lying an

1	hi'gĕñ· that one it is	ěⁿgāiĕnde'iăk it will know it (will be the sign of it)	he" where	niwadoshi'ne's just it year is in its course	ne" that	gāia'soⁿ· it is called	hi'gĕñ' this one it is
2	Deʻhoñnoñt'gwĕⁿ·. They are dancing.	Da', So,	'ă·'soⁿ· still	sgăt' one it is	ne" that	ne'wă' next in order	hi'gĕñ' this one it is
3	Ieniu"ciot. She is sitting.	Ne" That	na'eʻ verily	hi'gĕñʻ this one it is	ěⁿwĕñne"seg it will accompany them	nigĕⁿ" that is to say	ne" the	
4	haditgwă"dā'. they (m.) are a cluster (fixed).	Naⁿganiă"goⁿ· Beaver (Rodcutter)	Ga'sä'doⁿ· It spread skin is	ne" that	ěⁿgaiaso'oñg it will be called	bi'gĕñʻ this it is.	
5	Ganio" So soon as	gĕñ's customarily	dĕⁿioñthă'ăk one will start to travel	ne" that	ěⁿioñtgā'ioⁿ· one will watch it	bi'gĕñʻ this it is	dĕⁿioñda- one will
6	wĕñ'nieʻ travel	ne" the	soñ'eʻ." night (it is)."	Gaiñ'gwă· Somewhat	niio'weʻ so it is distant	a'eʻ again	wă'e'snie"cioñ' she spoke repeatedly
7	ne" the	Eiă'dagĕⁿ"tcĭʻ, She Ancient bodied (is),	wă'a'gĕⁿ·: she it said:	"Ĕⁿ"hadinaⁿgeg' "They (m.) will dwell habitually	ne" the	oñ'gweʻ man-being(s)	
8	we'ĕⁿʻ far	he'oñweʻ. the place where.	Da', So,	o'iă' it other (is)	khoʻ and	ěⁿganaⁿge'g it (z.) will dwell habitually	ne" the	naⁿganiă"goⁿ· it beaver
9	hoñwē'-gwăʻ place direction	he'oñweʻ the place where	tgĕⁿ"hănde'nioⁿ·." there it stream is plurally present."	Dogĕⁿ's It is true	ne""hoʻ thus	niia· so it		
10	wĕⁿ"oⁿʻ came to pass	ne" that	ne" the	gaioñ'niʻ it it causes	he" for that (where)	Iewĕñni'io' She Master (is)	sĕⁿ"ĕⁿʻ it matter of fact (is)	ne" the
11	Eiă'dagĕⁿ"tcĭʻ. She Ancient-bodied (is)							
12	Da', So,	o'nĕⁿʻ now	gaiñ'gwă· somewhat	nă'ioñ'nishe't so it is (long) lasted	o'nĕⁿ· now	we'so' much (it is)	iegowa'nĕⁿʻ she large (is)	
13	nĕñ'gĕñʻ this it is	ne" the	iagoñ'gweʻ she man-being,	Eiă'dagĕⁿ"tcĭ· She Ancient-bodied	goa'wăk. her offspring.	Da', So,	o'iĕⁿ now	
14	khoʻ and	we'so' much (it is)	gaʻhā'dāiĕⁿ·. it forest lies.	Da', So,	o'nĕⁿʻ now	do'sgĕñ'oⁿ"shoñʻ near by only,	ne"ho, there	

uprooted tree, whereon it was that she, the child, was always at play. Customarily she swung, perhaps; and when she became wearied she would descend from it. There on the grass she would kneel down. It was exceedingly delightful, customarily, it is said, when the Wind entered; when she became aware that the Wind continued to enter her body, it was delightful.

Now sometime afterward the Ancient-bodied watched her, musing: "Indeed, one would think that my [man-being] offspring's body is not sole [i. e., not itself only]. "Ho," she said, "hast thou never customarily seen someone at times?" "No," said the girl child. Then she, the Ancient-bodied, said: "I really believe that one would think that thou art about to give birth to a child." So now, the girl child told it, saying: "That [I say] there [at the swing] when, customarily, I would

gāiěñga'sä'de'	ne"	ne"	he'oñwe'	diiot'goñt	gotga'nie'	ne"	
it upturned tree	that	the	the place where	at all times	she is playing	the	1
ieksä"ä'.	Ne'	gĕñ's	godoñwi'dä"do"'	ioñ".	O'nĕ"'	gĕñ's	
she child.	That (it is)	customarily	she it was swinging on	perhaps.	Now	customarily	2
gotcĕ"'do"'	o'nĕ"'	ie"ho'	wä'ĕñdiä"dĕ"t.		Ogeo'djä"ge'	ie"'ho'	
she was wearied	now	there	she descended (lay down)		On the grass	there	3
o'dioñdoshō'doñ'.		Odo'kdä"gï',	ia'gĕ",	gĕñ's	os'gas	ne"	
she got on her knees.		It is at the extreme,	it is said,	customarily	it gives pleasure	that	4
io'iĕ"'	dagä'iïnt,	ne"'ho'	o'nĕ"'	gĕñ's	wä'ĕñni'na"dog	ne	
the time (now)	it it entered,	there	now	customarily	she it noticed (felt)	the	5
o'nĕ"'	eiä"dägoñ'	hewē'thä'	ne"	gä"hä',	ne" ne"	os'gas	
now	her body in	thither it is entering	the	It wind,	that the	it gives pleasure.	6
O'nĕ"',	gaiñ'gwä'	nä'ioñni'she't	o'nĕ"'		wä'ega'ĕñ'ioñ'	ne"	
Now,	somewhat	so it lasted	now		she it watched	the	7
Iegĕ"'tcï'	wä'ĕñ'	agwa's	äiĕñ"	thĕ"'ĕ"'	de'djiagoiä'do'sgä'ä'		
She Ancient One	she mused	just	one would think	not it is	her body is sole		8
ne"	khe'a'wäk.	"Hō',"	wä'a'gĕ",	"Hĕ"'ĕ"	gĕ"' ·	dewĕñ'do"'	
the	my (anthropic) child.	"Oh,"	she it said,	"Not	is it	not ever	9
gĕñ's	de'soñga"	de'she'gĕ"'?"	"Thĕ"'ĕ"',"	wä'a'gĕ"	ne"	eksä"ä'	
customarily	someone	thou seest one customarily?"	"Not it is,"	she it said	the	she child.	10
O'nĕ"'	wä'a'gĕ"	ne"	Iegĕ"'tcï':	"Āiĕñ"shoñ'	ĕ"'sade"doñ',	gi"	
Now	she it said	the	She Ancient One:	"One would think only	thou wilt give birth to a child,	I think,	11
äñ'	noñ"."	Da',	o'nĕ"'	wä'oñthiu'wï'	ne"	eksä"ä',	wä'a'gĕ"·
perhaps,	probably."	So,	now	she it told	the	she child	she it said:	12
"Ne"	ne"	ne"'ho'	gĕñ's	ne"	o'nĕ"·	o'gade'nio'so'dĕ"'	ne"'ho'
"That	the	there	customarily	the	now	I knelt down on my knees	there	13
gĕñ's	o'geni'na"dog	he"	o'wade'no"'dä·	ne"	gä"hä'	ne"	
customarily	I it felt	where	it itself buried	the	It wind	the	14

kneel down, I became aware that the Wind inclosed itself in my body." So now, she, the Ancient-bodied, said: "If it be so, I say as a matter of fact, it is not certain that thou and I shall have good fortune."

So sometime afterward then, seemingly, [it became apparent] that two male children were contained in the body of the maiden. And now, verily, also they two debated together, the two saying, it is said, customarily: "Thou shalt be the elder one," "Thee just let it be," so it was thus that they two kept saying. Now, one of them, a male person who was very ugly, being covered with warts, said: "Thou shalt be the first to be born." Now the other person said: "Just let it be thee." Now he, the Warty, said: "Just let it be thee to be the first to be born." "So let it be," said the other person, "thou wilt fulfil thy duty, perhaps, thou thyself." "So be it," verily said he, the Warty. Now, he who was the elder was born. And then in a short time she [the Ancient-bodied] noticed that, seemingly, there was still

---

1	giä'da'goñ'."	Da',	o'nĕⁿ'	wä'a'gĕⁿ	ne"	Iegĕⁿ"'tcï':	"Ne" ne"ho'
	my body in."	So,	nov	she it said	the	She Ancient One	"That it matter of fact
2	ne"	diĕñgwä"'shoñ'		äioñgiadää'shwiio"'he't		de'oi'wado'gĕñ'."	
	the	if that only be		it us good fortune would give		it is an uncertain matter."	
3	Gaiñ'gwä'	nä'ioñni'she't	o'nĕⁿ'	ne"	gwä"	ne"	deiksä''ä'
	Somewhat	so it lasted	now	that	seemingly	the	they (m.) are two children
4	dei"noⁿt	ne"	ne"	eiä'da'goñ'	ne"	eiä"'dase'.	Da', o'nĕⁿ'-kho'
	they (m.) two are gestating	that	the	her body in	the	she maiden.	So, now and
5	na'e'	deodii''hwăge'hĕⁿ'.	Ia'doⁿ',	gi"oⁿ',	gĕñ's:	"I's	ĕⁿsego-
	verily	they (m.) two are contending in dispute.	They (m.) two it said,	it is said,	customarily:	"Thou	thou wilt
6	waneñ'oñg."	"I's	gwä"',"	nigĕⁿ"	gĕñ's	ia'doⁿ'.	O'nĕⁿ' ne"
	be the larger (elder) one."	"Thou	just,"	that is to say	customarily	they (m.) two said.	Now the
7	shäiä"'dăt	ne"	agwa's	hăet'gĕⁿ,	ne" ne"	honoⁿ'hi"dăe'	waĕñ"·
	one he is person	that	very	he is ugly,	that the	he is covered with warts (pimples)	he it said·
8	"I's	ĕⁿtcadie'ĕⁿt	ĕⁿ'seññaⁿ'gät."	O'nĕⁿ'	ne"	shäiä"'dăt	waĕñ"·
	"Thou	thou wilt take the lead	thou wilt be born."	Now	the	one he is a person	he it said:
9	'I's	gwä"'."	O'nĕⁿ'	ne"	Honoⁿ'hi"dăe'	waĕñ"':	"I's gwä"
	"Thou	just."	Now,	the	He Warty	he it said;	"Thou just
10	ĕⁿtcadie'ĕⁿt	ĕⁿ'sĕññaⁿ'gät "	"Nio","	waĕñ"	ne"	shäiä"'dăt,	
	thou wilt be the first	thou wilt be born."	"So be it."	he it said	the	one he is a person,	
11	"ĕⁿ'si'wäie'is	gwä",	noñ"	iăⁿ'	i's'ä'."	"Nio","	na'e' waĕñ".
	"thou it vilt fulfill	just,	perhaps,	this	thou personally."	"So be it,"	verily he it said
12	ne"	Honoⁿ'hi"dăe'.	O'nĕⁿ'	waĕññaⁿ'gät	nigĕⁿ"	ne"	hago'wanĕⁿ'.
	the	He Warty.	Now	he is born	this it is	the	he large one.

another to be born. The other had been born only a short time when this one was also born. They had been born only a very short time when their mother died. There, verily, it is said that he, the Warty, came forth from the navel of his mother. So now, verily, she, the Ancient-bodied, wept there. Not long after this, verily, she gave attention to the twins. As soon as she finished this task she made a grave not far away, and so she there laid her dead offspring, laying her head toward the west. So now, moreover, she talked to her. She, the Ancient-bodied, said: "Now, verily, thou hast taken the lead on the path that will continue to be between the earth here and the upper side of the sky. As soon as thou arrivest there on the upper side of the sky thou must carefully prepare a place where thou wilt continue to abide, and where we shall arrive." Now, of course, she covered it.

Dä'djiä·'	o'nĕⁿ'-kho'	wä'ĕñni'naⁿdog	ne·'	o'iä'	gwā·'	'ä·'soⁿ·	1
In a short time	nov	and	she it noticed	the	it other	seemingly	still	
ĕⁿnaⁿ'gät.	Dä'djiä''shoñ'	honaⁿgä'doⁿ·	o'nĕⁿ'	ne·'	ne'wä'		2
he will be born.	In a short time only	he is born	nov	that	next in order		
waĕñnaⁿ'gät.	Dä'djiä''shoñ'	ninaⁿgä'doⁿ·	o'nĕⁿ'	wä'äi'ē'	ne·''		3
he was born.	In a short time	they (m.) two are born	now	she died	the		
shagodino''ĕⁿ·.	Ne''ho·	na'e',	gi''oⁿ',	ne·''	Honoⁿ'hi''dāe'		4
she their mother is.	There,	verily,	it is said,	the	He Warty		
daäiä'gĕⁿ't	he''	diiago'she''dot	ne·'	hono''ĕⁿ·.	Da',	o'nĕⁿ'	na'e'	5
he came forth	vhere	just she has her navel	the	his mother.	So,	nov	verily	
wä'oñ'sdaĕⁿ'	ne·'	Eiä'dagĕⁿ·'tcï·.	Thĕⁿ'ĕⁿ'	dä'aoñni'she'oⁿ'	o'nĕⁿ'		6
she wept	the	She Ancient-bodied.	Not it is	it lasted	nov		
na'e'	o'thoñwadï'snie'	ne''	dei'khĕⁿ'.	Ganio''	wä'oñdiĕñno''kdĕⁿ'		7
verily	she them cared for	the	they (m.) two are twins.	So soon as	she completed her task		
o'nĕⁿ·	na'e'	wä'eiadoñ'nï'	dosgĕñ'oⁿ'shoñ',	da',	ne''ho'	wä'ago	8
nov	verily	she made a cave (hole)	just near by,	so,	there	she	
iä''shĕñ'	ne·''	goä'wäk-gĕñ'oñ',	he·''	gää'gwĕⁿ''s-gwä'	ne''ho'		9
her laid	the	her offspring	was,	where	it sun sets	direction	there	
wä'agogoĕñ''.	Da',	o'nĕⁿ·	dï'q	wä'agothā'hăs.	Wä'a'gĕⁿ'	ne·''	10
she her scalp (head) laid.	So,	now,	moreover	she her talked to.	She it said	the	
Eiä'dagĕⁿ·'tcï·:	"O'nĕⁿ'	i's	na'e'	o'sathä'hoñ'dĕⁿ'	nĕñ'gĕñ'	he·	11
She Ancient-bodied:	"Now,	thou	verily	thou it path hast taken	this it is	where	
ioĕñ'djāde'	gäoñ'hiä''ge·	hĕⁿiothä'hinoñ'oñg.	Ganio''	ne''ho·		12
it earth is present	sky on	it path will have its course.	So soon as	there		
hĕⁿ·'cioⁿ'	ne·'	gäoñ'hiä''ge·	ĕⁿ'se'cioñnia'noñ'	he'oñwe·	ĕⁿ'si'di-	13
thou wilt arrive	the	sky on	thou wilt make preparations	the place where	thou wilt	
oñ'däk,	i''-kho·	he'oñwe'	hĕⁿiagwä'ioⁿ'.''	O'ĕⁿ·	wai'i·	14
continue to abide, .	we two (we and)	the place where	there we shall arrive.''	Now	of course	

So, now, only this was left, that she customarily cared for the twins, the two children.

Again, after some time, it is said, the two male children were of large size, and verily, too, they ran about there, customarily. Afterward, the elder one, being now a youth, questioning his grandmother, asked: "Oh, grandmother, where, verily, is my father? And who, moreover, verily, is the one who is my father? Where, moreover, is the place wherein he dwells?" She, the Ancient-bodied, said: "Verily, that one who is the Wind is thy father. Whatever, moreover, is the direction from which the wind is customarily blowing, there, truly, is the place where the lodge of thy father stands." "So be it," replied the youth. So now, verily, the youth stood out of doors, and now he, moreover, observed the direction of the wind, whence it was blowing; and this too he said: "I desire to see my father, and the reason is that

1. wa'oñwe"sä'. Da',' o'nĕⁿ· ne"shoñ' we'gĕñ· dĕⁿwadi"snic' nigĕⁿ"/
   she it covered. So, now that only it is left she will attend to two persons that it is

2. ne" dei'khĕⁿ·, ne"' dei'ksä'ä'.
   the they (m.) two are twins the they (m.) two are children.

3. Gaiñ'gwă' a'e' nä'ioñni'she't o'nĕⁿ·, gi"oⁿ·, deigowa'nĕñ ne"
   Somewhat again so it lasted now, it is said, they (m.) two are large the

4. dei'ksä'ä·, o'nĕⁿ·-kho' na'e· deidak'he's. Thä'gĕñ"oⁿ· o'nĕⁿ·
   they (m.) two are children, now and, verily, they (m.) two run about. Afterward now

5. waäda'oñ'doñ· ne"' hagowa'nĕñ·, o'nĕⁿ· na'e· haksä'däse"ä'
   he it asked the he (is) large, now, verily, he (is) a youth.

6. O'shago'oñ'doñ· ne"' ho'sot' waĕñ"·: "Aksot', gaiñ"· di'q na'e'
   He her asked the his grandmother he it said: "My grandmother, where moreover, verily,

7. ne"' ha'nī'? Soñ"' di'q kho"' na'e· nigĕⁿ"/ ni"' ne"' ha'nī'?
   the he is my father? Who moreover and verily that it is the I the he is my father?

8. Gawe"' di'q noñ"' gwä'gwä· thanaⁿ'ge'?" Wä'a'gĕⁿ ne"'
   Where, moreover, perhaps, in direction there he dwells?" She it said the

9. Eiä'dagĕⁿ·'tcī': "Ne" wai'i' hi'gĕñ· ne"' iä"ni ne"' Gä"hä'
   She Ancient-bodied: "That of course this it is the he is thy father the It Wind.

10. Gaiñ·"' di'q gwa'gwä· gĕñ's diioägoñt' ne"' noñ"' ne"'ho'-gwä'
    Where moreover, in direction customarily there it wind is fixed that perhaps there direction

11. thonoⁿ·"'sot ne"' iä"ni." "Nio·'," waĕñ"' ne"' haksa'dase"ä'
    there his lodge stands the he is thy father." "So be it," he it said the he youth.

12. Da', o'nĕⁿ· na'e· as'de' o'tha'dä't ne"' haksa'dase"ä', o'nĕⁿ·
    So, now, verily, out of doors he stood the he youth, now

13. di'q waätga'ioñ· he'oñwe'-gwä· diioägoñt'; ne"' kho"' ne"'
    moreover he it watched the place where in direction there it wind is coming; that and the

14. ha'doⁿ·· ne"' ne"' dewagadoĕñdjoñ'nī· ae'gĕⁿ ne"' lia'nī', ne"'
    he it kept saying that the I it need I him should see the he my father is,

he would give me aid." Now, he said: "Far yonder stands the lodge of my father, the Wind; he will aid me; he will take the bodies of all the kinds of animal [man-beings]; and by all means still something else that will be an aid to me." So now he started. He had not gone far when in the distance he saw the place where stood the lodge of his father. He arrived there, and there a man-being abode who had four[a] children, two males and two females. The youth said: "I have now arrived. O father, it is necessary that thou shouldst aid me. And that which I need are the game [animals] and also some other things." They were all pleased that they saw him. So now he, the Ancient, their father, said: "So let it be. Truly I will fulfil all of thy require-

diioi'"wă' there it is reason	ne'' the	aũgiă'dage'·hă'." he me should aid."		O'něn‘ Now	waěñ'': he it said:	"Hoñwe'-gwă‘ "Where in direction	1
thonon'so't there his lodge stands	ne'' the	hă'nī' he is my father	ne'' the	Gă''hă', It Wind,	ne'' that	ěn'gie'nanwa's he me will aid,	2
ěn'a·cioñnī' he it will make	ne'' the	hă'deganio''dăge‘; every it animal kind (is) in number;		tgagon'' by all means	'ă''son-kho‘ still and		3
hă'gwĭsděn'' something	gie'' some of them	ne'' the	o'iă', other that it is,	ne''	gagwe'gon it all	ěnagiă'dage'·hă'.' he me will aid."	4
Da', So,	o'něn‘ now	waă''děñdī'. he started.		Thěn''ěn‘ Not it is	de·we'ěn far away	deawe'noñ· he went	o'něn‘ now	5
waă'gěn he it saw	hoñwe'-gwă‘ where in direction	tgano'so't. there it lodge stands.		O'něn‘ Now	ne''·ho‘ there	waă'ion he arrived	ne''·ho‘ there	6
hěn''dion he abode	ne'' the	boñ'gwe‘, he man-being is,	ge'ĭ'a four	ni‘oksa'dă'iěn, so many he has children,	deiias'he‘ they (m.) two are persons	deidji' they (m.) two are male	7
na‘,	degiias'he· they (f.) two are persons	degnī'on·. they (f.) two are female.		Waěñ'' He It said	ne'' the	haksa'dase''ă‘: he youth:	"O'něn‘ "Now	8
o·gion''; I have arrived;	hă'nī', oh, my father,	ne'' that it is,	ne'' the	dewagadoěñdjoñ'nī· It me is necessary for		ăsgiă'dage'·hă· thou me shouldst aid.	9
Ne'' That	ne'' the	dewagadoěñdjoñ'nī‘ it me is necessary for	ne'' the	ganio'shoñ''on‘ it game (collective.)		ne''kho‘ that and	ne'' the	10
hă''gwĭsděn anything	gie'' some of them	ne'' the	o'iă'." it other."	Gagwe'gon It all		waěñnădon‘hă'ěñ‘ they were pleased		11
ne'' the	wă'oñwagěn''. they him saw.	Da', So,	o'něn‘ now	waěñ'' he it said	ne'' the	Hagěn‘'tcī‘ He Ancient	ne'' the	12

---

[a] The use of the number four here is remarkable. It seems that the two female children are introduced merely to retain the number four, since they do not take any part in the events of the legend. It appears to the writer that the visiting boy and his warty brother are here inadvertently displaced by the narrator by the substitution of the two girls for the reason given above, owing to his or a predecessor's failure to recall all the parts of the legend. This form has emphasized the importance of the twins to the practical exclusion of the other brothers. In the Algonquian Potawatomi genesis narrative, which, like those of its congeners, appears to be derived from a source common to both Iroquoian and Algonquian narrators, four male children are named as the offspring of the personage here called Wind. For the Potawatomi version consult De Smet, Oregon Missions, page 347.

r e nts in coming here. In the first place, however, I will that these here, ye m y children, severally shall arouse yourselves somewhat by running a race. I have a flute for which ye shall contend one with another, whereby ye shall enjoy yourselves. And I say that ye shall take a circuit of this earth here present, and also that ye shall take this flute." So now they stood at the line whence they should start. Now the visiting youth said: "I desire that here shall stand he, the Defender[a] [the False-face, He-defends-them], that he may aid me." Truly, it thus came to pass; the Defender came and stood there. And now, moreover, the youth said: "And I say that thou must put forth thy utmost speed for that I am going to trail thy tracks." So now truly it did thus come to pass that at all times they two [males] were in the lead throughout the entire distance covered in making the circuit [of the earth]. As soon as they started running he trailed him, and the pace was swift. In a short time now they made a circuit of it. Much did they two [males] outfoot the other two. Now he that

1	hoñwa″'nī: he their father is:	"Nio'. "So be it.	Do'gĕⁿs Truly	ne″'ho' thus	ĕⁿgi'wāie'is I will fulfill the matter	na″ot such kind of thing	se'he'die'. thou desirest in coming.	
2	Ne″ That	gwă″ seemingly	ia'e' in the first place	i″ I	ĕⁿtgĕñnoⁿ⁽'doⁿ⁾ I it will will		osthoñ' it little	ĕⁿswatga'nie' ye will amuse yourselves
3	něñ'gĕñ' this it is	gwaāwă'kshoñ'oⁿ' I am parent of you children		ne″ that	ne″ the	dĕⁿswĕñĕⁿ⁽'dat. ye will run (a race).		Agiĕⁿ″ I it have
4	ne″ the	ieo'dawās'thă' one uses it for blowing (a flute),	ne″ that	ne″ the	ĕⁿswasge⁽'hă' ye it will contend for	ne″ that	ne″ the	ĕⁿswadĕñdoñ'nĭă't.
5		Ne″ That	ne″ the	dĕⁿswathwada'se' ye will make a circuit of it	něñ'gĕñ' this it is	he″ where	ioĕñ'djāde', it earth is present,	
6	ne″kho' that and	ne″ the	ĕⁿswa'ā' ye will take with you	něñ'gĕñ' this it is	ne″ the	ieo'dawas'thă'.″ one uses it for blowing (a flute)."	Da', So,	
7	o'nĕⁿ' now	ne″'ho' there	o'thadi'dă't they (m.) stood up	he'oñwe' the place where	ĕⁿthĕñnĕⁿ″'sgā'. they (m.) will start from the line.	Da', So,	o'nĕⁿ' now	
8	waĕñ″ he it said	ne″ the	haksa'dase″ă'· he youth:	"Ne″ "That	ne″ the	dewagadoĕñdjoñ'nĭ' it me is necessary for		
9	ne'kho' here	daā'dă't he should stand	ne″ the	Shagodiowe'go'wā He Them Defends (He Whirlwind)	ne″ that	ne″ the	aāgiă'dagie' he should aid me."	
10	'hă'.″	Do'gĕⁿs It is true	ne″'ho' thus	nă″awĕⁿ'; so it came to pass·	ne″'ho' there	o'tha'dă't he stood up	ne″ the	
11	Shagodiowe'go'wa. He Them Defends (He Whirlwind)	O'nĕⁿ' Now	dĭ'q moreover	waĕñ″ he it said	ne″ the	haksa'dase″ă': he youth:		
12	"Ne″ "That it is	ne″ the	ĕⁿtsadia'noāt thou must exert thy best speed	ne″ that	nigĕⁿ″ so it is	ne″ the	ĕⁿgoñia'nondă' ″ I will trail thy tracks."	
13	Da', So,	o'nĕⁿ' now	do'gĕⁿs it is true	ne″'ho' thus	nă'a'wĕⁿ' so it came to pass	ne″ that	diiawĕⁿ″oⁿ' continually	hiiĕñ'de' they (m.) two were in the lead.

---

[a] This is the Seneca name for the Hadu″'l' of the Onondagas.

carried the flute gave it to his father. Now he, the Ancient, took it and also said: "Now, of course, truly thou hast won from me all the things that thou desirest that I should do for thee." Now, moreover, he there laid down a bundle, a filled bag that was very heavy. So now, verily, he gave to his son, to the one who came from the other place, this bundle and also this flute that he had won, and he also said: "I say that this shall belong to you both equally, to thee and thy younger brother." So now the youth took up the bundle and bore it on his back by means of the forehead burden strap. So now he traveled along to a place where he became tired and the sack began to be heavy. So now he exclaimed, "It may be, perhaps, that I should take a rest." And so now he sat down and also examined it [the bag]. He thought, "Let me, indeed, view them; for indeed they belong to me anyway."

ne'' the	he'' where	niio'we' so it is distant	waĕñnoñthwäda'se'. they (m.) made a circuit of it.	Ganio'' So soon as	o'iĕⁿ' the time (nov)	o'thĕñnĕⁿ'' they (m.) ran,	1
dat, he doubled his tracks	waodianondä''	osno'we'. it is swift.	Dä'djiä'' In a short time	o'nĕⁿ' now	waĕñnoñthwada'se' they (m.) made a circuit of it.		2
We'so' Such (it is)	wä'oñwañdiiatgĕñ'nï' he them overmatched		ne'' the	sniiä''dat. they (m.) two are persons (other).	O'nĕⁿ' Now	ne'' the	haä'wï' he it bore	3
ne'' the	ieo'dawas'thä' one it uses for blowing	da'oñ' he it gave to him	ne'' the	ho''ri. he his father (is).	O'nĕⁿ' Now	waä'ienä', he it took,	ne'' that	4
kho'' and	ne'' the	waĕñ'' he it said	ne'' the	Hagĕⁿ''tcï'': He Ancient	"O'nĕⁿ' "Nov	wai'i' of course	do'gĕⁿs it is true	5
o'sge''niä' thou me hast v on from	he'' where	ni'ioñ so it is in amount	desadoĕñdjoñ'nï' it thee is necessary for		ne'' the	nägoñiadie'ä's.'' so I thee should do for.''		6
O'nĕⁿ' Nov,	dï'q moreover	ie''ho' thus	waäthenaⁿ'iĕñ' he his bundle laid down	ne'' the	gaiä'' it bag	ganaⁿ'hoⁿ', it is full,		7
oi'nosde'. it is a heavy pack.	Da', So,	o'nĕⁿ' nov	na'e' verily	dä'oñ' he it gave to him	ne'' the	hoa'wăk his offspring	ne'' the	oiä'djï' elsewhere	8
thawe''doⁿ thence he came	nigĕⁿ'' that it is	ne'' the	ganĕⁿnos''hä', it bundle,	ne'' that and	kho'	ne'' the	nĕñ'gĕñ' this it is	9
ne'' the	ieo'dawas'thä' one it uses to blow	daoñwä'iĕⁿ', he it gave to him,		ne'' that	kho'' and	ne'' the	waĕñ': he it said:	10
"Ne'' "That	nĕñ'gĕñ' this it is	desniawĕⁿ''-gĕñ'oñg ye two it will own		will be	ne'' the	he'se''gĕñ'' he thy younger brother is.''	Da', So,	11
o'nĕⁿ' now	o'thathē'năk, he his bundle took up,	waätge''dat he bore it on his back by the forehead strap	ne'' the	baksa'dase''ä'. he youth.		Da'. So,	o'nĕⁿ' now	12
he'' where	niäthä'i'ne' there he was on his way	o'nĕⁿ' now	wa'os, he got tired,	ne'' that	kho'' and	ne'' the	hosda'ne'. it him weighed down.	13
Da', So,	o'nĕⁿ' now	wä'e': he decided:	"Agadoñïs''hĕñ' "I myself should rest.''	gi'' I think	ĕñ' it seems	noⁿ''.'' perhaps.''	Da', So,	14
I'' I	wai'i' of course	nigĕⁿ'' so it is	aga'wĕⁿ'.'' I own it (it is mine).''	O'nĕⁿ' Now	na'e' verily	ie''ho' there	waäwä·hä''sï', he it unwrapped,	15

Now, verily, he there unwrapt it and uncovered it. Just as soon as he opened it there were repeated shovings. Now, moreover, there all the various kinds of animals that his father had given him came forth. He was taken by surprise that all the animals so suddenly came forth. Thus it came to pass as soon as he fully opened the sack. And there, moreover, they severally trampled upon him. So the last one to come forth was the spotted fawn. Now he there shot it. On the front leg, a little above the place where the hoof joins the leg, there he hit it. It escaped from him, verily, moreover. So now he said: "Thus it will be with thee always. It will never be possible for thee to recover. And the wax [fat] that will at all times be contained therein will be a good medicine. And it will continue to be an effective medicine As soon as anyone customarily shall have sore eyes, one must customarily anoint them with it, binding it thereon; then, customarily it will be possible for one to recover.

1. waāwe'sä'go'-kho'. Ganio"-shoñ wä'hodoñ'go' o'nĕⁿ' dawa'djaĕñ"-
   he uncovered it and. So soon as just he it uncovered now it pushed up repeatedly.

2. cioñ'. O'nĕⁿ' dī'q dawadiia'gĕⁿ't ᵉ"ho' ne" hä'deganio"däge' ne"
   Now moreover thence they (z.) came forth there the every it animal in number (is) that

3. ne" ho'wi' ne" ho'ii. Waādiĕñgwä"shoñ', dawadiiagĕⁿ"däk ne"
   the he it gave to him the he his father is. He was surprised just, they (z.) came out suddenly the

4. hä'deganio"däge'. Ne"ho' na'a'wĕⁿ' ganio" we'so' o'tha'hagwĕñ'dat.
   every it animal in number (is). There (thus) so it happened so soon as much he it opened.

5. Ne"ho' dī'q o'nĕⁿ' o'thoiä'daiqda'noñ'. Da', ne" agwa's ne"
   There, moreover, now it trampled on him severally. So, that very the

6. naⁿ'gĕñ"shoñ o'gāia'gĕⁿ't ne" djïsda'thiĕñ'o"'. O'nĕⁿ' ᵉ"ho'
   very last (hindmost) it came forth the spotted fawn. Now there

7. waä"iak. Oĕñdoñ'-gwä', ga'si'noⁿge', osthoñ" he'tgĕⁿ'' ne"
   he it shot. Front side, its leg on, it little above (it is) the

8. odjienĕⁿ"dä'ge' he'oñwe' ga'si'not ne"ho' waä'si's. Wao"nia
   its ankle on the place where its leg is fixed there he it hit. It escaped from

9. gĕⁿ's dī'q na'e'. Da', o'nĕⁿ' waĕñ"': "Ne"ho' ii's
   him moreover verily. So, now he it said· "There the thou

10. nĕⁿio'dĕñ'oñg diiotgoñt'. Thĕⁿ"ĕⁿ' dä"aoñ' wĕñ'doⁿ' oñsa'sa'doⁿ'.
    so it will continue to be always. Not (it is) it is possible ever again thou thyself shouldst recover

11. Ne" ne" onoⁿgwä"shä'-gĕñ'oñg hoi'gĕñ' oi'sä' ne" ᵉ"ho'
    That the it medicine it will be that it is it fat (wax) the there

12. diiotgoñt' ĕⁿwañ'dä'k. Ne" ne" ĕⁿionoⁿgwä'tchi'ioäg. Ganio"
    always it will be contained. That the it medicine will continue to be a good. So soon as

13. gĕñ's songä" ĕⁿiagoganoñ'waⁿk ne" gĕñ's ne"ho' ĕⁿiago"gä',
    customarily anyone it will sicken one's eyes that customarily there one it will anoint,

14. ĕⁿioñdiĕⁿ"sāoⁿ', o'nĕᵘ' gĕñ's ĕⁿwa'doⁿ' ne" ĕⁿdjoñ'doⁿ'."
    one will bind it on one's self, now customarily it shall be possible the again shall one recover."

So then he departed again from that place. When he again arrived at the place where their lodge stood, he told his younger brother, saying: "Do thou look at what the father of us two has given us two." When he again arrived where his grandmother was, he said: "Now I have been to the place of my father on a visit. He granted me a most important matter. So do ye again go out of doors. Ye will hear the great noise [made] by all the several kinds of animals." Now they went out, and they listened to the loudness of the noise made by all the kinds of animals. Now there, their grandmother, the Ancient-bodied, she stood up, and she talked, saying: "Let it stand here; that is the elk, which this thing shall be called. Here also let another stand, one that is just a little smaller, which shall be called a deer. Now also another thing, let it stand here, and that

Dā′,	o′nĕⁿ·	ne"·ho·	saä·dĕñ′dī·.	Saä′ioⁿ·	he′oñwe·	thodi	1
So,	now	there	again he departed.	Again he arrived	the place where	their (m.)	
noⁿ·sot′	o′nĕⁿ·	dī′q	woō′wī·	ne"	ho"gĕñ·	ne"	Othägwĕⁿ"′dä′,	2
lodge stood	now	moreover	he him told	the	he his younger brother is	the	It Flint,	
waĕñ":	"Satga"′tho·	ne"	shoñgia′wī·	ne"	shedi"ni·."	O′nĕⁿ·	3
he it said:	"Do thou look at it	the	he it has given to us two	the	he is the father of us two."	Now	
ne"·ho·	saä′ioⁿ·	ne"	ho·sot′ge·	waĕñ":	"O′nĕⁿ·	ne"·ho·	4
there	again he arrived	the	his grandmother at	he it said:	"Now	there	
ho·ga"′gēt	ne"	ha·nī′ne·.	Oi·owa′nĕñ·	o·thagiä′dowe"′dĕⁿ".	Dā′,	5
I have been	the	at my father's.	It is a great matter	he me granted to.	So,	
o′nĕⁿ·	waä′dieñ′,	wääk′doñ′-kho·.	Wä′e·:	"Gekdoñsa"·-shoñ	6
now	he himself seated,	he it examined	and.	He thought:	"Let me go to view them	several.	
o′nĕⁿ·	saswäia′gĕⁿ·t.	Eⁿswathoñ′deg	he·"	nigäi′sdowanĕñ·	7
now	do ye go forth.	Ye it will hear	where	so it sound great is	
hä′de·ioñ·	ne"	ganio"shoñ′oⁿ·."	O′nĕⁿ·	waädiia′gĕⁿ·t,	o′nĕⁿ·-kho·	8
every one in number	the	it animal is severally."	Now	they (m.) went out,	now and	
wäiathoñ′dat	he·"	niiotkai"′ni	ne"	onoñdi·s′dä·	ne"	hä′deganio"·-	9
they (m.) listened	where	so it is loud	the	they (z.) are making noise	the	every it animal is in number.	
dage·.	O′nĕⁿ·	ne"·ho·	o·die′dä·t	ne"	shagodi"·sot,	ne·"	10
	Now	there	she stood up	the	she their grandmother is	the	
Eiä′dagĕⁿ"′tcī·,	wä·oñthiu′wī·,	wä·a′gĕⁿ·:	"Ne·kho·	dĕⁿgä′dä·t	11
She Ancient-bodied,	she it told,	she it said:	"Here	it will stand up	
nigĕñ"′	ne"	djinaĕñ"′dä·,	ne"	na′e·	nĕñ′gĕñ·	ne"	ēⁿgäiasō′oñg.	12
so it is	the	elk	that	verily	this it is	that	it will be named.	
Ne·kho·	o·iä′-kho·	ne"·ho·	dĕⁿga′dä·t.	ne·"	ne·"	heio·sthoñ·	13
Here	It other and	there	it will stand up,	that	the	it is just little	
niiagä"′ä·,	ne"	na′e·	nĕñ′gĕñ·	ne·ogĕⁿ"	ēⁿgäiasō′oñg.	O′nĕⁿ·	14
so it is small(er),	that	verily	this it is	deer	it will be named.	Now	

next in turn shall, verily, be called a bear. Now, also, another thing, next in order, let him stand here, and that next in order of time shall be called a buffalo. So that, verily, is just the number of [game animals] which are large in size. As soon, verily, as man-beings shall dwell here, those, verily, shall be the names of the different animals; when the man-beings dwell [here], then they shall give names to all the other animals."

So, verily, now, he, the youth, said: "I desire that there shall be a hollow here [in the ground], and that it shall be full of oil." Verily, it thus came to pass. Now, moreover, he said: "Hither let him [anthropic], the buffalo, come." In just a short time it then stood there. Now he said: "Therein do thou plunge thyself." Thus, truly, did it come to pass. On the farther side it landed from the oil pool, having become as fat as it is possible for it to be. So now again he

1	o'iä'-kho'	ne'wä'	ne'kho'	děⁿgä'dä't,	ne"	ne"	ne'wä'	ne"
	it and other	next in order	here	it will stand up,	that	the	next in order	the
2	nia'gwai'	ěⁿgāiasō'oñg	ne"	na'e'.	O'něⁿ'	o'iä'	kho'	ne'wä'
	bear	it will be called	the	verily.	Now	it other	and	next in order
3	ne'kho'	ne"	děⁿhä'dä't,	ne"	ne'wä'	de'giiä'goⁿ'	ěⁿgāiasō'oñg	
	here	the	he (m.) will stand up,	that	next in order	buffalo	it will be named.	
4	Da',·	ne"	na'e'	ne"ho'	niwěñ'nandī'	ne'	gä'niō'	ne"
	So,	that	verily	there	so many they are in number	the	it game	the
5	wadigo'waněⁿ's.	Ganio"	na'e'	ěⁿienaⁿge'g	ne'kho'	ne"	oñ'gwe',	
	they (z.) are large ones.	So soon as	verily	they will dwell	here	the	man-being,	
6	da',	ne"	na'e'	ěⁿwadiiä'shoñ';	ne"	no'něⁿ'	ěⁿadinaⁿ'geg	ne"
	so,	that	verily	they (z.) will be named severally;	that	the time	they (m.) will be dwelling	the
7	oñ'gwe'	o'něⁿ'	gagwe'goⁿ'	ěⁿadi'señ'noⁿ'	ne"	hä'deganio"dage' "		
	man-being	time now	it all	they (m.) them names will give	the	every it animal in number (is)."		
8	Da,'	o'něⁿ'	na'e'shoñ'	ne"ho'	o'něⁿ'	waēñ"	ne"	haksa'-
	So,	now	verily just	there	now	he it said	the	he
9	dase"ä':	"Dewagadoěñdjoñ'nī'	ne'kho'	dāio'dädä'gwěñ'oñg,	ne"			
	youth:	"It it causes me to desire	here	it hollow place should be,	that			
10	ne"	ō'noⁿ'	ne"ho·	ěⁿganaⁿhoñ'g."	Ne"'ho'	do'gěⁿs	naⁿ'a'wěⁿ'.	
	the	it oil	there	it will be full of it."	Thus	it is true	so it came to pass.	
11	O'něⁿ'	dī'q	waēñ":	"Ga'o'	it'het	ne"	degiiä'goⁿ'."	Dä'djiä'-
	Now	moreover	he it said:	"Hither	let him (anthr.) come	the	buffalo."	In a short time just
12	shoñ"	o'něⁿ'	ne"ho'	o'tgä'dä't.	O'něⁿ'	waēñ"·	"Ne"'ho'	
		now	there	it stood up.	Now	he it said ·	"There	
13	ho'sade"sgo'."	Ne"'ho'	do'gěⁿs	naⁿ'a'wěⁿ'.	Ho'gwä'	ho'wade'-		
	thither do thou plunge thyself."	Thus	it is true	so it came to pass.	That side	thither it		
14	sgo'go'	he"	niiogwe'nioñ'	o'sěñ".	Da',	o'něⁿ'	a'e'	waēñ":
	landed	where	so it is possible	it fat (is).	So,	now	again	he it said:

said: "Hither let him [anthropic] come next in order of time, the bear." In a short time now the bear stood there. Moreover, he now said again: "Therein do thou, next in order, plunge thyself into that oil." Thus, truly, did it come to pass. On the farther side it landed from the oil pool, having become as fat as it is possible for it to be. So now he said: "What is it thou wilt do, and in what manner, to aid [human] man-beings?" "This, seemingly, is all; I shall just flee from him," it said. So now he loaded it by inserting meat into its legs. And now, verily, its legs are very large. So now he said: "Let the deer next in order stand here." As soon as it stood there, he said: "There into that oil thou shalt plunge thyself." Now of course he [anthropic] cast his body therein, and landed from the oil pool on the other side, and it [zoic] was as fat as it was possible for it to be. So now he said: "With what and in what manner wilt thou aid the [human]

"Ga'o'	it'het	ne"	ne'wă'	ne⁽ⁱ	nia'gwai' "	Dă'djiă'shoñ⁽'	
"Hither	let him come	that	next in turn	the	bear."	In a short time just	1
o'něⁿ⁽	ne"'ho⁽	o'tga'dă't	ne"	nia'gwai'.	O'něⁿ⁽	di'q a'e'	
now	there	it stood itself	the	bear.	Now	moreover again	2
waěñ"·	"Ne"'ho⁽	i's	ne'wă'	ho'sade"'sgo⁽	bi'gěñ⁽	o'noⁿ'ge⁽."	
he it said·	"There	thou	next in turn	thither do thou plunge thyself	this it is	it oil in."	3
Ne"'ho⁽	do'gěⁿs	naⁿ'a'wěⁿ⁽		Ho'gwā⁽	ho'wade'sgo'go'	he"	
Thus	it is true	so it came to pass.		That side	thither it landed	where	4
niiogwe'nióñ⁽	o'sěñ".	Da',	o'něⁿ⁽	waěñ"·	"Ā'	naⁿ'o"těⁿ'ěñ⁽	
so it is possible	it fat (is).	So,	now	he it said;	"What	so it is kind of thing	5
ni's	něⁿ'cie"	ne"	ěⁿ'sheiă"dăge'"hă'	ne"	oñ'gwe⁽?"	"Ne"	
the thou	so wilt thou do it	the	thou them wilt aid	the	human beings?"	"That	6
gwā"	ne"	i"	ěⁿgade"'go',"	o'gěⁿ'.	Da',	o'něⁿ⁽	waoñdäni-	
seemingly	the	I	I will flee,"	it (z.) it said.	So,	now	he it inserted	7
oñ'soñ"	ne"	o'wā"	ne"	ga'si'năgoñ⁽	O'něⁿ⁽	na'e⁽	dea"'sinō-	
severally	the	it meat	the	its leg in.	Now	verily	his legs are	8
waněⁿs	Da',	o'něⁿ⁽	waěñ":	"Neo'gěⁿ"	ne'wă'	ne'kho⁽	
large.	So,	now	he it said:	"Deer	next in turn	here	9
děⁿga'dă't.	Ganio"	ne"'ho⁽	o'tga'dă't	o'něⁿ⁽	waěñ":	"Ne"'ho⁽	
he shall stand."	So soon as	there	it itself stood	now	he it said:	"There	10
hěⁿ'sade's'go⁽	bi'gěñ⁽	o'noⁿ'ge⁽."	O'něⁿ⁽	wai'i⁽	ne"'ho⁽	
thou wilt plunge thyself	this it is	it oil in."	Now	of course	there	11
waādiă'do"'iak	ho'gwā⁽-kho⁽	waā'do'go',	ne"-kho⁽	ne"	
he his body cast,	that side and	he came up,	that and	the	12
he"	niiogwe'nióñ⁽	o'sěñ".	Da',	o'něⁿ⁽	waěñ":	"Ā'	naⁿ'o⁽	
where	so it is possible	it fat (is).	So,	now	he it said:	"What	such kind	13
těⁿ"'ěñ⁽	ne"	i's	něⁿ"'cie⁽	ne"	ěⁿ'sheiă"dage'"hă'	ne"	oñ'gwe⁽?"	
of thing	the	thou	so thou wilt do it	the	thou them wilt aid	the	human beings?"	14

man-beings?" "As for me, I shall not flee from him," it said. He said: "With what, and in what manner, moreover, wilt thou just do it?" "I will just bite them repeatedly," it replied. So now he, the youth, said: "Thus, just so, and only so, shall it be with thee," and now, moreover, he removed severally its upper teeth. Then he said: "Now the bodies of all those things which have horns, the buffalo, and the elk, etc., inherit the effect of this change." That is the reason that they [anthropic] have no upper teeth. All these several small things, the raccoon, woodchuck [or badger], porcupine, and also the skunk, all cast their bodies therein; therein they [zoic] plunged themselves. So only that is the number of those who were received. So next in order are those (z.) who were not accepted. I say that these, the Fisher, the Otter, and the Mink, and the Weasel [were

1	"Ne" That	ne" the	i' I	thĕⁿ"ĕnⁿ not it is	thagade"go'," I should flee,"	o'gĕⁿ". it said.	Waĕñ": He said:	"A' "What
2	naⁿ·o·tĕⁿ"ĕñⁿ such kind of thing		dï'q-shoñⁿ more- only over	nĕⁿ"cie'?" so thou wilt do it?"	"Ĕⁿkhegai'-shoñⁿ," "I them will bite only,"			o'gĕⁿ" it it said.
3	Da', So,	o'nĕⁿⁿ now	waĕñ" he it said	ne" the	haksa'dase"ä': he youth:	"Nĕñ'dă' "This	gwa"-shoñⁿ seem- ingly just	
4	ne" the	i's thou	nĕⁿio'dĕñ'oñg," so it shall continue to be,"	o'nĕⁿⁿ now	dï'q more- over	waono'djodagwā'oñ' he its teeth removed plurally		ne" the
5	he'tgĕñ'-gwā' upper side.	Oⁿnĕⁿⁿ Now		waĕñ"· he it said:	"Ne" "The		gagwe'goⁿⁿ it all	o'nĕⁿⁿ now
6	wā'odiiā'dadiio'wäs their (z.) bodies shared the change		ne" the	degiiā"goⁿ, buffalo,		kho" and	ne" the	djonaĕⁿ"dă', elk,
7	kho" and	ne" the (ones)	deiodinoⁿ"geoñt." they (z.) have horns."		Ne" That	gaii'oñ'nĭ' it causes the matter	thĕⁿ"ĕnⁿ not it is	deadi they (m.)
8	noⁿⁿ"djot have teeth	ne" the	he'tgĕñ"-gwā'. upper side.		Gagwe'goⁿⁿ It all	nĕñ'gĕñⁿ this it is	ne" the	niĕñna' so they (z.) small are
9	să'-shoñⁿoⁿ, severally,	ne" that	ne" the	djo'ä'gă', raccoon,	the"dooⁿ, woodchuck (badger?),	ga'he"dă', porcupine,		ne"kho' that and
10	ne" the	se'noñⁿ, skunk,	ne" that	gagwe'goⁿⁿ it all	ne""ho' thus		o'wĕñnadiä'do"iak they (z.) cast their bodies'	
11	ne""ho' there		o'wĕñnade's'gok. they (z.) plunged.	Da', So,	ne""ho'-shoñⁿ thus only	ni'ioⁿ· so they many (are)	ne" that	ne" the
12	hoñwañdi'gwĕⁿⁿ. they (m.) were accepted.							
13	Da', So,	ne' that	ne'wă' next in order	ne" the	thĕⁿ"ĕnⁿ not	deawañdi'gwĕⁿⁿ: they were accepted:	Ne" That (it is)	ne" the
14	sgaiaⁿna"ne'gĕⁿⁿ, fisher,		ne" the	odawĕñ'doⁿ, otter,	kho" and	ne" the	djio'dä'gă', mink,	kho" and

the ones]. So that was the number of those who were excluded, [being set] aside, and who assembled there near by. So the Mink now cast his body into the oil. As soon as he came up out of it the youth seized him there, and he held him up, and he stripped his body through his hands, and that is the reason that his body did become somewhat longer. Now, verily, again it thus came to pass. Their bodies shared the change [into the character they now have], namely, those of the Fisher, and the Otter, and the Mink, and the Weasel. And this is the number of those [zoic] whose bodies next shared this transformation there—the Wolf, and the Panther, and the Fox. All these were excluded, being set aside.

So now the two male children were in the habit of going away. Day after day they two went to a great distance; there far away they two were in the habit of setting traps. So then day after day they two

ne‘'	hanoñ'got.	Da',	ne"‘ho‘	niwĕñnâñdī·'	wak'ä·'	wa'odiis,	
the	weasel.	So,	thus	so many they (are) in number	aside	they were excluded,	1
nĕ"‘ho·	wak'ä·'	waodiiä'däieī·'.		Da',	o'nĕⁿ·	ne‘'	djio'dä'gä·
there	aside	they (z.) assembled.		So,	now	the	mink
							2
ne"‘ho·	waädiä'do"iak		ne‘'	o'noⁿ'ge‘.	Ganio"-shoñ‘	daä'do'go'	
there	he cast his body		the	it oil in.	So soon as just	he landed therefrom	3
o'nĕⁿ·	ne‘'	haksa'dase"ä‘		ne"‘ho‘	waäie'naⁿ·,	kho‘'	ne‘'
now	the	he youth		there	he it caught,	and	the
							4
he·tgĕⁿ·'	waä'dat,	kho‘'	ne‘'	waä·'djiiu'äk,	ne"	ne‘'	gail·-
up high	he it held,	and	the	he stripped it through his hands,	that	the	it makes
							5
oñ'nī‘	gaiñ'gwä‘	nä·gäiä'des'he·t.		O'nĕⁿ·	na'e‘	a'e‘	ne"‘ho·
matter	somewhat	so its body became long.		Now	verily	again	there
							6
naⁿ·a'wĕⁿ·.	Wä·'odiiä'dadiio'äs		nĕñ'gĕñ‘	sgäianane'gĕⁿ·,	kho‘'	ne‘'	
so it came to pass.	Their bodies shared the change		this it is	fisher (marten),	and	the	7
odawĕñ'doⁿ·,	kho‘'	ne‘'	djio·'dä'gä·,	kho·'	ne‘'	hanoñ'got;	da'.
otter,	and	the	mink,	and	the	weasel;	so.
							8
ne"‘ho·	niwĕñnâñdī·'	he·'	wa·'odiiä'dadiio'äs.	Ne"	ne'wä·	ne‘'	
there (thus)	so many they (z.) are in number	where	their (z.) bodies shared the change.	That	next in order	the	9
othäioñ'nī·,	kho‘'	ne‘'	hĕñ'es,	ne‘'	kho‘'	ne‘'	noⁿ·gwat'gwä·,
wolf,	and	the	panther (longtail),	that	and	the	fox.
							10
gagwe'goⁿ·	wak'ä·'	wa'odi'is.					
it all	aside	they were excluded.					11
Da'.	o'nĕⁿ·	ne‘'	deiksa·"ä·	o'nĕⁿ·	gĕñ's	ia·dĕñ'dioⁿs.	O·hĕⁿ·-
So,	now	the	they (m.) two children	now	customarily	they (m.) two were in the habit of going away,	Day after
							12
cioñ'nioⁿ‘	hoūwe'-gwä·	henēt'hä·;	we'ēⁿ·	ne"	ne‘'	hī'eo'dä·ne's	
day plurally	far direction	they (m.) two go habitually;	far	that	the	they (m.) two go to set traps,	13

were in the habit of going away. So for some time now they [masc. anthropic] who severally had otgon*a* natures, and they also whose bodies were otgon in nature, hated them [the two boys]. Now, of course, they two, verily, in going away, were in the habit of going together. So that [I say], moreover, one day the elder one said: "Thou alone, for the time being, go thither. Thou alone next in time shalt view our several set traps." So moreover [I say], that truly it did thus come to pass. As soon now as he was far away they [masc. anthropic] whose bodies are otgon by nature killed him there. So now he, the elder one, became aware that they had killed his younger brother. So now he began to cry. And [I say] that when it made him weep the most, when he said in his crying, "ĕñ‛, ĕñ‛‛, 'ĕñ‛‛, 'ĕñ‛‛," then there were noises made in several places in the sky that is present. So now they [mase. anthr.] who are severally

1	Da', So,	o'nĕⁿ‛ now	o‛hĕⁿ‛cioñ'nioⁿ‛ day after day plurally	ia‛dĕñ'dioⁿs. they (m.) two went away habitually	Da', So,	gaiñ'gwā‛ somewhat
2	na‛ioñni'she‛t so long it lasted	o'nĕⁿ‛ now	hoñwadi‛swā'aiⁿs they (m.) them hated	ne‛' the	hoñnoñtgoⁿ‛shoñ''oⁿ‛ they (m.) are otgon*a* plurally	
3	ne'' that	ne‛' the	hoñnoñdiā‛dat'goⁿ‛s. their (m.) bodies are otgon plurally	O'nĕⁿ‛ Now	he‛' where	ia‛dĕñ'dioⁿs diia- they (m.) go away con- habitually
4	wĕⁿ''oⁿ‛ tinually	na'e‛ verily	gĕñ's custom- arily	i‛ne's. they (m.) two go together customarily.	Da', So,	ne'' that	dĭ'q more- over	ne‛' the	swĕñni's‛hä't one it day is
5	o'nĕⁿ‛ now	ne'' that	waĕñ'' he it said	ne‛' the	hagowa'nĕⁿ‛: he large one:	"I's-shoñ‛ "Thou	ia'e‛ only	ne''‛ho‛ for the time being	there
6	hoñ''set. thither do thou go.	Soñ‛hā‛ge'ă‛ Thou just alone (by thyself)	ne'wā' next in turn	ĕⁿ‛sekdoñ'ioⁿ thou wilt go to see them	ne‛' the	oñgni'eo‛doⁿ''." thou I have set traps."
7	Da', So,	ne'' that	dĭ'q more- over	do'gĕⁿs it is true	ne''‛ho‛ thus	iaⁿ'a'wĕⁿ‛. so it will come to pass.	Ganio'' So soon as	io'nĕⁿ‛ . the time
8	we'ĕⁿ‛ far	hē''s he is going about	o'nĕⁿ‛ now	ne''‛ho‛ there	waoñwa'nio' they (m.) him killed	ne‛' that	ne‛' the	hoñ their (m.)
9	noñdiā‛dat'goⁿ‛s. bodies are otgon plurally.	Da', So,	o'nĕⁿ‛ now	waānināⁿdo'g he (m.) it noticed	ne‛' the	hagowa'nĕⁿ‛ he large one is
10	ne‛' the	hoñwa'nio' they (m.) him killed	ne‛' the	ho‛gĕñ'' he his younger brother is.	Da', So,	o'nĕⁿ‛ now	o‛tha‛sĕñt'ho‛. he wept.	Ne'' That
11	ne‛' the	no'nĕⁿ‛. when (the now)	do'gĕⁿs it is true	waode‛hăsdoñ's, it used great strength on him,	ne‛' that	io'nĕⁿ‛ when (the now)	o'gĕⁿ'' it it said	ne‛' the
12	hăsdā‛‛hă‛, he is weeping,	ne'' that	ne‛' the	"ĕñ‛', "henh,	'ĕñ‛', henh,	'ĕñ‛', henh,	'ĕñ‛'," henh,"	o'nĕⁿ‛ now
13	wa'otgaiia‛'soñ' it began to give out sounds	he‛' where	gä'oñ‛hiăde'. it sky is present.	Da', So,	o'nĕⁿ‛ now	ne‛' the	hoñnoñtgoⁿ‛- they (m.) are otgon

a Otgon signifies malefic. It denotes specifically the evil or destructive use of orenda, or magic power.

ŏtgoⁱ, and also they [zoic] whose bodies are severally otgoⁱ, now, verily, became alarmed. Now, moreover, they said: "In just a short time only, we believe, the sky will fall, perhaps, as soon, we think, as he weeps much; it is preferable that he, his younger brother, shall return; nothing else [will stop it]." So now of course the youth became ashamed because such a large number of persons severally became aware that he was weeping. So now verily he did close up his lodge, all places therein where there were openings [crevices]. So now just after he had completed his task of closing up the openings, in just a short time, now thence, from the outside, Flint spoke, saying: "Oh, elder brother, now I have returned." So now he the elder one, who was shut up indoors, said: "It can not be that thou shouldst come in. Thou shalt just depart, thou thyself. Thou shalt take the lead on the path whereon went the mother of us two. There

shoñ'ʼoⁿ·,	ne''	kho·	ne·' onañdiă·datgoⁿˑshoñ''oⁿⁱ,	o'nĕⁿ·	na'e·	1
plurally,	that	and	the their (z.) bodies are plurally otgon,	now	verily	
wäˑo'noⁿˑdioⁿˑk.	O'nĕⁿ·	di'q	waĕñ'nī:	"Hăˑdjigwăs'-shoñ·		2
they (z.) began to fear.	Now	moreover	they it said:	"Just soon only		
ĕⁿdwä''sĕⁿ't,	gi'' ĕñ' ioñ'',	he·'	gä'oñˑhiăde· ganoⁿ ĕñ'	noⁿ''		3
it will drop down,	I think it may perhaps,	where	it sky is present so soon as it may be,	perhaps,		
we'so·	ĕⁿoñs'dăĕⁿˑ;	ne·'	sä''gwä·	ne·'	ĕⁿshadonˑhet'-shoñ·	ne·'	4
much	he will weep;	that	it is better (preferable)	the	he will again come to life	just the	
hoˑgĕñ''." Da',	o'nĕⁿˑ	wai'i·	ne·'	ne·' baksa·dase''ă·	waădeˑ'hĕⁿ·		5
he his younger brother is." So,	now	of course	that	the he is a youth	he became ashamed		
so''djīˑ	geñdioˑ'gowanĕñ·	o'nĕⁿ·	waĕññĕññinandogˑhoñ''		ne·'	6
because (too much)	it body of people large is	now	they became aware of it plurally		the	
băsdă'ˑhä·.	Da'.	o'nĕⁿⁱ	na'e·	waäˑho'doñ·	he·'	honoⁿˑso't,	7
he is weeping.	So,	now	verily	he it closed up	where	his it lodge stands,	
gagwe'goⁿ·	he'oñwe·	deioˑhăgwĕñde'nioⁿ. Da',		o'nĕⁿ·	wae·'		8
it all	the place where	it has openings plurally.		So,	now afterward		
shoñ·	waädiĕññoˑ''kdĕⁿ·	ne·'	waädjiodoññioñ'',	o'nĕⁿⁱ	dăˑ'djiă·'-shoñ·		9
just	he his task finished	the	he shut up the several openings,	now	soon after just		
o'nĕⁿⁱ	daä'snie't	ne·'	Othä'gwĕⁿ''dă·	ne·'	a'sde·ⁱ.	waĕñ''	10
now	thence he spoke	the	It Flint	the	out of doors,	he it said:	
"Hăˑ'djī''.	o'nĕⁿⁱ	sägioⁿ'' "	Da',	o'nĕⁿ· waĕñ''	ne·'	hagowa'nĕⁿ·	11
"My elder brother,	now	again I have returned."	So,	now he it said	the	he is large	
ne·'	ne·'	oñgie·'	bäˑ''noñt:	"Dä'a'oñ·	aoñdaˑ''cioⁿ.	Ĕⁿˑsaˑdĕñdī'-	12
that	the	indoors	he is contained:	"It can not be	thou shouldst enter here.	Thou shalt depart	
shoñ·	ne·'	i's.	Ne·'	ne·'	ĕⁿsathaˑoñ'dĕⁿ·	he'oñwe·	ieiagawe'noñⁱ	13
just	the	thou.	That	the	thou shalt take up the path	the place where	hence she has gone	
ne·'	ethinoˑ''ĕⁿ·-geñ'oñ·.	Ne·''hoˑ	i's-khoⁱ	ĕⁿcianoñ'dăk.	Ne·'	ne·'	14
the	she our mother it was.	There	thou and	thy track shall be present.	That	the	

thou too shalt print thy tracks. I say that thou shalt trail the tracks of her who was our mother. Moreover, not far hence, there thou shalt seat thyself. So there now thou shalt observe the kind of life that customarily the human man-beings will live who will dwell on the earth. So now there, moreover, the path will divide itself where thou wilt abide. One of the ways will lead thither to the place where is the abode of His-word-is-master,[a] and the other will lead to the place where abides He-dwells-in-caves.[b] And also thou wilt have servants, they-[masc.]-dwell-in-caves. So that, moreover [I say], thou shalt take this thing-to-blow, this flute, and that thou shalt constantly continue to blow it. Just as soon, customarily, as one's breath ends, one shall hear customarily from what direction speaks the flute.

Sometime afterward the youth now began to wonder, soliloquizing: "What is, perhaps, verily, in great measure, the reason that my grandmother does not eat wild potatoes?" Now, verily, he asked her,

ěⁿ'sheianěñ'oñ'	ne''	ethino''ěⁿ'-gěñ'oñ'.	Thěⁿ''ěⁿ'	dǐ'q	de'we'ěⁿ'	
1 thou shalt follow the path	the	she our mother it was.	Not it is	more-over	far (it is)	
ne''ho'	ěⁿ'sa'dieñ.	Da',	ne''ho'	o'něⁿ'	ěⁿ'satgū'ioñ	he''
2 there	thou shalt sit down.	So,	there	now	thou shalt watch	where
niio''děn	gěñ's	ne''	ioěñdjä''ge'	ěⁿiagon''heg	ne''	oñ'gwe'.
3 such it is in kind	custom-arily	the	it earth on	one shall be living	the	human beings.
Da',	ne''	dǐ'q	ne''ho'	děⁿwathä'ho'gěñ'	he'oñwe'	ěⁿ'si'-
4 So,	that	more-over	there	it path will divide into two	the place where	thou
dioñ'dǎk.	Ne''	ne''	sga't	Hawěñniio''ge'-gwā'	hěⁿiotha'hino'oñg,	
5 shalt continue to abide.	That	the	one it is	He Master at	direction thither it path shall lead.	
kho''	ne''	sga't	Hanisheonoⁿ''ge'-gwā'	hěⁿiotha'hino'oñg.	Ne''-	
6 and	the	one it is	He Cave-dweller at	direction thither it path shall lead.	That	
kho''	ne''	ěⁿsa'hǎ'shāieñ'dǎk	ne''	hadinishe'onoⁿ.	Da',	ne''
7 and	the	thou shalt have servants	the	they (m.) are cave-dwellers.	So,	that
dǐ'q	ne''	něñ'gěñ'	hěⁿ'shā'	něñ'gěñ'	ne''	ieo'dawās'thä',	ne''-
8 more-over	the	this it is	thou shalt take it	this it is	the	one uses it to blow,	that
kho'	ne''	diiawěⁿ''oⁿ'	ěⁿseño'dǎdō'oñg.	Ganio''-shoñ'	gěñ's	
9 and	the	continually	thou shalt keep on blowing it.	So soon as	just	custom-arily
ěⁿioñdoñi'swe''děⁿ'	o'něⁿ'	kho''	gěñ's	ěⁿiagothoñ'deg	he'oñwe'	
10 one's breath becomes exhausted (=dies)	now	and	custom-arily	one it shall hear	the place where	
diio'thä'	ne''	ieo'dawas'thä'.				
11 there it is speaking	the	one uses it to blow.				
Gaiñ'gwā'	nǎ'ioñnis'he't	o'něⁿ'	waodianoñ'the's,	ne''	ne''	
12 Somewhat	so long it lasted	now	he wondered at it,	a (it is)	the	
hě'he':	"Ā',	noñ''	na'e'	gō'wā'	de''es	ne''	oněñnoⁿ''dǎ'	ne''
13 he it thinks:	"What,	per-haps,	verily	great it is	not she it eats	the	it wild potato	the

---

[a] This is the name of the God of the Christians. [b] This is the name of the devil of the Christians.

saying: "Oh, grandmother, what is it, verily, and why dost thou not in great measure eat wild potatoes?" "I customarily, all alone, by myself eat food," she said; "I eat it [food], as a matter of fact." Now he mused, "Now, verily, I will watch her in the night, now just soon to be." So now he made an opening in his robe. Now, verily, he laid himself down, pretending to be asleep. Thence, nevertheless, he was looking, out of the place where he had made a hole in his robe. Now, moreover, he was looking out of the place where he had made an opening in the robe, and he was watching the place where his grandmother abode customarily. So now, she, the Ancient-bodied, went out. Now, moreover, she looked in the direction of the sunrising. Now the Star, the Day-bringer, was risen. Now she, the Ancient-bodied, said: "Now of course, so it is, I will remove my pot sitting [over the fire]." So now truly she removed the pot

aksot'.	O'nĕⁿ·	na'e·	o·shago·oñdoñ'.	Waeñ'·	"Aksot'.	ā'
my grand-mother?	Now	verily	he her questioned.	He it said:	"My grand-mother,	what,
noñ''	na'e·	gō'wā·	ne·'	i's	de''ses	ne·'	onĕñno'''dā'?"
perhaps,	verily	great it is	the	thou	not thou it eatest	the	it wild potato?"
"I'-shoñ·	gĕñ's,	agoñ·hoⁿ·ge'ā·	o'gadekhoñ'nī',"			wā'a'gĕⁿ·.
"I only	customarily,	I am wholly alone	I my food eat,"			she it said,
"i'ges	ne·''ho·.	O'nĕⁿ·	wā'e:	"O'nĕⁿ·	na'e·	ĕⁿkheiatgā'ioñ'.
"I it eat habitually	as matter of fact."	Now,	he resolved:	"Now,	verily,	I her will watch,
ne·'	ne·'	ha·djigwās'	ĕⁿio''gā·.	Da'.	o'nĕⁿ·	waogaiiĕñ'dĕⁿ·	ne·'
that it is	the	just soon now	it will be night."	So,	now	he it hole in it made	the
ha·gwās'thā·.	O'nĕⁿ·	na'e·	waadiās'hĕñ',	iā'geⁿ'oⁿ·,	hodā''oⁿ·
he it to wrap himself uses.	Now	verily	he lays himself down,	pretending,	he is asleep.
Ne·'ho·,	sĕⁿ''ĕⁿ·	nigĕⁿ''	dethaga'ne·	he'oñwe·	ne·'	thaogai'ieñt.
There,	nevertheless	so it is (however)	thence he is looking	the place where	the	there he it hole in it made.
O'nĕⁿ·	dī'q	na'e·	ne·'	haiās'hĕñ	ne·''ho·	o'nĕⁿ·	dethaga'ne'
Now	moreover	verily	the	he lay supine	there	now	thence he was looking
he'oñwe·	thaogai'ieñt	ne·'	i'ios,	o'nĕⁿ·	ne·''ho·	deagā'ne'
the place where	he has it hole in it made	the	robe,	now	there	his eyes were fixed on it
he'oñwe·	ie''dioⁿ·	ne·'	ho·sot'.	Da'.	o'nĕⁿ·	wā'eiā'gĕⁿ·t	ne·'
the place where	she was seated	the	his grandmother.	So,	now	she went out	the
legĕⁿ·'tci·	O'nĕ·	dī'q	wā·oñtgat'ho·	ne·'	tgāā·gwitgĕⁿ·'s'-gwā·.
She Ancient One.	Now,	moreover,	she looked	the	thence it luminary comes up direction
O'nĕⁿ·	diioā·gwitgĕⁿ·'oⁿ·	ne·'	Tgĕñdĕñwit'hā·	(Gadjī·soⁿ·'dā'.
Now	there it planet is risen	the	Thence it brings day	It Star (is).
O'nĕⁿ·	ne·'	legĕⁿ·'tci·	wā'a'gĕⁿ·:	"O'nĕⁿ·	wai'i·	nigĕⁿ·''
Now	the	She, Ancient One	she it said·	"Now,	of course	so it is
ĕⁿgnaⁿ·djodā'go·	ne·'	agnaⁿ·djot.''	Da',	o'nĕⁿ·	do'gĕⁿs
I pot will remove	the	I have set up the pot (on the fire).''	So,	now	truly,

[from the fire] and also put the wild potatoes in a bowl of bark, and there was just one bowlful. So now, next in order, she rummaged among her belongings in a bag which she pulled out, and now, verily, she there took out corn. So now she parched it for herself. Now, moreover, it popped. There was quite a pile of the popped corn. Now, verily, she took out a mortar of small size. Moreover, she struck repeated blows on the mortar, and the mortar grew in size, and it grew to a size that was just right. Now she took out the upper mortar[a] [pestle] from her bag. Now again she struck it repeated blows and it, too, increased in size. So now she pounded the corn, making meal. So now again she searched in her bag. She took thence again a small pot, and she, too, again did in like manner, striking repeated blows upon it, and it, too, increased in size. Now

1	wa'enaⁿ'djodā'go' she pot removed	ne" kho' that and	ne" the	gadjiĕⁿ"'ge‘ it bowl in	wā'e'ĕⁿ' she it placed	ne" the	oñeñ- it
2	noⁿ''dā', sgaksat'-shoñ‘ potatoes, one it dish only	o'wā'doⁿ'. it became.	Da', So,	o'nĕⁿ' now	ga'oñ‘hoⁿ' she herself	ne'wā' next in turn		
3	o'diagoda‘noⁿ''dai‘ she rummaged her belongings	ne" that	ne" the	gaiā'' it bag	wā'oñdieñ'tho'. she it pulled forth,	o'nĕⁿ' now		
4	na'e‘ verily	ne"‘ho‘ there	wā'eda''go' she it took out of	ne" the	oñeñ'oⁿ'. it corn.	Da'. So,	o'ñĕⁿ' now	
5	wā''oñdĕⁿ'soñ'. she parched it for herself.	O'nĕⁿ' Now	dī'q moreover	o'wa‘dādoñ'go'. it popped (burst).	O'nĕⁿ' Now			
6	gaiñ'gwā‘ somewhat	niio‘so'djes. so it pile is high.	O'nĕⁿ' Now	na'e‘ verily,	a'e' once more	wā'eda''go' she it took out	ne" the	
7	niwā''ā‘ so it small in size is	ne" the	ga'niga''dā'. it mortar.	O'nĕⁿ' Now	dī'q moreover	ne"‘ho‘ there	wā'eiĕⁿ''da'noñ', she it struck repeatedly,	
8	ne" ne" that the	ga'niga''dā' it mortar	o'wado'diāk, it grew,	ho'gowa''he‘t, it became larger, in size	agwa's very	ne‘ho"tcī‘ just right (exactly)		
9	naⁿ''waⁿ"‘he‘t. so it became in size.	O'nĕⁿ' Now	he‘tgĕñ'oñ' upper (one)	ne" the	ga'niga''dā' it mortar	wā'eda''go' she it took out		
10	ne" the	goiā'goñ'. her bag in.	O'nĕⁿ' Now	a'e' once again	wā'eiĕⁿ'dā'noñ', she it struck repeatedly,	o'nĕⁿ' now	ha'e'gwa‘ also	
11	ho'gowa''he‘t. it became large in size.	Da', So,	o'nĕⁿ' now	ne"‘ho‘ there	wā'e'the‘t, she it pounded,	othe"'shā' it meal	wā'e‘ she it	
12	cioñ'nī'. made.	Da', So,	o'nĕⁿ' now	a'e' once more	nĕⁿ" this way	hwā''eie' she it did	ne" the	goiā'goñ‘. her bag in.
13	Ne"‘ho‘ There	wā'eda''go'· she it took out	a'e' once more	niwā''ā‘ so it is small in size	ganaⁿ''djā', it pot,	ne"-kho‘ that and	ne" the	
14	ne"‘ho‘ there	a'e' once more	naⁿ'e'ie' so she it did	wā'eiĕⁿ'dā'noñ', she it struck repeatedly,	ho'gowa''he‘t-kho‘ it became large and	a'e' once more.		

[a] This term goes back to the time when upper and lower grinder had the same name.

she there set up the pot, and also made mush therein. So, as soon as it was cooked she again rummaged in her bag. So now she took from it a bone, a beaver bone. Now again, verily, she scraped the bone, and she poured the bone-dust into the pot, and now, moreover, at once there floated oil on its surface. Now, of course, she took the pot from the fire. So now she ate the food. Verily, now, the youth went to sleep. Now early in the morning again [as usual] she, the Ancient-bodied, went away to dig wild potatoes. As soon as she disappeared as she went, then he went to the place where his grandmother customarily abode. Now, moreover, he began to rummage [among her belongings]. He took out an ear of corn which had only a few grains left fixed to it, there being, perhaps, only three and a half rows of grains left. So now he began to shell the corn; he shelled it all.

O'nĕⁿ·	ne"·ho·	wā'enaⁿdjaniioñ'dĕⁿ',	o'nĕⁿ·	nĕ"·ho·	wā'edjĭsgoñ'nĭ'-			1
Now	there	she it pot fastened up,	now	there	she mush made			
khoⁱ.	Da'.	ganio"	ho·gā'i·	o'nĕⁿ·	a'e·	wā'dienoⁿ·'dai"	nigĕⁿ"	2
and.	So,	so soon as	it was cooked	now	once more	she it rummaged	so it is	
ne·'	goïā'goñⁱ.	Da'.	o'nĕⁿ·	ne"·ho·	wā'eda'go·	o'nĕñ'iā·		3
the	her bag in.	So,	now	there	she took it out	it bone		
naⁿgaⁿniā"goⁿ	o·nĕñ'iā'.	O'nĕⁿ·	a'e·	na'e·	wā'e·gēt.	O'nĕⁿⁱ	ne"·ho⁴	4
beaver	it bone.	Now	once more	verily	she it scraped.	Now	there	
wā'ā'oñtho·	ne·'	o·doñniĕⁿ"'shā'.	o'nĕⁿ·	dī'q	iogoñdā'dic·	o'gā'nñ'.		5
she it poured	the	it scrapings.	now	moreover	it at once	it caused oil to float.		
O'nĕⁿⁱ	wai'i·	wā'enaⁿdjoda'go·	ne·'	ganaⁿdjo't.	Da',	o'nĕⁿ·		6
Now	of course	she it pot removed	the	it pot sets up.	So,	now		
wā'oñdekhoñ'nĭ'.	O'nĕⁿ·	na'e·	wao'dā·	ne·'	haksa·da·se"ā⁴.	Ne·'		7
she it food ate.	Now,	verily	he went to sleep	the	he youth	That		
no'nĕⁿ·	sede·'tciā·	o'nĕⁿ·	a'e·	wā'oⁿ·'dĕñdī·	ne·'	Iegĕⁿ·'teï·		8
the time	early in the morning	now	once more	she departed	the	She Ancient One		
wā'ĕñnĕñnoⁿ'dogwat'hā'.	Ganio'·shoñ·	ho·wa·'doⁿ·	he·'	hwā'ĕⁿ·				9
she wild potatoes went to dig.	So soon as just	thither it disappeared	where	she went onward				
o'nĕⁿⁱ	ne"·ho·	wā'e·	he'oñ'weⁱ	ioñdiĕñdāk'hwā'	ne·'	ho·sot'.		10
now	there	thither he went	the place where	she it uses to remain	the	his grandmother.		
O'nĕⁿ·	dī'q	waā·'sāwĕⁿ·	ne·'	o'thanoⁿ·'dai·.	O'nĕⁿ·			11
Now	moreover	he it began	the	he it rummaged.	Now			
waāda·"go·	ne·'	o'nis'dā·	doga·ā·'·shoñ	nidjonĕñ'ot,	'āsĕⁿⁱ'			12
he it look out	the	(it) ear of corn	a few	only	so many it corn-grains remain on it,	three		
gi"shĕⁿⁱ	nidjoaā'ge·	hā'deswa·sĕñ'noⁿⁱ.	Da',	o'nĕⁿⁱ	waā·'sāwĕⁿ·			13
probably,	so many it row is in number	just it is one-half.	So,	now	he it began			
wao'gĕñ·	ne·'	oñĕñ'oⁿ.	gagwe·'goⁿ·	waās"ā·t.	Da'.	o'nĕⁿ·		14
he it shelled	the	it corn,	it all	he it exhausted.	So,	now		

So now he parched it for himself. Now, moreover, it popped, bursting iteratively, there being quite a heap, quite a large amount of it. Again he rummaged. Again he there took out a mortar of small size and also an upper mortar [pestle]. So now he used this to strike that, and now, moreover, both increased in size. And now he poured the parched corn. So now he in the mortar pounded it, and now verily it became meal. Now again he searched in her bag, and he took therefrom a small pot, and now used something else to strike upon it blows; then it, too, increased in size. Now, verily, he there set up the pot [on the fire] and also put water in it. So now he therein poured all this meal. Now, of course, he made mush. So now again he searched in the bag of his grandmother, and therefrom he took a bone, and he put it therein, and the mush became abundant.

waādĕⁿ'soñ'.	O'nĕⁿ'	dī'q	o'wa'dădoñ'go',	gaiñ'gwā'	niio''sōdjä'	
1 he it parched for himself.	Now	moreover	it popped by bursting.	somewhat	so it pile is in size.	
ne"kho'	ne''	gaiñ'gwā'	nä'ioñ"he't.	O'nĕⁿ'	a'e'	o'thanoⁿ''dai'
2 that and	the	somewhat	so it amount became.	Now	once more	he it rummaged.
O'nĕⁿ'	a'e'	ne''ho'	waada''go'	ne''	ga'niga''dä'	niwä''ä' ne"kho'
3 Now	once more	there	he it took out	the	it mortar	so it size is small that and
ne''	he'tgĕñ'oñ'	ne''	ga'niga''dä'.	Da',	o'nĕⁿ'	ne'' waāiä''dăk
4 the	upper (one)	the	it mortar (pestle).	So,	now	that he it used
waāiĕⁿ'dä'noñ',	o'nĕⁿ'	dī'q	o'gowa''he't	dedjä'oⁿ'.	Da',	o'nĕⁿ
5 he it struck repeatedly,	now	moreover	it became large	both	So,	now
ne''ho'	waiauñ'tho'	ne''	oneñ'soⁿ''gwā'.	Da',	o'nĕⁿ'	ne''ho'
6 there	he it poured	the	it parched corn.	So,	now	there
waāt'he't,	o'nĕⁿ'	wai'i'	othe''shä'	o'wā'doⁿ'.	O'nĕⁿ'	dī'q a'e'
7 he it pounded,	now	of course	it meal	it became.	Now	moreover once more
waāk'doñ'	ne''	goiä'goñ',	o'nĕⁿ'	ne''ho'	waāda''go'	ne'' niwä''ä'
8 he it searched for	the	her bag in,	now	there	he it took out	the so it is small in size
gana'''djä',	o'nĕⁿ'	hä'gwis'dĕ"'	a'e'	o'iä'	waāiä''dăk	waāiĕⁿ'da'noñ',
9 it pot,	now	something	once more	it other	he it used	he it struck repeatedly.
o'nĕⁿ'	a'e'-kho'	ho'gowa''he't.	O'nĕⁿ'	na'e'	ne''ho'	waāna'''dja-
10 now	once more and	it became large.	Now	verily	there	he it pot
nioñ'dĕⁿ,	waä'hnegä'eñ'-kho'.	Da',	o'nĕⁿ'	ne''ho'	wäauñ'tho'	
11 hung up,	he placed water in it and.	So,	now	there	he it poured	
neñ'geñ'	ne''	othe's'hä'	gagwe'go'''.	O'nĕⁿ'	wai'i'	waādjīsgoñ'nī'
12 this it is	the	it meal	it all.	now	of course	he mush made.
Da',	o'nĕⁿ'	a'e'	wäe''sak	ne''	goiä'goñ'	ne'' ho''sot. Ne''ho'
13 So,	now	once more	he it looked for	the	her bag in	the his grandmother. There
waāda''go'	ne''	o'nĕñ'iä',	o'nĕⁿ'	ne''	ne''ho'	wä'o', odoⁿ'hoñ'doⁿ'-
14 he took it out	the	it bone,	now	that	there	he put it in it abundant became

"Ho‘ho‘,'' he kept chuckling. "It tastes good." Now soon thereafter his grandmother returned. She said: "Well, what manner of thing art thou doing?" "I have made mush," the youth said, "and it is pleasant, too. Do thou eat of it, so be it, oh, grandmother. There is an abundance of mush." So now she wept, saying: "Now, verily, thou hast killed me. As a matter of fact, that was all there was left for me." "It is not good," he said, "that thou dost begrudge it. I will get other corn and also bone."

So now the next day he made his preparations. When he finished his task, he said: "Now it is that I am going to depart." So now, verily, he departed. He arrived at the place where dwell man-beings. As soon as he arrived near the village he then made his preparations. I say that he made a deer out of his bow, and, next in order, a wolf

kho‘	o'wā'doⁿ·	ne‘'	odjīs'gwā'.	"Ho‘ho‘,''	"Oga"oⁿ·''	kho‘,	ha'-	1
and	it became	the	it mush.	"Aha!''	"It tastes good''	and,	he	
doⁿ‘.	O'nĕⁿ·	dā'djiā'-shoñ·	sāie'ioⁿ·	ne‘'	ho‘sot.	Wā'a'gĕⁿ·:	"Gwĕ'.	2
kept saying.	Now	soon after	just	again she returned	the	his grandmother.	She it said:	"Well.
Aⁿnaⁿ·'ot	ni‘sadie‘'hā'?		"Agedjīsgoñ'ni‘,''	waĕñ',	ne‘'	haksa‘-	3
What manner of thing	so thou art doing?		"I mush am making.''	he it said,	the	he	
dase‘'ā‘:	"Agwa's	awĕñdetgā'de‘-kho‘.	Sadekhoñ'nī‘,	nio‘'.	4
youth:	"Very	it is pleasant and.	Do thou eat,	so be it.	
aksot'.	Odoⁿ·'hoñ'doⁿ·	ne‘'	odjīs'gwā'.''	Da'.	o'nĕⁿ·	wā'oⁿs'daeⁿ·,	5
my grandmother.	It is abundant	the	it mush.''	So,	now	she wept,	
ne‘'	ne‘'	wā'a'gĕⁿ·:	"O'nĕⁿ·	na'e·	noñ‘'	o'sgi'io‘.	Ne‘'ho‘-shoñ‘'	6
that	the	she it said:	"Now	verily,	probably,	thou hast killed me.	So much just	
ne‘'ho·	niwagiĕñ'dāk‘'	"Wā.'	De'wi'io,''	waĕñ',	"Sa‘sĕⁿ·'se‘.	7
as matter of fact	so it I have had.''	"Oh.	It is not good,''	he it said,	"Thou dost begrudge it.	
Oiā‘'-shoñ·	i‘'	ĕⁿgie'gwā'	ne‘'	oneñ'oⁿ·	kho‘'	ne‘'	o'neñ'iā‘.''	8
It other just	I	I it will get	the	it corn	and	the	it bone.''	
Da',	no'nĕⁿ·	wā'o‘'hĕñ't	o'nĕⁿ·	waādecioñniā'noñ‘.	No'nĕⁿ·	9
So,	the time	it day became	now	he his preparations made.	The now	
waādiĕnno‘k'dĕⁿ·	o'nĕⁿ·	waĕñ':	"O'nĕⁿ·	nigĕⁿ·	ĕⁿga·'dĕñdī‘.''	10
he his task finished	now	he it said:	"Now	that it is	I will depart.''	
Da'.	o'nĕⁿ·	na'e·	waā·dĕñ'dī.	Ne‘'ho‘	waa'ioⁿ·	he'oñwe·,	11
So,	now	verily	he departed.	There	he arrived	the place where	
ienañ'ge·	ne‘'	oñ'gwe·.^a	Ganio‘'	ne‘'ho·	waā'ioⁿ·	ne‘'	12
they (indef.) dwell	the	man-being.	So soon as	there	he arrived	the	
ganoñdak‘'ā·	o'nĕⁿ·	ne‘'ho·	waādecioñnia'noñ‘.	Ne‘'	ne‘'	13
it village beside	now	there	he preparations made.	That	the	
ho‘ĕñ'nā‘	waāde‘cioñ'ni‘	ne‘'	ne'ogĕⁿ·.	o'nĕⁿ·	ne‘'	ne'wā·	ne‘'	14
his bow	he it made for himself	the	deer,	now	that	next in order	the	

^aSee footnote on page 141.

out of his arrow; he made these for himself. Now he said: "Whenever it be that ye two run through the village it will customarily be that one will be just on the point of overtaking the other." Next in order he himself made into an Ancient-bodied one. So now he went to the place where they [masc.], the man-beings, abode. So now, sometime after he had arrived there, then, verily, they gave him food, gave to the Ancient-bodied. During the time that he was eating they heard a wolf approach, barking. One would just think that it was pursuing something. So now they all went out of doors. They saw a wolf pursuing a deer which was approaching there, and saw that, moreover, it was about to seize it. So now all ran thither. So now he was alone, and the Ancient-bodied ate. As soon as they had all gone, he now thrust his body into the place where, severally, the

ho″no^{n.}	ne″	ne′wă·	thāioñ′nĭ‘	ne‘′	ne″	waāde‘cioñ′nĭ‘.	O′nĕ^{n‘}
1 his arrow	that	next in order	wolf	the	that	he it made for himself.	Now
ne″‘ho·	waĕñ″:	"Thō′‘hă‘	gĕñ′s	ĕⁿgoñwā′âñt	no′nĕ^{n‘}		ganoñda-
2 there	he it said:	"Nearly	customarily	one it will overtake	the time		it village
goñ′·′shoñ·	hĕⁿsnidăk′hē'."		Ne″	ne‘′		ne′wă·	ha′oñ·hwaⁿ
3 in along	thither ye two will run."		That	the		next in order	he himself
(ha′oñ‘hoⁿ″)	ne‘′	hagĕⁿ″‘tcĭ·	waādadoñ′nĭ‘.	Da′,	ne″‘ho‘		waā′ioⁿ″
4 he himself	the	he ancient one	he himself made.	So,	there		he arrived
he′oñwe‘	gano^{n‘}′sot	ne‘′	thĕñni″dioⁿ·	ne‘′	hĕñnoñ′gwe‘.		Da′,
5 the place where	it lodge stood	the	there they (m.) severally abode	the	they (m.) (are) man-beings.		So,
o′nĕ^{n‘}	gaiñ′gwā‘	nă′ioñ′nishe‘t	ne″‘ho‘	bo′io^{n‘}	o′nĕ^{n‘}		wai′i‘
6 now	somewhat	so long it lasted	there	he has arrived	now		of course
waoñwakhwā′noñt	(? waoñkhwā′noñt)			ne‘′	hagĕⁿ″‘tcĭ·.		Ne″
7 they (m.) him food gave	they (m.) him food gave			the	he ancient one.		That
nă′ioñ′nishe‘t	ne‘′	hodekhoñ′nĭ·	o′nĕ^{n‘}	hoñnoñthoñ′de·			dăga
8 so long it lasted	the	he is eating	now	they (m.) it heard			thence
ni′ne′	ne‘′	thāioñ′nĭ‘.	Āiĕñ″-shoñ·	ha′gwisdĕⁿ″	dăgăs′he·.		Da′,
9 it came barking	the	wolf.	One would just think	something	thence it it is pursuing.		So,
o′nĕ^{n‘}	gagwe′go^{n‘}	waādiia′gĕⁿ·t.		Waĕñnoñtgat′ho·	ne‘′		thāioñ′nĭ‘
10 now	it all	they (m.) went out.		They (m.) saw	the		wolf
dăgas′he′	ne‘′	ne′ogĕⁿ′,	o′nĕⁿ·	di′q	thō′‘hă·	agūie′nâⁿ″.	Da′,
11 thence it it pursued	the	deer	now	more-over	nearly	it it could seize.	So,
o′nĕⁿ·	gagwe′go^{n‘}	ne″‘ho‘	o‘thĕñnĕñ′ĕⁿ‘dat.		Da′,		o′nĕ^{n‘}
12 now	it all	there	they (m.) ran.		So,		now
haoñ‘hoⁿ″geā‘′-shoñ‘		hodekhoñ′ni	ne‘′	hagĕⁿ″‘tcĭ‘.			Ganio″
13 he (was) all alone	just	he is eating	the	he ancient one.			So soon as
wă′oñs″ă·t	o′nĕ^{n‘}	ne″‘ho‘	waādiă′do″iak	he′oñwe‘			gasdĕⁿ″säni
14 they themselves exhausted	now	there	he his body cast	the place where			it corn string hangs

strings of corn hung. Two strings of corn he took off, and now, moreover, he placed them on his shoulder and he went out at once. He was running far away when they noticed [what he had done], but, verily, they did not at all pursue him. Again he arrived at their lodge. So now he cast them down where his grandmother abode. "Here," he said: "Thou wilt do with this as seems good to thee. Thou mayest decide, perhaps, to plant some of it." When it was day, he said: "Well, I will go to kill a beaver." Now, moreover, he went to the place that his grandmother had pointed out, saying that such things would dwell there. So he arrived there, and then, also, he saw the place where the beavers had a lodge. Then he saw one standing there. He shot it there and killed it. So then he placed its body on his back by means of the forehead pack-strap and then, moreover, he departed for home. Some time afterward he arrived

ioñ'doⁿ.	Deiosdëⁿ'säge·	waäniioñdä'go',	o'nëⁿ·	dï'q	hanëⁿshä'ge·.	
severally.	Two it corn string in number	he them removed.	now	moreover	his shoulder on	1
wao'dä·,	o'nëⁿ·	dï'q	waäiagëⁿ·'däk.	We'ĕⁿ·	waädäk'he·	o'nëⁿ.
he them hung,	now	moreover	he went out at once.	Far	he was running away	now	2
waëñnëñni'naⁿdog.	thëⁿ'ëⁿ·	na'e·	kho·'	de'osthoñ·'	deoñwä'cioñ·	
they (m.) became aware of it,	not it is	verily	and	it is a little	they him pursued.	3
Hoñsaä'ioⁿ·	he·'	thodinoⁿ'sot'.	Da',	o'nëⁿ·	ne''·ho·	wao'dï·
There he again arrived	where	there their lodge stands.	So,	now	there	he it cast	4
he'oñwe·	ie''dioⁿ·	ne·'	ho·sot'.	"Gwä'."	waëñ'',	"ëⁿ·sëñnoⁿ'doñ·
the place where	she was seated	the	his grandmother.	"Here,"	he it said,	"thou thyself wilt please	5
ï's he·'	nëⁿ·sadie'ä't	nëñ'gëñ·.	Ëⁿ·sē',	gi''shëⁿ·,	·gie·'	gieñtwä't''
thou where	so thou it wilt use	this it is.	Thou wilt decide	it may be,	some	I it will plant."	6
No'nëⁿ·	wä'o'·hëñ't	o'nëⁿ·	waëñ'':	"Gwä·',	Ëⁿgiioshä''	ne·'
The now	it became day	now	he it said:	"Well,	I it will go	the to kill	7
naⁿgaⁿniä''goⁿ.''	O'nëⁿ·	dï'q	ne''·ho·	hwä'e·	he'oñwe·	tgëⁿ'·hoñde'
beaver."	Now	moreover	there	thither he went	the place where	there it river flows	8
ne·'	gaoñwaⁿñt'	ne·'	ho·so't.	ne·'	ne·'	ga'wëñ·	ne·'	ne''·ho·
the	she it pointed out	the	his grandmother	that	the	she it has said	the	there	9
ëⁿganoñ'gek	ne·'	na''ot.	Da'.	o'nëⁿ·	ne''·ho·	waä'ioⁿ·,	o'nëⁿ·-kho·,
it will be abundant	that	such kind of thing.	So,	now	there	he arrived,	now -and	10
waa'gëⁿ·	he'oñwe·	odinoⁿ'sot'	ne·'	naⁿgaⁿniä''goⁿ.	O'nëⁿ·	
he it saw	the place where	they (z.) have their lodge	the	beaver.	Now	11
waa'gëⁿ·	ne''·ho·	gä'ät.	O'nëⁿ·	ne''·ho·	waä''iak,	kho·'	ne·'
he it saw	there	it stood.	Now	there	he it shot,	and	the	12
waä'nio·	Da',	o'nëⁿ·	waädiä'tge·'dat,	kho·'	ne·'	o'nëⁿ·	dï'q
he it killed.	So,	now	he placed its body on his back by forehead band,	and	the	now	moreover	13
saä''dëñdï·.	Gaiñ'gwä·	nä'ioñ'nishe't	o'nëⁿ·	ne''·ho·	saä''ioⁿ·	
again he departed.	Somewhat	so long it lasted	now	there	again he arrived	14

at the place where their lodge stood. Thus, also, again did he do; there where his grandmother was sitting he cast it. "Here," he said "So be it," she, the Ancient-bodied, said.

So now out of doors they two skinned it. They two held its body in many places. So when they two were nearly through their task there was a pool of blood on the green hide. So then she, the Ancient-bodied, took up a handful of the blood and cast it on the loins of her grandson. "Ha'ha'," she, the Ancient-bodied, said, "now, verily, my grandson, thou becomest catamenial." "Fie upon it," said the youth, "it is not for us males to be so affected as a habit; but ye, ye females, shall be affected thus habitually every month." Now, again he took up a handful of clotted blood and cast it between the thighs of his grandmother, and now, he said: "Thou, of course, verily, hast

1	he'oñwe‘ the place where	thodinoⁿ'sot'. there their lodge stands.	Ne"'ho‘ There	kho" and	a'e' once more	naāⁿ'ie'; so he it did;	ne"'ho‘ there
2	he'oñwe‘ the place where	ieniu"'ciot she is sitting	ne'' the	ho'sot' his grandmother	ne"'ho‘ there	wao'dī'. he it threw.	"Gwă"," "Here,"
3	waēñ". he it said.	"Niiawĕⁿ"'hă'," "I am thankful,"	wă'a'gĕⁿ she it said	ne'' the	Eiä'dageⁿ"'tcī‘. She Ancient-bodied One.		
4	Da', So,	o'nĕⁿ' now	as'de‘ out of doors	ne"'ho‘ there .	waniiēñ"'se'. they (m.) it skinned.	Deniienawă"'khoⁿ They two one the the other aided	
5	ne'' the	gāiä'dä"'ge. its body on.	Da', So,	ne'' that	no'nĕⁿ the now	tho'hă‘ nearly	ĕⁿiadiĕñno"'kdĕⁿ they (m.) two it task will complete
6	ga'hne'gă' it liquid	ne'' the	gă'cio‘să"'ge‘ it green hide on	ne'' the	otgwĕⁿ"'să'. it blood.	Da', So,	o'nĕⁿ now	ne'' the
7	Eiä'dageⁿ"'tcī‘ She Ancient-bodied One	o'dioⁿ"tcagäk' she handful took up	ne'' the	otgwĕⁿ"'să', it blood,	kho" and	ne'' the	ne"'ho‘, there
8	wăago'dī' she it threw	ne'' the	hoa'să"'ge‘ his loins on	ne'' the	hoñwañ'dē'. her grandson.	"Ha‘ha'," "Alas,"	
9	wă'a'gĕⁿ she it said	ne'' the	legĕⁿ"'tcī'' She Ancient One:	"O'nĕⁿ' "Now,	wai'i‘ of course	wă'sa"'diawĕñt, thou hast the menses (=dost abstain)	
10	gwā'dē'." my grandson."	"Tcisnĕñ'," "Fie upon it,"	waēñ" he it said	ne'' the	haksa'dase"'ā‘. he youth.	"Thĕⁿ"ĕⁿ‘, "Not it is	
11	ɪ"'ā‘ we personally	ne'' the	agwadji'nă‘ we males	ne"'ho‘ thus	nāiawĕñ"'seg; so it will be happening;	i's ye	dĕⁿ"gwae'' though	ne'' the
12	sweoⁿ"-shoñ"'oⁿ‘ ye females	ne"'ho‘ thus	nĕⁿiawĕñ"'seg so it will be happening	ne'' the	swĕñni'dă'-shoñ' " each month just."		
13	O'nĕⁿ' Now	oñsaā‘tcagäk' again he it handful took up.	ne'' the	o'tgwā' it clotted blood	o'nĕⁿ' now	dī'q moreover	ne"'ho‘ there	wao'dī' he it cast
14	ne'' the	deieo'gĕñ‘ between her thighs	ne'' the	ho'sot', his grandmother,	o'nĕⁿ' now	dī'q moreover	na'e‘ verily	waēñ · he it said:	"I's "Thou

now become catamenial." So now, she, the Ancient-bodied, began to weep, and she said: "Moreover, customarily, for how long a period will it be this as an habitual thing?" Then the youth said: "[As many days] as there are spots on the fawn. So long, verily, shall be the time that it will continue to be this." Now again she began to weep, the Ancient-bodied. So now she said: "It is not possible for me to consent that it shall be thus." "How many, moreover, then, shall they be?" he said. "I would accept the number of stripes on the back of a chipmunk," she said. "So be it," said the youth. So then he said: "Customarily, four days shall a woman-being remain out of doors. Then, customarily, as soon as she has washed all her garments, she shall reenter the place where they, her ohwachira[a], abide."

wai′i·	na′e·	o′nĕⁿ·	o·sa·″dia·wĕñt."	Da′,	o′nĕⁿ·	o·dioⁿ·sĕⁿt′ho·	
of course	verily	now	thou hast thy menses."	So,	now	she wept	1
ne·″	Iegĕⁿ·″tcī·,	o′nĕⁿ·	dī′q	wā·a′gĕⁿ·:	"Gaiñ·"	dī′q	gĕñ′s	
the	She Ancient-bodied One.	now	more-over	she it said	"Where	more-over	customarily	2
he·″	nĕⁿioñ′nishe·t	ne·″	ne·″·ho·	nĕⁿio′dĕñ′oñg?"	O′nĕⁿ·	ne·″	
where	so long it will last	the	thus	so it will continue to be·"	Now	the	3
haksa·dase·″ā·	waĕñ″:	"Ne·″	ne·″	he·″	ni′ioñ·	ne·″	niiodia·″gwā·	
he youth	he it said:	"That	the	where	so many it is	the	so many it spots has	4
ne·″	djĭsda·thiĕñ′ā·.	Ne·″·ho·	na′e·	nĕⁿioñ′nishe·t	ne·″·ho·	gĕñ′s	
the	spotted fawn.	There	verily	so long it will last	thus	customarily	5
nĕⁿio′dĕñ′oñg."	O′nĕⁿ·	a′e·	o·dioⁿ·sĕⁿt′ho·	ne·″	Iegĕⁿ·″tcī·.	Da′,	
so it will continue to be."	Now	once more	she wept	the	She Ancient-bodied One.	So,	6
ne·″	ne·″	wā·a′gĕⁿ·:	"Dā·a′oⁿ·	ne·″	agi·wani′ät	ne·″	ne·″·ho·	
that	the	she it said:	"It is not possible	the	I it will assent to	the	thus	7
naia′wĕⁿ· "	"Do′,	dī′q	noñ·″?"	waĕñ″.	"Ne·″	dī′q	noñ·″	
so it should come to pass."	"How,	more-over	perhaps?"	he it said.	"That	more-over	perhaps	8
age′go·	ne·″	djo·ho·″gwais	he·″	ni′ioñ·	ne·″	oianoⁿ·″doⁿ·	ne·″	
I it would accept	the	chipmunk	where	so many it is	the	it is lined	the	9
ga′swe·noⁿ·″ge·″,"	wā·a′gĕⁿ·	"Nio′,"	waĕñ″	ne·″	haksa·dase·″ā·.	
its back on,"	she it said.	"So be it,"	he it said	the	he youth.	10
Da′,	ne·″	waĕñ″:	"Ge′i·	gĕñ′s	nĕⁿio′dā·	as′de·	gĕñ′s	ne·″·ho·	
So,	that	he it said:	"Four	customarily	so many it will be days	out of doors	customarily	there	11
ĕⁿie·dioñ′dāk.	O′nĕⁿ·	ganio·″	gĕñ′s	gagwe′go·	ĕⁿienoⁿ·″āe·″·hoñ·	
one will continue to be.	Now	so soon as	customarily	it all	one will wash them plurally	12
ne·″	go·cioñnias′hā·	o′nĕⁿ·	gĕñ′s	dĕⁿdie′ioⁿ·	he′oñwe·	
the	one's raiment	now	customarily	thence one will come indoors	the place where	13
hĕñni·″dioⁿ·	ne·″	ago·watci′ā·."	
they (m.) are abiding	the	her ohwachira."	

---

[a] See first note on page 255.

So some time afterward she, the Ancient-bodied, said repeatedly: "And there shall be mountains, seemingly, over the surface of the earth here present." And now, verily, it did this come to pass. "And, too, there shall be rivers on the surface of the earth," again she said. Now, of course, truly it did thus come to pass.

Now the youth said: "Now I think that thou and I should return home; that thou and I should go to that place which my mother has made ready for us; that there thou and I should remain forever." "So be it," she, the Ancient-bodied, said.

So then it was true that his grandmother and he departed. So then, verily, they two went up on high. So this is the end of the legend.

1	Da', So,	o'něⁿ· now	gaiñ'gwā· somewhat	nā'ioñ'nishe't so long it lasted	o'něⁿ· now	ne·' the	Eiä'dageⁿ·'tcī' She Ancient-bodied One
2	ioñ'doⁿ·: she kept saying:	"Ěⁿionoñdade'niong "There will be mountains standing,		gwā·' seemingly	kho·' and	he·' where	ioěñdjadā'die' " it earth is present."
3	O'něⁿ· Now	do'gěⁿs it is a fact	ne·''ho' thus	naⁿ'a'wěⁿ'. so it came to pass.	"Ne·''-kho' "That and	ne·' the	ěⁿgěⁿ'hoñ- it river will be
4	de'nioñg present plurally	he·' where	ioěñdjā'ge', it earth is present,"	wä'a'geⁿ'-kho' she it said and	a'e'. another time.	O'něⁿ· Now	wai'i' of course
5	ne·''ho' thus	do'gěⁿs it is a fact	ne·''ho' thus	naⁿ'a'wěⁿ' so it came to pass.			
6	O'něⁿ' Now	ne·' the	haksa'dase·''ä' he youth	waěñ·': he it said:	"O'něⁿ· "Now	ěñ·' I suppose	ne·'' the	i'' we
7	aesediä'děñ'dī'. thou and I should return home.	Ne·''ho' There	bae·'ne' thou and I should go	he'oñwe' the place where	diiagode'sa'oⁿ· there she is ready	ne·'' the	
8	no·''iěⁿ·. my mother.	Ne·''ho· There	dae'ni'dioñdäk thou and I should be	āio'i'wadädie' " it should be a continuing matter."	"Nio·''," "So be it,"		
9	wä'a'geⁿ' she it said	ne·' the	Eiä'dageⁿ·'tcī· She Ancient-bodied One.				
10	Da', So,	o'něⁿ· now	do'gěⁿs it is a fact	waiä·''děñdī' they two departed	ne·' the	ho'sot'. his grandmother.	Da', So,	o'něⁿ' now
11	na'e' verily	he'tgěⁿ·'' up high	wā·'ne'. they two went.				
12	Da', [So,	ne·''ho' there	nigagai'is. so it legend is long.]				

A MOHAWK VERSION

In the regions above there dwelt man-beings who knew not what it is to see one weep, nor what it is for one to die; sorrow and death were thus unknown to them. And the lodges belonging to them, to each of the ohwachiras[a] [families], were large, and very long, because each ohwachira usually abode in a single lodge.

And so it was that within the circumference of the village there was one lodge which claimed two persons, a male man-being and a female man-being. Moreover, these two man-beings were related to each other as brother and sister; and they two were dehninō'taton[b] [down-fended].

Ratinak'ere'	ne'	ē'nekĕⁿ	ne'ne·	iä'·	de·hatiiĕñtē'ri·	ne'ne·	
They (m.) dwell	the	place above	(the that) who	not	they (m.) it know	the that	1
āioⁿ·shĕñt'ho·	no'k·	o'nï·	ne'	āiāi''heie'.	Ne'	o'nï·	ne'	dji'
one should weep, lament	and	also	the	one should die.	The	also	the	where	2
rotinoⁿ·so'toⁿ·	ne'	ska·hwădjirat'shoⁿ·,		kanoⁿ·sowa'nĕⁿ·.		nĕñ'	
their (m.) lodge stand one by one	the	one it ohwachira each (is)		lodge large (is)		now	3
tä·hnoⁿ·'	ĕⁿ's	kanoⁿ·se's	ne'	dji'	iati'teroⁿ·,	a·'se·kĕⁿ·'	
besides	customarily	it lodge long (is)	the	where	they (m.) abide,	because	4
ie·hwădjirowa'nĕⁿs	akwe'koⁿ	ĕⁿ's	skanoⁿ·sä·'ne·	ie'teroⁿ·.			
one's ohwachira large (are) plurally	(it all) whole,	customarily	one it lodge in	they (indef.) abide.			5
Ne'	kä'tï·	ne'	dji'	nikanā'tä·	skanoⁿ·'sä·	iakaoñkwe'tāiĕⁿ·,	
The	so then	the	where	so it village large (is)	one it lodge (is)	they (indef.) have person(s)	6
roñ'kwe·	no'k·	iakoñ'kwe·,	nĕñ'	tä·hnoⁿ·'	iatĕⁿno·'sĕⁿ·'·hä·	nĕñ'	
he manbeing (is)	and	she a manbeing,	now	besides	they two brother and sister are	now	7
tä·hnoⁿ·'	te·hninō'tātoⁿ·.						
besides	they (m.) two downfended are.						

---

[a] An ohwachira in its broadest and original sense denotes the male and female offspring of a woman and their descendants in the female line only. In its modern and narrowed meaning it is equivalent to family; that is, a fireside group, usually composed of a parent or parents and offspring.

[b] The epithet (in the dual form) dehninō'taton is descriptive of the requirement of an ancient custom now almost, if not wholly, obsolete among the Iroquois. It consisted in the seclusion of a child from the age of birth to puberty from all persons except its chosen guardian. The occasion of this seclusion was some omen or prodigy accompanying the birth of the child, which indicated that the child was uncanny, possessing powerful orenda, or magic power. It seems that children born with a caul were thus secluded, and the presence of the caul itself may have given rise to the custom. Persons thus secluded were usually covered with corn husks in some nook whence they came forth only at night in the care of their guardian. Moreover, the down of the spikes of the cat-tail was carefully sprinkled about the place of seclusion, the disarrangement of which would indicate an intrusive visit. Hence the epithet "down-fended," which is the signification of the Amerindic epithet.

In the morning, after eating their first meal, it was customary for the people to go forth to their several duties.

All the lodges belonging to the inhabitants of this place faced the rising and extended toward the setting sun. Now then, as to the place where these two down-fended persons abode, on the south side of the lodge there was an added room wherein dwelt the woman-being; but the man-being lived in an added room on the north side of the lodge.

Then in the morning, when all had gone forth, the woman-being habitually availed herself of this opportunity to pass through her doorway, then to cross the large room, and, on the opposite side of it, to enter the place wherein abode the man-being. There habitually she dressed his hair, and when she had finished doing this, it was her

	Ne′	ka′tĭ‵	ĕⁿ's	ne′	nĕñ′	orhoⁿ'ge′ne‵	wă'hatikhwĕñ′tă′ne'
1	The	so then	custom-arily	the	now	it morning in	they (m.) (ceased from food) had eaten
	e'tho′ɩe‵	nĕñ′	ĕⁿ's	wă'eiakĕñ′seroñ′.			
2	at that time	now	custom-arily	they (indef.) went out of doors individually			
	Ne′	kĕⁿ'i′kĕⁿ‵	ratinak'ere'	ne′	dji′	ɩotinoⁿ'so′toⁿ'	akwe′koⁿ
3	The	this is it	they (m.) dwell	the	where	their (m.) lodge stand one by one	it all (is)
	dji′	tkara'kwi′nekĕⁿ's		ɩo'k‵	ne′	dji′	iă'tewatchot'ho's
4	where	there it sun rises		and	the	where	there it sets (immerses itself)
	nitioteno ⁿ‵sāierā′tă′nioⁿ'						
5	thus there they (z.) self lodge severally faced.						
	Ne′	ka′tĭ‵	kĕⁿ'i′kĕⁿ	te'hnino'tătoⁿ'		ne′	dji′	noñ'we‵
6	The	so then	this is it	they two down-fended are		the	where	the place
	te'hni′teroⁿ'.	Ieionoⁿ‵'soñte'	ĕⁿtiĕ″ke‵	nă'kanoⁿ‵'sătĭ‵	e‵'	ɩoñ'we‵
7	they two (m.) abode.	There it lodge possesses	at the south (midday at)	such it lodge side of (is)	there	the place
	niie′teroⁿ'	ne′	iakoñ'kwe'	ɩo'k‵	ne′	roñ'kwe‵	othore′ke‵
8	there she abode	the	she man-being (is),	and	the	he man-being (is)	at the north (it cold at)
	ɩoñka′tĭ‵	ne′	dji′	ieionoⁿ‵'soñte'	e‵'	ne′	noñka′tĭ‵	rĕñ′teroⁿ'
9	side of it	the	where	there it lodge possesses	there	the	the side of it	he abode
	ne′	roñ'kwe‵.						
10	the	he man-being (is).						
	Ne′	ka′tĭ‵	ĕⁿ's	ne′	nĕñ′	akwe′koⁿ	wă'eiakĕñ′seroⁿ'	ne′
11	The	so then	custom-arily	the	now	(it all) whole	they (indef.) went out of doors severally	the
	orhoⁿ'ge′ne‵	e'tho′ne'	ĕⁿ's	ne′	iakoñ'kwe‵	ne′	nĕñ′
12	it morning in	at that time	custom-arily	the	she man-being (is)	the	now
	toñtakanho'hi'iă'ke',	kanoⁿ'sowanĕñ′ne‵	e‵'	noñka′tĭ‵	ĕⁿ's
13	thence she crossed the threshold,	it lodge (room) large into	there	the side of it	custom-arily
	iă'hoñta′weiă'te'	dji′	noñ'we‵	thĕñ′teroⁿ'	ne′	roñ'kwe‵.	E‵'
14	thither she it entered	where	the place	there he abides	the	he man-being (is).	There
	iă'hokerothi′ie'	ne′	dji′	niio′re'	ĕⁿ's	wă'kă‵'să',	e'tho′ne'	nĕñ′
15	thither she his hair handled	the	where	so it is far (is time)	custom-arily	she it finished,	at that time	now

custoı to come foıth and cıoss oveı to the otheı side of the lodge wheıe was her own abidıng place. So theı, in this ıaı ıeı it was that she daily devoted her attentıoı to hıı, dıessıng and aııaıgıng his haiı.

Theı, afteı a time, it caıe to pass that she to whoı this feıale peıson beloıged peıceived that, ındeed, it would seeı that she was in delicate health; that one would ındeed thıık that she was about to give biıth to a child. So theı, afteı a tiıe, they questioned her, sayıng: "To whom of the man-beıngs living withıı the boıdeıs of the village art thou about to have a child?" But she, the giıl child, did not aıswei a sıngle woıd. Thus, then, it was at otheı tiıes; they questioıed her ıepeatedly, but she said ıothıg in aıswei to theiı queıies.

At last the day of her coıfiıeıeıt caıe, and she gave biıth to a child, and the child was a giıl; but she peısisted in ıefusıng to tell who was its fatheı.

těⁿtkāiā′kěⁿ ne᾽	tä·hnoⁿ′	e·′	iěn̄sewata′weiä´te᾽	dji′	non̄ka′tī·	ne′
thence she (z.) will come forth	besides	there	thither she it will reenter	where	the side of it	the	1

a′oñ·hä᾽ tiio′näkte᾽. E·′ ka′tī ni′io᾽t ne′ niiä᾽tewe·ni·sera′ke·
it (she) her- self / there her own mat (room) is. / Thus, so then / so it stands / the / each it day in number (is) 2

ne′ te·ho′snie· ne′ rokerothi′iä·s
the / she him attends to / the / she his hair handles. 3

No′k· hakare· ka′tī něñ′ ne′ akaon̄kwe′tä᾽ wä·oñt′toke· ne′
And / after a while / so then / now / the / her (indef.) parent (is) / she (indef.) noticed it / the 4

iä·′ ne′′-kěⁿ· ä·ıio·′ skěñ′noⁿ᾽ te·iako′n·he᾽ ne′ akoiěñ′′ä·.
not / that is it / indeed / well in health / not she lives / the / her offspring. 5

Aiěñ′re᾽ ěⁿiakoksä᾽täiěñ′tä᾽ne᾽. No′k· hä′kare· ka′tī něñ′
One would think / she a child will have. / And / after a while / so then (therefore) / now 6

wä·kon̄wari·hwanon′toⁿ᾽se· oⁿ·′kä ne′ dji′ nikana′tä· ne′
she her questioned / who (it is) / the / where / so it village (is) in size / the 7

ratinak′ere· ne′ ratiteron̄′toⁿ· ne′ rotiksä·täiěñta′sere·. No′k·
they (m.) dwell / the / they (m.) abide severally / the / they (m.) are about to have child. / But 8

iä·′ skawěn̄′uä· thaon̄taion̄ta′tī· ne′ eksa᾽a·′. E·′ ka′tī ıi′lo᾽t
not / one it word (is) / she it answered back / the / she child. / Thus / so then / so it stood 9

oiä· skon̄wari·hwanon̄ton̄′ni·. Iä·′ othe′noⁿ· thakěñ′roⁿ·
it (is) other / she her questions repeatedly. / Not / anything / she (z.) it would say. 10

No′k‘ hä′kare· něñ′ iä᾽akote·niseri′·he·se᾽ něñ′ wä᾽akoksä᾽
But / after a time / now / her day arrived for her / now / she became 11

täiěñ′tä᾽ne·, tä·hnoⁿ·′ iakon̄′kwe· ne′ eksa᾽a·′ (eksä′)ᵃ. O′k· o′ ıěⁿ·
possessed of a child, / and / she a man- being (is) / the / she a child. / Only / now (it is) 12

dji′ ni′io᾽t iä·′ thāion̄thro′rī oⁿ·′kä ro·ni′·hä·.
where / so it stood / not / she it would tell / who (it is) / he it is father to (her). 13

ᵃ This is a contracted form of the preceding word and is very much used.

258   IROQUOIAN COSMOLOGY   [ETH. ANN. 21

But in the time preceding the birth of the girl child this selfsame man-being at times heard his kinsfolk in conversation say that his sister was about to give birth to a child. Now the man-being spent his time. in meditating on this event, and after awhile he began to be ill. And, moreover, when the moment of his death had arrived, his mother sat beside his bed, gazing at him in his illness. She knew not what it was; moreover, never before had she seen anyone ill, because, in truth, no one had ever died in the place where these man-beings lived. So then, when his breathing had nearly ended, he then told his mother, saying to her: "Now, very soon shall I die." To that, also, his mother replied, saying: "What thing is that, the thing that thou sayest? What is about to happen?" When he answered, he said: "My breathing will cease; besides that, my flesh will become cold,

1	No'kʻ	oʻhĕñ'toⁿ	ne'	dji'	niio're'	ne'	nĕñ'	shä'ĕñnak'erate'
	But	before, in front of it	the	where	so it is distant	the	now	when she is born
2	ne'	eksa''ä'	kĕⁿ'i'kĕⁿ'	roñ'kweʻ	rothoñ'teʻ	ĕⁿ's	ne'	raoñkwe'täʻ
	the	she child (is)	this it is	he man-being (is)	he heard it	customarily	the	his people (relatives)
3	ne'	iakothɪo'ɪĭʻ	ne'	dji'	iakoksä'täiĕñtä'sere'	ne'	iatĕⁿno'sĕⁿ'häʻ
	the	they (indef.) are telling it	the	where	she child is about to have	the	they two brother and sister are.
4	Nĕñ'	ne''	rĕñnoⁿ'toñ'nioⁿʻ.		Hä'kaieʻ	nĕñ'	toñtä'sawĕⁿ	nĕñ'
	Now	that it (is)	he was thinking about it.		After a time	now	thence it began	now
5	wä'honoⁿ'hwăk'tĕⁿʻ.		Ne'	o'nĭ'	ne'	ciiä'kaʻ'heweʻ	ne'	ĕⁿ'rĕⁿ'he'ieʻ
	it caused him to be ill.		The	also	the	there it brought it (it was time for it)	the	will he die
6	ne'	ro'nĭstĕⁿʻ'häʻ	raonak'täktä'	eʻʻ	ie'teroⁿ'	teiekan'ere'	ne'
	the	his mother	his mat beside	there	she abode,	she it looked at	the
7	dji'	ronoⁿ'hwăk'tänĭʻ.	Iäʻ'	teieiĕñte'rĭ;	iäʻ'	o'nĭ'	noñwĕñ'toⁿ
	where	it causes him to be ill.	Not	she knows it;	not	also	ever
8	teiakotkä''thoⁿ	ne'	aiakonoⁿ'hwăk'tĕⁿ',	a'se'kĕⁿʻ'	iäʻ'	seʻ'
	she has looked at it	the	it would cause one to be ill,	because	not	as a matter of fact
9	noñwĕñ'toⁿ	oⁿʻ'käʻ	teiakawĕⁿʻhe'ioⁿʻ	ne'	dji'	ratinäk'ereʻ.	Ne'
	ever	someone	one has died	the	where	they (m.) dwell.	The
10	ka'tĭ'	ne'	nĕñ'	oⁿʻhwä'djok	iä'tĕⁿʻhatoñri'seratkoñ'tĕⁿ'	nĕñ'
	so then	the	now	very soon	thither his breath will remain away	now
11	wä'shakawĕⁿʻ'häʻseʻ		ne'	ro'nĭstĕⁿʻ'häʻ,	wä'hĕñ'roⁿʻ:	"Nĕñ'
	he her addressed		the	his mother,	be it said:	"Now
12	oⁿʻhwä'djok	ĕⁿki'ʻheiäʻ.''	Ne'	o'nĭ'	ne'	ro'nĭstĕⁿʻ'häʻ	wä'i'roⁿʻ·
	very soon	I shall die.''	The	also	the	his mother	she it said:
13	"O''	ne'	nä'ho'tĕⁿ'	ne'	dji'	nä'ho'tĕⁿ'	sä'toⁿ'?	O''	ne''
	"What (is it)	the	kind of thing (is it)	the	where	kind of thing	thou it art saying?	What (is it)	that
14	nĕⁿiä'wĕñneʻ?''	Ne'	o'nĭ'	ne'	toñtä'hata'tĭ'	wä'hĕñ'roⁿʻ·
	so it will take place?''	The	also	the	thence he replied	he it said:
15	"Ĕⁿwä''tkäʻweʻ	ne'	dji'	katoñrie'seʻ,	tä'bnoⁿ''	ĕⁿkawis'toʻte'
	"It will cease, will leave it	the	where	I breathe, am breathing	besides	it will make it cold

and then, also, the joints of my bones will become stiff. And when I cease breathing thou must close my eyes, using thy hands. At that time thou wilt weep, even as it itself will move thee [that is, thou wilt instinctively weep]. Besides that, the others, severally, who are in the lodge and who have their eyes fixed on me when I die, all these, I say, will be affected in the same manner. Ye will weep and your minds will be grieved." Notwithstanding this explanation, his mother did not understand anything he had said to her. And now, besides this, he told her still something more. He said: "When I am dead ye will make a burial-case. Ye will use your best skill, and ye will dress and adorn my body. Then ye will place my body in the burial-case, and then ye will close it up, and in the added room toward the rising sun, on the inside of the lodge, ye will prepare well a place for it and place it up high."

ne' the	kieroñ'ke·, my flesh on,	neñ' now	tä·hnoⁿ·' besides	ěⁿio·hnir'·hä'ne· it will become hard	ne' the	dji' where	1
tewäksthoñteroñ'nioⁿ·. I am jointed severally, have joints.		Ne' The	o'nä· also	ne' the	neñ' (now) when	ěⁿwä·'tkä·'we· it will cease. will leave it	ne' the	2
dji' where	katoñ'rie·se· I breathe,	těⁿskeroñ'weke· must thou close my eyes		se·snoñ'ke· thy hand with	ěⁿ·sats'te'. thou must use it.	E·tho'ne· At that time	3
neñ' now	těⁿsä·shěⁿ'tho· must thou weep	o'k· just	thěⁿtewěñnoⁿ·'toⁿ·. it will come of its own accord.		No'k· And	ho'nï' also	ne' the	4
otiä·ke·'shoⁿ· others each of	ne' the	kanoⁿ·'säkoⁿ· it house in	ěⁿie·teroñ'täke· will they abide		ne' the	těⁿiekan'erake· they it will look at	5
ne' the	neñ' (now) when	ěⁿki·'heie·, will I die,	akwe'koⁿ it all	shä·těⁿiäwěñ'ne· likewise it will happen too		těⁿsewä·shěñt'ho· must (will) ye weep	6
tä·hnoⁿ·' besides	ěⁿsewä·nikoⁿ·rä'ksěⁿ·.'' will your minds be grieved.''		No'k· And	iä·'' not	ki'' I think	othe'noⁿ· anything	7
ne' the	ro'nïstěⁿ·'·hä· his mother		thiieiako·nikoⁿ·rä·iěñtä·'oⁿ thither it she understood		ne' the	dji' where	8
nä·ho'těⁿ· kind of thing (it is)	wä·hěñ'roⁿ·. he it said.	Něñ' Now	tä·hnoⁿ·' besides	sěⁿ·'bä· somewhat farther	i'sï yonder	noñ'we· the place	dji' where	9
nä·ho'těⁿ· the kind of thing	wä·shako·hro'rï'. he it told her.		Wä·hěñ'roⁿ·: He it said:		''Ne' ''The		neñ' now	10
ěⁿwaki·he'ioⁿ· it will have caused me to die	ěⁿsewaroñto·tseroñ'nï·, will (must) ye make a case,			ne' the	ěⁿtisewateweiěñ'toⁿ· will ye it do with care		11
ne' the	ěⁿ·skwäiä·tä·seroñ'nï·. will ye my body finely array.		e'tho'ne· at that time	neñ' now	oroñto·tsera'koⁿ· it case in		12
ěⁿ·skwäiä'ti'tä·, ye my body will place in (it).	no'k· and	ho'nï' also	e'tho'ne· at that time	ěⁿtisewanoñ'teke·, will ye it cover,	tä·hnoⁿ·' besides		13
ne' the	dji' where	tkarä·kwi'nekěⁿ·s thence it sun comes out (east)	noñkä'tï· side of it	ne' the	dji' where	ieionoⁿ·'soñte·, there it possesses a room (lodge)	14
kanoⁿ·säkoⁿ·' it room in	noñkä'tï· the side of it	ěⁿsewakwata'ko· will ye it prepare well		ē'nekěⁿ· high up	ěⁿsewä'rěⁿ·.'' will ye it place.''		15

So then, verily, when he had actually ceased breathing, his mother closed his eyes, using her hands to do this. Just as soon as this was accomplished, she wept; and also those others, including all those who were onlookers, were affected in just the same manner; they all wept, notwithstanding that never before this time had they known anyone to die or to weep.

Now then, indeed, they made him a burial-case; then there, high up in the added room in the lodge, they prepared a place with care, and thereon they put the burial-case.

And the girl child lived in the very best of health, and, besides that, she grew in size very rapidly. Moreover, she had now reached that size and age when she could run hither and thither, playing about habitually. Besides this she could now talk.

1. To'kĕⁿske' ka'tĭ' ne' nĕñ' dji' iă'thatoñrī'serătkoñ'tĕⁿ' ne'
   In truth   so then   the   now   where   thither his breathing did depart   the

2. ro'nĭstĕⁿ'‘hă‘ wă‘thoñwaroñ'weke' iesnoⁿ'‘ke‘ wă'oñts'te'. Ne'
   his mother   she his eyes closed   her hands on   she it used.   The

3. kă'tĭ' he' kară'tie' wă‘tioⁿ‘shĕñt'ho' no'k‘ ho'nĭ' ne' otiă'ke‘‘shoⁿ'
   so then   there   it it accompanied   she wept   and   also   the   others each of

4. ne' dji' ni'koⁿ' ne' teiekan'ere' o'k‘ shă'tia'wĕñne': akwe'koⁿ
   the   where   so it is in number   the   they it looked at   just   equally it happened;   it all

5. wă‘tioⁿ‘shĕñt'ho': ne'ne' iă‘' noñwĕñ'toⁿ te‘hatiiĕñte'ri ne'
   they wept;   the that   not   ever   they (m.) it know   the

6. o‘bĕñ'toⁿ‘ dji' niio're' ne' e'tho'ne' ne' oⁿ‘'kă' o'k‘ āiăi‘'heie'
   before   where   so it is distant   the   at that time   the   someone   only   one should die

7. ne' tĕⁿ'‘s ne'ne‘ āioⁿ‘shĕñt'ho'
   the   or   the that   one should weep.

8. Nĕñ' ka'tĭ' to'kĕⁿske' wă‘hoñwaroñto‘tseroñ'nioⁿ', nĕñ' o'nĭ'
   Now   so then   in truth   they (m.) case made for him,   now   also

9. tăioñteweiĕñ'toⁿ' ne' dji' wă‘hoñwāiă'tă‘seroñ'ni'. E'tho'ne' nĕñ'
   they (indef.) it did with care   the   where   they (m.) his body finely arrayed.   At that time   now

10. oronto'tsera'koⁿ' wă‘hoñwāiă'ti'tă'. E'tho'ne' nĕñ' ne' dji'
    it burial case in   they his body placed.   At that time   now   the   where

11. ieiotenoⁿ‘'soñte' kanoⁿ‘'săkoⁿ‘ noñka'tĭ' ē'nekĕⁿ· wă‘hati‘'rĕⁿ'.
    there it has a room attached   it house in   side of it   high up   they it placed.

12. No'k‘ ne' eksa‘'ă‘ akwă‘' o'k‘ skĕñ'noⁿ', nĕñ' tă‘hnoⁿ'/
    But   the   she a child   very   only   well,   now   besides

13. io'sno're' ne' dji' iakote‘hiă‘roñ'tie'. No'k‘ ne' nĕñ' e‘¹
    it is rapid   the   where   she is increasing in size.   But   the   now   there

14. citiako'iĕⁿ‘ ne' nĕñ' e'rok tcietăk'he's, iakotkă‘ri'tseroñni‘hă'tie'se',
    thence she arrived   the   now   everywhere   she runs about repeatedly,   she goes about making amusements for herself,

15. nĕñ' o'nĭ' ioñtă'tĭ'
    now   also   she talks.

Suddenly those in the lodge were greatly surprised that the child began to weep. For never before had it so happened to those who had children that these would be in the habit of weeping. So then her mother petted her, endeavoring to divert her mind, doing many things for this purpose; nevertheless she failed to quiet her. Other persons tried to soothe her by petting her, but none of their efforts succeeded in quieting her. After a while the mother of the child said: "Ye might try to quiet her by showing her that burial-case that lies up high, yonder, wherein the body of the dead man-being lies." So then they took the child up there and uncovered the burial-case. Now of course she looked upon the dead man-being, and she immediately ceased from weeping. After a long time they brought her down therefrom, for she no longer lamented. And, besides this, her mind was again at ease.

Wä'oñtie're^{n}· They were surprised	o'k' just	ne' the	kano^{n}·'säko^{n}· it house in	ie'tero^{n}· one abides	(ieteroñ'to^{n}·) they abide one by one	1
neñ' now	wä'tio^{n}·sheñt'ho· she wept	ne' the	eksa'ä·'. she a child. is	Ne'ne' The that	iä·' not	noñweñ'to^{n}· e·' the ever thus	2
thoñtäio'to^{n}·hä'tie· hither so it has been coming	ne' the	iakoksa'täieñ'to^{n}· they have children individually		ne' the	täio^{n}·sheñtho·'seke· they should cry as a habit.	3
Neñ' Now	ka'tï' so then	ne' the	o·ni'ste^{n}·hä· its (z.) mother	wä'tiakorho'toñ'nio^{n}·, she her comforted,	wä'tiako'niko^{n}· she her mind	4
raweñ'rie·. diverted.	O'iä· Other (it is)	o'k' just,	nä'tetioie're^{n}·· repeatedly so she it did do	ne' the	äiako'niko^{n}·raweñ'rie· might she her mind diverted.	5
Iä·' Not	ki'' it seems	thaoñ'to^{n}· it sufficed	ne' the	täioñto'tate·. she it would cease from.	O'ne^{n}· Now	o'iä· other (it is)	o'k' just	6
tcioñtatarho'toñ'nï·, again one her comforts,	iä·' not	ki'' it seems	tewa'to^{n}·s it suffices	täioñto'tate·. she it would cease from.	No'k· And	7
hä'kare· after a time	neñ' now	ne' the	akoksteñ'ä· she elder one	wä'i'ro^{n}·: she it said:	"Aietciiate'nieñ'te^{n}·. "Ye her should try there.	8
iäietchinä'toñ·'hä·se· thither ye it should show to her	ne' the	i'sï (far) yonder	e·'neke^{n}·· high up	tkaroñto'tserä·'here· there it burial-case lies	ne' the	9
dji' where	räiä'tï· his body it fills	ne' the	rawe^{n}·he'io^{n}·." he is dead."	E'tho'ne· At that time	katï'' so then	neñ' now	iä·akotiiä- thither they	10
tarat·'he^{n}ste· upbore her body	tä·hno^{n}·' besides	wä'koñtinoñtek'sï·. they it uncovered.		Neñ Now	wä·'hï verily	wä'oñtkät'ho· she it looked at	11
ne' the	rawe^{n}·he'io^{n}. he is dead.	Ne' The	ka'tï' so then	ne' the	ok'sä· at once	o'k' just	wä'o^{n}·'tkä·we· she ceased from it	ne' the	12
dji' where	teio^{n}·sheñt'ho·s. she was crying, weeping.	Akwä·'' Very	ka'tï' so then	ke^{n}·'' this	nä·he''. length of time	o'ne^{n}·· now	13
toñtäiakotiiä·'tats'ne^{n}·te·. thence they her body down brought,	neñ' now	iä·' not	thä·'teteio^{n}·sheñt'ho·s. not she is weeping.	Ne' The	o'nï also	14
ne' the	e·' thus	ni'io't so it stood	skeñ'no^{n}· (it is) well	tcieñno^{n}·toñ'nio^{n}· again she is in mind. (thinks iteratively)		15

It was so for a very long time. Then she began to weep again, and so, this time, her mother, as soon as possible, took her child up to where the dead man-being lay, and the child immediately ceased her lamenting. Again it was a long time before one took her down therefrom. Now again she went tranquilly about from place to place playing joyfully.

So then they made a ladder, and they erected the ladder so that whenever she should desire to see the dead man-being, it would then be possible for her to climb up to him by herself. Then, when she again desired to see the dead person, she climbed up there, though she did so by herself.

So then, in this way matters progressed while she was growing to maturity. Whenever she desired to see the one who had died, she would habitually climb up to him.

1	Akwă'' Very	wă'kari'ʻhwes it matter long became	něn' now	a're' again	toñsăioⁿʻshěñt'ho'. once again she wept.		Něñ Now	ka'ti' so then
2	ioñ'wă' at this time	ok'să' at once	o'kʻ just	ne' the	o'nistěⁿ'ʻhă' its (her) mother	iă'hoñtatiă'tarat'hěⁿste' thither she upbore her body		ne' the
3	oñtătiěñ''ăʻ her offspring	ne' the	dji' where	tka'ʻhere' there it lay on it	ne' the	rawěⁿʻhe'ioⁿʻ, he is dead,	ne' the	o'nĭ' also	ok'săʻ at once
4	o'kʻ just	wă'tioñto'tate' she ceased from it	ne' the	dji' where	teioⁿʻshěñt'hoʻs. she is weeping.		Akwă'' Very	ka'ti' so then	a're' again
5	kěⁿ'' this,	nă'he'', length of time,	něñ' now	a're' again	toñtăioñtatiă'tatsʻněⁿʻte'. thence again they her body down brought.		Něñ' Now	a're' again
6	skěñ'noⁿʻ well, contentedly	thitcakotkă'ri'tseroñniʻhă'tie'se'. again she herself goes about amusing.						
7	Něñ' Now	ka'ti' so then	e'tho'ne' at that time	něñ' now	wăʻhatinekotoñ'ni' they made a ladder (onekota)		ne' the	o'nĭ' also
8	wăʻhatinekoto'těⁿ'. they set up the ladder (onekota.)	Ne' The	ka'ti' so then	ne' the	kat'keʻ whenever	těⁿiakotoⁿʻhwěñ'tcioʻ'se' it will be needful for her		
9	ne' the	ăioñtkă'tho' she should look at it	ne' the	rawěⁿʻhe'ioⁿʻ he is dead	ěⁿwa'toⁿ, it will be possible,	ki'', I believe,	ne' the	akaoñʻhă''ăʻ she herself
10	iěⁿierat'hěⁿ'. thither she will ascend.	Ne' The	ka'ti' so then	ne' the	něñ' now	a're' again	toñsăiakotoⁿʻhwěñ'tcioʻ'se' again it was needful for her	
11	ne' the	aʻhoñwa'kěⁿʻ she should see him	ne' the	rawěⁿʻhe'ioⁿʻ he is dead	iă'erat'hěⁿ' thither she climbed,	ki'' I believe,	akaoⁿʻhă''ăʻ she herself.	
12	E'ʻ Thus	ka'tĭ' so then	niio'toⁿʻhă'tie' so it continued to be	ne' the	dji' where	iakoteʻhiă'roñ'tie'. she continued to increase in size.		Kat'keʻ Whenever
13	těⁿiakotoⁿʻhwěñ'tcio:se' she will need it	ne' the	ăioñtkă'ʻtho' she should look at it	ne' the	rawěⁿʻhe'ioⁿʻ he is dead			
14	iă'erat'hěⁿ' thither she climbed,	ki'' I think.	ěⁿ's. customarily.					

MOHAWK VERSION

In addition to these things, it was usual, when she sat on the place where the burial-case lay, that those who abode in the lodge heard her conversing, just as though she were replying to all that he said; besides this, at times she would laugh.

But, when the time of her maturity had come, when this child had grown up, and she had again come down, as was her habit, from the place where the dead man-being lay, she said: "Mother, my father said"—when she said "my father," it then became certain who was her father—"'Now thou shalt be married. Far away toward the sunrising there he lives, and he it is who is the chief of the people that dwell there, and he it is that there, in that place, will be married to thee.' And now, besides this, he said: 'Thou shalt tell thy mother that she shall fill one outer basket with bread of sodden corn, putting

Neñ'	tä'hnoⁿ''	ne'	ěⁿ's	ne'	neñ' 'e''	ieietskwä''here'	ne'	dji'
Now	besides	the	custom-arily	the	now thus	there she sits up high	the	where

1

tkaroñto'tserä''here'	iakothoñ'te'	eⁿ's	ne'	kanoⁿ''säkoⁿ'	ie'teroⁿ'
there it burial case lies up	they it heard	custom-arily	the	it house in	they (indef.) abide

2

ne'	iako''thäre'	ne'	dji'	ñi'io't	ne'	aoñta'ho'thä'räke'	ne'
the	she is conversing	the	where	so it stands	the	thence he would be talking	the

3

raweⁿ'he'ioⁿ'	no'k'	o'nï'	aoñtäiakori'hwä'seräkweñ'hä'tie'.	neñ'
he is dead	but	also	thence she continued to reply.	now

4

tä'hnoⁿ''	sewatie'reⁿ'	neñ'	täiakoie'shoⁿ'.
besides	sometimes	now	thence she would laugh.

5

No'k'	ne'	neñ'	ciiä'kä''hewe'	neñ'	shä'oñte'hia'roⁿ'	keⁿ'i'keⁿ'
But	the	now	there it arrived	now	there she matured	this (here) (it is)

6

eksa''ä'	ne'	neñ'	a're'	toūtäioñts'neⁿ''te'	ne'	dji'	tkä''here'	ne'
she a child	the	now	again	thence she descended	the	where	there it lies upon it	the

7

raweⁿ'he'ioⁿ'	wä'i'roⁿ':	"Isteñ''hä'	(isdä''),ᵃ	wä'heñ'roⁿ'	ne'
he is dead	she it said:	"Oh, Mother,		he it said	the

8

rake'ni''hä'	(ne' dji' niio're'	wä'i'roⁿ'	räke'ni''hä'	e'tho'ne'	neñ'
he my father (is)	(the where so it is far	she it said	he my father (is)	at that time	now

9

wä'katō'keⁿ'ne'	oⁿ''kä'	roñwä'ni''hä'	ne'	eksa''ä):	'Neñ'	eⁿ'saniä'ke'
it became known (as true)	who (it is)	he her father (is)	the	she a child (is)	'Now	thou shalt marry.

10

I'noⁿ'	ne'	dji'	tkarä'kwi'nekeⁿ's	noñka'tī'	e''	thanak'ere'.
Far (far away)	the	where	there it sun rises	side of it	there	there he dwells.

11

ne're'	thoñwakowa'neⁿ'	ne'	thatinak'ere'	ne' e''	eⁿseni'niäke'.'
the that	there he their chief (is)	the	there they dwell	the there	thou and he shall marry.'

12

Neñ'	tä'hnoⁿ''	wä'heñ'roⁿ'·	'Eⁿ'she'hro'ri'	ne'	sä'nisteⁿ''hä'
Now	and	he it said:	Thou her shalt tell	the	thy mother

13

ne're'	akwä''	eⁿtioñteweieñ'toⁿ',	kä'hi'k	teⁿie'ieste'	ne'	kaneⁿ'ha
the that	very	she shall do it the best possible,	it fruit	she it shall mix with it	the	it corn softened

14

ᵃ This is a shortened form of the next preceding word.

forth her best skill in making it, and that she shall mix berries with the bread, which thou wilt bear with the forehead strap on thy back, when thou goest to the place where he dwells to whom thou shalt be married.'"

Then it was that her mother made bread of corn softened by boiling, and she mixed berries with the corn bread. So then, when it was cooked, she placed it in a burden basket, and it filled it very full.

It was then, at this time, that the young woman-being said: "I believe I will go and tell it to my father." It was then that she again climbed up to the place where the dead man-being lay. Then those who were in the lodge heard her say: "Father, my mother has finished the bread." But that he made any reply to this, no one heard. So then it was in this manner that she conversed there with her dead father. Sometimes she would say: "So be it; I will." At other times

#					
1	nawĕⁿ‵'toⁿ‵ by boiling	(?kanĕⁿ‵sto'‵hare‵) it corn washed	ĕⁿienä'taroñ'ni', she bread shall make.	ioñtke'‵tats one bears it on the back by the forehead strap	ä't'here' it basket
2	ĕⁿkanä'noⁿ‵ it it shall fill	ne' the	iĕⁿ‵satke'‵tate' thither thou shalt bear it on thy back by the forehead-strap	ne' the	nĕñ' now	iĕⁿ‵'se' thither thou shalt go	dji' where	noñ'we‵ the place
3	thĕñ'teroⁿ‵ there he abides	ne' the	ĕⁿseni'niake'.'" thou he shall marry.'"					
4	E'tho'ne‵ At that time	nĕñ' now	ne' the	o‵nistĕⁿ‵'hä‵ its (her) mother	wä'enä'taroñ'ni' she it bread made	ne' the	kanĕⁿ‵ha it corn softened
5	nawĕⁿ‵'toⁿ‵, by boiling,	akwä‵' very	tewä'hiäies'toⁿ‵. one it has mixed with fruit.	Ne' The	ka'tï' so then	ne' the	nĕñ' now
6	shä'ka'ri‵ when it was cooked	e‵' there	wä'ake'tä' she it placed in it	ioñtke‵tats'thä‵ one uses it to bear it on the back by the forehead strap	a'therä'koⁿ‵, it basket in,	akwä‵'' very
7	wä'kä'nä‵ne‵. it filled it.					
8	E'tho'ne‵ At that time	nĕñ' now	ne' the	eiä'tase‵'ä‵ she new-bodied one (is)	wä'i'roⁿ‵: she it said:	"Iĕⁿ‵shi'hro'ri' "There I shall tell him,	ki" I think
9	ne' the	rake‵ni'‵hä‵." he is my father."	E'tho'ne‵ At that time	nĕñ' now	ioñsäierat'hĕⁿ‵ thither again she ascended	dji' where	noñ'we‵ place
10	tkä'‵here' there it lies upon it	ne' the	rawĕⁿ‵he'ioⁿ‵. he is dead.	Ne' The	o'ni' also	ne' the	iakothoñ'te' they it heard
11	ne' the	kanoⁿ‵'säkoⁿ‵ it lodge in	ie'teroⁿ‵ they abide	dji' where	wä'i'roⁿ‵: she it said:	"Rake'ni‵ "He my father (is)	nĕñ' now
12	wä'enä'tari'sä‵ she it bread has finished	ne' the	istĕñ‵'ä‵." my mother."	No'k‵ And	ne' the	aoⁿta‵hota'tike' he should have replied	iä‵' not	nä‵'' that thing
13	ne'' that one	oⁿ‵'kä‵ anyone	teiakothoñte‵''oⁿ‵. one it has heard.	E‵' Thus	ka'tï' so then	ni'io‵t so it is (stands)	tiiako‵'thare', just she was talking.
14	sewatie'rĕⁿ‵ sometimes	wä'i'roⁿ‵: she it said:	"Io‵," "Yes,"	sewatie'rĕⁿ‵ sometimes	nĕñ' now	täiakoie'shoⁿ‵. there she would laugh.

she would laugh. So after a while she came down and said: "My father said: 'To-morrow very early in the morning thou shalt start.'"
So then, when the next day came, and also when they had finished eating their morning meal, the young woman-being at this time said: "Now I believe I will start; but I will also tell my father, I believe." At this time she now went thither where stood the ladder, and, climbing up to the place whereon lay the burial-case of the dead man-being, she said: "Father, I shall now start on my journey." So then again it was from what she herself said that it was learned that he was her father.

It was at this time that he told her all that would befall her on her journey to her destination, and, moreover, what would happen after her arrival. So then, after she again came down, her mother took up for her the burden basket which was full of bread, and placed it on

Hā'kare'	ka'tĭ'	něñ'	toñtāioñtsněⁿ''te'		tä'hnoⁿ''	wä'i'roⁿ''	1
After a while	so then	now	thence again she descended		besides	she it said:	
"Wä'hěñ'roⁿ"	ne'	rake'ni''hä'	ěⁿio'r'hěⁿ'ne'		něñ'	ěⁿkä'těñ'tĭ'	2
"He it said	the	he my father (is)	it day will dawn		now	shall I start	
orhoⁿ'ke''djĭ'"							3
it morning early."							
Ne'	ka'tĭ'	ne'	něñ'	shä'or'hěⁿ''ne'	ne'	o'nĭ'	ne'	něñ'
The	so then	the	now	when day dawned (daylight came)	the	also	the	now	4
sä'hatikhwěñ'tä'ne'	ne'	or'hoⁿ'ke''ne'	wä'thoñtskä''hoⁿ'		e'tho'ne'	5
again they finished eating their food	the	it morning in	they fed themselves		at that time	
ne'	eiä''tāse'	wä'i'roⁿ':	"Něñ'	ki''	ěⁿkä'těñ'tĭ';	no'k'	o'nĭ'	něñ'
the	she the new-bodied one,	she it said:	"Now,	I think,	I will start;	but	also	now	6
iěⁿ'shi'hro'rĭ'	ki''	ne'	rake'ni''hä'.''	E'tho'ne'	něñ'	a'ie'	e''
thither I him will tell,	I think,	the	he my father." (is)	At that time	now	again	there	7
niioñsä'iěⁿ'	dji'	noñ'we'	tkaneko'tote'	tä'hnoⁿ''	iä'erat'hěⁿ'
just there again she went	where	the place	there it ladder stands	besides	thither she it ascended	8
dji'	noñ'we'	tharoñto'tserä''here'	ne'	rawěⁿ'he'ioⁿ',	tä'hnoⁿ''
where	place	there he a burial-case lies upon it	the	he is dead,	besides	9
wä'i'roⁿ':	"Rake''nĭ'	něñ'	ěⁿkä'těñ'tĭ'.''	Ne'	ka'tĭ'	ne'	dji'
she it said:	"He my father	now	I will start."	The	so then	the	where	10
ioñthro'rĭ'	ne'	aka'oⁿ'hä'	ne'ne'	ro'ni'hä'.		11
she it tells	the	she herself	the that	he her father (is).		
E'tho'ne'	akwe'ko'	wä'shako'hro'rĭ'	ne'	dji'	něⁿiawěⁿ''seroⁿ'	12
At that time	it all	he it told her	the	where	so it will happen serially	
ne'	dji'	niio're'	niiěⁿ'hěñ'iěⁿ'	no'k'	ho'nĭ'	ne'	iěⁿ'ioñwe'.	Ne'
the	where	so it is far	so thither she will go	and	also	the	there she will arrive.	The	13
ka'tĭ'	ne'	něñ'	shä'toñtāioñts'něⁿ'te',	e'tho'ne'	něñ'	ne'
so then	the	now	when thence she descended,	at that time	now	the	14
o'nistěⁿ''hä'	něñ'	wä'tioñtate''kwěⁿ'	ne'	ioñtke'tats'thä'	ä't'here'
its (her) mother	now	she it raised up for her	the	one uses it to bear it on the back by the forehead strap	it basket	15

the back of the young woman-being, to be borne by means of the forehead strap, and then the young woman-being went forth from the lodge and started on her journey, the path extending away toward the sunrising; and thither did she wend her way.

So it was surprising to her what a short distance the sun had raised itself when she arrived at the place where her father had told her there was a river, where a floating log served as a crossing, and at which place it was the custom for wayfarers to remain over night, as it was just one day's journey away. So the young woman-being now concluded, therefore, that she had lost her way, thinking that she had taken a wrong path. She then retraced her steps. Only a very short distance again had the sun gone when she returned to the place whence she had started, and she said: "I do not know but that I have lost my way. So I will question my father about it again." She

1	kană'taranā'non‘	ne'ne‘	eiă'tase'	wă'oñtat'therake‘'tăte'	neñ'
	it full of bread (is)	the that	she new-bodied (is)	she her caused to bear it on her back by the forehead strap	now
2	tă‘hnon'' iă'eiă'kĕn'ne'	neñ'	wă'on'teñ'tī'	dji'	tkară‘kwi'nekĕn's
	and hence she went forth	now	she started	where	there it sun habitually comes out
3	niiothă‘hāierā'ton‘	e‘'	niiă‘hā'ĕn'.		
	so it itself road faces	there	just thither she went.		
4	Ne' ka'tī' ne'	ione‘hră'kwă‘t	niiore''ă‘	ioteră‘kwakaratā'ton‘	
	The so then the	it is wonderful	so it is little distant	it sun had raised itself	
5	no'k‘ e‘' iă‘hā'oñ'we'	dji'	noñ'we‘ ne'	ro'ni‘'hă‘ ne'	iă'wĕn‘
	and there there she arrived	where	the place the	he her father (is) the	he it has said
6	tkă‘hion‘hată'tie' wă‘'tă'	karoñ'to'	ne' dji'	teieia‘hiak'thă'.	E‘'
	there it river extends along maple	it tree floats	the where	they use it to cross the stream.	There
7	ĕn's noñ'we‘ iă'oñnoñ'wete',	a‘se'kĕn'‘'		sewe‘hni'seră‘	dji'
	customarily the place there one would-stay over night,	because		one day	where
8	niwathă‘binoñ'tserese'. Neñ'	ka'tī'	ne'	eiă'tăse'	wă'ĕn‘'re'
	so it journey is long. Now,	so then	the	she new-bodied one (is)	she it thought
9	ori‘hwi'io' wă'eiă'tă‘'ton'ne',a wă'ĕn'‘re'		to'kă'	ion'wă'	wă'tekhă‘-
	it is true matter she her way has lost, she it thought		perhaps	this time	I it path
10	hanē'ră'ke'. E'tho'ne' ka'tī'	neñ'	sāion‘'kete'.	Nakwă‘'	oñ'wă'
	mistook. At that time so then	now	she started back.	The very	this time
11	kĕn'' o'k niio're'	niioteră‘kwă'teñ'tion‘		no'k‘	ion‘sā'ionwe'
	here only so it is distant	so it sun had moved		but	there again she arrived
12	ne' dji' tiiako‘teñ'tion‘	tă‘hnon''	wă'i'ron'':	"To'kă'	ion'wă'
	the where thence she started	and	she it said:	"Perhaps,	this time
13	wă'kiă'tă‘'ton'ne'.b Ĕnsheri‘hwanoñ'ton'se'		ka'tī'	ne'	rake'ni‘'hă‘
	I my way have mistaken. I him will again ask		so then	the	he my father (is).

a Literally, she lost her body.   b Literally, I lost my body, thereupon climbed up again to the place where her father lay in the burial-case. Those who were in the house heard her say: "Father, I came back thinking that, perhaps, I had lost my way, for the reason that I arrived so quickly at the point thou describedest to me as the place where I should have to remain over night; for the sun had moved scarcely any distance before I arrived where thou hadst told me there would be a river which is crossed by means of a log. This, then, is the aspect of the place whence I returned." At this time, then, he made answer to this, and she alone heard the things that he said, and those other people who were in the lodge did not hear what things he said. It is told that he replied, saying: "Indeed, thou hadst not lost thy way." Now it is reported that he said: "What kind of a log is it that is used in crossing there?" She answered, it is said: "Maple is

---

1. E'tho'ne' ka'ti' nĕñ' ioñsāierat'hĕⁿ' dji' noñ'we' tharoñto'-
   At that time / so then / now / thither again she ascended / where / the place / there he lies

2. tserä'here' ne' ro'ni'hä'. Iakothoñte'nioⁿ' ne' kanoⁿ'säkoⁿ'
   a burial-case / the / it her father (is) / They severally heard it / the / house in it

3. ieteroñ'toⁿ' ne' dji' wä'i'roⁿ': "Rake'nī', toñtakä'kete' so'djī'
   they one by one abide / the / where / she it said: / "He my father, / thence I turned back / for (too much)

4. wä'kere' to'kä' noñ'wä' wä'kiä'tä'toⁿ' ne' dji' so'djī' io'sno're'
   I thought it / perhaps / this time / I have strayed / the / where / for (too much) / it is rapid

5. e'' ia'hä'kewe' dji' niwatoⁿ'hwĕñdjiō'tĕⁿ' ne' dji' tak'hro'rī'
   there / there I arrived / where / such land kind (is) of / the / where / thou didst tell it me

6. dji' noñ'we' iĕⁿkĕñnoñ''hwete', a'se'kĕⁿ' iä'' othe'roⁿ' akwä'
   where / place / there I will stay over night, / because / not / anything / very

7. teioterä'kwä'tĕñ'tioⁿ' ro'k' e'' iä'hä'kewe' ne' dji' tak'hro'rī'.
   it sun had moved / and / there / there I arrived / the / where / thou didst tell it me

8. tkä'hioⁿ'hata'tie' karoñtä'ke' teieia'hiäk'thä'. E'' ka'ti' ni'io't
   there it river extends along / (the) log on / one uses it to cross the stream. / There / so then / so it is

9. dji' roñ'we' toñtakä''kete'. E'tho'ne' ka'ti' tä'hari·hwä'serä'ko'
   where / place / thence I turned back. / At that time / so then / thence he made answer

10. ne' akaoñ'hä' o'k' iakothoñ'te' dji' nä'ho'tĕⁿ' wä'hĕñ'roⁿ'; iä''
    the / she herself / only / she heard it / where / such kind of thing / he it said; / not

11. re're' otiä'ke''shoⁿ' ne' kanoⁿ'säkoⁿ' ie'teroⁿ' teiakothoñte''oⁿ'
    the that / it other every one / the / house in / they it (indef.) abide / they it did hear

12. ne' dji' nä'ho'tĕⁿ' wä'hĕñ'roⁿ'. Wä'hĕñ'roⁿ', ia'kĕⁿ': "Iä''tĕⁿ' se''
    the / where / such kind of thing / he it said. / He it said, / it is said: / "Not at all / indeed

13. tesāiä'tä'toⁿ''oⁿ'." Nĕñ' wä'hĕñ'roⁿ', ia'kĕⁿ': "O'' nä'karoñto'tĕⁿ'
    thou hast strayed." / Now, / he it said, / it is said: / "What / such it tree kind of

14. re're' karoñ'to' ne' dji' teieia'hiäk'thä'?" Wä'i'roⁿ', ia'kĕⁿ':
    the that / it tree floats / the / where / one uses it to cross the stream?" / She it said, / it is said:

15. "Wä''tä' nä'karoñto'tĕⁿ' ne' dji' teieia'hiäk'thä', no'k' o'ho''serä'
    "Maple / such it tree kind of / the / where / one uses it to cross the stream, / but / it basswood

the kind of log that is used at the crossing, and the log is supported by clumps of young saplings of basswood and ironwood, respectively, on either side of the stream." He replied, it is said: "That appears to be accurate, indeed; in fact, thou didst not lose thy way." At this time, then, she descended and again started on her journey.

And again, it seems, the sun had moved only just a little before she again arrived at the place whence she had returned. So she just kept on her journey and crossed the river.

So, having gone only a short distance farther on her way, she heard a man-being in the shrubbery say therefrom: "Ahen!" She of course paid no attention to him, but kept on her way, since her father had told her what would happen to her on the journey. Thus, in this manner, she did nothing except hasten as she traveled on to her destination. Besides this, at times, another man-being would say from out

---

1	tä'hnon" and	skarontäkäs'tä· ironwood (durable it tree)	nä'karonto'ten" such it tree kind of	oterontonni"ä' it sapling		iotho"ko- it clump
2	ton'nion" stands one by one	tedjia'ron· both	nonka'tï sides of it	e" there	ka'tï so then	karontawe'thär"hon· " one has infixed the log."
3	Wä·hěñ'ron", He it said,	ia'kěn· it is said:	"Ne" "That	e", there,	ki", I believe,	tkāie'rï se"; iä"těn" there it is indeed; not at all correct
4	se" indeed	tesāiä'tä'toñ'on"." thou hast strayed (lost thy body)."		E'tho'ne' At that time	ka'tï then	něñ' tontāiěnts'něn"te now thence she descended again
5	no'k' and	a're' also	tciako'těn'tion' again she started away.			
6	Nakwä" The very	ki" I believe	a're' again	o'sthoñ"hä' it small (is)	o'k' only	thiiotera'kwä'těn'tion" no'k' it sun has moved but
7	nä' that one	e" there	ion"sä'ionwe' again there she arrived	dji' where	non'we' place	tetiakok'ton", thence she had returned, o'k' ka'tï only, so then
8	e're̊n· beyond	ci'iěn" there she kept going	wä'tieiä"hiä'ke'. she crossed the stream.			
9	Iä" Not	ka'tï so then	so'dji' so very (too much)	i'no"· far	thiieiakawe'no"· thither had she gone	něñ' ka'tï iakothoñ'te' now so then she it hears
10	roñ'kwe' he a man-being (is)	o'ska'wäkon" it shrubbery in	tä'huta'ti' thence he spoke	tä'bě·ï'ro"·: thence he it said:	"Hěñ'm." "Ahem."	Iä" Not
11	ka'tï so then	othe'non" anything	thiieiakotsteris'to". thither did she heed give.		Iako'těntion"hä'tie' She kept on going	něñ' ne", now that
12	a'se·kěn·· because	ne' the	ro'ni'·hä' he her father	te'shako·bro'rï· he her had told it	dji' where	e" něn"iawě·ï'ne' there so it will happen.
13	E" Thus	ka'tï so then	ni'io't so it stood	ne' the	o'k' only	ne' iako'storoñ'tie' ne' dji' the she hastened onward the where
14	iontha'hi'ne'. she her path moved along.	Ne' The	o'ni' also	ne' the	o'iä' other	o'k' ěn"s ne' roñ'kwe· ne' only custom- the he a the arily man-being (is)

of the shrubbery: "Ahem!" But she kept on her course, only hastening her pace as much as possible as she continued her journey. But when she had arrived near the point where she should leave the forest, she was surprised to see a man-being coming toward her on the path, and he, when coming, at a distance began to talk, saying: "Stand thou, for a short time. Rest thyself, for now thou must be wearied." But she acted as though she had not heard what he said, for she only kept on walking. He gave up hope, because she would not even stop, so all that he then did was to mock her, saying: "Art thou not ashamed, since the man thou comest to seek is so old?" But, nevertheless, she did not stop. She did not change her course nor cease from moving onward, because her father had told her all that would happen to her while she trudged on her journey; this, then, is the reason that she did not stand. So then, after a while, she reached a grassy clearing—a

o'ska'wākoⁿˑ it shrubbery in	toñtāˑhĕñ'roⁿˑ thence he it said:	"Hĕñ'm." "Ahem."	No'kˑ But	kato'kĕnˑ it unchanged (is),	ki" I believe,	1
ni'io·t so it stood	nitiakoie'rĕⁿˑ so she continued to do	ne' o'kˑ the only	ne' the	iakostoroñ'tieˑ she hastened onward	ne' dji' the where	teia- she 2
kot'hā·hā·kwĕⁿˑ'hā'tieˑ it path continues to travel onward.	Ne' The	ka'ti' so then	ne' the	nĕñ' now	ak'tāˑ nearly	ne' nĕñ' the now 3
iāˑtaier·ho'tkā·we· thither side she it forest would leave	wā·oñtie'rĕⁿˑ she was surprised	o'kˑ only	ka'ti' so then	ne' the	roñ'kwe· he a man-being (is)	o·hā·hāˑ- it path 4
ke"shoⁿ on along	tāˑre· thence he is coming.	Ne' The	ka'ti' so then	ne' the	she'koⁿˑ still	kĕⁿ"āˑ short way	niio're· so it is distant	tāˑie· thence he is coming 5
no'kˑ and	tāˑho'thară'tieˑ, thence he came talking,	ra'toⁿˑ he it is saying:	"Tes'tāˑne· "Stand thou,	nā·he·āˑ. a short length of time.	Satoñris'hĕⁿˑ, Thou thyself rest 6
nĕñ' now	oⁿ"'teˑ probably	tesa·hwīshĕⁿ·he'ioⁿˑ." thou art weary (thy strength is dead)."	No'kˑ And	nakwāˑ" the very	dji' where	ni'io·t so it stood 7
ne' the	iāˑ" not	teiakothoñ'teˑ, she it hears.	ne' the	o'kˑ only	ne' the	iako·tĕñtioñ·hā'tieˑ. she keeps on going onward.	Wāˑ- He 8
hĕⁿ"nikoñ'riā·keˑ failed in his purpose (he his mind broke)	iāˑ" not	seˑ" indeed	thāˑtāietāˑ"ne·. there she did stand.	No'kˑ But	ne' the	o'kˑ only	ne' the 9
sashakote·hā·ta'nioⁿ, he taunted her with shame repeatedly,	na'toⁿˑ he it said:	"Iāˑ" "Not	tesate·hĕⁿ"seˑ art thou of thyself thus,	e·" ashamed	nihokstĕñ"āˑ so he old (is) 10
ne' the	wā'tseniĕñ"teˑ." thou him goest to seek."	No'kˑ And,	ki" I believe,	iāˑ" not	thāˑteiakotāˑ"oⁿˑ. there she did stand.	Kato'kĕⁿˑ. One certain way 11
nitiakoie'rĕⁿˑ so she continues to do	iako·tĕñtioñ·hā'tieˑ, she keeps on going onward,	āˑse'kĕⁿˑ" because	ro'niˑ"hāˑ he her father	akwe'koⁿ it all 12
seˑ" indeed	wāˑ"hīˑ verily	te·shako·hro'rīˑ he it her told	dji' where	nĕⁿiawĕⁿ"·seroⁿ so it will happen serially	ne' the	dji' eˑ" where there 13
ĕⁿioñthā·hi'neˑ, she will be traveling,	ne' the	ka'ti' so then	karī·hoñ'nīˑ it it causes	iāˑ" not	thāˑteiakotāˑ"oⁿˑ. she did stand.	No'kˑ And 14

clearing that was very large—in the center of which there lay a village, and the lodge of the chief of these people stood just in the middle of that village. Thither, then, to that place she went. And when she arrived at the place where stood his lodge, she kept right on and entered it. In the center of the lodge the fire burned, and on both sides of the fire were raised beds of mats. There the chief lay. She went on and placed beside him her basket of bread, and she said: "We two marry." So he spoke in reply saying: "Do thou sit on the other side of the fire." Thus, then, it came to pass, that they two had the fire between them, and besides this they uttered not a word together even until it became dark. Then, when the time came, after dark, that people retire to sleep habitually, he made up his mat bed. After finishing it he made her a mat bed at the foot of his. He then said: "Thou shalt lie here." So thereupon she lay down there, and he

---

1 hä'kare' after a time	neñ' now	iä'e'hĕñtä'rä'ne' thither she it field reached	kä'hĕñtowa'nĕⁿ'. it large field. (is)	Shä'tekä'hĕñt'hĕⁿ' Just it field in the middle of
2 eⁿ' tkanä'taiĕⁿ there it village lies	tä'hnoⁿ'! besides	ne' the	roñwäkowa'nĕⁿ' their chief	akwä'' shä'teka- the very just it village in the middle
3 iät'hĕⁿ' of	noñ'we' place	ni'honoⁿ''sote'. there his lodge stands.	E'' ka'ti' There so then	niiä'hä'ĕⁿ'. Ne' neñ' thither she The now went.
4 ka'ti' so then	dji' where	iä'hä''oñwe' there she arrived	ne' dji' the where	ronoⁿ''sote' o'k' ci'iĕⁿ tä'hnoⁿ'' his lodge stands only just she besides kept going
5 iä'hoñta'weiä'te'. thither she entered it.	Shä'tekanoⁿs'hĕⁿ' Just in the middle of the lodge	niiotek'hä' there it burns	tä'hioⁿ'' and	tedjia- on both
6 roⁿ''kwĕⁿ' sides	nä'kadjiĕⁿ''hätī' such it the fireside of	kanak'täiĕⁿ'. it couch (or bed) lay.	E'tho' There	räiä'tioñ'nī', his body lay supine,
7 o'k' ci'iĕⁿ' just just she kept going	wä'hoñwa'theräiĕⁿ''hä'se' she set the basket for him	ne' the	kanä'taroⁿk it bread	tä'hnoⁿ'' and
8 wä'i'roⁿ': she it said:	"Wä'oñkeni'niäke'." "Thou and I marry now."	Tä'hata'tī' He replied	ka'ti' so then	wä'hĕñ'roⁿ' he it said:
9 "E'rĕⁿ' "Yonder	nä'kadjiĕⁿ''hätī' such it fire side of	käsatiĕⁿ''." there do thou sit."	E'' ka'ti' There so then	nä'ä'wĕⁿ' wä'tii so it they it happened fire had
10 djiĕⁿ''hoñtĕⁿ' between them	tä'hnoⁿ'' besides	iä'' hĕⁿ'ska' not one (it is)	thä'teshoti''thare' did they talk together again	o'k' eⁿ'' only there
11 hiä'ōkarä''hwe'. it became evening.	Ne' The	ka'ti' so then	ne' dji' neñ' the where now	iä'kä''hewe' ne' dji' it was time the where
12 nitio'karä''oⁿ' there it is far in the evening	ne' the	neñ' now	dji' niiako'tä's where there they go to sleep customarily	neñ' wä'hatĕñnitska- now he prepared for himself
13 iä'seioñ'nī'. his mat.	Wä'hä''sä' He it finished	e'tho'ne' at that time	neñ' now	wä'shakotska'r'hä'se' dji' he it mat her spread for where
14 iä'te'hä'sī'täiĕⁿ there his feet lie.	Ne' The	ka'ti' so then	wä'beñ'roⁿ': he it said:	"Kĕⁿ'' ĕⁿ'sä'rate'." "Here thou shalt lie."

also lay down. They did not lie together; they only placed their feet together [sole to sole].

And when morning dawned, they two then arose. And now he himself kindled a fire, and when he had finished making the fire he then crossed the threshold into another room; he then came out bearing an onoia [string of ears] of white corn. He said: "Do thou work. It is customary that one who is living among the people of her spouse must work. Thou must take a bushel of hulled corn." So she thereupon shelled the corn, and he himself went to bring water. He also got a pot, a pot that belonged to him, and that was very large. He poured the water into the pot and hung it over the fire.

And when she had finished shelling the corn, she hulled it, parboiling the corn in the water. And when the corn was parboiled, she then poured the grains into a mortar. She then got the pestle from where

E'tho'ne'	ka'tĭ	nĕñ'	e''	wă'oñ'rate'	no'k'	ho'nĭ'	ne'	raoñ''hă'	1
At that time	so then	now	there	she lay down	but	also	the	he himself	
wă'ha'rate'.	Iă''	te'hoñnara'ton',	ne'	o'k'	ne'	wă'tiară·sītarī'ke'.			2
he lay down.	Not	they did lie together,	the	only	the	they joined their feet (sole to sole).			
No'k'	ne'	nĕñ'	că'or·hĕⁿ''ne'	nĕñ'	wă'hiatkets'ko'.	Nĕñ'	ne'		3
But	the	now	it became daylight	now	they two raised themselves.	Now	the		
ia'oⁿ·hă'	wă·hate'kă'te'.	Ne'	ka'tĭ'	ne'	nĕñ'	că'hadjiĕⁿ·hi·'să'			4
he himself	he it fire kindled.	The	so then	the	now	he it fire finished			
e'tho'ne'	iă'tha·nho'·hiiă'ke'	că'toñta·hāiā'kĕⁿ·ne'	skano'ră·	oıĕⁿ					5
at that time	thither he it threshold crossed	thence he came forth again	one string of corn	it white					
stakĕñ'ră·	shanorĕⁿ·hā'wī'.	Nĕñ'	wă·hĕñ'ron':	"Sāio''tĕⁿ·					6
grain	he string of corn brought.	Now	he it said:	Do thou labor.					
Iakoio''te'	ĕⁿ's ne'	ie·hnĕⁿ·hwă'·shĕⁿ'.	Ĕⁿsdjiskoñ'nī'	kanĕⁿ·hana-					7
One labors	customarily the	she lives in the family of (her) spouse.	Thou must make mush	it corn softened (soaked)					
wĕⁿ''toⁿ·.''	E'tho'ne'	ka'tĭ'	nĕñ'	wă'enĕⁿstaroñ'ko'	no'k'	ne'			8
by parboiling."	At that time	so then	now	she it corn shelled,	but	the			
ia'oⁿ·hă'	wă·ha·hnekako'·hă'	tă·hnoⁿ''	iă·hană·djā'ko'	ne'	raoñ'tă·k				9
he himelf	he water went to fetch	besides	there he it kettle got,	the	his pot				
kană·djowā'nĕⁿ·,	tă·hnoⁿ''	wă·ha·hnekĭ·hā'rĕⁿ'.							10
it kettle large	and	he it liquid hung (over the fire).							
No'k'	ne'	nĕñ'	că'ē's'ă'	wă'enĕⁿstaroñ'ko'	e'tho'ne'	wă-			11
And	the	now	wherein she finished it	she it corn shelled	at that time				
enĕⁿstana'wĕⁿ·te'	no'k'	ne'	nĕñ'	că'kanĕⁿstana'wĕⁿ'	e'tho'ne'				12
she it corn softened by parboiling	but	the	now	wherein it corn became soft by parboiling	at that time				
nĕñ'	kă·nikă''takoⁿ·	iă'enĕⁿsta'weroⁿ',	nĕñ'	iă'ecică''totā'ko'	nĕñ'				13
now	it mortar in	there she it corn grains poured,	now	she it pestle took from an upright position	now				
o'nĭ'	wă'et'he'te'.	Ĕn'skă'	o'k'	tāiecică''tĕⁿ·te'	no'k'	wă'ethe'se-			14
also	she it pounded.	One	only, just	she it pestle brought down	and	she finished			

it stood, and pounded the corn to meal. She brought the pestle down only once, and the meal was finished. The chief marveled at this, for he had never seen one make meal in so short a time. When she finished the meal, the water in the pot which he had hung over the fire was boiling. She, thereupon, of course, was about to put the meal into it, but he said: "Do thou remove thy garments." So she then divested herself of her garments. She finished this work, and then put the meal into the water. Now she stirred it, using a pot stick for the purpose. But the man himself lay alongside on the mat bed, having his eyes fixed upon her as she worked. So, of course, as the mush continually spattered, drops of it fell continually in divers places on her, all along her naked body. But she acted just as though she did not feel this. When the mush was sufficiently cooked, her whole naked body was fully bespattered with mush. At this moment he himself now removed the pot from the fire, and then, moreover, he opened a door not far away and said: "My slaves,

1	ii"să'. it meal.	Wă'rori'hwane'hra'ko' He it matter marveled at		ne' the	dji' where	iă" not	nonwĕñ'to^{n'} ever
2	te'hotkă"tho^{n'} he it has looked at	ne' the	niio'sno're' so it is rapid	āiethe'seri"să'. one it meal could finish.	Ne' The	ka'tĭ' so then	ne' the
3	nĕñ' now	că'ethe'seri"să' wherein it meal she finished	nĕñ' now	teio'hnekoñ'tie'se' it boils (casts liquid to and fro)	ne' the	ronă'dji''hare' he kettle has hung up.	
4	Nĕñ' Now	wă''hi' verily	nĕñ' now	iĕⁿiĕthe'sero''hwe', thither she it meal will immerse,	wă'hĕñ'roⁿ': he it said:	"Satseroñnia' "Do thou thy garments	
5	cioñ'ko'." remove."	E'tho'ne' At that time	ka'ti' so then	nĕñ' now	wă'oñtseroñnia'cioñ'ko'. she her garments removed.	Wă'e'să' She it finished	
6	e'tho'ne' at that time	nĕñ' now	ia'ethe'sero''hwe' thither she it meal immersed	nĕñ' now	teioñwĕñ'rie' she it stirred	kă'serawĕñ'rie' it pot stick	
7	ioñts'thă'. she it uses	No'k' And	ne' the	ra'oⁿ'hă' he himself	kanăktă'ke' it couch on	ne' the	thāia'tioñ'nĭ' there his body lay supine
8	te'shakokan'ere' he her watched	nĕñ' now	iakoio"te'. she is working.	Ne' The	ka'ti' so then	ne' the	dji' where	watdjĭs- it
9	kwătoñ'kwăs mush sputters	iako'stara'rā'sero^{n'} it drop impinges on her serially		ne' the	ie'hāiĕⁿ'să'ke"shoⁿ'. her naked body on along.	Nakwă" The very	
10	dji' where	ni'io't so it is (stands)	ne' the	iă" not	teiakoteriĕñ'tare'. she it knew.	Iă'tkāie'rī' It sufficient (is)	wă'kadjĭs'kwărĭ' it mush was cooked
11	nĕñ' now	ne' the	rakwă" the very	o'k' just	dji' where	niiebāiĕⁿ"să' so her naked body large (is)	iodjĭs'kware'. it mush is present.	E'tho'ne' At that time
12	nĕñ' now	ra'oⁿ'hă' he himself	wă'hană'dji'barā'ko', he unhung the kettle,	nĕñ' now	tă'hnoⁿ'' and (besides)	kĕⁿ'' here	roñ'we' the place
13	iă'ha'n'hotoñ'ko' there he moved the door-flap aside	tă'hnoⁿ'' and	wă'hĕñ'roⁿ': he it said:	"Aketsenĕⁿ''shoⁿ' "My slaves each one	ka'sene'." do ye two come."		

do ye two come hither." Thereupon there emerged two animals;
they were two large dogs. He said: "Do ye two wipe from along
her naked body the rush spots that have fallen on her." Thereupon
his slaves, two individuals in number, and besides of equal size,
went thither to the place where she was standing. Now, of course,
they two licked her naked body many times in many places. But, it is
said, their two tongues were so sharp that it was just as if one should
draw a hot rod along over her naked body. It is said that wherever
they two licked the blood came at once. So it is said that when they
two had finished this work, she stood there bathed in blood. He
thereupon said: "Now, do thou dress thyself again." And she did
redress herself. But, it is said, he said to his two slaves: "Come,
my slaves, do ye two eat, for now the food that was made for you is
cooked." So then the two beasts ate. And when they two had

E'' ka'ti'	takeniia'kĕⁿ'ne'	teknikowa'nĕⁿ·	e'r·hä·r.	Wä·heñ'roⁿ:		1
There so then	thence they two came forth	they two large are	dog(s).	He it said:		
"Säsenira'ke'f	(? oñsasenira'ke·w)ᵃ	ie·häiĕñsä'ke''shoⁿ	iodjĭskware'-			2
"Do ye two wipe it away again		her naked body on along	it mush is be- spattered			
nioⁿ.''	E'tho'ne'	ne'	raotsenĕⁿo'koñ'ä·	tekeniiä''she'	nĕñ'	3
sever- ally."	At that time	the	his slaves individually	they two individ- uals in number	now	
tä·hioⁿ·'	dji'	nä'tekenikowa'nĕⁿ·	e''	niiä·hä'kene'	ne' dji'	4
and	where	so they two (are) large	there	just thither they two went	the where	
i'tiete',	nĕñ' se''	o'k' wä''hi'	wä'akoti·häiĕⁿ·säkanĕñt'hoⁿ.	E'' se''		5
there she stood,	now in- deed	only verily	they her naked body licked repeatedly.	There in- deed,		
ia'kĕⁿ'	niionĕñ'nä·'säte't	dji'	ni'io't ne'	ioroñwaratari''hĕⁿ·	e''	6
it is said.	so their tongues sharp (are)	where	so it is the	it rod hot (is)	there	
naoñtäie'sere'	ie·häiĕⁿ·sä'ke''shoⁿ,	ne'	ĕⁿ's	ia'kĕⁿ' ne' dji'		7
so it one would draw along	her naked body along on,	the	custom- arily,	it is said. the where		
ioñ'we'	nakakä'noñte'	nakwä·'	o'k' e''	kanekwĕⁿ·sara'tie'.	Ne'	8
the place	so they licked	the very	just there	it blood came along with it.	The	
ka'ti' ia'kĕⁿ',	ne' nĕñ'	cä'keni·'sä'	nakwä·'	o'k' thidjene-		9
so then, it is said,	the now	they two it finished	the very	only she blood (just) stood		
kwĕⁿ·'sote'.	E'tho'ne' nĕñ'	wä·heñ'roⁿ:	"Nĕñ'	säsatseroñ'ni·."		10
forth.	At that time now	he it said:	"Now	do thou thyself dress again."		
E'tho'ne'	nĕñ'	säioñtseroñ'ni'.	No'k'	ne' raotsenĕⁿokoñ''ä·		11
At that time	now	she herself again dressed.	And	the his slaves individually		
wä·'rĕñ''hä·'se',	ia'kĕⁿ:	"Aketsenĕⁿokoñ''ä·,	hau'',	tedjitskä''hoⁿ·.		12
he it said to them,	it is said:	"My slaves individually,	come,	do ye two eat.		
Nĕñ' wä·'hi'	wä·ka'ni·	ne'	ietchikhoñniĕñ'ni·."	E'tho'ne'	nĕñ'	13
Now, verily	it is cooked	the	she you two food has prepared for."	At that time	now	

ᵃ This is the more correct form of the preceding term.

finished eating, he said to them: "Now do ye two reenter the other room." Thereupon they two reentered the other room, and moreover he shut them up therein.

Then, it is reported, he said: "It is true, is it not, that thou desirest that thou and I should marry? So, now, thou and I do marry."

So then the things that came to pass as they did during the time she was there were all known to her beforehand, because her father had indeed foretold all these things to her; hence she was able with fortitude to suffer the burns without flinching, when the mush spattered on her while she was cooking. If she had flinched when the drops of hot mush fell on her, he would have said to her: "I do not believe that it is true that it is thy wish that thou and I should marry." Besides this she bore with fortitude the pain at the time when the two

1. wă'tkiatskă'hoⁿ. No'k· ne' něñ' că'kenikhwěñ'tă'ne' wă'hěñ'roⁿ·
they two (anim.) ate. And the now they two it food finished he it said:

2. "Něñ' skă'n'ho''hătĭ· ioñsasadjiata'weiă'te'." E'thone' něñ'
"Now beyond it door-flap thither again do ye two enter." At that time now

3. skă'n'ho''hătĭ· ioñsakiata'weiă'te', něñ' tă'hnoⁿ' ioñsashako·n·ho'toⁿ
beyond the door-flap thither they two entered, now and thither again he them shut up.

4. E'tho'ne', ia'kěⁿ, něñ' wă'hěñ'roⁿ": "To'kěⁿske' wă'hĭ' e"
At that time, it is said. now he it said: "It is true verily thus

5. nitisă'nikoⁿ'hro'těⁿ· ne' āioñkeni'niake'. Něñ' ka'tĭ· wă'oñke
so thus thy mind (is) kind of the thou-I should marry. Now so then. thou-I do

6. ni'niake'."
marry."

7. Ne' ka'tĭ· ne' dji' nă'awěⁿ''seroⁿ' ne' dji' něñ' ıă'he" e"
The so then the where so it happened iteratively the where now length of time there

8. ieia'ko. Akwe'koⁿ· o'hěñ'toⁿ· tiiakoterıěñ'tare', a·se''kěⁿ·' ne'
there she arrived. Whole (all) beforehand (in front) there she it knew of, because the

9. ro'ıi'hă· akwe'koⁿ· se" te·shako·hro'rĭ· ne' karĭ'hoñ'nĭ·
he her father all, indeed, he her told the it it caused

10. wă'ekwe'nĭ' wă'oñtă·kats'tate' ne' dji' niio'tarĭ''hěⁿ· că'akodjis
she it was able to do she herself nerved to endure it the where so it hot (is) it her mush

11. kwatoñ'ko' ne' něñ' ciiakodjisko''hoⁿ·, a·se'kěⁿ·' to'kă' aoñtă
spattered on the now she it mush boiled, because if she it had

12. iakotoⁿ''noⁿ' ne' něñ' că'ako·stara'ră'ne' ne' iodjiskwatarĭ''hěⁿ·
shrunk from the now it drop her adhered to the it mush (is) hot

13. ă'hawěñ'ke', kĭ": "Iă" to'kěⁿske' e" tetisă'nikoⁿ'hro'těⁿ· ne'
he would have said, I believe: "Not it is true thus such there thy mind is kind of the

14. āioñkeni'niake'." No'k· o'ıi' ne' dji' wă'oñtă·kats'tate' ne'
thou-I should marry." And also the where she herself nerved to endure it the

dogs licked the rush from her body. If she had flinched to the point of refusing to finish her undertaking, it is also certain that he would have said: "It is of course not true that thou desirest that thou and I should marry."

And when his two beasts had finished eating, he then, it is said, showed her just where his food lay. Thereupon she prepared it, and when she had completed the preparation thereof, they two then ate the morning meal.

It is said that she passed three nights there, and they two did not once lie together. Only this was done, it is reported: When they two lay down to sleep, they two placed their feet together, both placing their heads in opposite directions.

Then, it is said, on the third morning, he said: "Now thou shalt again go thither to the place whence thou hast come. One basket of dried venison thou shalt bear thither on thy back by means of the fore-

Něñ'	ne'	shoūsāiakotidjiskokewa'nioⁿ.		To'kā'		aoñtāiakotoⁿ'/noⁿ'	1
now	the	again they (two) it mush in many places wiped off of her.		If		she it had shrunk from	

ne'	dji'	ne'	āiakokarā'rĕñ'/oⁿ'	ne'	ki''	o'nī'	ne'	a'ha'wĕnke'	2
the	where	the	she it would have been in fear of	the,	I believe,	also	the	he would have said:	

"Iā'' wă''hī to'kĕⁿske' te'se're' āioñkeni'niake'."
"Not   verily   it is true   thou it desirest   thou-I should marry."

No'k'	ne'	nĕñ'	cā'kenikhwĕñ'tā'ne'	ne'	raotsenĕⁿ'okoñ''ā'	4
And	the	now	they two their food finished	the	his slaves individually	

e'tho'ne',	ia'kĕⁿ,	nĕñ'	wā'shakonā'toñ''hā'se'	dji'	noñ'we'	5
at that time,	it is said,	now	he her it showed to	where	place	

nikake''roⁿ	ne'	rao'khwā'.	E'tho'ne',	nĕñ'	wā'ekwata'ko'	dji'	6
so it is piled	the	his food.	At that time	now	she it made ready	where	

niio're'	wā'e'sā'	nĕñ'	wā'tiatskā''hoⁿ'	ne'	o'r'hoⁿke'ne'	
so it is distraut	she it finished	now	they two ate	the	it morning at.	

'Ā''sĕⁿ'	ia'kĕⁿ	nā'oñnoñ'wete'	tā'hnoⁿ''	iā''	ĕⁿ'skā'	te'hoñna-	8
Three,	it is said,	so she stayed over the night	and	not	one (time)	they did lie	

ra'toⁿ'.	Ne'	o'k'	ĕⁿ's	ia'kĕⁿ	ne'	wā'tiarā'sītari'ke'	ne'	dji'	9
together.	The	only	customarily	it is said	the	they their feet joined	the	where	

wā'hoti'tā'we',	tenidjia'roⁿ'	e'rĕⁿ'	noñka'tī'	iā'teñiatkoñ''hĕñ'.	10
they slept,	both they two	yonder (elsewhere)	side of it	there they two their heads rest.	

Ne'	ka'tī	ia'kĕⁿ	ie'ne'	o'r'hoⁿke'ne'	nĕñ'	wā'hĕñ'roⁿ':	11
The	so then	it is said,	the that	morning in	now	he it said:	

"Nĕñ'	e''	iĕⁿ'se''se'	ne'	dji'	noñ'we'	tisā'tĕñ'tioⁿ''.	Sewā'the'rat	12
"Now	there	there again thou shalt go	the	where	the place	just thou didst depart.	One it basket	

ne'	ioñtke'tats'thā'	o'skĕñ'noñtoⁿ'	tekāiā'tanetā''kwĕⁿ'	io'wā'rāt'hĕⁿ'	13
the	one uses it to carry by the forehead strap	it deer	one its body has unlined (from fat)	it meat (is) dry	

iĕⁿ'se'satke''tate'.	Ěnkhe'wāra'noñte'	ne'	soñkwe'tā'.	No'k'	ho'nī	14
thither thou it wilt hear by the forehead strap.	I them meat will give	the	thy people.	And	also	

head strap. I will give some meat to thy people. Moreover, the entire village of people with whom thou dwellest in one place must all share alike in the division of the meat when thou arrivest there."

Thereupon, it is told, he climbed up above and drew down quarters of meat that had been dried. It is said that he piled it very high in the lodge before he descended. He then put the meat into her burden basket until it was full. Then, it is told, he took up the basket, and he shook the basket to pack the meat close. It actually did settle so much, it is told, that there was but a small quantity [apparently] in the basket. Now, he again began to put meat into the basket. It was again filled. And he again shook it to cause it to settle, and again it settled until it occupied but a very small space in the basket. Thus he used all the meat thrown down, and yet the basket was not full. Thrice, it is told, he drew down the quarters of

---

1. ne' o'k‘ iekanatakwe'ko$^{n\text{‘}}$ ne' skä‘'ne‘ tisewanak'ere' akwe'ko$^{n\text{‘}}$
   the only just it village whole the one in (place) just there ye dwell all

2. shä'tĕ^{n}ia'wĕñne‘ ĕ^n‘hatiiä'kho$^{n\text{‘}}$ ne' o'wä'ro$^{n\text{‘}}$ ne' nĕñ' iĕ^n‘se‘'sewe'''
   equal it shall happen they (m.) it will share the it meat the now there thou wilt arrive.''

3. E'tho'ne', ia'kĕ^n, nĕñ' iä'harat'hĕ^n‘ ē'nekĕ^n‘ tä'hä'wa'rani‘'se
   At that time, it is said, now thither he climbed high (place) he quarters

4. iĕ^n‘té' ne' io'wä'rat'hĕ^n‘. Ä'e'rĕ^n‘, ia'ke^n‘, nä'otoñwes'hä'ne' ne'
   of meat got down the it meat dry (is). Far yonder, it is said, it pile became large the

5. kano^n‘'säko$^{n\text{‘}}$ ne' nĕñ' toñta'hats'nĕ^n‘te'. E'tho'ne' nĕñ' ako'the-
   it lodge in the now thence he descended. At that time now he her

6. ia'ko$^{n\text{‘}}$ ne' ioñtke'tats'thä' e‘' wä'ha'wa'ra'tä' dji' niio're'
   basket In the one uses it to bear it by the forehead strap there he placed the meat in (it) where so it is distant

7. wä'kä'nä'ne'. E'tho'ne' ne' ia'kĕ^n‘, wä'tha'therä‘'kwe' tä'hno$^{n\text{''}}$
   it it filled. At that time the, it is said, he it basket took up and

8. wä'tha'therakarĕñ‘'ro^n‘ iä'hä'djio'roke‘. To'kĕ^{n}ske‘, ia'kĕ^n,
   he basket rocked from side to side. he it caused to settle down. It is true, it is said,

9. oñtä'djio'roke', nakwä‘' o'sthoñ‘'hä‘ o'k‘ te'tkäre'. Nĕñ' a're'
   it itself settled, the very it small is only there it is present (is left) Now again

10. toñtä'hatä‘'säwĕ^n‘ sä'hä'wa'rä'tä' ne' a'thera'ko$^{n\text{‘}}$. Saka'nä'ne'
    there again he began again he it meat put into the it basket In. Again it became full

11. a'ré'. E'tho'ne' nĕñ' a're' sä'ha'djio'roke' ne' a're' nakwä‘'
    once more. At that time now again again he it caused to settle the again the very

12. o'sthoñ‘'hä‘ o'k‘ te'tkäre'. E‘' thiiä'hä's'ä‘te' ne' o'wa'ro$^{n\text{‘}}$ iä‘'
    it small is only there it remains (is left). Thus, until he used it all the it meat not

13. teiona'noñ‘'o$^{n\text{‘‘}}$. Ä‘'sĕ^n‘, ia'kĕ^n‘ nä'ha'terätste' ta'ha'wä'rani'serĕ^n‘te'.
    it it filled. Three, it is said, so he repeated it he got down quarters of meat.

r eat, and each time, it is said, did the r eat nearly fill the lodge. Not until then was the basket filled. So then, when the basket was full, it is told, he said: "When thou arrivest there, thou and the inhabitants of the place r ust asse r ble in council, and the r eat shall be equally divided a r ong you. Moreover, thou r ust tell the r that they severally must remove the thatched roofs fro r their lodges when the evening darkness co r es, and that they r ust severally go out of the r. And they must store all the corn [hail] that will fall in the lodges, for, indeed, verily, it will rain corn [hail] this very night when thou arrivest there. So now thou r ust bear on thy back by r eans of the forehead strap this basket of dried venison." Thereupon he took up the basket for her, and he said: "Thou r ust carefully adjust the burden strap in the proper place, because it will then not be possible for thee to r ove the burden strap to a new place, no matter how tired soever

Tho'·hä·	ĕⁿ's,	ia'kĕⁿ·.	wä'kä'nä·ne'	ne'	dji'	nikanoⁿ'·sä'.	Oñ'wa'	1
Nearly	usually,	it is said,	it it filled.	the	where	so it lodge-large (is).	Just now	
wä'ka'nä·ne'.	Ne''	ka'tï'	ne'	nĕñ'	cä'kä'nä·ne'	e'tho'ne',	ia'kĕⁿ'.	2
it it filled.	The	so then	the	now	just it was filled	at that time,	it is said,	
wä·hĕñ'roⁿ':	"Ne'	nĕñ'	iĕⁿ·se·'sewe'	ĕⁿietchiiätkĕñnis'ä·'te'			ne'	3
he it said:	"The	now	there thou wilt arrive	they you shall assemble in			the	
ienäk'ere'	tä'hnoⁿ''	·ĕⁿietchiiäk'hoñ''hä'se'		ne'	o'wä''roⁿ'',			4
they dwell	and	they it shall divide among you		the	it meat,			
shä'tĕⁿiawĕñ'ne'	akwe'koⁿ·.	Tä·hnoⁿ''	ĕⁿietchi·hro'rï'				ne'	5
equal·so it will happen	all.	And	will one-you tell				the	
ĕⁿioⁿskwä·roñ'ko'	ne'	dji'	iakonoⁿ·sō'toⁿ'	ne'	nĕñ'	ĕⁿtio'kärä·hwe'		6
will they remove bark-roofs	the	where	their lodges stand severally	the	now	again will it become dark		
ne'	o'nï'	ne'	ĕⁿieiakĕñ''seroⁿ'.	Ne'	akwe'koⁿ·	ĕⁿioñteweiĕñ'toⁿ'		7
the	also	the	they will go out of doors.	The	all	they it will care for		
ne'	o'nĕⁿste'	ne'	kanoⁿ''säko'''	ĕⁿkake·roñ'tä·ne'.	a·'se'kĕⁿ·''		ne'	8
the	(it corn) hail	the	it lodge in	it will pile up.	because		the	
se''	wä·'hï'	ne'	o'nĕⁿste'	ĕⁿiokĕñ'nore'	ne'ne·	dji'	wä·soñ'tate'	9
indeed	verily	the	(it corn) hail	will it rain	the that	where	it night (is) extant	
ne'	nĕñ'	iĕⁿ·se·'sewe'.	Nĕñ	ka'tï'	iĕⁿ''se·sata·therake·'tate'			10
the	now	there thou wilt arrive.	Now	so then	thither again thou wilt bear (it) basket on thy back by the forehead strap			
kĕⁿ'i'kĕⁿ·	o·skĕñnoñ'toⁿ'	io'wä·rat'bĕⁿ·''.		E'tho'ne'	nĕñ'			11
this it is	it deer	it meat (is) dry.''		At that time	now			
wä·te·shako·therä·''kwĕⁿ'	ne'	o'nï'	wä·hĕñ'roⁿ':	"Akwä''	kasate-			12
he it basket for her took up	the	also	he it said:	"Very	do thou it do			
weiĕñ'toⁿ·	dji'	noñ'we·	nĕⁿwatke·to''hetste',	a·'se'kĕⁿ·''	iä·'	se''		13
with care	where	place	it forehead strap will pass,	because	not	indeed		
e'rĕⁿ·	thäsketä·'kwi·te'	iaweroñ·hä'tiĕⁿ	to'	nä·tĕⁿshwi·shĕⁿ·'heie'				14
in another place	thou it it forehead strap shalt move,	it matters not	how	so thou wilt die in thy strength become wearied				

thou mavest become, until thou indeed arrivest there. Now, at that time thou must remove thy burden." So then, when she had completed her preparations, she adjusted the burden strap so that it passed over her forehead at the fittest point. She then said: "Now I believe I have completed my preparations, as well as chosen just where the burden strap shall pass." Thereupon he released his hands from holding up the basket for her, and now, moreover, she started on her journey homeward.

Now, moreover, the basket she carried on her back was not at all heavy. But when she had gone perhaps one-half of the way back on her journey, the burden began to be heavy in a small measure. Then, as she continued her journey, it gradually became heavier. The instant she reached the inside of the lodge, the burden strap became detached and the basket fell to the ground, and the dried meat fell out of it. The meat filled the space within the lodge, for did she not bring much

	dji′	niio′re·	se″	wă·ˈhĭ′	iĕⁿ·se·ˈsewe′.	E·tho′ne·	nĕñ′
1	where	so it is distant	indeed	verily	there thou wilt arrive.	At that time	now

	ĕⁿ·se·satke·tă·ˈsĭ′."	Ne·	ka′tĭ·	ne′	dji′	nĕñ′	wă·eweiĕñnĕñ·tă·ne′
2	thou wilt take it from bearing it on thy back by the forehead strap."	The	so then	the	where	now	she task completed

	wă·ekwata′ko·	dji″	noñ′we·	nĕⁿwatke·to′·hetste·	wă·i′roⁿ·:	"Nĕñ′,
3	she it adjusted with care	where	the place	there it forehead strap will pass	she it said:	"Now,

	kĭ″	wă·keweiĕñnĕñ·tă·ne′	dji′	noñ′we·	nĕⁿwatke·to′·hetste·."
4	I believe,	I it task have completed	where	the place	there it forehead strap will pass."

	E·tho′ne·	wă·ha·ˈtkă·we·	ne′	dji′	ro·therakarā′tatoⁿ·	tă·hnoⁿ′
5	At that time	he it let go	the	where	he it basket held up	and

	e·tho′ne·	nĕñ′	sāioⁿ·tĕñ′tĭ′.			
6	at that time	now	she started homeward.			

	Nĕñ′	tă·hnoⁿ″′	iă·″	othe′noⁿ·	teiok′ste·	sāioñta·therake·′tate·.
7	Now	and	not	anything	it heavy is	again she it basket bears on her back by the forehead-strap.

	To′kă′	oⁿ″′te·	shă·tewă·sĕñ′noⁿ‘	dji′	niio′re·	niieiăkawe′non	nĕñ′
8	If	perhaps	just it (is) middle	where	so it is distant	just there she had gone	now

	toñtă·′săwĕ″′	o‘sthoñ′·hă‘	wă·okstĕñ′·ne·.	Ne′	ka′tĭ·	ne′	dji′
9	there it began	it (is) small	it heavy became.	The	so then	the	where

	niiako·tĕñtioñ·hă′tie·	tăiokstĕñ·′sere·.	Iă·ˈtkaie′rĭ·	kanoⁿ·′sakoⁿ‘
10	just so she traveled along	it became heavier increasingly.	It sufficient is	it lodge in

	ioñsāiera′tă·ne·	nĕñ′	toñ·ˈtke·totari·′sĭ′	tă·hnoⁿ′	e·ˈtă·ˈke‘	iă·hoⁿthe
11	there again she stood	now	it forehead-strap became unfastened	and	down, on the ground	there it

	răiĕñ·tă·ne·	tă·hnoⁿ′	oñweroñ·tă·ne·	ne′	io·wă·ˈrat·hĕⁿ·.	Wă·ˈkă′
12	basket fell	and	it spilled	the	it meat dry (is).	It it filled

	wă·ra′nă·ne·	ne′	dji′	niionak′tă·	ne′	kanoⁿ·′sakoⁿ‘.	E′so′	se″
13	with meat	the	where	so its room large (is)	the	it lodge in.	Much	indeed

ı eat on her back? For thrice, is it not true, he had pulled down ı eat in his lodge when he was putting the ı eat into her basket at the time when he was ı aking up her burden? It was then that she told the ı that they ı ust remove the thatched roofs from their lodges when it became evening.

Then she said: "He has sent you some ı eat. Now then, my kinsfolk, take up this meat lying in the lodge." Then at that ti ı e her people took up the dried ı eat, and so they all carried it away. She then said: "Ye ı ust remove the thatched roofs from the lodges that severally belong to you the first ti ı e ye go to sleep, because ı y spouse has sent word that he will give you so ı e white corn [white grains] during the time that ye will again be asleep. It will rain white grains while ye again are asleep." So, when it beca ı e dark,

wä´·hĭ̆	ne´	djiako'wä·rake'´te`,	a·se·kĕⁿ·´	ä·´sĕⁿ·	se´´	wä´·hĭ̆	
verily	the	she meat bore on her back by the forehead-strap.	because	three	indeed	verily	1
nä·bakar·hätĕ´nĭ̆	ne´	raonoⁿ·sakoⁿ·´	ne´	nĕñ´	cä·hä`wä·rä´tä`	ne´	
so many he turned (or threw) it down	the	his lodge in	the	now	since he meat placed in it	the	2
ako·thera´koⁿ·	ne´	nĕñ´	säshako·rie·nŏñ´niĕⁿ.		E·tho´ne`	ka´tĭ̆	
her basket in	the	now	he it her burden made for.		At that time	so then	3
nĕñ´	wä·oñt‘hro´rĭ̆	ne´	ĕⁿio·skwä·hroñ´ko`	ne´	dji´	iako-	
now	she it told	the	they will (must) take off tire bark-roof plurally	the	where	their	4
noⁿ·´so´toⁿ·	ne´	nĕñ´	ĕⁿio·karä·sne´·hä`.				
lodges stand plurally	the	now	it will become somewhat dark.				5
E·tho´ne`	wä·i´roⁿ·:	"E·tchisewä·waranoñtĕⁿ·hä´tie`		Nĕñ´	ka´tĭ̆		
At that time	she it said:	"He meat you has sent along to		Now	so then		6
ne´	kwanoⁿ·kwe·o´koⁿ·	te´sne·kwe`	kĕⁿ·i´kĕⁿ·	kä´wa·rake´·hroⁿ·			
the	ye my kindred severally	do ye it take up	this it (is)	it meat lying in a pile			7
kanoⁿ·´sakoⁿ·"	Ta´,	e·tho´ne`	nĕñ´	ne´	akaoñkwe´tä`	nĕñ´	
it lodge in."	So,	at that time	now	the	her kindred	now	8
wä´tie·kwe`	ne´	io·wä·rat´hĕⁿ·.	Ne´	ka´tĭ̆	ne´	nĕñ´	akwe´koⁿ·
they it took up	the	it meat dry (is).	The	so then	the	now	all (it is)	9
iä·e´·häwe`,	e·tho´ne`	nĕñ´	wä·i´roⁿ·:	"Ĕⁿtcia·skwä·hroñ´ko`		ne´	
thither they it bore away,	at that time	now	she it said:	"Ye will remove it bark-roof plurally		the	10
dji´	sewanoⁿ·´so´toⁿ·	ne´	ĕⁿtwatie´rĕⁿ·te`	nĕñ´	ĕⁿsewĕñ´tä´we`,		
where	your houses stand one by one	the	it will be the first	now	ye will sleep,		11
a·se·kĕⁿ·´	rawĕñ·hä´tie`	ne´	teiakeni´teroⁿ·	onĕⁿ·stakĕñ´rä·	ĕⁿietchi-		
because	he it said along, sent word	the	one I with whom abide	it corn white	he you corn		12
sewanĕⁿ·stanoñ´te`.	Onĕⁿ·stakĕñ´rä·	ĕⁿiokĕñ´nore`	dji´	nä´·he`			
will give.	It corn white	it will rain	where	it lasts (so long)			13
ĕⁿtciswĕñtä´seke`."							
again ye will sleep."							14

it showered corn [hail] during the entire night, and so by this means they had much grain [hail] when day dawned.

Then, in truth, they removed the roofs from their several lodges, and they retired to sleep. So, when they awakened, in truth, then there was very much corn [hail] lying in the lodges. The white corn [grain] lay above one's knees in depth. Thus lay the white corn, for so long as they slept it showered white corn [grain]. The reason that he gave her people corn was because he had espoused one of their people.

After a suitable time she started back, going to the lodge of her spouse. Verily she again made the journey in the same time that it took her the first time she went thither. So then, when she arrived there, she of course at that time related to him all that had happened

1	Ne′ The	ka′tī′ so then	ne′ the	nĕñ′ now	tāiokara′·hwe′ then it became dark	wa̱·okĕñ′nore′ it rained	o′nĕⁿ·ste′ it corn (hail)	
2	ä·sontăkwe′koⁿ·. it night entire.	E·′ There	ka′tī′ so then	nontontie′rä·te′ it did it by this means		wä·rotinĕⁿ·staka̱′tĕⁿne′ their corn (hail) became abundant for them		
3	ne¹ the	nĕñ′ now	cä·o·r′·hĕⁿ·. it (became) morning.					
4	To′kĕⁿske′ It is true	ka′tī′ so then	wä·oñ·skwä·hroñ′ko′ they removed bark-roof plurally	nĕñ′ now	e′tho′ne′ at that time	wä·ho they		
5	tī′tä·we′. fell asleep.	Ne′ The	ka′tī′ so then	ne′ the	nĕñ′ now	shoñsa·hatī′ie′ again they awoke	to′kĕⁿske′ it is true	ka′tī′ so then
6	iawe·towa′nĕⁿ· it is a quantity great	kanoⁿ·′säko′·′ it lodge in	kä′iĕⁿ·. it lay.	E′nekĕⁿ· Above	nä·akokwits′·hätī·′ so one's knee side of			
7	e·′ there	nī′tio· so it is deep	ne′ the	onĕⁿ·stakĕñ′rä· it corn white	a′se·kŏⁿ·′ because	dji′ where	nä′·he· it lasts (so long)	roti′tä′s they slept
8	e·′ there	nä′·he· it lasted	onĕⁿ·stakĕñ′rä· it corn white	iokĕñ′noroⁿ·. it has rained.	Ne′ The	tiiori′·hwä· it is reason	wä·sha- he it them	
9	kä′oⁿ· gave to	ne′ the	o′nĕⁿ·ste· it corn (hail)	ne¹ the	akaoñkwe′tä· her kindred	ne′ the	dji′ where	rotinia′koⁿ· they (are) married
10	ne′ the	raoñnoñkwe′tä′, his kindred,	tä·hnoⁿ·′′ and	ne·′tho· such	ni·hatiri′ho′tĕⁿ·. so their custom was.			
11	Akwä·′′ Very	ē′tho· enough	dji′ where	nä′·he· it lasts	nĕñ′ now	säioⁿ·tĕñ′tī′, (again she started) she went home	e·′ there	säiĕⁿ·′′te′ again she went
12	ne′ the	dji′ where	thonoⁿ·′sote′ there his lodge stands	ne¹ the	io′ne′. be her spouse.	E·′ There,	ki′′ I believe,	a′re′ again	nä′·he· it lasts	toñsäi- again she up
13	oñtha′·hä·kwe′ her journey took	dji′ where	ni·io′t· so it stands	ne′ the	tiiotierĕⁿ·′toⁿ· so it was first	e·′ there	cä·ĕⁿ·′te′. where she went.	Ne′ The
14	ka′tī′ so then	ne′ the	nĕñ′ now	ciioñsä′ioñwe′. there again she arrived.	Ta′, So,	e·tho′ne′ at that time	wä·′hī′ verily	nĕñ′ now
15	sä·hoñwä·hro′rī′ again she him told	akwe′koⁿ· it all	dji′ where	nä·awĕⁿ·′′seroⁿ′ it happened serially	ne¹ the	dji′ where	säie- again	

to her during her journey to and from home. Of course they two now abode together, for the reason, of course, that they two were espoused.

After a time he then said: "I am ill." So then, his people marveled at what he said, for the reason that they did not know what it was for one to be ill. So, therefore, at the time when they comprehended what had occurred in regard to him, they, of course, individually, as was customary, studied the matter, and informed the man who was ill what to do. It would seem, one would imagine, that his illness did not abate thereby, even though many different persons made the attempt, and his recovery was yet an unaccomplished task. So thus it stood; they continued to seek to divine his Word. Then, therefore, when they failed to cure his illness, they questioned him, saying: "How, then, perhaps, may we do that thou mayest recover from thy

kwăt'ho'.	Ta',	něñ'	ne"tho·	ni'io't	wă'·hī'	skă·'ne⁴	niteroⁿ'.		1
she is visited.	So,	now	thus	so it stands	verily	together (at one)	they two abode,		
1o'ne·	se'·	wă'·hī'.							2
his spouse (she is)	in-deed	verily.							
A'kaie·	něñ'	wă·běñ'ro'":	"Wăkenoⁿ·hwăk'tanī'."	Ta',	e·tho'ne·				3
After a time	now	he it said:	"I am ill."	So,	at that time				
něñ'	ne'	raoñkwe'tă·	wă·hotine·hrā'ko·	ne'	dji'	nă·'ho'těⁿ"			4
now	the	his people	they marveled	the	where	such kind of thing			
rā'toⁿ'.	a·se·kěⁿ·'	iă·'	te·hatiiěñte'ri·	o·'	ne'	nă·ho'těⁿ"	ne'		5
he it said,	because	not	they it knew	what	the	such kind of the thing (it is)	the		
āiakoněⁿ·hwăk'těⁿ".	Ne'	ka'tī'	ne'	dji'	něñ'	wă·hoti·nikoⁿ·hrāiěñ'-			6
one should be ill	The	so then	the	where	now	they it understood			
tă'ne·	dji'	niioteri·hwătiē'rěⁿ·	ne'	raoⁿ·hā'ke⁴.	Něñ	wă'·hī'			7
where	so it matter was done		the	he himself at (himself to)	Now	verily			
shatiiă·tats'hoⁿ"	dji'	ěⁿ's	ni'io't	dji'	těⁿ·bāiă·to're·'te·	wă·ho·hro'rī'			8
they every person one by one	where customarily	so it (is)	where	he it will judge of	he him told				
ěⁿ's	ne'	ronoⁿ·hwăk'tanī·	ne'	dji'	nă·hā'iere'.	Iă·'	hoⁿ·'te·kěⁿ"		9
cus-tomarily	the	he is ill	the	where	so he it should do.	Not	perhaps-is it		
ta·hoñsa·hāie·wěñ'tā·ne·,	wă·thoñttenioñ'ko·	iă·'	ki"	tewaā'toⁿ·s					10
again he recovered his health,	they took turns plurally	not,	I believe,	it it is able to do					
aoñsa·hāie·wěñ'tā·ne·.	Ta',	e''	ni'io't	hotěⁿ"'niote·	ē'tho·	hoñwa-			11
should again he recover his health.	So,	thus	so it (is)	he it feast holds	there	they			
wěñni·'saks.	Ne'	ka'tī'	a'kaie·	ne'	dji'	něñ'	wă·hoññā·ta'ko·		12
sought to divine his Word continually).	The	so then	after a time	the	where	now	they it failed to do		
ne'	aoñsa·hoñwatcoñ'toⁿ"	e·tho'ne·	něñ'	wă·hoñwari·hwănoñ'toⁿ"se'.					13
the	again they his health restore	at that time	now	they him asked questions,					
wă·hoñni'roⁿ"':	"O"	ka'tī'	oⁿ·'te·	nāiakwā'iere·	ne'	aoñsa·sie'-			14
they it said:	"What	so then	may it be	so we it should do	the	again thou shouldst			

illnĕss?' Then he answered the 1, saying: "I am thinking that, perhaps, I should recover from my illness if ye would uproot the tree standing in 1 y dooryard [on my shade], and if there beside the place from which ye uproot the tree I should lay 1 yself in a position recu 1 bent."

So thereupon his people uprooted the tree that stood in his dooryard. This tree belonged to the species wild cherry [dogwood; in Tuscarora, Nakwĕnnĕⁿˈiĕñthuç], and was constantly adorned with blossoms that gave light to the people dwelling there; for these flowers were white, and it was because of this that the blossoms gave light, and, therefore, they were the light orb [sun] of the people dwelling there.

So when they had uprooted the tree, he said to his spouse: "Do thou spread for me so 1 ething there beside the place where stood the tree." Thereupon she, in fact, spread something for hi 1 there, and

1	wĕñ'tä'ne'?" recover thy health?"	Ta', So,	e'tho'ne', at that time,	la'kĕⁿˈ, it is said,	thotä'tī· he replied	ne' the	o'nīˀ also	wäˈ he
2	hĕñ'roⁿˈˈ: it said:	"I'keˈie' "I it think	oⁿˈˈte' it may be	aoñsakie'wĕñ'tä'ne' I would recover my health		to'käˈ if	aesewaroñ you it tree should	
3	tota'ko' uproot	ne' the	akwatĕñno'serä'keˈ my yard in	i'kĕⁿˢ it is	keˈiˈˈhite', it tree stands,		tä'hnoⁿˈˈ and	e" there
4	iĕⁿkatiä'tioñ'nite' there I my body supine will lay	ak'täˈ near beside it	dji' where	noñ'weˈ the place	nĕⁿsewaroñtota'ko'." ye it tree will uproot."			
5	Ta', So,	e'tho'ne' at that time	ne' the	raoñkwe'täˈ his people	wäˈhatiroñtota'ko' they it tree uprooted	ne' the	keˈiˈˈhite' it tree stands	
6	ne' the	dji' where	raotĕñno'sera'keˈ, his yard in	o'rä'toⁿˈˈ it wild cherry	nä'karoñto'tĕⁿˈˈ such it kind of tree (is)	ne' the	keˈiˈˈhite' it tree stands	
7	tiio'tkoⁿˈˈ always, continuously	iotci'tcoñte' it bears flower as part of itself	ne', the,	iaˈkĕⁿˈ, it is said,	teio'swathe'täˈˈkoⁿˈˈ it causes it to be light thereby		ne' the	dji' where
8	eˈˈ there	ratinăk'ereˈ; they dwell;	aˈseˈkĕⁿˈˈˈ because	kĕñra'kĕⁿˢ it white (is)	nikatcītco'tĕⁿˢ such it flower kind of (is)			ne' the
9	aoriˈˈhwäˈ its cause	teio'swat'he' it (is) light	ne' the	aotcī'tcäˈ its flowers	ne' the	dji' where	kĕñra'kĕⁿˢ it (is) white	ni'loˈt. so it (is), stands.
10	Ne' The	näˈˈ that it is	raotirä'ˈkwäˈ their it sun (is)	ne' the	eˈˈ there	noñ'weˈ place	niˈhatinăk'ereˈ. just there they dwell.	
11	Ne' The	ka'tī so then	ne' the	neñ' now	ciˈhotiroñtotä'kwĕⁿˈˈ they had uprooted the tree		wäˈshakawĕⁿˈˈˈhäˈse' he her it said to	
12	ne' the	iō'ne': his spouse:	"Eˈˈ "There	iä'takitskarˈˈhäˈse' thither do thou me spread a mat for	ăk'täˈ near beside it	ne' the	dji' where	keˈiˈˈhītäˈ- it tree
13	kweˈ." stood."	E'tho'ne' At that time	tō'kĕⁿske' it is true	eˈˈ there	iäˈboñwĕⁿtskarˈˈhäˈse', there she spread a mat for him,		tä'hnoⁿˈˈ and	

---

a Several different kinds of trees and plants are named by various narrators as the tree or plant thus uprooted. Here the narrator intended the dogwood, although he gave the name for wild cherry).

he then lay down on what she had spread for him. And so, when he lay there, he said to his spouse: "Here sit thou, beside my body." Now at that time she did sit beside his body as he lay there. He then said to her: "Do thou hang thy legs down into the abyss." For where they had uprooted the tree there came to be a deep hole, which extended through to the nether world, and the earth was upturned about it.

That, then, it is true, came to pass, that while he lay there his suffering was mitigated. All his people were assembled there, and moreover, they had their eyes fixed on him as he lay there ill, marveling at this thing that had befallen him himself; for the people dwelling here did not know what it is to be ill. So then, when he had, seemingly, recovered from his illness, he turned himself over,

e'tho'ne'	e''	iä·ha'rate'	dji'	noñ'we'	wä·hoñwĕⁿtskar'·hä·se'.		1
at that time	there	there he lay down	where	the place	she him mat spread for.		
Ne'	ka'tī	wä'·hī'	ne'	dji'	nĕñ' e'' rāiä'tioñ'nī'	wä·shakawĕⁿ'·'hä·se'	2
The	so then	verily	the	where	now there his body was extended	he her it said to	
ne'	io'ne':	"Kĕⁿ''	sa'tiĕⁿ'	kiä'täk'tä'."	E'tho'ne'	nĕñ'	3
the	his spouse:	"Here	do thou sit	beside my body."	At that time	now	
to'kĕⁿske'	e''	wä·oñ'tiĕⁿ'	ne'	dji'	rāiä'täk'tä'	ne'	dji'	4
it is true	there	she set herself	the	where	his body beside	the	where
rāiä'tioñ'nī'	Nĕñ'	wä·hĕñ'roⁿ'':	"Iä'tesatchi'no'ⁿ'te'	o·shoñ'wäkoⁿ·,"			5
his body was extended.	Now	he it said:	"Thither do thou hang thy legs	it hole in,"			
a·se'kĕⁿ''	io'shoñwe''oⁿ',	iotoⁿ'hwĕñdjiate·tha'roⁿ'	ne'	dji'	nika'-		6
because	it became a hole,	it tore up the earth	the	where	so it is		
tĕñs	ne'	e''	tiioⁿ'hwĕñdjia'te'.				
thick	the	there	thither it earth stands forth.				
Ne'	ka'tī	wä'·hī'	ne'	dji'	nĕñ' e'' rāiä'tioñ'nī'	nĕñ'	toñ-
The	so then	verily	the	where	now there his body was extended	now	thence it
tok'tĕⁿ'	ne'	dji'	ni·horoⁿ'hia'kĕⁿ'.	Akwe'koⁿ·	ne'	raoñkwe'tä'	9
diminished	the	where	so he is suffering.	It all	the	his people	
e''	iakotkĕñni·''soⁿ'	ne'	o'nī'	te·hoñwakan'ere'	ne'	dji'	ni'io't	10
there	they are assembled	the	also	they watched him	the	where	so it is
dji'	ronoⁿ'hwäk'tanī'	rotiri·hwane·hrako''oⁿ'	ne'	dji'	niioteri-	11
where	he is ill	they marveled at the matter	the	where	such it matter	
'hwätie'rĕⁿ'	ne'	raoⁿ'·hä'ke',	a·se'kĕⁿ''	iä·'	te·hatiiĕñtĕ'rī'	ne'	12
had taken place	the	himself to,	because	not	they knew it	the	
e'tho·	thatinak'ere'	o·''	ne'	nä·ho'tĕⁿ'	ne'	āiakonoⁿ·hwak'tĕⁿ'	13
there	there they dwell	what it is	the	such kind of thing	the	one should become ill.	
Ne'	ka'tī	ne'	dji'	nĕñ'.	ä'nio·' sa·häie'wĕñ'tä'ne'	ne'	dji'	14
The	so then	the	where	now	seemingly again he recovered his health	the	where
ronoⁿ'hwäk'tanī',	e'tho'ne'	nĕñ'	wä·hatkar·hat'ho'	tä·hnoⁿ''	wä-	15
he is ill.	At that time	now	he turned over	and	he	

turning upon his side, and then, resting himself on his elbows, he at the same time looked into the hole. After a while he said: "Do thou look thither into the hole to see what things are occurring there in yonder place." He said this to his spouse. Thereupon she bent forward her body into the hole and looked therein. Whereupon he placed his fingers against the nape of her neck and pushed her, and she fell into the hole. Then he arose to a standing posture, and said to his people: "Now do ye replace the tree that ye have uprooted. Here, verily, it lies." They immediately reset the tree, so that it stood just as it did before the time they uprooted it.

But as to this woman-being, she of course fell into the hole, and kept falling in the darkness thereof. After a while she passed through it. Now when she had passed through the thickness thereof to the other

	'hatiă'tokoñroñ'tate'	tä'hnoⁿ'	e'tho'ne'	neñ'	wă'thathio'sotoñ'nioⁿ		
1	turned his body on its side	and	at that time	now	he rested on his elbows		
	e[,]	iă'te'hakan'ere'	ne'	o'shoñ'wăko^{n,}	A'kare'	neñ'	wă'heñ'roⁿ
2	there	thither he looked	the	it hole in.	After a time	now	he it said:
	"Iă'satkăt'ho·	ne'	o'shoñ'wăko^{n,}	o[,]	nă'ho'teⁿ		nitiotie'reⁿ,
3	"Thither do thou look	the	it hole in,	what is it	such kind of thing		there so it is doing
	ne'	i'sĭ'."	Ne'	wă'shakoñ''hă'se'	ne'	ro'ne'.	E'tho'ne'	neñ'
4	the	far yonder."	The	he said to her	the	his spouse.	At that time	now
	iă'tioñtsă'kete'	o'shoñ'wăkoⁿ	e[,]	iă'teiekăn'ere'.		E'tho'ne'	dji'	
5	thither she bent forward	it hole in	there	thither she was looking.		At that time	where	
	ieniă·ka'roñte'	e[,]	iă'theñnisno^{n,}sa'reⁿ		no'k·	iă'shako'reke'		
6	her nape of the neck (is)	there	there he placed his fingers		and	thither he her pushed		
	tä'hnoⁿ'	o'shoñ'wăko^{n,}	iă'eiă''teⁿ.	E'tho'ne'	neñ'	să'hatkets'ko'		
7	and	it hole in	thither her body fell.	At that time	now	again he arose		
	tä'hnoⁿ'	wă'shakawe^{n,}'hă'se'	ne'	raoñkwe'tă:	"Neñ'	săswaroñ-		
8	and	he said to them	the	his people:	'Now	again do ye set		
	to'te^{n,}	ne'	sewaroñtota'kwe^{n,}.	Keⁿ'	wă''hĭ'	kă'icⁿ'"	E'tho'ne'	
9	up (the) tree	the	ye tree have uprooted	Here	verily	it lies."	At that time	
	neñ'	să'hatiroñto'teⁿ.	Akwă·'	o'k'	he^{,,}	ni'tcio·t	ne'	dji' niio'-
10	now	again they it tree set up.	Verily	just	thus	so it again (is)	the	where so it
	toñ'ne'	āre'kho'	ci'hotiroñtota'kwe^{n,}.					
11	was	before	they it tree had uprooted.					
	Ne'	wă''hĭ'	ke^{n,}i'ke^{n,}	iakoñ'kwe·	neñ'	wă''hĭ'	nă''	ne'' iă'eiă'-
12	The	verily	this it is	she a man-being	now	verily	that one	the that thither her
	te^{n,}'ne'	o'shoñ'wăko^{n,}	tiio'kară·s	wă'eiă'toñ'tie'.	A'kare'	neñ'	iă'tĭoñ	
13	body fell	it hole in	there it is dark	thither her body floated.	After a time	now	thither she	
	to''hetste'	neñ'	wă''hĭ'	iă'eia'ke^{n,}'ne'	ne'	dji'	nika'teñs	ne' e^{,,}
14	passed out of it	now	verily	thither she emerged	the	where	so it is thick	the there

would, she of course looked about her in all directions, and saw on all sides of her that everything was blue in color; that there was nothing else for her to see. She knew nothing of what would, perhaps, happen to her, for she did not cease from falling. But after a time she looked and saw something; but she knew nothing of the thing she saw. But, verily, she now indeed was looking on a great expanse of water, albeit she herself did not know what it was.

So this is what she saw: On the surface of the water, floating about hither and thither, like veritable canoes, were all forms and kinds of ducks (waterfowl). Thereupon Loon noticed her, and he suddenly shouted, saying: "A man-being, a female one is coming up from the depths of the water." Then Bittern spoke in turn, saying: "She is not indeed coming up out of the depths of the water." He said: "She is indeed falling from above." Whereupon

---

1. Tiioⁿʻhwĕndjiäʹteʻ. Nĕñʹ wäʻhiʻ wäʻtioñtkäʻthoñnioñʹʻhweʻ täʻhnoⁿʹʹ
   there it earth stands forth. | Now | verily | she did look about in all directions | and

2. wäʻeʹkĕ^{nʻ} oʹkʻ thäʹtetcioʻkwataʹseʻ neʹ oʹkʻ neʹ oroñʹʻhiäʻ niʹioʻt.
   she it saw | only | just it it surrounds completely | the | only | the | it blue sky | so it (is), stands.

3. Iäʹʹ otheʹnoⁿ oʹiäʻ thäioñtkätʹʻhoʻ. Iäʹʹ otheʹnoⁿ teiakoteriĕñʹ
   Not | anything | other | she it could see. | Not | anything | she knows it

4. taieʻ oʹʹ kiʹʹ oʹkʻ oⁿʹʻteʻ nĕⁿiakoiäʻtaʹwĕñneʻ, aʻseʻkĕⁿʹʻ oʹkʻ tiio
   what, I believe, | only | perhaps | so it her body will happen to, | because | only | it

5. tkoñtäʻʹkwĕⁿʻ ieiäʻtonʹtieʻ. Noʹkʻ aʹkaieʻ nĕñʹ iäʹoñtkätʹhoʻ oʹʹ
   continues | her body is falling. | And | after a time | now | thither she looked (to see) | what it is,

6. kiʹʹ, oʹkʻ nitiotieʹrĕⁿʻ. Iäʹʹ otheʹnoⁿ teiakoteriĕñʹtareʻ djiʹ näʹ-
   I believe, | only | so it is done (it state of things is). | Not | anything | she it knows | where | such

7. hoʹtĕⁿ iäʻoñtkätʹhoʻ. Noʹkʻ nĕñʹ seʹʹ wäʻhiʻ käʻhnekowaʹnĕⁿʻ
   kind of thing | thither she it saw. | And | now | indeed | verily | it great (water) liquid

8. neʹ iäʻteiekanʹereʻ noʹkʻ kiʹʹ neʹ akaoⁿʻhäʻ iäʹʹ teieiĕñteʹriʻ
   the | thither she it saw | and | I believe | the | she herself | not | she knows it

9. neʹ näʻhoʹtĕⁿ
   the | such kind of thing.

10. Neʹ kaʹtiʻ neʹ oʻhnekaʹkeʻ iotiʻhoñwäʻkeroñnioñneʹʹseʻ niiäʻte
    The | so then the | it water on | they boats drift about plurally from place to place | all it

11. käʻsoräʹtseraʹkeʻ. Eʹthoʹneʻ neʹ Teoñniatarĕñʹtoⁿ neʹ wäʻhatʹtokeʻ
    kind of duck in number. | At that time | the | Loon | the | he it noticed

12. wäʻthoʻhĕñʹreʻteʻ, wäʻhĕñʹroⁿ: "Oñʹkweʻ täʹiĕⁿ kanoñʹwäkoⁿʻ."
    he shouted. | he it said: | "A man-being | she is coming | it water in the depths of."

13. Noʹkʻ eʻthoʹneʻ Teʻkäʻʻhoⁿ taʻhataʹtiʻ, wäʻhĕñʹroⁿ: "Iäʹʹ seʹʹ
    And | at that time | Bittern | he replied, | he it said: | "Not | indeed

14. kanoñʹwäkoⁿʻ thoñtäʹiĕⁿ.'' Wäʻhĕñʹroⁿ: "Eʹnekĕⁿ seʹʹ täieiäʹ-
    it water in the depths of | thence does she come." | He it said: | "Above | indeed | thence her body

they held a council to decide what they should do to provide for her welfare. They finally decided to invite the Great Turtle to come. Loon thereupon said to him: "Thou shouldst float thy body above the place where thou art in the depths of the water." In the first place, they sent a large number of ducks of various kinds. These flew and elevated themselves in a very compact body and went up to meet her on high. And on their backs, thereupon did her body alight. Then slowly they descended, bearing her body on their backs.

Great Turtle had satisfactorily caused his carapace to float. There upon his back they placed her. Then Loon said: "Come, ye who are deep divers, which one of you is able to dive so as to fetch up earth?" Thereupon one by one they severally dived into the water. It was at

1	toñ'tie'." is drifting."	E'tho'ne˙ At that time	nēñ' now	wa·hatitcie⁽ⁿ⁾·ha'ie⁽ⁿ⁾ they held a council	ne' the	dji' where	iä·hatī'lere' so they should do it
2	ne' the	dji' where	ä·shakonateweieñ'toⁿ·. they her should prepare for.		Iä'thotiri·hwāieñ'tä'se˙ There they decided for themselves		ne' the
3	Raniä·tēⁿ‘ko'wä‘ he Great Turtle		iä·honwaroⁿ·ieⁿ⁾·häre'. thence they invited him,		e'tho'ie' at that time	ka'tī˙ so then	ne' the
4	Teoñniatareñ'toⁿ⁾ Loon	nēñ· now	wa·hēñ'roⁿ·: he it said ·	"Ä·satiä'täkerä·'kwe' "Thou thy body shouldst cause to float		ne' the	dji' where
5	kēⁿ⁾· here	sī'teroⁿ· thou art, (sittest)	kanoñ'wäkoⁿ·." it water depths of."	No'k· And	tiiotiereⁿ⁾·'toⁿ⁾‘ it is the first thing		iä'shakotoñ'- thither they them
6	nie·te' sent	iotitio·kowa'nē⁽ⁿ⁾‘ they are a large body	ne' the	sorä·hokoñ'ä·. ducks plurally.	Wä·tkoñti'tēⁿ⁾ They flew		tä·hnoⁿ⁾· and
7	wä·koñthära'täte˙ they themselves caused to ascend	tä·hnoⁿ⁾· and	ionathwe·noñni·hä'tie˙ they themselves caused to be in a close body		tä·hnoⁿ⁾· and		iä·tia- thither
8	konate'rä‘te' they her went to meet	ē'nekēⁿ‘. above.	E·' There	tāieiä'tä'rä'ne' her body alighted		ne' the	koñti·shoñ'ne˙. their backs on.
9	E'tho'ie' At that time	nēñ' now	skēñnoñ'·ä· slowly	toñtakoñtsnēⁿ⁾·'te' thence they descended		iakotiiä'tēⁿ⁾·hawī', they her body bore,	
10	koñti·shoñ'ne· their backs on	ieiä'tarä'tie'. her body rested coming.					
11	Iä'tkāie'rī˙ Very correctly	ne' the	Raniä·'tēⁿkowä· he Great Turtle	nēñ' now	roti'nowä'kerä·'koⁿ‘. he his carapace causes to float.		E'tho‘ There
12	rä'nowä'ke· his carapace on	e·' there	iä'akoti'teroⁿ·. there they her set down.	E'tho'ne' At that time	ne' the	Teoñniatareñ'toⁿ⁾· Loon	
13	wä·hēñ'roⁿ·: he it said:	"Hau", "Come,	ne' the	sewä'thoñrio·kats'te's ye stout-breathed ones		oⁿ·'kä· who (is it)	rokwe'nioⁿ‘ he is able to do it
14	ne' the	ēⁿ·hä·thoñ'ro' he will dive (into the water)	ēⁿ·roⁿ·hwēñdjiäko''hä'?" he earth will go to bring?"		Ta', So,		e'tho'ne' at that time
15	skat'shoⁿ· one by one	toñte'rä‘te' thence it it did thereby	wä·hoⁿ·thoñroñ'nioⁿ·. they dove into the water one by one.		E'tho'ne' At that time		Djiēñni'to‘ Beaver

this time that Beaver made the attempt and dived. The time was long
and there was only silence. It was a long time before his back
reappeared. He came up dead, his breathing having failed him.
Thereupon they examined his jaws, but he had brought up no earth.
Then Otter said: "Well, let it be my turn now; let me make another
attempt." Whereupon he dived. A longer time elapsed before he
came to the surface. He also came up dead in his turn. They then
examined his jaws also. Neither did he, it is said, bring up any
earth. It was then that Muskrat said: "I also will make the desperate
attempt." So then he dove into the water. It was a still longer
time that he, in turn, was under water. Then, after a while, he
floated to the surface, coming up dead, having lost his breath. Thereupon, again, they examined the inside of his jaws also. They found
mud. He brought up his jaws and his mouth full of mud.

wăˑhateˈniĕñˈtĕⁿˑ	wăˑhaˑthoñˈroˑ.	Karīˈhweseˑ	oˈkˑ	thăˈteiotĕñˈtoñniˑ.	1
he it attempt made	he dived into the water.	It was a long matter	only	it is very still.	
Wăˈkarīˈhweseˑ	nĕñˈ	săioˈnowăˈˈkerăˑkweˑ	raoⁿˑheioⁿˈhăˈtieˑ	wăˑha	2
It was a long matter	now	again its back came to the surface	he came up dead	his	
thoñriōkˈtĕⁿˑ.	Eˈthoˈneˑ	wăˑhoññēˈˈsăkeˑ	răˑsnoⁿˑsoˈkoⁿˑ	iăˈˈ	3
breath gave out.	At that time	they it searched for	his hand in	not	
kăˈrekăˑ	tesroⁿˑhwĕñdjiĕⁿˑhaˈwīˈ.	Eˈthoˈneˑ	Tawiˈneˑ	wăˑhĕñˈroⁿˑ:	4
anywhere	(again) he earth brought.	At that time	Otter	he it said:	
"Toˈ, iˈˈ	noñˈwăˑ	skateˈniĕñˈtoⁿˑ"	Eˈthoˈneˑ	nĕñˈ	wăˑhăˑthoñˈroˑ.	5
"Well, I	this time	again I try it." let me try it	At that time	now	he dived into the water.	
Sĕⁿˈˈhăˑ	năˈkarīˈhweseˑ	nĕñˈ	săˑhatiăˈtăˈkerăˑkweˑ,	rawĕⁿˑhei	6
More	so it (is) a long matter	now	again he his body floated	he came	
oⁿˑhăˈtieˑ	oˈnīˑ	năˈˈ	neˈˈ.	Eˈthoˈneˑ	oˈnīˑ	năˈˈ	neˈˈ	wăˑhoññēˈˈ	7
up dead	also	(the) that	that one	At that time	also	(the) that	that one	they it sought	
săkeˑ	răˑsnoⁿˑsoˈkoⁿˑ.	Iăˈˈ	kiˈˈ	oˈˈ	năˈˈ	neˈˈ	tesroⁿˑhwĕñdjiĕⁿˑhaˈwīˈ	8
for	his hand in.	Not,	I think,	too	(the) that	that	he earth brought back.	
Eˈthoˈneˑ	Anōˈkiĕⁿˑ	wăˑhĕñˈroⁿˑ:	"Iˈˈ	oˈnīˑ	ĕⁿwakăˑtaˈkōˑ."	Nĕñˈ	9
At that time	Muskrat	he it said:	"I	also	I will attempt the hopeless."	Now	
kaˈtīˑ	wăˑhăˑthoñˈroˑ.	Sĕⁿˈˈhăˑ	năˈˈ	neˈˈ	wăˈkarīˈhweseˑ	10
so then	he dived into the water.	More	that one	the that	it matter was a long	
roˑthoñroˈˈhoⁿˑ.	Noˈkˑ	aˈkareˑ	nĕñˈ	săˑhatiăˈtăˈkerăˑkweˑ	rawĕⁿˑhe-	11
he has dived in the water.	And	after a time	now	his body again floated	he came	
ioⁿˑhăˈtieˑ	oˈnīˑ	năˈˈ	neˈˈ.	Wăˑhathoñriōˈktĕⁿˑ.	Eˈthoˈneˑ	nĕñˈ	12
up dead	also	that one	the that.	His breath gave out.	At that time	now	
aˈreˑ	wăˑhoññēˈˈsăkeˑ	răˑsnoⁿˑsoˈkoⁿˑ;	wăˑhatitsĕñˈrīˑ	onawăˈtstăˑ	13
again	they it sought for	his hand in;	they it found	it mud	
răˑtcăˈnĕⁿˈˈhăweˑ.	roˈkˑ	oˈnīˑ	ronhoskwaˈnˑhoñteˑ	neˈ	onawăˈtstăˑ.	14
he it handful brought,	and	also	he it mouthful had	the	it mud.	

It was then that they made use of this mud. They coated the edge of the carapace of the Great Turtle with the mud. Now it was that other muskrats, in their turns, dived into the water to fetch mud. They floated to the surface, dead. In this way they worked until they had made a circuit of the carapace of the Great Turtle, placing mud thereon, until the two portions of the work came together. Thereupon Loon said: "Now there is enough. Now it will suffice." Thereupon the muskrats ceased from diving to fetch up mud.

Now, verily, this man-being sat on the carapace of the Great Turtle. After the lapse of sufficient time, she went to sleep. After a while she awoke. Now then, the carapace of the Great Turtle was covered with mud. Then, moreover, the earth whereon she sat had become enlarged in size. At that time she looked and saw that willows had grown up to bushes along the edge of the water. Then also, when

---

1 E'tho'ne' neñ' ne'' wă'boñts'te' thi'kĕⁿ' onawāts'tă'. Wă'ha-
   At that time now the they it used this it is it mud. They
                      that

2 tinawatstă'r''ho' kă'nowăktă'tie' ne' Ranĭă'tĕⁿ''kowă'. Nĕñ' ĕⁿ's
   mud placed (smeared) it it carapace along the he Great Turtle. Now customarily
   over it   edge of

3 o'iă' o'k· ne' Ano'kiĕⁿ' sa'hă'thoñ'ro' wă'hanawatstako''hă'
   other only the Muskrat again he dove he mud went to bring.
                              into the water

4 Să'hatiă'ta'kerā'kwe' ĕⁿ's rawĕⁿ'heioⁿ'hă'tie'. E·' thi'hatī'iere'
   Again his body would float customarily he came up dead. There so they it did

5 dji' niio're' wă'thoñte'nowatā'se' ne' Ranĭă'tĕⁿ''kowă' wă'ha
   where so it is they it carapace made the he Great Turtle they
          distant   a circuit of

6 tinawatsta'r''ho', iă'toñsakiate'rā'ne'. E'tho'ne' ne' Tcoñniatarĕñ'toⁿ'
   it mud daubed there again they two joined. At that time the Loon

7 nĕñ' wă'hĕñ'roⁿ': "Nĕñ' e'tho·. Nĕñ' ŏⁿkakwe'nĭ'." Nĕñ' o'nĭ'
   now he it said: "Now enough. Now it will be able to do it." Now also

8 ne' ano'kiĕⁿ'hokoñ''ă' wă'hoñ''tkă'we' ne' dji' roñ'thoñroñ'nioⁿ's
   the muskrats plurally they stopped work the where they dove into the water plurally

9 ratinawă'tstako''he's.
   they mud went to bring up.

10 Nĕñ' wă''hĭ' kĕⁿ'i'kĕⁿ· iăkoñ'kwe' e·' ietskwă''here' Ranĭă'-
    Now verily this it is she man-being (is) there she sat he

11 tĕⁿ'kowă· rā'nowa'ke·. Akwă'' he''tho· dji' nă'karī''hwese'
    Great Turtle, his carapace on. Very enough where so it was a long matter

12 nĕñ' ka'ti' wă'ako'tā'we'. No'k· a'kare· nĕñ' sāie'ie'. Nĕñ'
    now so then she fell asleep. And after a time now again she awoke. Now

13 ka'tĭ' oⁿ'hwĕñ'djiă' iote'r'hō'roⁿ' ne' kă'nowă'ke' ne' Ranĭă·
    so then it earth it covered itself the it carapace on the He

14 tĕⁿ''kowă·, nĕñ' tă'hnoⁿ'' iote'hia'roⁿ' dji' niwatoⁿ'hwĕñ'djiă' ne'
    Great Turtle, now and it has grown where so it earth (is) large the

15 dji' le'teroⁿ'. E'tho'ne' nĕñ' wă'oñtkă'tho' ō'se· iotkwiroñ'nĭ'
    where she sits. At that time now she it looked at willow it shrubs grew to

she again awoke, the carcass of a deer, recently killed, lay there, and now besides this, a small fire burned there, and besides this, a sharp stone lay there. Now, of course, she dressed and quartered the carcass of the deer and roasted some pieces thereof, and she ate her till. So, when she had finished her repast, she again looked about her. Now, assuredly, the earth had increased much in size, for the earth grew very rapidly. She, moreover, saw another thing; she saw growing shrubs of the rose-willow along the edge of the water.

Moreover, not long after, she saw a small rivulet take up its course. Thus, then, things came to pass in their turn. Rapidly was the earth increasing in size. She then looked and saw all species of herbs and grasses spring from the earth, and also saw that they began to grow toward maturity.

---

dji′	tewatcä·ktä′tie′.	Nĕñ	tä·hnoⁿ·′	ne′	shoñsāie′ie·	o·skĕñnoñtoⁿ·′	1
where	it water at the edge of.	Now	and	the	again she awoke	it deer	
e·′	käiä′tioñ′nĭ·	ä′se·	käɹ′io·.	nĕñ′	tä·hnoⁿ·′	e·′ iotek′hä′	2
there	its body lay extended	new	one it has killed.	now	and	there it burns	
nikadjieⁿ·hä′′ä·.	nĕñ′	tä·hnoⁿ·′	e·′	kä′iĕⁿ·	oŭĕñ′iä·	io·hio·thi′ie·.	3
so it fire (is) small,	now	and	there	it lies	it stone	it is sharp-edged.	
Nĕñ′	wä′′hĭ′	wä·tkoñwäiä′täɹi·′te·		ne′	o·skĕñnoñtoⁿ·′.	Nĕñ′	4
Now	verily	she its body (broke) quartered		the	it deer.	Now	
wä′·hĭ′	o′nĭ′	wä·oñte·skoñtoñ′nioⁿ·.	Nĕñ′	o′nĭ′	wä·tioñtskä′·hoⁿ·.		5
verily	also	she made for herself several (pieces).	Now	also	she ate.		
Ne′	ka′tĭ·	nĕñ′	cä·ekhwĕñ′tä·ne·	toñsāioñtkä·thoūnioñ′·hwe·.	Nĕñ′		6
The	so then	now	where she her food finished eating	again she looked around repeatedly.	Now		
ka′tĭ·	sĕⁿ·′bä·	iaoⁿ·hwĕñdjiowa·nhä′′oⁿ·.	a·se·kĕⁿ·′	io·sno′re·			7
so then	more,	it earth had grown large,	because	it is rapid			
iote·hiä′roñ′tie·	ne′	oⁿ·hwĕñ′djiä·.	Nĕñ	tä·hnoⁿ·′	thika′te·	o′iä·	8
it is increasing in size	the	it earth (is).	Now	and	it is different	other it is	
wä·e′kĕⁿ·	iotkwiroñ′nĭ·	ne′	atcä′ktä′tie·	ne′	oŭekwĕⁿ·′täɹä·		9
she it saw	it itself shrubs made	the	water along edge of	the	it red color		
nikakwiro′tĕⁿ·	iotoñ′nĭ·.						10
such it kind of shrub	it itself grew.						
Ne′	o′nĭ′	ne′	iä·′	tekaɹī′·hwes	wä·oñtkät′ho·	wä·ka·hioⁿ·-	11
The	also	the	not	it (is) a long matter	she it saw	it a stream caused	
hoñ′ko·′te·	nikä·hioⁿ·hä′′ä·.	E·′	ka′tĭ·	ni′io·t	dji′	wathawiñoñ′tie′.	12
to pass on its course	so it stream (is) small.	There	so then	so it is	where	at different times (it bears itself along severally).	
Io·sno′re·	iotoⁿ·hwĕñdjiate·hiä·roñ′tie·.	Nĕñ′	o′nĭ′	wä·oñtkät′ho·			13
It is rapid	it earth is increasing in size.	Now	also	she it saw			
niiä·tekahōñ′täke·	wä·tkoñnoⁿ·hwĕñdjiot′kä·we·	ne′	o′nĭ′	toñtakoñt			14
all kinds it plants in number	they left (it) earth	the	also	they it			
·hoñtate·hiä′roⁿ·.							15
plants increased in size.							

Now also, when the time had come for her to be delivered, she gave birth to a female man-being, a girl child. Then, of course, they two, mother and daughter, remained there together. It was quite astonishing how rapidly the girl child grew. So then, when she had attained her growth, she of course was a maiden. They two were alone; no other man-being roved about there in any place.

So then, of course, when she had grown up and was a maiden, then, of course, her mother was in the habit of admonishing her child, saying, customarily: "Thou wilt tell me what manner of person it is who will visit thee, and who will say customarily: 'I desire that thou and I should marry.' Do not thou give ear to this; but say, customarily: 'Not until I first ask my mother.'"

Now then, in this manner, matters progressed. First one, then another, came along, severally asking her to become his wife, and she

1	Ne' The	o'nĭ' also	ne' the	nĕñ' now	iă'kă''hewe' it is time there it it brought	nĕñ' now	wă'akoksă'tāiĕñ'tă'ne' she child brought forth
2	iăkoñ'kwe' she man-being (is)	ne' the	eksā''ă'. she child (is).	Nĕñ Now	wă''hĭ' verily	e'' there	keni'teron' they two abode	ne' the
3	akoiĕñ''ă'. she has a small one.	Akwă'' Very	.ione'hră'kwă't it is marvelous		io'sno're' it is rapid	dji' where	iakote'hiă'- she increased
4	roñ'tie' in size	ne' the	eksā''ă'. she child (is).	Ne' The	ka'tĭ' so then	ne' the	nĕñ' now	ciiakote'hiă'roñ'tie' where she increased in size
5	nĕñ' now	wă''hĭ' verily	eiā'tāse' she (is) maid	oñ'ton'. it became.	Ionon'hă'tci'wă'; They two (were) entirely alone;	iă.' not	on''kă' any- one	o'iă' other it is
6	kăn'ekă' anywhere	te'iĕn's one moved about	ne' the	oñ'kwe'. man-being.			
7	Ta', So,	ne' the	ka'tĭ' so then	wă''hĭ' verily	ne' the	dji' where	nĕñ' now	iakote'hiă'ron' she grew up	nĕñ' now
8	eiā'tāse' she is maid	i'kĕn', it is,	nĕñ' now	wă''hĭ' verily	ne' the	onistĕn''hă' her mother	ioñtat'hro'rĭs she her tells	ne' the
9	oñtatiĕñ''ă' her offspring	ion'ton' she it says	ĕn's: custom- arily:	"Ĕnsk·hro'rĭ' "Thou me shalt tell	o'' what	ni'hāiă'to'tĕn' such be kind of body has	ne' the
10	to'kă' if	ĕn'hiă'ktă''se' he thee will visit	ne' the	ĕn'baton''heke' he will keep saying	i'ke'hre' I it desire	āioñkeni'niăke'. thou I should marry.
11	To''să Do not	ĕn'sathoñ'tāte'. thou it shalt con- sent to.	Ĕn'sĭ'ron' Thou it wilt say	ĕn's: custom- arily:	'Nia're'kwe' 'Until first,	ki'' I be- lieve,	ĕnkhe- I her will
12	'hro'rĭ' tell	ne' the	istĕñ''ă' '' my mother.'"				
13	Nĕñ Now	ka'tĭ' so then	e'' there	niio'ton'hă'tiĕ'. so it continued to be.	O'iă' Another it is	o'k· only	ĕn's custom- arily	is're' again he comes	wă'shakori- he her asks
14	'hwanoñtoñ'nion' questions	ne' the	a'hoti'niăke'. they should marry.	Ne' The	e'' there,	·ki'' I believe,	ĕn's custom- arily	wă'i'ron' she it said:

customarily replied: "Not until I first ask my mother." When she would tell her mother what manner of person had asked her to marry him, her mother would answer, saying customarily: "No; he is not the person." But, after a while the maiden said: "One who has a deep fringe along his legs and arms paid a visit." The elder woman said: "That is the one, I think, that it will be proper for you to marry." Thereupon she returned to the place where the young man stood. She said: "We should marry, she says." The young man answered, saying: "When it is dark, I shall return." So then, when the appointed time arrived, he also came back. Then it was that he paid court to her. But, I think, they two, he and the maid, did not lie together. When she lay down so that she

"Nia'rekwe"	ěⁿkhe·hro'rī	ne'	istěñ''ă·."	Ne'	ka'tī	ěⁿ's	wă·'hī	
"Until first	I her shall tell	the	my mother."	The	so then	customarily	verily	1
ne'	něñ'	wă·'oñtat·hro'rī	ne'	o·nistěñ''ă·	ne'	dji'	ni·hăiă'-	
the	now	she her told	the	her mother	the	where	such he kind of body	2
to'těⁿ	ne'	wă·shakori·hwanoñtoñ'nī	ne'	a·hoti'niăke·;	tăieri·hwă'-			
has	the	he her has asked questions	the	they should marry;	she			3
sera'ko·	ěⁿ's	ne'	o·nistěñ''ă·	wă·i'roⁿ	ěⁿ's:	"Iă'	ne'	tě'kěⁿ·"	
replied	customarily	the	her mother	she it said	customarily:	"Not	that	it is."	4
No'k·	ă'kare·	něñ'	wă·i'roⁿ	ne'	eiă'tăse·:	"Wă·hakwat'ho·	ne'	
And	after a time	now	she it said	the	she maid (is):	"He paid a visit	the	5
roñ'kwe·,	teiotarotă'tie·	ne'	ra·'sina'ke·,	no'k·	o'nī	ne'	ranoñ-	
he man-being (is),	it fringe showed along	the	his legs on,	and	also	the	his	6
tsă'ke·."	Wă·i'roⁿ	ne'	akokstěñ''ă·:	"Ne''	ki''	ěⁿkăie'rite·	ne'	
arms on."	She it said	the	she elder one (is):	"That,	I believe,	it will be proper	the	7
ěⁿseni'niăke·."	E·'tho'ne·	něñ'	e·'	să'iěⁿ·'te·	dji'	noñ'we·	i'trate·	
ye two will marry."	At that time	now	there	again she went	where	place	there he stands	8
ne'	ranekěⁿ·'teroⁿ.	Wă·i'roⁿ	ne'	eiă'tăse·:	"Aioñkeni'niăke·,			
the	he young man. (is)	She it said	the	she maid (new-bodied)·	"Thou-I should marry,			9
iă·'kěⁿ·."	Tă·hari·hwă·'sera'ko·	ne'	ranekěⁿ·'teroⁿ	wă·hěñ·'roⁿ:				
it is said."	He replied	the	he young man (is)	he it said:				10
"Ne'	něñ'	ěⁿtio'karas	e'tho'ne·	něñ'	těⁿ'tke·."	Ne'	ka'tī	ci-	
"The	now	it will become dark	at that time	now	I will come."	The	so then	there	11
iă·kă·'hewe·	dji'	noñ'we·	ni·hona'toⁿ	e·'tho'ne·	ka'tī	sa'rawe·.		
it arrived	where	the place	just where he it appointed	at that time	so then	he again arrived.		12
Něñ	ka'tī	wă·'shakotehinatoⁿ·'hă·'se·.	No'k·	iă·'	ki''	te·'hoñna		
Now	so then	he "courted" her.	And	not,	I believe,	they two have		13
iă'toⁿ·	ne'	eiă'tăse·.	Ne'	něñ'	shă·'oñtiă·'tioñ'nite·	ne'	ěⁿiako'-	
lain together	the	she maid (new-bodied).	The	now	she lay supine	the	she will	14
tă·'we·	ěⁿs'kă·	ne'	raoiěñ'kwire·	ena·'skwăk'tă·	ě·'	wă·hă'iěⁿ	
sleep	one (it is)	the	his arrow	her breast beside	there	he it laid.	15

could sleep, he laid one of his arrows beside her body. Thereupon he departed. Then, at his return, he again took his arrow and departed again, carrying the arrow away with him. He never came back afterward.

After a while the elder woman became aware that the maiden was growing in size, caused by the fact that she was pregnant.

So when the day of her delivery had come, she brought forth twins, two male infants. But during the time that she was in travail, the maiden heard the two talking within her body. One of them said: "This is the place through which we two shall emerge from here. It is a much shorter way, for, look thou, there are many transparent places." But the other person said: "Not at all. Assuredly, we should kill her by doing this thing. Howbeit, let us go out that other way, the way that one, having become a human being, will use as an exit. We will turn around and in a downward direction we two will

	E'tho'ne'	nĕñ'	säˑhäˑtĕñ'tĭ'.	Ne'	ka'tĭ'	ne'	nĕñ'	shoñsa'rawe'
1	At that time	now	again he departed.	The	so then	the	now	again he returned

	toñsä'räˑkwe'	ne'	raoiĕñ'kwire'	nĕñ'	täˑhnonˑ'	säˑhäˑtĕñ'tĭ'	ioñsäˑ
2	he it took up again	the	his arrow	now	and	he again departed	he it took

	häˑ'häwe'	ne'	raoiĕñ'kwire'.	Iäˑ'	noñwĕn'tonˑ	thäˑtethawe'noñˑ
3	away with him	the	his arrow.	Not	ever	did he return (retrace his steps).

	A'kaie'	ka'tĭ'	ne'	akokstĕñ''äˑ	nĕñ'	wäˑoñt'toke'	nĕñ'
4	After a time	so then	the	she elder one (is)	now	she it noticed	now

	iakoteˑbiäˑroñ'tie'	ne'	eiä'täse'	ne'	kariˑhoñ'nĭ'	dji'	iene'ronˑ.
5	she is increasing in size	the	she maid, new-bodied is	the	it it causes	where	she is pregnant.

	Ne'	ka'tĭ'	ne'	nĕñ'	ciiä'akoteniˑseri''heˑse'	wäˑakoksäˑtäiĕñˑ'täˑne'
6	The	so then	the	now	where her day arrived to her	she became possessed of offspring

	teˑ'nikˑ'hĕnˑ.	No'kˑ	dji'	näˑ'ˑhe'	wäˑ'hĭ'	nĕñ'	iakorĕñˑhia'kĕnˑ
7	they two are twins.	And	where	it lasts (while)	verily	now	she was in pain

	iakothoñ'te'	ne'	eiä'täse'	tetˑhotĭ'thäre'	eiä''takonˑ.	Shäiä''täˑ
8	she it heard	the	she new-bodied(is)	there they conversed together,	her body in.	He one person

	iä'tonˑ:	"Kĕnˑ'	noñ'we'	tĕntĕniiakĕnˑ'täˑkwe'.	Sĕnˑ'häˑ	ne'
9	he it said:	"Here (it is)	the place	thou I will use it to go out.	More	the

	niio're'aˑ	aˑ'seˑkĕnˑ'	satkätˑ'hoˑ	oˑ'kˑ	thiiäˑ'teioˑ'swathe'nionˑ.''	No'kˑ
10	so it is little distant	because	do thou look	just	it is transparent in places.''	And

	ne'	shäiä'täˑ	ra'tonˑ:	"Iäˑ'tĕnˑ.	Ĕnˑiethi'rio',	wäˑ'hĭ'	näˑ'	ne'
11	the	he one person	he it said:	"Not at all.	Thou I will kill her,	verily	that one	the that.

	Eˑ'	kiˑ'	noñka'tĭ'	tĕn'teniiakĕnˑ'täˑkwe'	dji'	noñ'ka'tĭ'	ĕnˑieiakĕnˑ'täˑkwe'
12	There, I believe,		side of it	thou I will use it to go out	where	side of it	one will use it to go out

	ne'	oñ'kwe'	ĕnˑiakotonˑ'onˑhäˑ'tie'.	Tĕntiatkärˑhate'ıĭ'	eˑ'ta'ke'	noñka'tĭ'
13	the	man-being	one having become it will come.	Thou I will turn ourselves around	down, under	side of it

go." So then the former one confirmed what this one had proposed, when this one said: "This it shall continue to be." But, however, he now contested another matter. He did not comply when the second one said: "Do thou take the lead." He said: "Not at all; do thou go ahead." So then it was in this manner that they two contended, and he who said: "Right in this very place let us two go straight out, for assuredly this way is as real as that," gained his point. Finally, the other agreed that he himself should take the lead. At that time, then, he turned about, and at once he was born. So at that time his grandmother took him up and cared for him. Then she laid him aside. At that time she again gave attention to her [the daughter], for now, indeed, another travail did she suffer. But that other one emerged in another place. He came out of her armpit. So, as to him, he killed his mother. Then, his

niiěn'heñt'ne'."	Něñ'	ka'tĭ'	ne'	shāiā'tā·	wä·hari·hwä·ni'rate·	ne'
thither thou I will go."	Now	so then	the	he one person	he it matter confirmed	the
dji'	nä·ho'těⁿ·	ia'toⁿ:	"Ne'	e·'	nāioton"·häke'."	
where such kind of thing	he it said:	"The	thus	so it should continue to be."		
No'k·	o'iä·	ki''	ioñ'wä·	iä·ho'těⁿ·	toñsä·hari·hwake·'nhä'.	Iä''
And	other (thing),	I believe,	this time	such kind of thing	again he it matter debated for.	Not
te·hat·hoñ'tats	ne'	shāiä'tä·	dji'	ra'toⁿ:	"I'se'.	shěñ't."	Ra'toⁿ:
he it consents to	the	he one person (is)	where	he it says:	"Thou,	do thou take the lead."	He it says:
"Iä·'těⁿ".	I'se'.	shěñ't."	E·	ka'tĭ'	ni'io·t	dji'	te·hotiri·hwa
"Not at all.	Thou,	do thou take the lead."	There	so then	so it is	where	they two matter
ken'hěⁿ·,	iok·	wä·hateri·hwatkwe'nĭ·	ne'	ra'toⁿ:	"O'k·	kěⁿ·'
debated (matter)	and	he his point won	the	he it says:	"Only	here it is
ioñ'we·	ietiattakwari·'siä't	ne'	wä·'hĭ'	niiore·'ä·	nä·'	ne·'."
the place	hence let us two go straight out	the	verily	it is not far	that one	the that."
Ta',	e·tho'ne·	něñ'	ne'	shāiä'tä·	wä·hathōñ'tāte·	iaOⁿ·'hä·
So,	at that time	now	the	he one person	he consented to it	he himself
ěⁿ·hä·'heñte·.	E·tho'ie·	něñ'	wä·thatkär·hate'nĭ·	iä·hakoñtätie·'te·	
he will take the lead.	At that time	now	he turned himself around.	he without stopping	
wä·heñnä'kerate·.	Ta',	e·tho'ne·	ne'	ro·sot'hä·	wä·thoñwäiä'tä·kwe·
he was born.	So,	at that time	the	his grandmother	she his body took up
wä·hoñwakwata'ko'.	E·tho'ie·	i·'sĭ'	iä·'e·'iěⁿ'.	E·tho'ie·	a·'re·
she him cared well for.	At that time	far yonder	there she it laid.	At that time	again
toñsäioñtate·'nia'rä·'ne·	a·'se·kěⁿ·'	něñ'	se''	a·'re·	o'lä·	toñtäie
again she her her hands set to	because	now	indeed	again	other it is	she had
roⁿ·hiä'kěⁿ·.	No'k·	äk'te·	ne'	ioñ'we·	wä·hāiakěⁿ·'tä·kwe·
travail.	And	aside	the	the place	he it emerged by.
E·nhoⁿ·ro'koⁿ·	wä·hāiakěⁿ·'tä·kwe·.	Ta',	wä·shako'rio·	nä·''	ne·''
Her armpit in	he it emerged.	So,	he her killed	that one	the that

grandmother took him up and attended to his needs also. She completed this task and laid him alongside of the one who had first come. So thereupon she devoted her attention to her child who was dead. Then, turning herself about to face the place where she had laid the two infants, she said: "Which of you two destroyed my child?" One of them answered, saying: "Verily, he himself it is, I believe." This one who had answered was a very marvelously strange person as to his form. His flesh was nothing but flint.[a] Over the top of his head there was, indeed, a sharp comb of flint. It was therefore on this account that he emerged by way of her armpit.

But the flesh of the other was in all respects similar in kind to that of a man-being. He spoke, saying: "He himself, indeed, killed her." The other one replied, saying: "Not at all, indeed." He again

1. ro·nistĕñ″ă·. E·tho′ne‧ wă·thoñwăiă′tă‘kwe‧ wă·hoñwakwată′ko‧
   his mother. At that time she his body took up she cared for him well

2. o″ nă″ ne″. Wă·es″ă‧ nĕñ′ skă·″ne‧ wă·hoñwatiiă′tioñ′nite‧ ne′
   too the that She it finished now one at (place) she lay their bodies extended the
   that one.

3. tho‘hĕñ′toⁿ‧. Ta′, e·tho′ne‧ nĕñ′ wă·tioñtate′niă′ră′ne‧ ne′
   thence he came So, at that time now she her her hands set to the
   first.

4. iakaoñ·he′ioⁿ‧ ne′ oñtatiĕñ″ă‧. E·tho′ne‧ nĕñ′ e″ noñka′tĭ‘
   she is dead the her offspring. At that time now there side of it

5. nĕⁿsăioñtie′ră′te‧ dji′ noñ′we‧ ni·hoñwatiiă′tioñ′nitoⁿ‧ tă‘hnoⁿ″
   again she herself turned where the place she them laid extended and
   toward it

6. wă′i′roⁿ: "Oⁿ″kă′ ne′ teseniiă″she‧ wă·shakō′rio′ ne′ kheiĕñ″ă‘?"
   she it said: "Who is it the ye two individuals he her killed the my offspring?"

7. Shăia′tă‧ tă‘hată′tĭ′ wă‘hĕñ′roⁿ: "Raoⁿ″·hă‧, kĭ″, wă′‘hĭ′."
   He one thence he he it said: "He himself I be- "verily."
   person answered (it is), lieve,

8. Kĕⁿ′i′kĕⁿ‧ tă‘hata′tĭ′ ione‘hră′kwă‘t rotoñkwe′tătie′roⁿ ne′ dji′
   This it is thence he it is marvelous his person ugly (is) the where
   replied

9. ni·hăiă′tō′teⁿ. Aō′skoⁿ‧ tawĭ′skară‧ ne‧ raoieroñ′ke‧. Teiotaro-
   such his body It is wholly flint (crystal) the his flesh on. It has a ridge
   kind (is) chert (along it)

10. ta′tie‧ raonoñdjistăkĕñ′iate‧ io‘hio′thi′ie‧ tawĭ′skară′ se″. Ne″
    his head crest of it is sharp flint (crystal) indeed. That
    it is

11. wă′‘hĭ′ kari‘hoñ′nĭ′ ie‘nhoro′koⁿ‧ wă·hăiakĕⁿ″tă‘kwe‧
    verily it it causes her armpit in he it used to emerge.

12. No‘k‧ ne′ shăia′tă‧ ne′ tkăie′rĭ′ ne′ oñ′kwe‧ ni·hăieroñto′tĕⁿ‧.
    And the he one the it is the man-being such his flesh kind
    person correct of is.

13. Tă‘hata′tĭ′ wă‘hĕñ′roⁿ: "Raoⁿ″·hă‧ se″ wă·shakō′rio′." Toñtă
    Thence he he it said: "He himself indeed he her killed." Thence he
    replied (it is) again

14. ‘bata′tĭ′ ne′ shăia′tă‘ wă‘hĕñ′roⁿ: "Iă″tĕⁿ se″." Să‘hĕñ′roⁿ:
    spoke the he one he it said: "Not at all indeed." Again he it said:
    person

---

[a] It is for this reason that he is called Tawiskaroⁿ′, which is the Mohawk name for flint or chert. Consult The Cosmogonic Gods of the Iroquois, Proc. Am. Ass. Adv. Sci., v. 44, pp. 241 and following, 1895.

said: "Indeed, he himself killed her." Thus then, in this manner, the two debated. But he who was guilty of killing her did not swerve from his denial, and so then he finally won his point. Whereupon their grandmother seized the body of him whose flesh was verily that of a man-being and with all her might cast him far into the bushes. But the other, whose flesh was flint, was taken up and cared for by her. And it was also wonderful how much she loved him.

Now, in its turn, she again laid her hands on the flesh body of her girl child, who was verily now not alive. She cut off her head and said: "Even though thou art now dead, yet, albeit, thou shalt continue to have a function to perform." And now she took up the flesh body and hung it on a tree standing hard by her lodge, and she said: "Thou shalt continue to give light to this earth here present. But the head also she hung in another place, and she said: "Thou also

"Se"	raon'ha'	wa'shako'rio'."	E''	ka'ti'	ni'io't	wa'thniri·hwa-	1
"Indeed,	he himself (it is),	he her killed."	There	so then	so it is	they two it matter	
ke'nha'.	Thori·hwakonta''ko'''·	dji'	raton·hi''·ha'	no'k·	ho'ni'	ne'	2
disputed.	He continued to assert it	where	he it denied	and	also	the	
shaia'ta·	dji'	ka'ien	ne'	shako'rio·	ne'	ka'ti'	wa·hateri·hwa-	3
he one person	where	it lies	the	he her killed	the	so then	he his (matter)	
tkwe'ni'.	E'tho'ne·	ne'	roti·sot'ha·	wa'thoñwaia'ta·'kwe·	ne'ne·		4
point won.	At that time	the	their grand- mother	she his body took up	the that		
tkaie'ri	oñ'kwe·	ni·haiero''to'te''·	ta·hno'''	ia'tioñte'shen'nia'te·			5
it is correct	man-being	such he flesh has kind of	and	she employed her whole strength			
o·hoñ'tako''·	ia·hoñwaia'toñ'ti'.	No'k·	ne'	shaia'ta·	ne'	tawi'skara'	6
it shrubbery in	thither she his body threw.	And	the	he one person	the	flint (crystal)	
raiero'''tota·'ko''·	wa'thoñwaia'ta·'kwe·	ne'	wa·hoñwateweien'to''',				7
he is fleshed thereby.	she his body took up	the	she him cared for well,				
no'k·	ho'ni'	akwa·'	ione·hra'kwa·	dji'	ni·hoñwanoro'''khwa'.		8
and	also	very	it is marvelous	where	so she him holds dear.		
Neñ'	non'wa·	ne'	ke'''	niioñsaie'iere·	ne'	akoieron'ta·	ne'	9
Now	this time	the	here (it is)	so again she touched it	the	her flesh	the	
oñtatien''a·-keñ·ha'	ne'	wa·'hi'	neñ'	ia·'	tetciakon·'he·.	Wa·oñta-	10
her offspring	it was	the	verily	now	not	still she lives.	She	
tenia·'ria'ke'	ta·hno'''	wa'i'ro'':	"Iawero''ha'tien·,	dji'	neñ'	11
her head cut off	and	she it said:	"Even though (no matter)	where	now	
son·he'io''·	sen·'ha'	ki''	o'k·	en·sateri·hoñ'take·."	Neñ	ta·hno'''	12
thou art dead,	more,	I believe,	just	thou it duty wilt have to perform."	Now	and	
watie·'kwe·	ne'	oieroñ'ta·	ne'	akono'''sa'kta·	ke·r·'hite·	e·'	13
she it took up	the	it flesh	the	her house beside	it tree stands	there	
wa·e·ha'reñ'	ta·hno'''	wa'i'ro'':	"Teñ·sa·shwathe'to'''hake·	ne'	14
she it hung up	and	she it said:	"Thou it wilt continue to light	the	
ken''	wato'''hweñdjia'te·,	no'k·	ho'ni'	ne'	onoñ'dji·	ak'te·	ne'	15
here	it earth is extant,	but	also	the	it head	elsewhere	the	

shalt continue to have a function. Thou shalt have less power to give light." Thus then she completed her arrangements for supplying herself with light. Now, assuredly, she had made fast the sun for herself, and also the moon. She imposed on them the duty of furnishing her with light for their part. Verily, indeed, it was the head of her girl child who was dead that she used to make the moon, but her body she made into the sun. They were to be fixed always in one place, and were not to be moving from place to place. Now, besides this, she restricted them to herself and her grandson, saying: "We two, entirely alone, shall ever be supplied by this light. No other person shall use it, only we two ourselves."

When she had now, indeed, finished all of her task, she was surprised by the moving of the grasses at the spot whither she had cast the other one of her grandchildren. He was alive; he had

1. noñ'we‘   nä‘e‘hä'rĕⁿ’   tä‘hnoⁿ’’   wä’i'roⁿ’:   "Ĕⁿ‘sateri‘hoñ'täke‘   o’’
   the place   she it hung up and   she it said: "Ever thou it duty wilt have too
                                                                                        to perform

2. ni'se’.   Ka’ıo‘   ni'se’   dji’   nŏⁿ‘se‘shats'teke‘   ne’   dji’   tĕⁿ‘se‘shwathe   Less   the   where   thy power shall be   the   where thou it shalt cause
   thou.   thou   effective

3. the’’tĕⁿ’."   Nĕñ’   wä’‘hï’   wä’eweiĕñnĕñ'tä'ne‘   dji’   nĕⁿio‘toⁿ’‘häke‘
   to be   Now   verily   she it manner finished   where   so it will continue
   light."   of it   to be

4. dji’   tĕⁿiakot‘shwathe’’tĕⁿ’.   Nĕñ’   wä’‘hï’   iakoterä‘kwanĕñtäk’toⁿ‘,
   where it her will cause it to be   Now   verily   she has set up it sun for herself,
          light for.

5. ĕⁿ‘hnï'tä’   o'nï’,   koñwari‘hoñta'nï‘   tĕⁿiako‘shwathe‘toⁿ’‘häke‘   nä’’
   it moon   also.   she her duties gave it will cause it to be light that
                                                                             one

6. ne’’.   Ne’   se’’   wä’‘hï’   ne’   oūtatiĕñ’’ä‘   ne’   iakaoⁿ‘he’ioⁿ‘
   the   The   indeed verily   the   her offspring the   she is dead
   that.

7. akonoñ'djï‘   ne’   ĕⁿ‘hnï'tä’   wä’akoñ'niä‘te’,   no‘k‘   ne’   akoie'roūtä’
   her head   the   it moon   she used it to   and   the   her flesh
                                    make it,

8. kaiä’’kwä’   nä’’   ne’’.   Tiiotkoⁿ‘’   katō'kĕⁿ‘   ŏⁿiorä'nĕñ'täkoⁿ’’,   iä‘’
   it sun   that   the   Always   it is certain it will be attached, not
                one   that.   way

9. tĕⁿkiä‘tĕñtië’seke’.   Nĕñ’   tä‘hnoⁿ’’   wä’oñtathwe‘noñ'niĕⁿ’   wä’i'roⁿ’:
   they two will travel about Now   and   she restricted them   she it said:
   habitually.   herself

10. "Oñkenoⁿ‘hä’’ä‘   tĕⁿioñkiat‘shwathe‘toⁿ’’‘häke‘.   Iä‘’   oⁿ’‘kä’   ne’
    "Thou I only   thou I will give light for us.   Not   anyone   the

11. o'iä’   thäioñts'te’,   ne’   o‘k‘   ne’   oñkenoⁿ‘hä’’ä‘."
    other   one will use it, the   only   the   thou I only."
    it is

12. Nĕñ’   wä’‘hï’   akwe'koⁿ‘   wä’eweiĕñnĕñ'tä'ne‘   wä’oñtie'rĕⁿ’   o‘k‘
    Now   verily   it all   she finished its manner she was surprised only
                                 of doing

13. kä'tï’   tetio‘hoñti‘shoⁿ’‘khwä‘   dji’   noñ'we‘   ie‘honwaıä'toñ'tioⁿ‘
    so then there it grass moves to   where   the place   there she his body threw
             and fro

14. ne’   shäiä’’tä‘   ne’   roñwatere’’ä‘,   roⁿ’‘he‘.   Iä‘’   te‘hawĕⁿ‘he’ioⁿ‘
    the   he one   the   her grandson,   he is   Not   he has died.
          person   alive.

not died; for she thought when she had cast him far away that he would, of course, die, but, howbeit, he had not died. He walked about there among the bushes. But after a while he came thence toward the lodge of his grandmother, but she ordered him away, saying: "Go thou far off yonder. I have no desire whatever to look on thee, for thou it is, assuredly, who hast killed my girl child. So, then, therefore, go thou far off yonder." Verily, he then went from there. But, albeit, he was moving about in a place not far from the place where the lodge stood. Besides this, the male child was in good health, and his growth was rapid.

After awhile he made for himself a bow and also an arrow. Of course he now went about shooting from place to place. He went, indeed, about from place to place, for now, of course, the earth was indeed of considerable size. The earth, indeed, verily

a'se'kĕⁿ·'	wă'ĕñ·'re'	dji'	i'sĭ'	ie·hoñwäiä'toñ'tioⁿ·	ĕⁿ·rĕⁿ·'heie'	1
because	she it desired	where	far, yonder	there she his body cast	he will die	
wä'hĭ'.	no'k·	iä·'	ki''	te·hawĕⁿ·he'ioⁿ·.	E·' hi'tre'se' o·hoñtä-	2
verily,	but	not,	I believe,	he has died.	There there he moved about	
koⁿ·'shoⁿ'.	No'k·	a'kaie·	e·'	nä·toñta're'	dji' iakonoⁿ·'sote' ne'	3
it grass in, along	And	after a time	there	thence he came	where her house stands the	
10·sot'hä·.	no'k·	sä·hoñwanĕⁿnia'nĭ'	wä·i'roⁿ·:	"I'sĭ'	noñ'we·	4
his grandmother,	and	she him drove away again	she it said:	"Yonder	place	
niiä·hä'se·	iä·'	othe'noⁿ·	thä·tewakatoⁿ·hwĕñdjioñ'nĭ·	ne'	takoñkäⁿ'	5
thither do thou go.	Not	anything	I am in need of it	the	I thee should	
erake·.	a·se'kĕⁿ·'	i'se·	wä'hĭ'	she'rio· ne'	kheiĕñ·'ä·. Wä·s',	6
see,	because	thou	verily	thou her the didst kill	my offspring. Go, ·	
nio·''	kä'tĭ·,	i'sĭ'	noñ'we·	niiä·ha'se·."	To'kĕⁿske· kä'tĭ· i'sĭ'	7
so be it	so then,	far, yonder	place	thither do thou go."	It is true so then far, yonder	
noñka'tĭ·	ioñsa're·.	No'k·	e·'	ki'' i'ie'se·	iä·' i'noⁿ· te'kĕⁿ·	8
the side of it	again he went.	And	there,	I believe, he went about	not far it is	
ne'	dji'	kanoⁿ·'sote·	noñ'we·,	tä·hnoⁿ·'	rotä'kari'te' ne'	9
the	where	it house stands	place,	and	he was well the	
raksä·''ä·	io·sno're·	dji'	rote·hiä·roñ'tie·.			10
he child	it is rapid	where	he is increasing in size.			
A'kare·	nĕñ'	wä·hatä'ĕñnoñ'nĭ'	(?wä·hatä'ĕñnoñ'niĕⁿ'),[a]		kāiĕñ'-	11
After a time	now	he made a bow for himself			it	
kwire·	o'nĭ'	wä·roñ'nĭ'.	Nĕñ'	wä·hĭ'	roiĕⁿ'ĕⁿ·hä'tie'se·. E'iok	12
arrow	also	he it made.	Now	verily	he went about shooting it. Everywhere	
is're·	se·'',	a·se'kĕⁿ·'	nĕñ'	se·''	wä·hĭ' akwä·' kĕⁿ·' niwatoⁿ·-	13
again he went	indeed,	because	now	indeed	verily very here so it earth	
·hwĕñ'djiä·.	Iote·hiä·roñ'tie·	se·''	wä·hĭ'	ne'	oⁿ·hwĕñ'djiä·. Ne'	14
large (is).	It continued to increase in size	indeed	verily	the	it earth. The	

[a] This is the usual form of the text preceding term.

continued to grow in size. So at times he would return to the side of the lodge. The other boy, his younger brother, looked and saw that he had a bow and also an arrow. Then he spoke to her, his grandmother, saying: "Thou shouldst make for me a bow and also an arrow, so that I also should have them." So, thereupon, she made him a bow and also an arrow; and, then, therefore, they both had bows and arrows.

So now, verily, they two wandered about shooting. So then he whose body was exactly like that of a man-being went in his shooting along a lake shore, even at the water's edge. There stood a clump of bushes there, whereon rested a flock of birds. He shot at them and they flew over the lake, but the arrow fell into the water. Thereupon he went thither to the water's edge, and cast himself into the lake; he desired to go and recover his arrow. So when he leaped into the

1 kā'tī' so then	sewatie'rĕⁿ· sometimes	kanoⁿ·sāk'tā' house beside	sa're·te'. again he would go.	Wä'hatkät'ho· He looked	ne' the	
2 shāiā'tā· he one person	ne' the	iā·tāte·kĕñ''ā· they two are related as brothers	ro'ĕñ'nāiĕⁿ· he it bow has	kāiĕñ'kwire· it arrow	o'nī'. also.	Nĕñ' Now
3 wā'shakawĕⁿ'·hā'se· he her said to	ne'ne' the that	ro·sot'hā· his grandmother	wā'hĕñ'roⁿ: he it said:	"A'skwā'ĕñ- "Thou it bow shouldst make		
4 noñ'niĕⁿ· for me	no'k' but	o'nī' also	ne' the	kāiĕñ'kwire', it arrow.	aoñkiĕñ'tāke· I it'should have	o'nī' also	ni''." the I."
5 Ta', So,	e·tho'ne· at that time	nĕñ' now	wā·hoñwā'·ĕñnoñ'niĕⁿ· she it him bow made	no'k' and	o'nī' also	ne' the
6 kāiĕñ'kwire·. it arrow.	Ta'. So,	nĕñ' now	wā·'hĭ' verily	tenidjia'roⁿ· they both	ronā'ĕñ'nāiĕⁿ· they bow had	no'k' and
7 o'nī' also	ne' the	kāiĕñ'kwire· it arrow.				
8 Ta', So,	nĕñ' now	wā·'hĭ' verily	te·hoñnatawĕñ'rie·. they traveled about.	rotiiĕⁿ'ĕⁿ·hā'tie·se· they went about shooting.	Ta', So,	
9 ne' the	ka'tī' so then	ne' the	tkāie'rī' it is correct	oñ'kwe' manbeing	ni·hāiā'to'tĕⁿ· such his body kind of (is)	dji' where	roiĕⁿ'ĕⁿ·ha'tie·se', he goes about shooting,
10 kaniatarāktā·'tie· it lake along side of	i're· he walks	dji' where	teio·hnekāk·'te'. it liquid (water) ends (= water's edge).	E·' There	io'hiano·'kote it clump of bushes stood	
11 tä'hnoⁿ' and	e'' there	kĕⁿtho·kwā'·here· it bunch rested on	tci'tĕñ''ā'. bird.	Wā·hā'iā'ke·. He shot.	tä'hnoⁿ and	
12 kaniatarā'ke' it lake on	niiā'kā'tie· thither it flew	tä'hnoⁿ' and	awĕñ'ke· it water in	iā·hā'·ho' there it immersed itself	ne' the	
13 raoiĕñ'kwire·. his arrow.	E·tho'ne· At that time	e'' there	niiā·'ha're· thither he went	dji' where	teio·hnekāk·'tā it liquid (water) ends	
14 tä'hnoⁿ' and	o'k' only,	iā·'hatiā·toñ'tī' thither he his body cast	kaniatarā'ke·, it lake on,	wā're·'re· he it intended	oñsekko·''hā' I it will go after again	

water, he did not feel that he had plunged into the water, because he fell supine on the ground. There was no water there. He arose and was surprised that a lodge stood there, and that he had arisen beside the doorway. He looked into the lodge and saw a man sitting therein. The man who was sitting in the lodge said: "Enter thou here." So then he entered, and he who sat therein said: "Thou hast now arrived. I assuredly invited thee that thou shouldst come here. Here, then, lies the reason that I sent for thee. It is because I hear customarily the kind of language thy grandmother uses toward thee. She tells thee that she does not love thee, and the reason of it is that she believes that what Tawǐ'skaroⁿ customarily says is true. He says, customarily, of course, that thou killedst her who was the mother of

---

1. ne' raoień'kwire. Ne' kā'tǐ dji' neñ' iǎ'theñnitcoⁿ·'kwǎ·kwe·
   the   his arrow.   The   so then where now   thither he leaped

2. o·hnekā'ke· iǎ" te·hottō'kĕⁿ‘ ne' ia·ho·sko''oⁿ· ne' o·hnekā'ke·.
   it liquid on not he it noticed the thither he had the it liquid on,
                                         fallen into water

3. a·se·kĕⁿ·' oⁿ·hweñdjia'ke· iǎ·hāshā'tā'ne'. Iǎ·' kan'ekā· teka·hne'ko'.
   because   it earth on   there he fell   Not   anywhere   it liquid con-
                            supine.   rained.

4. Sa·hatkets'ko· neñ' wǎ·hatie'rĕⁿ· o'k e·' kanoⁿ·'sote· dji'
   Again he arose now   he was surprised only there it house   where
                                                        stands

5. ka·n·hokā'roñte· ak'tā· e·' noñ'we· oñsa·hatkets'ko'. Neñ' iǎ‘
   it doorway is open nearby there place again he arose. Now there

6. hatkāt'ho· kanoⁿ·'sakoⁿ· wǎ·ho'kĕⁿ' roñ'kwe· e·' theñ'teroⁿ·
   he looked it house in   he him saw   he man-   there there he
                                          being (is)   rested.

7. Neñ wǎ·heñ'roⁿ· ne' kanoⁿ·'sākoⁿ· theñ'teroⁿ·: "Kasatau'eiǎ'te·."
   Now he it said   the it house in   there he   "Thence do thou
                                          rested: enter."

8. Ta', e·tho'ne' neñ' iǎ·hatau'eiǎ'te·. tā·hnoⁿ·' neñ' wǎ·heñ'roⁿ·
   So,   at that   now   there he entered. and   now   he it said
         time

9. ne' theñ'teroⁿ·: "Neñ', wǎ·'sewe·. I·' wǎ·'hǐ iekoⁿ·hnoñ'koⁿ·
   the there he   "Now,   thou hast   I   verily   hence I thee sent
        abides: arrived.   for

10. ne' aoñta·'se·. Kĕⁿ·' ka'tǐ kari·hoñ'ni' dji' iekoⁿ·hnoñ'koⁿ·
    the thou shouldst Here so then it it causes where hence I thee sent
         come.   it is   for

11. a·se·kĕⁿ·' wǎkathoñ'te· ĕⁿ's ne' sa·sot'hā· dji' nikari·ho'tĕⁿ·
    because   I it hear   custom- the thy grand- where such it matter
                            arily   mother   kind of

12. iako·'thǎre· ne' ise'ke·. Iesa·hro'rǐ's dji' iǎ·' teiesanoroⁿ·'khwǎ·.
    she speaks the thou (thee) she thee tells where not she thee loves (esteems).
                     to.

13. ne' tiiori·'hwǎ dji' ne' tiiakawe·tā·'koⁿ· ne' Tawǐ'skaroⁿ dji
    the just it it is cause where the so she it firmly believes the Flint (Crystal) where
         of

14. nǎ·ho'tĕⁿ· ĕⁿ's ra'toⁿ·. Ra'toⁿ· ĕⁿ's wǎ·'hǐ i'se· she'rio· ne'
    such kind of custom- he it says. He it says custom- verily thou thou her the
    thing   arily   arily   (it is) didst kill

15. ietchi'nisteñ·'ǎ·kĕⁿ·hā'. Ta', iǎ·' to'kĕⁿske· te'kĕⁿ‘ dji' nǎ·ho'tĕⁿ·
    she of you two was. So, not it is true it is where such kind of
    mother   thing

you two. Now, what he customarily says is not true, and the grandmother of you two firmly believes the things that he says; so that is the reason that I desire that thou shouldst come hither. For the fact is, she discriminates between you two, loving him, but not thee. Here, then, I have made a bow and an arrow as well for thee. Here, then, take them." So thereupon he accepted them. They were marvelously fine in appearance. He said: "Thou must make use of these as thou goest about shooting, for sometimes thou hast asked thy grandmother to make thee a bow somewhat better than the one thou madest for thyself, yet she would, customarily, not give ear to it, and besides that she would habitually refuse, and then order thee away. She would customarily say: 'Go thou from here. I have no desire to be looking at thee, for thou art the one assuredly who killed my girl child.' Now this, customarily, was the kind of discourse she spoke. So now, then, another thing. Here, of course, are two

1	ĕⁿ's ra'toⁿ; cus- he it says; tomarily	no'k' and	ne' the	ietchi'sot'hă· your two grand- mother	ne' the	tiiakawe'tä·"koⁿ' so she it firmly believes	ne' the	dji' where
2	nă·ho'tĕⁿ' such kind of thing	ra'toⁿ; he it says;	ta', so,	ne' that	tiiori·"hwă· so it reason is	wăke'roⁿ' I it pur- posed	kĕⁿ'' here	ĕⁿ'te'se'te'. thou wilt come.
3	Ne' The	dji' where	teiakoti·"hĕⁿ' she one to the other prefers	raoⁿ·"hă· he him- self	roñwanoroⁿ"khwă', she him loves,		no'k' and	ni'se' the thou
4	iä·'tĕⁿ'. not at all.	Kĕⁿ'' Here it is	kä'tĭ' so then	koñiä'ĕñnoñnĭĕⁿ'nĭ', I thee it bow have made for,		no'k· and	o'nĭ' also	ne' the
5	kaiĕñ'kwire'. it arrow.	Ko'' Here (it is)	kä'tĭ'." so then."	Ta', So,	e·tho'ne' at that time	nĕñ' now	wă'hăie'nă'. he it took.	
6	Akwä'' Very	ione·hrä'kwä·t it is marvelous	iorä'se'. it is fine in appearance.	Wä·hĕñ'roⁿ' He it said:	"Ne" "That one		ĕⁿ'sats'thăke' thou it shalt use habitually	
7	ne' the	dji' where	säiĕⁿ·ĕⁿ·hä'tie'se', thou goest about shooting,	a·se·kĕⁿ'' because	sewatie're·ⁿ' sometimes	wä·sheri·hwanoñ'- thou her askedst		
8	toⁿ'se' question	ne' the	sa·'sot'hä· thy grand- mother	ne' the	äiesä'ĕñnoñ'nĭĕn· she it bow should make for thee		ne' the	sĕⁿ·"hă' more
9	äioian'ereke' it would be good	ne' the	dji' where	ni'io·t so it is	ne' the	satatsä·ä'nĭ·, thou thyself didst make for,	iä·' not,	ki' I believe,	ĕⁿ's custom- arily
10	thäioñthoñ'tate' she it would consent to		nĕñ' now	tä·hnoⁿ·'' and	äiesate'kwä'te'. she thee would order away.		Wä·'i'roⁿ' She it said	ĕⁿ's· custom- arily:
11	"I'sĭ' "Far yonder	noñ'we' the place	iä·ha'se' there do thou go.	Iä·'' Not	thä'tewakatoⁿ·hwĕndjioñ'nĭ' I it desire, (it is needful for me)			ne' the
12	takoñkan'ereke'. I thee should see.	I'se' Thou	wä·'hĭ' verily	se' indeed	she'rio' thou her didst kill	ne' the	kheiĕñ'ä·. my off- spring.	Ta', So,
13	e'' thus cus- tomarily	ĕⁿ's such her tale is	niieri·ho'tĕʰ where	dji' she is talking.	iako·''thăre'.	Ta', So,	nĕñ' now	a're' o'iä'. again other it is.
14	Kĕⁿ'' This	wä·'hĭ' verily	tekanoⁿ·kwĕñ·''iake· two it ears of corn in number		tekoñteroñ'weks white = (shriveling)		o'nĕⁿ·ste' it-corn	ne' the

ears of sweet corn. These thou must take away with thee. One of the ears is not yet ripe; it is still in its milky state, but, as to the other, it is mature. Thou must take them with thee. As to the one in the milky state, thou must roast it for thyself; but as to the one that is mature, it shall be for seed corn." Thereupon, then, when he had finished speaking, telling him all things, he said: "Here they are, then." Whereupon he took them.

It was at this time also that he told him, saying: "But, as to that, I am thy parent." That was said by him whose lodge stood there and who is the Great Turtle. Then the young man departed.

So then when he had returned home in traveling, he would habitually run along the lake shore and would say, customarily: "Let this earth keep on growing." He said: "People call me Maple Sprout

iĕⁿ·se'shāwe·. hence it thou shalt take.	Ne' The	skanoⁿ·kwĕñ'´iät one it ear of corn	iä´ not	teiotoñni's´oⁿ·, it has ripened,	se'koⁿ· still	1
okoⁿ·seroñ'tä· it milky is	(?okä·sero'tä·)ᵃ	i'kĕⁿ·, it is,	no'kʻ and	ne' the	ĕⁿ·´skä· iotoñni's´oⁿ· the one it is ripe	2
nä´ that one	ne´´, the that	ne'ne· the that	iĕⁿ·ses'hāwe·. hence thou shalt take it.	Ne' The	okoⁿ·seroñ'tä· ĕⁿsatenĕⁿ·s it is milky thou thyself shalt roast corn for	3
toñ'tĕⁿ· that one	nä´ the that	ne´´, and	no'kʻ the	ne' one	ĕⁿ·´skä· ne'ne· iotoñni's´oⁿ· the that it is ripe	4
ĕⁿieiĕntho·´thäke· one will use it to plant (for planting)."	nä´ that one	ne´´.´´ the that	E·tbo'ne· At that time	ka'tï´ so then	dji' nĕñ´ where now	5
wä·hari·hō'ktĕⁿ· he it matter ended	akwe'koⁿ· it all	wä·ho·hro'rï· he him told	nĕñ´ now	wä·hĕñ'roⁿ·: he it said:		6
"Ko·´. "Here it is,	ka'tï·." so then."	E·tho'ne· At that time	nĕñ´ now	wä·häie'nä· he them took.		7
Nĕñ Now	o'nï· also	e·tho'ne· at that time	nĕñ´ now	wä·ho·hro'rï· he him told	wä·hĕñ'roⁿ·: "I" nä´ he it said· "I that it is one	8
koñiĕñ'´ä·." I am thy parent."	Ne·´´ That	nä´ that one	wä·hĕñ'roⁿ· he it said	ne' e·´ the there	ni·honoⁿ·´sote· ne'ne· just his lodge the stands that	9
Haniä·tĕⁿ·´kowä· He Turtle Great	kĕⁿ·i'kĕⁿ·. this it is.	Ta´, So,	e·tho'ne· at that time	nĕñ´ now	sa·hä·tĕñ'tï· ne' he started the again	10
ranekĕⁿ·´teroⁿ·. he young man.						11
Ne' The	kä'tï so then	ne' the	nĕñ´ now	ciiehe'sro· there he reached home	nĕñ´ wä·'hï· dji' te·hota- now verily where he	12
wĕñ'rie·, travels,	kaniatarakta'tie· it lake alongside of	ĕⁿ/s customarily	niiä·hatak'he·. ust he would run,	ra'toⁿ· he it says	ĕⁿ/s· customarily:	13
"Iote·hiä·roñ'tie· "Let it increase in size	ne' the	kĕⁿ·i'kĕⁿ· this it is	iotoⁿ·hwĕñ'djiäte·." it earth (is) present here,"	nĕñ´ now	tä·hnoⁿ·. and	14

ᵃ This is the usual form of the next preceding term.

[Sapling]." Verily, as far as he customarily ran, so far the earth grew anew, and, besides that, maple saplings customarily would produce themselves. So then, it was his custom to do thus. On whatever side in turn he would run along the shore of the lake, just as far as he would run, just so far would this come to pass: new earth would form itself, and also maple saplings formed themselves into trees. He also said, customarily, as he ran along: "Let the earth increase in size" and: "Maple Sapling will people habitually call me." Thus it was, by means of this kind, that the earth became enlarged to the size it now has when we look at the size of this world.

So then, at this time, in turn, he formed severally the various bodies of the animals. Therefore, Sapling customarily would take up a handful of earth, and would cast it upward. Customarily, many hundreds of living things, as many as the handfuls he threw up,

1. "Wă'tă´ Oteroñtoñni'ă· ioñ'kiats." Ne' kă'tĭ ne' dji' ĕⁿ's
   "Maple It Sapling (it itself made small tree) they me name habitually." The so then the where customarily

2. niio're' niiă·hatak'he· e·" hĕⁿ's niio're' ă'se· oñtoⁿ·hwĕñdjioñ'nĭ,
   so it is distant so thither he ran there customarily so it is distant it new (is) it itself earth made.

3. nĕñ' tă·hnoⁿ·' wă·'tă´ oteroñtoñii'ă· ĕⁿ's oñteroñtoñ'nĭ. E'tho·
   now and maple it sapling (it itself made small tree) customarily it itself made into tree. Thus

4. kă'tĭ ni·hăier'·hă' dji' o'k· noñka'tĭ· ĕⁿ's niiă·hatak'he· karia-
   so then so it he does where only the side of it customarily so thither he ran it lake

5. taraktă'tie· dji' niio're' niiă·hatak'he· e·" hĕⁿ's nă·ă'wĕⁿ·, ne'
   alongside of where so it is distant so thither he ran there customarily so it happened, the

6. ă'se· oñtoⁿ·hwĕñdjioñ'nĭ, no'k· ho'nĭ ne' wă·'tă´ oñteroñtoñni'ă·.
   it new (is) it itself earth found, and also the maple it made itself into small tree.

7. Ne' ĕⁿ's o'nĭ· ratoñ'ne· ne' nĕñ' ratak'he·: "Iote·hiăroñ'tie·
   The customarily also he went saying the now he ran: "Let it increase in size

8. ne' oⁿ·hwĕñ'djiă·," ne' o'nĭ· ne' "Oteroñtoñni'ă· ioñ'kiats."
   the it earth." the also the It Sapling one me calls habitually"

9. Ta', ē'tho· nitioiera'toⁿ· ne' dji' ioⁿ·hwĕñdjiiowa·n·hă·'oⁿ· ne'
   So, thus so it did by means of this the where it earth became large the

10. dji' nĭ'io·t ne' dji' tewakan'ere· ne' dji' niwatoⁿ·hwĕñ'djiă'.
    where so it is the where· we it see the where so it earth large (is).

11. Ta', e'tho'ne· ne' ioñ'wă' koñtirio'o'koⁿ· wă·shakotiiă'toñii-
    So, at that time the this time they animals, he their bodies

12. ă'nioⁿ·. Ne' kă'tĭ ne' Oteroñtoñni'ă· oⁿ·hwĕñ'djiă· ĕⁿ's
    made plurally. The so then the It Sapling it earth customarily

13. wă·thă·tca'nă·kwe· no'k· ē·'iekĕⁿ· ĕⁿ's iă·ho'tĭ. E'so· ĕⁿ's
    he it handful picked up and high up customarily there he it threw. Many customarily

14. tekoñ'niă·we· a·e·rĕⁿ· ĕⁿ's wă·koñtitienoñ'tie· dji' ni'koⁿ· iă·ho·-
    they hundreds (are) in all directions customarily they went flying where so it numbers thither

flew away in different directions. He customarily said: "This shall continue to be your condition. When ye wander from place to place, ye must go in flocks." Thereupon a duty devolved upon this species of animals; for example, that they should habitually take roosts. Now, of course, different animals were severally asked to volunteer to aid man. Whichever of them would give ear to this, would say to it: "I, I think, will volunteer." Thereupon they would customarily ask him, saying: "Well then, permit us to see in what way thou wilt act when thou protectest thy offspring." The Bear, therefore, volunteered. Now then he acted so rudely that it was very marvelously terrifying. The manner in which he would act ugly would, I think, kill people. Thus, indeed, he exhibited to them how he would defend his offspring. They said: "Not at all, we think, shouldst thou volunteer." Whereupon, of course, others

tca'non'tī'.	Wă·hĕñ'ro^n·	ĕ^n's:	"E·',	ni'se·	nĕ^{n}io·to^n'·hăke·	ne'	1
he handfuls threw.	He it said	customarily:	"Thus,	the thou	so it will continue to be	the
dji'	tĕ^{n}teiatawĕñrie'·hăke·		ĕ^{n}tciĕñnitio·kwaratiĕ'seke'."		E'tho'ne·		2
where	she will continue to travel		ye will go about in groups (bodies)."		At that time	
noñ'we'	wă·oñnateri·hwāiĕñ'·hă'se·		ne'	koñtirio'o'ko^n·	o^n·'kă·		3
place	it them duty became for		the	they animals	who (it is)	
ĕ^{n}ie·nă·kwă·r·ho·'seke'.	Nĕñ'	wă·'hī'	ne'	koñtirio'o'ko^n·	o'iă'	o'k·	4
one roosts will form.	Now	verily	the	they animals	other	only
ĕ^n's	shoñwari·hwanoñtoñ'nī'	ne'	a·hathoñkăr'iă'ke'.		O^n·'kă·	o'k'	5
customarily	he them duties assigns to	the	he should volunteer to do it.		Who	just
ĕ^n's	wă·hathoñ'tate·	wă·'hĕñ'ro^n·:	"I'	ki''	ĕ^{n}kathoñkă'riă'ke'."		6
customarily	he would consent to it	he it said:	"I (it is),	I believe,	I will volunteer to do it."	
E'tho'ne·	ĕ^n's	wă·hoñwari·hwanoñ'to^n'se·		wă·hoñni'ro^n·		ĕ^n's:	7
At that time	customarily	they him asked		they it said		customarily:
"To',	kă'tī'	iakwatkăt'ho·	to'	nĕ^{n}te·'siere·	ne'	nĕñ'	ĕ^n·sate-
"How	so then	let us see	how	so thou wilt do it	the	now	thou wilt 8
wirake·'nhă'."	O·kwa'rī',	ki''.	wă·hathoñkă'riă'ke'.		E'tho'ne·		9
thy young defend."	Bear,	I believe,	he volunteered (scored stick).		At that time	
nĕñ'	wă·hateri·hwă'ksă'te·.	Akwă·'	ione·hră'kwă't,		teiotĕno^n·hi-		10
now	he his matter acted ugly.	Very	it is marvelous,		it is aston-	
ani·'to^n·,	iotte·'ro^n·.	A·shako'rio'	ki''	ne'	oñ'kwe·	dji'	na·hă'iere· 11
ishing,	it is frightful.	It one would kill,	I believe,	the manbeing	where	so he would act	
dji'	wă·hateri·hwak'să'te·.	Nĕñ'	wă·'hī'		wă·shakonă'toñ'·hă'se·		12
where	he his matter acted ugly.	Now ·	verily		they him showed	
dji'	nĕ^{n}thă'iere·	ne'	ĕ^n·hatewirake·'nhă'.		Wă·hoñni'ro^n·:	"Iă·'	13
where	so he will act	the	he his young will defend.		They it said:	"Not,
ki''	i'se·	thă·sathoñka'riă'ke·."	Ta'.	nĕñ'	wă·'hī'	o'iă'	o'k· 14
I believe,	thou	thou shouldst volunteer to do it."	So,	now	verily	other	only it is

offered themselves as volunteers. Nevertheless, none were acceptable, because their methods of defending their offspring were terrible. So one after another volunteered. After a while the Pigeon said "It is time now, I think, that I should volunteer." Whereupon, assuredly, they said: "How then wilt thou do when thou protectest thy offspring? Let us see." Then Pigeon flew hither and thither, uttering cries as it went. Then sometimes it would again alight on a bough of a tree. In a short time it would again fly, winging its way from place to place, uttering cries. So then they said: "Now, this will be suitable." At the same time they had lying by them a dish containing bear's oil; they therein immersed Pigeon, and they said: "So fat shall thy offspring customarily be." It is for this reason that the young of the pigeon are as fat as a bear usually is.

---

1 ěⁿ's   shothoñkariā'koⁿ·.   Iā·'   ki"   thakāie'rite·   sō'djĭ·   ěⁿ's   noti-
   custom- again he volunteers. Not,   I   it would be   because   custom- their
   arily   believe, correct   arily

2 weiěññätsā'nĭ·   ne'   wä·hatewirăke·'nhă'.   Ta',   e·'   kā'tĭ·   wä·'hĭ'
   manner of acting the   he his young would   So,   thus so then verily
   (is) frightful   defend.

3 ni'lo·t   o'iä·   o'k·   shothoñkariā'koⁿ·.   No'k·   hā'kare·   něñ'   ori'te'
   so it is other   only   again he volunteers to   And   after a   now   it pigeon
             it is   do it.   time

4 wä·hěñ'roⁿ·:   "Něñ'   ki"   i"   ěⁿkathoñkar'iä'ke·."   E'tho'ne·   wä·'hĭ'
   he it said: "Now,   I   I,   I will volunteer to do it   At that   verily
                  believe,   (score stick)."   time

5 wä·hoñni'roⁿ·:   "To',   kā'tĭ·   iakwatkät'ho'   dji'   ieⁿte·'siere·   ne'
   they (m.) it said: "How,   so then let us see it   where   so thou wilt   the
                                                                                act

6 něñ'   ěⁿ·satewirăke·'nhă'?   E'tho'ne·   něñ'   ne'   ori'te'   wä·katie·'soⁿ'
   now   thou thy young wilt   At that   now   the   it pigeon   it flew about from
          defend?"   time   place to place

7 io'tharătie·'se'.   Sewatie'rěⁿ·   něñ'   a're'   okwirā'ke·   shěññits
   it went about   Sometimes   now   again   it shrub   again it
   uttering cries.   (branch) on

8 kwa'rěⁿ·.   Nä·he·'ä·   o'k·   ěⁿ's   no'k·   ha'ie'   toñsakā'těⁿ',
   would alight. In a short only   custom- and   again   again it would
                  time   arily   fly,

9 sakatie·'soⁿ'   io'tharä'tie·'se'.   Něñ'   wä·hoñni'roⁿ·:   "Něñ'   ne'
   again it flew from it went about   Now   they (m.) it said: "Now   that
   place to place   uttering cries.

10 ieⁿkāie'rite'."   E'tho'ne·   něñ'   ronnatek'sāieⁿ'   o·kwa'rĭ·   kěñ'ie'
   it will be correct At that   now   they a vessel for it bear   it oil
                      time   themselves have set

11 i'kare'   e·'   kā'tĭ·   iä·hoñwä·'sko'   ne'   ori'te',   něñ'   tä·hnoⁿ·'
   it con-   there so then there they him   the   it pigeon,   now   and
   tains   immersed

12 wä·hoñni'roⁿ··   "E·'   ěⁿ's   ni'se·   něⁿionare·'sěⁿ·'häke'   ne'   shei
   they (m.) it said: "Thus   custom- the   so they will be fat   the   thy
                               arily   thou

13 ěñ'okoñ·'ä·."   (Ne'   kā'tĭ·   kari·hoñ'nĭ·   ne'   ori'te'   aotiwi'rä'   e·'
   offspring."   (The   so then   it reason is   the   it pigeon   their off-   thus
                                                                    spring

14 niionarē·'sěⁿ·   dji'   ni'io·t   ěⁿ's   ne'   o·kwa'rĭ·   io're'sěⁿ·.)
   so they fat (are)   where so it is custom- the   it bear   it is fat.)
                                        arily

During this time Tawī'skaron" was watching what Sapling was doing. Thereupon he began to imitate him by also making animal bodies. But this work was too difficult for him to allow his doing it correctly. He failed to make correctly the bodies of the animals just as they are. He formed the body of a bird as he knew it. So, when he had finished its form, he let it go, and now, I think, it flew. Forsooth, it succeeded in flying, but it flew without any objective point. And, I believe, it did not become a bird. Now then he had completed the body of what we know as the bat. So then, when he, Sapling, had completed in their order the bodies of the marvelously various kinds of animals, they began to wander over the face of the earth here present.

Then, as Sapling was traveling about over the face of the earth, he, after a while, marveled greatly that he could not in any

Ne'	ká'tĭ	ne'	Tawī'skaron'	e·'	te·hakan'ere'	ne'	dji'	ni·ha-	1
The	so then	the	Flint (Ice, Crystal)	there	he it watched	thew	here	so he	
tie·r'‘hă̆	ne'	Oterontoñni''ă'.		Ñeñ'	tă·hnon''	wă‘hĭ'		tă‘horá̤-	2
is doing	the	It Sapling.		Now	and	verily		he him imitated	
ke'rĕn'	nĕñ'	wă‘hāiằ'toñnia'nion'		o'nĭ'.		Nă''	ne'	ɩo'k‘	3
now		he their (z.) bodies plurally made		also.		The that	that one	and	
wă‘hono'ron'se'		aoñta‘hoieri'ton·hăke'		ne'	dji'	nikoñtiiă'to'tĕn·se'			4
he it failed to do		he it should have done correctly		the	where	so their kinds of body plurally.			
Tci‘tĕñ''ă̆'	wă‘hāiă̆'toñ'nĭ'		ne'	dji'	roteriĕñ'tăre'.	Ne'	ká'ti'	ne'	5
Bird	he its body made		the	where	he it knows.	The	so then	the	
dji'	nĕñ'	wă‘hāiă̆'tis''ă̆'		wă‘ha·''tkă̆'we·,	nĕñ''	ki''	wă'tka'tĕn''		6
where	now	he its body finished		he it let go,	now,	I believe,	it flew.		
To'kĕn̆ske'	ki''	oñ'ton'	wă'tka'tĕn'.	O'k‘	kĕn''	thiiă̆'ka'tie'		ɩo'k‘	7
It·is true,	I believe,	it was successful	it flew.	Just	here it is	just thither it went flying		and	
iă̆''	ki''	tci·tĕñ''ă̆'	teiotoñ''on‘.	Ne'		wă‘hĭ'	wă‘hāiă̆'tis''ă̆'		8
not,	I believe,	bird	it has become.	The		verily	he its body finished		
ɩoñ'wă̆'	ne'	tewāiĕñte'rĭ'	iakohon·''tariks		koñwa'iats.	Ne'	ká'ti'		9
this time	the	we it know	it bites one's ears (bat)		they it call.	The	so then		
ne'	nĕñ'	ne'	Oteroñtoñni''ă̆'	sa‘has'ă̆'	akwe'kon·	wă‘shakoiă̆-			10
the	now	the	It Sapling	again he it finished	it all	he made			
toñniă̆'nion'		ne'	koñtirio'o'kon'	ne'	ione‘hra'kwă̆·t		e'so'		11
their body plurally		the	they animal (are)	the	it is wonderful		many		
niionon·hwĕñdjia'ke·.		Ñeñ'	wă‘·hĭ'	wă'tkoñtawĕñ'rie'	ne'	dji'			12
they lands (kinds) in number (are.)		Now	verily	they traveled about	the	where			
ion·hwĕñdjiă̆'te'.									13
it earth present (is).									
Ne'	ká'ti'	ne'	Oteroñtoñni''ă̆·	ne'	dji'	te‘hotawĕñ'rie·		ne'	14
The	so then	the	It Sapling	the	where	he traveled		the	
dji'	ion·hwĕñdjiă̆'te'	ă'kaɩe·		nĕñ'	wă‘hori·hwane·hra'ko·		iă̆''		15
where	it earth present is	after a time		now	he matter was astonished at		not		

place still see the different kinds of animals. Thereupon he traveled about over the face of the earth seeking for them. He also thought, forsooth: "This is an astonishing matter; where, perhaps, have they gone—they, the animals whose bodies I have made?" So then, while he went from place to place, and while he was looking for the animals, he was startled. Near him a leaf made a noise, and looking thither he was surprised to see a mouse peering up there along the leaves. The mouse that he saw is called the Deer-mouse, and, of course, he had intended to shoot it, but the Deer-mouse spoke to him, saying: "Do thou not kill me. I will tell thee then where have gone those things thou art seeking, the animals." So then in truth he resolved not to kill it, and then he spoke and said: "Whither then have the animals gone?" Thereupon the Deer-mouse said: "In that direction there is

kăn′ekă′	thaoñsă'ha′kĕⁿ'	ne′	koñtirio′o′koⁿ'.	Nĕñ′	wă′'hĭ'	
1 anywhere	again he them could see	the	they (z.) animals (are).	Now	verily	
wă'thatawĕñ′rie'	wă'shakoiă'ti′săke'.	Ne′	o′nĭ'	i′re're':	"Hă′nio"	
2 he traveled	he their bodies sought to find.	The	also	he thought:	"Forsooth,	
iori'hwane'hra′kwă't,	kă'	oⁿ''te'	niieione′noñ	ne′	kheiă''tis''oⁿ	
3 it it matter astonishing is,	where it is	perhaps	just there they have gone	the	I their (anthr.) bodies have formed	
ne′	koñtirio′o′koⁿ'?	Ne′	kă′ti'	wă′'hĭ'	ne′	dji′ te'hotawĕñrie
4 the	they (z.) animals (are)?"	The	so then	verily	the	where he went about
ɔă′tie′se'	ne′	dji′	shăiă′ti'saks	ne′	koñti′rio'	wă'hatie′rĕⁿ' o′k'
5 traveling	the	where	again he their bodies seeks to find	the	they animals (are)	he was surprised just.
Kĕⁿ''	ioñ′we'	e''	wă'onera'tak′are'	e''	iă'hatkăt′ho'	wă'ha
6 Here it is	the place	there	it leaf made a sound	there	there he looked	he was
tie′iĕⁿ'	o′k'	tcinō′wĕⁿ'	e''	toñtke′to′tĕⁿ'	onera''tōkoⁿ'.	Tso-
7 surprised	just	mouse	there	it peeped up	it leaf among. (it leaves among)	Deer-
tshot′hoⁿ'	koñwă′iats	ne′	tcino′wĕⁿ'	wă'ha′kĕⁿ'.	No′k'	wă′'hĭ'
8 mouse	they it call	the	mouse	he it saw.	And	verily
nă''	raweroñ′ne'	ĕⁿ'hă′iă′ke'	io′k'	kĭ''	toñta′tĭ'	ne′ tcino′wĕⁿ'
9 that one	he had intended	he it will shoot	and,	I believe,	thence it spoke (to him)	the mouse
ne′	o′nĭ'	wă′kĕñ′roⁿ':	"To'′să'	takeri′io'.	Ĕnkoⁿ''hro′rĭ'	kă′tĭ'
10 the	also	it it said:	"Do not do it	thou me kill.	I thee will tell	so then
kă''	noñ′we'	niieione′noñ	ne′	tciă′ti'saks	ne′	koñtirio′o′koⁿ'.''
11 where	the place	there they have gone	the	thou their bodies seekest to find	the	they animals (are).''
To′kĕⁿske'	kă′tĭ'	wa′re're'	iă''	thakri′io',	nĕñ′	tă′hnoⁿ'' ta'hata′tĭ'
12 It is true	so then	he it thought	not	I it should kill,	now	and he spoke
wă'hĕñ′roⁿ':	"Kă''	kă′tĭ'	niieione′noñ	ne′	koñti′rio'?"	E′tho′ne'
13 he it said:	"Where it is	so then	just there they have gone	the	they animals are?"	At that time
nĕñ′	wă′kĕñ′roⁿ'	ne′	Tsotshot′hoⁿ'	tcino′wĕⁿ':	"E''	noñ′we'
14 now	it it said	the	Deer Mouse	mouse:	"There	place

a large of great mountains of rock. There in the rocks they abide,
and are indeed shut up. If, when thou arrivest there, thou lookest,
thou wilt see a large stone placed over the cavern, which stone one
has used for the purpose of closing it up. It is Tawĭ'skaroⁿ· himself and his grandmother who have together done this; it is they
who imprisoned the animals." So then, therefore, he went thither.
It was true then that a stone lay over the place where was the opening into the rock; it was closed therewith. So he then removed
the stone from it, and he now said: "Do ye all come forth. For,
assuredly, when I caused you to be alive, did I intend that ye
should be imprisoned here? Assuredly, I intended that ye should
continue to roam from place to place over this earth, which I have
caused to be extant." Thereupon they did in fact come forth.
There was a rumbling sound, as their feet gave forth sounds while

tiionontätä'tie·	otstĕñ'rä·	e·'	iotstĕñräka'roñte·-kowa'nĕⁿ·.		e'tho·	1
just there it mountain stands extended	it rock (is)	there	it rock cavern great (is)		there	
otstĕñ'räkoⁿ·	iekoñti'teroⁿ·	koti·n·ho'toⁿ·	se'.	To'kä·	nĕñ'	e·'	2
it rock in	there they abide	they are shut up	indeed.	If	now	there	
iĕⁿ·'sewe·	ĕⁿ·satkät'ho·	kĕⁿtstĕñrowä'nĕⁿ·	e·'	ka'·)eıe·	dji'	3
there thou wilt arrive	thou wilt look	it rock large	there	it lies on it	where	
iotstĕñräka'roñte·	ne''	ka·n·hotoⁿ·'kwĕⁿ·.	Raoⁿ·'hä·	ne'	Tawĭ'skaroⁿ·	4
it rock cavern (is)	the	one it used to close it.	He himself	the	Flint (Ice, Crystal)	
ro·'k·	ne'	ro·sot'hä·	ne'	e·'	ni·hotiie'reⁿ·	niñ·ho'toⁿ	ne'	5
and	the	his grand-mother	the	thus	so they it did	they two shut them up	the	
koñti'rio·."	Ta',	e'tho'ne·	nĕñ'	e·'	wa're·te'.	To'kĕⁿske·	kä'tĭ·	6
they animals (are)."	So,	at that time	now	there	thither he went.	It is true	so then	
e·'	kĕⁿtstĕñra'·here·	dji'	noñ'we·	dji'	iotstĕñräka'roñte·	7
there	one it rock placed on it	where	place	where	it rock cavern (is)	
kan·ho'toⁿ·.	Ta',	e'tho'ıe·	nĕñ'	sa·hĕⁿtstĕñrä·hra'ko·	nĕñ'	8
one closed it.	So,	at that time	now	again he rock took off	now	
tä·hnoⁿ·'	wä·)ĕñ'roⁿ·:	"Toñtasewäia'kĕⁿ·ne·	akwe'koⁿ·	Iä·'	9
and	he it said:	"Hence do ye come forth	it all	Not	
se·'	wä·'hi·	tewake'roⁿ·	ne'	dji'	kion·he'toⁿ·	kĕñt'ho·-kĕⁿ·'	10
indeed	verily	I it intended	the	where	I thee caused to live	here, is it	
ĕⁿ·senin·hotoⁿ·'häke·	(ĕⁿsewan·hotoⁿ·'häke').[a]	Wäke'roⁿ·	wä·'hi'	11
ye will remain shut up.		I it intended	verily	
tĕⁿtciatawĕñrie·'häke·	ne'	dji'	wäkoⁿ·hwĕñdjia'tatĕⁿ·."	Ta',	12
ye will continue to travel about	the	where	I it earth made to be present."	So,	
e'tho'ne·	nĕñ'	to'kĕⁿske·	toñtakoñtiia'kĕⁿ·ne·.	Teio'toⁿ·hare'nioⁿ·	13
at that time	now	it is true	thence they came forth.	It sound spread forth	
ne'	dji'	wä·tionoñniakä're·re·	ne'	dji'	nĕñ'	tcotiiakĕⁿ·'oⁿ·hä'tie·	14
the	where	their feet (hoofs) sounded	the	where	now	again they were coming forth.	

[a] This is the usual form of the next preceding term.

they kept coming forth. So, at this time, the grandmother of
Tawĭ′skaroⁿ said: "What thing, perhaps, is now happening? There
is a rumbling sound." She thus addressed her grandson, Tawĭ′skaroⁿ.
Before Tawĭ′skaroⁿ could reply, she spoke again, saying: "It is true,
undoubtedly, that Sapling has found there there where thou and I
have the animals imprisoned. So then, let us two go at once to
the place wherein we two imured them." Then at once they two
went out, and without delay ran thither. So when they two arrived
there, it was even so; the Sapling stood there, having opened the
cavern in the rock, and verily a line of animals ever so long was
running. The two rushed forward and took up the stone again, and
again shut in those that had not come out, and these are animals great
in size and now dwelling therein.

	Ta′,	e′tho′ne′	noñ′we‘	Tawĭ′skaroⁿ	ro‘sot′hă‘	wă′i′roⁿ:	"O"
1	So,	at that time	place	Flint (Ice, Crystal)	his grand- mother	she it said:	"What
	nă‘ho′těⁿ	oⁿ‘‘te‘	niioteri‘hwătie′rěⁿ‘		kěⁿ′i′kěⁿ‘		teio′toⁿ′‘hāre' "
2	kind of thing	perhaps	there it matter is being done		this it is		it sound is present."
	wă‘boñwěⁿ′‘hă‘se'	ne'	roñwatere′′ă‘	Tawĭ′skaroⁿ		Iă′′	hā′re’kho'
3	She it him said to	the	her grandson	Flint (Ice, Crystal)		Not	yet
	tethotā′tĭ‘	ne'	Tawĭ′skaroⁿ.	Toñtāioñtā′tĭ'	wă′i′roⁿ:		"Ori‘hwi′io'
4	again he talked	the	Flint (Ice, Crystal.)	Thence again she talked	she said:		"It is certain
	noñ′wă'	ne'	Oteroñtoñ′ni′′ă‘	iă‘hatsěñ′rĭ'	dji'	noñ′we‘	niiethi-
5	this time	the	It Sapling	there he it found	where	place	there we them have shut
	n‘ho′toⁿ	ne'	koñti′rio'.	Ne'	kā′tĭ'	nakwă′′	iokoñta′tie' e‘‘
6	up	the	they (are) animals.	The	so then	the very	at once there
	iet′ene‘	dji'	noñ′we‘	niiethin‘ho′toⁿ’."	E′tho′ne'	něñ'	iokoñtă′tie'
7	thither let us two go	where	place	there we them have shut up."	At that time	now	at once
	iă′niiakěⁿ′′tă′tci’,	nakwă′′	o‘k‘	e‘‘.	iă′tiara′′tăte'	Ne'	kā′tĭ' dji'
8	thither they two went out,	the very	just	there	thither they two went running.	The	so then where
	něñ'	iă‘hā′newe'	to′kěⁿske‘	kā′tĭ'	e‘‘	i′iate' ne'	Oteroñtoñni′′ă‘,
9	now	there they two arrived	it is true	so then	there	he stood the	It Sapling,
	sho‘n‘hotoñ′kwěⁿ‘	ne'	iotstěñraka′roñte’,	ne′′	nakwă′′	o‘k‘	he‘‘
10	he had opened closed place	the	it rock cavern (is),	that	the very	just	yon- der.
	thă’tekaněñ′res	koñtităkhenon′tie'		ne'	koñti′rio'.	Nakwă′′	o‘k‘
11	there its line (is) long	they were along running		the	they animals (are).	The very	only
	ci-niiă’takoñtă′tie'	toñsa‘nitstěñ′ră‘kwe'		sa‘nin′ho′toⁿ		ne'	iă′′
12	they went without stopping	again they two stone took up		again they two it closed		the	not
	thă’tetiotiiakěⁿ′′oⁿ‘,	nakwă′′	i′kěⁿ‘	kario’towa′něⁿ′′se'		ne'	kā′tĭ'
13	then they had come out,	the very	it is	it animal great (are)		the	so then
	ne'	o‘k‘	he′′	niiesăkon‘′hese'.			
14	the	just	there	just there again they live.			

Sapling kept saying: "Do ye two not again immure the 1." Nevertheless, Tawĭ'skaroⁿ' and his grand 1 other just placed thereon other stones. So then the kinds of ani 1 als that we know are only those that ca 1 e out again.

So then it ca 1 e to pass that Sapling, as he traveled fro 1 place to place, went, after a while, along the shore of the lake. There, not far away, he saw Tawĭ'skaroⁿ', 1 aking for hi 1 self a bridge of stone [ice] across the lake, which already extended far out on the water. Thereupon Sapling went to the place where he went on working. So then, when he arrived there, he said: "Tawĭ'skaroⁿ', what is this that thou art doing for thyself?" He replied, saying: "I am 1 aking a pathway for 1 yself." And then, pointing in the direction toward which he was building the bridge, he added: "In that direction there is a land where dwell great ani 1 als of fierce dispositions. As soon as I co 1 plete 1 y

Ne'ne'	Oterontoñni''ä'	ra'toⁿ:	"To''sä'	sasenin'ho'toⁿ'."	1
The that	It Sapling	he it says:	"Do not do it	again you two it close."	
Sĕⁿ''bä'	o'k·	toñtanitstĕñra'rĕⁿ'	ne'	Tawĭ'skaroⁿ' no'k'	ne'	2
More	only	they two rock laid on it	the	Flint (Ice, Crystal) and	the	
ro'sot'hă'	Ne'	kă'tĭ' ne' dji'	noñ'wă'	niionoⁿ'hwĕñdjia'ke'	ne'	3
his grandmother.	The	so then the where	this time	so they lands (kinds) in number are	the	
koñti'rio'	ne'	tewăiĕñte'rĭ' e''	ni'koⁿ'	ne' tciiotiiakĕñ''oⁿ'.		4
they animals (are)	the	we them know thus	so they number	the again they emerged.		
Ta', ne'	kă'tĭ'	wă''hĭ' ne'	Oterontoñni''ä·	dji' te'hotawĕñrie'-		5
So, the	so then	verily the	It Sapling	where he traveled		
ha'tie'se'	ā'kare'	nĕñ' kaniatarăk'tă'	niiă'ha're'.	E'' wă'hotkă''		6
about	after a time	now it lake beside	thither he went.	There he him saw		
tho' ne'	Tawĭ'skaroⁿ'	thă'onĕñ'ă' e'rĕⁿ'	kaniatară'ke''shoⁿ'	otstĕñ'rä'		7
the	Flint (Ice, Crystal)	already far	it lake on along	it rock (ice)		
wă'hotaskoñniă'tă'kwĕⁿ'hă'tie'.	"	E'tho'ne' ne'	Oterontoñni''ä'	e''		8
thither he it bridge goes on making of it for himself.		At that time the	It Sapling	there		
niiă'ha're'	dji'	noñ'we' wă'boio'tă'tie'.	Ne'	kă'tĭ' ne' dji'		9
thither he went	where	place he working went ahead.	The	so then the where		
nĕñ'	e''	iă'hā'rawe' wă'hĕñ'roⁿ':	"Tawĭ'skaroⁿ',	o'' ne'		10
now	there	there be arrived he it said:	"Flint, (Ice, Crystal)	what (is it) the		
ni'satie·r''hă'?"	Tă'hari·hwă'sera'ko'	wă'hĕñ'roⁿ':	"Wăkathă'hoñni-		11
thou art doing?"	Thence he replied	he it said:	"I road am making for myself."		
'hă'tie'."	Iă'hă'tca'tĕⁿ'	dji' noñ'kă'tĭ'	nă'hoierä'toⁿ'hă'tie'	wă-		12
	Thither he pointed	where side of it	thither he his way was making	he	
'hĕñ'roⁿ':	"E''	noñ'we'	tiioⁿ'hwĕñdjiă'te'	koñtirio'towa'nĕⁿ'se'		13
it said:	"There	the place	there it earth (is) present	they animals large (are)		

ᵃThis incident shows definitely that Flint, or rather Ice-coated or Crystal, is the Winter power. There is here a substitution of rock for ice, just as there has been in the name of this important nature force.

pathway to that other land, thereon will they habitually come over. Along this pathway will they be in the habit of coming across the lake to habitually the flesh of human beings who are about to be [who are about to dwell here] on this earth." So then Sapling said to him: "Thou shouldst cease the work that thou art doing. Assuredly the intention of thy mind is not good." He replied, saying: "I will not cease from what I am doing, for, of course, it is good that these great animals shall be in the habit of coming hither to eat the flesh of human beings who will dwell here."

So, of course, he did not obey and cease from building the bridge for himself. Thereupon Sapling turned back and reached dry land. So along the shore of the sea grew shrubs. He saw a bird sitting on a limb of one. The bird belonged to the class of birds that we

1 koñti'sero'‘hĕⁿ'se' e‘¹ noñ'we‘ tkanak'ere'. Kawĕñni'io' nĕñ'
  they fierce are   there place   there they . So soon as now
                                       inhabit:

2 ĕⁿkathä‘hĭs'‘ă' ne' nĕñ' e‘' iĕñ'wawe' thi'kĕⁿ: tiioⁿ'hwĕñdjiä'te'
  I shall complete the now there there it will that it is   there it earth stands
  my road   reach

3 e‘' tĕⁿtkoñne'thäke' o‘hä‘hä'ke'‘shoⁿ' tĕⁿkoñtiiä'iäk'seke' ne'ne‘
  there thence they will con- . it path on along . thence they will habitually the that
  tinue to come   cross the stream

4 ĕⁿtkoñti'wä‘hrakhe'seke' ne' oñ'kwe‘ᵃ ioñnakerät'he' ne' kĕⁿ'
  thence they meat will habitually the man-being they are about to the here
  come to eat   inhabit   it is

5 ioⁿ'hwĕñdjiä'te'." Ta', e'tho'ne' ne' Oteroñtoñni''ä‘ nĕñ'
  it earth is present." So, at that time the It Sapling   now

6 wä‘hawĕⁿ'‘hä‘se' ne' Tawĭ'skaroⁿ': "Ä‘sä'‘tkä'we‘ dji' satie'rĕⁿ‘
  he it said to him the Flint: "Thou it shouldst where thou art at
                         (Ice, Crystal)   cease from   work.

7 Iä‘' wä'‘hi' teioiän'ere' dji' ni‘sa'nikoⁿ'hrō'tĕⁿ‘." Tä‘hari‘hwä'se
  Not verily it is good   where so thy mind is shaped." He replied

8 ia'ko' wä‘hĕñ'roⁿ': "Iä‘' thaka''tkä'we, dji' nä‘ho'tĕⁿ'
  he ti said: "Not   I it should cease where such kind of
                                from   thing

9 nikatie'r'‘hä'. Ioian'ere' se'' wä'‘hi' thoi'kĕⁿ‘ koñtirio'towa'nĕⁿ'se'
  such I am doing. It is good indeed verily this it is they animals large (are)

10 ĕⁿtkoñti'wä‘rakhe'seke' ne' oñ'kwe‘ ne' kĕⁿ'' ĕⁿienäk'ereke'."
   thence they will habitually come the man-being the here they will continue
   to eat meat   (human)   it is   to dwell."

11 O'nĕⁿ‘ wä'‘hi' iä'' te‘hotboñta'toⁿ‘ ne' a‘hä''tkä'we' ne' dji'
   Now   verily not he it consented to the he it would cease the where
                                                             from

12 rotä‘skoñni'‘hä'tie'. E'tho'ne' ne' Oteroñtoñni''ä‘ nĕñ' sä‘hä''kete'
   he it bridge is making for At that the It Sapling   now   again he turned
   himself.   time   back

13 aoⁿ'hwĕñdjiathĕñ''ke‘ ioñsa'rawe'. Ne' kä'tĭ' ne' kaniataräktä'tie'
   it earth is dry at   there again The so then the it lake it side of along
   (to dry land)   he arrived.

14 iokwirarät'ie', tci'tĕñ''ä‘ wä‘ha'kĕⁿ' e‘' kĕñtskwa'‘here' okwira'ke‘.
   it brush grew   bird   he it saw there it it sat on   it branch on.
   along,

ᵃ This refers to human beings, which, it was understood, were about to inhabit the earth.

are accustomed to call the bluebirds. Sapling then said to the Bluebird: "Thou shalt kill a cricket. Thou shalt remove one hind leg from it, and thou shalt hold it in thy mouth, and thou shalt go thither to the very place where Tawï'skaroⁿ' is working. Hard by the place where he is working thou shalt alight, and thou shalt cry out." The bird replied, saying: "Yo'' [very well]."

Thereupon it verily did seek for a cricket. After a while it found one, and killed it, too. Then it pulled out one of its hind legs and put it into its mouth to hold, and then it flew, winging its way to the place where Tawï'skaroⁿ' was at work making himself a bridge. There it alighted hard by him at his task. Of course it then shouted, saying: "Kwe', kwe', kwe', kwe', kwe'."[a] Thereupon Tawï'skaroⁿ' upraised

Ne'	dji'	nä'ho'těⁿ'	koñwä'iats	ne'	tci'těñ''ä'	Swiwi'ko'wä'.[b]	1
The	where	such kind of thing	one it calls	the	bird	Great Bluebird.	
Něñ'	ne'	Oterontoñni''ä'		wä'rěⁿ'·hä'se'		ne' Swiwi'-	2
Now	the	It Sapling		he it her said to		the Great	
ko'wä':	"Tarak'tarak		ěⁿ'seri'io'	tä'hnoⁿ''		ěⁿsnitshotä'ko'	3
Bluebird:	"Cricket		thou it wilt kill	and		thou its thigh shalt take off	
ěⁿ''skä'	ne'	ěⁿ'sate'nhoñ'tä'		no'k'	he''	iěⁿ''se' dji'	4
one	the	thou it shalt hold in thy mouth		and	there	there thou shalt go where	
noñ'we'	ne'	Tawï'skaroⁿ'	wä'hoio'tä'tie'		äktä''ä'	dji' roio''te'	5
place	the	Flint (Ice, Crystal)	he goes on working		near by	where he is working	
e''	iěⁿ'sěñnitskwa'rěⁿ',		no'k'	těⁿsa'hěñ're'te'."		Toñtä'tï' ne'	6
there	there thou shalt sit,		and	thou shalt shout."		It spoke in the reply	
tci'těñ''ä'	wä'kěñ'roⁿ':	"Io''."					7
bird	it it said:	"So be it."					
E'tho'ne'	něñ'	tō'kěⁿske'	wä'oiä'tï'sake'		ne'	tarak'tarak	8
At that time	now	truly	it its body sought		the	cricket.	
Ä'kaie'	něñ'	wä'oiä'tatsěñ'rï'	tä'hnoⁿ''	wä'oie'nä'	ne'	o'nï' ne'	9
After a while	now	it its body found	and	it it seized	the	also the	
wä'o'rio'.	E'tho'ne'	něñ'	wä'o'nitshota'ko'		ěⁿ''skä',	tä'hnoⁿ''	10
it it killed.	At that time	now	it its thigh took off		one,	and	
e'tho'ne'	něñ'	ěⁿte'nhoñ'tä'.	Něñ	tä'hnoⁿ''		wä'tka'těⁿ', e''	11
at that time	now	it it put into its mouth.	Now	and		it flew, there	
niiä'kä'tie'	dji'	noñ'we' ne'	Tawï'skaroⁿ'	wä'hotäskoñnioⁿni'hä'tie'			12
there it went flying	where	the place the	Flint (Ice, Crystal)	he it bridge kept on building for himself.			
E''	iä'hěñnitskwa'rěⁿ'	ak'tä'	dji'	roiō''te',	něñ'	wä''hï'	13
There	there it alighted	near by	where	he was working,	now	verily	
wä'tiio'hěñ'ie'te'	wä'kěñ'roⁿ':	"Kwē'',[a]	kwē'',	kwē'',	kwē''.		14
it uttered a cry	it (z.) it said:	"Kwē''.	kwē'',	kwē'',	kwē''.		

[a] This is approximately the death cry or halloo of the Iroquois.

[b] The bluebird is here mentioned as it is among the first of the migratory birds to return in the spring, which is a token that the spring of the year has come, and that the power of the Winter power is broken.

his head and looked and saw a bird sitting there. He believed from what he saw that it held in its mouth the thigh of a man-being, and also that its mouth was wholly covered with blood. It was then that Tawī'skaroⁿ' sprang up at once and fled. As fast as he ran the bridge which he was making was dissipated.[a]

Now then, verily, the father of Sapling had given him sweet corn, and now he roasted this corn. A great odor, a sweet odor, was diffused. So when the grandmother of Tawī'skaroⁿ' smelt it, she said: "What other thing again is Sapling roasting for himself?" She addressed Tawī'skaroⁿ' saying: "Well, let us two go to see it, where he has his fire built." Now, of course, they two had at once uprisen, and they

kwē''.''	E'tho'ne'	něñ'	wă'hěñnoⁿ'kets'ko'	ne'	Tawī'skaroⁿ'	
1 kwē''.''	At that time	now	he his head raised	the	Flint (Ice, Crystal)	
tä'hnoⁿ''	wă'hatkă''tho'	wă'ha'kěⁿ'	tci'těñ''ă·	e·'	kěⁿtskwä''here'.	
2 and	he looked	he it saw	bird	there	it sat.	
Wä''re're'	dji'	ni'io't	dji'	wă'hatkăt'ho'	oñ'kwe'-kěⁿ''hă'	
3 He thought	where	so it is	where	he it looked at	man-being it had been	
io'hnitsa'nhoñ'te'	něñ'	tä'hnoⁿ''	ne'	dji'	ka'saka'roñte'	
4 it thigh in its mouth held.	now	and	the	where	its mouth	
onekwěⁿ'sōs'koⁿ'.	E'tho'ne'	ne'	Tawī'skaroⁿ'	toñtă'hatěⁿstä'tcī'		
5 it is wholly blood.	At that time	the	Flint (Ice, Crystal)	thence he quickly arose		
10'k·	bāiă'takoñtă'tie'	shote'kwěⁿ·.	Dji'	niio'sno're'	ne'	dji'
6 and	his body did not stop	again he fled.	Where	so it is rapid	the	where
ratăk'he·	e·''	nitcio'sno're'	tcioteri'sioñ'hă'tie'	ne'	hotăskoñni	
7 he ran	thus	so again it is rapid	again it disappeared (came to pieces)	the	he it bridge had been making	
oñni'hătiē'ne'.						
8 for himself.						
Ne'	kā'ti'	wă''hi'	ne'	Oteroñtoñni''ă·	10'ui''hă·	thō'wi·	ne'
9 The	so then	verily	the	It Sapling	his father	he him gave	the
tekoñteroñ'weks	o'něⁿ'ste·	ne'	kā'ti'	wă'hateněⁿ'stoñ'těⁿ'.		
10 white (shriveled)	corn	the	so then	he corn roasted.·		
Kă'serowa'něⁿ'	kă'sera'koⁿ'	oⁿte'se'rărěⁿ'.	Ne'	kā'ti'	ne'	
11 It odor (is) great	it odor (is) pleasant	it odor took on.	The	so then	the	
Tawī'skaroⁿ'	ro'sot'hă·	wă'akos'ho'	tä'hnoⁿ''	wă'i'roⁿ':	"O·''	hā're'
12 Flint (Ice, Crystal)	his grand-mother	she it smelled	and	she it said:	"What (is it)	again
nä'ho'těⁿ'	ne'	Oteroñtoñni''ă·	rotēs'koñte'?''	Wă'hoñwěⁿ''hă'se'		
13 such kind of thing	the	It Sapling	he it roasts for himself?''	She said it to him		
ne'	Tawī'skaroⁿ'	wă'i'roⁿ':	"To',	tiatkěⁿ'se'ra·	ne'	dji'
14 the	Flint	she it said:	"Well,	let us two go to see it	the	where
thotekā'toⁿ·.''	Něñ'	se·''	o'k·	wă''hi'	toñtatitěⁿstä'tcī'	10'k·
15 there he has fire.''	Now	so it is	just	verily	they two quickly arose	and

---

[a] That is, so fast as winter recedes, so rapidly the ice on rivers and lakes disappears.

two ran. They two arrived where he had kindled his fire, and they two saw that it was true that he was roasting for himself an ear of sweet corn. Verily, the fatness was issuing from it in streams on the grains, along the rows of grains until only the cob was left, so fat was the corn. The grandmother of Tawĭ′skaro[n] said: "Whence didst thou bring this?" He replied: "My father gave it to me." She answered, saying: "Thou dost even intend that the kinds of men who are to dwell here shall live as pleasantly as this, here on this earth." And just then she took up a handful of ashes, and she cast them on the ear of corn that was roasting. At once the fat of the corn ceased from issuing from the roasting ear. But Sapling very severely rebuked his grandmother for doing this. Whereupon he again took up the ear of corn and wiped off the ashes that had fallen upon it. Then he again set it to

te'hoñnara'tā'to[n].	Iă'ha'newe'	dji'	thotekā'to[n].	wă'hiatkăt'ho'	1
they two ran.	There they two arrived	where	there he has fire	they two looked	
to'kĕ[n]ske'	kā'tī'	rote'skoñte'	skă'hrā''tă'	tekoñteroñ'weks	2
truly	so then	he is roasting it for himself	one it ear (of corn)	white (, shriveled)	
o'nĕ[n]'ste'.	Nakwă''	kĕñ'ie'	io'hnawĕ[n]toñ'nio[n]	tiiotiiakĕ[n]'/o[n].	ne'	3
it corn.	The very	it oil	it streams flows down	they come forth	the
onĕ[n]'stā'ke'	nakwă''	nĕñ'	ne'	kĕ[n]''	niio'nhoñwa'tă'	skă'hrā'tā'iĕ[n]	4
it grain on	the very	now	the	here	so (many) it rows has	just it ear of corn lies (is left)
e''	niionĕ[n]stare''sĕ[n].	Wă'i'ro[n]	ne'	ro'sot'hă':	"Kă''	ni'să'hā?''	5
there	so it corn fat (is).	She it said	the	his grandmother:	"Where is it	thence thou it didst bring?"
Tă'hĕñ'ro[n]:	"Rake'ni''hă'	rakwa'wĭ'.''	Toñtāioñta'tī'	wă'i'ro[n].	6
He replied:	"He my father (is)	he it gave to me.''	Again thence she spoke	she it said:	
"Akwă''	i''se'ie'	e''	nĕ[n]iakoto'nhā'reke'	ne'	oñ'kwe'	ne'	7
"Just	thou it intendest	thus	so well they will live	the	man-being(s) (= humans)	the
ĕ[n]ienakerenioñ''hăke'	ne'	dji'	io[n]hwĕñ'djiate'.	Nĕñ'	so'k	8
they will dwell in places (as tribes)	the	where	it earth present (is).	Now	at once
wă'tewă'tcia'na'kwe'	o'se''haiă'	e''	wă'tio'iă'ke'	ne'	o'se''harā'	9
she handful took up	it ashes	there	she it cast against	the	it ashes
ono[n]'kwĕ[n]''āke'	ne'	e''	rotes'koñte'.	Iă'hoñteri''siă'te'	ne'	dji'	10
it ear (of corn) on	the	there	he it is roasting for himself.	It ceased at once	the	where
kĕñ'ie'	iotiiakĕ[n]'o[n]'hā'tie'	ne'	e''	rotes'koñte'.	No'k.	ne'	11
it oil	they (z.) oils keep coming forth	the	there	he it is roasting for himself.	and	the
Oteroñtoñni''ā'	akwă''	ione'hrā'kwā't	wă'shakori'hwās'tĕ[n]'	ne'	12
It Sapling	very	it is remarkable	he her chided	the
ro'sot'hă'	dji'	nā'e'iere'.	E'tho'ne'	nĕñ'	toñsā'ra'kwe'	ne'	13
his grandmother	where	so she it did.	At that time	now	again he it took up	the
o'nĕ[n]'ste'	să'harā'kewe'	ne'	dji'	io'se'hā'rare'.	E'tho'ne'	14
it corn	again he it wiped	the	where	it it had ashes on.	At that time

roast; but it was just possible for it to exude only a small amount of fatness again, as it is now when one roasts ears for himself. It is barely visible, so little does the fatness exude.

Now the grandmother of Sapling fetched ripened corn that Sapling had planted, and she shelled it. Then she poured it into a mortar. And now she took the pestle and with it pounded the corn, and she made haste in her pounding, and she said: "Verily, thou wouldst have a mankind exceedingly well provided. Verily, they shall customarily be much wearied in getting bread to eat. In this manner then shall they customarily do with the mortar and also the pestle." She herself had finished then. Whereupon Sapling rebuked her for what she had done. He, in regard to this matter, said: "That which thou hast done is not good."

Then, verily, while Sapling was traveling, he was surprised to find

---

1 sa'hate'skoñ'tĕⁿ' a'ie' akwă" e" ho'k' thoñsakakwe'nĭ' osthoñ"hă'
  again he it roasted / again / very / thus / just / as much as it was possible / it is small
  for himself

2 o'k' thoñsawĕñieno'tĕⁿ' (ne' noñ'wă' dji' ni'io't ne!
  only / again it oil put forth / (the / this time / where / so it is

3 āioñte'skoñ'tĕⁿ' akwă" ne' o'k' ne' wă'he'ne'ne' tawĕñiäno'tĕⁿ').
  one would roast it for one's self / very / the / just / the / it is visible, / thence it oil would exude).

4 E'tho'ne' ne' ro'sot'hă' iă'e'ko' ne' iotenĕⁿ'stĭs"oⁿ' ne'
  At that time / the / his grandmother / thence she it got / the / it corn has matured / the

5 Oteroñtoñni"ă' roiĕñt'hĕⁿ', wă'enĕⁿ"staroñ'ko'. E'tho'ne' kă'ıi-
  It Sapling / he it has planted, / she it shelled. / At that time / it mortar

6 kă"takoⁿ' iă'oñ'weroⁿ'. Nĕñ' wă'"hĭ' iă'e'sisă'tota'ko' wă'et'he'te'
  in / thither she it poured, / Now / verily / there she got the pestle / she it pounded

7 wă'tiako'sterĭ''hĕⁿ' ne' dji' wă'ē'the'te' tă'hnoⁿ'' wă'i'roⁿ''·
  she made haste / the / where / she it pounded / and / she it said:

8 "Akwă" i''se'ıe' tō'-kĕⁿ'' nĕⁿtiakokwatstoⁿ''hăke' ne' oñ'kwe'
  "Very / thou desirest / how is it / so they will be living at ease / the / man-beings. (humans)

9 Akwă'' ĕⁿ's āieroⁿ''hiă'kĕⁿ'tcĭ' ne' dji' ĕⁿienă'tarake'. E"
  Very / customarily / one should struggle utterly / the / where / one bread will eat. / Thus

10 hĕⁿ's nĕⁿieier''hăke' ne' kă'nikă''tă' ıo'k' ho'ıi' ne' a'si'să' "
  customarily / so one it will habitually do / the / it mortar / and / also / the / it pestle."

11 Akaoⁿ''hă' ne' iakos''oⁿ'. Ta', e'tho'ne' ne' Oteroñtoñni''ă'
  She herself / the / she them finished. / So, / at that time / the / It Sapling

12 wă'shakori'hwăs'tĕⁿ' ne' dji' nă'e'iere', wă'hĕñ'roⁿ': "Iă"
  he her matter it rebuked in / the / where / so she it did / he it said: / "Not

13 wă'"hĭ' teioia'nere' ne' dji' nā''siere'."
  verily / it is good / the / where / so thou it didst do."

14 Ne' kă'tĭ' wă'"hĭ' ne' Oteroñtoñni''ă' dji' te'hotawĕñ'ıie'
  The / so then / verily / the / It Sapling / where / he travels

that it became dark. So then he mused, saying: "Why, this seems to be a marvelous matter, this thing that takes place." Thereupon he returned homeward. Arrived there, he found the sun in no place whatsoever, nor did he find Tawĭ′skaroⁿ and his grandmother. It was then that he looked about him. So then he looked and saw a light which was like the dawn. Therefor he understood that the sun was in that place. He therefore sought servants who would accompany him to fetch the sun. Spider volunteered; so also did Beaver; so also did Hare; so also did Otter. So at this time they made themselves a canoe. When they had completed the canoe, they all then placed themselves in the canoe, and they then of course began to paddle, directing their course toward the place where the dawn shone forth, toward the

wă·hatie′rēⁿ·	o′k·	nēñ′	tāiokara′·hwe′.	Ta′,	e·tho′ne·	wā′re·re′:	1
he was surprised	only	now	thence it became dark.	So,	at that time	he thought:	
"A′ⁿio"	iori·hwane·hrā′kwā·t		dji′	nā′ā′wēⁿ."	E·tho′ne′	nēñ′	2
"Well,	it matter is wonderful		where	so it happened."	At that time	now	
sa·hā·tēñ′tī′.	Ia·sā′rawe·	iā·′	kā′tī′	kăn′ekā·	ne′	karā·′kwā·.	3
he went back (home).	There he arrived	not	so then	anywhere	the	it sun.	
Tawĭ′skaroⁿ·	ⁿo′k·	ho′ⁿi	ne′	ro·sot′hā·	iā·′	ho" ne"	kăⁿ′ekā′.	4
Flint (Ice = Crystal)	and	also	the	his grand- mother	not too	the	anywhere.	
E·tho′ne·	ne′	nēñ′	wā·thatkā·′toñ′nioⁿ·.		Wā·hatkāt′ho′	kā′tī′	5
At that time	the	now	he looked about in different ways.		He looked	so then	
tetio‘shwāt′he·	dji′	ni′io·t	ne′	tetiawēñ′tote′.	Nēñ′	e·tho′ne′	6
there it is light	where	so it is	the	there it daydawns.	Now	at that time	
wā·ho·nikoⁿ·rāiēñ′tā·ⁿe·		e·′	noñ′we·	iekā′iēⁿ·	ne′	karā·′kwā·.	7
he it understood		there	the place	there it lies	the	it sun.	
Ta′,	e·tho′ne′	nēñ′	ne′	wā·ha·nhā·tserī′sāke·		ne′	a·ɔōñ′ⁿe·	8
So,	at that time	now	the	he assistants sought for		the	they him should accompany	
a·hoñsa·hatiko·′·hā·	ne′	karā·′kwā·.	Takwā·ā·′sā·r		wā·hathoñka′-	9
they should go after it again	the	it sun.	Spider		he volunteered,	
riā·′ke·,	ⁿo′k·	ha′ⁿe·	Tsoni′to·,	ⁿo′k·	ha′ⁿe·	Tā·hoⁿ·tane′kēⁿ·,	10
	and	again	Beaver,	and	again	Hare,	
ⁿo′k·	ha′ⁿe·	Tawĭ′ne·.	Ta′,	e·tho′ne′	nēñ′	wā·hoñthoñioñ′nī′	11
and	again	Otter.	So,	at that time	now	they themselves it boat made for.	
Ne′	kā′tī′	dji′	nēñ′	wā·hoñthonwis·′ā′	e·tho′ne′	nēñ′	akwe′koⁿ·	12
The	so then	where	now	they their boat finished	at that time	now	it all	
kā·hoñ′wākoⁿ·	wā·hoñtī′tā′,	nēñ′	tā·hnoⁿ·′	wā·′hī′	wā·hati′kawe′	13
it boat in	they embarked,	now	and	verily	they paddled	
e·′	na·hatiie′rā·te·	dji′	noñ′we·	tiiawēñ′tote·.	Ne′	kā′tī′	ne′	14
there	thither themselves directed	where	the place	there it day dawns.	The	so then	the	

place where lay the sun. The trees stood together, and on their tops lay the sun. So then Sapling said: "Thou, Beaver, do thou cut down the tree; and thou, Spider, shalt climb the tree, and at the top of the tree thou shalt fasten thy cord. Then thou shalt descend, hanging by thy cord, until thou reachest the ground." And he said to Hare: "As soon as the tree falls, thou must seize the sun. Thou art assuredly an adept at skulking through the underbrush. No matter how difficult the ground be, thou art able of course to flee by stealth, if at this time it so be that one pursue thee from place to place." He said: "But thou, Otter, shalt care for the canoe. If it be so that we all get aboard the canoe, thou shalt turn back the canoe at once."

1	něñ' time	ciia'hati'ra'r''ho' there they arrived	ne' the	dji' where	tkawe'note' there it island stands	dji' where	noñ'we' the place	iekā'iěⁿ' there it lies
2	ne' the	kaiă''kwă'. it sun.	Ěⁿskā''ne' One (place) in	ne' the	dji' where	ke'r''hi'toⁿ it tree stand plurally		karěñ'hakěñ'iate' it tree top of	
3	e'' there	ieka''here' it it lies upon	ne' the	kaia''kwă'. it sun.	E'tho'ne' At that time	ne' the	Oteroñtoñni''ă' It Sapling		
4	wă'hěñ'roⁿ: he it said:	"I'se' "Thou	ne' the	Tsoni'to' Beaver	ěⁿseroñ'tiă'ke', thou it tree shalt cut down,	io'k' but	ii'se' the thou		
5	Takwă'ă''sa'r Spider	ěⁿserāt'hěⁿ thou shalt climb it	ne' the	karoñta'ke' it tree on	karěñ'hakěñ'iate' it tree top of	e'' there			
6	ěⁿtesne'rěñke' thou shalt it tie	ne' the	sa'se'riie'. thy cord.	E'tho'ne' At that time	těⁿtesăts'něⁿ'te' thence thou shalt descend	ěⁿtesatiă' thou thy body shalt fasten			
7	taniiěñ'toⁿ to it	ne' the	sa'se'riie'ke' thy cord on	dji' where	niio're' so it is far	oⁿhwěñdjiā'ke' it ground on			
8	ěⁿse'serā'tă'ne'." again thou it wilt reach"	No'k' And	wă'hawěⁿ'hă'se' he him said to	ne' the	Ta'hoⁿtane'kěⁿ Hare				
9	wă'hěñ'roⁿ: he it said:	"Kawěnni'io' "So soon as	něñ' now	ěⁿkaroñtie'noⁿne' it tree shall fall	i'se' thou it is	těⁿse''kwe' thou it shalt pick up			
10	ne' the	kaia''kwă'. it sun.	Seweiěñ'te't Thou art skillful	wă''hĭ' verily	ne' the	ěⁿsatkwatoñ''hwe' thou shalt flee in zigzag lines	ne' the		
11	o'skawakoñ''shoⁿ. it bushes among.	Iaweroⁿhă'tiěⁿ' It matters not		to' how	nă'teiaoⁿhwěñdjianoñ- so it land forbidding (is)				
12	nia'ni't thou art able to do it,	sakwe'nioñ I believe,	ki'' verily	wă''hĭ' the	ne' thou shalt flee in zigzag lines	ěⁿsatkwatoñ''hwe' the	ne'		
13	to'kă' if	ioñ'wă'-kěⁿ'' this time is it	āiesă'sere''soⁿ. one thee would pursue about.	No'k' And	ne' the	Tawi'ne' Otter	ka'hoñ it boat		
14	we'iă' the thou	ii'se'	ěⁿsate'nikoⁿra'roⁿ. thou it wilt attend to.	To'kă' If	wă''hĭ' verily	něñ' now	akwe'koⁿ' it all		
15	ěⁿtciakwati'tă' again we shall embark	iokoñtă'tie' at once (it follows)	ěⁿsattă'kwă'te' thou it wilt turn	ne' the	ka'hoñwe'iă'." it boat."				

All this, then, came to pass. Beaver, of course, worked there, biting out pieces from the tree; and Spider, for his part, climbed to the tree top, and having reached the top, he then, verily, fastened his cord about it. Thereupon he let himself down, and again alighted on the earth. So then, when there was, of course, little to cut, and the prospect was encouraging that it would be possible to fell the tree, then Spider pulled on the cord. Then, in fact, the tree toppled over. Thereupon Hare rushed forward and seized the sun, for, indeed, Tawī′skaroⁿ′ and his grand mother both came running up. It was then that Hare fled, taking the sun away with him. Now, of course, they pursued him in many places; he fleetly scurried through the shrubbery. After a time he directed his course straight for the canoe; for then,

E′thoʻ	kā′tī′	to′kĕⁿske′	naʻā′wĕⁿ′.		Tsoni′toʻ	wăʻʻhī′	nĕñ′	eʻ′
Thus	so then	truly	so it happened.		Beaver	verily	now	there	1
wăʻhoioʻ′tă′	wăʻhatekhwanioñ′koʻ		neʻ	karoñta′keʻ,		noʻkʻ		neʻ
he worked	he it bit repeatedly		the	it tree on,		and		the	2
Takwăʻă′′saʻr	iăʻharat′hĕⁿ′		nă′,	neʻʻ	neʻ		karĕñʻhakĕñ′iateʻ
Spider	there he climbed		that one	the that	the		it tree top of	3
iăʻha′raweʻ,	nĕñ′	wăʻʻhī′	eʻʻ	tăʻbaʻhwan′rakeʻ		neʻ	raoʻseri′ieʻ.
there he arrived.	Now	verily	there	he it wrapped		the	his cord.	4
E′thoʻneʻ	nĕñ′	toñtaʻhatiăʻtoñ′teʻ,		saʻhara′tăʻneʻ	oⁿʻhwĕñdjiăʻkeʻ.
At that time	now	thence he his body suspended,		again he reached it	it earth on.	5
Neʻʻ	kā′tī′	wăʻʻhī′	neʻ	nĕñ′	eʻʻ	hoʻkʻ	năʻtetcioiă′saʻ	neʻ	nĕñ′
That	so then	verily	the	now	there	only	so it is narrow	the	now	6
ioʻrʻbā′ratsteʻ	nĕñ′	ĕⁿwa′toⁿ	ĕⁿkaroñtienoⁿʻ′neʻ		e′thoʻneʻ	neʻ
it is very hopeful	now	it will be possible	it tree will fall		at that time	the	7
Takwăʻă′′saʻr	nĕñ′	tăʻhaʻseriieʻtati′roñtoⁿ′.		Toʻkĕⁿskeʻ	kā′tī′
Spider	now	he it cord pulled on.		Truly	so then	8
wăʻkaroñtienoⁿ′′neʻ.	E′thoʻneʻ	neʻ	Ta hoⁿʻtăne′kĕⁿ	tăʻhāiăʻtakoñtā-
it tree fell.	At that time	the	Hare	thence his body followed instantly	9
tieʻʻteʻ	wăʻtrăʻkweʻ	neʻ	kaiaʻʻkwă′.	Nĕñ′	seʻʻ	wăʻʻhī′	oʻkʻ	eʻʻ
he it took up	the	it sun.		Now	indeed	verily	just	there	10
teʻhnitakʻheʻ	neʻ	Tawī′skaroⁿ′	noʻkʻ	hoʻnī′	neʻ	roʻsot′băʻ.	Nĕñ′
they two ran	the	Flint (Ice, Crystal)	but	also	the	his grandmother.	Now	11
wăʻʻhī′	Tăʻhoⁿʻtăne′kĕⁿ	wăʻhate′koʻ,	ioñsaʻhaʻʻhăweʻ	neʻ	kaiaʻʻ
verily	Hare	he fled,	hence he it bore	the	sun.	12
kwă′.	Nĕñ′	wăʻʻhī′	wăʻhoñwaʻsereʻ′soⁿ′.	Rotkwatoñʻhweʻtieʻseʻ
	Now	verily	they him pursued from place to place.	He fled in devious courses	13
neʻ	oʻskawakoⁿʻ′shoⁿ′.	Ā′kaieʻ	nĕñ′	iăʻhakoñtătieʻ′teʻ	djiʻ	noñ-
the	it bush(es) among.	After a time	now	thither he went directly	where	the side	14
kā′tīʻ	tkăʻhoñwăʻiĕⁿ′,	nĕñ′	seʻ′	wăʻʻhī′	neʻ	roñnatiăʻ′keʻ	nēʻ
of it	there it boat lies,	now	indeed	verily	the	they others	the	15

indeed, the others, his friends, were aboard the canoe. He came thither on the bound, and got aboard the canoe. At the same time with this, Otter pushed off the canoe, and they again began to paddle.

So then, as they rowed back, Otter, it is said, did verily continue to talk. They forbade him, but he did not obey. Then a person struck him a blow with a paddle on his mouth. (It is for this reason that now the mouth of the Otter is such that one would think that it had been broken off long ago. His lower jaw is shorter than the upper. It is plain where one struck him with a paddle.)

So when they had arrived at home, Sapling said: "It shall not continue to be thus, that a single person rules over the sun." Then it was that he cast the sun up to the center of the sky, saying: "There where the sky is present, thereto must thou keep thyself

---

1	roñteñ'ro' they his friends are	ieshatiiä'tĭ' there again they are embarked	ka'hoñ'wakoⁿ' it boat in.	O'k' Just	cihatak'he' there he ran along	ioñsa'- again he
2	hati'tä'. embarked.	E'tho'ne' At that time	iokoñtä'tie' at once (it follows)	ne' the	Tawi'ne' Otter	sa'hatä'kwä'te' he it turned back again	ne' the
3	ka'hoñwe'iä', it boat,	neñ' now	wä''hĭ' verily	sa'hati'kawe'. again they paddled.			
4	Ne' The	kä'tĭ' so then	ne' the	dji' where	neñ' now	shoti'hoñwakerä'ne' again their boat floats along	Tawi'ne', Otter,
5	ia'kĕⁿ, it is said,	to'kĕⁿske' truly	dji' where	ro'thará'tie'. he kept on talking.	Roñwana'hris'thä', They him forbade,	no'k' and	iä'' not
6	te'hothoñta'toⁿ'. he obeyed.	Neñ' Now	e'tho'ne' at that time	shäia'tä' he one person	ä'kawe' it paddle	wä'ho'iĕⁿ'te' he him struck	
7	dji' where	rä'saka'roñte' his mouth (is)	wä'hanoⁿ'hwar'iä'ke'. he him it blow struck.	(Ne' (The	tiiori''hwä' it is reason	ne' the	
8	noñ'wä' present time	ne' the	Tawi'ne' Otter	e'' thus	ni'io't so it is	dji' where	ra'saka'roñte' his mouth	äieñ're' one would think
9	o'k' just	tetkäiä'ktci''hoⁿ'. one it had broken.	Ni'ha'qhiots'hes'ä' So his jaw (is) short	ne' the	e'tä'ke' lower	noñkä'tĭ', side of it,	
10	we'ne' it is plain	dji' where	e'' there	käiĕⁿ''toⁿ' one it struck	ä'kawe' it paddle	wats'toⁿ'.) one used it.)	
11	Ta', So,	ne' the	kä'tĭ' so then	wä''hĭ' verily	ne' the	neñ' now	ciioñsa'hoñ'newe' there again they arrived	ne' the	Oteroñtoñ- It Sapling
12	ni''ä' he it said:	wä'heñ'roⁿ':	"Iä' "Not	e'', thus,	thĕⁿio'toⁿ''hake' thus it will continue to be	ne' the	tcieiä'tä' one person	ho'k' only
13	aieweñniiō''hake' one it should control	ne' the	kara''kwä.'' it sun."	Ta', it so,	E'tho'ne' at that time	neñ' now	
14	sä'tewä'señ'noⁿ' just its middle	ne' the	dji' where	karoñ''hiate' it sky is present	e'' there	iä'ho'tĭ' he it threw	ne' the
15	kara''kwä' it sun	tä'hnoⁿ'' and	wä'heñ'roⁿ': he it said:	"E'tho' "There	dji' where	karoñ''hiate' it sky is present	e'' there

attached, and, besides this, thou shalt continuously journey onward." He pointed thither, and said: "'The place where it plunges itself into the deep [that is, the west]' people will habitually call the place whither thou shalt habitually descend, the place wherein thou shalt habitually be immersed. At these times, verily, darkness will come upon the earth present here; and 'The place where the sun rises [that is, the east]' people will habitually call the place whence thou wilt habitually peer out, and people will say, 'Now the Sun has come out.' Then shalt thou raise thyself upward therefrom. Thus thou shalt continue to have this function to perform. Thou shalt continue to give light to this earth." Besides this he said: "Whensoever mankind mention thee, they will ever say customarily: 'He is the Great Warrior who supplies us with light.'" So then, in its turn, now came of course the luminary, the Moon, which was his mother's head,

ĕⁿ‵satiä''tanĕñ'takto"'‵häke'	nĕñ'	tä‵hnoⁿ‵'	o'k	ĕⁿtiotkoñtä'‵kwĕⁿ'
wilt thou thy body attach (as a fixture)	now	and	just	it shall be continuous
ĕⁿ‵sa'tĕñtioñhä'tie'."	lä‵ha‵tca'tĕⁿ'		wä‵hĕñ'roⁿ':	" Dji' iä'tewat-
thou shalt move along."	Thither he pointed		he it said:	"Where there it sets
tchot'ho‵s	ĕⁿkoñwäiats'heke'	dji'	ĕⁿ's	noñ'we‵ iĕⁿ‵sats'noⁿ‵te'
(immerses itself)	will they call it habitually	where	customarily	the place there thou shalt go down
iĕⁿ‵sanoñwi're‵te'.	E‵tho'ne'	wä'‵hï'	nĕñ'	ĕⁿtiokä'ra‵hwe' ne' dji'
there thou shalt be immersed.	At that time	verily	now	it shall become dark the where
ioⁿ‵hwĕñdjiä'te'.	Dji'	tkara‵kwi'nekĕⁿ's		ĕⁿkoñwäia'tsheke',"
it earth is present.	Where	there it sun comes out		shall it they call habitually,"
(iä‵hä''tcatĕⁿ' dji'	noñka'tï‵)	"eⁿ' hĕⁿ's	noñka'tï‵	tĕⁿsake'to‵te' ne'
(thither he pointed where	the side of it)	"there customarily	side of it	there thou shalt the peer over
ĕⁿiai'roⁿ' ne'	oñ'kwe‵	nĕñ'	takara‵kwi'nekĕⁿ'ne'.	Ta', e‵tho'ne'
one it will the say	man-being (human)	now	it sun has come up.	So, at that time
toñtesatharä'tate'. E''	ni'se'	ni'io‵t dji'	ĕⁿ‵sateri‵hoñ'take‵,	tĕⁿssh-
thence thou shalt raise There thyself.	the thou	so it is where	thou duty wilt have it,	thou
wathe''täke' ne'	dji'	ioⁿ‵hwĕñdjiä'te'."	Nĕñ	tä‵hnoⁿ‵' wä‵hĕñ'roⁿ'‵
it wilt make the light	where	it earth is present."	Now	and he it said:
"Kat'ke‵ ne'	oñ'kwe‵	i'se'	ĕⁿiesanä'toⁿ'	ĕⁿioñtoⁿ‵'heke' ĕⁿ's‵
"Whenever the	man-being (human)	thou	one thee shall designate	one shall continue to say customarily:
'Ro‵skĕⁿ'rake‵te''kowä''	ne'	teshoñkwa‵shwathe''tĕñni‵s "		
'He Great Warrior (is)	the	he us causes it to be light for.'"		
Ta', e‵tho'ne'	nĕñ'	noñ'wä'	ne'ne‵ ĕⁿ‵hni'tä'	ne' wä'‵hï' ne'
So, at that time	now	the present time	the it moon that	the verily the
räoⁿ‵‵hä'	ro'nistĕñ‵‵hä'-kĕⁿ‵hä'	akonoñ'djï‵	ne'	ro‵sot'hä' dji'
he himself	his mother it was	her head	the	his grandmother where

1
2
3
4
5
6
7
8
9
10
11
12
13

and which his grandmother had also placed on the top of a standing tree. This, too, he threw up to the sky, saying: "The power of thy light at night shall be less." He added: "At times they will see thee in full. Every night thy size shall diminish until it is gone. Then again, thou shalt every night increase in size from a small beginning. Every night, then, thou shalt grow until the time comes when thou hast completed thy growth. So now, thus it shall be as to thy mode of existence." Moreover he said: "Whenever mankind who shall dwell here on earth mention thee, they will keep saying customarily: 'Our Grandmother, the luminary pertaining to the night.'"

Then Sapling now formed the body of a man[a] and also that of a woman [of the race of mankind]. His younger brother, Tawĭ′skaroⁿ',

line									
1	ke·rhi′te'	o′nĭ'	nă″	ne″	e‛¹	iako‛hā′re',	e′tho‛	ho′nĭ'	nă″
	it tree stands	also	the that	that one	there	there she it fastened at the top,	there	also	the that
2	ne″ iă‛ho′tĭ'	ne'	dji'	karoñ′‛hiate',		wă‛heñ′roⁿ':		"Ĕⁿtiioto′ktăke'	
	that there he it threw	the	where	it sky is present,		he it said:		"It will be lacking	that
3	ne' ni′se'	ne'	dji'	tĕⁿ'se‛shwathe′tĕⁿ			ne'	a‛soñtheñ′ne‛."	
	the the thou	the	where	thou shalt cause it to be light			the	it night (time) in.	
4	Wă‛heñ′roⁿ':	"Sewatie′rĕⁿ‛	eⁿkană′noⁿ'‛hăke'			ne'	dji'	tĕⁿiesa-	
	He it said:	"Sometimes	it shall be full			the	where	one	
5	kan′ereke'.	Niuă′tewă‛soñta′ke‛	ĕⁿtiiostho'oⁿ‛hă′tie'		ne'	dji'	ni″să'		
	thee look at shall.	Every night (every night in number)	it shall continue to grow smaller		the	where	thou art large		
6	dji'	niio′re'	iĕⁿwa′ts'ă‛te'.	E′tho′ne'	nĕñ	a′re'	niwā″ă‛	dji'	
	where	so it is far	it shall all disappear.	At that time	now	again	so it is small in size	where	
7	tĕⁿtesate‛hia′roⁿ'	sewa‛soñtats′hoⁿ'	o′nĭ'	nă″	ne″	ne'	dji'		
	thence thou shalt grow larger	one it night apiece	also	the that	that one	the	where		
8	tĕⁿtesate‛hia′roⁿ'	dji'	niio′re'	tĕⁿtkăie′ri′ne'	ĕⁿsesate‛hia′roⁿ'.	Ta',			
	thence thou shalt grow larger	where	so it is distant	it shall be correct	again thou shalt grow to maturity.	So,			
9	e‛″ ni′se'	nĕⁿio′toⁿ'‛hăke'	ne'	dji'	ĕⁿsiă′ta′teke'."	Nĕñ'	tä‛hnoⁿ''		
	thus the thou	so it shall continue to be	the	where	thou shalt exist."	Now	and		
10	wă‛beñ′roⁿ':	"Ne'	ka′tke‛	i′se'	ĕⁿiesana′toⁿ'	ne'	oñkwe		
	he it said:	"The	whenever	thou	one thee shall designate	the	man- (human)		
11	‛ho′koⁿ'	ne'	ĕⁿienak′ereke'	ne'	dji'	ioⁿ‛hwĕndjia′te'	ĕⁿioñtoⁿ‛'-		
	being plurally	the	they will be dwelling	the	where	it earth is present	one shall habitually		
12	heke‛	ĕⁿ's	Iethi‛sot′hă‛	ne'	a‛soñtheⁿ'‛khă'	kaia″kwă'."			
	say	customarily	she our grandmother	the	nocturnal (it night middle of the)	it luminary."			
13	Ne'	ka′tĭ'	ne'	Oteroñtoñni″ă‛	nĕñ'	wă‛hoiă′toñ′niă'	ne'		
	The	so then	the	It Sapling	now	he his body made	the		
14	roñ′kwe·	no′k‛	ho′nĭ'	ne'	ioñ′kwe‛.	E‛″	te‛hakan′ere'	ne'	
	he man-being (a man)	but	also	the	she man-being. (a woman)	There	he it looked at	the	

---

[a] This incident is evidently taken from Genesis in the Christian Bible.

watched him there. So then, when he had, of course, caused them to live, he placed them together.

Then it was that Sapling started upon a journey to inspect the condition of the things he had finished on the earth then standing forth. Then, at that time, he came again to review those things and to see what things man [of the human race] was doing.

Then he returned to the place in which he had given them liberty. So then he found the two doing nothing except sleeping habitually. He merely looked at them, and went away. But when he came again their condition was unchanged; they slept habitually. Thus then, in this manner matters stood the very few times he visited them; the condition was unchanged; they slept customarily. Thereupon he took a rib from each, and substituted the one for the other, and replaced each one in the other body. Then, of course, he watched them,

iǎ·tate'kĕñ"ǎ·	Tawī'skaroⁿ".	Ne'	kā'tĭ'	wǎ'·hĭ'	ne'	dji'	nĕñ'
his younger brother	Flint.	The	so then	verily	the	where	now

1

wǎ·shakao'n·hete'	skǎ·'ne'	wǎ·shako"teroⁿ".	
he them caused to live	in one (place)	he them placed.	

2

Nĕñ'	wǎ'·hĭ'	ne'	Oterontoñni"ǎ·	wǎ'hǎ'tĕn'tī'	sǎ·hatkĕⁿ'se-
Now	verily	the	It Sapling	he started away	again he went

3

nioⁿ'·hǎ'	dji'	ni'io't	ne'	dji'	ros'ā'·hoⁿ"	ne'	dji'	watoⁿ·hwĕñ-
to view them	where	so it is	the	where	he things has finished	the	where	it earth is

4

ejiǎ'te'.	Ne'	kā'tĭ'	ne'	dji'	nĕñ'	tonta·shakoñtkĕⁿ'se'roⁿ'
present.	The	so then	the	where	now	again he them viewed in order

5

'othe'noⁿ"	kĕⁿ·	ni·hatie·r'·hǎ'	ne'	oñ'kwe·
something	is it	so he is doing	the	man-being. (human)

6

Ne'	kā'tĭ'	dji'	nĕñ'	sa'rawe·	dji'	noñ'we·	ni·shakotka'wĕⁿ·
The	so then	where	now	again he arrived	where	place	just he them left

7

iǎ·'	kā'tĭ'	othe'noⁿ"	teiatie·r'·hǎ'	ne'	o'k·	ne'	roti'tǎ's.	Ne'
not	so then	anything	they two were doing	the	only	the	they slept.	The

8

o'k·	ne'	wǎ·shakotkǎt'ho'	ak'te·	noñ'we·	noñka'tī·	niioñsa're·
only	the	he them looked at	elsewhere	the place	side of it	just again he went.

9

Ne'	kā'tĭ'	ne'	nĕñ'	a're·	sa'rawe·	katō'kĕⁿ·	ni'io't	roti'tǎ's
The	so then	the	now	again	again he arrived	unchanged	so it is	they slept habitually.

10

E·'	kā'tĭ'	ni'io't	akwǎ·'	to·kā'·ǎ·	noñterats'te·	ne'	wǎ·sha-
Thus	so then	so it is	very	few	it is repeated	the	he

11

ko·k'tǎ·se·	katō'kĕⁿ·	ni'io't	roti'tǎ's.	Ta',	e'tho'ne·	nĕñ'
them visited,	unchanged	so it is	they slept habitually.	So,	at that time	now

12

skat'shoⁿ"	wǎ·shakote·karota'ko',	nĕñ'	tǎ·hnoⁿ"'	wǎ·thate'nĭ'	dji'
one each	he them rib took out of,	now	and	he them exchanged	where

13

sa·shakote·karo'tĕⁿ".	Nĕñ	wǎ'·hĭ'	wǎ·shakote·nikoⁿ·rā'rĕⁿ"	wǎ're're':
again he it rib fixed into them.	Now	verily	he them watched	he it thought:

14

thinking of what perhaps right now happen. It was therefore not long before the woman awoke. Then she sat up. At once she touched the breast of the man lying at her side, just where he had placed her rib, and, of course, that tickled him. Thereupon he awoke. Then, of course, that matter was started—that matter which concerns mankind in their living; and they also started that matter for which in their kind their bodies are provided—that matter for which reason he is a male human being and she a female human being.

Then Tawĭ'skaroⁿ also formed a human being, but he was not able to imitate Sapling, as the form of the human being he poorly made showed. Tawĭ'skaroⁿ addressed Sapling, saying: "Do thou look, I also am able, myself, to form a human being." So when Sapling looked at that which

1	"O'" "What is it	ci' this	kĕⁿ'' is it	ne' the	nĕⁿia'wĕⁿ?" so it will happen?"	Iă'' Not	kā'tĭ so then	tekari'hwes it is a long matter	ne' the
2	iakoñ'kwe' she man-being (woman)	nĕñ' now	wă'e'ie'. she awoke.	E'tho'ne' At that time	wă'oñtkets'ko'. she sat up.	Nakwă'' The very	o'k just		
3	ciieiă'takoñta'tie' her body followed along	ne' the	rāiă'tioñ'nĭ' his body lay extended	ne' the	roñ'kwe' he man-being (man)	e'' there	kĕⁿ'' where		
4	niiă''eiere' just she it touched	dji' where	noñ'we' place	ni'hote'karota'kwĕⁿ' there he rib has removed	rană'ă'tā'ke' his flank on				
5	wă'thoñwanĭs'tekă'te' she him tickled	wă'hĭ'. verily.	E'tho'ne' At that time	nĕñ' now	wă'hā'ie'. he awoke.	Nĕñ' Now			
6	wă'hĭ' verily	ĕⁿteri'hwă'tĕñ'tĭ' it matter started	dji' where	niiakoteri'hwăte' just one it duty has	ne' the	oñ'kwe' man-beings			
7	ne' the	iako'n'be' they live	no'k' and	ho'nĭ' also	nĕñ' now	wă'hiateri'hwă'tĕñ'tiă'te' they matter started	dji' where		
8	nă'ho'tĕⁿ' such kind of thing	niiă'tāiĕñta''kwĕⁿ' just their bodies it are designed for	dji' where	nă'ho'tĕⁿ' such kind of thing	kari'hoñ'nĭ' it it causes	ne' the			
9	roñ'kwe' he man-being (man)	i'kĕⁿ'' it is	no'k' and	ho'nĭ' also	ne' the	dji' where	ioñ'kwe' she man-being (woman)	i'kĕⁿ' it is.	
10	Tawĭ'skaroⁿ' Flint (Ice, Crystal)	kā'tĭ' so then	o'nĭ' also	wă'roñ'nĭ' he it made	ne' the	oñkwe'; man-being;	no'k' but	iă'' not	
11	te'hokwe'nioⁿ' he is able to do it	ne' the	a'honă'ke'ranĭ' he him should imitate	ne' the	Oteroñtoñni''ă' It Sapling	dji' where	nă'' the that		
12	ne'' that one	niioñkweto'tĕⁿ' just kind of man-being	ne' the	wă'hā's'ă', he it finished,	a'se'kĕⁿ'' because	ne' the	Tawĭ'skaroⁿ' Flint (Ice, Crystal)		
13	wă'hawĕⁿ'hă'se' he him spoke to	ne' the	Oteroñtoñni''ă': It Sapling:	"Satkăt'ho' "Do thou look at it	wakkwe'nioⁿ' I it am able to do				
14	se'' indeed	o'nĭ' also	ni'' the I	ne' the	oñ'kwe' man-being (human)	ĕⁿkoñ'nĭ'." I it will make."	Ne' The	kā'tĭ' so then	ne' the

made hi say "I am able to for a hu an being," he saw that what he had for ed were not human beings at all. The things he for ed were possessed of hu an faces and the bodies of otkon [onste s], subtly ade otkon. Sapling spoke to him, saying: "That assuredly is the reason that I forbade thee, for of course thou art not able to do as I yself am doing continually." Tawī'skaroⁿ answered, saying: "Thou wilt nevertheless see that I can after all do as thyself art doing continually, because, indeed, I possess as uch power as thou hast." Now, verily, at this ti e they two separated. And now, Sapling again traveled fro place to place on the surface of the earth. He went to view things that he had co pleted. After a while, then, Sapling pro enaded along the shore of the sea. There he saw Tawī's-

Oterontoñni'ằ	dji'	neñ'	wă‘hatkăt'ho'	ne'	ra'toⁿ	ne'	1
It Sapling	where	now	he it looked at	the	he it says	the	
wakkwe'nioⁿ·	ne'	oñ'kwe·	eⁿkoñ'nī'	iă·'	boñ'kwe·	te'kĕⁿ·	ne'	2
I it am able to do	the	man-being (human)	I it will make	not	he man-being (man)	it is	the	
ro‘sā'oⁿ.	Ne'ne'	o'k·	ne'	oñ'kwe·	kakoⁿsoñtă'‘koⁿ·		neñ'	3
he them has finished.	The that	just	the	man-being	he is faced therewith		now	
tă‘hnoⁿ'	ot'koⁿ	kāiă'toñtă·'koⁿ,	ka'rio',	oñī'tat'ko^m	ka'rio',	ne'	4
and	otkon (malefic)	it is bodied therewith,	animal, (it is)	subtly otkon	animal,	the	
wă·'hī'	wa‘hāiă'ti's'ā'.	Tă‘hata'tī'	ne'	Oterontoñni'ằ	wă‘heñ'roⁿ·:		5
verily	he its body finished.	He spoke	the	It Sapling	he it said:		
"Ne'	wă‘hī'	kari‘hoñ'nī'	koⁿn‘he'se·	ne'	dji'	iă·''	se''	wă‘hī'	6
"The	verily	it it causes	I thee caution	the	where	not	indeed	verily	
tesakwe'nioⁿ·	ne'ne·	nae·'siere·	ne'	i·'	dji'	niwakiereⁿ‘hă'tie'."		7
thou art able to do it	the that	so thou it shouldst do	the	I	where	so I it keep on doing."		
Neñ	wă‘hī'	toñtă‘hata'tī'	ne'	Tawī'skaroⁿ·	wă‘heñ'roⁿ·:	"Eⁿ·sa-	8
Now	verily	thence he answered	the	Flint (Ice, Crystal)	he it said:	"Thou	
tkăt'ho'	ki''	dji'	eⁿkkwe'nī'	se''	e·''	neⁿkie're·	dji'	9
it wilt see,	I think,	where	I it shall be able to do	indeed	thus	so it I shall do	where	
ni‘sāiereⁿ‘hă'tie·	ne'	i'se',	a‘se'kĕⁿ·'	e·''	se''	niwake‘shatstĕⁿ·'serā'	10
so thou art carrying on work	the	'thou,	because	thus	indeed	so my power is large	
dji'	ni'io't	ne'	i'se'.''	Neñ'	wă‘hī'	e'tho'ne'	toñsa‘hiatekhă'‘sī'.	11
where	so it is	the	thou	Now	verily	at that time	they two again separated.	
Neñ'	a're'	wă‘hī'	ne'	Oterontoñni'ằ·	toñsa‘hataweñrie'‘sā'	ne'	12
Now	again	verily	the	It Sapling	he went traveling about	the	
dji'	ioⁿ‘hweñdjiă'te'.	Să‘hatkĕⁿ'senioⁿ·'‘hā·	ne'	dji'	ni‘ho‘sa'-	13
where	it earth is present.	Again he went to see the things plurally	the	where	he things has	
ā'n‘hoⁿ.	Ā'kare·	kā'ti'	ne'	Oterontoñni'ằ·	kaniataraktă'tie·	e·''	14
made severally.	After a time	so then	the	It Sapling	it lake along	there	
i're'.	E'tho·	kā'ti'	wă‘ho'kĕⁿ·	ne'	Tawī'skaroⁿ	e·''	rata'tie'se'.	15
he is walking.	There	so then	he him saw	the	Flint (Ice, Crystal)	there	he stood about here and there.	

karon stanbing about in different places. At the water's edge lay the body of a man-being who was as white as foam.[a] When Sapling arrived there, he said: "What is this that thou art doing?" Tawĭ'skaron replied, saying: "Assuredly, I have made the body of a male man-being. This person whose body lies here is better-looking than is the one whom thou hast made." Assuredly, I have told thee that I have as much power as thou hast; yea, that my power is greater than is thy power. Look thou, assuredly his body is as white as is the body of the one whom thou hast formed." Sapling answered, saying: "What thou sayest is assuredly true. So then, if it be so, let me be looking while he makes movements of his body and arises. Well, let him stand, and also let him walk." Whereupon Flint said: "Come! Do thou

1	Ne' The	dji' where	teio'hnekak'te' it water's edge at	roñ'kwe‘ he man-being	e‘’ there	rāiă'tioñ'nĭ', his body lay extended,	e‘’ there	ni‘hara'kĕn‘ so he is white
2	dji' where	ni'io·t so it is	ne' the	o‘hwats'tă'. it foam.		Wă‘hĕñ'ron He said	ne' the	Oterontoñni''ă‘ It Sapling
3	ne' the	dji' where	nĕñ' nov	e‘’ there	ia'rawe': there he arrived:	"O‘’ "What is it	ne' the	ni‘satie‘r‘‘hă'?" so thou art doing?"	Tă‘hata'tĭ' He answered
4	ne' the	Tawĭ'skaron (Ice, Crystal)		wă‘hĕñ'ron': he it said ·		"Wă‘hiiă'toñ'nĭ' "I his body made		wă‘‘hĭ' verily	ne' the
5	roñ'kwe‘. he man-being.	Kĕn'i'kĕn‘ This it is		rāiă'tioñ'nĭ' he an extended body lies,	sĕn‘‘hă' more		niiora'se‘ so it is fine-looking	dji' where	ni‘hă- so he his
6	iă'to'tĕn' kind of body	dji' where	ni'se‘ thou	ni'io‘t so it is	ne' the	sheiă'tis''on. thou his body hast made.	Kon‘hro'rĭ‘ I thee told	wă‘‘hĭ' verily
7	dji' where	e‘’ thus	niwake'shatstĕn‘'serā' so my power is large		dji' where	ni'se‘ the thou	ni'io‘t. so it is.	Nĕñ' Nov	tă‘hnon' and
8	sĕn‘‘hă' more	o'nĭ' also	i'sĭ' beyond	noñ'we‘ place	niwake'shatstĕn‘'serā' so my power is large		dji' where	ni'se‘ the thou
9	ni'io·t. so it is.	Satkăt'ho‘ Do thou look	wă‘‘hĭ' verily		kara'kĕn‘ it (is) white	ne' the	ni‘hāiă'to'tĕn' such his body kind of (is)		dji' where
10	ni'se‘ the thou	ni'io‘t so it is	sheiă'tis''on‘." thou his body hast finished."		Tă‘hata'tĭ' He replied		ne' · the	Oterontoñni''ă‘ It Sapling
11	wă‘hĕñ'ron': · he it said :	"To'kĕnske‘, "Truly,		wă‘‘hĭ' verily	ne' the	dji' where	nă‘ho'tĕn' such kind of thing	sā'ton'. thou it sayest.
12	To', Well,	kă'tĭ' so then	tekkan'erak let me look on	ratoria‘neroñ'ko‘ let him make movements		nĕñ' nov	tă‘hnon' and	a‘hat let
13	kets'ko' him arise.	To', Well,	a‘hă'tă'ne let him stand up		no'k‘ and	ho'rĭ' also	ă‘hă‘tĕñ'tĭ'." let him walk."	Ta', So,
14	e'tho'ne‘ at that time	ne' the	Tawĭ'skaron Flint (Ice, Crystal)		wă‘hĕñ'ron': he it said :	"Hau", "Come,	satkets'ko‘." do thou arise."

[a] This man-being was Snow, Winter's handiwork. The life with which this man-being was endowed by Sapling is that which enables the snow to return every winter. Otherwise it could never have returned.

arise." But he that lay there did not take a single movement. Then, of course, Tawĭ′skaroⁿ put forth all his skill to cause this being to live and then to arise. He did everything possible to do it but he could not effect his purpose and failed to cause him to come to life, for he did not come to life. Then Sapling said: "Is this not what I have been saying, that thou art not able to do as I can do?" He added: "What purpose, in its turn, will be served by having his body lying here, having no life? Is it only this, that he shall always lie here? That is the reason that I habitually forbid thee to make also the things that thou seest me making; for, assuredly, thou art not able to do the things that I am doing." So then, of course, Tawĭ′skaroⁿ said: "Well, then, do thou cause that one there to live." So, in truth, Sapling consented to this. He drew near to the place where the man

Iă′′	othe′noⁿ˙	te‛hotoria′′neroⁿ˙	ne′	rāiä′tioñ′nĭ˙		Něñ′	wä′‛hĭ˙	1
Not	anything	he himself moved	the	his body lies extended.		Now	verily	
ne′	Tawĭ′skaroⁿ˙	dji′	o′k‛	nä′tethore′rěⁿ˙	ne′	a‛hato′n‛hete`,		2
the	Flint (Ice, Crystal)	where	just	so he did everything	the	he should come to life,		
e‛tho′ne′	a‛hatkets′ko`.	Nakwä′′	dji′	o′k‛	nä′tethori‛hwāiera′toⁿ˙			3
at that time	he should arise.	The very	where	just	he did all manner of things			
no′k‛	wä‛hono′roⁿ˙se`	ki′′	ne′	a‛hoton‛he′toⁿ˙.		E‛tho′ne′	ne′	4
and	he it failed to do,	I think,	the	it would come to life for him.		At that time	the	
Oterontoñni′′ä‛	wä‛hěñ′roⁿ˙·	"Ne′′	wä′‛hĭ˙	cika′toⁿ˙.		Iă′′	se‛	5
It Sapling	he it said:	"That one	verily	where I keep saying.		Not, indeed,		
wä′‛hĭ˙	e˙′′	tesakwe′nioⁿ˙	dji′	ni′′	ni′io′t."		Wä‛hěñ′roⁿ˙·	6
verily	thus	thou art able to do it	as	the I	so it is."		He it said	
"Nä‛ho′těⁿ˙	ioñ′wä′	ěⁿwate‛s′te`	ne′	kěⁿ′′	rāiä′tioñ′nĭ˙	iä′′		7
"What kind of thing	this time	it will be of use	the	here it is	he his body lies extended	not		
tero′n‛he`.	Ne′	o′k‛-kěⁿ˙	ne′	tiiot′koⁿ˙	e˙′′	ěⁿ˙hāiä′tioñ′nike`?		8
he lives.	The	only is it	the	always	there	his body will lie extended ever?		
Ne′	wä′‛hĭ˙	kari‛boñ′nĭ˙	koñiä‛ris′thä′	ěⁿ˙s	ne′	dji′	nä‛ho′těⁿ˙	9
The	verily	it it causes	I thee chide	customarily	the	where	what kind of thing	
wa‛satkät′ho`	wä‛koñ′nĭ′	no′k‛	ha‛ie′	i′se`	wä‛soñ′nĭ˙.	Iă′′,		10
thou didst see	I it made	and	again	thou	thou it madest.	Not		
se′′,	wä′‛hĭ˙	tesakwe′nioⁿ˙	ne′	naä′′sie′re`	dji′	nikatie′r′hă′.′′		11
indeed,	verily	thou art able to do it	the	so thou it shouldst do	where	so I do things."		
Ta′,	e‛tho′ne`	wä′‛hĭ˙	ne′	Tawĭ′skaroⁿ˙	wä‛hěñ′roⁿ˙:	"To′,	kä′tĭ˙	12
So,	at that time	verily	the	Flint (Ice, Crystal)	he it said:	"Well,	so then	
i′se`	e˙′′	tco′n‛het.′′	To′kěⁿske`	kä′tĭ˙	ne′	Oterontoñni′′ä˙		13
thou	there	do thou cause it to live.′′	Truly	so then	the	It Sapling		
wä‛hatboñ′tate`.	E˙‛	kä′tĭ˙	niiä‛ha′re`	dji′	rāiä′tioñ′nĭ˙	tä‛hnoⁿ′′		14
he it consented to.	There	so then	so thither he went	where	his body lay extended	and		

lay, and bent over and breathed into his nostrils, and he at once
began to breathe, and lived. He said to him: "Do thou arise and also
do thou stand, also do thou keep traveling about on this earth." The
body of a woman had he also formed at that place. Sapling caused
both of them to live.

Tawï'skaron' spoiled and undid some of the things that Sapling had prepared. The rivers to-day in their different courses have been changed, for, in forming the rivers, Sapling provided them with two currents, each running in a contrary course, currents made for floating objects in opposite directions; or it may be that it is a better explanation to say that in the middle of the river there was a division, each side going in a direction contrary to that of the opposite side, because Sapling had intended that mankind should not have, as a usual thing, any difficult labor while they should be traveling. If, for any reason, a

---

	iă'thatsa'kete'	ră'nion'sa'ko^{n.}	e^{ɛ,}	iă'hatoñ'rï'	ne'	o'nĭ'	ne'
1	there he bent forward.	his nose in	there	thither he breathed	the	also	the

	iokoñtă'tie'	tă'hatoñ'rï'	wă'hato'n'hete'.	Wă'hĕñ'roⁿ:	"Satkets'-
2	at once (it follows)	thence he breathed	he came to life.	He it said:	"Do thou

	ko',	ne'	o'nĭ'	tes'tă'ne'	ne'	o'rï'	ne'	tesatawĕñrie''hăke'
3	arise,	the	also	do thou stand	the	also	the	do thou keep traveling about

	dji'	ion'hwĕñdjia'te'."	Ioñ'kwe'	o'nĭ'	o'k'	skă''re'	dji'	shako-
4	where	it earth is present."	She man-being.	also	just	in one place	where	he made

	iă'toñ'ni'.	Ne'	Oteroñtoñni''ă·	tetcia'ro^{n,}	shakaon'he'to^{n'}.
5	her body.	the	It Sapling	both	he them caused to live.

	Ne'	Tawï'skaro^{n'}	o'tiăke'	shohetkĕⁿ''to^{n'},	shorï''sio^{n,}	ne'	dji'
6	The	Flint (Ice, Crystal)	some (things)	he spoiled them again,	he dis-arranged	the	where

	nă'ho'tĕⁿ	rokwătă'kwĕ^{n'}	ne'	Oteroñtoñni''ă·	Ne'	ioñ'wă'-kĕ^{n'}
7	such kind of things	he has put in order	the	It Sapling.	The	this time is it

	ne'	dji'	kaqhion'hate'nio^{n.}.	a'se'kĕ^{n''}	ne'	Oteroñtoñni''ă·	dji'
8	the	where	it river present in several places,	because	the	It Sapling	where

	roqhion''hoñnia'nioⁿ	teio'hnekĕⁿ''to^{n,}'kwĕ^{n'},	ne'	tĕⁿ''s	ne'	acte-
9	he rivers made several	it has two currents either flowing in an opposite direction	the	or	the	we

	wĕñ'roⁿ	teio'hnekĕⁿ''hawi''to^{n'},	ro'k	kĕ^{n,}	ki''	kā'iĕⁿ	sĕⁿ''hă'
10	should say	either it has two currents bearing in an opposite direction,	and	here it is,	I believe,	it lies	more

	io'nikon''hrăiĕñ'tă't	ne'	aetewĕñ'roⁿ	să'tekaqhion''hi''hĕ^{n'}	tekia-
11	it is comprehensible	the	we should say	it river middle of it	they

	tek'hĕ^{n'},	tetcia'ro^{n'}	e'rĕn'	teio'hnekĕⁿ''hawi''to^{n'},	a'se'kĕ^{n''}	ne'
12	two join,	they two both	else-where	two it current flow, either in an opposite course,	because	the

	Oteroñtoñni''ă·	rawĕ'ro^{n'}	iă''	thĕⁿ'iakoron''hiakĕñ'''hăke'	ne'
13	It Sapling	he it intended	not	they will be greatly distressed	the

	oñ'kwe'	dji'	tĕⁿ'iakotawĕñrie'''hăke'.	To'kă'	othe'noⁿ	ĕⁿkari'-
14	man-beings (human)	where	they will keep on traveling about.	If	anything	it it will

person would wish to descend the current, it would indeed not be a difficult matter simply to place himself in a canoe, and then, of course, to descend the current of the river; and then, if it should be necessary for him to return, he would, of course, paddle his canoe over to the other side of the river, and just as soon as he passed the division of the stream then, of course, his canoe would turn back, and he would then again be descending the current. So that is what Sapling had intended; that mankind should be thus fortunate while they were traveling about on rivers, but Tawī'skaroⁿ· undid this.

Now, moreover, Tawī'skaroⁿ· himself formed these uplifted mountains: these mountains that are great, and also these divers rocky cliffs—he himself made them, so that mankind who would dwell here would have cause to fear in their continual travelings.

hoñ'nī·	ĕⁿiĕⁿ·hnawĕⁿ·'te·	ka·hoñweiā'ke·	iā·'	ki''	wă·'hī·	
cause	one stream will descend	it boat on	not,	I believe,	verily	1
othe'noⁿ·	tewĕñ'to're·	ne'	o'k·	āioñti'tā·	ne'	ka·hoñ'wako ·
it anything	it is difficult	the	only	one himself should embark	the	it boat in	2
nĕñ'	wă·'hī·	ĕⁿioⁿ·hnawĕⁿ·'te·	No'k·	to'kă·	tĕⁿiakotoⁿ·hwĕñ'djio·'se·	
now	verily	one it current will descend.	And	if	it one will be necessary for	3
ne'	aoñsāioⁿ·'kete·	ne'	ki''	o'k·	wă·'hī·	ne'	e'rĕⁿ·	nā·kaqhioⁿ·ha'tī
the	one should return again	the	I think	only	verily	the	other (side)	such it river side of	4
niiĕⁿie·hoñ'ioñtie·	dji'	o'k·	niio·'sno're·	ne'	nĕñ'	tāioñto·'hetste·	
thither one his boat will steer	where	only	so it is rapid	the	now	one it will pass	5
dji'	tekia·hnekăk'hĕⁿ·	nĕñ',	ki'',	o'k·	wă·'hī·	ĕⁿsewă·'kete·	ne'
where	they two waters join	now,	I believe,	only	verily	it will go back again	the	6
ako·hoñwe'iā·,	io·hnawĕⁿ·toⁿ·hā'tie·	a're·.	Ta',	ne'	rawe'roⁿ·	
one's boat,	it is going down stream	again.	So,	the	he it intended	7
ne'	Oteroñtoñni·'ā·	e·'	nĕⁿ·'watiesĕⁿ·'hăke·	ne'	oñ'kwe·	ne'
the	It Sapling	thus	some one will be contented	the	man-being(s) (= humans)	the	8
kaqhioⁿ·'hăkoⁿ·	dji'	tĕⁿiakotawĕñrie·'hăke·.	No'k·	ne'	Tawī'skaroⁿ·	
it river in	where	one will be habitually traveling.	And	the	Flint (Ice, Crystal)	9
sho·hetkĕⁿ·'toⁿ·,	shori·'sioⁿ·.					
again he it spoiled,	again he it disarranged.					10
Nĕñ'	tă·bnoⁿ·'	ne'	Tawī'skaroⁿ·	kĕⁿi'kĕⁿ·	ionontĕ'nioⁿ·	ionontŏ·
Now	and	the	Flint (Ice, Crystal)	this it is	it mountain stands plurally	it mountain	11
wa'nĕⁿ·se·	teiotstĕⁿ·'re'nioⁿ	o'nī·,	raoⁿ·'hā·	e·'	ni·hoie'rĕⁿ·	
large (are)	it rock stands high plurally	also,	he himself	thus	so he has done it.	12
Ne'	oñ'kwe·	ĕⁿienakerenioñ'·hăke·	ĕⁿiakotswatani·'heke·	dji'		
The	man-being(s) (human)	they will be dwelling in diverse places	it them will keep troubling	where		13
tĕⁿiakotawĕñrie·'hăke·.						
they will be traveling about.						14

Now, moreover, Sapling and also Tawĭ'skaroⁿ' dwelt together in one lodge, each occupying one side of the fire opposite to that of the other. It was then, verily, usual when they two had returned to abide in the lodge, that Tawĭ'skaroⁿ' kept questioning Sapling, asking him what object he feared, and what would most quickly kill him. Sapling replied: "A weed that grows in the swampy places, a sedge called 'it-cuts-a-person,' is one thing. I think, when I do think of it, that that weed struck against my body by some one would cut it. I do believe that it would cut through my body." Then Tawĭ'skaroⁿ' replied, saying: "Is there no other object which gives thee fear?" Sapling, answering, said: "I usually think that the spike of a cattail flag would kill me if one should strike me on the body with it." (These two things that Sapling spoke of, his father had told him to say, when he had been at his father's lodge.)

1. Něñ' tähnoⁿ'' ne' Oteroñtoñni''ă' io'k ho'nĭ' ne' Tawĭ'skaroⁿ'
   Now   and   the It Sapling   and also the Flint (Ice, Crystal)

2. skanoⁿ'să''ne' nĭ'teroⁿ', te'hotitciěⁿ''hoñte' (te'hotitciěⁿ'harets'toⁿ')
   one it house in there they two abide, they are on opposite sides of the fire (they fire have between them.)

3. Ne' kă'tĭ' wă''hĭ' ěⁿ's ne' něñ' ieshoti'iěⁿ' kanoⁿ''sakoⁿ'
   The so then verily , customarily the now there again they have entered it house in

4. sni'teroⁿ' něñ' ěⁿ's wă''hĭ' ne' Tawĭ'skaroⁿ' rori·hwanoñtoñ'nĭ'
   again they two abide now customarily verily the Flint (Ice, Crystal) he him questions asks

5. ne' Oteroñtoñni''ă', ra'toⁿ': "Oʻ'' hěⁿ's nă'ho'těⁿ'. ne' iaoⁿ''hă'
   the It Sapling,   he it says: "What (is it) customarily kind of thing the he himself

6. ratsa'ni'se' ne'ne' io'sno're' a'ho'rio'." Wă'hěñ'roⁿ' ne'
   he it fears the that it is quick it him would kill." He it said   the

7. Oteroñtoñni''ă': "O'să'kěñtă'ke' iotoñ'nĭ' o''boñte' iako'hre'nă's
   It Sapling: "It marsh land on it grows it weed   it one cuts, (a sedge)

8. i'ke'ne' koñwă'iats ěⁿ's. Thoi'kěⁿ' o''boñte' kiă'ta'ke' āie'iěⁿ'te'
   I believe, they it call customarily. That it is it weed my body on one it should strike

9. aoñk''hrene', tä'hnoⁿ'' i'ke'ne' iă'taoñtiak'te' ne' kiă'tă'ke'."
   it me would cut, and I think it would break in two the my body on."

10. Toñtă'hěñ'roⁿ' ne' Tawĭ'skaroⁿ': "Iă''-kěⁿ' othe'noⁿ' ne' o'iă'
    He spoke in reply the Flint (Ice, Crystal): "Not is it anything the other it is

11. te'shetsha'nĭ'se'?" Toñtă'hata'tĭ' ne' Oteroñtoñni''ă' wă'hěñ'roⁿ'·
    thou it dost fear?" He spoke in reply the It Sapling   he it said:

12. "Oro'tă' otcawěⁿ''să' ne' ěⁿ's i'ke'ne' aoñkeri'io' ne'ne'
    "It flag (cattail) its spike the customarily I think it me would kill the that

13. āioñkiěⁿ''te' kiă'tă'ke'." (Kěⁿ'i'kěⁿ' teiori''hwake' ne' dji'
    one me would strike my body on." (This it is two matter(s) in number the where

14. nă'ho'těⁿ' wă'hěñ'roⁿ' ne' Oteroñtoñni''ă' ro'ni''bă' ro'hro'ri'
    such kind of thing he it said the It Sapling his father he it him has told

At that time Sapling said: "What thing then dost thou fear?" Tawiskaron said: "Yellow flint, and also the horns of a deer. I suppose, when I do think of it, that I should perhaps die at once should one strike me with either."

So after that when Sapling traveled, if he saw a stone of the yellow chert kind, he would customarily pick it up and place it high on some object, and also, if he saw a deer's horn, he would pick it up and would place it high on some object.

Then, verily, it came to pass that they two had again returned home. The height of one side of their lodge was not great, but the height of the other side was greater. Sapling occupied the side which had the greater and Tawi'skaron the side which had the lesser height. Then it

ne'ne'	a'hĕñ'roⁿ	e[']	ciiä'hakwăt'ho'	dji'	thonoⁿ''sote'	ne'	1
the that	he should say	there	he visited there	where	there his house stands	the	
ro'ni'ʻbäʻ.)	E'tho'ne'	ne'	Oterontoñni''äʻ	wä'hĕñ'roⁿ:	"O''	kă'tĭ'	2
his father.)	At that time	the	It Sapling	he it said:	"What	so then	
ni'se'	nă'bo'tĕⁿ'	setsba'ni'se'?"	Wä'hĕñ'roⁿ	ne'	Tawi'skaroⁿ:		3
the thou	kind of thing	thou it fearest?"	He it said	the	Flint: (Ice, Crystal)		
"Okarakĕñ'räʻ	onĕñ'iäʻ	no'kʻ	ha'ne'	o'ksĕñnontoⁿ''	oua'karäʻ		4
"It white-grained (yellow chert)	it rock	and	again	it deer	its horn		
i'keʻne'	ĕⁿ's	ne'	āioñ'kiĕⁿ'teʻ	iaki'he'iăʻteʻ	oⁿ''teʻ."		5
I think	customarily	the	one me would strike	I would die at once	perhaps."		
Ta',	e'tho'ne'	ne'	dji'	te'hotawĕñ'rieʻ	ne'	Oteroñni''äʻ toʻkă'	6
So,	at that time	the	vhere	he traveled	the	It Sapling if	
wä'hatkăt'ho'	kanĕñ'iäiĕⁿ'	ne'	okarakĕñ'räʻ	wä''träʻkwe'	ĕⁿ's		7
he it saw	it stone lies	the	it white-grained (flint)	he it picked up	customarily		
ē'nekĕⁿ'	wä'hä'rĕⁿ	no'kʻ	ho'nĭ'	ne'	o'skĕñnontoⁿ''	oua'karäʻ	8
up high	he it placed up	and	also	the	it deer	its horn	
ne'	wä'hatkăt'ho'	wä''trăʻkwe'	ē'nekĕⁿ'	iä'ha'rĕⁿ'.			9
the	he it saw	he it picked up	up high	he it placed up.			
Ta',	ne'	kă'tĭ'	wä'ʻhi'	ne'ne'	a're'	iesho'tĭʻ Ska'tĭ' ne'	10
So.	the	so then	verily	the that	again	there again they are together. One side of it the	
dji'	rotinoⁿ''sote'	nă'teioʻnhoⁿ'tesʻäʻ'	no'kʻ	ne'	ska'tĭ'	teio[']n-	11
vhere	their lodge stands	its side is low	and	the	one side of it	its side	
boⁿ''tes	nä''	ne''.	Dji'	kă'tĭ'	ne'	nonka'tĭʻ ne' teioʻnhoⁿ''tes	12
is tall (high)	that one	the that.	Where	so then	the	the side of it the its side is tall	
e[']	nonka'tĭʻ	ne'	Oterontoñni''äʻ	ĕⁿ's	rĕñ'teroⁿ	no'kʻ ne'	13
there	the side of it	the	It Sapling	customarily	he abides	and the	
Tawi'skaroⁿ	dji'	ne'	nonka'tĭʻ	nă'teioʻnhoⁿ'tesʻäʻ'	nă''	ne''.	14
Flint (Ice, Crystal)	where	the	the side of it	its side is low	that one	the that.	

wăs that Sapli͏ng i͏ncreased the i͏nte͏nsit͏y of the fire b͏y putti͏ng hicko͏ry ba͏rk o͏n it. The͏n, assu͏redl͏y, it beca͏me a hot fi͏re, and the͏n, assu͏redl͏y, the legs of Tawĭ'skaroⁿ· bega͏n to chip and flake off f͏ro͏m the i͏nte͏nse heat of the fi͏re. The͏n, of cou͏rse, Tawĭ'skaroⁿ· said: "Thou hast ͏made too g͏reat a fire. Do thou ͏not put a͏nothe͏r piece of ba͏rk o͏n the fire." But Sapli͏ng ͏ne͏ve͏rtheless put o͏n the fire a͏nothe͏r piece of ba͏rk, and the͏n, of cou͏rse, the fire beca͏me g͏reate͏r. Now the fire was i͏ndeed hot, and now, too, Tawĭ'skaroⁿ's whole bod͏y was ͏now flaki͏ng off in che͏rt chips. Now, too, he was a͏ng͏ry, because Sapli͏ng kept putti͏ng ͏mo͏re ba͏rk on the fire, and, besides that, his side of the lodge ha͏vi͏ng o͏nl͏y a slight height, he had o͏nl͏y ͏ve͏ry little space i͏n which to abide. Now he w͏rithed i͏n the heat; i͏ndeed, Tawĭ'skaroⁿ· beca͏me so a͏ng͏ry that he ran out at o͏nce, and

1	Něñ' Now	wă'·hĭ' verily	ne' the	Oterontoñni''ă· It Sapling	wă·hatciěⁿ·howa'nă·te'. he caused the fire to be great.	Onéñno'' It hickory
2	ka͏rǎ· it bark	o'hwā'tcĭste'	ne' the	wă·hrĕñt'ho'. he put it on the fire.	Něñ' Now	wă'·hĭ' verily	to'kěⁿske' truly
3	wă'otciěⁿ·hatari''hěⁿ·, it hot fire became it,		něñ' now	tă'hnoⁿ'' and	wă'·hĭ' verily	toñta'·săwěⁿ· there it began	ne' the
4	Tawĭ'skaroⁿ· Flint (Ice, Crystal)	raniěñtā'ke'· his leg on		wă·tatoñ'kwă·s it flakes off iteratively	ne' the	dji' where	so'tcĭ· too much
5	wă'otciěⁿ·hatari'·hěⁿ·. it hot fire it became.	Něñ' Now	wă'·hĭ' verily	ne' the	Tawĭ'skaroⁿ· Flint (Ice, Crystal)	ra'toⁿ·· he it says:
6	"So'tcĭ' "Too much	nă·satciěⁿ·howa'nă·toⁿ·. thou it fire hast caused to be great.	To''să' Do not do it	o'iă' other it is	sase·hwātcĭstoñt'ho'·. again thou bark put on fire.
7	No'k' And	ne' the	Oterontoñni''ă· It Sapling	sěⁿ·'hă' more	o'k' only	ěⁿ·s customarily	sa·hahwā'tcĭstoñ'tho'. again he bark put on fire.
8	Něñ' Now	ěⁿ·s customarily	wă'·hĭ' verily	sěⁿ·'hă' more	wă·katciěⁿ·howa·''nhă'. it fire became great.	Něñ' Now	wă'·hĭ' verily
9	to'kěⁿske' truly	iotciěⁿ·hata'ri·hěⁿ· it hot fire is it	něñ' now	tă·huoⁿ'' and	ne' the	Tawĭ'skaroⁿ· Flint (Ice, Crystal)	něñ' now
10	o'k' only	dji' where	ni·hāiā'tă' just his body large (is)	wă·tatoñ'kwă·s it flakes off in chips	ne' the	tawĭ'skarǎ'. chert (crystal).	Něñ' Now	o'nĭ' also
11	ronă'khwěñ''oⁿ'. he has become angry	Ne' The	kă'tĭ' so then	ne' the	Oterontoñni''ă· It Sapling	ne' the	dji' where	o'iă' other it is
12	o'k' just	ěⁿ·s customarily	să·hate'kă'te' again he it kindled	něñ' now	tă'hnoⁿ'' and	ne' the	dji' where	nă'teio·'nhoⁿ·tes'ă'' its side is low
13	ne' the	kari·hoñ'nĭ' it it causes	niionaktā''ă· it room is small	͏nǎ'' that one	ne'' the that	ne' the	Tawĭ'skaroⁿ· Flint (Ice, Crystal)	dji' ͏where
14	nonka'tĭ' side of it	rĕñ'teroⁿ·. he abides.	Něñ' Now, I believe,	ki''	te·hot·hěⁿ·takěñ'rie'. he is rolling about in the heat.	Něñ', Now,	ki'', think,
15	wă'·hĭ' verily	e'' there	nă·honā'khwěⁿ·'ne' so he became angry	ne' the	Tawĭ'skaroⁿ· Flint (Ice, Crystal)	ne' the	iă·hāiakěⁿ·tā'tcĭ' he went out of doors at once

running into the marsh, he there broke stalks of the sedge called "it-cuts-a-person." Then he came thence on a run to the lodge, and then said: "Sapling, I now kill thee," and then struck him blows with the stalks he had brought back. So then they two now began to fight, the one using the stalk striking the other blows. But after a while Tawĭskaron° became aware that his blows against Sapling did not cut him. Whereupon he then darted out again, and then went to get this time the spike of the cattail flag. So then, as soon as he returned, he rushed at Sapling and struck him blows. Again his blows failed to cut him. Then it was that Tawĭskaron° fled, and then Sapling pursued him. Now, of course, they two ran. In every direction over the entire earth they two ran. So whenever Sapling saw a yellow flint stone or a deer horn on a high place he would customarily seize it suddenly, and would hit

o'sä'këntä'ke'	niiä'hatak'he',	e''	iä'hä'iä'ke'	ne'	iako·hre'nä·s	1
it marsh on	so there he ran,	there	there he it cut off	the	it one cuts	
o''hoñte'.	E'tho'ne'	nëñ'	e''	toñta'hatak'he'	dji'	rotino^n'sote'.	2
it here	At that time	now	there	again hither he ran	where	their lodge stands.	
Kaweñni'io·	e'tho·	sä'rawe·	e'tho'ne'	wä·hëñ'ro^n:	"Oteroñtoñni''ä·	3
So soon as	there	again he arrived	at that time	he it said	"It Sapling	
nëñ'	wä'koñ'rio'."	Ne'	kä'tï	wä'hoië^n'ta'nio^n'	ne	o''hoñte'	ne'	4
now	I thee kill."	The	so then	he him struck repeatedly	the	it herb	the	
sha'ha'wï.	Ta'.	nëñ'	wä''hï'	wä'hiateri'io',	ne'ne·	o''boñte'	5
again he it brought.	So,	now	verily	they two fought	the that	it herb	
ne'	shä'ha'wï	ne'	wä'hoië^n'ta'nio^n'.	No'k·	ä'kare·	ne'	6
the	again he it brought	the	he him struck repeatedly.	And	after a time	the	
Tawï'skaro^n	wä'hat'toke·	iä·''	ne''-kë^n·	teka·hre'nä·s	dji'	7
Flint (Ice, Crystal)	he noticed it	not	the is it that	it it cuts	where	
roië^n''thä'.	E'tho'ne·	nëñ'	sa'hāiakë^n'tä'tei'	ne'	noñ'wä·	ne'	8
he strikes him repeatedly.	At that time	now	again he went out suddenly	the	this time	the	
onō'tä·	otcawë^n·'sä·	ne'	sä'hako·'hä·.	Ne'	kä'tï	nëñ'	dji'	9
it flag (reed),	its spike	the	again he went after it.	The	so then	now	where	
sä'rawe·	o'k·	ci·hāiä'takoñta'tie·	ne'	wä·hoië^n'ta'nio^n'	Iä·''	ha'ie·	10
again he returned	just	there his body did not stop	the	he him struck repeatedly.	Not	again	
teiotoñ''o^n·	ne'	a·ho·hrena'nio^n·ke'.	E'tho'ne·	ne'	Tawï'skaro^n·	11
it succeeded	the	he him could cut repeatedly.	At that time	the	Flint (Ice, Crystal)	
wä'hatē'ko'.	Nëñ'	ne'	Oteroñtoñni''ä·	wä'ho·'sere'.	Nëñ	12
he fled.	Now	the	It Sapling	he him pursued.	Now	
wä·'hï'	wä'tiara·'tāte'.	O^n·hwëñdjiakwe'ko^{n}ʻ	nä'toñtä·hnitakhe·'te'.	13
verily	they two ran.	It earth (is) whole	again thence they two it overran.	
Ne'	kä'tï	ne'	kat'ke·	ne'	Oteroñtoñni''ä'	wä·hatkät'ho·	ne'	14
The	so then	the	whenever	the	It Sapling	he it saw	the	

Tawï′skaroⁿ' therewith. Customarily chert chips would fly when he hit him. Thus then he hit him as they went running. Whenever Sapling saw a horn or a yellow chert stone he would seize it suddenly and hit Tawï′skaroⁿ' with it. Then after a while he killed him. Now, at this time, toward the west, where the earth extends thitherward, there lies athwart the view a range of large mountains that cross the whole earth. There, so it is said, his body lies extended. He fell there when he was killed. Now, besides, it is plain, when we consider in what condition the earth is, that when we look about we see that the surface is uneven, some places being high, even ranges of mountain, while some are for their part low. This was, of course, done by the two as they ran from place to place, fighting as they went. That is the reason that the surface of the earth is uneven.

1	okarakeñ′rä‘ it yellow chert	oneñ′iä’ it stone	ne' the	tĕⁿ'′s or	ne' the	o‘skĕñnoñtoⁿ'′ it deer	ona′karä’ it horn
2	ne' the	ĕⁿ′s customarily	tä‘ha‘hra′kwä‘te’ he it took up at once	ne' the	wä‘ho‘iĕⁿ‘te’. he him hit (with it)	Wä′tewato′ko' It chipped off	ĕⁿ′s customarily
3	ne' the	tawï′skarä’ chert	ne' the	neñ′ now	wä‘tho‘kwä′'te’. he him hit.	E‘′ There	kä′tï so then	ni′io‘t so it is
4	roiĕⁿ‘tanioñ′ne’ he him went hitting along	dji′ where	te‘hnitak′he’se’. they two went running about.	Kat′ke‘ Whenever	ne' the	a′re’ again	wä‘hatkä- he it saw
5	t′ho’ the	ne'	ona′karä’ it horn	ne' the	tĕⁿ′'s or	ne' the	okarakĕñ′rä‘ it yellow chert	oneñ′iä’ it stone	tä‘ha- he it took
6	‘hra′kwä‘te’ up at once	ĕⁿ′s customarily	ne' the	wä‘ho‘iĕⁿ‘te’. he him hit.	Ä′kare’ After a time	kä′tï so then	neñ′ now	iä‘ho′rio’ there he him killed.
7	Ne' The	kä′tï so then	noñ′wä‘ present time	ne' the	dji′ where	iä′tewatchōt′ho‘s there it sets, at the west	noñka′tï‘ the side of it	iaoⁿ‘hwĕñ it earth
8	djioñtie‘′toⁿ‘ extends	e‘′ there	tetionontä′roⁿ‘hwe’ there it mountain extends athwart	ionontowa′nĕⁿ‘ it mountain large (is)	teiaoⁿ‘hwĕñ it crosses
9	djiiak′toⁿ‘ world	ne′ne‘ the that	iä′kĕⁿ‘ it is said	räiä′tatä′tie’. his body extends along.	E‘′ There	noñ′we‘ the place	ni‘boiä’ his body
10	tieneñ′′oⁿ‘ has fallen	ne' the	neñ′ now	shä‘ho′rio’. he killed him.	Nĕñ′ Now	tä‘hnoⁿ′′ and	wĕ′ne‘ it is plain	ne' the
11	tĕⁿtwäiä‘to′re‘te’ we it shall consider	ne' the	dji′ where	ni′io‘t so it is	ne' the	dji′ where	ioⁿ‘hwĕñdjiä′te’ it earth is present
12	ĕⁿtewatkät′ho’ we it shall see	tekoñtti‘ha′nioⁿ′. they differ among themselves.	O′tiä‘ke‘ Some	ē′nekĕⁿ‘ high	tiioⁿ‘hwĕñ- it earth stands
13	djiä′te’, out,	ionontä‘hro′nioⁿ′. it mountain is in ranges.	O′tiä‘ke‘ Some	e‘tä′ke‘ low	nä′′ that one	ne′′. the that.	Ne′ The
14	wä‘′hï′ verily	ne' the	neñ′ time	sä‘te‘bnitak′he’se’ they two ran about	roññaterīio‘hä′tie′se‘ they two went about fighting	ne' the	e‘′ there
15	ni‘hotiie′roⁿ‘ they two it did	ne' the	dji′ where	tekiatoⁿ‘hwĕñdjiati‘ba′nioⁿ′. two earth differ from each other plurally.

Now then, as it was the custom of Sapling to travel, he met a male man-being. Sapling said: "What dost thou as thou goest?" He replied, saying: "I come inspecting the earth, to see whether it is just as I put it forth." Sapling replied, saying: "Verily, indeed, this is a marvelous matter about which thou art now on thy way, for the reason that assuredly it was I, myself, who completed this earth." The other person answered and said: "Not at all; for I myself have completed this earth." Whereupon Sapling replied, saying: "Well then, if it be so, let it be made plain verily, that thou didst complete this earth. He added: "At our two backs, at a distance, there is a range of high mountains of rock which is in appearance like a wall, so perpendicular are the rocks. Hither must thou move them close to thy body. If, perhaps, thou art able to do this, it will be certain

Ne'	kā'ti'	ne'	Oterontoñni''ā·	ěⁿ's	ne'	dji'	te·hotawěñ'rie,	
The	so then	the	It Sapling	customarily	the	where	he traveled	1
e''	wă·ho'kěⁿ',	roñ'kwe'.	Wă·hěñ'roⁿ'		ne'	Oterontoñni''ā':	"O''	
there	he him saw	he man-being (is).	He it said		the	It Sapling:	"What	2
ni·satierěⁿ·hā'tie'?"		Tă·hari·hwă'sera'ko'		ne'	shāia'tă·		wă·hěñroⁿ'·	
so thou goest about doing it?"		He answered		the	he one person (the other)		he it said:	3
"Sewakatkěⁿ'se·bā'tie'.		Katokěⁿ'-kěⁿ'		ni'io't	ne'		wakoⁿ'hwěñdji-	
"I it come again viewing.		Unchanged	is it	so it is	the		I it earth have caused to be	4
ā'tatoⁿ'."	Tă·hari·hwă'sera'ko'		ne'	Oterontoñni''ā·		wă·hěñ'roⁿ'·		
extant."	He answered		the	It Sapling		he it said:		5
"Iori·hwane·hra'kwă·t		wă·'hī'		ne'	dji'	ni·satierěⁿ·hā'tie',		
"It matter is marvelous		verily		the	where	so thou it comest doing,		6
a·se·kěⁿ·'	i''	wă·'hī'	wāks''oⁿ·	ne'	kěⁿ·'	ioⁿ·hwěñdjiā'te'."		
because	I (it is)	verily	I have finished it	the	here it is	it earth (is) present."		7
Toñta·bata'tī'·	ne'	shāiā'tă·	wă·hěñ'roⁿ':		"Iă·'těⁿ'.	I''	se''	
Thence Again he replied	the	he one person (other person)	he it said:		"Not at all.	I (it is)	indeed	8
wakoⁿ·hwěñdjīs''oⁿ·."	E'tho'ne'	ne'	Oterontoñni''ā·			toñta·hěñ'roⁿ':		
I it earth have finished."	At that time	the	It Sapling			again he said in reply:		9
"Ni·hěⁿ'nio·,	kiā'ā'sā',	katō'kěⁿ'ne'	a·shī'kěⁿ·		to'kěⁿske'	i'se'		
"So there now,	come,	let it be shown	if it may be		truly	thou it is		10
ěⁿsas''oⁿ'	ne'	kěⁿ·'	ioⁿ·hwěñdjiā'te'."		Wă·hěñ'roⁿ':	"Tsoñ'ne·		
thou it mayst have made	the	here it is	it earth is present."		He said:	"At our two back(s)		11
noñka'tī'	e·'	tiionontătā'tie'		otstěñ'rā'	ē'nekěⁿ·	tiiot'te'	dji'	
the side of it	there	there it mountain extends along		it rock	high	there it stands out	where	12
ni'io't	ne'	dji'	tewa·'soⁿ·'tote'	e·'	niiottakwari''sioⁿ·	ne'	dji'	
so it is	the	where	it is a standing wall	thus	so it is vertical	the	where	13
teiotstěñ're'.	Ka'io'	tciā'tak'tă'	ěⁿteskwi''te'.		To'kā'	ěⁿskwe'nī'		
it rock is present.	Hither	thy body beside	thou it shalt move hither.		If	thou shalt be able to do it		14

that thou didst indeed complete this earth; if thou wilt only speak, telling that mountain range to move itself hither." He added: "Now do it then." Thereupon the other person said: "Thus it will, I think, come to pass." Then he called out, saying: "Come thou, yon mountain range, move thyself hither. Do thou stand beside my body." But the mountain range remained there; the mountain was still there unchanged. It did not move thence. Sapling spoke and said: "There, that is exactly what I have been saying, that thou hast not established this earth." The other person again replied, saying: "Well then, let it become evident, if it be true, that thou hast established the earth. Come then, do thou move that rock mountain hither." Sapling replied and said: "Thus then will I do." Thereupon he called out to the range of mountains. He said: "Come, move thyself hither." Then, verily, it moved itself

1	to′kĕⁿske′, truly,	ki′′, I think,	wă′‘hi′ verily	i′se′ thou	soⁿ‘hwĕñdjis′′oⁿ′. thou it earth hast finished.	Ne′ The	o′k‘ just	ne′ the
2	oñte‘sata′tĭ′ thou shalt speak	ne′ the	ka′io’ hither	aoñtoñt′kwi‘te′ it itself should move	ne′ the	thoi′kĕⁿ‘ that it is	ionontătă′tie′." it mountain extends along."
3	Wă‘hĕñ′roⁿ‘: He it said:	"Nĕñ "Now	kā′tĭ′." so then."	E′tho′ne′ At that time	wă′‘hi′ verily	ne′ the	shāiă′tă‘ he other person (one he body.)
4	wă‘hĕñ′roⁿ‘: he it said:	":E·', "Thus,	ki′′, I think,	nĕⁿia′wĕⁿ′ne′." so it will come to pass."	E′tho′ne′ At that time	ne′ the	nĕñ′ now
5	iă‘hatā′tĭ′ thither he spoke	wă‘hĕñ′roⁿ‘: he it said:	"Hau′′, 'Come,	thoi′kĕⁿ‘ that it is	nisenon′tăte′ there thou art a standing mountain	ka′io′ hither
6	kăsat′kwi‘te′. hither do thou thyself move.	Kiă′′tăk′tă′ my body beside	e′′ there	te′stă′ne′." do thou stand."	No′k‘ and	e′′ there	tiionon′tăte’ there it mountain stood
7	kato′kĕⁿ‘ unchanged	ne′ the	ni′io‘t so it is	ne′ the	e′′ there	tiionon′tăte′. there it mountain stood.	Iă′‘ Not	ka′io′ hither	tetiotkwi′toⁿ‘. it itself has moved.
8	Nĕñ′ Now	wă′‘hi′ verily	ne′ the	Oteroñtoñni′′ă‘ It Sapling	tă‘hata′tĭ′ thence he spoke	wă‘hĕñ′roⁿ‘: he it said:	"Ta′, "So,
9	ne′ the	wă′‘hi′ verily	cika′toⁿ‘, where I have said.	‘Iă′′tĕⁿ‘ Not at all	se′′ indeed	wă′‘hi′ verily	i′se′ thou	tesoⁿ‘hwĕñdjis′′oⁿ′." thou earth hast finished." (it is)
10	Ne′ The	shāiă′tă‘ he other person (one he body)	toñta‘hata′tĭ′ again he replied	wă‘hĕñ′roⁿ‘: he it said:	"To′, "Well,	kā′tĭ′ so then	kato′kĕⁿne′ let it be shown
11	to′kĕⁿske′-kĕⁿ‘ truly is it	ne′ the	i′se′ thou	soⁿ‘hwĕñdjis′′oⁿ′. thou earth hast finished.	I′se′ Thou	kiă′′ăsă′ come	kă′io′ hither
12	kăs′kwi‘te′ hither do thou it move	thoi′kĕⁿ‘ that it is	tetiiotstĕñ′re′." there it has set rock(s) up."	Toñta‘hata′tĭ′ He spoke again	ne′ the	Oteroñtoñ- It Sapling
13	ni′′ă‘	wă‘hĕñ′roⁿ‘: he it said:	"E′′ "Thus	ka′tĭ′ so then	nĕⁿ′kiere′." so I it shall do."	E′tho′ne′ At that time	nĕñ′ now
14	iă‘hata′tĭ′ thither he spoke	ne′ the	dji′ where	tetiionontătă′tie′, there it mountain extends along,	wă‘hĕñ′roⁿ‘· he it said:	"Hau′′, "Come,	ka′io′ hither

thence. Close to his body, at his back, did it come to a standstill. The cliff even lightly grazed his shoulder blades. Then Sapling said: "Now turn thyself around to the opposite side and look where the range of mountains is." Whereupon he turned about and the rock struck his nose and, as to him, his nose became awry. Then at that time he spoke, saying: "Truly, indeed, thou hast established this earth here present. It was not at all I who did it. If, then, thou wilt consent to it that I may live, I will then ever continue to aid thee. I will protect at all times thy people who are to dwell on this earth." Sapling replying said: "Truly it shall thus come to pass. Mask shall mankind ever call thee, and also Grandfather."

Then, verily, during the time that Sapling was again traveling to

---

kasat′kwi′te′." E′tho′ne′ ka′ıo̱̱ toñt′kwi′te′. Rāiă′tak′tă′ ra·sho′n̄′-
hither do thou thyself   At that time   hither   it itself moved.   His body beside   his   1
move."
ne‘ e‘' wă′tka′tă′ne′   ne′   dji′   ionontătă′tie′.   Wă·ho·so·nien̄·to·'-
back there   it stood   the   where   it mountain ex-   It his shoulder blades   2
at   tends along.   grazed
seıe· ne′ dji′ teiotsteñ′re′.   E′tho′ne′   ne′   Oterontoññi′′ă‘
       the   where it rock has set   At that time   the   It Sapling   3
                    up.
wă·heñ′ron̄· "Nĕñ′ te‘satkă‘r‘hate′nī‘. Ia̍′satkăt′ho‘ ne′ dji′
he it said: "Now   do thou thyself turn   Thither do thou   the   where   4
                       around.   look
niionontătă′tie′."   E′tho′ne′   nĕñ′   wă′thatkă‘r‘hate′nī′   tä·bnon̄·'
there it mountain stands   At that time   now   he himself turned around   and   5
up along."
wă′tiotsteñro′ien̄·te·   ne′   ra′nioñ′ke·   tä·bnon̄·'   wă·ha′nioñsakareñ′re·
it him rock struck   the   his nose on   and   his nose became awry   6
nă′' ne·''. Ta′. e′tho′ne· tethota′tī· wă·heñ′ron̄, ia′kĕn̄:
that   the   So,   at that time   thence he spoke   he it said.   it is said: 7
one   that.
"To′kĕn̄ske· wă·'hī· i′se′ să′son̄ ne′ dji′ ion̄·hwĕñdjiā′te·. Iă·′
"Truly   verily   thou thou it hast the   where   it earth is present.   Not   8
                             it is   finished
i·'' te′kĕn̄·. To′kă′t kā′tī′ ĕn̄·sathoñ′tate· ne′ akon′·heke·
I   it is.   If   so then   thou shalt consent   the   I should live   9
ĕn̄·konienawa·se′·heke· kā′tī′. Ĕn̄tekhe·nhe·hătiē′seke· ne′ soñkwe′tă·
I thee will continue to aid   so then.   I them will go about protecting   the   thy people 10
ne′ ĕn̄ienakere′nioñke· ne′ dji′ ion̄·hwĕñdjiā′te·." Tă·hata′tī ne′
the   they shall dwell in groups   the   where   it earth is present."   He spoke   the   11
Oterontoñni′′ă‘ wă·heñ′ron̄· "To′kĕn̄ske· ki·'' e·'' nĕn̄iā′wĕn̄·ne·.
It Sapling   he it said: "Truly,   I   thus   so it will come   12
                                                think,   to pass.
Akoñ′wăıă· ne′ oñ′kwe· ĕn̄iesana′ton̄·'khwăke· nĕñ′ tä·hnon̄·'
It Mask   the   man-being   they thee it will use to indicate   now   and   13
                  (human)
oñkwă·sot′hă‘ o′nī·."
our Grandfather   also."   14

Ne′ kā′tī′ wă·'hī ne′ Oterontoñni′′ă· ne′ dji′ nă·'he· wă′thata
The   so then   verily   the   It Sapling   the   where   it lasts   he traveled 15

inspect anew the things that he had finished on this earth, then he saw another male man-being. He addressed him, saying: "What art thou doing on thy way?" The other said: "It seemed that it became necessary for me to see thee." Sapling replied: "That is undoubtedly true." The other person answered and said: "I desire that thou shouldst consent to permit me still to live. If thou wilt then consent to what I say, I will give assistance to thee; I will watch over their bodies, and I will also give them life and support and, moreover, I will continue to defend mankind, whom thou wilt cause to dwell on this earth which thou hast completed." Replying, Sapling said: "Let me see what kind of power thou hast." Thereupon the male man-being, whose name of old is Hi'noⁿ' [Thunder], started upon a run and went up into the clouds. Now, verily, rumblings were

1. wĕñ'rie' ne'ne' shotkĕⁿ'se'hä'tie' ne' dji' ne' ho'sa'an''hoⁿ' ne'
   the that again he it went about viewing / the / where / the / he them made / the

2. dji' ioⁿ'hwĕñdjia'te' e'' kä'tĭ' o'iä' ne' roñ'kwe' wä'ho'kĕⁿ.
   where / it earth is present / there / so then / other it is / the / he man-being (is) / he him saw.

3. E'tho'ne' wä''hĭ' ne' Oteroñtoñni''ä' wä'hĕñ'roⁿ': "O''
   At that time / verily / the / It Sapling / he it said / "What is it

4. nisatierĕⁿ'hä'tie'?" Wä'hĕñ'roⁿ' ne' shäiä'tä': "Wä'tewakatoⁿ
   just thou art going about doing?" / He it said / the / other person: / "It me became necessary for,

5. 'hwĕñdjio''se' ki'' ne' akoñ'kĕᵐ'." Wä'bĕñ'roⁿ' ne' Oteroñtoñni''ä':
   I think, / the / I thee should see." / He it said / the / It Sapling:

6. "To'kĕⁿske' wä''hĭ'." Toñta'hata'tĭ' ne' shäia'tä' wä'hĕñ'roⁿ':
   "Truly / verily." / He spoke in reply / the / other person / he it said:

7. "I'ke're' a'sathoñ'tăte'-kĕⁿ' ne' ako'n'heke'. To'kă't kä'tĭ'
   "I it desire / thou shouldst consent to it / caust thou / the / I live should. / It / so then

8. sathoñ'tătoⁿ' dji' nä'ho'tĕⁿ' ka'toⁿ' ĕⁿkoñie'năwä'se'. Ĕⁿkheiä'-
   thou it consentest to / where / that kind of thing / I it say / I thee will aid. / I their bodies

9. tä'nikoⁿ'ra'rĕⁿ' ne' o'nĭ' ne' ĕⁿtekhe''nhe' nĕñ' tä'hnoⁿ'' ĕⁿkheiä'-
   will watch over / the / also / the / I them will protect / now / and / I them will

10. taken'hĕⁿ''häke' ne' oñ'kwe' nē' ĕⁿsheiĕñnak'eratste' ne' dji'
    continue to aid / the / man-being (human) / the / thou them wilt cause to dwell / the / where

11. ioⁿ'hwĕñdjiä'te' ne' dji' wä'soⁿ'hwĕñdjis''ä'." Toñtä'hata'tĭ' ne'
    it earth is present / the / where / thou earth hast completed." / He spoke in reply / the

12. Oteroñtoñni''ä' wä'bĕñ'roⁿ': "To', kä'tĭ' katkăt'ho' ne' dji'
    It Sapling / he it said: / "Well, / so then / let me see it / the / where

13. nisa'shatstĕⁿ'sero'tĕⁿ'?" E'tho'ne' ne' roñ'kwe', Hi''noⁿ' ni'ha'
    thy kind of power?" / At that time / the / he man-being, / The Thunder / such (is)

14. sĕnno'tĕⁿ' ori'hwakäioⁿ'ne''hă', wäthä'rä'tate' ē'nekĕⁿ' niiä'ha're'
    his name / in the manner of ancients, / he ran / high / there he went

heard; it thundered in the clouds, and lightnings were also emitted, and moreover many flashes shot forth, seeming as though only one from their rapidity. So then the man-being descended again where Sapling was standing, and he said: "Now assuredly thou didst see what kind of power I have." Sapling, replying, said: "It is true indeed that thou art able to do just as thou didst tell me not long ago." Then he continued: "Art thou able to cast water habitually on this earth as the summers come?" The other answered, saying: "I am able to do so." Sapling said in reply: "So then let me see how thou wilt do this." The other person replied: "Yo'; so be it." Now he again ascended on high where the clouds are present. Now then again it thundered, and besides, the lightning flashed, and the clouds

otsa'tākoⁿ· *it cloud is,*	Nēñ' *Now*	wä'·hī' *verily*	wä'tio'toⁿ·hä'rere' *it rumbled*	ne' *the*	otsa'takoⁿ, *it cloud in,*	1
wä'ka'we're' *it spoke*	ne' *the*	o'nī' *also*	ne' *the*	tewēñnere'kara'·hwä·s, *it lightened (it winked),*	nēñ' *now*	tä·hnoⁿ' *and*	2
wä'ote'seroñtie'·'seroⁿ·, *it shot strokes repeatedly,*	nakwä' *the very*	o'kⁱ *only*	sha'kä· *one it is*	iä'hoñ'nī'. *there it made it.*	Ta', *So,*	3
e'tho'ne' *at that time*	nēñ' *now*	toñta·hats'nēⁿ·te' *he again came down*	ne' *the*	roñ'kwe·, *he man-being,*	e·' *there*	sa'rawe' *again he arrived*	dji' *where*	4
noñ'we· *place*	ne' *the*	Oteroñtoñni'·ä· *It Sapling*	ni·'iate·, *just he stands,*	nēñ' *now*	tä·bnoⁿ' *and*	wä·bēñ'roⁿ: *he it said:*	5
"Nēñ' *"Now*	wä'·hī' *verily*	wä·satkät'ho· *thou it didst see*	dji' *where*	niwake'shatstēⁿ·sero'tēⁿ·." *such my kind of power (is)."*		6
Toñta·hata'tī' *He spoke in reply*	ne' *the*	Oteroñtoñni'·ä· *It Sapling*	wä·hēñ'roⁿ: *he it said:*	"To'kēⁿske· *"Truly*	wä'·hī' *verily*	7
sakwe'nioⁿ· *thou art able to do it*	ne' *the*	e·' *thus*	nōⁿ·'siere· *so thou wilt do it*	ne' *the*	dji' *where*	nä·ho'tōⁿ *that kind of thing*	wä'sekhro'rī' *thou me didst tell*	8
ne' *the*	oⁿ·wä'tcī·." *not long ago."*	No'kⁱ *And*	ioñsä·hēñ'roⁿ: *further he it said:*	"Sakwe'nioⁿ·-kōⁿ· *"Thou art able to do it*	ne' *the*	9
ēⁿ·sa'hnekoñtiē'seke· *thou shalt cast water habitually*	ne' *the*	dji' *where*	ioⁿ·hwēñdjia'te· *it earth is present*	ne' *the*	dji' *where*	10
wakēⁿ·nhate'nioⁿ·," *it summer is present plurally?"*	Toñta·hata'tī' *He spoke in reply*	ne' *the*	shäia'tä· *other person*	wä·hēñ'roⁿ· *he it said:*	11
"Wäkkwe'nioⁿ·." *"I it am able to do."*	Toñta·hēñ'roⁿ *He said in reply*	ne' *the*	Oteroñtoñni'·ä·: *It sapling:*	"To', *"Well,*	12
kā'tī' *so then*	katkät'ho· *let me see it*	dji' *where*	nēⁿ·'siere·" *so thou it wilt do."*	Toñta·hata'tī' *He spoke in reply*	ne' *the*	shäia'tä· *one he person (is)*	13
wä·hēñ'roⁿ: *he it said·*	"Io'." *"So be it."*	E'tho'ne' *At that time*	nēñ *now*	ē'nekēⁿ· *high*	nioñsä're· *there again he went*	dji' *where*	14
noñ'we· *the place*	tiiotsa'tāre'. *there it cloud is present.*	Nēñ' *Now*	a're· *again*	wä'·hī' *verily*	saka'we're· *again it spoke*	nēñ' *now*	15

21 ETH—03——22

became thick, and besides this they became black. Then it came forward, from the sea did it come over the dry land, raining as it came. It was marvelous as it came along. Then of course the rain passed. Then he again returned to the place where Sapling was moving about. So then Sapling spoke to him, saying: "What thou art able to do is satisfactory. So it will indeed come to pass. It shall follow closely the course pointed out in thy request. So now, indeed, it will be thy duty to travel continually, for it was thou thyself that requested this. Do thou not then ever fail to do thy duty. Thou must, of course, ever be vigilant; if at whatever time it be there come dangers to the lives of men because great serpents move from place to place in the depths of this earth and also in the sea; if it come to

1	tä'hno"' and	tewĕññere'kara''hwä's it lightened (it winks)	nĕñ' now	tä'hno"' and	wä'kĕⁿtsatatĕ"s''hä'ne' it cloud became thick	
2	nĕñ' now	tä'hno"'' and	wä'ka'hoñ'tci'ne'. it black became	E'tho'ne' At that time	nĕñ' now	toñ'tĕñ'tï' thence it started
3	kaniatara'ke' it lake on	takäiĕⁿ'ta'kwe' it entered thereby	oⁿ'hwĕñdjiatbĕñ''ke' it dry land on	noñta'we' thence it came	iokŏñno it moved	
4	roⁿ'hä'tie'. raining along.	Ione'hrakwä'toⁿ'hä'tie'. It goes along marvelously.	Ne' The	kä'tï' so then	wä''hï' verily	ĕⁿtkĕñno it
5	ra'sero''hetste'. rain passed.	E'tho'ne' At that time	nĕñ' now	e'' there	sa'rawe' again he arrived	dji' where	noñ'we' the place
6	ni''re'se' he is going about	ne' the	Oteroñtoñni''ä'. It sapling.	Ta', So,	e'tho'ne' at that time	ne' the	Oteroñtoñni''ä' It sapling
7	tetbota'tï' thence again he spoke	hawĕñ'': he it said:	"Tkäie'rï' "It is proper	ne' the	dji' where	ni'io't so it is	ne' the	dji' where
8	sakwe'nio"'. thou art able to do it.	E' There,	ki'' I think,	nĕⁿia'wĕⁿ'ne' so it will happen	ĕⁿtioianĕ"''häwe' it manner will follow of it	ne' the	dji' where
9	ni'lo't so it is	ne' the	dji' where	wä'seri'hwanoñ'toⁿ'. thou matter hast requested.	Nĕñ' Now	kä'tï' so then	wä''hï' verily	e'' thus
10	ni'se' the thou	nĕⁿio''toⁿ' so it will be come	dji' where	tĕⁿ'satawĕñrie''häke', thou shalt keep traveling about,	a'se'kĕⁿ'' because	i'se' thou	wä''hï' verily
11	e'' thus	ni'lo't so it is	dji' where	wä'seri'hwanoñ'toⁿ'. thou matter hast requested.	To''sä' Do not do it	kä'tï' so then	noñwĕñ'toⁿ, ever
12	kasä'serĕñ'noⁿ'te' thou be remiss.	Ĕⁿ'se'nikoⁿ''raräke' Thou it shalt watch ever	wä''hï' verily	to'kä' if	kat'ke' sometime
13	teioterĭĕⁿ'thä'ra'tä'ne' it is mind-entangling	ne' the	oñ'kwe' man-beings (human)	dji' where	iako'n'he', they are living,	a'se'kŏ'ⁿ' because
14	teionatawĕñ'rie' they do travel	o'niare'ko'wä' it great serpent	onä'koⁿ' inside	ne' the	dji' where	ioⁿ'hwĕñdjia'te' it earth is present
15	no'k' and	ho'ni' also	ne' the	kaniatara'koⁿ. it sea in.	Ne' The	wä''hï' verily	ne' the	to'kä't if	kat'ke', sometime

pass that at some time these great serpents desire to seize people as they severally travel from place to place, thou must at once kill such serpents, and when thou killest them, they will be that on which thou shalt feed. Other animals also, equal in otkon orenda [malefic magic power][a] to these, all such shall fare like them. Thou wilt ever have these to watch—have these as thy adversaries. Now then, of course, I have finished this matter. Now then such is the office thou hast assumed. Mankind will name thee "Our Grandfather whose-voice-is-customarily-uttered-in-divers-places." Then, indeed, they two parted company. There the legend ends.

ne'	o·niare'ko'wä·	ĕⁿwe·''ie'	ĕⁿiakoie'nä'	ne'	oñ'kwe·ho'koⁿ·		ne'
the	it serpent great	it it will desire it	it one will seize	the	people		the	1
dji'	tĕⁿiakotawĕñrie'·häke'		i'se'	iokoñtä'tie'	ĕⁿ·seri'io',	no'k·	ne'
where	they will keep traveling about		thou	it follows at once	thou it shalt kill,	and	the	2
nĕñ'	ĕⁿ·seri'io'	ne''	i'se'	ĕⁿson·he·kwĕⁿ'·hake'.		Tekoñtiiä'tate'nioⁿ·
now	thou it shalt kill	that our	thou it is	thou shalt continue to live thereby.		They (z.) bodies have severally different	3
o'nï'	ne'ne·	shä'teioñnat'koⁿ'se'[a]		akwe'koⁿ·	ki''	shä'tĕⁿio·toⁿ'·häke'.
also	the that	equally they are otkon		it all,	I think	alike so it shall continue to be.	4
I'se'	nä''	ne''	ĕⁿ·sateri·hwäiĕñni'·häke'		ne'	tĕⁿ·sewa·hnio'täke'.
Thou	the that	that one	thou thy task shalt have it habitually		the	ye shall be adversaries habitually.	5
Nĕñ'	kä'tï'	wä'·hï·	wä·keri·hō'ktĕⁿ'.	Nĕñ'	kä'ti·	ni'se·	e·''
Now	so then	verily	I matter have ended.	Now	so then	the thou	thus	6
ni'io·t	dji'	wä·sateri·hoñ'tĕⁿ'.		Ne'	oñ'kwe·	ĕⁿiesanä'toⁿ'·khwäke'
so it is	where	thou it duty art charged with.		The	man-being (human)	they shall continue to name thee	7
ne'	"Raksot'hä·	ne'	Rawĕñnota'tie'se'."				
the	"He my grandfather is	the	His-voice-goes-about-sounding.'				8
E'tho'ne·	wä'·hï'	nĕñ'	toñsakiatekhä'sï·				
At that time	verily	now	they two separated.				9
E'tho·	nika'kares						
There	so it legend is long.						10

[a] See p. 224 and Orenda and a Definition of Religion, by J. N. B. Hewitt, Am. Anthropologist (n. s.), vol. 4, p. 33, 1902.

WILLIAM HENRY FISHCARRIER, A CAYUGA CHIEF (AGE 88), CANADA

ROBERT DAVID ('GADJI-NONDA'HE'), A CAYUGA CHIEF, CANADA

WILLIAM SANDY, ALEXANDER HILL,
WILLIAM HENRY FISHCARRIER, ROBERT DAVID

WILLIAM SANDY (BORN FISHCARRIER), CAYUGA WARRIOR, CANADA

JOHN BUCK, ONONDAGA CHIEF AND FIRE-KEEPER, CANADA

WILLIAM WEDGE, CAYUGA HEAD CHIEF AND FIRE-KEEPER, CANADA

INDEX

	Page
Aaltû fraternity, ceremonies celebrated by.	23
Abbreviated katcina dances, description of	56
fraternities taking part in	23
See Soyohim katcinas.	
Abote, appearance of, in Palülükoñti	52
in Powamû festival	36
description of	99
Ahül, advent of, in Powamû festival	33–35
common derivation of Ahülani and	122
description of, in representations of Hopi katcinas	67
identity of, with Tawa wüqtaka	28, 122
with Wûwûyomo	28
participation in Powamû festival by	67
regular appearance of	17
relation of, to the Katcina clan	65
resemblance of, to Pautiwa	59
similarity of acts of, to those of Pautiwa	26
Ahül katcina, substitution of, for Ahülani.	122
Ahül mask, resemblance of, to that of Wüwäyomo	65
Ahülani, appearance of, in Soyaluña	24
common derivation of Ahül and	122
connection of, with sun worship	122
description of	121, 122
personation of sun god by	24
Soyal katcina, derivation of	124
substitution of, by Ahül	122
Ahülti, derivation of Ahül and Ahülani from	122
Aiwahokwi, identity of	26
Alaska, field work in	IX, XII
Algonquian dialects of Nova Scotia and Cape Breton	XI, XXIV
Algonquian languages, comparative vocabulary of	XI, XXIV
Alo mana, derivation of	125
description of	108, 109
Alosaka, derivation of	125
description of	121
Hopi germ god	24
See Muyiñwû.	
Alphabet used in spelling Hopi names	126
Altars, absence of, in buffalo dance	30
in Pamürti	26
in Tawa Paholawû	31
in winter Lakone Paholawû	39
appearance of, in Hopi festivals	57
in house of the Patki clan	29
in Pamürti festival	28
in representations of Hopi katcinas.	28
in Soyaluña	25

	Page
Altars, use of, in Hopi festivals	55, 56
American aborigines equally divided in culture stages	XXII
Amulet, appearance of, in pictures of Hopi katcinas	101
Aña, derivation of	125
Aña katcina manas, ceremonial grinding of meal by	49
Ancient-bodied, a female man-being in Iroquoian cosmology.	228
Ancient clan masks, description of	109–112
ownership of	109
Ancients, Hopi, personation of	16
See Katcinas.	
Animism, significance of	15
Anklets, appearance of, in representations of Hopi katcinas	68
Ankwanti, appearance of Hahaï wûqti in	68
appearance of Wupamau in	91, 92
See Palülükoñti.	
Announcement days of Hopi elaborate festivals	20
Anote, ceremony led by	69
Cìfoto helmet kept in house of	95
East mesa Natacka masks of Tobacco clan kept by	70
Antelope katcinas, association of, with Kwewû	103
Antennæ in pictures of Hopi katcinas	81
Añwuei, personation of, in Tcivato kiva	30
Anwücnaco taka, derivation of	125
Añya, dance of Añya katcinas at Walpi called	45
Añya katcina manas, description of	93, 94
Añya katcina masks, resemblance of, to Hokyaña	94
Añya katcinas, appearance of, in dramatization of growth of corn	93
in picture of the Nakopan hoya	117
dance of, in Palülükoñti	50
introduction of, by Patki	45
probable derivation of, from Patki clans	94
public dance of, in Walpi plaza	54
resemblance of, to Zuñi Kokokci	94
Añya manas, similarity of masks of, to those of Soyal manas	24
resemblance of masks of, to those of Sio manas	107
Apache katcinas among Hopis	17
Ape in Iroquoian cosmology	214
Argentina, field work in	IX
Arizona, field work in	IX, XI, XVIII
Armor, find of European	X
Armstrong, John, annalist	137

341

342 INDEX

Arrow, appearance of, in pictures of Hopi
katcinas 61,
66, 69, 72, 75, 76, 78, 81, 82, 90, 91,
98, 99, 103, 106, 108, 110, 111, 113
use of, by Hopi katcinas 85, 86
Arrow clan. *See* Pakab clan.
Artificial flowers, appearance of, in apparel
of Hopi katcinas 85
Asa clan 61, 62
affiliation of, with Zuñi 29
celebration of advent of katcinas of, in
Pamürti 57
dramatization of return of ancients of. 16
house of, display of masks in ... 28
entrance of Pamürti procession into. 27, 28
introduction of East mesa Natackas into
Tusayan by 71
katcina return dance of the 62
Kokopelli introduced by 86
origin of 26
participation of, in Pamürti ceremony. 21
representation of return of ancients of. 26–29
Atocle, derivation of 71, 125
description of 75, 76
participation in Powamû festival by... 67
Aurora Borealis, a man-being in Iroquoian
cosmology 156, 172, 175
Avatc hoya, appearance of, in connection
with Humis katcina, in Pamürti . 27
Awatobi, certain monsters derived from... 71
germ god of 38
introduction of Owakülti into. 58
massacre at..................... 74
people of, migration of, to the Middle
mesa 104
representation of Deer katcinas from .. 103
See Pakab clan.
Awatobi maid, birth of child by.... 104
meeting of Alosaka with....... 121
Awatobi Soyok taka, derivation of. 71
description of 74
participation in Powamû festival by... 67
Awatobi Soyok wüqti, description of. 75
participation in Powamû festival by... 67
Aya, description of.................... 114
Aztec picture, suggestion of, by picture of
Kwahu 77
Badger clan, connection of, with Pamürti . 27
mask used in personating Nakiatcop
possessed by 86
See Honani clan.
Badge. *See* Tiponi.
Bandoleer, appearance of, in pictures of
Hopi katcinas.................. 91,
97-99, 104, 106–108, 111, 120
Barbarism characterized by male descent.. XXI
Bars, symbolic use of, in decoration of Hopi
katcinas 75
Barter katcinas, distinction of, from Huhuan 83
Bartlett, J. R., Seri vocabulary obtained by. XXV
Basket, use of, by Hopi katcinas............ 73, 74
in distribution of beans in Hopi ceremonies 70
in Lalakoñti festival. 58
Basket dance. *See* Lalakoñti.
Basket dance of Rain-cloud clans...... 22
Basket dances, Hopi 22, 23

Basket plaques, appearance of, in pictures
of Hopi katcinas 122
use of, in Masauû ceremony............. 37
Basketry, Hudson collection of . XXXIII
Beak, appearance of, in pictures of Hopi
katcinas...................... 67, 78–80
Bean, a female man-being in Iroquoian cosmology 174
Bean katcina. *See* Muzribi.
Bean-planting, mention of................. 22
See Powamû.
Beans, appearance of, in pictures of Hopi
katcinas.................... 68, 101
in Hopi ceremonies........... 31, 39, 70, 81
Bear, a man-being in Iroquoian cosmology........................... 174, 303
See Honau.
Bear clan, introduction of katcina by member of............. 111
Bear family of Hano, mask owned by 112
Bear family of Walpi, similarity of mask of,
to that of Ke Towa Bisena 112
Bear katcinas, personation of, in Hopi festivals............................ 41
similarity of symbolism of, to those of
the badger..................... 95
Bear paws, appearance of, in pictures of
Hopi katcinas.................. 95, 112
Bear skin, appearance of, in pictures of
Hopi katcinas 112
Beard, appearance of, in pictures of Hopi
katcinas........72, 84, 86, 88, 99, 110–112
Beast gods, definition of................. 135
Beaver, a man-being in Iroquoian cosmology 174, 202, 287, 315
Bee, imitation of, by Hopi katcinas........ 81
Beings not called katcinas, description of. 118-121
Beings, primal, in Iroquoian thought....... 135
Bell, appearance of, in pictures of Hopi
katcinas..................... 89
ringing of, in Hopi festivals............ 37
use of, by Hopi katcinas 77
Berendt, C. H., Mayan studies of XXVI
Bird calls, imitation of, in Hopi festivals.. 43,
49, 88
Bird dance, performance of, in Powamû
festival 25
in Soyaluña festival.................. 25
Bird effigies, appearance of, in Hopi festivals............................ 49, 88
Bird's head, appearance of, in pictures of
Hopi katcinas 77
Bird tracks in Hopi katcina pictures...... 87
Birds, imitation of flight of, by Hopi katcinas. 78
personation of, in Powamû............. 32
pictures of, in Hopi festivals 41, 42
representation of, by Hopi katcinas.... 79
representation of, in Hopi festivals..... 47
representation of sun by 122
representation of sun god by........... 24
worship of............................ 29
Bison, connection of Calako horns with 110
imitation of hunt of, in Hopi festivals . 31
See Buffalo; Mucaias.
Bittern, a man-being in Iroquoian cosmology............................ 179, 285

	Page
Black Bass, a man-being in Iroquoian cosmology	225
Blanket, appearance of, in Hopi katcina representations	60
worn reversed by Hopi katcinas	84
use of, in Hopi festivals	37, 40, 42, 46, 47
Blindness, assumption of, by Sumaikoli	96
Bluebird in Iroquoian cosmology	311
Boas, Franz, new Chinook texts of	XXVII
Body of Zephyrs in Iroquoian cosmology	295
Bogies, occasional visits of, in Walpi Powamû festival	71
Bow, appearance of, in pictures of Hopi katcinas	61, 72, 76, 79, 81, 82, 90, 91, 98, 99, 103, 106, 108, 111, 113
use of, by Hopi katcinas	78, 86
Bowls, appearance of, in pictures of Hopi katcinas	83
Kokle, common design in modern	95
Bows and arrows, distribution of, in Powamû festival	31
Bread, marriage, reference to	263, 264
Breath, as a source of conception	167
use of words meaning, to represent spirit power	15
Bridge of stone in Iroquoian cosmology	312
Brinton, D. G., Mayan Dictionary transferred to Bureau by	XXVI, XXVII
Brush, appearance of, in pictures of Hopi katcinas	93
Buck, John, Onondaga chief and firekeeper, annalist	136
Buckskin, appearance of, in pictures of Hopi katcinas	60, 98, 102, 108, 111, 121
decorative use of, in Pamürti festival	28
use of, in apparel of Hopi katcinas	72, 73, 79, 85, 86, 87, 94
in making war implement for Hopi katcinas	90
Buckskin ball, appearance of, in pictures of Hopi katcinas	116
Buffalo. See Mucaias.	
Buffalo dance, appearance of Mucaias mana, in	92
celebration of	21
description of, in Palülükoñti festival	43
origin of	31
significance of appearance of eagle in	67
Woe katcina represented in	66
Buffalo maid, sun symbol worn by	93
See Mucaias mana.	
Buffalo shrine, offerings placed in, in buffalo dance	30
Buffalo skin, appearance of, in representations of Hopi katcinas	73
replacement of, by sheepskin	92
use of, in apparel of Hopi katcinas	73
Buffalo sun ceremony, derivation of Calako masks from tribes practising the	110
Buffalo youth. See Mucaias taka.	
Buli clans, introduction of Owakülti from Awatobi by	58
Buli manas, appearance of, in butterfly dance	58
derivation of	125
description of	119, 120

	Page
Bulitikibi, description of	58
Bull-roarer, appearance of, in Hopi festivals	30
in pictures of Hopi katcinas	97, 120
use of, by Tcolawitze	61
See Whizzer.	
Butterfly dance. See Bulitikibi.	
Butterfly maids. See Buli manas.	
Butterfly symbols, appearance of, in Hopi pictures	90, 92, 106, 119
Cactus, appearance of, in pictures of Hopi katcinas	106, 112, 113
Cactus katcina. See Yuña.	
Cactus maid, association of, with Cactus katcina	113
Cactus tongs, appearance of, in picture of Yuña mana	113
Caiastacana, appearance of, in Pamürti	27
derivation of	125
description of picture of	60
difference in designs of, and those of Hututu	61
Cakwa Cipikne. See Cipikne.	
Cakwahonaû, description of	95
Calako, identity of, with Macibol	87
masks of	28
identity of, with those of the sun	28
similarity of ancient masks to	109, 110
use of, in Pamürti festival	65
personation of, in Palülükoñti festival	49, 50
sun gods personated by	110
Calako horns, connection of, with those of the bison	110
Calendar, Hopi ceremonial	18–24
California, field work in	IX
California tribes, social system of, based on language	XXII
Cape Breton, ethnologic studies in	XI
Cardinal points, animals belonging to	25
colors of, corresponding to those of raincloud symbols	X, 47
representation of, in pictures of Hopi katcinas	103
worship of fire god at	96
Caribbean art, study of the importance of	X, XIII
Catawba dialect recorded as a type	XXIV
Cebollita valley, N. Mex., ruins of dressed stone in	XVIII
Cedar, appearance of, in representations of Hopi katcinas	65
use of, in pictures of Hopi katcinas	122
Cedar bark, use of, as hair, in dress of Hopi katcinas	86
as torch carried by Tcolawitze	61
in Hopi festivals	96
in Sumaikoli festival	96
Central America, ethnography of	XXIII, XXIV
Ceremonial days in Hopi elaborate festivals	20
Ceremonies, appearance of katcinas in	15
personation of gods in	13
Chavero, Alfredo, work of, concerning symbolism	13
Checker, decorative use of, in Hopi pictures	83
Cherokee, the, myths of	XXIX
Cherry, wild, in Iroquoian cosmology	282
Chevron, appearance of, in symbolism of Woe	66, 67

	Page
Chevron, in Hopi pictures	77, 79, 101, 119
Chicken katcina, introduction of, among Hopis	17
See Kowako.	
Chief's badge in pictures of Hopi katcinas	76
Child-flogging, ceremonials of, at Walpi and Hano	69
Children's dance. See Wahikwinema.	
Chipmunk, representation of, in Hopi katcina masks	116
stripes on, in Iroquoian cosmology	253
Chipmunk katcina. See Kona.	
Chorus, appearance of, in buffalo dance	30, 31
in Hopi festivals	44, 48, 77, 93
in pictures of Hopi katcinas	88
Cipikne, description of picture of	60
personation of, in Pamürti	28
representation of, in Pamürti	27
Cipomelli, description of	104
Citoto, appearance of, in Palülükoñti	52
description of	95
Citulilü, derivation of	125
description of	107, 108
dressed like Hopi Snake priests	108
Civics, primitive, investigated by American ethnologists	XXI
Ciwikoli, derivation of	125
description of	96, 97
Clan masks, sanctity of	109
unused, description of	109–112
Clans, classification of katcinas by	18
extinct, Hopi, disposal of masks of	17
introduction of katcinas by	17
relation of katcinas to	45
Clay balls, appearance of, in Hopi katcina pictures	115
Clay basket, use of, in Hopi festivals	107
Cloth screen, use of, in Hopi festivals	41, 42
Clowns, appearance of, in Hopi foot races	114
in Hopi katcina pictures	76, 78, 83
association of, with Piptuka	116
with Wiktcina	116
participation in Powamû dance by	33, 91, 92
personation of, in Pamürti	27
struggle of, with Great Snake effigy	87
See Tcukuwimpkya.	
Cock. See Kowako.	
Cold-bringing woman	83, 84
Color, variations of, in katcina representations	60, 82, 95
on parts of the body of Hopi katcinas	78, 80
Comanche, derivation of Türtumsi from the	99
Comb, chicken, appearance of, in pictures of Hopi katcinas	80
Conception, parthenogenetic, described	167, 229
influence of, in development of religion	138
Conical tinklers	61
Constellations, how formed and named	227, 228
Cooking pot, appearance of, in pictures of Hopi katcinas	104
Copper implements, aboriginal, collection of	XXXIII
Coral, use of, as necklace, in Hopi pictures	119

	Page
Corn, a female man-being in Iroquoian cosmology	174
appearance of, in Hopi pictures	68, 69, 82, 95, 98, 102, 106, 115, 119, 122
distribution of, in Soyaluña	24
dramatization of growth of	93
ear of, appearance of, in Hopi katcina pictures	102, 122
in katcina representations	68
roasted, in pictures of Hopi katcinas	106, 115
use of, in pictures of Hopi katcinas	98
in Powamû festival	71
symbolic use of, in Hopi festivals	41
use of, by Natackas	35
in Hopi foot races	114
Corncobs, appearance of, in Hopi pictures	118
Cornfield, imitation of, in Hopi festivals	40, 42, 46, 47
Corn flowers, appearance of, in Hopi pictures	119
Corn husks, appearance of, in Hopi pictures	65, 67, 74, 75, 83, 91, 100–101, 103, 106, 110, 111, 121
artificial flowers made of	85
use of, as necklace in dress of Hopi katcinas	100
Corn katcina. See Kae.	
Corn maiden, association of, with Hehea	73
representation of, by marionettes	87, 88
Corn-planting. See Palülükoñti.	
Cornstalk, appearance of, in pictures of Hopi katcinas	95, 98
Cosmologies not simple but composite	136
Cosmology, Iroquoian	127–339
Coto, description of	89
Cotokinuñwû, derivation of	124
description of	120
Cotton, appearance of, in pictures of Hopi katcinas	43, 59, 65, 70, 90, 92, 99, 102, 105, 106, 122
Coues, Elliott, death of	XXXVIII
search of, for documents in the pueblos	X, XXII
Cow katcina, introduction of, among Hopi	17
See Wakae.	
Cow's head, appearance of, in pictures of Hopi katcinas	113
Coyote. See Isauñ.	
Coyote clan, mask of. See Hopinyu.	
Coyote spring, location of	84
Creation, signification of, in development of religion	138
Crescent, appearance of, in pictures of Hopi katcinas	75, 78, 80, 82, 98, 99
Cricket in Iroquoian cosmology	311
Crook, appearance of, in pictures of Hopi katcinas	60, 68, 72, 86
Crosses, appearance of, as decorations of Tcukwaina yuadta	63
decorative use of, in pictures of Hopi katcinas	65, 67, 111
Crow feathers, appearance of, in Hopi katcinas	69
Cuba, field work in	IX, X
Culture, stages of, in aboriginal society	XXI

	Page
Curved sticks, use of, by girls in hair-dressing	62
Cushing, F. H., account of the life of	xxxv-xxxviii
archeologic researches of	xiii, xviii
collection made by	xiv
death of	xxxv
field work of	x
Cuskahimū, ceremonial day of Hopi festivals	20
Custala, ceremonial day of Hopi festivals	20
Cyclopedia of Native Tribes	xi, xxiii, xxxii
Dance day of Hopi elaborate festivals	20
Dances, absence of, in winter flute festival	29
See Ceremonies; Buffalo dance; Butterfly dance; Flute dance; Snake dance, etc.	
Dances, Powamû festival	32
Dawn katcina, resemblance of, to Nakiatcop	86
See Telavai.	
Daylight, a man-being in Iroquoian cosmology	174
Dead, the, of sky land converse with living	263
December, ceremonies celebrated in	21
Deer, a man-being in Iroquoian cosmology	173
appearance of, in picture of Hopi katcinas	95
Deer horn, appearance of, in Hopi pictures	60, 103, 121
Deer-hunter, legend of	104
representation of, in picture of Sowiñwû	103
Deer katcinas, association of, with Kwewû	103
See Sowiñwû.	
Deer-mouse, a man-being in Iroquoian cosmology	306
Deer scapulæ, appearance of, in pictures of Hopi katcinas	103
substitution of sheep scapulæ for	85
Defender, a man-being in Iroquoian cosmology	234
Dehninotaton. *See* Down-fended.	
Departure of the katcinas, prominence of Eototo in celebration of	77
See Niman.	
Disks, use of, as sun symbols in Hopi testivals	41, 43, 46
to represent buttons in dress of katcinas	88, 98
to represent sunflowers in pictures of Hopi katcinas	64
Dogs in Iroquoian cosmology	153
Dogwood, blossoms of, in Iroquoian cosmology	282
Dolls, distribution of, in Powamû festival	31, 39
Hopi representation of gods by	15
Down-tended, definition of	142, 255
Drum, appearance of, in pictures of Hopi katcinas	107
Drummer, appearance of, in Hopi festivals	94
Drumstick, appearance of, in pictures of Hopi katcinas	107
Duck, a man-being, in Iroquoian cosmology	175
Duck katcina. *See* Pawik.	
Eagle, embodiment of spirit of sun as	16

	Page
Eagle, representation of sun by	122
symbolic use of, in Hopi katcina pictures	77
symbolism of, in Hopi ceremonies	67
See Kwahu.	
Eagle feathers, appearance of in Hopi pictures	65, 68-72, 82, 84, 86, 90-92, 97-100, 102, 103, 106-108, 110-113, 117, 118, 119
breast, in representations of Hopi katcinas	68, 121
employment of, in dress of Hopi katcinas	66
peculiarity of, in dress of Kohonino	85
use of, as warrior symbol by Teakwaina	63
Eagle katcina. *See* Kwahu.	
Eagles, absence of, in public buffalo dance	43
personation of, in Palülükoñti festival	43
Eagle's head, appearance of, in pictures of Hopi katcinas	
Eagle symbol, appearance of, in pictures of Hopi katcinas	103
Ear pendants, appearance of, in pictures of Hopi katcinas	84
use of, in decoration of Teutckutû	67
Earth altar man. *See* Nanoikasi.	
Earth goddess, worship of	55
East mesa, performance of dance of Buli mana at	120
East mesa ceremony, appearance of Sio mana and Koyimsi in	107
East mesa Natackas, derivation of	71
derivation of Middle mesa Natackas from	71
Elk horns, appearance of, in Hopi katcinas	60
Elsmereland, ethnologic investigation in	xii
Embroidery, appearance of, in pictures of Hopi katcinas	92
Bototo, derivation of	125
description of	76, 77
identity of, with Masauū	38
origin of name	77
participation in Powamû festival by	67
Eskimauan migrations, study of	xii
Eskimo, Alaska, linguistic research among	xii
Eskimo, central, investigation of	xii
Ethics, primitive, original research in	xxi
Everette, W. E., linguistic investigations of	xii
Explorations, early, elucidated by Cherokee traditions	xxx
Eyes, appearance of, in representations of Hopi katcinas	
crescent shape of, in pictures of Hopi katcinas	43, 68, 71, 74, 90, 122
globular, appearance of, in pictures of H_{opi} katcinas	66, 81, 85
goggle, in pictures of Hopi katcinas	41, 89, 91, 99
lozenge-shaped, in pictures of Hopi katcinas	112
protuberant, in pictures of Hopi katcinas	75, 86
rectangular, in pictures of Hopi katcinas	78, 101

INDEX

	Page
Eyes, small, in pictures of Hopi katcinas...	76
stellate, in pictures of Hopi katcinas...	80
False arm, use of, by Macibol	87
Falsetto, use of, in Hopi festivals	33-35
Fasting on the part of Hopi katcinas	42, 53
Fawn, spots on, in Iroquoian cosmology	253
spotted, a man-being in Iroquoian cosmology	173, 236
Fawn skin, use of, in dress of Hopi katcinas.	107
Feast, serving of, in Pamürti festival	28
Feathered strings, appearance of, in Hopi pictures	56, 96
Feathers, appearance of, in pictures of Hopi katcinas	59, 60, 64, 65, 75, 81, 83, 86, 87, 93, 95, 96, 98, 100-103, 108, 112, 113, 117, 121, 122
ornaments of, absence of, on mask of Yomi	37
peculiar use of, in dress of Hopi katcinas	41, 66
prayer, use of, by Hopi katcinas	76
in flute ceremony	30
red, use of, in representations of Hopi katcinas	72
turkey, appearance of, in representations of Hopi katcinas.	67
use of, in Pamürti festival	28
in representing bird katcinas	25
in Sumaikoli	57
February, Hopi ceremony in	22, 85
Festivals, Hopi, classification of	19
abbreviated	20
elaborate	20
See Ceremonies.	
Fewkes, J. W., discovery of ruins by	XIX
field work of	XI
Hopi paintings obtained by	XXV
memoir by, on Hopi katcinas	13-26
studies of, among the Hopi	XV, XVI, XXX, XL
Fire, kindling of, in Hopi festivals	55, 96
symbolism of	24
worship of	24, 96
Firearms, use of, in Hopi festivals	31
Fire Dragon in Iroquoian cosmology	157, 164, 174, 223
Fire drills, use of, in Hopi festivals	55
Fire god, worship of	55
See Tcolawitze.	
Fire-tenders, part of, in Hopi festivals	40, 44-46
Fish, appearance of, in Hopi katcina pictures	113
Fisher, a man-being in Iroquoian cosmology	202
Fish katcina. See Pakiokwik.	
Fletcher, Alice C., field work of	XII
Pawnee ceremony recorded by	XXXI
Flint, a man-being in Iroquoian cosmology	188, 195, 201, 293, 294
Florida, wood and shell objects from	XIV
Flowers, artificial, use of, by Hopi katcinas	73, 76, 101
Flute, appearance of, in pictures of Hopi katcinas	80, 84, 101, 102
reference to	234, 235
use of, in Hopi ceremonies	30
Flute dance	22
fraternities taking part in	23

	Page
Flute dance, symbolism of Ahülani in	121
See Lelenti.	
Flute girl, identity of dress of, with that of snake girl	57
Flute katcina. See Lenya.	
Flute prayer-stick-making	21
Flute priests, festival of	29, 30
alternation of, with snake festival	19
Foods given to civilization by the Indians.	XX
Foot races, appearance of Natia in	104
in Hopi festivals	53
See Wawac.	
Fox, a man-being in Iroquoian cosmology.	202
Fox skin, appearance of, in pictures of Hopi katcinas	65, 68-70, 72, 75, 76, 82, 84, 97, 99, 112, 114
Fraternities, Hopi	23, 24
initiation of novices into	19
Frogs, representation of, in Hopi festivals..	47
symbolic use of, in prayer-stick-making	31
use of effigy of, in Tawa Paholawû	56
Gatschet, A. S., linguistic researches of.	XI, XXIV
Germ god, worship of	24
Germ goddesses, Soyal manas personations of	122
Germination, Masauû regarded as a god of.	38
Gibson, Chief John Arthur, annalist	137
Gifts, distribution of, by Hopi katcinas	82, 83
Gill, DeL., work of, in preparing illustrations	XXXII
Gill, Mrs., pictures by	47
Girdle, appearance of, in pictures of Hopi katcinas	80, 84
Glutton. See Paiakyamû; Tcutckutû.	
God, definition of the term	135
Gods, Hopi methods of representing	13, 15, 16
See Katcinas.	
Gourd, appearance of, in Hopi pictures	64, 68, 116, 120, 121
use of, by Hopi katcinas	37, 105, 112
as helmet, by Hopi katcinas	77
Grandfather. See Hadu'I'.	
Grandfather katcina. See Tacab yebitcai.	
Grandmother in Iroquoian cosmology	320
Grandmother woman. See So wüqtî.	
Green Bear. See Cakwahonau.	
Great Plumed Serpent, effigies of, carried in Palülükoñti	87
gourd decorated with masks of, in Palülükoñti	41
representation of, on kilt of Citulilü	108
spring sacred to	52, 53
See Palülükoñti.	
Hadu'I', a man-being in Iroquoian cosmology	197, 201
Hahai, appearance of, in Powamû festival.	71
Hahaiwuqti, appearance of, in Palülükoñti.	53
in picture of the Nakopan hoya	117
in Powamû festival	35, 67
description of	68
personation of, in Nacab kiva in 1893	50
Hair, arrangement of, in pictures of Hopi katcinas	42, 70, 73, 74, 82, 85, 88, 89, 93, 94, 113, 115, 117, 118
cedar bark used as, in dress of Hopi katcinas	86

INDEX 347

	Page
Hako ritual of the Pawnee	XXXI
Hakto, description of picture of	60
personation of, in Pamürti	27, 28
Hale, E. E., Trumbull dictionary obtained by	XXV, XXVI
Haliotis shell, representation of, in Hopi pictures	119
Hand, figure of, on Natia mask	104
Hand katcina. *See* Natia.	
Hand-tablet dance, Hopi	23
Hani, personation of pipe-lighter by	30
Hano, buffalo dance at	31, 43
corn-planting in plaza kiva of	52
East mesa Natacka masks in	70
extinction of Sun clan of	57
gathering of Palülükoñti katcinas at	52
Hopi katcinas derived from	126
house of Plumed Snake of	51
planting of beans at	31
Powamû child-flogging at	36, 69
resemblance between Walpi Sumaikoli celebration and that held at	55
resemblance of Walpi drama to that of	42
serpent effigies owned by	51
shrine on trail to	33
Sumaikoli and Kawikoli masks in	96
Sumaikoli summer ceremony at	57
worship of war gods of	21, 25, 26
Yohozro claimed by	84
Hano clans, introduction of East mesa Natackas into Tusayan by	71
Hano names for Hopi katcinas	122-124
Hare, a man-being in Iroquoian cosmology	315
appearance of, in pictures of Hopi katcinas	78
Hatcher, J. B., ethnologic material collected by	XII
Patagonian collection made by	XXXIII
Hatchways, habit of katcinas of calling down	88
Havasupai, figure of Kohonino derived from	85
Hawk, symbolic use of, in pictures of Hopi katcinas	77
See Kwayo.	
Hawk feathers, appearance of, in Hopi katcina pictures	74
Head, importance of, in representations of Hopi katcinas	15
See Masks.	
Head of Zephyrs in Iroquoian cosmology	295
Hehea, association of, with Wüwütcimtû and Tataukyamû	73
appearance of, in Palülükoñti	52, 54
in Powamû festival	39
with So wüqti	76
description of	73, 74
Hehea katcina, appearance of, in picture of the Nakopan hoya	117
in Powamû festival	39
in dramatization of growth of corn	93
in Palülükoñti festivals	44
Natackas accompanied by	72
Hehea mana, description of	74
participation in Powamû festival by	67
Héhée, description of	74
participation in Powamû festival by	67

	Page
Héhée, resemblance between representation of, and that of Teakwaina mana	63
He-holds-the-earth in Iroquoian cosmology	152, 178
Hele, derivation of	125
Helilulu, derivation of	125
personation of, in Pamürti	27
representation of, in Hopi katcinas	66
Hematite, use of, in decoration of Hopi katcinas	77
Hemico, derivation of	125
description of	115
Hewitt, J. N. B., determination of Seri as a distinct stock by	XXV
field work of	XI
report of, on Iroquoian cosmology	127-339
researches of, in Iroquoian mythology	XXIX, XXXII
Hilder, F. F., linguistic work of	XXXII
Hill, R. T., ethnologic collection of	XII, XIII
Hinon in Iroquoian cosmology	339
name for thunder in Iroquoian cosmology	336
Hodge, F. W., archeologic discovery by	XVIII
cyclopedic work of	XXXII
field work of	X
sociological researches of, among pueblo tribes	XXII, XXIII
Hoffman, W. J., death of	XXXVIII
ethnological labors of	XXXIX
Hokyaña, derivation of	125
description of	94
peculiar dancing step of	94
Hokyaña mana, description of	95
Holmes, W. H., esthetological researches of	XIII
field work of	X, XIII
Homovi, painting of pictures of katcinas by	14
personation of Pautiwa by	59
Honani, celebration of advent of katcinas of, in Pamürti	57
Honani clan, affiliation of, with Zuñi	29
celebration of return of ancients of	26, 28
figurines of Corn maidens possessed by	87, 88
Hopi katcinas derived from	125
house of, arrangement of masks in	28
display of masks in	66
entrance of Pamürti procession into	28
masks belonging to	65
origin of	26
participation of, in Pamürti ceremony	21
Zuñi masks in possession of	66
Honau, appearance of, in Palülükoñti festivals	52
picture of, in house of war god	25
Honau family of Walpi, mask of	112
Honyi, badge of, in flute ceremony	29
Tcabaiyo personated by, in Powamû festival	75
Hopak, derivation of, from eastern pueblos	89
Hopak katcina, appearance of, in Palülükoñti	54
derivation of	125
Hopak mana, derivation of	125
description of	89
Hopi Avate hoya, description of	83
Hopi Calako mana, derivation of	124

	Page
Hopi Calako mana, description of	119
mask of	119
Hopi, clan masks of, features common to	109
dramaturgy of	XIV
festivals of, description of	24
gods of, paintings of, discovered	XXV
language of, foreign words in	97
masks of, explanation of pictures on	114
mythology of, investigation of	XI
people of	111
birds personated by	32
personation of Navaho katcina by	97
personages of, comparison of, with other pueblos	62
snake priests of, costume of	108
symbolism of the, presentation of, in Palülükoñti	40
territory of, owned by Sikyatki	38
winter ceremonial of	XXX
Hopi katcinas, Hano names for	122-124
memoir on	13-126
Tanoan names for	122-124
Hopiñyû, derivation of	125
description of	111, 112
designation of, as a Sikyatki katcina	112
Horns, appearance of, in dress of Hopi katcinas	41, 43
in pictures of Hopi katcinas	60, 61, 66, 69, 71, 72, 81, 83, 85, 87, 89, 91, 92, 99, 101, 106, 110-112, 116, 118, 120, 121
Horsehair, appearance of, in Hopi pictures	60, 65, 68-70, 78, 80, 82, 95, 97, 100, 102, 103, 106, 110-112, 118, 120, 121
use of, in dress of Hopi katcinas	93, 108
Hospoa, description of	80
Hotca, appearance of, in Soyaluña	25
Hotcani, derivation of, from the Keresan	100
description of	100
Hotcauni, linguistic similarity of, to Hotcani	100
Hototo, derivation of	125
description of	99
Hotsko, appearance of, in Sovaluña	25
description of	79
personation of, in Powamû	32
Huhuan, description of	83
personation of, in Powamû dance	33
Huhuan katcina, appearance of, in Powamû festival	39
dance of, in Palülükoñti	50
Huik, appearance of, in Pamürti	27
description of picture of	61
Humming-bird. See Totca.	
Humis, derivation of	83
description of	82
meaning of	64
Humis katcina, representation of, in Pamürti	27
Hunting katcina. See Tcilikomato.	
Hututu, appearance of, in Pamürti	27
description of picture of	61
Ice. See Flint.	
Indian, pursuit of, by Hemico	115
Indian Territory, field work in	IX, XII
Initiation ceremonies, influence of, on Hopi calendar	16, 19
Iroquoian comparative mythology	XXXI

	Page
Iroquoian cosmology	127-339
Iroquoian traditions, study of	X, XXIV
Isba, spring near	84
Isauñ clan, mask of. See Hopinyû.	
Jamaica, field work in	IX, X
January, Hopi festival in	21
Jaw, Navaho gesticulation with the	88
Jenks, A. E., study of wild rice by	XIX, XX
John, Andrew, informant	137
Kae, description of	98
Kaisale, derivation of	125
description of	120
Kaisale mana, derivation of	125
description of	120
resemblance of to Zuñi maid	120
Kalektaka, ceremony of	23, 25, 26
peculiarity in dress of	65
Katcina, definition of	16, 44, 45
Katcina clan, Abtil the returning sun of	65, 122
ancients of	57, 70
celebration of return of ancients of	16, 22
description of	110
display of war-god image belonging to	25, 26
habitation of Kicyuba by	70
Hopi katcinas derived from	125
Powamû festival at Walpi controlled by chief of	31
Katcina fathers, appearance of, in Hopi festivals	56
Katcina fraternity, ceremonies celebrated by	23
Katcina mana, description of	70
participation in Powamû festival by	67
Katcinas, ancient, among Hopi	17
importance of, in classifying katcinas	18
beings not called	118-121
celebration of return of the	31
Hopi	17, 18
memoir on	13-126
nature of	15, 16
Navaho, appearance of, among Hopi	17
description of pictures of	97, 98
personation of, by the Hopis	97
use of disks in dress of	88
See Tacab katcinas.	
number of, known by Hopi	17, 59
return of, in Powamû	36
selection of, to be painted	14
times of appearance of	16, 17
variation in, in Great Serpent exhibition	49, 50
Kau, description of	101
Kawikoli, association of Sumaikoli masks with that of	55, 96
derivation of	125
description of	96
personation of, at Zuñi	96
Kecu, appearance of, in Soyaluña	25
description of	78
personation of, in Powamû	32
Kelemüryawû, ceremonies celebrated in	21
Keme, description of	100
Keres, derivation of Hotcani from	100
katcinas of, among Hopis	17, 18
personages of	62
Soyok derived from	71

INDEX

	Page
Kerwan, description of	70
participation in Powamû festival by	67
Ke Towa Bisena, derivation of	126
description of	112
Kicyuba, derivation of Tuñwup from	70
mask of Katcina clan brought from	110
sacredness of water from	125
See Katcina clan.	
Kilts, use of, by girls, in Hopi festivals	118
Kiowa, obscure social organization of	XXI
Kite. *See* Keea.	
Klahewe	120
Knife, use of, by Hopi katcinas	75
Kohonino, description of	85
Kokle, description of	95
facial markings of	95
Kokokci, probable derivation of, from Patki clans	94
resemblance of, to Áñya katcina	94
Kokop clan, war-god image belonging to	26
Hopi katcinas derived from	125
Kokop family, mask of Eototo possessed by	77
Kokopelli, derivation of	125
description of	86
introduction of, by Asa clan	62, 86
Kokopelli mana, derivation of	125
description of	86
Kokshi, dance of Áñya katcinas called	45
Kokyan. *See* Spider clan.	
Kokyan wüqti, appearance of, in Palülükoñti festival	43
description of	90
resemblance between, and Hahaiwüqti, worship of	68
	21, 25
Komantci. *See* Türtumsi.	
Komoktotokya, ceremonial day of	20
Kona, description of	115, 136
Kopitcoki, use of, in Paliülükoñti	53
Koroctû, derivation of, from the Keres	102
description of	102, 103
Kotka, badge of, in flute ceremony	29
mask of Honau clan kept by	111
similarity of mask of, to that of Ke Towa Bisena	112
to those of Wiki and Naha	109
Kowako, appearance of, in Soyaluña	25
comparison of, with others	81
description of	80
time of introduction of, into the katcina cult	84
Koyimsi, description of	107
participation in Powamû dance by	32
Koyona, description of	80
time of introduction of, into the katcina cult	81
Koyona mana, personation of, in Powamû	32
Koyona taka, personation of, in Powamû	32
Kiiküte clan, prayer sticks given to member of	30
house of, Tcakwaina masks in	29
entrance of Pamürti procession into	28
Kukutcomo, habitation of, by Isauù clan	112
Kumbi Natacka, description of	72
participation in Powamû festival by	67
Kutca, description of	106
Kutcahonauû, employment of, to draw pictures of katcinas	13

	Page
Kutca mana, description of	106
Kutca Natacka, description of	72
Kwacus Alek taka, derivation of	125
description of	108, 109
Kwahu, appearance of, in Soyaluña	25
description of	77
personation of, in Pamürti	27, 29
in Powamû	32
in Tcivato kiva	30
Kwakwantû fraternity, ceremonies celebrated by	23
Kwatoka, bird personation of, representative of sun	122
Hano name for	123
Kwayo, appearance of, in Soyaluña	25
comparison of, with others	81
personation of, in Pamürti	27, 29
Kwewû, derivation of	125
description of	103
picture of, in house of war god	25
Kyamüryawû, ceremonies celebrated in	21
Lakone girls, appearance of, in Lálakoñti festival	58
Lakone mana, derivation of	124
description of	118
variety in dress of, in different pueblos	118
Lakone prayer-stick-making	22
Lalakoñti, appearance of Lakone mana in	118
difference of, from butterfly festival	58
duration of	20
fraternities taking part in	23
introduction of, into Tusayan by the Patki clans	58
regular occurrence of, in September	22-58
Lalakoñtû, prayer-stick-making of	55
winter assemblage of	39
Lalakoñtû fraternity, ceremonies celebrated by	23
Language, Hopi, composite nature of	18
Lapûkti, description of	86
Lasso, appearance of, in pictures of Hopi katcinas	72-74, 76
Leather, use of, in dress of Hopi katcinas	107
for horns, in pictures of Hopi katcinas	83
in representing tongue	91
Leggings, appearance of, in representations of Hopi katcinas	61, 72, 73
Leleñti, description of	57
duration of	20
Leñpaki. *See* Leleñti.	
Lenya, description of	21, 101
See Flute.	
Lenya fraternity, ceremonies celebrated by	23
Letotobi, description of	114
Library Bureau, number of books and pamphlets in	XXXII
Lightning symbols, appearance of, in Hopi pictures	84, 90, 92, 95, 98, 102, 108, 120
in paraphernalia of Hopi katcinas	43
use of, in Hopi festivals	41, 42
Light orb, a man-being in Iroquoian cosmology	174
Little Colorado river, introduction of Añya katcinas from	45
ruins discovered near	XI, XIX
Loiica, derivation of	125

350 INDEX

	Page
Loiica, description of	61
introduction of, into Tusayan	62
Loon, a man-being in Iroquoian cosmology	179, 285
Long-hair dance. *See* Añya.	
Luctaia, ceremonial day of, in Hopi festivals	20
Macibol, description of	87
identity of, with Calako	49, 87
Macikwayo, personation of, in Pamürti	27, 29
Macmahola, picture of	116
McGee, W J, Seri language recorded by	xxv
study of the Seri by	xiv, xvii
Maine, field work in	ix, x
Makto, description of	113
Mallery, Garrick, inscriptions obtained by	xxv, xxxix
Malo, derivation of	125
description of	82
part taken by, in Pamürti festival	29
Malo katcina, appearance of, in Powamû festival	39
personation of, in Nacah kiva	30
Mumzrau festival, association of Heben with Corn maids in	74
Mamzrau mana, appearance of, in Mamzrauti	58
derivation of	125
description of	118
Mamzrauti, appearance of Palahiko mana in	118
description of	23, 58
difference of, from butterfly festival	58
duration of	20
fraternities taking part in	23
See Maraupaki.	
Mamzrautû fraternity, ceremonies celebrated by	23
Mamzrautû society, prayer-stick-making of	55
Man-being, definition of	141
Maple sprout, a man-being in Iroquoian cosmology	301
See Sapling.	
Marau fraternity. *See* Marau prayer-stick-making.	
Maraupaki, appearance of Mamzrau mana in	118
Marau prayer-stick-making, description of	22
Marati society, meeting of	23
March, Hopi ceremony in	22
appearance of Macibol in	87
appearance of Wukokotl in	85
ceremonies of	84
Marionettes, representation of Corn maids by	49, 87
use of, explanatory of the use of idols among the Hopi	49
Masauû, advent of	36–38
appearance of, in Palülükoñti	52
derivation of	38, 125
description of	76
identity of sash worn by, with that of Sumaikoli	96
personation of, in Palulukoñti	50
similarity between designs of, and those of Eototo	77

	Page
Mask, a man-being in Iroquoian cosmology	335
See Hadu'i'.	
Masks, Hopi use of, in representing gods	13
importance of, in pictures of Hopi katcinas	15, 59
individual, description of	112–114
introduction of, into Hopi festivals	109
Mastcomo, Hopi festival performed at	36
Maswik katcinas, appearance of, in Powamû festival	36, 38
chorus of	77
Matia, description of	104
Maya astronomy	xxxi
Maya calendar system	xxxi
Maya codices, relative excellence of Hopi pictures and	15
Maya language, dictionary of	xxvi
Meal, corn ground into, for Natackas	71
grinding of, in corn festival	94
offering of, in Powamû festival	39
symbolic use of, in Hopi festivals	30, 31, 33, 34, 37, 41, 44, 56, 60, 69, 103, 107, 118, 121
Meal-grinding, ceremony of, by Añya katcina manas	73
Meal plaque, appearance of, in representations of Hopi katcinas	69
Meal pouch, appearance of, in pictures of Hopi katcinas	59, 65, 68, 76, 121
Meat, offering of, in Powamû festival	39
Medicine, a man-being in Iroquoian cosmology	175
meaning of term	15, 16
Metate, appearance of, in corn festival	93, 94
in Hopi festivals	44, 94
Meteor, a man-being in Iroquoian cosmology	174
Mexican calendar and numerical systems	xxxi
Mexican codices, relative excellence of Hopi pictures and	15
suggestion from, in studying symbolism	13
Mexican tribes, classification of	xxiii, xxiv
Middle mesa, Awatobî migration to	104
derivation of Natackas of	71
effigies at pueblos of	51
Minnesota, field work in	ix
wild rice industry in	xix
Mishongnovi people, personation of Sowiñwû by	104
Mohawk version of Iroquoian cosmology	255
Moisture tablet, appearance of, in Hopi pictures	77, 79, 80, 121
Mole, offering of, in Powamû festival	39
Molina, Audomaro, collaboration of, on Mayan dictionary	xxvii
Momo, description of	81
personation of, in Powamû	32
Momtcita, description of	21, 25, 26
fraternities taking part in	23
Monkey in Iroquoian cosmology	214
Moñ kiva, assembling of sun priests near	56
corn-planting in	52
dance performed in	30
display of war-god images in	25, 26
Lalakoñtû winter assemblage held near	39
Masauû rite performed in	37

INDEX 351

	Page
Moñ kiva, participants from, in Pamtirti	27
prayer-stick-making near	31
Moñkohu, use of, in representations of Hopi katcinas	59
Months, Hopi	19
Moñwiva, Hano ceremonies performed at	52, 53
location of	84
Monwû, appearance of, in Soyaluña	25
description of	78
personation of, in Powamû	32
in Tcivato kiva	30
Monwû wüqti, association of, with Owl katcinas	79
description of	79
Moon, appearance of, in pictures of Hopi katcinas	99, 113
Mooney, James, Cherokee studies of	xxix, xxx
reference to photograph by	39
Mosili̇li. See Rattle.	
Motul, Mayan dictionary of	xxvi
Mountain-lion. See Toho.	
Mountain-lion skin, appearance of, in pictures of Hopi katcinas	66, 90, 96, 106
Mountain pueblo, derivation of Türkwinû from	105
Mountain-sheep katcina. See Pañwû.	
Mountaineer. See Türkwinû.	
Mucaias, appearance of, in Palülükoñti	52
Mucaias mana, derivation of	126
description of	92, 93
Mucaias taka, derivation of	126
description of	92
part taken by, in Pamürti festival	29
Mucaiasti, description of	30, 31
See Buffalo dance.	
Mudheads, appearance of, in Hopi festivals	46
in pictures of Hopi katcinas	107
participation in Powamû festival by	32, 33
See Clowns; Paiakyamû.	
Music, aboriginal, new light on	xxxi
Muskrat, a man-being in Iroquoian cosmology	184, 287
Muskwaki, transitional serial organization of	xxi
Muyiñ wüqtaka, identity of, with the Tanoan Nanoikusi	122
Muyiñwû, germ god of Awatobi	38
worship of	21, 24
Muzribi, description of	101
Mythology, development of	xxix, xxx
Naacnaiya, description of	21
duration of	20
fraternities taking part in	23
Naactadji, derivation of	126
Nacab kiva, bird dance in, in Pamürti festival	29
dances in, in Soyaluña	25
display of war-god image in, in Soyaluña	26
Palülükoñti festival at, in 1893	50
participants from, in Pamürti	27
personation of Malo katcina in	30
Powamû bird dance performed by men of	32
Naka, Powamû festival at Walpi controlled by	31

	Page
Naka, similarity of mask of, to those of Kotka and Wiki	109
Nakiatcop, description of	86
resemblance of, to Dawn katcina	86
Nakopan hoya, derivation of	125
Nakopan personages, description of	117
Nakopan picture, portrayal of ancient Hopi katcinas by	117
Nalucala, derivation of	126
Hopi name for Pohaha	111
Naluctala, ceremonial day of, in Hopi festivals	20
Nanatacka. See Natackas.	
Nanoikusi, identity of, with Muyiñ wüqtaka	122
Nanoiûkwia, indentity of, with Tuwapoñtumsi	122, 123
Natacka mana, appearance of, in Powamû festival	35, 39
description of	72
participation in Powamû festival by	67
Natacka naamû, appearance of, in Powamû festival	35
description of	71
Natacka taamd, participation in Powamû festival by	67
Natacka wüqti, description of	72
Natackas, association of, with Hehea, in Powamû festival	73, 74
children of Hahai wüqti	68
correspondence of, with Soyok taka	74
description of	70–73
monsters in Powamû festival	70
name Soyok given by Hopi to	71
regular appearance of	17
visitation of, to pueblos for food	39
visit of, in Powamû festival	35, 36
Natick vocabulary, publication of	xxvi
Navaho, common use of silver disks as ornaments among	62
katcinas derived from	126
similarity in dress of Hokyaña drummer to that of a	94
Navaho Añya katcinas, description of picture of	
personation of, by chorus in Palülükoñti festival	44
Navaho Añyas, similarity of masks of, to those of the Hopi	88
Necklaces, appearance of, in Hopi pictures	83, 88, 119
human bones used as, by Hopi katcinas	76
use of, in decoration of Teutckutû	67
New-fire ceremony, appearance of Wüwütcimtû and Tataukyamû in	73
description of	24
effect of, on Hopi ceremonial calendar	19
variations in	19
See Wüwütcimti.	
Newhouse, Seth, annalist	137
New Mexico, field work in	IX, XI, XVIII
New York, field work in	IX
Night, a man-being in Iroquoian cosmology	174, 224
Niman, abbreviated Katcina dances closed by the	56

352 INDEX

	Page
Niman, description of	22, 57
duration of	20
difference in, in different pueblos	57
fraternities taking part in	23
purpose of	16
Niman katcina, appearance of Tuñwup on altar of	70
Nova Scotia, field work in	ix
Novices' moon. *See* Kelemüryawû.	
November, Hopi ceremonies celebrated in	21
Nüvak, association of, with Yohozro wüqti	84
derivation of	126
description of	83, 84
regarded as a Hano katcina	83
October, Hopi ceremonies celebrated in	23
Hopi festival occurring in	118
Offerings, custom of making, to katcinas	77
Ohwachira, definition of	255
Oklahoma, field work in	ix, xii
Old-man cactus. *See* Samo wüqtaka.	
Old-man sun. *See* Abül; Tawa wüqtaka.	
Onondaga version of Iroquoian cosmology	141
Ontario, field work in	ix
Oraibi, description of Star katcina of	89
Natackas at	71
Powamû festival most complicated at	31
use of extramural receptacles for serpent effigies by	51
variant of Coto in	89
Orenda, definition of	339
Orozco y Berra, linguistic classification of, indicated	xxv
Otgon, definition of	197, 242
Otter, a man-being in Iroquoian cosmology	174, 180, 287, 315
Owa, description of	82
representation of, by Telavai	81
Owa katcina, appearance of, in Powamû festival	39
Owa katcina mana, derivation of	126
Owa katcina taka, derivation of	126
Owakül mana, derivation of	125
Owakülti, description of	23, 58
difference of, from butterfly festival	58
duration of	20
fraternities taking part in	23
introduction of, from Awatobi	58
resemblance of, to Lalakoñti	58
Owakül tivo, derivation of	125
Owakültû fraternity, ceremonies celebrated by	23
Owakültû society, dance of, in Palülükoñti	50
Owanozrozro, appearance of, in Powamû festival	36
description of	88, 89
Owl. *See* Monwû.	
Paho. *See* Prayer sticks.	
Paiakyamû, appearance of, in dramatization of growth of corn	93
in Hopi festivals	24
in picture of the Nakopan hoya	117
association of, with Kaisale mana	120
Painting, Hopi skill in	13, 15
katcina, Hopi fears about	14
Paintings, appearance of, in Powamû festival in 1900	81

	Page
Pakab clan, ceremony of	25, 26
Hopi katcinas derived from	125
introduction of Owakülti by	58
introdnotion of Teanaû into Walpi by	54
serpent effigies kept in house of	51
Teanaû introduced into Tusayan by	91
Pakatcomo. *See* Patki clan.	
Pakiokwik, description of	113, 114
Pakwabi, description of	108
Palabikuña, description of	115
Palahiko mana, derivation of	125
description of	118, 119
similarity of mask of, to that of Hopi Calako mana	119
personations of, in Hopi festivals	55
Palakwayo, description of	77
personation of, in Powamû	32
Palülükoñ, association of, with Nüvak	84
derivation of	124
description of	87
effigies of	50, 51
Walpi ceremonies performed at home of	52
Palülükoñti, appearance of Hahai wüqti in	68
application of name corn-planting to	52
description of	22, 40-55
katcinas appearing in	16, 87-95
occasional ceremonies connected with	48-50
variation in	19
Paluña hoya, derivation of	125
description of	90, 91
worship of	21, 25
Pamürti, celebration of advent of Zuñi katcinas in	57
ceremony of, led by Pautiwa	59
description of	21, 26-29, 59
fraternities taking part in	23
Hopi festival	24
katcinas appearing in	16
personation of Sio Humis taamû in	64
purpose of	16
significance of introduction of Teakwaina in	62
Pamüryawû, ceremonies celebrated in	21
Pañwû, description of	102
Papago, altruism of	xxvii
conquest of nature by	xxviii
Paper bread, appearance of, in pictures of Hopi katcinas	115
in representation of Tcutckutû	67
use of, in Hopi foot races	114
Paraphernalia used in Palülükoñti	50, 51
Parrot feathers, appearance of, in Hopi pictures	69, 70, 92, 95, 98, 100, 105, 106, 112, 120
Paski, description of	117
Patagonia, researches in	xii
Patcosk, description of	99
Patki, Ahûlani, the returning sun of the	122
introduction of Añya katcinas by	45
Patki clan, affiliation of, with Walpi	29
altar in house of	29
dramatization of return of ancients of	16
Hopi katcinas derived from	124
participants in Tawa Paholawû members of	31

	Page
Patki clan, prayer-stick-making at the old house of	31
throwing of meal at, by Pautiwa	26
clans, introduction of Lalakoñti into Tusayan by the	58
house of, entrance of Pamürti procession into	28
Lalakoñtû winter assemblage held in	39
serpent effigies kept in	51
probable derivation of Añya katcina and Zuñi Kokokcĭ from	94
Patszro, appearance of, in Soyaluña	25
description of	80
personation of, in Powamû	32
Patszro katcina, comparison of, with others	81
Patuñ, description of	116
Pautĭwa, appearance of, in Powamû festival	36
connection of, with Pakab clan	25
god, derivation of	125
description of picture of	59
personation of, in Pamürti	26, 27
personators from Tcivato kiva led by	48
resemblance between symbolic design of, and that of Cĭpikne	60
Pavaoakaci. See Moisture tablet.	
Pawik, appearance of, in Soyaluña	25
derivation of	125
description of	78
personation of, at Nacab kiva in 1893	50
in Pamürti	27
Pawnee Hako ceremony	xxxi
record obtained of	xii
Payne, E. J., on changes in languages	18
Phallic emblems, appearance of, in representations of Hopi katcinas	72–74
Phallic proceedings among the Hopi, significance of	24
Pictures of katcinas, arrangement of	18
description of	59
employment of Hopis to draw	13
purpose of	15
variations in, made by different persons	59
Pigments used by Hopis in painting katcina pictures	14
Pigeon, a man-being in Iroquoian cosmology	304
Piki. See Paper bread.	
Pima katcinas among Hopi	17, 18
Pinart, Alphonse, Seri vocabulary obtained by	xxv
Pine, appearance of, in pictures of Hopi katcinas	64, 79, 82, 83, 100, 102, 113
use of, as screens in Hopi festivals	46, 47
by Hopi katcinas	76, 97, 106
to represent hair and beard	105
Pine tree, appearance of, in pictures of Hopi katcinas	78, 95, 112, 119
Piñon nuts, use of, in Hopi festivals	30
Piokot, description of	105
Piptuka, description of	116
Plains Indians, connection of, with Tewas	111
similarity of leggings worn by Pohaha to those of	111

	Page
Planting katcina. See Puski.	
Planting stick, appearance of, in pictures of Hopi katcinas	116
use of, by Hopi katcinas	77
in Masauû ceremony	37
Plaza kiva of Hano, corn-planting in	52
Plumed Snake, consecration of Moñwiva to. house of	84
of	51
Pohaha, description of	111
Pompin, Tewa name of San Francisco mountains	105
Porto Rico, field work in	ix
ethnologic material from	xii
Potato, wild, the first of vines to grow	226
Pottery, Tusayan, excellence of painting on	15
Powa, derivation of	125
Powamû, appearance of Wupamau in	91, 92
application of name Bean-planting to	52
advent of ancients of Katcinas clans	57
bird dances in	25
description of	22, 31–39, 84, 85
duration of	20
fraternities taking part in	23
Hopi festival	24
katcinas appearing in	67
participation in Powamû festival by	67
resemblance of, to Pamürti	26
return of Ahül from	122
significance of	16
variation in	19
Powamû katcinas, festival of	38
Powamûryawû, Hopi ceremony in	22
Powell, J. W., field work of	x, xiii
sociological studies of	xx
work of, in comparative philology	xxiii
Prayer offerings, custom of making, in Hopi festivals	77
Prayer sticks, made by Flute chief in 1900	29
making of, in winter Jakoñe Pahólawû	39
use of, in Hopi ceremonies	30, 31, 53, 55, 57, 93
Praying, custom of, in Hopi festivals	53, 54
in Pamürti festival	28
Priest fraternities, Hopi, association of, with masked katcina observances	24
names of	23
Priests. See Fraternities.	
Prizes, use of, in Hopi foot races	114
Pueblo women, style of hairdressing of	89
Pueblos, correlated agricultural and social development of	xxii
Puma. See Toho.	
Purification, act of, in Hano child-flogging ceremony	69
days of, in Hopi festivals	20
Putckohu. See Rabbit sticks	113
Püükoñ, appearance of mother and grandmother of	43
derivation of	125
Kokyan wüqti, grandmother of	90
similarity in facial symbols of, to those of Keea	78
Püükoñ hoya, description of	90
Hopak, the sister of	89
Paluña hoya, twin brother of	90
similarity of symbols of Puukoñ katcina to those of	90

21 ETH—03——23

354 INDEX

	Page
Püükoñ hoya, worship of	21, 25
Püükoñ katcinas, dissimilarity of, and Buffalo katcinas	43
Püükoñki, description of	25
Rabbit skin, use of, as rug, by Hopi katcinas	50, 74, 76, 78, 79, 106
Rabbit sticks, appearance of, in pictures of Hopi katcinas	113, 116
Rabbit tails, use of, for necklaces, in decoration of Hopi katcinas	67
Raccoon, a man-being in Iroquoian cosmology	202
Racing katcina. See Wawac.	
Rain, representation on Hopi masks of symbols to bring	114
symbols of, in Hopi festivals	41, 42
Rainbow, symbols of, appearance of, in Hopi pictures	64, 102, 108, 121
legend of travel of Hopi gods on	121
Rain-cloud clan, basket dance of	22
katcinas of, celebration of advent of, in Soyaluña	57
See Patki clan; Water-house clan.	
Rain-cloud symbol, appearance of, in Hopi festivals	29, 41, 42, 47
in pictures of Hopi katcinas	59, 64, 66, 68, 80, 81, 84, 88, 90, 92-94, 98, 102, 105, 106, 108, 112, 118, 120
Rain priests, Zuñi, correspondence of, to katcina fathers	56
Rain symbols, appearance of, in Hopi pictures	47, 84, 88, 92, 105, 119
Rattle, a man-being in Iroquoian cosmology	174
appearance of, in pictures of Hopi katcinas	64, 72, 78-80, 83, 86, 92, 95, 96, 99, 102-104, 107, 114
distribution of, in Powamû festival	31
gourd, appearance of, in pictures of Hopi katcinas	82
turtle-shell, appearance of, in pictures of Hopi katcinas	82
use of, in flute ceremony	30
in Hopi festivals	37
in Pamürti	27
Rattlesnake, appearance of, in pictures of Hopi katcinas	107
Reed. See Pakab.	
Responsivity, ethnological principle of	xxviii, xxix
Return katcina. See Ahül.	
Rice, wild, extensive aboriginal use of	xix, xx
Rings, appearance of, in decoration of Hopi katcinas	83, 115
Rio Grande pueblos, dress of tablita dancers of	58
introduction of buffalo dance from	43
introduction of butterfly dance from	119
migration of Asa and Honani clans from	26
Roberts, E. W., authorization of bulletins procured by	xxvi
Rose-willow in Iroquoian cosmology	289
Sabi, mask of, kept by Walpi Pakab clan	95
Sa clan, serpent effigies kept in house of	51

	Page
Sahagun manuscript, suggestion of, concerning symbolism	13
part played by, in Nasauu ceremony	37
Salab Monwû, description of	79
Salamopias, identity of Cipikne with	60
Samo wüqtaka, association of, with Hopinyu	112
derivation of	125
Samo wüqtaka katcinas, appearance of, in Palülükoñti	52
San Francisco Mountains, name given to, by Tewas	105
Turkwinû derived from people of	95
Sapling, a man-being in Iroquoian cosmology	196, 201, 208, 218, 219, 302, 312, 315, 325, 328, 331, 333, 335
See Tharonhiawakon.	
Sash, appearance of, in pictures of Hopi katcinas	68, 75, 76, 78-80, 82, 86, 96, 99, 100, 108
dance, appearance of, in representations of Hopi katcinas	68
wearing of, on shoulder, by Hopi katcina	105
Savagery, matronymic system characteristic of	xxi
Seasons, Hopi	19
Secret ceremonies, absence of, in abbreviated Katcina dances	56
from butterfly festival	58
performance of, in Niman	56
Seeds, appearance of, in pictures of Hopi katcinas	107
Semicircular bands, use of, in decoration of Hopi katcinas	95
symbolic use of, in pictures of Hopi katcinas	80
Seneca version of Iroquian cosmology	221
September, annual occurrence of Lalakoñti in	58
Hopi ceremonies celebrated in	22
Seri, the, egoism of	xxvii
face-painting of	xiv
language of, not related to the Yuman	xxv
dialects of	xxv
maternal organization of	xiv
submission to nature of	xxviii
technology of	xvii
Sheep scapulæ, appearance of, in pictures of Hopi katcinas	61, 76, 106
use of, by Hopi katcinas	85
in accompaniment to dance in Hopi festivals	56
in making accompaniment for song in Hopi ceremonies	64
Sheep horns, appearance of, in pictures of Hopi katcinas	102
Sheepskin, appearance of, in dress of Hopi katcinas	43, 72, 73, 75, 83, 92, 93, 106, 117, 119
Sheepskin wig, appearance of, in picture of Woe	67
Shell rattle. See Rattle.	
Shells, appearance of, in pictures of Hopi katcinas	92

INDEX 355

	Page
Shell tinklers, representation of, in pictures of Hopi katcinas	68
Shrines, appearance of, in Pamürti	27
use of, in Hopi festivals, for reception of prayer sticks	31
Sichumovi, celebration of butterfly festival at	58
celebration of Owakülti at	58
celebration of Pamürti at	21, 26
derivation of katcinas in	125-126
East mesa Natacka masks in	70
figurines of Corn-maidens possessed by Honani clan of	87, 88
origin of people of	26
planting of beans at	31
serpent effigies owned by	51
visitation by Ahül to houses in	34
Sikya Cipikne. See Cipikne.	
Sikyahonauü, use of house of, in Pamürti	28
Sikyatki, derivation of Hemićo from	115
derivation of Masauü from	38
destruction of	115
excellence of painting of pottery from	15
Hopi territory owned by	38
introduction of Eototo from	77
legend connected with	117
people of, familiarity with katcina cult by	117
pottery from	112
See Kokop clan.	
Sikyatki katcina, designation of Hopinyü as a	112
Sipapu, appearance of, in Pamtirti festival	28
sacred badges placed in, in flute ceremony	29
use of, in addressing gods	55
Sio, derivation of	125
description of	107, 112
Sio Avato hoya, derivation of	125
description of picture of	64
difference of, from Hopi Avute Hoya	83
Sio Calako, derivation of	125
representation of, by Hopi katcinas	66
Sio Humis, derivation of	125
description of picture of	63
Sio Humis katcina, appearance of, in Powamü festival	39
Sio Humis taamü, description of picture of	64
Sio Humis taadta, derivation of	125
Sio katcinas, Powamü dance by	32
Sio mana, derivation of	125
description of	107
Sitgreaves, Lorenzo, ruined pueblo discovered by	XIX
Siwap, description of	100
Skin tablet, appearance of, in pictures of Hopi katcinas	101
Sky god. See Sun god; Wupamau.	
Sky, visible, in Iroquoian cosmology	141
Sky world in Iroquoian cosmology	175, 255, 282
Smoke, ceremonial, in Powamü festival	36
Smoke talk, ceremonial days of, in elaborate Hopi festivals	20
Smoking, custom of, in Hopi ceremonies	30, 53, 60
in Pamürti festival	28
Snake, effigies of, appearance of, in Hopi festivals	41, 42, 46, 51

	Page
Snake, heads of, appearance of, in pictures of Hopi katcinas	84
image of, in picture of Teanaü	91
Snake clan, overcoming of Masauü by chief of	38
Teabaiyo katcina owned by	75
See Teüa clan.	
Snake dance, description of	22
fraternities taking part in	23
suggestion of, by Teanaü katcina	54
See Teüatikibi.	
Snake festival, alternation of, with flute festival	19
Snake fraternity. See Teüa fraternity.	
Snake girl, identity of dress of, with that of flute girl	57
Snake prayer-stick-making, description of	21
Snake priests, meal bag of	91
resemblance of decoration of Macibol to snake symbol of	87
similarity of costume of, to that of Citulilü	108
tinklers worn by	61
Snares, use of, by Natackas	35
Snipe katcinas. See Patszro.	
Snout, varieties of, in pictures of Hopi katcinas	28, 59, 60, 62, 64-66, 74, 76, 82, 85, 86, 91, 95, 97, 99, 100, 102, 103, 105-108, 111, 114
Snow, a man-being made by Tawiskaron	324
Snow katcina, identity of some of the symbols of, with those of Huik	61
See Nüvak.	
Sociology, branches of	XX, XXI
Solar myths, association of flute with Tawan	101
Song, characteristic feature of, in Sumaikoli	55
movements of Corn maidens to rhythm of	88
rendition of, in Hopi festivals	31, 36, 37
use of, as accompaniment to meal-grinding in Hopi festivals	44
in flute ceremony	30
in Pamürti	27
Sorcery, accusation of, against painters of katcinas	14
Soul, meaning of term	16
Sowiñwü, derivation of	125
description of	103-104
similarity of symbolism of, to that of Teüb	103
So wüqti, appearance of, in festival of Powamü katcinas	38
description of	76
identity of Kokyan wüqti with	90
Soyal katcina. See Ahülani; Soyaluña.	
Soyal manas, appearance of, in Soyaluña	121
derivation of	124
relation of, to clan	45
See Soyaluñn.	
Soyaluña, appearance of Ahülani in	121
celebration of advent of rain-cloud katcinas in	57
description of	21, 24, 25
duration of	20
Images of war gods displayed in	25, 26

356 INDEX

	Page
Soyaluña, modifications in, corresponding to celebration of flute or snake dance	21
purpose of	16
variation in	19
Soyan ep, appearance of, in Palülükoñti	52
derivation of	125
description of	85
Soyohim katcinas, descriptions of pictures of	98-106
Soyok, derivation of name	71
Soyok mana, derivation of	125
personation of, at Walpi	74
See Natacka mana.	
Soyok taka, correspondence of, with Natacka	74
derivation of	125
personation of, at Walpi	74
Soyok wüqti, derivation of	71
participation in Powamû festival by	39, 67
See Natacka wüqti.	
Soyoko, description of	70, 71
See Natackas.	
Soyoko group, Tcabaiyo referred to	75
Soyol katcina. *See* Ahülani.	
Soyol manas, appearance of, in Soyaluña	24
Soyowa, derivation of	125
See Sio.	
Spider, a man-being in Iroquoian cosmology	315
embodiment of spirit of earth as	16
Spider clan	111
Spider woman. *See* Kokyan wüqti.	
Spirits, primitive belief in existence of, after death	15, 16
Spots, decorative use of, in pictures of Hopi katcinas	76, 103
Spring, sacred, use of water from, by Hopi katcinas	76
Sprout, Maple. *See* Tharonhiawakon.	
Sprouting seeds, symbolic use of, in pictures of Hopi katcinas	101
Spruce, appearance of, in Hopi pictures	89, 121
Squash, a female man-being in Iroquoian cosmology	174
appearance of, in pictures of Hopi katcinas	65, 78, 97, 107
blossom of, appearance of, in pictures of Hopi katcinas	63, 82, 92, 97, 102, 103, 112, 116, 118, 119
seeds of, appearance of, in representations of Hopi katcinas	64
Squash katcina. *See* Patuñ.	
Staff, appearance of, in pictures of Hopi katcinas	65, 68, 103, 121
Standard-bearer, figure of, in picture of Buli mana	120
Star, a female man-being in Iroquoian cosmology	174
Star katcina. *See* Coto.	
Stars, appearance of, in pictures of Hopi katcinas	65, 92, 99, 102, 111, 113
characteristic arrangement of, in picture of Coto	89
decorative use of, in Hopi festivals	47
Stephens, David, exposition of meaning of creation by	188

	Page
Stevenson, Matilda C., mention of Hotcanni by	100
on Zuñi claim to Sichumovi	26
Zuñi studies of	xxx
Stein, R., Eskimauan research of	xii
Stick, notched, use of, in Hopi festivals	56
Stone, bridge of, in Iroquoian cosmology	309
Stone images, representation of Hano warrior gods by	21
Stone implements, Steiner collection of	xxxiv
Sumaikoli, appearance of, in spring and summer festivals	96
association of Kawikoli mask with those of	96
ceremony of	22, 23
derivation of	125
description of	96
identity of sash worn by, with that of Masauû	96
spring ceremony of	55
summer ceremony of	57
Sumaikoli masks, capture of, in Navaho foray	57
preservation of, in Hano	57
similarity of Walpi to Hano	55
Summer, prayer-stick-making in	83
Summer sun prayer-stick-making, fraternities taking part in	23
Sun, bringing of Buffalo maid to Tusayan by	31
dramatization of return of	21
objective embodiment of spirit of	16
personation of, in eagle form	122
representation of, in Hopi pictures	120
similarity of symbolism of, to that of Wupamau	91
symbols of, in Hopi festivals	41-43
Sun clan of Haim, extinction of	57
Sun god, dramatization of the advent of	24
garment worn by, in picture of Ahül	68
representation of, in Pamürti	26
in Soyaluña	24
worship of	24
See Ahül; Calako; Pautiwa.	
Sun gods, Calako one of the	110
explanation of multiplicity of	101
similarity of attire of, to that of Sumaikoli	
Sunflower, a female man-being, in Iroquoian cosmology	174
appearance of, in Hopi pictures	64, 106, 112, 120
Sun fraternity. *See* Sun prayer-stick-making.	
Sun katcina. *See* Tawa.	
Sun ladders, appearance of, in Hopi festivals	43
in pictures of Hopi katcinas	93
Sun masks. *See* Wüwüyomo.	
Sun prayer-stick-making, description of	21, 22
See Tawa Paholawû.	
Sun priests, assembling of, in Tawa Paholawû	56
winter ceremony of	31
Sun spring. *See* Tawapa.	
Sun symbol, worn by girl in buffalo dance	67

INDEX

	Page
Sun tablet, appearance of, in pictures of Hopi katcinas	79
Sun worship, use of Cálako masks in	110
Swastika, appearance of, in pictures of Hopi katcinas	114
Symbolism, definiteness of, in pictures of Hopi katcinas	59
method of obtaining information about	14
predominance of, in primitive technique and decoration	xvi, xvii
Symbols on masks, Hopi skill in painting	13
Tablet, appearance of, as headdress, in pictures of Hopi katcinas	105
in Hopi pictures	64, 102, 112, 118-120
Tablita dancers, dress of	58
Tacab, description of	98
part taken by, in Pamürti festival	29
personation of, at Nacab kiva in 1893	50
representation of, by Telavai	81
resemblance of, to Tacab yebitcai	98
Tacab Añya, description of	88
Tacab Añya katcina manas, appearance of, in Palülükoñti festival	44
Tacab katcina, personation of, in Wikwaliobi kiva	30
similarity of mask of Teük to that of	108
Tacab katcinas, dance of, in Palülükoñti	50
Powamû dance by	33
Tacab naactadji, description of	97
Tacab tenebidji, description of	97, 98
Tacab yebitcai, description of	98
resemblance of, to Tacab	98
Tadpoles, appearance of, in pictures of Hopi katcinas	96
use of, in decoration in Hopi festivals	47
Takpabu, corn in picture of Yehoho called	106
Talakin, association of, with Natia	104
Tanik, mask of, kept by Walpi Pakab clan	95
resemblance of, to Wupamau	95
Tanoan Añya katcinas, dance of, in Palülükoñti	50
Tanoan colonists, introduction of East mesa Natackas into Tusayan by	71
Tanoan katcinas, adoption of, among Hopis	18
Nüvak regarded as one of the	83
Tanoan names for Hopi katcinas	122-124
Tanoan pueblo, buffalo dance at	43
Tañ towa. *See* Sun clan.	
Tatauk yamù, appearance of, in new-fire ceremony	73
Tatauk yamù fraternity, ceremonies celebrated by	23
Tateûkti, appearance of, in Hopi festivals	24
in picture of the Nakopan hoya	117
in Powamû festival	39
description of	87, 116, 117
Tawa, association of flute with	101
description of	100, 101
Tawa fraternity, ceremonies celebrated by	23
Tawa Paholawû, summer, description of	56
winter	31
See Sun prayer-stick-making.	
Tawa wüqtaka, identity of, with Ahül	122
Tawapa, meeting place in Pamürti	27
similarity of Walpi festival at, to those of March festival	84

	Page
Tawapa, ceremonies performed at	52
Tawawimpkya. *See* Sun priests.	
Tawiskaron, a man-being in iroquoian cosmology	305, 307, 309, 310, 324, 327, 332
Tcabaiyo	71, 75
Tcakwaina, derivation of	125
description of picture of	62
resemblance of, to Hehée	74
Tcakwaina clan, claim of, to Tcakwaina katcinas as clan ancients	
Tcakwaina katcinas, personages participating in dances of	62
Powamu dance by	33
Tcakwaina mana, derivation of	125
legend of	63
Tcakwaina masks, possession of, by Küküte clan	29
Tcakwainas, personation of, in Pamürti	27
Tcakwaina taadta, derivation of	125
Tcakwaina taamu, description of picture of	63
Tcakwaina yuadta, derivation of	125
description of picture of	63
Tcanaû, appearance of, in Palülükoñti	52
derivation of	125
description of	91
similarity of mask of Wupamau to that of	91
similarity of meal bag of, to that of snake priests	91
See Sabi.	
Tcanaû katcina, appearance of, in Palülükoñti	
Tcatcakwaina kokoiamû, personation of, by Tcakwaina katcinas	45
Tcatcakwaina mamantû, personation of, by Tcakwaina katcinas	45
Tcatcakwaina taamû, personation of, by Tcakwaina katcinas	45
Tcatcakwaina tatakti, personation of, by Tcakwaina katcinas	45
Tcatcakwaina yuamû, personation of, by Tcakwaina katcinas	45
Tcilikomato, description of	116
Tcivato kiva, bird personations in	30
corn-planting in	52
Hopi festival performed in	36
Tcolawitze, derivation of	125
description of picture of	61
personation of, in Pamürti	26, 27
Tcosbuci, derivation of	85, 125
description of	85, 86
Tcotcoyuñya, first ceremonial day of elaborate Hopi festivals	20
Tcüa, language of, different from modern Hopi	18
Tcüa clan, description of	110
serpent effigies kept in house of	81
Tcüa fraternity, ceremonies celebrated by	23
Tcüatikibi, description of	57
duration of	20
Tcüb, description of	103
Tcüb fraternity, ceremonies celebrated by	23
Tcüb katcina, similarity of symbolism of, to that of Sowiñwû	103
Tcüclawû, derivation of	125
Tcukapelli, description of	115

358   INDEX

	Page
Tcukubot, description of	91
Tcukuwĭmpkya, appearance of, in Hopi festivals	24
Tcutckutû, appearance of, in Hopi festivals.	24
description of	67
Technology, earliest stages of	XVII, XVIII
Te clan, mask of. *See* Pohaha.	
Teeth, prominence of, in mask of Yohozro.	84
Tehabi, description of	70
participation in Powamû festival by	67
Tehuelche tribe, investigation of	XII
Telavai, appearance of, in picture of the Nakopan hoya	117
in Powamû festival	39, 67
description of	81
Tenebidji, derivation of	126
Tenochio, Seri vocabulary furnished by	XXV
Tetañaya, description of	81
Teük, derivation of	125
description of	108
Tewa, buffalo dance introduced from	31
connection of, with Plains Indians	111
introduction of masks to the East mesa by colonists from	111
names of, for katcinas	123, 124
Teva kiva, Powamû dance in	32
Tewan clan, katcinas introduced by	62
Tharonhiawakon, meaning of creation of man and animals by	138
names of	138
reference to	137
See Zephyrs.	
Theatrical performance, Hopi	22
Thomas, Cyrus, Central American stocks classified by	XXIV
cyclopedic labor of	XXXII
Mayan and Mexican calendars investigated by	XXXI
Thomas, Jessie E., Mayan vocabulary, transcribed by	XXVII
Tiburon, Seri Indians of, study of	XIV
Tierra del Fuego, researches in	XII
Tihüni, Hopi ceremonial day of	20, 54
Tinklers, appearance of, in pictures of Hopi katcinas	96
Tin rattles, peculiar to dress of Helilülü	66
Tiponi, absence of, in Pamürti	26
appearance of, in flute festival	29
Tiwenu, description of	102
Tiyuna, Hopi ceremonial day of	20
Tobacco clan, East mesa Natacka masks kept by	70
Toho, description of	105, 106
picture of, in house of war god	25
Tokotci, picture of, in house of war god	25
Tokotcpatcuba, garment worn by Yehoho.	106
Tooth, the tree called	151, 176
Totca, description of	78
personation of, in Powamû	32
Totci, figurines of Corn maidens made by	88
Totokya, Hopi ceremonial day of	29, 52, 121
Triangular figures, appearance of, in pictures of Hopi katcinas	65–67, 79, 99–101
use of, as rain symbols	66
Triangular mouth, Hopak distinguished by.	89
Trifid symbol, appearance of, in representations of Hopi katcinas	71

	Page
Trumbull, J. H., Natick dictionary of.	XXV, XXVI
Trumpets, use of, in Hopi festivals	54
Tubeboli manas, pictures of, in Hopi festivals	42
Tumae, description of	104
Tumas, description of	68, 69
flogging by	36
member of Tuñwup group	70
participation in Powamû festival by	67
personation of, in Powamû dance	33
Tuñwup, derivation of	125
description of	69
function of, in Powamû festival	67, 68, 69
personation of, in Powamû dance	33
regular appenrance of	17
Tuñwup group, personages of	70
Tuñwup katcinas, flogging by	36
Tuñwup taadta, derivation of	125
Tuñwup taamu, description of	70
member of Tuñwup group	70
participation in Powamû festival by	67
Turkey. *See* Koyona	80
Turkey feathers, appearance of, in pictures of Hopi katcinas	71, 89, 100, 102, 103, 105, 107
use of, in Hopi festivals	46
Türkinobi	51
Turkwinû, derivation of	95, 105, 124
description of	105
mask of, kept by Walpi Pakab clan	95
Turkwinû mana, derivation of.	124
description of	105
Turpockwa, appearance of, in Soyaluña	25
description of	79
similarity of symbolism of, to that of Palakwayo	77
Turquoise, use of, as ear pendants, in Hopi pictures	113, 119
in picture of Woe	67
as ornaments, by Tcosbuci	85
Turtle, a man-being in Iroquoian cosmology	174, 180, 181, 286, 288, 301
Turtle shells, appearance of, in representations of Hopi katcinas	64
distribution of, in Powamû festival	31
Türtumsi, derivation of, from Comanche tribe	99
description of	99
Tusayan, bringing of Buffalo maid by Sun to	31
bringing of helmet of Tcakwaina to	62
ethnologic exploration of.	XL
germ god of	38
introduction of East mesa Natackas into	71
introduction of Lalakoñti into	58
introduction of Loiica and Kokopelli into	62
Tcanaû introduced by Pakab clan into.	91
Tuscaroras, adoption of, by League of the Iroquois	133
Tuwanacabi. *See* Honani clan.	
Twins, birth of, in Iroquoian cosmology	292
male, birth of	185, 230
Ucümüryawû. *See* March.	
Urcicimû, description of	106

INDEX 359

	Page
Visor, appearance of, in pictures of Hopi katcinas	95, 97, 98, 102, 103
Vocabularies, American, in archives of the Bureau	XXIII
Vroman, A. C	X
Wafer bread, appearance of, in pictures of Hopi katcinas	83
Wabikwinema, description of	30
Wakac, derivation of	126
description of	113
Wala, masking of katcinas at	52
shrine of	33
Walapai tribe, derivation of Teosbuci from	85
Walpi, bird gods personated by	29
child-flogging at	36, 69
corn-planting in Tciyato kiva of	52
departure of katcinas from	57
derivation of katcinas in	125, 126
destruction of Sikyatki by the	115
East mesa Natacka masks in	70
frightening of children by Soyok wüqti at	39
introduction of Sio from Zuñi into	112
Pakab clan of, introduction of Tcanaü by	54
mask of Citoto kept by	95
mask of Sabi kept by	95
mask of Tañik kept by	95
mask of Turkwinü kept by	95
participation of, in Pamürti	27
personators in Palülükoñti festival from	48
planting of beans at	31
plaza of, public dance of Añya katcinas in	54
Powamü festival at	31
serpent effigies made by, in 1900	51
serpent effigies owned by	51
similarity of mask of Bear family of, to that of Ke Towa Bisena	112
Sumaikoli and Kawikoli masks in	96
Sumaikoli summer ceremony at	57
variant of Coto at	89
visitation of Abül to houses in	34
Walpi katciñas, derivation of, from Awatobi	74
Walpi men, Sowiñwü katcina not recently personated by	104
War bonnet, appearance of, in pictures of Hopi katcinas	90
War implement, appearance of, in pictures of Hopi katcinas	90
Waring, Lucretia M., cataloguing of Bureau library by	XXXII
Warrior, representation of a	108
the Great, in Iroquoian cosmology	319
War gods, worship of	25, 26
Warrior maid, Hēhēe appearing as, in Powamü festival	74
Warty, a man-being in Iroquoian cosmology	230, 238
Wasp katcinas. See Tetañaya.	
Water, Fresh, a man-being in Iroquoian cosmology	175
prayer for, in Hopi festivals	53
squirting of, by Hopi katcinas	81

	Page
Waterfowl, man-beings in Iroquoian cosmology	182, 285
Water-house clan, germ goddesses of	122
Water of Springs, a man-being in Iroquoian cosmology	174
Wattles, appearance of, in pictures of Hopi katcinas	80
Wawac races, description of katcinas appearing in	114-117
Wealth, display of, in Pamürti festival	28
Wedding blankets, appearance of, in Hopi pictures	119
Whip, use of, in Hopi foot races	114
White bear. See Kutcahonauü.	
White katcina. See Kutca.	
Whites, influence of, on Hopi painting	13, 14
Whizzer, appearance of, in Hopi pictures	91, 108, 111, 120
See Bull-roarer.	
Wicoko, worship of	25
Wikteina, description of	116
Wikwaliobi kiva, Tacab and Woe katcinas personated in	30
Wild-cat. See Tokotci.	
Willow wands, use of, by Hopi katcinas	50
Wind, a man-being in Iroquoian cosmology	174, 224, 232, 233, 235
Spring, a man-being in Iroquoian cosmology	174
Wings, imitation of, by feathers	25, 27
Winship, G. P	X
Winter flute Paholawü, description of	23, 29, 30
Winter Lakone Paholawü, description of	39
fraternities taking part in	23
Winter Marau Paholawü, description of	23, 55
Winter prayer-stick-making, resemblance of, to that of summer	56
Winter snake ceremony, fraternities taking part in	23
Winter solstice ceremony, Hopi	24, 25
worship of war gods in, in Hano	25
of Walpi, appearance of Ahülani in	122
See Soyaluña.	
Winter sun prayer-stick-making, fraternities taking part in	23
Winter Tawa Paholawü, description of	31
Wisconsin, field work in	IX
wild-rice industry in	XIX
Woe, description of	66, 67
participation in Powamü festival by	67
part taken by, in Pamürti festival	29
Woe katcinas, appearance of, in Palülükoñti	52
personation of, in Wikwaliobi kiva	30
Wolf, a man-being in Iroquoian cosmology	171
Wolf katcina. See Kyewü.	
Women, Hopi, skill of, in painting	15
personation of, by men, in Hopi festivals	41, 43
Wood, H. S., editorial work of	XXXII
Wukokoti, appearance of, in Palülükoñti in Powamü festival	52, 36
description of	85
Wupamau, appearance of clown in company of, in Powamü	91, 92
appearance of, in Palülükoñti	52

	Page
Wupamau, derivation of,	125
description of	91, 92
resemblance of, to Tanik	95
similarity of mask of Tcanaû to that of.	91
Wüwükoti, ancient clan masks designated by the name of	109
appearance of beard and horns in pictures of	111
derivation of	125
Wüwütcimti, description of	21, 24
fraternities taking part in	23
Wüwütcimtû, appearance of, in new-fire ceremony	73
Wüwütcimtû fraternity, ceremonies celebrated by	23
Wüwütcimtû priests, face decoration of, in new-fire ceremony	74
Wüwüyomo, derivation of	125
description of	65
display of masks of, at Pamürti	66
masks of	28
participation in Powamû festival by	67
relation of, to Honani clan	65
resemblance of masks of, to that of Abül	65
Wuyok, appearance of, in Hopi Palülükoñti festivals	52
Yahgan tribe, investigation of	xii
Yaupa, description of	79
personation of, in Powamû	32
Yaya priests, appearance of, in spring and summer festival	96
description of	96
fraternity of, ceremonies celebrated by	22, 23
Kawikoli accompanied by	96
Walpi spring festival held by	55
Yebitcai, derivation of	126
Yeboho, description of	106
Yellowhammer, a man-being in Iroquoian cosmology	175, 202

	Page
Yohozro wüqti, derivation of	126
description of	84
Yucca, mouse trap of, in Powamû festival	71
whip of, appearance of, in pictures of Hopi katcinas	66, 69, 70, 72, 76, 89, 98, 106, 108, 115, 116
Yucatan, Mayan vernacular of	xxvi
Yuman katcinas among Hopis	18
Yuman tribe, derivation of Tcósbuci from a	85
style of hair-dressing of	85
Yuña, description of	113
Yuña mana, description of	113
Yuñya, Hopi ceremonial day of	20, 62
Zephyrs, a man-being in Iroquoian cosmogony	171, 183, 185, 295, 296
Zigzag lines, symbolic use of, in pictures of Hopi katcinas	72, 75, 76, 84, 87, 89
Zigzag sticks, use of, as lightning symbol, in pictures of Hopi katcinas	43, 92
Zuñi, Calako masks of, display of, at Pamürti	65, 66
claim of, to Sichumovi	26, 62
derivation of Alo mana from	109
derivation of Atocle from	71, 75
derivation of Kawikoli from	96
derivation of Kwacus Alek taka from	109
derivation of words from	97
hair of Hokyaña mana dressed in fashion of	95
Hopi katcinas derived from	60, 107, 108, 112, 125
appearance of, in Hopi festivals	17, 18
in Pamürti	26
celebration of advent of, in Pamürti	57
mythology of, reference to monograph on	xxx
style of women's ceremonial headdress of, identical with that of Hopak	89
resemblance of rain priests of, to katcina fathers	56
See Sio.